# of North
American
Sport

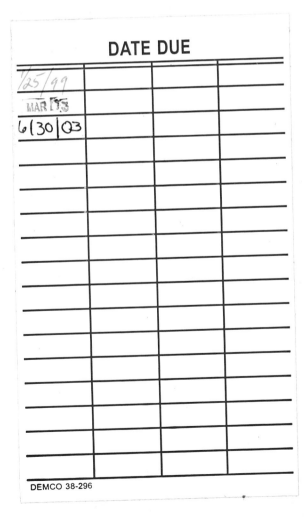

DATE DUE

/25/99			
MAR 03			
6/30/03			

# of North American Sport

SIXTH EDITION

Dr. D. Stanley Eitzen
Colorado State University

Dr. George H. Sage
University of Northern Colorado

Brown & Benchmark
PUBLISHERS

Madison, WI Dubuque Guilford, CT Chicago Toronto London
Mexico City Caracas Buenos Aires Madrid Bogotá Sydney

Book Team

Executive Managing Editor *Ed Bartell*
Project Editor *Theresa Grutz*
Production Editor *Donna Nemmers*
Art Editor *Rita L. Hingtgen*
Photo Editor *Rose Deluhery*
Proofreading Coordinator *Carrie Barker*
Production Manager *Beth Kundert*
Production/Costing Manager *Sherry Padden*
Production/Imaging and Media Development Manager *Linda Meehan Avenarius*
Visuals/Design Freelance Specialist *Mary L. Christianson*
Senior Marketing Manager *Pamela S. Cooper*
Copywriter *Sandy Hyde*

Basal Text *10/12 Times Roman*
Display Type *Bembo*
Typesetting System *Macintosh™ QuarkXPress™*
Paper Stock *50# Restore Cote*

Brown & Benchmark
PUBLISHERS

Executive Vice President and General Manager *Bob McLaughlin*
Vice President, Business Manager *Russ Domeyer*
Vice President of Production and New Media Development *Victoria Putman*
National Sales Manager *Phil Rudder*
National Telesales Director *John Finn*

A Times Mirror Company

Cover design by Elise Lansdon

The credits section of this book begins on p. 329 and is considered an extension of the copyright page.

Cover images (clockwise from top left): © Skjold Photographs; © Dave Frazier; © Skjold Photographs.
Back cover image: © Mark Richards/PhotoEdit

Copyedited by Anne Scroggin; proofread by Francine Buda Banwarth

Printed in the United States of America by Times Mirror Higher Education Group, Inc.,
2460 Kerper Boulevard, Dubuque, IA 52001

10 9 8 7 6 5 4 3 2 1

To Our Grandchildren:

D. S. Eitzen's grandchildren are Christopher,
Nicole, Jacob, Zachary, and Cooper;
G. H. Sage's grandchildren are Tyler,
Garrett, Lucas, and Elise

CONTENTS

preface xi

1 *The Sociological Analysis of Sport
in Society*   1
The Pervasiveness of Sport 2
The Discipline of Sociology 2
  Assumptions of the Sociological Perspective 4
  Problems with the Sociological Perspective 5
  Units of Sociological Analysis 6
  *Sociological Theories: Contrasting Ways to See
    and Understand Social Life 9*
  Research Perspectives of Sport Sociologists 13
Sport As a Microcosm of Society 14
  Common Characteristics of Sport and Society 14
Levels of Sport 16
  Informal Sport 16
  Organized Sport 16
  Corporate Sport 16
Summary 17
Notes 17

2 *Social and Cultural Sources of the Rise
of Sport in North America*   21
Colonial Traditions in North America 22
The Early Nineteenth Century: Early
    Industrialization and Technology 23
*Sport in the Early Nineteenth Century: Building
    a Framework for Modern Sport 23*
The Technological Revolution and Sport 25
The Latter Nineteenth Century: The
    Beginnings of Modern Society 26
*The Latter Nineteenth Century: The Rise
    of Modern Sport Forms 27*
The Twentieth Century: The Modern
    World 34
*The Twentieth Century: The Maturing
    of Modern Sport 34*
Summary 39
Notes 39

3 *Sport and Societal Values*   43
The American Value System 44
  Success 44
  Competition 45
  The Valued Means to Achieve 46
  Progress 46
  Materialism 47
  External Conformity 47
Societal Values and Sport 48
  Competition and Success in Sport 48
  The Valued Means to Achievement in Sport 52
  Progress in Sport 52
  Materialism in Sport 52
  External Conformity in Sport 53
Summary 54
Notes 54

4 *Children and Sport*   57
Youth Sports Programs: Something
    for Everyone 58
The Rise of Youth Sports Programs:
    The Take-Off and Expansion of a New
    Form of Sport 59
Objectives of Youth Sports Programs: What Do
    Young Athletes Want? What Do Their
    Parents and Coaches Want? 60
Socialization and Sport 61
Socialization into Sport: Why Do Children Get
    Involved in Organized Sports? 61
  Families 61
  Parents 62
  Siblings 63
  Peers 63
  Coaches 63
  Schools 63
  Mass Media 64
  Participants 64
Socialization via Sport 65
  Two Forms of Play 65
Development of Personal-Social Attributes
    Through Sport 70

Potential Psycho-Social Problems
    of Youth Sports 71
  Adult Intrusion 71
  Deviant Normative Behavior 72
  Disruption of Education 73
  Risk of Injury 74
  The "Winning Is the Only Thing" Ethic 74
Sports Alternatives for the Young Athlete 75
  Cooperative Games 76
  Youth Sports Coaches 76
  Bill of Rights for Young Athletes 76
Summary 77
Notes 77

5   *Interscholastic Sport*   *81*
The Status of Sport in Secondary Schools 82
The Consequences of Sport for Schools,
    Communities, and Individuals 83
  The Consequences of Sport for the School 84
  The Consequences of Sport for the Community 85
  The Consequences of Sport for the Participant 86
Problems, Dilemmas, and Controversies 89
  The Reinforcement of Gender Roles 89
  Cheating 90
  Autocratic Coaches 90
  Excessive Pressures to Win 90
  Elitism 91
  Sport Specialization 91
  Budget Shortfalls 91
  Corporate High School Sport 92
Efforts to Reform High School Sports 93
Summary 97
Notes 98

6   *Intercollegiate Sport*   *101*
College Sport As Big Business 103
  The Consequences of a Money Orientation
    in College Sports 105
  A Contradiction: Athletes As Amateurs in a Big
    Business Environment 109
The NCAA and Student-Athletes 109
  The Enforcement of "Amateurism" 110
  The Restriction of Athletes' Rights 111
The Educational Performance
    of Student-Athletes 112
  Intellectual Preparation of Student-Athletes
    for College 112
  Academic Performance 112
  Graduation Rates 112
  The Impediments to Scholarly Achievement
    by College Athletes 115

Reform 116
  The Administration of College Sports 117
  Emphasizing the Education
    of Student-Athletes 117
  Commitment to Athletes' Rights 118
Summary 118
Notes 119

7   *Social Problems and North American*
    Sport: Violence and Drugs   *123*
Violence in Sport: Which Is It—Violence
    or Aggression? Confusion
    in the Literature 124
Theories About the Connection Between
    Violent Behavior and Sport 124
Aggression Theories and Research
    on Sports 126
Violence and North America 127
  A History of Violence 127
  A Contemporary Culture of Violence 128
Violence in North American Sport 129
  Violent Behavior by Athletes As Part
    of the Game 129
  Borderline Violence 130
  Who or What Encourages Player Violence? 131
  Violence Against Athletes 133
Violent Behavior by Athletes off the Field
    of Play 133
  Why Do Athletes Assault Women? 134
Sports Fan Violence 135
  Factors Associated with Fan Violence 136
  Reducing Fan Violence 136
Substance Abuse and Sport 137
  The Scope of Substance Abuse in Sport 137
  Substance Abuse Not New to Sports 138
  Reasons for Substance Abuse Among Athletes 139
  Preventing Substance Abuse in Sports 141
Summary 143
Notes 144

8   *Sport and Religion*   *147*
Religion and Society 148
  Social Functions of Religion 148
The Relationship of Religion and Sport 150
  Primitive Societies 150
  Ancient Greece 150
  The Early Christian Church 150
  The Reformation and the Rise of
    Protestantism 151
  From the Seventeenth to the Twentieth
    Century 151

Twentieth-Century North America 153
Sport As Religion 153
Religion Uses Sport 155
  Churches 155
  Religious Leaders 156
  Church Colleges and Universities 156
Religious Organizations and Sports 156
  The Fellowship of Christian Athletes 157
  Sport and Missionary Work of Churches 157
  Athletes in Action 158
  Athletes As Evangelists 158
  The Promise Keepers: Sportianity, Gender,
      and Sexuality 158
  Sportianity and Social Issues 159
Value Orientations of Religion and Sport 159
  The Protestant Ethic 159
  Protestantism and Contemporary Sport 162
Sport Uses Religion 162
  The Use of Prayer 163
  The Use of Magic 165
  Magic and Its Uses in Sports 166
Summary 168
Notes 168

9 Sport and Politics 173
The Political Uses of Sport 175
  Sport As a Propaganda Vehicle 175
  Sport and Nationalism 177
  Sport As an Opiate of the Masses 179
  The Exploitation of Sport by Politicians 180
  Sport As a Vehicle of Change in Society 181
  Sport As a Socializing Agent 182
The Political Attitudes of Coaches and
      Athletes 183
  Coaches 183
  Athletes 185
The Political Olympics 186
  Political Problems 186
  A Proposal for Change 188
Summary 190
Notes 190

10 Sport and the Economy 193
Who Benefits Economically from Sports? 194
Professional Sport As a Business 198
  Professional Sport As a Monopoly 198
  Public Subsidization of Professional Team
      Franchises 199
  Ownership for Profit 203
The Relationship Between Owner
      and Athlete 205
  The Draft and the Reserve Clause 205
  Free Agency 207

  Salaries 212
  A Radical Question: Are Owners Necessary? 214
Amateur Sport As a Business 214
  The Economics of Collegiate Sport 215
Summary 217
Notes 218

11 Sport and the Mass Media 221
Social Roles of the Mass Media 222
  Prominent and Subtle Roles of the Media 222
The Symbiosis of Mass Media and Sport 222
  Linkages of the Mass Media and Sport 223
Television: The Monster of the Sports
      World 225
  Increasing TV Sports Coverage 226
  Economic Aspects of Televised Sports 226
Television's Influence on Sport 227
  Increases in Sport Revenue 227
  Popularity Shifts 228
  Professional Sports Franchise Location 229
  Intercollegiate Sport 229
  High School Sports 230
  Game Modifications for TV 231
  Redefining the Meaning of Sport 231
  Trash Sports 233
The Impact of Sport on the Mass Media 233
  Increased Sport in the Media 233
  Sports Privileged Treatment by the Media 234
  Sports Consumers and the Mass Media 234
Sports Journalism and the Mass Media 235
  Women and People of Color
      in Sports Journalism 237
Summary 240
Notes 240

12 Sport, Social Stratification,
      and Social Mobility 243
Social Class and Sport 244
  Adult Participant Preferences for Sports by
      Socioeconomic Status 244
  Youth Sport Participation by Socioeconomic
      Status 246
  Spectator Preferences for Sports
      by Socioeconomic Status 248
  Segregation in Sports by Social Class 250
Social Mobility and Sport 251
  Sport As a Mobility Escalator 251
  Demythologizing the Social Mobility Through
      Sport Hypothesis 253
Summary 258
Notes 258

13 *Race and Sport* 261

The History of African American Involvement
  in Sport 262
Black Dominance in Sport 264
  Race-Linked Physical Differences 264
  Race-Linked Cultural Differences 265
  Social Structure Constraints 265
Racial Discrimination in Sport 269
  Stacking 270
  Rewards and Authority 273
  Ability and Opportunity 275
Summary 276
Notes 276

14 *Gender in North American Sport:*
     Continuity and Change 279

The Heritage of Gender Inequality 280
Social Sources of Gender Inequality
  in Sport 282
  Parental Child-Rearing Practices
     and Gender Construction 282
  The School and Gender Construction 283
  The Mass Media and Gender Construction 284
  The Gendered Nature of Athletes
     As Role Models 285
Social Barriers to Female Participation in
  Sport 285
  Negative Stereotypes 285
The Opportunity and Reward Structure
  for Females in Sport 289
  From Boys-Only Youth Sport to Opportunities
     for Both Sexes 289
  Toward Gender Equity in High School Sports 290
  Toward Gender Equity in Intercollegiate
     Sports 292
  Gender Equity and High School and College
     Women's Coaching and Athletic
     Administration 296
  Why Have Men Been Hired to Coach
     and Administer Women's Sports? 297
  Gender and Careers at the Top Levels
     of Sport 297
Sport and Gender Identity for Males 299
Summary 300
Notes 301

15 *Contemporary Trends and the Future*
     of Sport in North America 305

Trends in Population Growth 306
  Population Composition 306
  Location of Population 307
  Population Trends and Sport 307
Trends in Industry and Technology
  and Sporting Activities 309
  An Information/Service North American
     Society 309
  The Information/Service Workplace and Sporting
     Activities 310
A Future Society and Sport 311
  Intellectual Sports of the Future 311
  Violent Sports of the Future 311
  Uses of Technology in Sport 312
  A Counterpoint to Technosports: Ecosports 314
The Future and Personal Fitness and Healthy
  Lifestyles 315
  Runners and Walkers 316
  Employee Fitness Programs 316
Trends in the Economy and Future Sports 317
  The Future of Professional Sports 317
  The Future of Televised Sports 317
  Intercollegiate Athletics and the Future 319
  Secondary School Sports and the Future 319
  Gambling and Sports 320
Trends in Social Values and Future Sport 320
  The Quest for Democracy and Equality 321
  Trends in Sports Values 321
Summary 323
Notes 324

Credits 329

Index 331

Introduction

Sport takes place in social settings and has a profound influence on the social life of large numbers of people of all ages, but the study of sport from a sociological perspective has not been prominent. Academic fashions are changing, however, and in the past decade the tools of sociology—its perspective, theories, and methods—have been increasingly employed in studying sport. As a consequence, a cumulative and systematic body of knowledge is beginning to take form. The literature has grown rapidly, beginning with anthologies and culminating in full-blown texts and periodicals. Also, international conferences on sport sociology have stimulated worldwide sociological study of sport, and this subject has had a prominent place in the convention programs of physical education meetings as well as of national and regional meetings of sociology associations. Finally, sport sociology classes are now commonly offered by sociology and kinesiology/physical education departments throughout the nation.

Purpose of This Text

Three goals guide our efforts in writing this book. In the analysis of the sport structure in societies, our first goal is to analyze sport critically and in so doing demythologize sport. Thus, the reader will understand sport in a new way. She or he will also incorporate implicitly the sociological perspective in his or her repertoire for understanding other parts of the social world.

Our second goal is to impress on our readers in kinesiology/physical education and sociology the importance of including the sociology of sport as a legitimate subfield in each of the two disciplines. We hope that this book will convince kinesiology/physical education students of the importance of social forces upon sports activities and organizations. Although the mechanical and physiological factors of sport are important, the social milieu in which participation is embedded is crucial with respect to who participates, when, where, and the consequences of such participation. Sport involvement is more than making use of the levers of the body and using strength and endurance to achieve the objective. To sociology students, our message is that sport is a social activity worthy of serious inquiry. It is a substantive topic as deserving of sociologists' attention as those standard specialties: the family, religion, and politics. Not only is sport a microcosm of the larger society, but sports phenomena also offer a fertile field in which to test sociological theories.

Our final goal is to make the reader aware of the positive and negative consequences of the way sport is organized in society. We are concerned about some of the trends in sport, especially the move away from athlete-oriented activities toward the impersonality of what we term "corporate sport." We are committed to moving sport and society in a more humane direction, and this requires, as a first step, a thorough understanding of the principles that underlie the social structures and processes that create, sustain, and transform the social organizations within the institution of sport.

All of the chapters in this edition have been revised and the content updated. We have tried to incorporate the salient research and relevant events that have occurred since the publication of the last edition of this book.

The focus of the first two editions was on sport in American society. Although that emphasis remains, the focus in the third, fourth, fifth, and now sixth edition has been broadened to include sport in Canadian society as well. There are many parallels with sport and society in these neighboring nations, as well as important differences that we will note where appropriate. Finally, we have made a special effort in this edition to incorporate race and gender throughout the text.

Organization

In chapter 1 we describe the focus of sociology as a discipline and identify the different analytic levels employed by sociologists. We identify and contrast the two major sociological theories on their interpretation of sport. Next we show how sport provides an ideal setting for utilizing certain sociological instruments and methodologies and affords a setting for the testing of sociological theories.

The phenomenon of sport represents one of the most pervasive social institutions in North America, and in chapter 2 we discuss the relationships between technological, industrial, and urban developments and the rise of organized sport. This chapter has undergone a complete revision for this edition.

The major theme of this book is that sport is a microcosm of society. Salient social values are identified in chapter 3, and we discuss how sport reflects and reinforces the core values, beliefs, and ideologies of the society.

For millions of people, involvement in sport begins in youth sports programs. In chapter 4 we describe how children are socialized into sport, and we discuss some of the consequences of these sports experiences.

Sport and education are inexorably intertwined in society. Chapter 5 examines interscholastic sport, focusing on the social sources responsible for the promotion of sports programs, the consequences of school sports programs, and the problems surrounding school sport.

Chapter 6 is devoted to big-time intercollegiate sport. Although this level of sport is extremely popular, we focus here on the many problems that compromise the integrity of the educational mission of universities.

Chapter 7 analyzes two major social problems in sport—violence (participant and fan) and substance abuse/use by athletes. Included here are such topics as athletes' abuse of women, violence against athletes, and athletes with eating disorders.

In chapter 8 we explore the relationship between religion, one of the oldest universal social institutions, and sport, one of the newest. We trace the changing relations between the two institutions and show how contemporary sport has many of the characteristics of a religion. We also describe how religious agents and agencies use sport to promote religion and how athletes employ magico-religious rituals, taboos, and fetishes in the hope of enhancing their performances.

Although the sport establishment publicly disavows any relationship between politics and sport, the fact is that the two are closely related. In chapter 9 we discuss the close ties between the two and show that there are several characteristics inherent in both institutions that serve to guarantee this strong relationship. In addition to updating, the topics of this chapter have been reordered for clarity.

Economic factors play an overriding role in much of contemporary sport. Not only have the growth of the economy and the emergence of unprecedented affluence, especially in the past two decades, influenced sports, but the enormous increase of interest in sport has had a dramatic economic impact. Chapter 10 describes the multidimensional aspects of economic considerations in sport. Emphasized in this chapter is the ongoing owner-player problem that results in strikes and lockouts.

There is a symbiotic relationship between sport and the mass media. In chapter 11 we review the social functions of the mass media and their relation to sport, the influence of the mass media on sport and of sport on the mass media, and the role of the sports journalist.

Sport is typically assumed to be an egalitarian and a meritocratic institution. In chapter 12 we examine these two assumptions as they relate to social class and social mobility. The analysis shows that these beliefs are largely myths.

Systematic and pervasive discrimination against African Americans has been a historical feature of North American society, but many North Americans believe that sport has been free of racism. Chapter 13 documents the historical and contemporary facts illustrating that sport has had and still has many of the same racial problems as the larger society.

The theme of chapter 14 is that the world of sport has been the exclusive domain of males and that sociocultural forces have combined to virtually exclude female sport involvement. We discuss how the opportunity structure is changing, yet problems of equity remain. Also included in this chapter for the first time are issues of sexuality as they relate to women and men athletes.

The final chapter speculates on the future of sport in North America. The basic theme in this chapter is that since sport reflects society, as the society changes, sport will also undoubtedly undergo some transformation. We discuss several current trends and possible future changes in society and discuss how each is likely to be manifested in sport changes.

Acknowledgments

The development of this edition has been a coordinated effort by both authors in that we have made contributions of one kind or another to each of the chapters. To expedite the writing of the chapters, however, a division of labor was necessary. D. Stanley Eitzen is primarily responsible for the chapters dealing with the sociological analysis of sport, sport and values, sport and education (interscholastic and intercollegiate), politics, economics, social stratification, and racism. George H. Sage is primarily responsible for the chapters on the rise of North American sport, sport and social problems, sport and youth, sport and religion, sport and the mass media, females in sport, and the future of sport. We had the advantage of having several conscientious reviewers who made a number of useful suggestions on the fifth edition:

Dr. Ralph Vernacchia
Western Washington University

Dr. Cynthia Pemberton
University of Missouri, Kansas City

Dr. Catriona Higgs
Slippery Rock University

Most of their suggestions were incorporated in our revision; some were not. Responsibility for the weaknesses that remain is shared by the authors.

About the Authors

We believe that our sports backgrounds and academic interests harmonize in such a way that we form a unique team for writing a book on sport sociology. Both of us are former high school and collegiate athletes. Eitzen has coached on the high school level and has been involved in various capacities in youth sports programs; Sage has coached at the youth, high school, and college level. We have conducted considerable research and published widely in sport sociology. Eitzen is known for his studies of racism in sport; his critiques of various aspects of the social organization of sport; and his anthology, *Sport in Contemporary Society,* now in its fifth edition. Sage is known for his studies of coaches; analyses of professional teams; his recent book, *Power and Ideology in American Sport;* and his anthology, *Sport and American Society.* Although Sage is a kinesiologist and Eitzen a sociologist, our approaches to the sociology of sport are remarkably similar.

D. Stanley Eitzen
George H. Sage

Chapter 1

The Sociological Analysis of Sport in Society

"Good sociology should begin with the application of radical skepticism and criticism to one's own society, to one's place in it, and, by extension, to all social behavior. Sociology should, in short, be alienating."

Pierre van den Berghe

The subject of this book is sport—an extraordinarily pervasive social phenomenon in North America. The sociological perspective is the analytical approach that we will use to examine this very important human activity. We begin with a brief description of the importance of sport in society, followed by an introduction to the discipline of sociology, and how the sociological approach aids in our understanding of sport.

The Pervasiveness of Sport

Social scientists are especially interested in sport because this phenomenon is so pervasive in the United States and Canada. While seemingly a trivial aspect of life, sport is important, particularly as society becomes increasingly leisure-oriented. Many millions of Americans and Canadians are vitally interested in sport. It constitutes much of their conversation, reading material, leisure activity, and discretionary spending. Over one-tenth of the *World Almanac* is annually devoted to sports. In fact, sports receive more coverage in the almanac than politics, business, or science. *USA Today,* the most widely read newspaper in the United States, devotes one-fourth of its space to sports. The sports section is, for many, the most closely examined part of the daily newspaper. Newspapers, in turn, devote more space to sports than to a variety of other topics, including business news, which should be of central importance in a capitalist economy. Evidence of sportsmania is also seen in the amount of television time devoted to sport, with some 15 percent of major network time devoted to sport, plus some cable networks providing twenty-four-hour sports coverage. Historically, the most watched television events are sports spectacles such as the Super Bowl.

Moreover, sport is big business with the gross national sports product estimated at $60 billion. Television networks bid billions of dollars for multiyear rights to televise college basketball tournaments, professional sports, and the Olympic games. Each team in the 1996 Fiesta Bowl received $12 million. Sports betting is staggering, with an estimated $70 million bet legally and $5 billion wagered illegally on just one event—the 1996 Super Bowl. Including all sports,

table 1.1 *Number of Spectators at Major Sports Events for 1992*

Sport	Number of Spectators
Horseracing (1990)	63,803,000
Major league baseball	56,852,000
College football	36,199,000
College basketball	
Men's	29,378,000
Women's	3,397,000
Greyhound racing	28,660,000
Professional football	17,784,000
Professional hockey (1991)	12,344,000

Source: U.S. Bureau of the Census, *Statistical Abstract of the United States: 1994,* 114th edition (Washington, D.C., 1994), p. 256.

gambling is likely some multiple of $100 billion. Table 1.1 shows the very large amount of sports spectatorship in the United States. When these numbers are multiplied by the average cost of tickets, parking, and refreshments, the amount generated by sports attendance is huge. Similarly, with about half of the U.S. population engaging in regular sports participation (see fig. 1.1), the amount spent on sports related equipment is enormous (about $50 billion just for recreational users).

Although sport is an important component of society worthy of serious sociological analysis, all too often it has been relegated to popular commentators because academics have tended to ignore it as a frivolous activity. Traditionally, the leading sociological journals have published few articles on sport. We hope to demonstrate throughout this book that sport merits scientific and critical analysis. We will use the tools of modern sociology to analyze sport in society.

The Discipline of Sociology

Sociology is the scientific discipline that describes and explains human social organization. The size of a human group under study can range from a couple to

Figure 1.1 Participation in ten most popular sports activities, by sex: 1992

Source: U.S. Bureau of the Census, *Statistical Abstract of the United States: 1994,* 114th edition (Washington, D.C., 1994), p. 248.

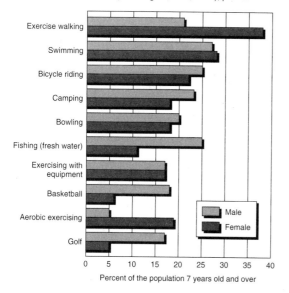

Percent of the population 7 years old and over

explain human behavior. Sociology is joined in this quest by other disciplines, especially biology and psychology. Biological explanations of human behavior focus on the structure (potentials and limitations) of the human body and the innate drives (hunger, thirst, sex, and comfort) that constrain humans. *Sociobiology,* by Edward Wilson, for example, presents the controversial but forceful argument that human genetic heritage explains much behavior, from the way human life is ordered in groups to the prevalence of violence.[2]

Psychological explanations of human behavior focus on mental processes and human behavioral characteristics. Psychology is helpful, for example, in explaining why particular individuals may be violent, self-destructive, criminal, humanitarian, saintly, prejudiced, alcoholic, or failure-prone.

Biological and psychological explanations are only partially useful, however, because they focus exclusively on the individual. The sociological approach, in contrast, stresses those factors external to the individual. These might be social conditions in the community or society such as varying degrees of unemployment, inflation, leisure time, urban blight, or restricted opportunities for minority groups. An extremely important external influence on human behavior is the understanding of meanings that the members of a social organization share. These shared meanings constitute *culture.* Under the rubric of culture are the standards used to evaluate behavior, ideology, customs, expectations for persons occupying various positions, and rules—all of which limit the choices of individuals, regardless of their biological heritage or their psychological proclivities. A final external source of control is an individual's *social location.* Each individual in society is—because of his or her wealth, occupation, education, religion, racial and ethnic heritage, and family background—ranked by others and by himself or herself. Placement in this complex hierarchy exerts pressures, subtle and blatant, on people to behave in prescribed ways.

Although sociology is typically superseded by psychological explanations, the goal of this book is to provide a purely sociological analysis and explanation of sport in North America. Such an inquiry, we hope, not only will be interesting and insightful but

a church, from a family business to a corporation, from a community to a society. The sociologist is interested in the patterns that emerge whenever people interact over periods of time. Although groups may differ in size and purpose, similarities exist in their structures and in the processes that create, sustain, and transform their structures. In other words, although one group may form to make quilts for charity while another forms with the goal of winning football games, they will be alike in many important ways. We know, for example, that through recurrent interaction certain characteristics emerge: (1) a division of labor; (2) a hierarchical structure of ranks (i.e., differences in power, prestige, and rewards); (3) rules; (4) punishment for the violation of rules; (5) criteria for the evaluation of things, people, ideas, and behavior; (6) a shared understanding of symbols with special meanings (specialized language such as nicknames, gestures, or objects); and (7) member cooperation to achieve group goals.[1]

Sociologists are interested not only in the underlying order of social life but also in the principles that

also will introduce the reader to a new and meaningful way to understand the social world and the phenomenon of sport.

Assumptions of the Sociological Perspective

We have seen that human behavior is examined through different disciplinary lenses and that each field of inquiry makes important contributions to knowledge. Of the disciplines focusing on human behavior, sociology is commonly the least understood. The implicit goal of this book is to introduce you to the sociological ways of perceiving and interpreting the role of sport in North America. Let us begin by enumerating the assumptions of the sociological approach that provide the foundation for this unique way of viewing the world.[3]

1. Individuals Are, by Their Nature, Social Beings

There are two fundamental reasons for the assumption that humans are naturally social beings. First, children enter the world totally dependent on others for their survival. This initial period of dependence means, in effect, that each individual is immersed in social groups from birth. Second, throughout history individuals have found it advantageous to cooperate with others (for defense, for material comforts, to overcome the perils of nature, and to improve technology).

2. Individuals Are, for the Most Part, Socially Determined

The assumption that individuals are socially determined stems from the first assumption of the sociological approach, that people are social beings. Individuals are products of their social environments for several reasons. During infancy, children are at the mercy of others, especially parents. These persons can shape the potential behaviors of infants in an infinite variety of ways, depending on their proclivities and those of the society. Parents will have a profound impact on their children's ways of thinking about themselves and about others; they will transmit religious views, attitudes, and prejudices about how other groups are to be rated. Children will be punished for certain behaviors and rewarded for others. Whether

children become bigots or integrationists, traditionalists or innovators, saints or sinners, athletes or nonathletes depends in large measure on parents, siblings, and others with whom they interact.

Parents may transmit to their offspring some idiosyncratic beliefs and behaviors, but most significantly they act as cultural agents, transferring the ways of the society to their children. As a consequence, a child is born not only into a family but also into a society, both of which shape the personality characteristics and perceptions of each individual. Sociologist Peter L. Berger summarized the impact of society on individual development, "Society not only controls our movements, but shapes our identity, our thoughts and our emotions. The structures of society become the structures of our own consciousness. Society does not stop at the surface of our skins. Society penetrates us as much as it envelopes us."[4] The individual's identity is socially bestowed and is shaped by the way he or she is accepted, rejected, and defined by others. Whether an individual is attractive or plain, witty or dull, worthy or unworthy depends on the values of the society and the groups in which the individual is immersed. Although genes determine an individual's physical characteristics, social environment, especially an individual's social class location, determines how those characteristics will be evaluated. Suggesting that people are socially determined is another way of saying that we are, in many ways, puppets dependent upon and manipulated by social forces. A major function of sociology is to identify the social forces that affect us so greatly. Freedom, as Reece McGee pointed out, can come only from a recognition of these unseen forces:

> Freedom consists in knowing what these forces are and how they work so that we have the option of saying no to the impact of their operation. For example, if we grow up in a racist society, we will be racist unless we learn what racism is and how it works and then choose to refuse its impact. In order to do so, however, we must recognize that it is there in the first place. People often are puppets, blindly danced by strings of which they are unaware and over which they are not free to exercise control. A major function of sociology is that it permits us to

recognize the forces operative on us and to untie the puppet strings which bind us, thereby giving us the option to be free.[5]

Accordingly, one task of sociology is to learn, among other things, what racism and sexism are and to determine how they work. This is often difficult, though, because we typically do not recognize their existence. Social forces may have prompted us to believe and to behave in racist and sexist ways.

To say that people are puppets is too strong, however. The assumption that individuals are shaped by their society is not meant to imply a total social determinism. The puppet metaphor is used to convey the idea that much of who we are and what we do is a product of our social environment. However, society is not a rigid, static entity composed of robots; there are nonconformists, deviants, and innovators as well. Although the members of society are shaped by their social environment, they also change that environment. Human beings are the shapers of society. This is the third assumption of the sociological approach.

3. Individuals Create, Sustain, and Change the Social Forms Within Which They Conduct Their Lives

Although humans are often puppets of their society, they are also puppeteers. In brief, the argument is that social groups of all sizes and types (families, peer groups, work groups, athletic teams, corporations, communities, and societies) are formed by their members. The group that interacting persons create becomes a source of control over them (i.e., they become puppets of their own creation), but the continuous interaction of the group's members also changes the group.[6]

Three important implications stem from this assumption that groups are created by persons in interaction. First, these created social forms have a certain momentum of their own that defies change. The ways of doing and thinking that are common to the group are accepted as natural and right. Although human-made, the group's expectations and structures take on a sacred quality—a sanctity of tradition—that constrains behavior in socially prescribed ways.

The second implication is that social arrangements, because they are a result of social activity, are imperfect.

Slavery benefits some segments of society by taking advantage of others. A competitive free-enterprise system creates winners and losers. The wonders of technology make worldwide transportation and communication easy and relatively inexpensive, but they also create pollution and waste natural resources. These examples show that both positive and negative consequences emanate from human organization.

The third implication is that through collective action individuals are capable of changing the structure of society and even the course of history. This process of humans coping with, adapting to, and changing social structures is called *social agency*.

Problems with the Sociological Perspective

Sociology is not a comfortable discipline, and therefore it will not appeal to everyone. Looking behind the "closed doors" of social life is dangerous. The astute observer of society must ask such questions as: How does society really work? Who really has the power? Who benefits under the existing social arrangements, and who does not? To ask such questions means that the inquirer is interested in looking beyond the commonly accepted explanations. Berger put it, "The sociological perspective involves a process of 'seeing through' the facades of social structures."[7] The underlying assumption of the sociologist is that things are not as they seem. Do school sports serve educational goals? Are athletes in big-time college programs exploited? Does participation in sport build character? Are sports free of racism? Are school sports sexist? Is sport a realistic mechanism of upward mobility for lower-class youth? Is success or failure the most common experience of athletes? To make such queries is to question existing myths, stereotypes, and official dogma. The critical examination of society tends to demystify and to demythologize. It sensitizes the inquirer to the inconsistencies present in society.

The sociological assumption providing the basis for this critical stance is that the social world is made by people and therefore is not sacred. A society's economic system, its law, its ideology, its distribution of power, and its sports institutions are all created and sustained by people. They can be changed by people as a consequence. If we wish to correct imperfections in our society, then we must truly understand how social phenomena work and learn what changes will help achieve our goals. The central task of this book is to aid in such an understanding of sport in North America.

The sociological perspective is also discomforting to many because understanding the constraints of society is liberating (traditional sex roles, for example, are no longer "sacred" for many persons). However, liberation from the constraints of tradition also means freedom from the protection that custom provides. The robotlike acceptance of tradition is comfortable because it frees us from choice (and therefore blame) and from ambiguity. The understanding of society is a two-edged sword, freeing us but also increasing the probability of our frustration, anger, and alienation.

A final source of discomfort is that the behavior of people is not always certain. Prediction is not always accurate because people can choose between options and because they can be persuaded by rational and irrational factors. The result is that even when sociologists know the social conditions, they can predict the consequences only in terms of probabilities. On the other hand, chemists know exactly what will occur if a certain measure of one chemical element is mixed with a precise amount of another in a test tube. Civil engineers, armed with the knowledge of rock formations, types of soils, wind currents, and temperature extremes, know exactly what specifications are needed to build a dam in a certain place. They could not determine these, however, if the foundation and the building materials kept shifting. That is the problem, and the source of excitement, for the sociologist. Social life is highly complex, and its study is beset by changes and uncertainties. Although the goal of the sociologist is to reduce the margin of error, its complete elimination is impossible as long as humans are not robots.

Units of Sociological Analysis

We have seen that sociologists are interested in social organizations and in how social forces operate to channel human behavior. The scope of sociology ranges from individuals sharing common social characteristics to small groups to society.

The Social–Psychological Approach

Some sociologists focus on human behavior rather than on social organizations. They direct their research to finding under what social circumstances people behave in predictable ways. Most commonly, research from this approach has focused on the behaviors and attitudes of people who share a common social characteristic or characteristics. For example, first-borns might be compared with latter borns on self-concept, accomplishments, or similarities with parents' political or religious views. Similarly, persons from different social classes, ethnic groups, or regions might be compared on divorce rates, work histories, or political behaviors.

Social-psychological research has been popular among sport sociologists. Typically, studies have compared athletes and nonathletes on a number of dependent variables (i.e., variables influenced by the effect of the independent variable). The assumption is that the athletic experience makes a difference in political and religious attitudes and in values, psychological attributes, and character.[8]

The Micro Level

At the micro level, the emphasis is on the structure of relatively small groups (e.g., families, friendship groups, and such organizations as the Friday Night Poker Club, the local Nazarene Church, the African Violet Society, and the Pretty Prairie High School football team). Some of the research questions of interest at this level are: What are the principles underlying group formation, stability, and change? What are the most effective forms of organization to accomplish group goals? Under what conditions is member cooperation maximized? Under what conditions is member behavior least predictable?

Sports teams are especially useful research settings in which to test theories about social organization. Sociologists of sport have researched, for example, the organizational characteristics correlated with success (leadership style, leadership change, homogeneity of members). They have examined where in sports organizations racial discrimination is most likely to occur.

As a final example of the micro level, sport sociologists have researched sports teams to examine the important social processes of competition and

Sports teams are a form of social organization, embodying competition and cooperation. They also have their own norms, values, roles, and forms of social control.

cooperation. Sport provides innumerable instances in which competition and cooperation occur separately and simultaneously. On the one hand, sports contests are instances of institutionalized conflict. Therefore, they may serve to control undesirable aggression and violence in socially acceptable channels. On the other hand, sports teams require cooperation to be effective. An important question (some would say the central question) in sociology is: What facilitates group cohesion? Under what conditions do members pull together, and when do they pull apart? The leaders of sports teams (coaches, managers, and athletic directors) spend a good deal of their time working to build group unity. Some are successful; others are not. Is it a matter of charisma, authoritarianism, homogeneity of personnel, winning, social control, or what?

The Macro Level

Small groups such as families, friendship groups, and sports teams illustrate nicely the process and components of social organization. Each of these groups, however, exists in a larger social setting—a context that is also structured—with its own norms, statuses, roles, and mechanisms of social control. These components of social structure constrain social groups and the attitudes and behaviors of individuals, regardless of their group memberships.

Societal Norms   There are societal prescriptions (*norms*) for how one should act and dress in given situations—for example, at a football game, concert, restaurant, church, park, or classroom. In other words, norms are situational. Clearly, behavior considered appropriate for spectators at a football game (e.g., spontaneous screams of exuberance or despair, the open criticism of authority figures, and even the ritual destruction of goalposts) would be inexcusable behavior at a poetry reading. We know what is expected of us in these different situations. We also know how to act with members of the opposite sex, with elders, with social inferiors, and with equals. Thus, behavior in society is patterned. We know how to behave, and we can anticipate how others will behave. This allows interaction to occur smoothly.

Values   As bases for the norms, values are also part of society's culture. *Values* are the criteria used in assessing the relative desirability, merit, or correctness of objects, ideas, acts, feelings, or events. This is the topic of chapter 3, so we will only state here that the members of society are taught explicitly and implicitly how to judge whether someone or something is good or bad, moral or immoral, appropriate or inappropriate. North Americans, for example, believe that winning (in school, in sports, in business, and in life) is the highest goal. They not only value success; they know precisely how to evaluate others and themselves by this critical dimension.

Status and Role at the Societal Level   Societies, like other social organizations, have social positions (*statuses*) and behavioral expectations (*roles*) for the occupants of these positions. There are family statuses (son, daughter, sibling, parent, husband, wife); age statuses (child, adolescent, adult, elder); gender statuses (male, female); racial statuses (African American, Hispanic, Native American, white); and socioeconomic statuses (poor, middle class, wealthy). For each of these statuses, there are societal constraints on behavior. To be a male or a female in American society, for example, is to be constrained in a relatively rigid set of expectations. Similarly, African Americans and others of minority status have been expected to "know their place." Historically, their "place" in sport was segregated as they were denied equal access to sports participation with whites. Due to racial integration, the "place" of racial minorities often remains unequal (at certain playing positions, head coaching, management).

Societal Institutions   One distinguishing characteristic of societies is the existence of a set of institutions. The popular usages of this term are imprecise and omit some important sociological considerations. An institution is not merely something established and traditional (e.g., a janitor who has worked at the same school for forty-five years). An institution is also not limited to a specific organization such as a school, a prison, or a hospital. An institution is much broader in scope and in importance than a person, a custom, or a social organization. *Institutions* are social arrangements that channel behavior in prescribed ways in the important areas of societal life. They are interrelated sets of normative elements, such as norms, values, and role expectations, devised by the persons making up the society and passed on to succeeding generations to provide "permanent" solutions for crucial societal problems.

Institutions are cultural imperatives. They serve as regulatory agencies that channel behavior in culturally prescribed ways. As Peter Berger has written: "Institutions provide procedures through which human conduct is patterned, compelled to go in grooves deemed desirable by society. And this trick is performed by making the grooves appear to the individual as the only possible ones." [9] For example, a society instills in its members predetermined channels for marriage. Instead of being allowed a whole host of options (e.g., polygyny, polyandry, or group marriage), sexual partners in the United States and Canada are expected to marry and to set up a conjugal household. Although the actual options are many, the partners tend to choose what society demands. In fact, they do not consider the other options valid. The result is a patterned arrangement that regulates sexual behavior and ensures a stable environment for the care of dependent children.

Institutions arise from the uncoordinated actions of multitudes of individuals over time. These actions, procedures, and rules evolve into a seemingly designed set of expectations because the consequences of these expectations provide solutions that help maintain social stability. The design is not accidental, however; it is a product of cultural evolution.

All societies face problems in common and are continually seeking solutions. Although the variety of solutions is almost infinite, there is a functional similarity in their consequences; that is, stability and maintenance of the system. All societies, for instance, have some form of family, education, polity, economy, and religion. The variations on each of these themes found in societies is almost beyond imagination. [10] (See table 1.2 for a list of common societal problems and the resulting institutions.)

Sport, too, is an institution. What societal needs are served by sport? Several have been identified by various writers: (1) sport serves as a safety valve for both spectators and participants, dissipating excess energies, tensions, and hostile feelings in a socially acceptable way; (2) athletes serve as role models, possessing the proper mental and physical traits to be emulated by other members of society; and (3) sport is a secular, quasi-religious institution that uses ritual and ceremony to reinforce the values of society, thereby restricting behavior to the channels prescribed by custom. [11]

Institutions are, by definition, conservative. They provide the answers of custom and tradition to questions of societal survival. For this reason, any attack on an institution is met by violent opposition. This is surely true for sport, as Harry Edwards has noted, "If this characterization is correct, one would expect that any attack upon the institution of sport in a particular society would be widely interpreted (intuitively, if not explicitly) as an attack upon the fundamental way of life of that society as manifest by the value orientations it emphasizes through sport. Hence, an attack upon sport constitutes an attack upon the society itself." [12]

Institutions provide the unity and stability crucial for the survival of society. While absolutely necessary, institutions in contemporary society are often outmoded, inefficient, and unresponsive to the incredibly swift changes brought about by

table 1.2 *Common Societal Problems and Resulting Institutions*

Societal Problems	Institution
Sexual regulation; maintenance of stable units that ensure continued births and care of dependent children	Family
Socialization of newcomers to the society	Education
Maintenance of order; distribution of power	Polity
Production and distribution of goods and services; ownership of property	Economy
Understanding the transcendental; search for the meaning of life, death, and humankind's place in the world	Religion
Understanding the physical and social realms of nature	Science
Providing for physical and emotional health care	Medicine

technological advances, population shifts, changing attitudes, and increasing worldwide interdependence. Institutions are made by women and men, therefore, they can be changed by these same persons. We should be guided by the insight that although institutions appear to have the quality of being sacred, they are not. They can be changed. Critical examination is imperative, however. Social scientists must look behind the facades. They must not accept the patterned ways as the only correct ways. Questioning patterned ways is part of the democratic heritage as defended in the U.S. Declaration of Independence, for example. Jerome H. Skolnick and Elliott Currie have noted:

Democratic conceptions of society have always held that institutions exist to serve man [sic], and that, therefore, they must be accountable to men [sic]. Where they fail to meet the tests imposed on them, democratic theory holds that they ought to be changed. Authoritarian governments, religious regimes, and reformatories, among other social systems, hold the opposite: in case of misalignment between individuals or groups and the "system," the individuals and groups are to be changed or otherwise made unproblematic.[13]

This book will focus on sport at the societal level. We will describe how sport reinforces societal values. We will analyze the reciprocal linkages with other institutions—sport and education, sport and religion,

sport and politics, sport and the economy. Although the level of analysis is macro, the research findings from social-psychological and micro studies will be included whenever appropriate.

Sociological Theories: Contrasting Ways to See and Understand Social Life

Each sociologist who gives scholarly attention to social phenomena is guided by a theoretical perspective. The focus of attention, the questions asked, the relationships sought, the interpretations rendered, and the insights unraveled are rooted in a theoretical base. Michael Harrington put it this way:

Truths about society can be discovered only if one takes sides. . . . You must stand somewhere in order to see social reality, and where you stand will determine much of what you see and how you see it. The data of society are, for all practical purposes, infinite. You need criteria that will provisionally permit you to bring some order into that chaos of data and to distinguish between relevant and irrelevant factors or, for that matter, to establish that there are facts in the first place. These criteria cannot be based on the data for they are the precondition of the data. They represent—and the connotations of the phrase should be savored—a "point of view." That involves intuitive choices, a value-laden sense of what is meaningful and what is not.[14]

Although there are several important theoretical perspectives that have been used fruitfully to understand sport, we will confine this discussion to functionalism and conflict theory, the two most common ones. Each of these theoretical perspectives presents a very different way of seeing and interpreting social life.

Functionalism

The functionalist perspective attributes to societies the characteristics of cohesion, consensus, cooperation, reciprocity, stability, and persistence.[15] Societies are viewed as social systems, composed of interdependent parts that are linked together into a boundary-maintaining whole. The parts of the system are basically in harmony with each other. The high degree of cooperation (and societal integration) is accomplished because there is a high degree of consensus on societal goals and on cultural values. Moreover, the different parts of the system are assumed to need each other because of complementary interests. Even though there are differences in resources by various groups in society, there are countervailing pressures that prevent abuse and domination by one group. The disadvantaged do not rebel because they accept the values of society and they believe the system is inherently just. All social change is gradual, adjustive, and reforming because the primary social process is cooperation and the system is highly integrated. Societies are therefore basically stable units.

For functionalists the central issue is: What is the nature of the social bond? What holds groups together? One way to focus on integration is to determine the manifest (intended) and latent (unintended) consequences of social structures, norms, and social activities. Do these consequences contribute to the integration (cohesion) and, therefore, the maintenance of the social system?

Functionalists focusing on sport look, for example, for the ways in which sport unifies. They assess how sport contributes to the socialization of youth. They show how sport serves as a model for the striving and achievement of excellence. Finally, they determine the ways sport serves as an inspiration.

Conflict Theory

The assumptions of conflict theory are opposite from those of functional theory. Conflict theory focuses on the social processes leading to disharmony, disruption, instability, and conflict. From this perspective, the basic form of interaction is not cooperation but competition, which often leads to conflict.[16] Conflict is endemic in social organizations because of social structure, especially class differences. The things that people desire, such as property, prestige, and power, are not distributed equally, resulting in a fundamental cleavage between the advantaged and the disadvantaged. Moreover, the powerful use their power to maintain their power and economic advantage. This is done sometimes through force but more often through control of the decision-making apparatus. More subtly, the powerful maintain their power by achieving ideological conformity through the media, schools, churches, and other institutions. This is a most effective means of social control because it results even in individuals defining conditions against their interests as appropriate, a condition that Karl Marx called *false consciousness.*

A prominent assumption of the conflict perspective is that the understanding of society or any of its institutions requires the analysis of the political economy. Power and wealth are inextricably intertwined, and they dominate the rest of society. Therefore, the conflict theorist must consider the type of economy, the ways that members are organized for production and consumption, the distribution of material goods, the way decisions are made, and the distribution of power.

Conflict theorists focusing on sport would, for example, examine intercollegiate athletics by focusing on the power of the National Collegiate Athletic Association (NCAA) over athletes, the cozy relationship between that organization and the television networks, the resistance of the NCAA and university administrators to implement Title IX (which requires equal treatment for women), big-time college sport as big-business, illegal tactics by coaches in recruiting athletes, and the exploitation of the athletes. Functional theorists, on the other hand, would focus on the integrating effects of intercollegiate sport for students, faculty, alumni, and community members. They would also look for the positive consequences for participants such as grades, self-esteem, character traits, career aspirations, and the career mobility patterns of former athletes.

Sport from the Functional and Conflict Perspectives

Functionalists examining any aspect of society emphasize the contribution that part makes to the stability of society.[17] Sport, from this perspective, preserves the existing social order in several ways. To begin, sport symbolizes the American way of life—competition, individualism, achievement, and fair play. Not only is sport compatible with basic American values, but it also is a powerful mechanism for socializing youth to adopt desirable character traits, to accept authority, and to strive for excellence. Sport also supports the status quo by promoting the unity of society's members through patriotism (e.g., national anthem, militaristic displays, and other nationalistic rituals that accompany sports events). Can you imagine, for example, a team that espouses antiestablishment values in its name, logo, mascot, and pageantry? Would we tolerate a major league team called the Atlanta Atheists? the Boston Bigamists? the Pasadena Pacifists? or the Sacramento Socialists? Finally, sport inspires us through the excellent and heroic achievements of athletes, the magical moments in sport when the seemingly impossible happens, and the feelings of unity in purpose and of loyalty of fans.

Clearly, then, sport from the functional perspective is good. Sport socializes youth into proper channels, sport unites, and sport inspires. Thus, to challenge or criticize sport is to challenge the very foundation of society's social order.

Conflict theorists argue that the social order reflects the interests of the powerful. Sport is organized at whatever level, whether youth, high school, college, or professional, to exploit athletes and meet the goals of the powerful (e.g., public relations, prestige, and profits).

Sport inhibits the potential for revolution by society's "have nots" in three ways. First, sport validates the prevailing myths of capitalism, such as anyone can succeed if he or she works hard enough. If a person fails, it is his or her fault and not that of the system. Second, sport serves as an "opiate of the masses" by diverting attention away from the harsh realities of poverty, unemployment, and dismal life chances by giving them a "high."[18] Third, sport gives false hope to blacks and other oppressed members of society as they see sport as a realistic avenue of upward social mobility. The high visibility of wealthy athletes provides

"proof" that athletic ability translates into monetary success. The reality, of course, is that only an extremely small percentage of aspiring athletes ever achieves professional status.

Conflict theorists agree with functionalists on many of the facts but differ significantly in interpretation. Both agree that sport socializes youth, but conflict theorists view this negatively since they see sport as a mechanism to get youth to follow orders, work hard, and fit into a system that is not necessarily beneficial to them. Both agree that sport maintains the status quo. Instead of this being interpreted as good, as the functionalists maintain, conflict theorists view this as bad because it reflects and reinforces the unequal distribution of power and resources in society.

A Comparison of the Functional and Conflict Perspectives

These theoretical perspectives present contrasting views of social life. (See table 1.3 for a summary of differences.) Neither perspective presents the complete answer to understanding social life. Each presents only one side. Society is inherently contradictory, exhibiting harmony as well as deep divisions. Social change can be slow or rapid, reforming or revolutionary. The functional perspective emphasizes the positive while the conflict perspective emphasizes the negative. The point is that both exist. Sport, for example, has both a positive and negative side. It promotes health, yet injuries occur. There is fairness as well as unfairness. Sport can unify or divide a school, community, or nation. Sport can lead to racial integration or maintain the secondary status for racial minorities. The behaviors of athletes can inspire observers as well as disgust them. Athletes can personally gain from sports participation, but they can also be exploited.

Although there is a duality in social life, this book uses conflict theory. We do so for three reasons. First, most students intuitively accept the functional perspective. They tend to accept the way things are uncritically. The conflict perspective assumes a different stance. From this view, there is a basic mood of skepticism about cultural and social patterns. There is a fundamental distrust of existing power arrangements since they

table 1.3 *Assumptions of Functionalism and Conflict Theory*

Functionalism	Conflict Theory

1. The social order
  a) The parts of society are in harmony.
 	
  b) Social order is based on complimentary interests and consensus on norms and values.
	a) The parts of society are in competition and conflict.
	b) Social order is based on coercion by the powerful and subtlely by achieving ideological conformity through schools, churches, and families.

2. Social stratification
  a) Differential rewards is a mechanism to insure that all the slots in the division of labor are filled.
  b) Classes are relative rankings involving economic success and social prestige.
	a) Unequal distribution of rewards reflects the interests of the powerful. It is unjust, divisive, and a source of social instability.
	b) Class divides society into two conflicting camps that contend for control.

3. Distribution of power
  a) The state works for the benefit of all.
 	
  b) Power is diffused among competing interest groups.
	a) The state exists for the benefit of the ruling class (the law, police, and the courts protect the interests of the wealthy).
	b) Power is concentrated in a power elite.

4. Social change
  a) Society is relatively stable.
  b) Change is gradual, adjustive, and reforming.
	a) Society is relatively unstable.
	b) Change can be abrupt and revolutionary.

5. Deviance
  a) People are deviant because they have been socialized to accept and obey the norms of society.
  b) The solution for deviance is to punish or rehabilitate deviants.
	a) The inequities of society generate the behaviors that the powerful label as deviant.
	b) The solution for deviance is to restructure society to eliminate inequities and to provide laws that reflect the interests of all groups.

6. Representative concerns in the study and analysis of sport
  a) How does sport contribute to the integration of schools, communities, and society?
  b) How does sport serve individuals positively (work habits, character, upward mobility)?
  c) How does sport inspire?
	a) How does sport maintain the interests of the power elite?
	
	b) How does sport contribute to alienation, manipulation of the masses, violence, racism, sexism, and unethical behaviors?
	c) How are the goals of sport distorted by commercialism, nationalism, and bureaucracies?

Source: D. Stanley Eitzen and Maxine Baca Zinn, *In Conflict and Order: Understanding Society,* 5th ed. (Boston: Allyn and Bacon, 1991), pp. 41, 200, 238, 401; and Jay J. Coakley, *Sport in Society: Issues and Controversies,* 4th ed. (St. Louis: Times Mirror/Mosby, 1990), p. 24.

are, by definition, oppressive to the powerless segments. Ideologies are questioned because they support the status quo. Myths are measured against reality. This critical examination of social structure and culture demystifies, demythologizes, and, sometimes, emancipates. This surely is an important goal of any sociology course.

Second, the conflict perspective directs attention toward social problems emanating from structural arrangements. The conflict theorist asks: Under these social arrangements who gets what and why? Who benefits from and who bears the social costs of change and stability? Sport, just like the core institutions of the economy, religion, and family, is an area where these kinds of questions typically are not asked. These are vital questions that must be asked in a sociology course on sport.

Third, since the conflict perspective looks critically at social structures, it directs our attention at changing those special arrangements that diminish the human condition.

Research Perspectives of Sport Sociologists

The scholarly interest in sport is growing rapidly throughout the world. Sport-oriented research by social scientists is being reported in sociological, psychological, and physical education journals in increasing quantities.[19] However, the scientific study of sport remains a relatively untapped area. We continue to be guided by myths and "common sense" interpretations.

Normative and nonnormative are the two basic approaches to research in the field of sport sociology.[20] The *normative orientation* is value-laden research done to prove a point. It starts with assumptions about the way things should be and searches for evidence that this is or is not the case.

There are three types of normative research. The first type is found among sociologists in totalitarian states. During the Cold War, this type of research was conducted in the Communist-bloc countries. This type of research is directed toward finding ways that sport can be organized and employed to meet the goals of the state. Thus, sport sociology has a mission to contribute to the betterment of society, as determined by the powerful in society.

A second type of normative research has been found primarily among physical educators in North America and western Europe. Research is focused on the demonstration of sport in building character (learning the values of hard work, competition, fair play, and teamwork).

A third type of normative research has a muckraking function. The researcher assumes beforehand that something is wrong (by his or her values) and sets out to prove it. An example of this type of research is setting out to prove that racism prevails in sport. For example, a book by Paul Hoch, written from a Marxist perspective, shows how sports are instrumental in maintaining capitalism by promoting competitiveness, elitism, sexism, nationalism, militarism, and racism and thus keeping the international working class divided against itself.[21]

The *nonnormative approach,* in contrast, is the scientific description and explanation of what is (not what ought to be). The basic tenet of this approach is that the researcher must be objective and, therefore, value neutral. Sport is neither a priori good nor a priori bad; the goals of sport are neither accepted nor rejected.

This research goal of objectivity, while laudable, is impossible to attain. Michael Harrington has argued, "I am . . . a deeply biased man, a taker of sides; but that is not distinctive at all. Everyone else is as biased as I am, including the most objective social scientist. The difference between us is that I am frank about my values while many other analysts fool both themselves and their audiences with the illusion that they have found an intellectual perch that is free of Earth's social field of gravity."[22] How the researcher does the research, chooses the problem, interprets and uses the findings are all affected by conscious and unconscious attitudes as well as one's theoretical perspective.[23] This is not to say, of course, that the researcher should stop striving to be objective; it only recognizes the formidability of the task in the social sciences. If sociology is a science, its practitioners must strive to be as objective as possible, thereby fulfilling the basic canons of science.[24]

A very serious problem of the value-neutral approach is that it does not take sides; it takes the way things are as a given entity (neither good nor evil).

Thus, research in the name of value neutrality supports the status quo. If racism and sexism exist in sport and if the athlete is being abused, the researcher cannot remain neutral. We cannot remain morally indifferent to injustice.

Robert W. Friedrichs argued that sociologists have tended toward one of two roles—priest or prophet.[25] The priestly role is one of fulfilling the canons of science. The prophetic role, on the other hand, involves making value choices and commitments. The choices that the sociological prophet makes are oriented in the direction of social reform, of constructing a better society.

The material in this book reflects both the normative and the nonnormative or the priestly and the prophetic perspectives. Our goal is twofold: (1) to report what is known about sport and society from social science research and (2) to make the case for reform. As social scientists, we are obliged to be as scientific as possible (using rigorous techniques and reporting all relevant findings whether they support our values or not). At the same time, however, we are committed to moving sport and society in a more humane direction.

To accomplish these goals, we will question established orthodoxies, demythologize sport, and point out the gaps between values and actual practices.[26] We intend, then, to combine a scientific stance with a muckraking role. The latter is important because it forces us to examine such social problems as drug usage in sports, the prevalence of racism and sexism in sports, illegal recruiting, the inhumane treatment of players by bureaucratic organizations and authoritarian coaches, and the perversion of the original goal of sport.[27] Only by a thorough examination of such problems, along with the traditional areas of attention, will we realistically understand the world of sport and its reciprocal relationship with the larger society.

Sport As a Microcosm of Society

The analyst of society is inundated with data. She or he is faced with the problems of sorting out the important from the less important and with discerning patterns of behavior and their meanings. He or she needs shortcuts to ease the task. To focus on sport is just such a technique for understanding the complexities of the larger society. Sport is an institution that provides scientific observers with a convenient laboratory within which to examine values, socialization, stratification, and bureaucracy to name a few structures and processes that also exist at the societal level. The types of games people choose to play, the degree of competitiveness, the types of rules, the constraints on the participants, the groups that do and do not benefit under the existing arrangements, the rate and type of change, and the reward system in sport provide us with a microcosm of the society in which sport is embedded.

Common Characteristics of Sport and Society

Suppose an astute sociologist from another society were to visit the United States and Canada with the intent to understand North American values, the system of social control, the division of labor, and the system of stratification. Although he or she could find the answers by careful study and observation of any single institution (i.e., religion, education, polity, economy, or family), an attention to sport would also provide answers. In the United States, it would not take that sociologist long to discern the following qualities in sport that are also present in the larger society.

The High Degree of Competitiveness

Competition is ubiquitous in North American society. North Americans demand winners. In sports (for children and adults), winning, not pleasure in the activity, is the ultimate goal. The adulation given winners is fantastic while losers are relatively forgotten. Consider, for example, the difference in how the winner and the loser in the Super Bowl are evaluated. Clearly, to be second best is not good enough. The goal of victory is so important for many that it is laudable even if attained by questionable methods.

The Emphasis on Materialism

Examples of the value North Americans place on materialism are blatant in sport (e.g., players signing multimillion-dollar contracts, golfers playing weekly for first-place awards of as much as five hundred thousand dollars, professional teams being moved to more economically fertile climates, and stadiums being built at public expense for hundreds of millions of dollars).

The Pervasiveness of Racism
Racist attitudes and actions affect the play, positions, numbers of starters, and futures of minority group members in North American sport. Just as in the larger society, racial minorities in sport are rarely found in positions of authority.

The Pervasiveness of Male Dominance
Sport contributes to the perpetuation of male dominance through four minimalizing processes: (1) defining—by defining sport as a male activity; (2) directly controlling—men control sport, even women's sport; (3) ignoring—by giving most attention to male sports in the media and through community and school budgets, facilities, and the like; and (4) trivializing—women's sports and women athletes are belittled and diminished.[28]

Mariah Burton Nelson reminds us that sport provides many subtle and not-so-subtle messages about the relative importance of men and the relative unimportance of women. She says:

We live in a country in which the manly sports culture is so pervasive we may fail to recognize the symbolic messages we all receive about men, women, love, sex, and power. We need to take sports seriously—not the scores or the statistics, but the process. Not to focus on who wins, but on who's losing. Who loses when a community spends millions of dollars in tax revenue to construct a new stadium and only men get to play in it, and only men get to work there?

Who loses when football and baseball so dominate the public discourse that they eclipse all mention of female volleyball players, gymnasts, basketball players, swimmers?

Who loses when coaches teach boys that the worst possible insult is to be called "pussy" or "cunt"?

Who loses when rape jokes comprise an accepted part of the game?[29]

The Domination of Individuals by Bureaucracies
Conservative bureaucratic organizations, through their desire to perpetuate themselves, curtail innovations and deflect activities away from the wishes of individuals and from the original intent of these organizations.

The Unequal Distribution of Power in Organizations
The structure of sport in the United States is such that power is in the hands of the wealthy (e.g., boards of regents, corporate boards of directors, the media, wealthy entrepreneurs, the United States Olympic Committee, and the National Collegiate Athletic Association). Evidence of the power of these individuals and organizations is seen in the antitrust exemption allowed them by Congress in dealing with athletes, in tax breaks, and in the concessions that communities make to entice professional sports franchises to relocate or to remain and incidentally, to benefit the wealthy of that community.

The Use of Conflict to Change Unequal Power Relationships
Conflict (in the forms of lawsuits, strikes, boycotts, and demonstrations) is used by the less powerful (e.g., African Americans, women, and athletes) to gain advantage in sport and in society.

Sport Is Not a Sanctuary; Deviance Is Found Throughout Sport
Since sport reflects society, bad actors and bad actions will be found in sport as they are in society. Both fairness and unfairness are found. There are ethical and unethical athletes, coaches, and athletic administrators. Focusing on the negative, E. M. Swift has argued:

In sports, certainly to North Americans, 1994 was an unusually disheartening year. Greed seemed to go unchecked. A baseball strike led to the cancellation of the World Series. An extended hockey lockout threatens the entire NHL season. It was a year of increasingly shocking violence away from the fields of play: the attack on Nancy Kerrigan by the Tonya

Harding camp; the gunning down of a Columbian soccer player who had accidentally scored against his own team in a World Cup loss to the U.S.; the O. J. Simpson indictment for a brutal double murder.

Against this tawdry backdrop we've again been forced to face up to the sad truth that sports isn't a sanctuary. It reflects, often too clearly, society. And, yes, today greed and violence are a big part of society.[30]

Levels of Sport

One final task remains for this first chapter. We need to establish at the outset the subject matter of this book. Our object of study is *sport,* which we define as any competitive physical activity that is guided by established rules. Competition, the first of the three characteristics of sport, involves the attempt to defeat an opponent. This opponent may be a mountain, a record, an individual, or a team. The second characteristic involves physical activity. One attempts to defeat an opponent through physical abilities such as strength, speed, stamina, and accuracy. (Of course, the outcome is also determined by the employment of strategy, not to mention chance.) Rules, the final characteristic of sport, distinguishes it from more playful and spontaneous activities. The scope, rigidity, and enforcement of the rules, however, vary by type and level of sport, as we shall see.

Our definition of sport is too broad to be entirely adequate. A pickup game of basketball and a game in the National Basketball Association (NBA) are examples of two related but at the same time very different activities that fall under our definition.[31] In the same way, an improvised game of one-on-one is sport; so is professional football—although it has been argued that professional football is not sport because of its big business aspects or because it is more like work than play for the participants. Clearly, there is a need to differentiate several levels: informal sport, organized sport, and corporate sport. The first and last of these distinctions were first made by Bil Gilbert, and many of the ideas that follow stem from his insights.[32]

Informal Sport

Informal sport involves playful physical activity engaged in primarily for the enjoyment of the participants. A touch football game, a neighborhood basketball game, and a game of workup (baseball) are examples of this type of sport. In each of these examples, some rules guide the competition, but these rules are determined by the participants and not by a regulatory body.

Organized Sport

The presence of a rudimentary organization distinguishes *organized sport* from informal sport. There are formal teams, leagues, codified rules, and related organizations. These exist primarily for the benefit of the players by working for fair competition, providing equipment and officials, scheduling, ruling in disputed cases, and offering opportunities for persons to participate. Young Men's Christian Association (YMCA) leagues, city leagues, Little League programs, interscholastic teams and leagues, and low-pressure college teams and leagues are examples of organized sport that have not lost the original purposes of the activity. A strong case can be made, however, that many Little League programs have become too organized to maintain the goal of fun through participation for the youth. If so, they belong in the "corporate sport" category.[33] Also with high school sport in some situations[34] as we will see in chapter 5.

Corporate Sport

Corporate sport has elements of informal sport and organized sport, but it has been modified by economics and politics. In Bil Gilbert's words, corporate sport is "a corrupted, institutionalized version of sport."[35] Here, we have sport as spectacle; sport as big business; sport as an extension of power politics. The pleasure in the activity for the participants has been lost in favor of extrinsic rewards for them and pleasure for fans, owners, alumni, and other powerful groups.

Whereas sports organizations at the organized sport level devote their energies to preserving the activities in the participants' interest, organizations at the corporate sport level have enormous power (often a monopoly).

As their power increases, they devote less and less of their energy to satisfying the needs for which they were created. They become more interested in perpetuating the organization through public relations, making profits, monopolizing the media, crushing opposing organizations, or merging leagues to limit opposition and to control player salaries. They also reduce their own risk by being inflexible and noninnovative. Professional sports leagues, big-time college athletics governed by the NCAA, and the International Olympic Committee are examples of the bureaucracies that characterize corporate sport and subvert the pleasure of participating for the sake of the activity itself.

These three levels of sport can be placed on a continuum from play to work. As one moves from informal to corporate sport, the activities become more organized with a subsequent loss of autonomy and pleasure for athletes. Corporate sport dominates sport in North America, therefore, we will focus on that level in this book. That level is but an extension of the organized sport level, however, so we will at times direct our attention toward noncorporate organized sport as well.

"Pseudosport" is another activity often included in the sports pages of newspapers, but one that we would claim falls outside even our broad definition. Professional wrestling, the Roller Derby, and activities involving teams such as the Harlem Globetrotters are examples of pseudosport. Although athletes are involved in these activities and the activities involve physical prowess, they are not sport because they are not competitive. They may be packaged as competition, but these activities exist solely for spectator amusement.

Summary

The perspective, concepts, and procedures of sociology are used in this book to describe and explain the institution of sport in society. The subject matter of sociology is social organization. Sport involves different types of social organizations, such as teams and leagues. These, in turn, are part of larger social organizations, such as schools, communities, international associations, and society. The task of this book is to understand the principles that underlie the structures and processes that create, sustain, and transform these social organizations. Most importantly, this undertaking requires that the observer examine the social arrangements of sport from a critical stance. Some sample questions that must direct the serious investigator are: How does the organization really work? Who really has the power? Who benefits, and who does not?

The two fundamental themes of this book have been introduced in this chapter. The first is that sport is a microcosm of society. Perceiving the way sport is organized, the types of games people play, the degree of emphasis on competition, the compensation of the participants, and the enforcement of the rules is a shorthand way of understanding the complexities of the larger society in which sport is embedded. The converse is true also. The understanding of the values of society, of its types of economy, and of its treatment of minority groups, to name a few elements, provides important bases for the perception or understanding of the organization of sport in society.

The second theme is that the prevailing form of sport—the corporate level—has corrupted the original intentions of sport. Instead of player-oriented physical competition, sport has become a spectacle, a big business, and an extension of power politics. Play has become work. Spontaneity has been superseded by bureaucracy. The goal of pleasure in the physical activity has been replaced by extrinsic rewards, especially money.

Notes

1. See Muzafer Sherif and Carolyn W. Sherif, *Groups in Harmony and Tension* (New York: Octagon Books, 1966); William F. Whyte, *Street Corner Society* (Chicago: University of Chicago Press, 1943); and Elliot Liebow, *Tally's Corner: A Study of Negro Street Corner Men* (Boston: Little, Brown, 1967).

2. Edward O. Wilson, *Sociobiology: The New Synthesis* (Cambridge, Mass.: Belknap Press, 1975).

3. For an elaboration of the discipline of sociology and the sociological perspective, see D. Stanley Eitzen and Maxine Baca Zinn, *In Conflict and Order: Understanding Society*, 7th ed. (Boston: Allyn and

Bacon, 1995), chaps. 1–2 ; Anthony Giddens, *Introduction to Sociology* (New York: Norton, 1991), chap. 1; John Walton, *Sociology and Critical Inquiry: The Work, Tradition, and Purpose,* 2d ed. (Belmont, CA: Wadsworth, 1990); Randall Collins, *Sociological Insight: An Introduction to Non-Obvious Sociology,* 2d ed. (New York: Oxford University Press, 1992); Peter L. Berger, *Invitation to Sociology: A Humanistic Perspective* (Garden City, N.Y.: Doubleday Anchor Books, 1963); and C. Wright Mills, *The Sociological Imagination* (New York: Oxford University Press, 1959).

4. Berger, *Invitation to Sociology,* 121.

5. Reece McGee, *Points of Departure: Basic Concepts in Sociology* (Hinsdale, Ill.: Dryden Press, 1975), x–xi.

6. Marvin E. Olsen, *The Process of Social Organization,* 2d ed. (New York: Holt, Rinehart and Winston, 1978).

7. Berger, *Invitation to Sociology,* 31.

8. For examples of this approach to sport, see the articles appearing in the *Journal of Sport & Exercise Psychology* (Champaign, Ill.: Human Kinetics).

9. Berger, *Invitation to Sociology,* 87.

10. The discussion on institutions is taken from Eitzen and Baca Zinn, *In Conflict and Order,* 41–43.

11. See Harry Edwards, *Sociology of Sport* (Homewood, Ill.: Dorsey, 1973), 84–130.

12. Ibid., 90.

13. Jerome H. Skolnick and Elliott Currie, "Approaches to Social Problems," in *Crisis in American Institutions,* ed. Jerome H. Skolnick and Elliott Currie (Boston: Little, Brown, 1970), 15.

14. Michael Harrington, *Taking Sides* (New York: Holt, Rinehart and Winston, 1985), 1.

15. This description of the functional perspective is taken from Eitzen and Baca Zinn, *In Conflict and Order,* chap. 3. For more detail on the functional perspective, see James H. Frey, "College Athletics: Problems of a Functional Analysis," in *Sport and Social Theory,* eds. C. Roger Rees and Andrew W. Miracle (Champaign, Ill.: Human Kinetics, 1986), 199–209.

16. This description of the conflict perspective is taken from Eitzen and Baca Zinn, *In Conflict and Order,*

chap. 3. For more detail, see D. Stanley Eitzen, "Conflict Theory and the Sociology of Sport," *Arena Review* 8 (November 1984): 45–54; and George H. Sage, *Power and Ideology in American Sport: A Critical Perspective* (Champaign, Ill: Human Kinetics, 1990).

17. This section is taken from Eitzen and Baca Zinn, *In Conflict and Order,* 41–43. It is dependent in part on Jay J. Coakley, *Sport in Society: Issues and Controversies,* 5th ed. (St. Louis: Mosby, 1994), chap. 2.

18. Paul Hoch, *Rip Off the Big Game* (New York: Doubleday, 1972).

19. For summary descriptions and bibliographies of the sociology of sport, see George H. Sage, "Pursuit of Knowledge in the Sociology of Sport: Issues and Prospects," *Quest* 39 (December 1987): 255–81; Jay J. Coakley, "Sociology of Sport in the United States," *International Review of the Sociology of Sport* 22 (1987): 63–79; and James H. Frey and D. Stanley Eitzen, "Sport and Society," *Annual Review of Sociology* 17 (1991): 503–22. For the history of the sociology of sport as a discipline, see John W. Loy, Jr., Gerald S. Kenyon, and Barry D. McPherson, "The Emergence and Development of the Sociology of Sport as an Academic Specialty," *Research Quarterly* 51 (March 1980): 91–109; and *Arena Review* 8 (November 1984), entire issue.

20. See John W. Loy, Jr. and Gerald S. Kenyon, "Frames of Reference: Overview," in *Sport, Culture and Society,* ed. John W. Loy, Jr. and Gerald S. Kenyon (New York: Macmillan, 1969), 9–11; and George H. Sage, "Sport Sociology, Normative and Nonnormative Arguments: Playing the Same Song Over and Over and . . . ," in *Sociology of Sport: Diverse Perspectives,* ed. S. L. Greendorfer and Andrew Yiannakis (West Point, N.Y.: Leisure Press, 1981), 7–14.

21. Hoch, *Rip Off the Big Game.*

22. Harrington, *Taking Sides,* 2.

23. Although we have taken the position that value neutrality is impossible in the social sciences, the issue is not a simple one and has encouraged considerable debate. For a summary of various positions, see George Ritzer, *Sociology: A Multiple Paradigm Science,* rev. ed. (Boston: Allyn and Bacon, 1980), chap. 1.

24. See Howard L. Nixon II, "A Normal Science Imperative for Sport Sociology: Issues of Objectivity, Bias, and Knowing," *Journal of Sport and Social Issues* 18 (August 1994): 249–58; and John C. Phillips, *Sociology of Sport* (Boston: Allyn and Bacon, 1993), chap 2.

25. Robert W. Friedrichs, *A Sociology of Sociology* (New York: Free Press, 1970).

26. For an elaboration of the various sports myths, see Eldon E. Snyder and Elmer Spreitzer, "Basic Assumptions in the World of Sports," *Quest* 24 (summer 1975): 3–9.

27. A strong case has been made for this muckraking approach by Merrill J. Melnick, "A Critical Look at Sociology of Sport," *Quest* 24 (summer 1975): 34–47.

28. Lois Bryson, "Sport and the Maintenance of Masculine Hegemony," *Women's Studies International Forum* 10 (1987): 349–60.

29. Mariah Burton Nelson, *The Stronger Women Get, the More Men Love Football: Sexism and the American Culture of Sports* (New York: Harcourt Brace & Company, 1994), 8.

30. E. M. Swift, "Giving His All," *Sports Illustrated,* 19 December 1994, 88.

31. For elaborate discussions on the differences between play, game, and sport, see Johan Huizinga, *Homo Ludens: A Study of the Play Element in Culture* (Boston: Beacon Press, 1955); Roger Caillois, *Man, Play and Games* (London: Thames and Hudson, 1962); John W. Loy, Jr., "The Nature of Sport: A Definitional Effort," in *Sport in the Socio-Cultural Process,* ed. M. Marie Hart (Dubuque, Iowa: Wm. C. Brown Publishers, 1972), 50–66; Edwards, *Sociology of Sport,* 43–61; John W. Loy, Jr., Barry D. McPherson, and Gerald S. Kenyon, *Sport and Social Systems* (Reading, Mass.: Addison-Wesley, 1978), 3–26; and Allen Guttmann, *From Ritual to Record* (New York: Columbia University Press, 1978), 1–14.

32. Bil Gilbert, "Gleanings from a Troubled Time," *Sports Illustrated,* 25 December 1972, 34–46.

33. John Underwood, *Spoiled Sport* (Boston: Little, Brown, 1984), 151–73.

34. See H. G. Bissinger, *Friday Night Lights: A Town, A Team, and A Dream* (Reading, Mass.: Addison-Wesley, 1990).

35. Gilbert, "Gleanings from a Troubled Time," 34.

Chapter

*Social and Cultural Sources of the Rise
of Sport in North America*

$\mathbf{A}$ main theme of this book is that there is a close relationship between sport and society. It is also our contention that a study of sport based solely on the present will result in an incomplete picture of this cultural practice. The forms of sport in any given society are rooted in historical, social, and cultural traditions and can be understood only through a familiarity with those traditions. Thus one who studies the sociology of sport without studying sport's history will never truly understand the social and cultural forces that underpin contemporary sport. In this chapter we shall briefly examine the changing sociocultural conditions of Canadian-American society over the past four hundred years and attempt to show how these conditions have affected and influenced the rise and current state of North American sport.

The United States and Canada have experienced similar stages of historical development. Each went through a period of British control; each had a period of westward expansion; each experienced a massive influx of immigrants from Europe; and each witnessed urbanization and industrialization during the late nineteenth century. The countries share a common language; they share a border for over three thousand miles, and about 85 percent of the Canadian population lives within one hundred miles of the American-Canadian border. It is hard to imagine any two countries in the world having closer social and cultural ties than Canadians and Americans.[1]

Over the past four centuries, the United States and Canada have grown from a few widely scattered and disunited settlements located along the eastern seaboard of part of North America into two of the most modern and industrially advanced nations in the world. They have also become two of the leading nations in sports. Fostered by a variety of historical, social, and economic conditions, sports have become a major national pastime for the people of both countries. From agrarian societies whose inhabitants had little time for games and sports, except on special occasions, North Americans have become a population of urbanites who watch ten to twenty hours of sports on television each weekend and consider it almost a duty to participate in some form of exercise or sport for recreation. To understand the conditions responsible for this transformation of sport, we must examine the changing sociocultural nature of North America since its European colonization.

Colonial Traditions in North America

Although it seems unimaginable, there were no organized participant or spectator sports during the pre-1800 period in North America. In the first place, people actually had very little leisure time or opportunity to engage in sports. The harsh circumstances of wresting a living from the environment necessitated continual work. Colonists had to devote most of their efforts to basic survival tasks. A second factor restricting sports involvement was the church (the subject of religion and sport is examined more fully in chapter 8). Religion was the most powerful social institution in the North American colonies. Puritanism was prominent in New England, and other Protestant religions dominated social life in the middle and southern colonies.

All of these religious groups placed severe restrictions on play and games, with the Puritans being the most extreme. They directed attacks at almost every form of amusement: dancing for its carnality, boxing for its violence, maypoles for their paganism, and play and games in general because they were often performed on the Sabbath. Moreover, their religious criticisms were closely bound to the dislike for playful activities of any kind. Honest labor was the greatest service to God and a moral duty; any form of play or amusement signaled time-wasting and idleness and was therefore defined as wicked. Everyone having a calling to work hard was a first premise of Puritanism. They believed that it was not leisure and amusement but diligent work that represented glorification of God.

Laws prohibiting a form of social behavior and the actual social customs and actions of a people rarely coincide. In the case of the colonies, religious and legal strictures failed to eliminate the urge to play among the early North Americans. Although frequently done in defiance of local laws, sports such as horse racing, shooting matches, cockfights, footraces, and wrestling matches were engaged in throughout the colonies to break the monotony of life. Moreover, farm festivals in which barn raisings, quilting bees, and cornhusking activities took place also provided occasional amusement and entertainment. The most popular sports of the colonial gentry were cockfighting, hunting, dancing, and most popular of all, horse racing. Other recreational activities were popular for those who frequented the taverns. The tavern was a social center, primarily for drinking but also for all manner of popular pastimes, such as cards, billiards, bowling, and rifle and pistol shooting.[2]

As colonial settlement moved west into the hinterland in the eighteenth century, religious restrictions against sport were rather ineffective. Men and women in the backcountry enjoyed a variety of competitive events when they met at barbecues and camp meetings. They gambled on these contests, especially horse races, cockfights, and bearbaiting. The sports and games that marked these infrequent social gatherings were typically rough and brutal. Two popular activities were fistfights, which ended when one man could not continue, and wrestling, in which eye gouging and bone-breaking holds were permitted.[3] Horse racing was the most universal sport on the frontier, for every owner of a horse was confident of its prowess and eager to match it against others. Both men and women were skillful riders. The other constant companion of the frontiersman, his rifle, engendered a pride in marksmanship, and shooting matches were a common form of competition.[4]

The Early Nineteenth Century: Early Industrialization and Technology

The major catalyst for the transformation of North American sport was a series of inventions in England in the late eighteenth century that completely changed the means by which goods were produced. These inventions made possible technological advances that ushered in two of the most important developments in human history—the industrial revolution and the technological revolution.

The major characteristic and social consequence of the industrial revolution was the factory system. The initial impact was seen in the textile industry. The spinning of thread and the weaving of cloth had traditionally been done at home on spinning wheels and hand looms, but new methods for performing these tasks enabled them to be done in factories by power-driven machinery. By 1820 the Lowell loom had been developed, making possible the spinning and weaving of cotton in the same factory. The sewing machine of Elias Howe revolutionized the making of clothes, shoes, and various leather goods.

Other industries emerged. The successful smelting of iron with the aid of anthracite coal was perfected around 1830; by 1850 improved methods of making steel had been developed. Steel production was the backbone of industrial development because the machinery for factories was primarily made from steel. Moreover, the rapidly growing railroad system depended on steel for track and for railcars.

Artisans and craftspersons were transformed into an industrial workforce. As figure 2.1 shows, the proportion of the workers engaged in agriculture steadily decreased from approximately 90 percent in 1800, to 40 percent in 1900, to less than 10 percent in 1990. Industry needed a plentiful supply of labor located near plants and factories, so population shifts from rural to urban areas began to change population characteristics and needs.[5] Urbanization created a need for new forms of recreational activities, and industrialization gradually supplied the standard of living and the leisure time necessary to support broad-based forms of recreation and organized sport.

Sport in the Early Nineteenth Century: Building a Framework for Modern Sport

In the first few decades of the nineteenth century, North Americans enjoyed essentially the same recreations and sports as they had during the colonial period. Those turbulent, expansive years brought important changes though, and an increasing number of early nineteenth century North Americans found time for amusements and sport.

As conditions changed from rural to an urban population and from home trades and individualized

Figure 2.1 Percentage of labor force in agriculture

Source: U.S. Bureau of the Census, *Historical Statistics of the U.S., Colonial Times to 1970,* Bicentennial ed., Parts I and II. Washington, D.C., 1975; and U.S. Bureau of the Census, *Statistical Abstract of the United States: 1990.* Washington, D.C., 1990.

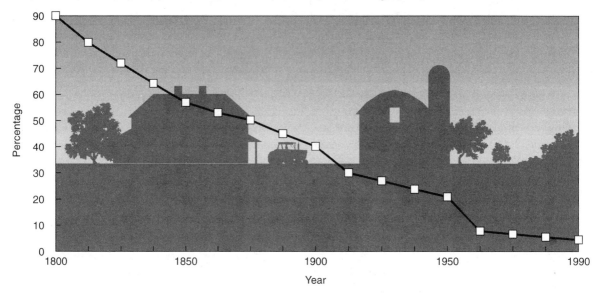

occupations to large-scale industrial production, a growing interest emerged in spectator sports, especially rowing, prizefighting, footracing (the runners were called pedestrians), and similar activities; but the sport that excited the most interest was horse racing. With its traditions going back to early colonial days, horse racing was the favorite of the popular spectator sports. In May of 1823 a horse race between Eclipse and Sir Henry attracted one of the largest crowds ever to witness a nineteenth-century sporting event in North America. A crowd estimated at seventy-five thousand overwhelmed the race course. Thoroughbred racing was not the only popular form of horse racing. It has been claimed that harness racing was the first modern sport in North America.[6]

Horse racing was much in demand in Canada. In *Canada's Sporting Heroes,* S. F. Wise and Douglas Fisher described its popularity in Quebec. "Almost from the outset of British rule in 1763 French Canadians took readily to . . . horse racing. . . . By 1829, interest was so great that special boat trips were laid on to bring Montrealers to Quebec for the races, and the Montreal newspaper *La Minerve* held its presses in order to bring

its readers the latest results. . . . By the 1850s . . . regular race meetings were held in forty towns and villages throughout the province. . . ."[7]

Native American, French, and British traditions contributed to Canada's other sporting interests in the early nineteenth century. Native American games of lacrosse, snowshoeing, and canoe activities were adopted by the settlers. British and French settlers also took enthusiastically to physical activities that could be played in the cold northern climate, so sleighing, ice skating, and curling were popular in the winter, while hunting, fishing, fox hunting, and horse racing were popular in the short Canadian summers.[8]

The enthusiasm for horse racing in early nineteenth century North America is illustrated by the song "Camptown Races," published in 1850 by Stephen Foster, one of America's most famous composers. This was the first North American song of enduring popularity composed around a sporting theme. The lyrics end, "I'll bet my money on da bobtail nag. Somebody bet on da bay."

The transformation from occasional and informal sport to highly organized commercial spectator sport began for both countries in the period before the U.S. Civil War. Thus, the framework of modern sport was established during the first half of the nineteenth century, setting the stage for the remarkable developments in mass popular sport and professional sport in the last half of the century.

The Technological Revolution and Sport

One of the most significant forces to transform sport from informal village festivals to highly organized sports was the technological revolution. Beginning in the early nineteenth century, technological advances made possible the large-scale manufacturing that is characteristic of industrialization. Through technology, the practical application of science to industry, many kinds of machines, labor-saving devices, and scientific processes were invented or perfected. Of course, the technological revolution was only one of the determining factors in the rise of modern sport, but ignoring its influence would result merely in superficial understanding of contemporary sport forms.

Transportation

One area in which technological innovation had an enormous impact on the rise of sport was transportation. Travel of any kind was difficult and slow in the pre-1800 period. A distance that today takes hours to travel took more than the same number of days in those times. Modes of transportation were limited to foot, horse, and boat. Roads, when they existed, were primitive, dangerous, and often blocked by almost impassable rivers.

The first notable technological breakthrough in transportation came in the early nineteenth century with the development of the steam engine. This invention and its use on boats made it possible to fully develop river traffic. The first successful steamboat in North America, the Clermont, was built by Robert Fulton, and in 1807 it chugged 150 miles up the Hudson River from New York to Albany in about thirty hours. In time, steamboats stimulated the building of canals and the enlarging of rivers, thus opening new areas that had previously been isolated and cut off from commerce and trade.

The steamboat did not solve all the transportation problems; river travel was of no help to people who did not happen to live near large rivers. Furthermore, it was not a particularly fast mode of transportation because the large steamers sometimes had to thread their way carefully through very narrow or shallow water. A new form of transportation began to compete with river transportation about the time that canal building reached its peak. This was the railroad. A fourteen-mile stretch of the Baltimore and Ohio Railroad was opened in 1830. Railroad construction expanded rapidly—mostly short lines connecting principal cities—and by 1840 nearly three thousand miles of track were in use in the United States.

It was the steamboats and railroads of the antebellum era that had the first significant impact on nineteenth-century sport. As one of the first products of the age of steam, steamboats served as carriers of thoroughbred horses to such horse racing centers as Vicksburg, Natchez, and New Orleans, all located along the Mississippi River. Crowds attending horse races or prizefights were frequently conveyed to the site of the events via steamboats. The riverboats on the Mississippi and the St. Lawrence also served as carriers of racing or prize fight news up and down the river valleys.

More important to the development of organized sport was the railroad. In the years preceding the Civil War, the widespread interest in thoroughbred and harness races was in great part nurtured by railroad expansion, as horses and crowds were transported from one locality to another. Similarly, participants and spectators for prizefights and footraces were commonly carried to the sites of competition by rail. Scheduling the fights where they would not be disrupted by the authorities frequently became necessary because prizefighting was outlawed in many cities. This meant that spectators often had to use the railroad to get to the site of the bout.

Communication

As important as transportation was to the rise of North American sport, the new forms of communications over the past century and a half have been equally significant. The invention and development of the telegraph was the most important advance in communication during the first half of the nineteenth century. Samuel F. B. Morse perfected an electrical instrument by which combinations of dots and dashes could be transmitted along a wire, and the first telegraph line was built between Baltimore and Washington, D.C. in 1844. Morse transmitted the message, "What hath God wrought?" and thereby started a new era in communication. Soon telegraph lines stretched between all the principal cities, and by 1860 some fifty thousand miles of line existed east of the Rockies. Meanwhile, Western Union was extending its lines to the Pacific coast, putting the Pony Express out of business a little more than a year after it was founded.

From its invention in 1844, the telegraph rapidly assumed a significant role in the dissemination of sport news because newspapers and periodicals installed telegraphic apparatus in their offices. Only two years after its invention, the *New York Herald* and the *New York Tribune* had telegraphic equipment. By 1850 horse races, prizefights, and yachting events were being reported over the wires.

Simultaneous with the development of the telegraph, a revolution in the dissemination of news occurred with improvements in printing presses and in other processes of newspaper and journal production. The telegraph and the improved press opened the gates to a rising tide of sports journalism, but the journalistic exploitation of sports did not actually take off until the decade following the Civil War.

While advances in electrical forms of communication were instrumental in the rise of sport, other communications media supplemented and extended sport publicity. In the early years of the nineteenth century, sports were more directly aided by magazine and book publishers than they were by newspapers. However, the rise of sports journalism was closely tied to new inventions in printing processes, as well as to the telegraph network that spanned the continent in the mid-1800s. As early as the 1830s, several of the largest newspapers were giving extensive coverage to prizefights, footraces, horse races, and other sports. What was perhaps the most notable newspaper concerned with sports in the United States appeared in 1831 and survived until 1901. The paper was called the *Spirit of the Times*.[9]

The Latter Nineteenth Century: The Beginnings of Modern Society

Before 1850 U.S. industry had been largely concentrated in New England and the mid-Atlantic states, but by 1900 industrialization and manufacturing spread out to all parts of the country. Industry began to move westward. New industries were created. The meat-packing industry developed in Chicago and Kansas City, and in the plains states the production of wood products became prominent.

Before the Civil War in the United States, factories were small. The most common forms of business organization were partnerships, owned by two or more individuals, and proprietorships, in which a single person owned the entire business. As the factory system took root, however, a capitalistic class began to emerge, and a new form of business ownership, the corporation, became the dominant form of organization. By the 1890s, corporations produced nearly three-fourths of the total value of manufactured products in the United States.

The large corporations developed mass-production methods and mass sales, the bases of big business, because of the huge amounts of money that they controlled. They were also able to drive out small businesses and acquire control over the production and the price of goods and services in a given field of business. For example, by 1880 the Standard Oil Company controlled 90 percent of the country's petroleum business. When the U.S. Steel Corporation was founded near the turn of the century, it controlled some 60 percent of the iron and steel production of the nation, from the mining of the ore to the distribution of the finished products.[10]

Meanwhile, the conflict over control of the vast Canadian expanse of the continent, which had remained unresolved throughout the sixteenth, seventeenth, and eighteenth centuries, was finally settled with the Confederation of Canadian Provinces in 1867. Canada became the first federal union in the British empire, and the latter half of the nineteenth century was a period of consolidation of provinces within the union. Canadian industrialization was proceeding along a similar trajectory.

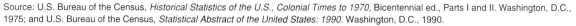

Figure 2.2 Percentage of U.S. population in urban areas

Source: U.S. Bureau of the Census, *Historical Statistics of the U.S., Colonial Times to 1970*, Bicentennial ed., Parts I and II. Washington, D.C., 1975; and U.S. Bureau of the Census, *Statistical Abstract of the United States: 1990.* Washington, D.C., 1990.

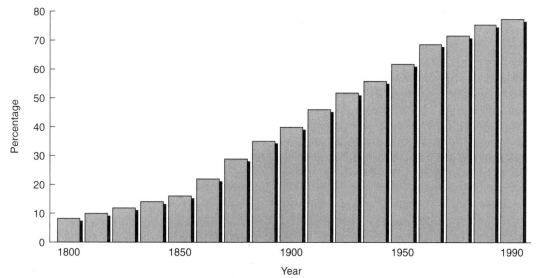

At the time of Confederation, manufacturing in Canada was still primarily of a local handicraft nature requiring very little capital, and much of the trade was based on farming, fishing, and timber products. Beginning in the 1870s, though Canadian manufacturing received an impetus from the new industrial revolution of steel and railroads. Moreover, advanced technology, corporate organization, and low-cost transport fostered a unified market and a factory system of specialized mass production to serve it.

As technology increased the means of industrial production in North America, more and more people gave up farming and came to the cities to work in the factories and offices. They were joined by a seemingly endless stream of immigrants who sought a better life in North America. Factories multiplied, and towns and cities grew rapidly. The first United States census, completed in 1790, recorded a population of nearly 4 million, about 6 percent of whom were classified as urban; by 1900 the population had risen to 76 million, with some 40 percent living in urban areas.

Figure 2.2 shows the pattern of growth in urban population. Chicago's population tripled between 1880 and 1900, and Boston's increased threefold—from 177,840 to 560,892—between 1860 and 1900. From 1860 to 1910 the number of U.S. cities with populations over 100,000 increased from nine to fifty. The 1871 census of Canada reported that there were only twenty communities with over 5,000 residents; by 1901 there were sixty-two, and twenty-four of those had a population of over 10,000.[11]

The Latter Nineteenth Century: The Rise of Modern Sport Forms

The gathering storm of dissension over slavery in the southern United States eventually erupted into civil war in 1861. Although the war momentarily slowed the growth of sporting practices, the stimulus it gave to manufacturing and industrial expansion served as the economic foundation for subsequent rapid advances in sport in the latter part of the nineteenth century.

Urbanization

Urban influences on the world of sport made their appearance in the mid-nineteenth century. By 1860 the increasing concentration of city populations and the monotonous and wearisome repetition of industrial work created a demand for more recreational outlets. Urbanization created favorable conditions for commercialized spectator sports, while industrialization gradually provided the leisure time and standard of living so crucial to the growth and development of all forms of recreation.[12]

Towns and cities were natural centers for organizing sports. The popular sport of horse racing centered in New York, Boston, Charleston, Louisville, and New Orleans, and the first organized baseball clubs were founded in such communities as New York, Boston, Chicago, St. Louis, and Toronto. Yachting and rowing regattas, footraces, billiard matches, and even the main agricultural fairs were held in or near the larger cities.[13]

Diffusion of Sport from the Upper to the Lower Classes

No transformation in the recreational and sport scene was more startling than the sudden spread of sporting activities from the wealthy class into the upper-middle, the middle, and even the working class. Millionaires pursued horse racing, yachting, lawn tennis, and golf. Working women and young ladies of the middle class turned to rowing and cycling, and the working class played pool, fished, hunted, backed their favorite boxers, and gradually tried their hands at the sports of the affluent classes.

Wealthy farmers, plantation owners, and businessmen were highly influential in stimulating public interest in such sports as cricket, yachting, fox hunting, and horse racing and trotting. In the southern United States, the seasonal nature of the crops permitted recreation in the lull periods of each year, and the slack seasons were spent enjoying a wide variety of sports activities. Northern gentlemen, affluent from commercial or manufacturing interests, also turned to various sports.

During the latter half of the nineteenth century people tried to adapt to the new urban-industrial society by forming subcommunities based on status. One type of status community was the athletic club, formed by younger, wealthy men who shared a common interest in sports. The private clubs were a major stimulus to the growth of yachting, baseball, lawn tennis, golf, track and field, and country clubs.[14] Essentially the same pattern of upper-class promotion of organized sport through social elite sports clubs existed in Canada.[15] Thus, members of the social elite in both the United States and Canada deserve much credit for early sporting promotion and patronage.

New sports introduced by the wealthy were often adopted by the working class. Baseball is a classic example of this pattern. From an informal children's game played throughout the eighteenth century, baseball developed codified rules in the 1840s, and groups of upper-social-class men organized clubs, taking care to keep out lower-social-class persons. The first of these baseball clubs, the Knickerbockers of New York, was primarily a social club with a distinctly upper-class flavor; it was similar to the country clubs of the 1920s and 1930s before they became popular with the middle class. A baseball game for members of the Knickerbockers, was a genteel amateur recreational pursuit, with an emphasis on polite social interactions rather than an all-out quest for victory.[16]

The Civil War wiped out this upper-class patronage of the game, and a broad base of popularity existed in 1869 when the first professional baseball team, the Cincinnati Red Stockings, was formed. This was followed in 1876 by the organization of the first major league, and baseball became firmly entrenched as the national pastime by the end of the century.

Baseball attracted the interest of Canadians as well, and by 1859, Torontonians had begun playing the game, spurring an expansion of play to other cities. In the mid-1880s clubs from Toronto, Hamilton, London, and Guelph had formed Canada's first professional baseball league. By the end of the nineteenth century, baseball play in Canada was solidly embedded in Canada's sporting culture.[17] At about the same time, ice hockey, which was to become Canada's national pastime, was making its own early history. It seems to have been played in its earliest unorganized form in the mid-1850s, but the first public showing of the game took place in 1875.[18] Ice hockey quickly became a favorite sport of Canadians.

As cities grew, an element of the population that journalists referred to as "rabble" and "rowdies" stimulated organized sports interest. Wherever sports events were held, this group could be found gambling on the outcome and generally raising the emotional atmosphere of the event by wildly cheering their favorites and booing or attempting to disconcert those whom they had bet against. Although sports organizers publicly condemned the actions of this unruly element, they secretly spurred them on because this group often helped insure the financial success of sporting events.

The Role of Immigrants

Immigrants also contributed to the rise of sport in a variety of ways. First, many immigrants settled in the cities and became a part of that urban population who sought excitement through sport and recreation as an antidote to the typically dull and monotonous jobs they held. Second, since a great many of these mid-nineteenth-century immigrants did not possess the strict religious attitudes toward play and sport of the fundamental Protestant sects, they freely enjoyed and participated in sports of all kinds. Third, the immigrants brought their games and sports with them to North America. Cricket, horse racing, and rowing were widely popular with the British immigrants. The Germans brought their love for lawn bowling and gymnastics. German turnverein (gymnastic clubs) were opened wherever Germans settled; by the time of the Civil War, there were approximately 150 American turnverein with some ten thousand members.[19] In Canada in 1859, German migrants had organized a turnverein in what is now Kitchener, and a Turner Association with forty members was active in Toronto in 1861. The Scots pioneered in introducing track and field sports to North America with their annual Caledonian games. In a definitive study, Gerald Redmond quite convincingly showed that the "emigrant Scots" were a dominant force in the development of Canadian sport in the nineteenth century.[20] The Irish seemed to have a particular affinity for the prize ring, and some of the most famous nineteenth-century boxers in North America were immigrants from Ireland. Two Irish-American boxing champions, John L. Sullivan and James J. Corbett, were among the most popular sports heroes of the century.

Muscular Christianity and Intellectuals

The grasp of religion on the mid-nineteenth-century mind was so strong and conservative that sport could penetrate only the periphery of social life. Reaction to the Puritan belief that pleasure was the companion of sin emerged, however, when liberal and humanitarian reform became a major concern. One aspect of the social reform movement was the effort to improve the physical health of the population. The crusaders noted that a great deal of human misery was the result of poor health, and they believed that people would be happier and more productive if they engaged in sport to promote physical fitness and enhance leisure.

Leaders in what became known as the "Muscular Christianity Movement" were highly respected persons, willing to risk their positions and reputations on behalf of exercise and sport. Beecher family members, famous for their Christian reform positions, were among the active crusaders for exercise and sport. Catharine Beecher wrote a book in 1832 entitled *Course of Calisthenics for Young Ladies,* but her most influential book was *A Manual of Physiology and Calisthenics for Schools and Families,* published in 1856. This book not only advocated physical exercise for girls as well as for boys but also promoted the introduction of physical education into American schools.

Support for physical activity came from other respected persons as well. Noted author Oliver Wendell Holmes was "convinced that greater participation in sport would improve everything in American life from sermons of the clergy to the physical well-being of individuals." Equally vigorous in his advocacy of sport was the renowned Ralph Waldo Emerson, and his status in the intellectual community served to increase the impact of his support. The combined attention of the clergy, social reformers, and intellectuals to the need for physical fitness and wholesome leisure had a favorable effect upon public attitudes because sport suddenly became important to many people, especially the young, who had previously shunned it.[21]

The Beginnings of Intercollegiate Athletics

Intercollegiate athletics began in the United States in 1852 with a rowing match between Harvard and Yale, but it was not until the 1870s and 1880s that intercollegiate sports became an established part of higher education and contributed to the enthusiasm for athletic and sporting diversions. From a spectator standpoint, football became extremely popular. During this era, football was a sport for the affluent classes rather than for the masses because it largely reflected the interests of the college students and alumni; the pigskin game, nevertheless, did develop into a national sport by 1900.[22]

After students organized teams, collegiate sports revolutionized campus life, serving as a major source of physical activity for many students and a significant source of entertainment for other students, alumni, and the general public. In the United States, intercollegiate athletics gradually became more than merely a demonstration of physical skills between rival institutions. The students, alumni, and public began to regard victory as the measure of a college's prestige. Campus and commercial editors increased their coverage, and sports events became featured items in newspapers and magazines. As a result, this increased coverage focused attention on winning and made contest results appear to be an index of an institution's merit.[23]

Thus, a belief emerged throughout American colleges that winning teams favorably advertised the school, attracted prospective students, enhanced alumni contributions, and in the case of state-supported universities, increased appropriations from the state legislature. The notion that successful teams brought renown to the college (and to its president) must surely have been in the mind of University of Chicago President William Rainey Harper when he hired Yale All-American Amos Alonzo Stagg in 1890. He asked Stagg to "develop teams which we can send around the country and knock out all the other colleges. We will give them," wrote Harper, "a palace car and a vacation too."[24]

Technological Innovation and Sport: Transportation

The growth of the railroad industry continued throughout the latter part of the nineteenth century. By 1860 more than thirty thousand miles of track carried about two-thirds of the internal trade of the country. It was,

however, the decade just after the Civil War that witnessed the completion of a transcontinental line. In 1869 the Central Pacific and Union Pacific workers laid the final rail to complete the first transcontinental line. Other lines followed in the latter three decades of the 1800s. Similar events were occurring in Canada. In November 1885 the transcontinental Canadian Pacific Railway was completed.

The railroad played an instrumental role in staging the first intercollegiate athletic event, a rowing race between Harvard and Yale. According to sport historian, Ronald A. Smith, "the offer by a railroad superintendent to transport and house the crews of the two most prestigious colleges [Harvard and Yale] at a vacation spot over a hundred miles from the Cambridge campus and nearly twice that distance from New Haven was the beginning of . . . college sport in America."[25] The offer was accepted, and the Boston, Concord, and Montreal Railroad transported the participants and fans to New Hampshire's Lake Winnipesaukee for the event.

In 1869 the first intercollegiate football game between Rutgers and Princeton was attended by students riding a train pulled by a "jerky little engine [that] . . . steamed out of Princeton, New Jersey, on the memorable morning of November 6, 1869." The historic McGill-Harvard football match of 1870, which pitted a Canadian university against a North American university, would not have been played without the convenience of railway transportation. Throughout the final decades of the nineteenth century, intercollegiate athletic teams depended upon the railroad to transport teams and supporters to football, baseball, and rowing events, as well as to other collegiate athletic contests.

The fledgling professional baseball clubs made use of the rapidly expanding railroad network in the 1870s, and the organization of the National League in 1876 became possible primarily because of the continued development of connecting lines. As major league baseball developed, the formation of teams followed the network of rail lines, a pattern that remained basically undisturbed until the late 1950s when teams began to travel by air.

Many other sporting pursuits were fostered by railroad development after 1865. Widespread interest in thoroughbred and trotting racing was in large part sustained by the expansion of the railway system. Interregional races became possible, and horses and spectators were carried from all over the country to track races. Realizing the financial advantage of encouraging horse racing, many railroads transported horses at reduced prices. The rail lines capitalized on public interest in prizefighting, too, despite its illegality, and frequently scheduled excursion trains for important bouts. The popularity of America's first heavyweight champion, John L. Sullivan, was acquired by his train tours to various parts of the country.

The role played by the railroads in the promotion of sport in the United States was being duplicated in Canada. According to one sport historian, "The Canadian Pacific Railway company had a special interest in the Montreal Baseball Club and offered full exemption for team managers, and special half-fare rates to teams willing to play the club. . . . The popularity of rowing was [also] encouraged by the railroads as there were many generous concessions granted to rowing enthusiasts."[26]

Technological Innovation and Sport: Communication

The Atlantic cable, successfully laid in 1866 by Cyrus Field, did for intercontinental news what the telegraph had done for national communication. The cable reduced the time necessary to send a message between Europe and North America from ten days (by steamship) to a moment or so. This advance in communication was a boon to sports enthusiasts, for it overcame the frustration of having to wait two or three weeks to get sports results from England and Europe. In 1869, when the Harvard crew traveled to England to row against Oxford on the Thames River, enormous national interest centered on the match. Along the sidewalks in New York, the Harvard-Oxford race was the main topic of conversation. The results of the race were "flashed through the Atlantic cable as to reach New York about a quarter past one, while the news reached the Pacific Coast about nine-o'clock, enabling many of the San Franciscans to discuss the subject at their breakfast tables, and swallow the defeat with their coffee."[27] All this was the culmination of a campaign in transatlantic news coverage that began months earlier and served as the first real test of the Atlantic cable. The combination of telegraph and Atlantic cable aroused great interest in international sport.

The major communications breakthrough in the latter part of the nineteenth century was the telephone, which was first exhibited at the Centennial Exposition in Philadelphia in 1876. There, Alexander Graham Bell demonstrated that an electrical instrument could transmit the human voice. Although at first most people thought of the telephone as a plaything, business and industrial leaders saw its possibilities for maintaining communication with their far-flung interests. In 1900 there were slightly more than 1 million telephones in use; today there are hundreds of millions. With less than 8 percent of the world's population, the United States and Canada possess more than half the world's telephones.

Newspapers were one of the first businesses to make extensive use of telephone service, and the sports departments founded by many of the newspapers in the last two decades of the nineteenth century depended on the telephone to obtain the results of sports events. By the end of the century, the telephone was an indispensable part of sports journalism.

The expansion of sports journalism in the latter three decades of the nineteenth century related not only to the universal use of telegraphy by publishers, which made possible instantaneous reporting of sports events, but also to the realization by editors of the popular interest in sports. Indeed, sport emerged as such a standard topic of conversation that newspapers and magazines extended their coverage of it in the 1880s and 1890s. At the same time, the number of United States newspapers increased sixfold between 1870 and 1900 (from 387 to 2,326), and their combined circulation rose from 3.5 million to 15 million. Publishers and editors recognized the growing interest in sport and began to cater to it to win large circulations. New York papers such as the *Herald,* the *Sun,* and the *World* devoted enough attention to sports that a new form of reporter, the sports journalist, emerged. It remained, however, for William Randolph Hearst to develop the first sports section for his paper, the *New York Journal.*[28]

The publication of various kinds of books about sports increased in the mid-nineteenth century, too. Athletic almanacs and dime novels extolling the exploits of athletes and sportsmen grew in popularity. Two books by Thomas Hughes, *Tom Brown at Rugby* and *Tom Brown at Oxford,* were responsible for a rising desire for sports fiction. In 1896 Gilbert Patten began pouring out a story a week of the heroic achievements of a fictional athlete by the name of Frank Merriwell to meet the demand for boys' sports stories. Before he was through, Patten had produced 208 titles, which sold an estimated 25 million copies.[29]

Other Technological Breakthroughs and Sport

Other technological advances had a marked, though perhaps less obvious, influence on the transformation of sport. Improvements in photography developed rapidly in the years following the Civil War, as cumbersome equipment was replaced by the more mobile Eastman Kodak, which also produced clearer pictures. Indeed, sport played an important role in the early development and popularization of the camera. In 1872 Eadweard Muybridge, with the prodding of Leland Stanford, made the first successful attempt to record the illusion of motion by photography. He was interested in discovering whether a trotting horse left the ground entirely at some point in its gait (it does). By setting up a battery of cameras that went off sequentially, he successfully photographed the movements of the horse. The clarity of these pictures led Muybridge to realize that his technique could be extended to analyze the movements of all kinds of species. He subsequently photographed a host of walking and running animals. His monumental eleven-volume study entitled *Animal Locomotion* (1887) included thousands of pictures of horses, birds, and even human athletes. Other experimenters gradually perfected the techniques that gave birth to the true motion picture.

We have already described how advances in the use of electricity led to important developments in communication, but the use of electricity to produce light had an equally significant impact on sport. When Thomas A. Edison invented the incandescent bulb in 1879, he inaugurated a new era in the social life of North Americans. With the invention of the light bulb, sports events for the first time could be held at night. Within a few years, electric lighting and more comfortable accommodations helped lure athletes and spectators into school and college gymnasiums and into public arenas and stadiums. Prizefights, walking contests, horse shows, wrestling matches, basketball games, ice hockey games, curling matches, and other sports began to be held indoors in lighted facilities. Madison Square Garden in New York City had electric lights by the mid-1880s (the current Madison Square Garden is its third incarnation), where they were used for a variety of sports events. Much of the appeal of indoor sporting events was directly attributed to the transformation that electric lighting made in the night life of the cities.

One final example of the part an invention has played in sport is the vulcanization of rubber by Charles Goodyear in the 1830s. It eventually influenced equipment and apparel in every sport. Elastic and resilient rubber balls changed the nature of every sport in which they were used; equipment made with rubber altered many tactics and techniques. The pneumatic tire developed in the 1880s revolutionized cycling and harness racing in the following decade, and it played a vital role in the rise and spectacular appeal of auto racing.

Equipment to Play Modern Sports

Modern sports are dependent upon inexpensive and dependable equipment for their popularity. Mass production of goods and corporate organization developed in sport just as they did in other industries. Although the manufacturing and merchandising of sporting goods were still in the pioneer stage of development in the late nineteenth century, much of the growing popularity of sport and outdoor recreation was due to the standardized manufacture of bicycles, billiard tables, baseball equipment, sporting rifles, fishing rods, and numerous other items.

The first major sporting goods corporation was formed in 1876 by Albert G. Spalding, a former pitcher for the Boston and Chicago baseball clubs. Beginning with baseball equipment, he branched out into various sports. By the end of the century the A. G. Spalding and Brothers Company had a virtual monopoly in athletic goods. Department stores, led by Macy's of New York City, began carrying sporting goods on a large scale around the early 1880s. Sears, Roebuck devoted eighty pages of its 1895 catalog to sporting equipment.[30]

With the rising popularity of numerous sports in the twentieth century, with advances in technology making possible the introduction of newer and better equipment, and finally with improved manufacturing and distribution methods, the sporting goods industry has become a multimillion-dollar-a-year industry. Several large corporations control a major portion of the business, but with the proliferation of sports, many small companies as well produce a variety of sports equipment.

Social Philosophy and Modern Sport

The profound changes in interpersonal relations created by the technological and industrial revolutions required that moral and social justifications be sought for the role of capitalism in human affairs. The captains of industry found their chief justification in two related ideas, the gospel of wealth and social Darwinism. According to the gospel of wealth, money and success are the just rewards of industry, thrift, and sobriety; the mass of humanity remains poor because of their own laziness and natural inferiority. Government, according to this notion, should merely preserve order and protect property; it should leave control over the economy to the natural aristocracy, who had won and held their leadership in competitive struggle.

Social Darwinism, probably the most important social philosophy in the latter third of the nineteenth century, supplied a biological explanation for the gospel of wealth. As an integrated philosophy, it was largely the product of the fertile mind of the British sociologist Herbert Spencer. Spencer was profoundly impressed by Charles Darwin's findings in the field of biology, and he constructed his system on the principles of the survival of the fittest. Darwin had reported that in the animal world an ongoing, fierce struggle for survival destroys the

weak, rewards the strong, and produces evolutionary change. Struggle, destruction, and the survival of the fit, Spencer argued, were essential to progress in human societies as well. The weak threaten the road to progress and deserve to perish. The strong survive because they are superior. Although social Darwinism repudiated the humane and Christian principles on which democratic tradition rested, Spencer's theories had great popularity and markedly penetrated North American thought. This was the case for several reasons but perhaps chiefly because social Darwinism was made to order to suit the needs of the ruling business interests. It justified the "success ethic" in the name of progress; it justified economic warfare, poverty, exploitation, and suffering as the survival of the fittest.[31]

The chief North American expositor of Social Darwinism was William Graham Sumner, who in 1875 at Yale taught one of the first sociology courses in North America. Sumner based his sociology on the notion that human life encounters formidable obstacles and threats to its survival. There is a fundamental struggle to "win" (a favorite word of Sumner's) under the conditions imposed by nature. In this process humans always compete with others. Sumner argued, "Every man who stands on the earth's surface excludes every one else from so much of it as he covers; every one who eats a loaf of bread appropriates to himself for the time being the exclusive use and enjoyment of so many square feet of the earth's surface as were required to raise the wheat."[32]

Sumner linked competition to the emergence of virtues, such as those of perseverance and hard work, that were presumed to be answers to the struggle against nature. Winning was seen as the just reward of the superior individual; losing was viewed as the overt manifestation of inferiority.

The actual extent to which Social Darwinism became a part of North American sport is debatable, but a number of observers have noted that the rise of highly organized sport coincided with the emergent popularity of Social Darwinism and that the high degree of emphasis on winning games demonstrated in North American sport is an orientation congruent with this social philosophy. American football players often remark that success in their sport is like "the law of the jungle" or "the survival of the fittest." Similar opinions about ice hockey are sometimes expressed by Canadian hockey players.

The Twentieth Century: The Modern World

The United States witnessed a veritable population explosion in the twentieth century, with a population in excess of 265 million and an urban population of around 83 percent of the total. Canada experienced a similar trend. In 1867 its population was approximately 3.5 million, with less than 20 percent living in towns and cities; in the 1990s Canada had a population of over 27 million, more than 60 percent of whom were urbanites.

The concentration of large groups of people in towns that soon would become thriving cities made it possible for sport to be transformed from informal and spontaneous events to organized, highly competitive activities. In other words, industrialization and urbanization were major contributors to the rise of sport, greatly enhanced, of course, by the revolutionary transformations in communication, transportation, and other technological advances.

In the twentieth century the corporate form of business expanded and extended into virtually every form of goods and service operation. In 1995 the two hundred largest industrial corporations in the United States controlled over 64 percent of the total assets held by all manufacturing corporations.[33] Some economists called the twentieth century the "century of the corporation."

The Twentieth Century: The Maturing of Modern Sport

The final three decades of the nineteenth century saw the rising tide of sports begin to take a place in the lives of North Americans, but it was in the first thirty years of the twentieth century that the athletic spirit became a prominent part of the social life of large numbers of people. Between the 1890s and World War II, sport became the most pervasive popular cultural practice in North America.[34]

Urban areas fostered sport through better transportation facilities, a growing affluent class, a higher standard of living, more discretionary funds for purchasing sporting equipment, and the ease with which leagues and teams could be organized. The wealthy were no longer the only people with the leisure and the means to enjoy recreational pursuits. Working-class persons gradually won shorter working hours and higher wages, enabling them to spend larger sums of money on entertainment, one form of which was sport. Thus, sport discarded its aristocratic trappings and rapidly emerged as a popular form of entertainment and recreation. James Bryce, a British observer of North American life in 1905, wrote, "[Sport] occupies the minds not only of the youth at the universities, but also of their parents and of the general public. Baseball matches and football matches excite an interest greater than any other public events except the Presidential election, and that comes only once in four years. . . . The American love of excitement and love of competition has seized upon these games."[35]

No single event heralded the beginning of what has been designated as the era of modern sports, but the Roaring Twenties acted as a bridge connecting the old pastimes to contemporary sport. Sport seemed to be the most engrossing of all social interests in the 1920s; it became a bandwagon around which rallied students and alumni, business and transportation interests, advertising and amusement industries, cartoonists and artists, novelists and sports columnists. Indeed, the 1920s are still looked upon by some sport historians as sport's golden age. Some of America's most famous athletes rose to prominence during those years: Babe Ruth, the "Sultan of Swat"; Knute Rockne and the "Four Horsemen of Notre Dame"; Jack Dempsey, heavyweight boxing champion; Bill Tilden and Helen Willis Moody in tennis; and Bobby Jones and Glenna Collett in golf. In Canada, Howie Morenz, James Ball, and Ethel Catherwood thrilled the masses with their achievements. These are only a few of the coaches and athletes who contributed to the growing popularity of sports.[36]

From the 1920s onward, sport became a pervasive part of North American life, penetrating into every level of the educational systems and into the programs of social agencies and private clubs. This has become especially true of the business world; sport affects such areas of the economic system as finance, fashion, mass media, transportation, communication, advertising, the sporting goods industry, and a variety of marginal enterprises that profit from sport.

North American business and labor organizations contributed to the rise of sport through organized industrial recreation programs for millions of workers. During the nineteenth century most industrial leaders showed little interest in the health and welfare of their employees; by the beginning of this century, however, voices inside and outside industry were pleading for consideration of the worker as a human being, with special focus on the worker's physical and mental health. Business and labor leaders began to realize that perhaps opportunities for diversion, whether in intellectual or recreational directions, might enhance employee health and morale and increase productivity. The idea of providing company-sponsored recreation as a phase of business management caught on, and programs of all sorts came into existence. In 1913 a United States Bureau of Labor Statistics survey found that half of the companies surveyed had some form of recreation program for their employees. A similar survey of 319 companies in 1927 found that 157 maintained baseball diamonds or athletic fields; 50 had tennis courts; 13 had established golf courses; 223 sponsored baseball teams; and 41 had soccer teams. By the 1950s some 20,000 companies were sponsoring various forms of industrial recreation with more than 20 million employees participating.[37] From 1930 to 1950, the best amateur teams in basketball, baseball, and softball were company-sponsored teams. The National Industrial Basketball League included the Phillips 66ers, the Goodyear Wingfoots, and the Peoria Caterpillars. Championships in the National Baseball Congress and Amateur Softball Association were dominated by company-backed teams.

Industrial employee recreation programs have grown enormously over the past fifty years, and today more than 2 billion dollars a year is spent on employee recreation. Indeed, industry spends more on sports equipment than all schools and colleges combined. More than 125 golf courses are owned by corporations, and industry is probably the biggest user of bowling lanes; table tennis tables; and volleyball, basketball, and softball equipment in the country. Three-fourths of all firms employing more than one thousand people have some form of exercise and athletic program, and more than ten thousand companies now have full -or part-time recreation managers.[38]

Labor unions, originally formed to acquire better pay and working conditions for industrial employees, gradually broadened their interests to include the health and mental welfare of their members. The United Automobile Workers (UAW) established a recreation department in 1937 based on a strong policy of organized recreation for all ages. Other unions have programs that include almost everything in the way of leisure-time activities: Among these are team and individual sports, social functions, dancing instruction, handicrafts, orchestras, and hobby clubs. Some unions have acquired large tracts of land on which they have built elaborate recreational facilities for the use of their members.

Two major developments in sport characterize the past thirty years: the colossal expansion of amateur and professional spectator sports and the boom in participant sports. Amateur sports, from youth to intercollegiate athletic programs, have multiplied at a bewildering pace. Baseball and football in the United States and ice hockey in Canada were once about the only sports sponsored for youngsters, but there are over twenty-five sports with organized youth programs, from swimming to motor bicycling, and it is possible for children as young as six years of age to win a national championship. The limited high school and collegiate programs featuring three or four sports for males have now been expanded to include twelve to fifteen sports for both males and females.

Professional sports teams are forms of corporate organizations that function very similarly in many respects to corporations of any other kind, albeit with certain tax and monopolistic advantages not given to other businesses.[39] In 1922 the United States Supreme Court exempted baseball from antitrust legislation. Since that time owners of baseball and other professional sports teams have used that decision, and more recent ones, to define their special legal and economic position. (The legal and economic position of corporate sport is more fully discussed in chapter 10.)

The first professional baseball team was player-owned and player-controlled, but major league teams were organized into business corporations in the latter part of the nineteenth century and continue as business enterprises made up of separate corporations under a cartel. Professional football began in the 1920s, and industry had a hand in its development. The Acme Packing Company in Green Bay, Wisconsin, sponsored a local team, which was fittingly called the Packers; and in Decatur, Illinois, the A. E. Staley Manufacturing Company started the team that became known as the Chicago Bears. From these humble beginnings, professional football is now a $600-million-a-year business, and each franchise in the National Football League (NFL) is worth in excess of $80 million.[40]

On-site spectator sports in the United States have gross paid admissions of over 600 million dollars a year. Some 70 million admissions are paid to horse racing, 57 million to professional baseball, 37 million to college football, and about 17 million to professional football.[41] These figures are, of course, dwarfed by the number of people who watch televised sports events.

Participant sports, the second main development of the past generation, have been products of increased leisure and income. The construction of facilities and the manufacture of equipment inexpensive enough for the large mass of working-class people have had an important impact on participant sports. Moreover, a concerned awareness of the increasingly sedentary lifestyle of persons in all socioeconomic strata and of the rise in diseases related to this lifestyle has stimulated mass participation in sport and exercise. One national poll reported that approximately 78 percent of the adult North American population engage in some form of exercise or sport each week.[42] The number of sports participants is impressive. It is estimated that in a single year 64 million persons swim, almost 24 million play golf, 17 million play tennis, 15 million ski, and bicyclers far outnumber all but swimmers.[43]

Other sports have their devotees as well. Perhaps most remarkable is the running boom that has swept North America. There are over 22 million runners/joggers. Virtually every major city has a marathon that draws thousands of runners (e.g., Boston, New York,

Atlanta).[44] Even allowing for a considerable margin of error in the participation reports, sport involves an enormous number of people. Increased leisure and income are undoubtedly the main causes for the extraordinary development of participant sport in the current generation.

The Technological Revolution and Sport: Transportation

By the turn of the century, almost every realm of sport shared in the powerful impact of the railroad, and in the years up to World War II this influence continued unabated. Perhaps one of the most significant contributions of the railroad to sport in the twentieth century has been the opening of new areas for recreation. For example, the initial stimulus for the popularization of skiing was the "snow train." The first snow train left Boston's North Station in 1931. Four years later such trains were leaving New York's Grand Central Station with thousands of ski enthusiasts on board, intent on spending a weekend on the slopes of New England. Railroads were responsible for the development and promotion of a number of North America's most popular winter sports resorts in the western states and provinces.

As important as the steam engine was to improving transportation and stimulating industrialization, its impact on the social life and transportation habits of North Americans was minuscule in comparison to that of the development of the internal combustion engine. This invention made possible the automobile and the airplane, two modes of transportation that completely revolutionized travel and numerous other aspects of life. In addition to their contributions to transportation, the automobile and airplane created totally new industries involving billions of dollars in capital and employing millions of workers. They stimulated the construction of millions of miles of highways, and they spawned many industries and occupations related to auto and aircraft, production and use. For example, the prosperity of the oil, rubber, steel, and electronic industries depend to a large extent on these two forms of transportation. The growth of metropolitan areas, especially suburban and satellite towns outside large cities, was also stimulated by the automobile.

Inventors in Europe and the United States had successfully developed an internal combustion engine powered by gasoline by the last decade of the nineteenth century. Initially, however, there was little general interest in the converted bicycles that were the first automobiles because they were used either for racing or as a toy for the rich. Then a young man, Henry Ford, saw the potential of the automobile as a means of popular transportation. Realizing that he would have to gain financial backing for the auto through racing, he built a huge-engined racing car, the "999," and hired a professional bicycle rider by the name of Barney Oldfield to race it. After the "999" easily won against its challengers, Ford wrote: "the '999' did what it was intended to do: It advertised the fact that I could build a fast motorcar. A week after the race I formed the Ford Motor Company." [45] In 1895 there were four registered autos in the United States; by 1915 the number had grown to 2.5 million, and by 1996 there were over 100 million.

Racing was the first and foremost attraction of the automobile in the days when its usefulness for any other purpose was questioned. In 1895 H. H. Kohlsaat, publisher of the *Chicago Times-Herald,* sponsored the first automobile race in America; automobile races had already become the fad in Europe. Early automobile manufacturers recognized the commercial value of races and used them as a major marketing technique to win public interest. This particular aspect of automobile racing continues. Throughout the twentieth century automobile racing has grown in popularity and now includes a bewildering array of forms including midget autos, stock cars, hot rods, drag, and so forth. [46]

The automobile contributed to the rise of sport in many ways beyond racing. For countless millions, the auto progressively opened up broader horizons of spectator and participant sport. It provided an easy means of transportation from city to city and from the country to the town or city. Thus, large stadiums and other sports facilities could be conveniently reached by large groups of people. Also, for the first time, golf courses, ski resorts, tennis courts, bathing beaches, and areas for such field sports as fishing, camping, and hunting were within practical reach of large masses of the population. All this would have been impossible without the transportation provided by the automobile.

In 1903 Orville and Wilbur Wright successfully flew an airplane, but it was not until World War I that airplanes were used on any large scale, first for scouting enemy movements and later in actual combat. During the 1920–1940 era, aircraft design was improved, airports were constructed, and regular passenger, mail, and express lines were established. World War II provided for further development, and soon the airplane became the prominent mode of long-distance public transportation. Airplanes have in effect shrunk the continent by reducing traveling time.

Airplane races have never held the spectator appeal of auto racing, but air transportation has had a significant impact on sport in other ways. Until about the mid-1950s, most professional and collegiate athletic teams traveled by rail. With improvements in all phases of air transportation, the airplane became the common carrier of teams. The expansion of professional sports franchises from the East and Midwest into the West and the South and the increased number of pro sports teams could only have been achieved with air travel. Interregional collegiate football and basketball games were rare until air travel made it possible to take long trips in a short period of time. Interregional contests then became a part of the weekly schedule of collegiate sports.

The Technological Revolution and Sport: Communication

In 1896 an Italian scientist, Marchese Guglielmo Marconi, patented the wireless technology and showed the possibility of telegraphy without the use of wires. Within a few years, wireless telegraphy was carrying messages to all parts of the world. One of the first stories to be covered by wireless was a sports event: Marconi was hired by the Associated Press in 1899 to report on the international yacht race involving Sir Thomas Lipton's *Shamrock* and America's *Columbia.* Thus, wireless communication took its place along with the telegraph and the telephone in intensifying public interest in sport and stimulating the rise of sport.

The next important step in electrical communication was the radio, which until 1920 was mainly a toy for amateur scientists. However, in 1920 a radio station in Pittsburgh began broadcasting, and the start of a new communication medium and industry was under-way. More than 98 percent of North American homes have radios, with an average of five per household. Radio's growth heyday was during the 1930s and 1940s, and the broadcasting companies claimed that all but 2 percent of the North American people were listeners. It was not until the early 1950s that television began to overshadow radio in providing information and home entertainment.

Radio broadcasting of sports events actually preceded the beginning of public broadcasting. On 20 August 1920 the radio station of the *Detroit News* went on the air to announce the results of the World Series baseball games. This was before the first public radio station in Pittsburgh made its initial broadcast in November of that year. Also in 1920, the first college football game was broadcast from a station in Texas.[47]

Radio came of age in the hectic 1920s, and while music and news broadcasts were the standard programs, sports events were rapidly absorbed into the entertainment schedule. One early historian of radio noted: "Sportscasting had no crawling or creeping stages. It jumped down from the obstetrical table, kicked its heels in the air, and started out to do a job."[48] Radio and sports were natural partners. Broadcasting, for the first time, brought all the drama of the diamond, ringside, gridiron, and racetrack into homes from coast to coast.

Persons under the age of forty in the 1990s were brought up watching television, the latest communications development. Indeed, some media experts claim that the 1990s college generation spent more waking hours watching television than doing any other single thing. Members of North American households watched an estimated average of forty-nine hours of television weekly.[49]

Although television had been experimentally developed prior to World War II, it was not until the late 1940s that technology and marketing combined to produce models for home use. The major television boom occurred in the early 1950s; the number of sets rose from 10 million to 60 million in a single decade, and the number of broadcasting stations rose from 100 to 700. By 1957 television was a fixture of most households and no longer a novelty.

As television sets became available to the public and the broadcasting of programs expanded, it quickly became evident that televised sports events would be immensely popular, and television continually expanded its coverage of sports. The three major national networks scheduled over sixteen hundred hours of sports per year by the mid-1990s. Cable TV scheduled several thousand more; and several national and regional cable networks telecasted only sports.

In the twentieth century the sports page has been an indispensable part of every newspaper. From a concentration on a few sports, such as baseball, college football, horse racing, and boxing, attention is now given to an enormously wide range of sports. Many newspaper publishers believe that the sports section is the most important factor in a newspaper's circulation.

Along with the newspaper, magazines and books have done much to attract attention to athletics in the past century and a half. Even before the U.S. Civil War, a host of turf journals appeared, plus many periodicals devoted to field sports and outdoor life. Sports journals proliferated greatly in the late nineteenth century, so that almost every sport had at least one periodical devoted to it. This trend has continued, and a substantial portion of shelf space in newsstands is occupied by magazines about sports (more will be said about this in chapter 11).

In its early years the motion picture industry concentrated primarily on boxing. The first commercial motion picture was a six-round bout between Young Griffo and Battling Barnett in 1895. Motion pictures of boxing championships were one of the most popular forms of spectator sport in the first three decades of the twentieth century and served to stimulate the public appetite for organized sports. The videotape has become an indispensable instrument for coaches for scouting opponents and for reviewing the performances of their own athletes. Collegiate and professional coaches of some sports spend as much time viewing films as they spend on almost any other coaching task. Undoubtedly, the motion picture has contributed to the remarkable advances in the technical aspects of sport.

The impact of the still camera cannot be overlooked, either. Beginning in the early years of the twentieth century, newspapers and magazines made extensive use of pictures to show the performance of athletes in the heat of competition or to illustrate the correct (or incorrect) method of performing a skill. The popularity of sports magazines, especially *Sports Illustrated,* is largely due to the superb photographs that are part of each issue. This has had the effect of further nurturing sports by keeping them in the public eye.

Other Technological Innovations and Sport

Although indoor sports were greatly stimulated by electric lighting, baseball, America's national pastime, did not discover the value of this invention until the 1930s. Social historians record 1930 as the year of the emergence of night baseball. The first such ventures took place in Des Moines and Wichita in the summer of 1930. Several minor leagues quickly adopted night baseball, but it was not until 1935 that Cincinnati introduced the first night game in the major leagues. Only in the 1940s did night baseball gain general acceptance in the major leagues; the first World Series night game was not played until 1975.[50] (The owner of the Chicago Cubs for many years, Phillip K. Wrigley, never accepted night baseball, and lights were not installed at Wrigley Field until the summer of 1988.)

Sport in Education

As stated previously, intercollegiate sport began as a form of student recreation, but rapidly grew in popularity among the general public. Indeed, during the latter part of the twentieth century it became a form of big business. The practice of using sport as the right arm of the public relations department of a college, which began in the late nineteenth century, continued. This system of intercollegiate sport is unique to the United States, and it has been one of the most significant forces in the development of American organized sports. High school sports are modeled on this system, and many nonschool youth sports programs have been organized as feeder systems to the high school and college programs. Finally, the intercollegiate programs serve as a farm system for many of the professional sports. (Chapters 5 and 6 will discuss the topic of sport in education in depth.)

Until the 1970s Canadian universities tended to model athletic programs after the British tradition,

meaning that programs were primarily sponsored and administered by students, and little emphasis was given to their commercial exploitation. However, an "American model" in intercollegiate sports has been increasingly adopted, causing some observers to claim that this is another example of the homogenization of American and Canadian cultures.[51]

Summary

In this chapter we have reviewed the rise of sport in North America. Social circumstances are related to events of the past; in the case of North American sport, changing sociocultural conditions provide excellent clues to understanding its present form.

Highly organized spectator and participant sports are products of the past century and a half, and the technological and industrial revolutions played major roles in the transformation of sport. Urbanization was also a significant factor, the evolution of sports became possible only with a large urban population. Finally, influential persons from the clergy and the intelligentsia, as well as social reformers, have contributed ideas that form the bases of attitudes, values, and beliefs about sport.

Notes

1. Richard L. Barton, *Ties That Bind: Canadian/American Relations: Politics of News Discourse* (Hillsdale, N.J.: Erlbaum, 1990). In 1995 a national poll of Canadians found that 74 percent of the respondents agreed that Canadians have a distinct character, but about 50 percent believe Canada is becoming more like the United States (reported in Anthony Wilson-Smith, "A Quiet Passion," *Maclean's* 108 [July 1, 1995]: 8–12).

2. Allen Guttmann, *A Whole New Ball Game: An Interpretation of American Sports* (Chapel Hill, N.C.: University of North Carolina Press, 1988); see also Benjamin G. Rader, *American Sports: From the Age of Folk Games to the Age of Spectators,* 2d ed. (Englewood Cliffs, N.J.: Prentice-Hall, 1990), 1–16; Nancy Struna, "Puritans and Sport: The Irretrievable Tide of Change," in *The Sporting Image: Readings in American Sport History,* ed. Paul J. Zingg (New York: University Press of America, 1988), 1–21, which discusses the changing attitude toward physical activity in Puritan society.

3. Elliott J. Gorn, "'Gouge and Bite, Pull Hair and Scratch': The Social Significance of Fighting in the Southern Backcountry," in *Sport in America,* ed. David K. Wiggins (Champaign, Ill.: Human Kinetics Publishers, 1995), 35–50.

4. Nancy L. Struna, "Gender and Sporting Practice in Early America, 1750–1810," *Journal of Sport History* 40 (spring, 1991): 10–30; for an excellent discussion of Canadian sports and other physical activity during this period, see Don Morrow, et al., *A Concise History of Sport in Canada* (Toronto: Oxford University Press, 1989).

5. David Brody, *In Labor's Cause: Main Themes on the History of the American Worker* (New York: Oxford University Press, 1993); Bruce Laurie, *Artisans Into Workers: Labor in Nineteenth-Century America* (New York: Hill and Wang, 1989).

6. Edward L. Bowen, *The Jockey Club's Illustrated History of Thoroughbred Racing in America* (Boston: Little, Brown, 1994); Nancy L. Struna, "The North-South Races: American Thoroughbred Racing in Transition, 1823–1850," *Journal of Sport History* 8 (summer 1981): 28–57; Melvin L. Adelman, "The First Modern Sport in America: Harness Racing in New York City, 1825–1870," in *Sport in America,* ed. David K. Wiggins (Champaign, Ill.: Human Kinetics Publishers, 1995): 5–32.

7. S. F. Wise and Douglas Fisher, *Canada's Sporting Heroes* (Don Mills, Ont.: General Publishing, 1974), 7.

8. Morrow et al., *A Concise History of Sport in Canada,* 1–22; see also Alan Metcalfe, *Canada Learns to Play: The Emergence of Organized Sport, 1807–1914* (Toronto: McClelland and Stewart, 1987).

9. Robert W. McChesney, "Media Made Sport: A History of Sports Coverage in the United States," in *Media, Sports, & Society,* ed. Lawrence A. Wenner (Newbury Park, Calif.: Sage, 1989), 50–52; see also Metcalfe, *Canada Learns to Play.*

10. Emmett Dedmon, *Challenge and Response: A Modern History of Standard Oil Company (Indiana)* (Chicago: Mobium Press, 1984); see also Howard J. Sherman, "The Concentration of Economic Power in the United States," in *Critical Perspectives in Sociology,* 2d ed., ed. Berch Berberoglu (Dubuque, Iowa: Kendall/Hunt, 1993).

11. Eric H. Monkkonen, *America Becomes Urban: The Development of U.S.: Cities and Towns, 1780–1980* (Berkeley: University of California Press, 1988); Gilbert A. Stelter and Alan F. Artibise, eds., *Power and Place: Canadian Urban Development in the North American Context* (Vancouver: University of British Columbia Press, 1986).

12. Steven A. Riess, *City Games: The Evolution of American Urban Society and the Rise of Sports* (Urbana, Ill.: University of Illinois Press, 1989); Morrow et al., *A Concise History of Sport in Canada.*

13. See for example Melvin M. Adelman, *A Sporting Time: New York City and the Rise of Modern Athletics, 1820–1870* (Urbana, Ill.: University of Illinois Press, 1986); Stephen Hardy, *How Boston Played: Sport, Recreation, and Community, 1865–1915* (Boston: Northeastern University Press, 1982).

14. Rader, *American Sports,* 85–95. In 1897 one of these clubs, the Boston Athletic Association, sponsored the first Boston Marathon, now one of the world's premier sports events.

15. Richard Gruneau, *Class, Sports, and Social Development* (Amherst, Mass.: University of Massachusetts Press, 1983), 91–136; see also Alan Metcalfe, "The Growth of Organized Sport and the Development of Amateurism in Canada, 1807–1914," in *Not Just a Game: Essays in Canadian Sport Sociology,* ed. Jean Harvey and Hart Cantelon (Ottawa, Ont.: University of Ottawa Press, 1988), 33–50.

16. Warren J. Goldstein, *Playing for Keeps: A History of Early Baseball* (Ithaca, N.Y.: Cornell University Press, 1989); George B. Kirsch, *The Creation of American Team Sports: Baseball and Cricket, 1838–72* (Urbana, Ill.: University of Illinois Press, 1989); Charles C. Alexander, *Our Game: An American Baseball History* (New York: Holt, 1991).

17. William Humber, *Cheering for the Home Team: The Story of Baseball in Canada* (Erin, Ont.: The Baseball Mills Press, 1983).

18. Richard Gruneau and David Whitson, *Hockey Night in Canada: Sport, Identities and Cultural Politics* (Toronto: Garamond Press, 1993).

19. Robert K. Barney, "Forty-Eighters and the Rise of the Turnervein Movement in America," in *Ethnicity and Sport in North American History and Culture,* eds. George Eisen and David K. Wiggins (Westport, Conn.: Greenwood Press, 1994), 19–42; see also Rader, *American Sports,* 57–58; Riess, *City Games,* 96–99.

20. Gerald Redmond, *The Sporting Scots of Nineteenth-Century Canada* (East Brunswick, N.J.: Fairleigh Dickinson University Press, 1982); see also Ann Donaldson, *The Scottish Highland Games in the United States* (Gretna, La.: Pelican, 1986).

21. Harvey Green, *Fit for America: Health, Fitness, Sport, and American Society* (New York: Pantheon, 1986); J. C. Whorton, *Crusaders for Fitness: The History of American Health Reformers* (Princeton, N.J.: Princeton University Press, 1982).

22. Ronald A. Smith, *Sports and Freedom: The Rise of Big-Time College Athletics* (New York: Oxford University Press, 1988).

23. Ibid, 118–46.

24. Amos Alonzo Stagg, quoting William Rainey Harper in a letter to his family, 20 January 1891, quoted in Richard J. Storr, *Harper's University: The Beginnings* (Chicago: University of Chicago Press, 1966), 179.

25. Smith, *Sports and Freedom,* 27–28.

26. Ian F. Jobling, "Urbanization and Sport in Canada, 1867–1900," in *Canadian Sport: Sociological Perspectives,* ed. Richard S. Gruneau and John G. Albinson (Reading, Mass.: Addison-Wesley, 1976), 65–66. For an excellent discussion of the relationship between railroads and Canadian sport, see Trevor Williams, "Cheap Rates, Special Trains and Canadian Sport in the 1850s," *Canadian Journal of History of Sport* 12 (December 1981): 84–93.

27. *Frank Leslie's Illustrated Newspaper* 29 (New York), 28 September 1869, p. 2; see also William G. Durick, "The Gentleman's Race: An Examination of the 1869 Harvard-Oxford Boat Race," *Journal of Sport History* 15 (spring, 1988): 41–63.

28. McChesney, "Media Made Sport," 53–54.

29. Rader, *American Sports,* 150; see also Morrow et al., *A Concise History of Sport in Canada,* 274–81.

30. Stephen Hardy, " 'Adopted by All the Leading Clubs': Sporting Goods and the Shaping of Leisure," in *For Fun and Profit: The Transformation of Leisure Into Consumption,* ed. Richard Butsch (Philadelphia: Temple University Press, 1990), 71–101.

31. Carl N. Degler, *In Search of Human Nature: The Decline and Revival of Darwinism in American Social Thought* (New York: Oxford University Press, 1991); Howard L. Kaye, *The Social Meaning of Modern Biology: From Social Darwinism to Sociobiology* (New Haven, Conn.: Yale University Press, 1986).

32. Albert Galloway Keller, ed., *Essays of William Graham Sumner,* vol. 1 (New Haven, Conn.: Yale University Press, 1934), 386.

33. *Census of Manufacturers* (Washington, D.C.: U.S. Government Printing Office, 1995).

34. Steven W. Pope, "Negotiating the 'Folk Highway' of the Nation: Sport, Public Culture and American Identity, 1870–1940," *Journal of Social History* 27 (winter, 1993): 327–40; see also Steven A. Riess, "Sports and Machine Politics in New York City, 1870–1920," in Wiggins, *Sport in America,* 163–84.

35. James Bryce, "America Revisited: The Changes of a Quarter-Century," *Outlook,* 25 March 1905, 738–39.

36. Mark Dyreson, "The Emergence of Consumer Culture and the Transformation of Physical Culture: American Sport in the 1920s," in Wiggins, *Sport in America,* 207–23.

37. Carol B. Grant, *Workplace Wellness: The Key to Higher Productivity and Lower Health Costs* (New York: Van Nostrand, 1992); Gareth M. Green and Frank Baker, eds., *Work, Health and Productivity* (New York: Oxford University Press, 1991); Juliet B. Schor, *The Overworked American: The Unexpected Decline of Leisure* (New York: Basic Books, 1991); *Fitness and Lifestyle at the Workplace* (Ottawa, Ont.: Minister of Supply and Services Canada, 1988); Richard G. Kraus, *Recreation and Leisure in Modern Society* (Glenview, Ill.: Scott, Foresman, 1988).

38. For an excellent discussion of current developments in employee recreation in the U.S., see Robert W. Patton et al., *Developing and Managing Healthy Fitness Facilities* (Champaign, Ill.: Human Kinetics, 1989); and for a discussion of programs in Canada, see Pierre Brodeur, "Employee Fitness: Doctrines and Issues," in *Not Just a Game,* ed. J. Harvey and H. Cantelon (Ottawa, Ont.: University of Ottawa Press, 1988), 227–42.

39. For excellent discussions of this issue, see Jerry Gorman and Kirk Calhoun, *The Name of the Game: The Business of Sports* (New York: Simon & Schuster, 1994); Kenneth M. Jennings, *Balls and Strikes: The Money Game in Professional Baseball* (New York: Praeger, 1990); Lee Lowenfish, *The Imperfect Diamond: A History of Baseball's Labor Wars,* rev. ed. (New York: Da Capo Press, 1991).

40. David Harris, *The League: The Rise and Decline of the NFL* (New York: Bantam, 1987); see also Warren Freedman, *Professional Sports and Antitrust* (New York: Quorum Books, 1987).

41. Bureau of the Census, *Statistical Abstract of the United States: 1994,* 114th ed. (Washington, D.C., 1994), 256.

42. "The Prevention Index: A Report Card on the Nation's Health," *Prevention Magazine.*

43. Bureau of the Census, *Statistical Abstract,* 258.

44. Ibid.

45. Henry Ford and Samuel Crowther, *My Life and Work* (Garden City, N.Y.: Doubleday, 1922), 51.

46. Ivan Randall, *The Checkered Flag: 100 Years of Motor Racing* (Secaucus, N.J.: Chartwell Books, 1993).

47. McChesney, "Media Made Sport," 54–59.

48. Francis Chase, Jr., *Sound and Fury* (New York: Harper, 1942), 303.

49. *The 1990 Nielson Report on Television* (Northbrook, Ill: Nielson Media Research, 1990).

50. Douglas A. Noverr and Lawrence E. Ziewacz, *The Games They Played* (Chicago: Nelson-Hall, 1983), 111.

51. Don Macintosh, "Intercollegiate Athletics in Canadian Universities: An Historical Perspective," in *The Role of Interuniversity Athletics: A Canadian Perspective,* ed. A. W. Taylor (London, Ont.: Sports Dynamics, 1986).

Chapter 3

Sport and Societal Values

"Nobody
remembers who came
in second."

Charles Schulz

If sport is a microcosm of society, then the types of sports, the way in which sport is organized, who participates and who does not all offer clues about the nature of the society. The study of sport, like the study of any institution, should provide important indicators about (1) a society's values, (2) a society's social structure (social stratification and social organization), and (3) a society's problems.

The objective of this chapter is to examine the reciprocal relationship between sport and societal values. The relationship is interdependent because societal values affect the kinds of sports that are played, the way they are organized, the way they are played, and the motivations for participation in them. However, the converse is also true in that sport affects values. Sport, like all institutions, is conservative primarily because it reinforces certain values.

Our description is limited to American values, but these resemble, albeit somewhat imperfectly, the predominant values of Canadians as well. The factors that work to differentiate Canadian values from American values are, first, that Canada has a long history of having accepted English rule after the Americans rebelled against it; second, that Canadians have two dominant religions, the Anglican religious heritage from the British and the Catholic heritage from the French, while Americans are more pluralistic; and third, that Canada wants to be different from its neighbor to the south. Strong factors also work toward a congruence of values: (1) Many Canadians have received their higher education in the United States, (2) Canadians typically watch television and movies and read American newspapers and magazines from the United States, and (3) American corporations have a strong presence in Canada.[1]

The American Value System

People are valuing creatures. That is, human beings live in an affectively charged world where some things are preferred over others. Some objects, people, or ideas are considered wrong, bad, or immoral; others are believed correct, good, or moral. Some goals are deemed worthy; others are not. Values are the bases for making decisions. *Values* are the culturally prescribed criteria by which individuals evaluate persons, behaviors, objects, and ideas as to their relative morality, desirability, merit, or correctness. The phrase "culturally prescribed" is an important qualifier in this definition because it implies that human beings are *socialized,* that is, taught the criteria by which to make such judgments. Children learn from their parents, peers, churches, schools, and the media what is right or wrong, moral or immoral, correct or incorrect.

Although individuals may have their own idiosyncratic criteria for evaluation, we will examine those values widely held in U.S. society. Several caveats should be mentioned at the outset, however. First, diversity in the United States precludes any universal holding of values. Some individuals and groups reject the dominant values, and members of certain ethnic and religious groups have very different values. Moreover, differences in emphasis of the dominant values exist because of region, social class, age, and size of community.

Second, the system of American values is not always consistent with behavior. For example, Americans have always valued hard work as the means to success, yet rich persons who may have inherited their wealth are highly esteemed in American society. Moreover, the value of equality of opportunity that all Americans verbally embrace is inconsistent with the injustices suffered by members of minority groups.

Third, the values themselves are not always consistent. How does one reconcile the coexistence of individualism with conformity or of competition with cooperation? Robin M. Williams, Jr., an eminent analyst of U.S. society, concluded: "We do not find a neatly unified 'ethos' or an irresistible 'strain toward consistency.' Rather, the total society is characterized by diversity and change in values. Complex division of labor, regional variations, ethnic heterogeneity, and the proliferation of specialized institutions and organizations all tend to insulate differing values from one another."[2] To minimize the problem of inconsistencies, we will present only the most dominant of North American values in this section.[3]

Success

The highly valued individual in American society is the self-made person. In other words, one who has achieved money and status through his or her own efforts in a highly competitive system. Our cultural heroes are persons like Abraham Lincoln, John D. Rockefeller, Oprah Winfrey, and Samuel Walton, each of whom rose from humble origins to the top of his or her profession.

Success can be achieved, of course, by outdoing all others, but to know the exact extent of an individual's success is often difficult. Hence, obvious economic success (income, personal wealth, and possessions) is the most commonly used measurement. Economic success, moreover, is often used to measure personal worth. As Williams has put it, "The comparatively striking feature of American culture is its tendency to identify standards of personal excellence with competitive occupational achievement."[4]

Competition

Competition is highly valued in U.S. society. It is not just competition, though, it is winning in competitive situations that is so highly valued. This winning is so highly valued that society heaps disproportionate rewards on these winners. Thus, we could be characterized as the "Winner-Take-All Society."[5] Most Americans believe it to be the one quality that has made the United States great because it motivates individuals and groups to be discontented with the status quo and with being second best. Motivated by the hope of being victorious in competition or by fear of failure, North Americans believe that the United States must not lose a war or the arms race, the Olympics, or the race to explore outer space. For the United States to have been the second nation to land its citizens on the moon would have been seen as a huge defeat.

Competition pervades almost all aspects of American society. The work world, sports, organizations like the Cub Scouts, schools, and even courtship thrive on competition. The pervasiveness of competition in schools is seen in the selection process for athletic teams, cheerleading squads, debate teams, choruses, bands, and play casts. In each case, competition among classmates is the basis of selection. Even the grading system is often based on the comparison of classmates with one another.

The Cub Scout program, because of its reliance on competition, is an all-American organization. In the first place, individual status in the den or pack is

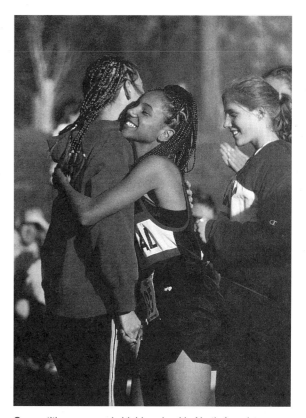

Competitive success is highly valued in North American culture and is sometimes associated with personal worth.

determined by the level one has achieved by the attainment of merit badges. Although all boys can theoretically attain all merit badges, the boys are pitted against one another to see who can obtain the most. Another example of how the Cub Scouts use competition is their annual event the Pinewood Derby. Each boy in a Cub pack is given a small block of wood and four wheels, which he is then to shape into a racing car. The race is held at a pack meeting at which one boy eventually becomes the winner. The competition is rarely questioned, even though nearly all of the boys go home disappointed losers. Why is such a practice accepted, indeed, publicized? The answer, simply, is that it is symbolic of the way things are done in virtually all aspects of American life.

An important consequence of this emphasis on the survival of the fittest is that some persons take advantage of their competitors in order to succeed. This is done rather routinely in political campaigns with "dirty tricks," misleading advertising, and illegal contributions to win elections.

The zeal to win has caused people to cheat. For example, it has been found that a common practice in livestock fairs is to pump animals with tranquilizers and steroids to calm their demeanors and to encourage weight gain and muscle tone in the hope that these animals will be declared "champions." In 1995 the last two champion steers at the National Western Livestock Show in Denver were disqualified after the animals tested positive for clenbuterol.

In the business world, theft, fraud, interlocking directorates, and price-fixing are techniques used by some individuals and corporations to get ahead.[6] A related problem, the abuse of nature for profit (although not a form of cheating) deprives others of limited resources and degrades the general quality of life so that the profiteer can pursue economic success. The ecology crisis is caused by individuals, corporations, and communities who find pollution solutions too expensive. Thus, in looking out for themselves, they ignore the short- and long-range effects on social and biological life. In other words, competition, although a constant spur for individuals and groups to succeed, is also the source of some illegal activities and social problems in the United States.

The Valued Means to Achieve

There are three related, highly valued ways to succeed in North American society. The first is hard work. North Americans, from the early Puritans to the present day, have elevated persons who are industrious and denigrated those who are not. Most Americans, therefore, assume that poor people deserve to be poor because they are allegedly unwilling to work as hard as persons in the middle and upper classes. This explanation places the blame on the victim rather than on a social system that systematically thwarts efforts by the poor. Hopelessness, brought on by a lack of education, by one's skin color or gender, or by a lack of experience, is interpreted as a fault and not as a function of the economic system.[7] This typical interpretation, moreover, is buttressed by the success of some members of the poor in the sports world. Athletic stars such as Nancy Lopez, Marshall Faulk, Michael Jordan, and others are presented as dramatic evidence that a meteoric rise in fame and fortune is possible through the blending of hard work and talent. One could argue that these persons succeed in the sports world because sport has become relatively immune to the racism present in the larger society. One could also argue, however, that these persons succeed not because of the openness of the system but because they managed somehow to overcome its roadblocks.

The two remaining valued means to success are continual striving and deferred gratification. Continual striving has meaning for both the successful and the not-so-successful. For the former, it means that a person should never be content with what she or he has; there will always be more land to own, more money to make, or more books to write. For the latter, *continual striving* means a never-give-up attitude, a belief that economic success is always possible, if not for oneself, at least for one's children.

Deferred gratification refers to the willingness to deny immediate pleasure for the sake of later rewards. The hallmark of the successful person in the United States has such a willingness, whether to stay in school or to work at two jobs or to go to night school. One observer has asserted, for example, that the difference between the poor and the nonpoor in this society is whether they are future- or present-time oriented.[8]

Superficially, this assessment appears accurate, but we argue that the lack of a future-time orientation among the poor is not a subcultural trait but basically a consequence of their hopeless situation due to structural constraints. Moreover, there is a question whether this value still prevails among the children of the nonpoor.

Progress

Societies differ in their emphasis on the past, on the present, and on the future. American society, while giving some attention to each time dimension, stresses the future. Americans neither make the past sacred nor remain content with the present. They place a central value on progress—on a brighter tomorrow, a better job, a bigger home, a move to the suburbs, a college education for their children, and self-improvement.

Americans are not satisfied with the status quo; they want growth (bigger buildings, faster planes, bigger airports, more business moving into the community, bigger profits, and new world records). Many want to change and conquer nature (dam rivers, clear forests, rechannel rivers, seed clouds, spray parks and residential areas with insecticides, and replace grass with artificial turf), although the ecological crises are leading more and more to question this value.

Although the belief in progress implies that change is good, some things are not to be changed, for they have a sacred quality: the political system, the economic system, American values, and the nation-state. Thus, Americans, even while valuing technological change, do not favor fundamental changes in the system.

Materialism

An American belief holds that "hard work pays off." The payoff is success not only in one's profession but also in economic standing, in income and in the acquisition and consumption of goods and services that go beyond adequate nutrition, medical care, shelter, and transportation. The superfluous things that we accumulate or strive to accumulate, such as country club memberships, jewelry, lavish houses in prestige neighborhoods, boats, second homes, pool tables, electric toothbrushes, and season tickets to the games of our favorite teams, are symbols of success in the competitive struggle. However, these have more than symbolic value; they are elements of what North Americans consider the "good life" and, therefore, a right.

The American emphasis on materialism is reflected in the motives of college students. In 1994 a survey of nearly 237,777 first-year college students found that 72 percent said a major reason for attending college was "to be able to make more money," up dramatically from the 39 percent in 1970 with this response (1970 was the height of the counter-cultural movement on college campuses).[9] This materialism is also seen indirectly in the choice of majors as 22 percent of all 1992–93 college graduates had a business degree.[10]

The emphasis on having things has long been a facet of U.S. society. This country has always been a land of opportunity and abundance. Although many persons are blocked from full participation in this abundance, the goal for most persons is to accumulate those things that bring status and that provide for a better way of life by saving labor or enhancing pleasure in their leisure time.

External Conformity

Societies cannot tolerate total freedom by individuals. Without a minimum of cooperation and of conformity to laws and customs, there is anarchy. To avoid disorder and lawlessness, society socializes individuals into acceptable beliefs and practices. For their part, individuals actually seek to be socialized. We seek the approval of our colleagues and therefore try to be successful by some shared standards of achievement or of conformity. Conformity, then, is a characteristic of all societies. The degree of conformity required, however, varies greatly from society to society.

Analytically, we can separate conformity in American society into two levels. At one level are the official expectations of behavior by the community, the state, and the nation: the customs and the laws individuals are expected to obey. Deviations from these expectations are punished by fines, imprisonment, gossip, or other negative *sanctions*. The threat of these sanctions is usually enough to ensure conformity. More than this, however, we are socialized to desire conformity.

At another more personal level, individuals tend to conform to the expectations of groups with which they closely identify: families, peers, ethnic groups, religious groups, and work groups. Thus, within the context of the society-wide expectations for behavior, there is great diversity: suburbanites conform to other suburbanites, as do ghetto residents, teenagers, the jet set, union members, and businesspersons with their peers. David Riesman has characterized Americans as being *other-directed*.[11] By this he meant that they are oversensitive to the opinions of others. In a sense, Americans continually have their antennas out, picking up signals from those important to them. Another observer, William H. Whyte, pointed to this same phenomenon in the organizational context of social life.

Whyte argued that the bureaucratic trend in American society forces many persons to conform. Rules must be followed, boats must not be rocked, if individuals are to get ahead in the bureaucracy.[12]

Bureaucratic organization is authoritarian and hierarchical. It is also rational. That is, it is based entirely on certain understood and accepted rules efficiently designed to serve the organization's goals. The interests of the organization are paramount in the development of these rules, and the formal aspects of a bureaucracy manifest these interests and rules.

The influence of bureaucracy is a source of norms regulating a large number of activities both within and beyond large-scale organization boundaries. So powerful and so pervasive are the organizations that employ bureaucratic methods that the value orientations engendered by this form of organization have attained the status of core values for American society. They so permeate the fabric of every social institution that the socialization process is largely devoted to conditioning youth to this orientation.

Societal Values and Sport

We have pointed out repeatedly that sport mirrors a society's basic structure and values. The relationship between American values and the forms of sport that prevail is the theme of this section.

Many reasons exist for the tremendous popularity of sport in the United States. The conditions of mass society constitute an important set of factors. Individuals living in an urban and bureaucratic society tend to feel *alienated;* in effect, they have feelings of isolation, powerlessness, self-estrangement, and meaninglessness. These persons need to identify with others in a cause that will give meaning to their existence and an escape from an otherwise humdrum world. Sports teams, each pursuing victories, representing factories, schools, neighborhoods, cities, or nations provide an important source of identification for individuals in American society who otherwise do not feel connected with others. They provide entertainment, diversion, and great expectations.

Another reason for the popularity of sport in the United States is that the masses have been influenced by sports publicists and the media. Television, newspapers, and magazines have generated interest in sports by creating heroes and by continually bombarding the citizenry with statistics, human-interest stories, and coverage of the sporting events themselves.

A third factor that partially explains the sports mania in the United States is the increased leisure time available to most Americans. This, coupled with the relatively high standard of living that many Americans enjoy, provides much of the basis for the rise in attendance figures at sports events and the rise in sport activity by Americans.

An important underlying factor, and one emphasized in this section, is the close relationship between American sport and American values. In learning the culture (through the socialization process), most Americans have internalized values that predispose them to be interested in the outcome of competitive situations; and competition is the *sine qua non* of sport.

Competition and Success in Sport

As in the larger society, there is a tremendous emphasis in American sport on competitive success. Winning is glorified by all who participate. The following epigrams by various coaches exemplify this emphasis on winning:

"Defeat is worse than death because you have to live with defeat."

Bill Musselman

"No one ever learns anything by losing."

Don Shula

"In our society, in my profession, there is only one measure of success, and that is winning. Not just any game, not just the big game, but the last one."

John Madden

"There are only two things in this league, winning and misery."

Pat Riley

"A tie is like kissing your sister."

Duffy Daugherty

"Our expectations are to play for and win the national championship every year. . . . Second, third, fourth, and fifth don't do you any good in this business."

Dennis Erickson (when head football coach at the University of Miami)

Americans want winners, whether winning is in school or in business or in politics or in sport. In sport, we demand winners. Coaches are fired if they are not successful; teams are booed if they play for ties. Inevitably, coaches faced with the option of taking a tie or gambling on winning (with a high probability of losing) will go for the win with the comment, "We didn't come down here to tie." The twenty-seven teams in the National Football League that do not win the Super Bowl in a given year are losers. Not even the members of the runner-up team consider themselves successful: They did not win the only game that really counts.

Coaches do all they can to socialize their athletes with the value of winning. They reinforce winners with praise, honor, and status. The primary goal of sports competition is to succeed (to win). Thus, coaches do all they can to instill in their athletes the character traits that they believe will bring team success (e.g., loyalty, enthusiasm, initiative, self-control, confidence, poise, hard work, and ambition). Negatively, they ridicule losers or quitters. As an example of a technique used to instill in athletes the desire to excel, one coach of a pony-league football team (fourth, fifth, and sixth graders) in Lawrence, Kansas, had his young boys yell "I'm a girl!" before they could let their legs touch the ground during a leg-lift exercise. This fear of humiliation kept many boys doing the exercise beyond their normal endurance and, the coach probably assumed, increased their potential for winning.

Another coaching technique to instill in their athletes the goal of winning has been to place slogans on the dressing room walls to exhort players to value certain behaviors. Commonly, such slogans espouse the competitive spirit:

"A quitter never wins, a winner never quits."

"When the going gets tough, the tough get going."

"It's not the size of the dog in the fight, but the size of the fight in the dog."

"Never be willing to be second best."

"The greatest aim in life is to succeed."

"Win by as many points as possible."[13]

The demand for winners is found at all levels of sport. Even among youngsters, winning is everything, as evidenced by the pressures commonly found in adult-sponsored children's sports such as baseball, football, soccer, and swimming. Another example of the emphasis on winning among youngsters can be seen in the contests sponsored by some business corporations. Gatorade Company sponsors a "Punt, Pass, and Kick" contest for youngsters eight through thirteen; Phillips Petroleum sponsors a similar "Pitch, Hit, and Throw" contest for baseball skills. In each case, winners are selected at the local level and proceed through the various state and regional tournaments until a winner is found for each age category. In one year, there were 1,112,702 entrants in the Punt, Pass, and Kick contest and only six winners. Why would an organization sponsor an event that produced six winners and 1,112,696 losers? Perhaps, the answer lies in that this, too, is a microcosm of the larger society.

The Soap Box Derby, sponsored by several major corporations, is another sport activity for youngsters. Here again, the ultimate winner is the one person who survives the tests from among the tens of thousands who initially enter the competition. This is clearly a situation of survival of the fittest. Unfortunately, the fittest is not always the winner, as attested by the scandal associated with the 1973 Soap Box Derby. In this case, victory was so important to the winning boy and his uncle that they used an illegal magnet to give the vehicle an unfair advantage at the start of each race. Moreover, a later investigation revealed that one-third of the final cars (and six of the top ten) had been altered to achieve an unfair advantage.

Such scandals are also found in the sports world, as we shall note throughout this book. Most visible is the illegal recruiting of athletes by colleges and universities. In the quest to succeed (i.e., win), some coaches have violated National Collegiate Athletic Association

box 3.1 *The Negative Consequences of Overemphasizing Competition in Sport*

When winning is the primary standard for evaluation, several negative outcomes result. Let me enumerate these, using sport for examples. First, in a competitive society there is a tendency to evaluate people by their accomplishments rather than their character, personality, and other human qualities. When "winning is everything," then losers are considered just that. One successful university basketball coach once counseled prospective coaches that if they wanted to be winners, then they should associate only with winners. Is this an appropriate guiding principle for conducting our lives?

Second, when winning is paramount, schools and communities organize sports for the already gifted. This elitist approach means that the few will be given the best equipment, the best coaching, and prime time reserved for their participating, while the less able will be denied participation altogether or given very little attention. If sports participation is a useful activity, then it should be for the many, not the few, in my view.

A third problem with the emphasis on winning is that parents may push their children beyond the normal to succeed. . . . In 1972 the national record for one-year-olds in the mile run was established by Steve Parsons of Normal, Illinois (the time was 24:16.6). [Is this an example] of child abuse or what?

A fourth problem with the primacy of winning is that coaches may push their charges too hard. Coaches may be physically or emotionally abusive. They may limit their players' civil rights. And, they may play their injured athletes by using pain killers without regard for their long-term physical well-being.

Fifth, when the desire to win is so great, the "end may justify the means." Coaches and players may use illegal tactics. Athletes may use performance enhancing drugs such as steroids and amphetamines to achieve a "competitive edge" or more subtly, but nonetheless unethical, using such means as blood doping or getting pregnant to get positive hormonal changes and then having an abortion. Both of these practices

---

(NCAA) regulations by arranging to have transcripts altered to ensure athletes' eligibility; by enrolling athletes in classes and obtaining for them academic credits for course work never taken; by allowing substitutes to take admissions tests for athletes of marginal educational ability; by paying athletes for nonexistent jobs; by illegally using government work-study funds for athletes; and by offering money, cars, and clothing to entice athletes to their schools.

When "winning is everything," players and coaches may turn to other forms of cheating. Many athletes take drugs to enhance their performance artificially. This practice is so commonplace, even expected in some sports, that we might call steroids that increase bulk and strength "vocational drugs." Players may try to gain an unfair advantage also by such practices as "doctoring" a pitch or "corking" a bat in baseball,

curving the blades of the stick beyond the legal limits in hockey, pretending to be fouled in basketball, or "boosting" the manifold pressure to gain a horsepower advantage in automobile racing.[14]

Winning is the great North American obsession. It dominates our lives, as we have seen. One of the problems with this hyperemphasis on winning is that it tends to warp sport. Sport, in its pristine form, emphasizes the playing of the contest with thrills achieved from strategy, luck, finesse, cunning, practice, and skill. When winning is everything, however, the playing of the game becomes secondary. In effect, the destination becomes more important than the journey. When this occurs, sport is diminished. As sportswriter Bill Shirley has lamented: "Our win-at-all-costs philosophy has so distorted our sense of values that we have reversed the precept of Baron Pierre de Coubertin

box 3.1 *Continued*

occur among endurance athletes. . . . So much, I would argue, for the myth that "sport builds character."

Sixth, when winning is all important, there may be a tendency to crush the opposition. This was the case when Riverside Poly High School girls basketball team played Norte Vista several years ago. Riverside won by a score of 179–15 with one player, Cheryl Miller, scoring a California record of 105 points. Was the Riverside coach ethical? . . . Will the Norte Vista girls be motivated to improve their performance or will this humiliating experience crush their spirit?

Seventh, many people in a competitive society have difficulty with coming in second. . . . [For example, a few years back, a football team, composed of fifth-graders, in Florida was] undefeated going into the state finals but lost there in a close game. At a banquet following that season each player on this team was given a plaque on which was inscribed a quote from Vince Lombardi:

There is no room for second place. I have finished second twice at Green Bay and I never want to finish second again. There is a second place bowl game but it is a game for losers played by losers. It is and always will be an American zeal to be first in anything we do and to win and to win and to win.

In other words, the parents and coaches of these boys wanted them to never be satisfied with being second. Second is losing. The only acceptable placement is first.

Finally, when "winning is the only thing" the joy in participation is lost. I have observed that organized sports from youth programs to the professional level is mostly devoid of playfulness. When the object is to win, then the primacy of the activity is lost. . . .

In other words, it's the process that is primary, not the outcome. White water rafters and mountain climbers understand this. So, too, do players in a pickup touch football game. Why can't the rest of us figure out this fundamental truth?

Source: Excerpts from D. Stanley Eitzen, "The Dark Side of Competition in American Society," *Vital Speeches*, 56 (January 1, 1990), 185–186.

when he founded the modern Olympic Games. Today, on all levels of sports—from Little League to the National Football League—the most important thing is not merely to take part but to win; the most important thing in life is not the struggle but the triumph; the essential thing is not to have fought well but to have conquered."[15] See box 3.1 for an elaboration on the negative consequences of competition.

Such a heavy emphasis on winning is not a natural phenomenon but rather a cultural one. Games of many societies have no competitive element but reflect a different emphasis because of their cultural values. For contrast, let us examine a game from another society that would never capture the enthusiasm of North Americans.

The Tangu people of New Guinea play a popular game known as taketak, which involves throwing a spinning top into massed lots of stakes driven into the ground. There are two teams. Players of each team try to touch as many stakes with their tops as possible. In the end, however, the participants play not to win but to draw. The game must go on until an exact draw is reached. This requires great skill, since players sometimes must throw their tops into the massed stakes without touching a single one. Taketak expresses a prime value in Tangu culture, that is, the concept of moral equivalence, which is reflected in the precise sharing of foodstuffs among the people.[16]

Another example is how the Zuni Indians treat an outstanding runner, as reported by anthropologist Ruth Benedict. "The ideal man in Zuni is a person of dignity and affability who has never tried to lead, and who has never called forth comment from his neighbors. Any conflict, even though all right is on his side, is held against him. Even in contests of skill like their foot races, if a man wins habitually he is debarred from running. They are interested in a game that a number can play with even chances, and an outstanding runner spoils the game: they will have none of him."[17]

These examples underscore our contention that a society's sports do mirror its basic values. Cooperative societies have sports that minimize competition, and aggressive societies have highly competitive games.

The Valued Means to Achievement in Sport

In sport, as in the larger society, the goal of individual achievement must be accomplished through continuous hard work and sacrifice. The work ethic is also the sports ethic. Someone wins with enough work and sacrifice or, conversely, someone loses without enough work. This is illustrated by the slogans that coaches use to inspire hard work in their athletes:

"The will to win is the will to work."

"Practice makes perfect."

"Success is 99 percent perspiration and 1 percent inspiration."

"No one ever drowned in sweat."

"By failing to prepare yourself you are preparing to fail."

"There is no substitute for hard work."

"It's better to wear out than to rust out."[18]

Americans do not like quitters in sports or in the other areas of social life. This is seen in the disdain accorded typically to school dropouts, panhandlers, persons who declare bankruptcy, persons who do not seek employment, and athletes who either quit the team or do not give a 100 percent effort even when the outcome of the game is no longer in doubt. Coaches, because they believe that success in sport and in life is dependent on sustained effort, do all in their power to instill in their athletes a never-give-up attitude.

Sport reinforces the success values of society for spectators as well. Susan P. Montague and Robert Morais made this point with special reference to football:

Football validates the success model by staging a real event in which the principles of success are shown to work as promised by society. The contest actually happens before the viewer's eyes. The reality of the event is then transferred to the ideology of the success model, which is presented as accounting for the winning team's superior performance. Of course, there is a sleight of hand going on here, because "the best team always wins." The team that wins is not necessarily best; it is best because it wins. In order to set the stage for the legitimacy of the assertion that the best team does indeed win, the teams must rigidly and publicly adhere to behaviors symbolic of the success model during their training [i.e., self-denial and hard work]. It can then be argued that a team's superior performance is consonant with the expectations of the success model. The burden of proof switches to the losers: If the team that abides by the rules wins, then the team that loses must have failed to dedicate itself seriously enough.[19]

Progress in Sport

Coaches, athletes, and fans place a central value on progress. Continued improvement (in mastering new techniques, in winning more games, or in setting new records) is the aim of all athletes and teams. As an example, track and field stars undergo great pressures to set new records each time they compete. The demands come from the fans, from the press, from promoters, and often from the athletes themselves.

Materialism in Sport

Although the value that Americans place on success in competitive situations has the most important impact on the way sport is organized in the United States, materialism also has an important effect. Professional teams especially are formed to make a profit. Owners make lucrative arrangements with television networks that have a dramatic effect on sports (e.g., scheduling, timing, and number of time-outs). Teams that do not show a high enough profit may be moved to another city in the search for more money. Professional leagues have also secured exemptions from federal antitrust legislation to protect their investments. High-powered university teams are just as involved in profits as the pros, but they are less obvious about their material interests.

Athletes, too, are plainly motivated by material concerns. Writing in 1972, when sport was not nearly as materialistic as now, Tom Meschery, former professional basketball player and coach lamented:

There was a time, and it was not so long ago, when things such as honor and loyalty were virtues in sport, and not objects of ridicule. It was a time when athletes drew pleasure and satisfaction from the essence of competition, not just from their paychecks. But somehow, with the introduction of big business, the concept of sports in this country has changed. The business psyche has invaded basketball and has made the players nothing but businessmen spurred by the profit motive. In some cases players make more money with their outside financial activities than they do on the court. Their sport becomes a mere showcase to keep them before the public, like an actor's guest appearance on a television talk show. The game no longer has its roots sunk into idealistic bedrock. It's just business: nine to five.[20]

Examples of the attitude Meschery described are common in all sports. After each Olympics so-called amateur athletes parlay their sports accomplishments into millions for endorsements, personal appearances, and the like. Free agents in professional sports commonly sign with the highest bidder and often try to renegotiate contracts before they expire. In such instances, team and fan loyalty are all but forgotten. Team owners typically have no loyalty to the cities that subsidize them. They move their teams to where more money can be made or threaten to move in order to receive even greater benefits from their host cities.

Athletes hire lawyers to negotiate for the highest possible bonuses and salary arrangements. They hold out individually and even strike collectively, on occasion, for better material comforts (see chapter 10). Furthermore, athletes often engage in activities calculated to increase attendance at contests. Boxers and their promoters (e.g., Mike Tyson and Don King) are well known for this. Star athletes also devote much of their energy to making money by endorsing products and projects, making personal appearances, and giving inspirational talks (basketball star Michael Jordan, for example, makes about $30 million just from endorsements).

Sports fans, too, are influenced by material considerations. They like plush stadiums with expensive scoreboards and other amenities. They are excited by athletes playing for large stakes (e.g., the difference between first and second place in a golf tournament may be as much as two hundred thousand dollars).

External Conformity in Sport

Conformity is highly valued in American sport. Coaches, generally, demand that their athletes conform to the behavior norms of the community in hairstyles, manner of dress, and speech patterns. This is probably the result of two factors (both of which we will elaborate later in this book): first, coaches feel that their precarious jobs may be in further jeopardy if they permit athletes to act outside community standards; second, coaches tend to be conservative.

Coaches of team sports place a high value on team unity, emphasizing subordination of self to team success. Athletes are expected to subordinate their wills to achieve team success, as the following coaching cliches indicate:

"There is no 'I' in team."

"There is no 'U' in team."

"A player doesn't make the team, the team makes the player."

"United we stand, divided we fall."

"Cooperate—remember the banana; every time it leave the bunch, it get skinned."[21]

Another aspect of external conformity, found in both sport and in the larger society, is the acceptance of authority. The system, the rules, and the structure of power are not challenged. Coaches typically structure coach-athlete relationships along authoritarian lines. They analyze and structure team positions for the precise specialization of the athletes, and they endeavor to control player behavior not only throughout practice and contest periods but also on a round-the-clock basis. Under this form of management, the athletes are the instruments of organizational goals. In most cases they are not consulted about team membership, practice methods, strategy, team rules, or any of the other dynamic functions of a team. In a biting critique of modern sport, Jean-Marie Brohm stated: "Sport is basically a mechanization of the body, treated as an automaton, governed by the principle of maximizing output. The organism is trained to sustain prolonged effort and maintain the necessary regularity of pace. . . . In the guise of a game which is supposed to freely develop the strengths of the individual, sport in fact reproduces the world of work."[22] Thus, play has been transformed into work. The playfulness, fun, and creativity of sport is controlled by the absolute control of coaches over their teams and players; if players wish to participate, they must conform to the coach's system. The typical coach's philosophy is "It's my way or the highway."

Summary

American values clearly affect American sport. Just as important is the insight that sport in society, through its organization and the demands and the emphases of those in power, reinforces societal values. This mutual reinforcement places sport squarely in the middle of society's "way of life." It is precisely because sport is so intertwined with the fundamental values of society that any attack on sport is usually interpreted as unpatriotic. Hence, criticism of sport is rarely taken seriously. We should keep this in mind as we examine the positive and negative consequences of sport in society. Any proposed changes in sport must be related to the values of society.

Notes

1. Craig Crawford and James Curtis, "English-Canadian-American Differences in Value Orientations: Survey Comparisons Bearing on Lipset's Thesis," *Studies in Comparative International Development* 14, nos. 3–4 (1979): 23–44.

2. Robin M. Williams, Jr., *American Society: A Sociological Interpretation,* 3d ed. (New York: Knopf, 1970), 451.

3. We have relied on three sources that were especially helpful for the delineation of North American values: Williams, *American Society,* 438–504; Cora Dubois, "The Dominant Value Profile of American Culture," *American Anthropologist* 57 (December 1955): 1232–1239; and Phillip Slater, *The Pursuit of Loneliness: American Culture at the Breaking Point* (Boston: Beacon Press, 1970).

4. Williams, *American Society,* 454–55.

5. Robert H. Frank and Philip J. Cook, *The Winner-Take-All Society* (New York: The Free Press, 1995).

6. See David R. Simon and D. Stanley Eitzen, *Elite Deviance,* 4th ed. (Boston: Allyn and Bacon, 1993).

7. See William Ryan, *Blaming the Victim,* rev. ed. (New York: Pantheon Books, 1976).

8. Edward C. Banfield, *The Unheavenly City: The Nature and Future of Our Urban Crisis* (Boston: Little, Brown, 1970). For a critique of Banfield's position, see William Ryan, "Is Banfield Serious?," *Social Policy* 1 (November-December 1970): 74–76.

9. *The Chronicle of Higher Education Almanac* 62 (1 September 1995): 17.

10. Ibid., 20.

11. David Riesman et al., *The Lonely Crowd* (New Haven, Conn.: Yale University Press, 1950).

12. William H. Whyte, Jr., *The Organization Man* (New York: Simon and Schuster, 1956).

13. Eldon E. Snyder, "Athletic Dressing Room Slogans as Folklore: A Means of Socialization," *International Review of Sport Sociology* 7 (1972): 89–102.

14. See D. Stanley Eitzen, "Ethical Problems in American Sport," *Journal of Sport and Social Issues* 12 (spring 1988): 17–20.

15. Bill Shirley, "Is It Really A Sin to Lose?" *The Denver Post,* 11 November 1983, sec. D, p. 1.

16. George B. Leonard, "Winning Isn't Everything: It's Nothing," *Intellectual Digest* 4 (October 1973): 45. See also, Alfie Kohn, "Sports Create Unhealthy Competition," in *Sports in America: Opposing Viewpoints,* ed. William Dudley (San Diego, Calif.: Greenhaven Press, 1994), 17–20.

17. Ruth Benedict, *Patterns of Culture* (New York: Mentor Books, 1934), 95; see also John Garrity, "A Clash of Cultures on the Hopi Reservation," *Sports Illustrated,* 20 November 1989.

18. Snyder, "Athletic Dressing Room Slogans as Folklore," 89–102.

19. Susan P. Montague and Robert Morais, "Football Games and Rock Concerts: The Ritual Enactment of American Success Models," in *The American Dimension: Cultural Myths and Realities,* ed. W. Arens and Susan P. Montague (Port Washington, N.Y.: Alfred Publishing, 1976), 42.

20. Tom Meschery, "There Is a Disease in Sports Now," *Sports Illustrated,* 2 October 1972, 56.

21. Snyder, "Athletic Dressing Room Slogans as Folklore," 89–102.

22. Jean-Marie Brohm, *Sport: A Prison of Measured Time* (London: Ink Links, 1978), 55.

Chapter 4

Children and Sport

More people participate in sport during their youth than at any other time in their lives. Although for many young boys and girls sports involvement is limited to informal, neighborhood play, an increasing number of North American youth participate in highly organized athletic competition. Youth sports programs have grown to include greater numbers of participants, and new programs have been created to include a bewildering variety of sports. Thus, a great deal of the social life of youngsters is spent playing sports.

Youth Sports Programs: Something for Everyone

Nonschool youth sports programs in North America are organized by more than twenty-five agencies and by thousands of local and regional sports organizations. Estimates of the total number of participants run to 20 million for American youth and some 2.5 million for Canadian youth.[1] Little League baseball is the largest of the youth sports organizations with twenty thousand leagues in over sixty countries and more than 3 million youngsters engaged in Little League annually. However, in terms of participants soccer has been growing faster than any other youth sport during the past decade. More than three thousand YMCAs in the United States provide some 3 million boys and girls the opportunity to participate in organized sports. The Junior Olympics Sports Program sponsors over two thousand local, state, regional, and national events in twenty-one different sports. Girls' participation in sports in the United States has been increasing over the past twenty years and represents about 40 percent of the participants; in Canada only about 27 percent of youth sport participants are females.

The programs are becoming more elaborate and are enlisting younger participants each year. There is a well-organized outlet for almost every child who has an interest in playing sports. Parents can enroll their children in age-group gymnastics and swimming programs at three years of age; ice hockey, soccer, football, T-baseball, and a half dozen other sports begin at age four. Indeed, an early start is

considered essential, if parents or children have professional or Olympic-level aspirations. Starting at ten or eleven years of age is considered too old in this case.[2]

The major promotional forces behind these youth sports programs have been parents and interested laypersons, while educators, physicians, and psychologists have tended to be less enthusiastic. Indeed, educators have rather effectively prohibited interscholastic sports in the elementary schools and have severely restricted school sports in the junior high schools. They have, however, been ineffectual in controlling nonschool programs.

As sports for children and adolescents have expanded and diversified, a wide variety of sponsors have emerged. The types of agencies that sponsor youth sport in the United States are quite varied, and an example of each is shown in table 4.1. Canadian youth sport funding comes from various sources. The major sources are the government, community fund-raising, private sponsorships, and registration fees. Virtually all of the national associations receive over half of their money from the federal government. At the local level, fund-raising and registration fees account for more than half of the total money.

Such a bewildering number of youth sports programs with varying structural arrangements exist that it is somewhat foolish to talk about them as though they were all alike. There are programs that emphasize participation and carefully regulate the type and extent of stress placed on the players. On the other hand, there are programs in which adults intrude enormously on the play of the youngsters; in many of these the purpose is simply to train children to become champions. An example of the former is the Nick Bollettieri Tennis Academy in Florida, which is quite clearly devoted to producing tennis champions. Accounts of the lives of many of the tennis prodigies at the Tennis Academy clearly demonstrate that their only goal in sports, or at least the goal of their parents and coaches, is to become a professional athlete. There are many academies and clubs in a variety of sports scattered across North America training athletes to become pros or Olympic-level competitors.[3]

table 4.1 *Categories of Agencies Who Organize Youth Sports*

Type of Agency	Example of Type
National youth sport organization	PONY Baseball
National youth agency	Boys Clubs of America
National governing body	U.S. Wrestling
National service organization	American Legion Baseball
National religious organization	Catholic Youth Organization
Regional youth sport organization	Soccer Association for Youth
State school activity association	Illinois High School Activity Association
Local school district	Hutchinson, Kans., Public School
Local service club	Champaign Optimist Club
Municipal recreation department	Champaign Park District
Private sports club	Urbana Wrestling Club

Source: Frank L. Smoll, Richard A. Magill, and Michael J. Ash, *Children in Sport,* 3d ed. (Champaign, Ill.: Human Kinetics, 1988), p. 19.

Despite variations in youth sports forms and functions, advocates of youth sports programs claim that they provide a means for the development of such personal-social attributes as self-discipline, cooperativeness, achievement motivation, courage, persistence, and so forth. Proponents of organized youth sports typically view them as good preparation for the realities of adult life. Additionally, advocates contend that the physical activity involved in playing sports promotes health and fitness.[4] On the other hand, critics of youth sports claim that excessive psychological and physical demands are frequently placed on participants. They also contend that the encroachment of adults into the world of young persons reduces the value of play as a spontaneous, expressive experience. Finally, critics observe that youth sports frequently seem to be conducted for the self-serving needs of parents and youth sports leaders. A workshop addressing intensive training and participation in youth sports sponsored by the American Orthopaedic Society for Sports Medicine asserted that pressure from parents and coaches is forcing many elite child athletes to strive for perfection. That pressure may be responsible for a host of physical and psychological ailments.[5]

The Rise of Youth Sports Programs: The Take-Off and Expansion of a New Form of Sport

Two independent but interrelated developments in the sociocultural milieu of North American society in the past two generations were primarily responsible for the rise and expansion of youth sports programs. The first was the rise of organized and corporate sport in all parts of the country. The first half of the twentieth century witnessed an enormous growth in popular spectator sports, such as major league baseball, collegiate football, professional ice hockey, boxing, and others. High school athletics became an integral part of North American education, and the overall obsession with these forms of organized sport eventually trickled down to preadolescent youth.

The second development promoting the growth of youth sports programs was that North Americans began to realize the need and importance of protecting and providing varied opportunities for children. Increasingly, childhood was seen as a particularly opportune time for nurturing attitudes and habits that would prepare youth for adulthood. Youth leaders urged the use of sports for the development of desirable personal-social skills. When the schools refused to sponsor sports for preadolescent youth, the task was left to voluntary agencies, and responsibility for sport competition for the preadolescent group was assumed by child-oriented organizations outside of the educational framework.[6]

Until the 1970s most organized youth sports programs were for boys only, but growing out of the attack by the women's movement on gender discrimination in all aspects of social life, exclusion of girls from organized sport became unacceptable. The Little League's ban against participation by girls was challenged in 1973, and after several lawsuits girls legally won the right to participate in Little League baseball. Over the past twenty years organized youth sport has become available in almost every sport in which girls have wished to participate. The initial reservations, and even objections, to girls' sports participation have gradually declined and have been replaced by enthusiastic endorsement by almost everyone. However, there are those who question the wisdom of merely incorporating females into the prevailing youth sport system. One critic of the traditional youth sports model, argues that, ". . . for many females, traditional youth sport programs do not offer a sociosymbolic system or structure conducive to creative development. In exploring the fictions of segregation and integration, we found that with integration our differences were not lost, nor with segregation our worlds separated. Both practices act as modalities of foreclosure in that females, as subjects, have little chance of inventing new configurations within the traditional system of youth sport."[7]

Objectives of Youth Sports Programs: What Do Young Athletes Want? What Do Their Parents and Coaches Want?

Regardless of the sponsoring agency, the objectives of most youth sports programs are quite similar. They are intended to provide young persons with an opportunity to learn culturally relevant sports skills. Inasmuch as sport is such a pervasive activity in North American society, developing sports skills becomes almost a public duty. Equally important in the objectives of these programs, however, is the transmission of attitudes and values through interpersonal associations with teammates and opponents and through deliberate actions on the part of coaches, officials, and parents. Thus, youth sports are viewed as an environment for promoting attitudes and values about such things as competition, sportsmanship, discipline, authority, and social relationships. The original certificate of the federal charter granted to Little League baseball illustrates the objectives of most youth sports programs: "To help and voluntarily assist boys in developing qualities of citizenship, sportsmanship, and manhood. Using the disciplines of the native American game of baseball, to teach spirit and competitive will to win, physical fitness through individual sacrifice, the values of team play, and wholesome well-being through healthful and social association with other youngsters under proper leadership."[8] Girls are now participants in Little League baseball, but its objectives are still the same.

In a popular book for parents, coaches, and athletes about youth sports, the author lists seven values of sports for young athletes. They are:

1. Helps a child's overall physical development.
2. Gives the child the opportunity to become familiar with his/her body and to learn the body's needs and limitations.
3. Is social as well as physical and thus teaches young athletes how to interact with his/her peers.
4. Teaches cooperation, teamwork, and how to follow rules.
5. Helps the child learn for him/herself if winning or losing is important.
6. Gives parents the opportunity of offering the child unqualified support.
7. Helps the child gain acceptance and credibility among his/her peers.[9]

Beyond the benefits that youth sports are believed to provide for participants, community-based programs may function to satisfy a community need by contributing what appears to be a link with symbols of stability, order, tradition, and a communal focus. The extent to which youth sports actually serve these functions is hard to quantify, but there is little doubt that substantial community financial and human resources are poured into the programs. Local merchants sponsor teams, coaches volunteer their time, groundskeepers, concession-stand operators, scorekeepers, and so forth facilitate the ongoing operations of the program; and parents turn out in large numbers to cheer their children. In addition, playing fields are built and maintained, and equipment is largely furnished, with taxpayers' money. Youth sports are indeed a significant community activity in towns and cities throughout North America.

Socialization and Sport

With youth sports as pervasive as they are in North America, questions about the social sources for the promotion of youth sports involvement are important for understanding how youngsters get into organized sports and what the consequences are of these experiences. In the broadest sense the process of becoming a young athlete is part of a socialization process.

Socialization is the process of learning and adapting to a given social system. In the context of society, the activity of socialization is called cultural transmission and is the means by which a society preserves its norms and perpetuates itself. At birth, infants are certainly living organisms, but they are not social beings. Humans raised in isolation develop only their animal nature, but those raised in human society demonstrate the human aspects that derive from social living. They also demonstrate the impact of their culture upon them, and this is called socialization.

Socialization begins at birth and continues throughout an individual's life cycle, but the years from birth to adolescence are considered critical, for in these years the basic cultural transmission takes place. Numerous people are involved in the socialization of an individual, but because of their frequency of contact, their primacy, and their control over rewards and punishments, the primary agents and agencies for socialization are families, peer groups, schools, churches, and mass media.

The outcomes of the socialization process are attitudes, values, knowledge, and behaviors that are related to the culture of which individuals are a part and to the roles that they will play in it. Thus, as children in a society interact with others through language, gestures, rewards, and punishments, they learn the attitudes, the values, and the expectations of various individuals in that society as well as the behaviors considered appropriate to the various situations of their social life. Socialization is, however, more than a one-way process from socializers (parents, peers, and so forth) to the children; a reciprocal interaction is also at work, and youngsters may affect the attitudes, values, and behaviors of adults.[10] Young athletes, for example, may influence the attitudes and behaviors toward sport of various socializing agents, including parents, coaches, teachers, and peers.

The topic of socialization and sport may be divided into two subtopics for analysis: (1) socialization into sports and (2) socialization via sports. In the first the focus is on the agents and agencies that attract, or draw, children into sports. That is, an analysis of the ways in which children become involved in sports. An analysis of socialization via sports concentrates on the consequences, or outcomes, of sports involvement. In the next section, we direct our attention to socialization into sport; socialization via sport is addressed later in this chapter.

Socialization into Sport: Why Do Children Get Involved in Organized Sports?

The study of socialization into sports roles is concerned with who gets involved in sport, which social agents and agencies are responsible for guiding people into such involvement, how persons learn sports roles, and what the social processes for becoming involved are.

Families

The family is the first and perhaps the most important social environment in a young person's life, and there is overwhelming evidence that the family—its social status, its structure, and its patterning of activities—is a significant influence in socializing boys and girls into sport.

One important influence on the sport involvement of youngsters is the structure of the family. Families vary in size from a single child to sometimes more than a dozen offspring; following divorce or the death of one parent, some families become single parent families. According to the 1990 Census, traditional families, meaning married couples with or without children, is at its lowest rate, 56 percent, in at least two hundred years. Almost half of all children are growing up without both natural parents in the household.[11]

Very little is known about the influence of any specific structural variable on sport socialization with the exception of ordinal position in relation to siblings. The term "ordinal position" refers to the numerical place of an individual's birth in the order of births in his or her family (such as firstborn or born third of five). Several research studies in sociology of sport found that participation in dangerous sports is a function of birth order, with later-borns being overrepresented in such dangerous sports as football, hockey, wrestling, skydiving, and rugby. Explanations of these findings have centered on the possibility of variations in parental behavior toward first- and later-born children. For example, developmental psychologists have found that parents pay more attention to their firstborns and are overly protective of them, with the result that firstborns become hesitant and fearful of situations of perceived physical harm or danger. Thus, firstborns may be more likely to avoid dangerous sports. Since later-borns are not monitored as closely, they may experiment more with risky endeavors and thus become less fearful of dangerous activities, including dangerous sports.[12]

Participation in youth sports programs cuts across all socioeconomic strata; however, as in adult sports involvement, children from working-class families are overrepresented in some youth sports, and children from upper-middle-class families in others. Parents socialize their children into sports that are deemed most appropriate for their socioeconomic status. For example, age-group tennis players, skiers, gymnasts, and swimmers tend to come from upper-middle-class families. On the other hand, youth baseball, boxing, wrestling, and football programs tend to attract youngsters from middle- and working-class families. (Chapter 12 deals with the social stratification aspects of sports in more detail.)

Parents

Children tend to adopt the attitudes and values of their parents. Parents who reward the acquisition of motor skills and who themselves engage in sporting activities tend to socialize their children to an interest in physical activity. Indeed, several investigators have found that parents are important agents of sport socialization for both their sons and their daughters.[13]

Parental influence appears to occur through their own participation (the modeling influence) and through their interest in and encouragement of their offspring's involvement in sport. Surveys of North American families have found that around 75 percent of parents engage in some kind of sports activity with their children.[14] Thus, research suggests that parental encouragement and actual participation are primary sources of sport socialization. A high percentage of fathers and mothers of young female athletes actually engaged in sport themselves, and overall, parents are the most salient social agents in encouraging female high school athletes to participate.[15]

Although parents have received considerable attention as a factor in influencing the sport involvement of their offspring, very little is known about the specific contributions that each parent makes. Some investigators have reported that the father was frequently the most significant socializing agent in the family and the most important predictor of sport participation for both boys and girls. Others have reported a tendency for the same-sex parent to have greater influence on sport involvement than the opposite-sex parent. More specifically, they have found that fathers' sports interests were more strongly related than mothers' interests to direct primary participation for both males and females.[16]

Parents who have been queried about their children's involvement in organized sports programs have expressed rather strong support. A five-part series by *USA Today* on children in sports revealed that parents see a variety of benefits from youth sports: 84 percent said it helped youngsters become physically fit, 83 percent said it provided fun for children, and 74 percent said it helped develop self-confidence. Three out of four parents of youth sport athletes rated the coaches as excellent or good. They generally felt that sports have had a positive effect on family life and view sports as supporting parents in socializing their children, in that they teach youngsters useful personal and social skills. Overall, parents were pleased with their community's sports programs and with their children's involvement.[17]

For those parents whose children are training for elite status, for instance to be an Olympic-level athlete or a professional athlete, there are fears, sacrifices, and constant pressures. Is the child being robbed of his/her childhood in the tightly structured training environment? Are the sacrifices of the child living away from home year-around worth it? Are the costs for coaching worth it? There is also the constant realization that unless the child continues to improve against the competition he or she will be dropped by the coach or the program or both.[18] When parents set for their child the goal of achieving professional standing, pressures are inevitably applied to the child's performance.

In the literature on socialization into sport, little attention has been given to the ways in which youths influence their parents to become involved. Instead, most research has presented a unidimensional socialization process in which the offspring are the learners and the parents are the socializers. Some sociologists have called for greater attention to the symbolic interactionist perspective, which sees social interacting as reciprocal and negotiable. In this view, analyses of parent effects need to be balanced by analyses of child effects and of the two-way "reciprocal-effects synthesis." With respect to sport, in addition to parental encouragement of offspring, some family adjustments may produce reverse socialization, with parents being socialized into sport through their children's participation. Indeed, many parents learn about sport and become involved in sport from their children. Therefore, the socialization between parents and their children is frequently bidirectional. Thus, although parents may initially steer their children into sport, the child's involvement often has behavioral and attitudinal consequences for the parents.

Siblings

A rather consistent association has been shown between parents' sports involvement, their support, and their encouragement and the involvement of their children in sport, but the influence of siblings is not so clear. It is probable that the example of an older brother or sister participating in organized sport spurs younger children to become involved. However, when sports participants are asked to list the persons most important in their own sport-role socialization, the influence of siblings is typically rated quite low. A broad base of familial support is probably present in most cases when children become involved in sport. The ability of siblings to influence the social environment apart from parents is quite circumscribed.[19]

Peers

As important as the family is, the neighborhood and the peer group also serve as powerful socializing agents for sport involvement, especially as youngsters move into adolescence. Typically, during adolescence less time is spent with the family, and more time is spent with peers. Interactions with peers in the neighborhood and at school almost force compliance with their interests and activities. When peers are involved in sports, young people frequently experience a great deal of pressure to become involved also or to give up cherished social relationships. Several studies examining the influence of socializing agents on the process of socialization of boys and girls into sports have found that peers are a major influence throughout childhood and adolescence.[20]

Coaches

Coaches are not often the persons responsible for initiating young boys and girls into sports, but for many youngsters an extremely close, emotional bond develops between athlete and coach, a bond that frequently becomes the main reason for continuing involvement. From the thousands of volunteer coaches to those who make their living coaching, coaches exert a tremendous influence on young athletes. Most young athletes perceive that the role of "coach" is socially admired. Also, young athlete's abilities, an important source of self-esteem, have been developed by their coach. The coach is, therefore, seen as someone who has helped the athlete acquire some of his/her most important possessions. Many ex-youth athletes, years after they have stopped competing, still consider their former coaches to be the most significant adults in their lives.

Schools

Of course, the school, with its physical education classes, is a significant socializing agent for North American children. Thanks to universal education and a physical education curriculum that typically puts a great deal of emphasis on learning athletic skills, most children are taught the rudiments of a variety of sports in school. (Chapter 5 deals further with sport in high school.)

Mass Media

The mass media must be mentioned with regard to the sport-role socialization of young boys and girls. Youngsters are virtually inundated with sports via newspapers, magazines, and especially television. It is obvious that the mass media bring sports to the attention of the young. Few youngsters do not know the names of the NFL, NHL, NBA, and major league baseball teams. A great many boys and girls have heroes among professional and Olympic athletes, and many of them have plastered their bedroom walls with sports posters.

Parents, siblings, peers, coaches, schools, and the media, then, are the sport-socializing agents and agencies that act on youth. They are so influential that it is a rare youngster who is not affected in some way by sport as he or she passes through childhood and adolescence.

Participants

Studies of participants in youth sports programs usually find that they have positive attitudes toward their experiences. When asked what they like most about their sports experiences, participants typically list the fun of being on an organized team, the chance to meet others and to make friends, and the opportunity to improve their skills. In a *USA Today* poll about children in sport, researchers asked participants why they participate. Eighty-eight percent said they participate in sports just to have fun.[21] The National Institute for Child Centered Coaching found that the four most important reasons kids play organized sport are:

1. To have fun.
2. To improve skills and learn new ones.
3. To be with friends and make new ones.
4. For the excitement of competition.[22]

Although millions of youngsters enthusiastically participate in organized youth sports each year and many continue for as long as they are eligible, a surprisingly large number do not continue to take part in sport; they become dropouts. Indeed, as many as one-third of youth sports participants voluntarily drop out of sport each year.[23] Seventy percent of kids by the age of thirteen drop out of youth sports programs. Researchers have tried to ascertain the motives for sports withdrawal. They have found that the disappointment of not getting to play, poor umpiring, and being scolded for mistakes by coaches, parents, or both, are the things that the young participants dislike most. In a study carried out by the Youth Sports Institute at Michigan State University that asked participants why they discontinued youth sports involvement, the top ten reasons were, in ranked order:

1. I lost interest.
2. I was not having fun.
3. It took too much time.
4. Coach was a poor teacher.
5. Too much pressure.
6. Wanted a nonsport activity.
7. I was tired of it.
8. I needed more study time.
9. Coach played favorites.
10. It was boring.[24]

In summarizing the research on youth sports withdrawal, sport psychologist Daniel Gould said:

> Former youth sport participants cite a number of varied personal and situational reasons for sport withdrawal. These include such diverse motives as interest in other activities, conflicts of interest, lack of playing time, lack of success, little skill improvement, lack of fun, boredom, and injury. Conflicts of interest and interest in other activities have been found to be the most consistently cited motives for sport withdrawal. Other more negative motives such as a lack of playing time, overemphasis on competition, boredom, competitive stress, dislike of the coach, and no fun have been rated as major motives for sport withdrawal by a smaller number of former participants. Some evidence reveals that these more negative motives play a more important role in the discontinuation of younger as compared to older dropouts.[25]

The picture that emerges from studying young athletes and their views of participation in youth sports is that they want to have fun and learn skills, but since many of them encounter pressures to train and win, some simply drop out of organized sport programs. For them, the promise of fun, sociability, and skill acquisition through sports is lost.

Socialization via Sport

The extent to which the attitudes, values, beliefs, and behaviors of North American young people are actually influenced by participation in organized youth sports programs is largely unknown because few investigations have been undertaken on this topic. Thus, little empirical evidence exists to substantiate the many claims that have been made for the contribution of sport to building character.[26] The major reason is because sport constitutes only one of the sets of forces operating on young people. Every child is subjected to a multitude of social experiences that are not sport related. Thus, much of what we think we know about the effects, or consequences, of sport participation is impressionistic, and this fact needs to be remembered in any discussion of the topic.

There are several principles of socialization theory, however, that probably hold true with regard to youth sports. In general, the influence of sports experiences will be stronger: (1) when the degree of involvement is frequent, intense, and prolonged; (2) when the participation is voluntary rather than involuntary; (3) when the socializer (e.g., the coach) is perceived as powerful and prestigious; and (4) when the quality of relationships is high in expressiveness.

Two Forms of Play

Several social scientists have suggested that the social context in which a sport activity takes place determines its social outcomes. The observational studies of several investigators indicate that there are two distinct social contexts in which youth sports activities take place: "peer-group" and "adult-organized." They have characterized and contrasted the potential socialization outcomes for these two forms of play in terms of their organization, process, impetus, and social implications.

Organization

In organized team sports the most salient characteristic is that both action and involvement are under adult control and the actions of the players are strictly regulated by specialized rules and roles. As Gary Fine noted in his insightful book *With the Boys: Little League Baseball and Preadolescent Culture,* "Little League games are organized as performance rather than play. . . . Little League is based solely on a structural concordance with professional leagues."[27]

Youth sport coaches are remarkably similar in the way they organize practice sessions. Activities during practice tend to be very rule-bound. Coaches allow little flexibility in the executing of skills or in the performing of other tasks associated with practice. The youngsters tend to wait to be told what to do, often waiting for directions on how to do things that are routine. Spontaneous behavior, when it occurs, consists of "horsing around" while waiting to practice some given task. Very few decisions on any aspect of the practice are made by the youngsters. Most decisions are made by the coaches, and the participants are expected to carry them out obediently. The emphasis in the organized setting tends to be on the development of sport skills, not on the development of interpersonal skills.

With respect to peer play, before the age of seven, children rarely play games spontaneously; if they play them at all, it is usually on the initiative of adults or older children. Thus, organized sports programs for youngsters under the age of seven are not organized extensions of what children of that age would be doing anyway; they are simply testaments to the power and influence adults have on young children.[28]

When peer play is found, usually among youngsters over the age of seven, it is player-controlled. Players rely on informal norms of conduct and informal rules to regulate the game. The youngsters make consensual decisions on groupings and game rules. Teams are usually organized informally; this is done quickly and typically with little friction. The games children choose in free play generally have fewer rules and fewer specialized roles than the games organized by adults, and children vary the rules in the process of play to suit the situation. According to

Peer play is player controlled and has fewer rules and fewer specialized roles than organized sport. The focus is on personal involvement. The purpose is to have fun.

Fine, "In informal 'sandlot' games the authority structure operates differently. It is not that there is no authority structure. Instead, the structure works not through role occupancy but by moral suasion."[29]

Process

The process of play in peer-group sport and adult-organized sport is also quite different. In the former, teams are chosen, and the game usually begins quickly. Field researchers of children's informal sports frequently note the efficiency with which the youngsters go about getting the teams chosen and the game under way. Arguments about rule interpretations or a "call," such as whether a player is "safe" or "out," when they do occur, usually cause only minimal delays. Shouts of "Let him have it" or "Play it over" usually settle the debate, and play is resumed.

In the informal, peer-group games the primary focus tends to be on the involvement in a combination of action, personal involvement, keeping the game close, and the reaffirming friendships. The quest for victory, or a "win," is not one of the salient outcomes; instead of a narrow focus on winning there is often a search for self-mastery; that is, attempting to create situations that require performing up to a personal standard of satisfaction.[30]

By contrast, in the play process of organized youth sports, there tends to be an emphasis on order, punctuality, respect for authority, obedience to adult directions, and a strict division of labor. Coaches typically insist on order, sometimes prohibiting participants from talking unless the coach speaks to them. The coach's concern for order and discipline often reduces the amount of playing time. Organizing the practice session or stopping practice to discuss mistakes or to punish misbehavior sometimes takes up significant portions of the practice session. The participants become so accustomed to following orders in an organized sport setting, that they frequently will cease to play altogether if the coach is absent or not directly supervising. Close observation by the coach is required to keep them playing.[31]

In organized youth sports the participants have no say in the rules; the rules are made by adults. In the programs of national sports agencies (such as Little League baseball), a national rule book is published to which all participants must conform. Thus, in this form of sport, participants are merely followers, not makers or interpreters, of the rules. Fine's comments are instructive: "The official rules of Little League baseball are given by adults—not subject to change by preadolescent negotiation. Little Leaguers are supposed to follow rules provided by the national organization, and coaches and umpires must be knowledgeable about these rules and enforce them without exception. . . . For a game as simple as preadolescent baseball, these rules are extensive, filling sixty-two pages in 1984."[32]

Winning is frequently the overriding goal in formal youth sports programs. By striving for league standings, by awarding championships, by choosing all-star teams, such programs send the not-so-subtle message to youngsters that the most important goal of sports is winning games.

Impetus

The impetus of peer play comes entirely from the youngsters; they play because they enjoy it. They are free to commence and terminate a game on the basis of player interest. Conversely, the impetus of play in organized sports programs comes from the coaches; they schedule the practices for a given time and end practices when they see fit. Games are scheduled by a league authority and are played in a very rigid time frame. The youngsters have no choice but to play in the way the adults wish them to play. Their own enjoyment appears to be of little concern to the adults. Fine argued that "there are components of the playing of Little League baseball that can usefully be seen as 'work', at least in a moral sense. Coaches and many players expect the participants to adhere to a Puritan work ethic, preparing themselves for adult

life."[33] One coach prodded his young players to "take pride in your work!" We summarize the dimensions of the various forms of youth play in table 4.2.

Social Implications

Adult-sponsored youth sport is basically an organized structuring of groupings, activities, and rules that are imposed upon the participants. Peer play, on the other hand, is a voluntary activity with a flexible process of social exchange based on consensus. Youngsters are therefore exposed to quite different experiences in what appear to be similar sport activities.

What are the social implications of these two different forms of organization of play activities for the socialization of youngsters? The application of arbitrary, adult-imposed rules in youth sport markedly contrasts with the spontaneous group-derived rules in peer-group play. This contrast is a function of the different roles of the peer group and of adults in the socialization process. The role of the peer group serves to bridge the gap between the individualistic world of children and the orientations of the wider society. The role of the organized team serves to emphasize the adult, universalist-achievement orientations deemed appropriate by the society. The differences between the goals of peer-group play and organized team effort become apparent in their emphasis on means and ends.

In the peer context, play is not overly concerned with ends; the essence of the play is the play—its fun, decisions, ritual, and personal interactions. In contrast, in organized sports, play tends to be incidental. For the adults who organize sport programs, play is identified with ends. That is, to win, to teach youngsters to play soccer, baseball, and so forth in the short run, and to develop certain attitudes and values toward social relationships and activities that in the long run tend to reproduce the requirements of occupational life by emphasizing punctuality, periodicity, and performance. Indeed, it has been argued that the organized sport experience is substantially influential in producing a bureaucratic personality.[34]

In peer play, there tends to be an elaboration of means either through varying the rules, particularizing relationships, or encouraging novelty. The games chosen in free play (in which less specialization of roles tends to occur) permit more elaboration of means. For example, the

table 4.2 *Dimensions of Experience in Spontaneous Play, Informal Competitive Games, and Organized Team Sport Events*

Dimensions of Experience	Spontaneous Play	Informal Games	Organized Team Sport Events
I. Basis of action	A search for mastery, a use of imagination, and a coincidental meshing of personal interests and/or role-playing activities	Prior experiences and existing social relationships coupled with the interpersonal and decision-making abilities of group members	Predesigned system of roles, adult leadership, and the collective role-learning abilities of team members
II. Norms governing actions	Emergent and created to meet personal standards, interest, and/or to simulate imagined role relationships	Carried over from past experience with changes and qualifications based on individual needs and maintenance of uncertainty	Highly formalized and specific, serving both organizational and formal team goals
III. System of social control	Internally generated and dependent on individual role-playing and role-taking interests and abilities	Generally internal and dependent on the collective vested interests in the game at hand	Partially internal but heavily maintained by formal standards enforced by external agents and dependent on the compliance of players
IV. Types of sanctions used	Self-imposed on a token basis or informally administered when a scene is disrupted	Informal and primarily used to minimize threats to the maintenance of action, personal involvement, and uncertainty	Both informal and formal and used for the preservation of values as well as order
V. Basis of group integration	Generally coincidental and dependent on a continual commitment to and overlap of the roles played by each of the individuals involved	Generally based on the strength of personal relationships combined with a process of social exchange between group members	Based on a combination of collective satisfaction and an awareness of and compliance with a formal set of norms and role expectations

children find many ways to use the same ball in their games. In organized sports the codified rules (enforced by coaches and officials) permit only one way to use a ball, a one-size field, a certain number of players to a side, and so forth. In organized sports programs, disputes about "calls" or about rules do not occur between players because they are made and applied by referees and coaches. Therefore, the experience in peer-play emphasizes interpersonal skills (negotiations and compromise), while the experience in organized sport is dominated by

a knowledge and dependence on strict rules and with the acceptance of the decisions of adults, who are in positions of legitimate authority.

Applying an empirically derived model of enjoyment of social experience, the Flow Model, to formal and informal sport settings, one group of researchers found a high positive correlation between challenges and skills in informal sports settings but not in adult-supervised settings. This finding "suggests that the flow experience is easier to achieve when adolescents

table 4.2   *Continued*

Dimensions of Experience	Spontaneous Play	Informal Games	Organized Team Sport Events
VI. Meanings attached to actions and events	Emergent, nebulous, and varying with each individual's conception of what is or should be going on	Personal, situational, and related to the intensity of action and the social implications of the experience	Often serious, assuming relevance beyond the game itself, and frequently related to instrumental concerns
VII. Nature of status structure	Intrinsic and varying with each individual's personal experience	Primarily intrinsic and dependent on each individual's assessment of personal involvement and success	Both intrinsic and extrinsic, related to the experience itself, the quality of performance and/or game outcomes
VIII. Basis of status structure	Combination of age, individual creative abilities, and arbitrary situational distinctions	Age combined with interpersonal and physical abilities	Physical abilities, contributions to team success, and conformity to the coach's expectations
IX. Extent of individual freedom	Limited only by self-imposed restrictions with involvement voluntary at all times	Variable with restrictions related to individual physical skills and prior status within the group	Variable but restricted to the range of behavior accepted within the rules and expectations of the coach
X. Amount of structural stability	Variable and depends on the time span over which collective involvement can be maintained	Relatively high and grounded in prior group experiences and the anticipation of future games	Very high and grounded in the endorsement of adults and the formal goals of the team

Source: Jay Coakley, "Play, Games, and Sport: Developmental Implications for Young People." In *Play, Games and Sports in Cultural Contexts*, ed. Janet C. Harris and Roberta J. Park (Champaign, Ill.: Human Kinetics, 1983), pp. 435–436.

are in control of the activity, probably because they can manipulate the balance between challenges and skills more easily in an informal setting."[35]

What is implied by an analysis of these two play forms is that play behavior in the peer group is quite different from play behavior in the youth sports program. We are not arguing that the adult-sponsored programs have no contribution to make to the socialization of youngsters. What we are emphasizing is that the variations in the social organization of children's play probably have different social consequences for them. However, little more than speculation is possible about the specific social outcomes of peer play and organized youth sports.

Development of Personal–Social Attributes Through Sport

As noted earlier in this chapter, the primary justifications of youth sports programs are the opportunities they provide for young boys and girls to learn culturally relevant sport skills and to develop desirable personal-social characteristics. Although the learning of attitudes, values, and moral behavior is a core aim of youth sports, very little empirical research has focused on the outcomes of sports participation.

There has been, however, a sustained interest in the effects of sports experiences on the orientations youth have toward sport. One of the orientations early sport sociologists focused on was whether participation in organized sport influences what participants think is most important about playing. Specifically, they studied orientations that emphasize the process (playing fair, playing for fun) and orientations that emphasize the product (playing to win); the latter was called a "professional" attitude.

Overall, there is a strong tendency for both males and females who have been involved in organized sports to have more professionalized orientations than their peers who have not been involved in organized sports. Among elite athletes, males and females are very similar in their orientations toward winning. These findings are probably not surprising, given the structural conditions of organized sport, which socializes youngsters into accepting and internalizing values of success-striving, of competitive achievement, of personal worth based upon sports outcomes, and of subjection of self to external control.[36] Although it is difficult to credit (or discredit) sports participation entirely for greater professionalized attitudes toward play, it seems that sport for fun, enjoyment, fairness, and equity are sacrificed at the altar of skill and victory as children move toward adulthood.

Playing by the rules and not taking unfair advantage of competitors is universally admired, but fair play sometimes conflicts with the quest for victory. Fairness may be promoted in youth sport, but on the other hand, victory in organized sports competition often carries more salient rewards. What attitudes do participants really acquire?

The research on this topic is sparse and has weaknesses, but it is consistent: Persons who have had extended experience in organized sports display more unfairness than those with less experience. In some youth sports leagues, the traditional practice of the players and coaches of both teams lining up and shaking hands has been abolished because it has led to ugly name calling and even brawls. This is one indication of the lack of fair play found in some youth sports programs.[37]

Of course, rule violations in sport are complex because the normative rules of competitive sports are those of consensus, legitimized by peer decree. They frequently foster intentional violations of the formal rules of the sport because such violations often increase the probability of a successful outcome and result in social and personal rewards to offenders. Only when positive reinforcement for rule violating is replaced by salient personal and social punishment will normative rules encouraging illegal behavior be repudiated.

Another approach to studying orientations toward sport has focused on the moral reasoning of athletes and nonathletes. Investigators have discovered that morality in sport is perceived differently from morality in daily life. Sport is often viewed as a part of life in which moral questions are irrelevant. The extent to which moral reasoning for sports is transferred into daily life is not clear, but since the sport culture is so dominant in the life of athletes, its values and norms might easily be seen as appropriate to nonsport situations.

Research on moral reasoning among young athletes and their nonathlete peers has found that the athletes have less mature levels of moral reasoning than nonathletes. Again, the reasons for such differences may or may not be related to sports experiences of the athletes. The results do suggest, however, that notions of youth sporting experiences universally developing positive personal-social characteristics are too simplistic.[38]

Competence in sports skills apparently does influence self-evaluation and social esteem with peers. Sports provide innumerable opportunities for the individual to perceive the feelings of others and their judgments. Thus, experiences in sports are instrumental in development of a self-image, or self-concept. Investigations show that sports abilities and interests are related to a positive self-concept, and research has consistently shown that young sports participants score higher in a variety of tests that measure mental health.[39]

Unfortunately, the research design of these studies makes it impossible to determine whether the differences found between athletic participants and nonparticipants are the result of participation or whether persons with certain personal-social characteristics are initially attracted to and remain involved in sports. Therefore, differences that exist between young athletes or skilled performers and the unskilled are not necessarily a consequence of sport involvement. Few persons dispute the potential contributions of sports competition to the psychosocial development of the participants. The actual effectiveness of participation in promoting such development is still an unanswered question, however.

Potential Psycho–Social Problems of Youth Sports

Study of problems in youth sports has become quite active, with educators, concerned parents, and even professional athletes expressing their apprehension about potential harm to youngsters in organized sports. Although sport literature is rich with those authors who have axes to grind or converts to proselytize, the fact is they often make some very telling points. There is little doubt that some very abusive practices are taking place in the world of youth sports. Having said this, we wish to reemphasize the point we made in the previous section, namely that many young people experience positive personal-social growth experiences through youth sports. The kinds of outcomes experienced by youngsters are primarily contingent upon parents and coaches, for they are the most powerful "significant others" in the lives of young boys and girls.

In this section we discuss some of the most common problems of youth sports. We make no specific accusations. We merely suggest that social experiences of a certain kind may have social consequences that are perhaps unintended and unwanted.

Adult Intrusion

There is overwhelming agreement that one of the major problems of youth sports is the intrusion of adults into the play of youngsters. The rationale behind the organization of youth sports programs is admirable: to provide young boys and girls with structure for their sports, opportunities for wide participation, proper equipment for their safety, and adult coaching to help them learn the fundamental skills. Many parents and coaches live vicariously through the youngsters, living out their unfulfilled sports dreams through the children, making considerable emotional and, sometimes, financial investments in the young athletes. Therefore, they expect a payoff and that payoff is athletic achievement by way of victories and championships. When a youngster achieves, parents and coaches see that success as, in a way, their own personal achievement. If the child fails to live up to performance expectations, he or she may feel like a personal failure, as well as feeling he or she didn't fulfill the expectations of others. These pressures on a young athlete are described quite articulately for Jennifer Capriati, who turned professional at age thirteen, shortly before she dropped out of pro tennis four years later: "The costs of living the fast-forward life of a tennis pro are worth questioning, and Capriati is doing just that. Is trying to be No. 1 worth missing out on school and girlhood? Are adulation and money enough compensation for having to play out your adolescence and family dramas in the *National Inquirer*?"[40]

For parents and coaches whose aspirations are national rankings and a professional sports career for the youngsters involved, youth sports are not play and games; they are a way of life. One father totally committed to making his daughter a professional tennis star, sold his house and piled the entire family into the family car, which was used to travel from tournament to tournament. As one of her former coaches observed, "She is under tremendous pressure to do well. Tremendous pressure to perform for her father." During one tournament, her father yelled from the stands, "Mary, kill the bitch," meaning his daughter's opponent. The father admits "maybe I'm trying to live my youth now."[41] This father finally had to be barred from admission to professional tennis matches where his daughter was playing because of his obnoxious behavior toward his daughter and her opponents during matches.

Marv Marinovich virtually devoted his life to the athletic development of his son, Todd. From birth,

Todd was placed in full-time training, groomed to be a pro quarterback. Experts in exercise physiology, biomechanics, vision development, and dietetics were employed. At one time, Marv bragged that Todd "might become the greatest NFL quarterback of all time." Todd had a very brief career as an NFL quarterback; he didn't measure up and is no longer in the NFL. Marv has opened the Marv Marinovich Performance Training Institute and enrolls children whose parents want to place them in full-time training for sports.[42]

The long-term consequences of competitive stress on young athletes has not been studied in any detail, but several studies document that youth sport athletes do indeed experience pre- and postcompetition stress. It is likely that the more adults pressure youths to perform and to win, the greater will be the stress. Statements made by friends at the time tennis prodigy Jennifer Capriati was arrested for possession and use of drugs in 1994 illustrate the pressures that sometimes become unbearable. One friend noted: "Everybody sure wanted to take credit [for her successes] when things were going well. When she had problems, people scattered." Another said: "She explained it to me: She loves tennis; the happiest moments of her life are when she's playing. But as soon as it got to be 'Number 1, Number 1, Number 1,' it was too stressful. They were running her life. Her dad. Her coaches. She didn't make money just for herself. A lot of people were depending on her."[43]

Certainly, children who are sent to private clubs in another part of the country to train, are coached by well-known coaches, compete in national and international sports events or turn professional during their adolescence are under immense pressures for they are competing to live up to their parents, coaches, media, and their own expectations, and it is a heavy burden.

Adult intrusion into the world of youth sports is potentially dysfunctional in another way. It can rob the young participants of some of the greatest potential of sports and that is the opportunity to have fun and to develop self-discipline and responsibility for one's own actions. Many youth sports programs are dominated by the coaches, who make all the decisions; they decide who plays and what plays to run. The youngsters are the "hired help," who carry out the orders and do not ask questions if they do not want to be labeled "problem athletes."

Although facts are scarce, the imposition of adult decisions on youth programs appears to do little to develop self-discipline and self-responsibility in children. While it is not fair to condemn all youth sports programs, the ways in which many are directed by adults tend to conflict with the true spirit of play by exaggerating the importance of technique, efficiency, and winning, and thus, some programs may take away fun and other play elements from the youngsters (see box 4.1).

Deviant Normative Behavior

A second major problem in youth sport socialization has to do with norm learning. If we accept the notion that children learn normative behavior from sports and if we agree that social-norm deviance is widespread in sport, clearly, youth sports programs may be providing patterned reinforcement of attitudes, values, and behaviors that are at variance with our social norms. Deviation from the ideal norms occurs frequently in sports (e.g., incidents of athletes physically attacking one another during games, the booing of officials, and even the incorporation of deviance as part of the strategy of the game, such as spearing in football, illegal body checking in hockey, and so forth). There are well-planned, deliberate violations of the norms to make winning difficult for the opponent in most sports. Perhaps the epitome of deviant behavior in the interest of winning was the vicious attack on ice skater Nancy Kerrigan planned by another ice skater, Tonya Harding, and carried out by her accomplices just before the U.S. Figure Skating Association championships in 1994.[44]

Such acceptance of the use of deviant normative behavior is associated with the obsession to win. This is not to suggest that winning should not be an objective of competitive sports. When we say obsession, we are talking about those who make winning the overriding purpose of youth sports.

Although one may question the extent to which deviant normative patterns learned in sports are generalized to larger social relations, one certainly must consider the possible social effects on athletes who play under coaches who encourage unethical behavior. Convincing evidence from social learning experiments

To the Tribune:

Is it possible to be appalled but not surprised by what I read in *The Tribune*? Strange question, but the answer is a most resounding YEAH! Somehow nothing that adults do amazes me anymore. Perhaps, I, too, am becoming callous to the facts of our society.

I read with sadness that the City Recreation Department canceled the remaining adult soccer games for the season due to violence on the playing field and toward designated officials. Sad? Yes. Surprising? Hardly.

As the mother of three children who have participated in various Young America, Greeley Recreation and Little League programs over the years, let me share some painfully accurate observations:

1. The most juvenile, infantile, and disgusting behavior at games comes from the parents and adults in attendance.
2. The most filthy, ungodly, foul language at games comes from the parents and adults.
3. The most unsportsmanlike conduct witnessed at any given athletic event which involved small children comes from the fathers, mothers, grandparents, etc., of those impressionable children on the field, in the gym or at the pool.
4. Anyone wishing lessons on how to act like a brainless animal can see this concept modeled each week at various parks around

town. No, it does not come from the children competing against each other, but from the parents and guardians whose job it is to instill values and healthy attitudes about competition and fair play.

I have witnessed children dissolved to tears by fathers (and mothers) who attack them verbally after a game because they weren't aggressive enough, didn't hit hard enough, did a poor job and therefore "helped" their team to lose. These same children are told, "Forget what your coach says, play to win." Could it be that these very same parents grew up to play Greeley soccer?

What a sad commentary on our society when adult recreation programs are interrupted because a few people have not figured out that athletes are not gladiators, that fair play is not an oxymoron, and that competition can be friendly, healthy and growth producing rather than an operational definition of what happens when spoiled little brats grow up to be competitors.

How sad for Greeley and its outstanding programs, that many have to suffer for the sake of a few mental midgets. How sad for the children of Greeley that there are role models such as those people.

And then we wonder where children learn the violent behavior they demonstrate.

Shirley Henry-Lowe
Greeley

Source: Used with permission of the author and *The Greeley (Colorado) Tribune*. Published October 11, 1989, p. A10.

demonstrates that youngsters do model the attitudes and behaviors of those whom they respect and admire, and young athletes almost universally have high regard for their coaches.

Disruption of Education

For young boys and girls who are being groomed for national championships and professional careers, normal school attendance becomes impossible. At first the athletic career and school may

coexist peacefully, but when young athletes must practice six to eight hours per day, travel to distant cities and even foreign countries to participate in competition, and perhaps move from one region of the country to another to receive the desired coaching, normal educational routines must be disrupted. One example of this situation is professional tennis, where more and more of the touring pros are forsaking formal education for a shot at fame and fortune. Three of four of the women's tour have not finished high school, and in 1991 none of the women's top fifty and only one of the men's top fifty had a college degree.[45]

This situation extends beyond tennis. Other sports, especially swimming, figure skating, speed skating, skiing, and gymnastics require most of those who hope to become national and international level performers to train with the best coaches. There are so few of them in each sport that most athletes have to leave their home and take up residence sometimes thousands of miles away to be near the best coaches and facilities.[46]

Several solutions have emerged to meet the needs of young athletes who are in full-time training. One solution is the employment of tutors for the youngsters. Increasingly, however, such informal arrangements are giving way to more formal academies where children live, train, and go to school in one complex. Perhaps the most well-known of these "sport schools" is the Nick Bollettieri Tennis Academy in Bradenton, Florida. It enrolls some two hundred students, ages ten to eighteen, each year. Basic costs for board, coaching, and private schooling range from $25,000 to $50,000. There are more than 300 tennis training academies in the United States alone, and there are others for skiing, figure skating, swimming, and several other sports.[47]

Most of the sport schools will point with some pride to the academic records of their students. Of course, these students are almost uniformly from upper-middle-class families, and they receive tutorial instruction or are in classes with a low student-to-teacher ratio. While these alternatives may result in a good education for such youngsters, a question can be raised about the disruptive effects of having to go to school in a "special" environment and about the restricted interpersonal relationships present in such an environment. This leads to a fundamental question: Is sport involvement so important during the growing-up years that children must be robbed of the normal experiences of childhood? Undoubtedly, some parents and coaches answer "yes," and for those very, very few who become Olympic champions or successful professionals, this assessment may be justified. For the vast majority of young athletes who endure this lifestyle and do not achieve the desired goal, however, a childhood may be lost. Even Nick Bollettieri concedes, "Sure, it's a false trail" to the professional ranks. "How many reach that level? It exists, but the chances of reaching that level are slim and none."[48]

Risk of Injury

Daily living has risks and the potential for injury. Going through childhood and adolescence without risk and injury would be like missing a part of one's life. Given this, there are nevertheless some activities in which the chance of injury is greater than normal, and when these activities are forced on youngsters by adults, the issue of abuse is present. Medical concern for the young athlete has a long history, and most persons associated with youth sports have heard the arguments about "Little League elbow" and about the dangers of tackle football and ice hockey for preadolescent youngsters.

There is, however, a growing concern that goes beyond Little League elbow and broken bones in football or hockey to "swimmer's shoulder" and "gymnast's back." The accelerated training regimens of many current youth athletes that extend up to six hours per day, six days a week, throughout the year, raise serious questions about physical injury. Physicians are seeing a dramatic increase in overuse injuries among children in organized sports. According to one physician who specializes in sports injuries, "One third of U.S. children who participate in sports suffer some kind of injury requiring attention from parents, physicians, or both."[49] Those who are striving for elite status in a sport are at greatest risk of serious overuse injury.

The "Winning Is the Only Thing" Ethic

The final problem we shall describe, one that lurks throughout youth sports and is virtually a given with elite youth athletes, is what we call the "Winning Is the Only Thing" ethic. Although this notion is widely accepted for child athletes thrown into the big business of professional sports, such an ethic really does not belong in youth sport organizations whose purpose is education and personal development. Such an

ethic is inappropriate because it makes conditional persons out of participants. They become defined by win-loss records, and the records become the basis for assigning worthiness to individuals. Winners are accorded prestige and honor; losers suffer disdain and ridicule.

The criterion for success, winning, can become a terrible burden for a young athlete. To be labeled a loser is the epitome of criticism in our society. When victory is stressed above all else, athletes cannot always cope with being the second best in the country or the world. Teenage tennis champion Jennifer Capriati felt the pressures of her father, her coaches, her sponsors, and her friends, and it took its toll. She dropped out of tennis, was arrested for possession of drugs, and has been in drug rehabilitation programs at least twice.[50] The pressures on Tonya Harding to win the 1994 U.S. Figure Skating championships and position herself favorably to win the Olympics became so overwhelming that she and her ex-husband planned and executed an attack on her main rival, Nancy Kerrigan. Granted, Tonya Harding was no teenager when this took place, but she had been a participant in youth sports throughout her teen years.[51]

With more and more professional athletes making huge salaries, and top amateur athletes earning money and getting considerable media attention, more and more junior and age-group athletes are in training to become professional or Olympic-level athletes, and the pressures have become even more intense on these youngsters. What for most boys and girls is play becomes a job for some young athletes. In spite of the hours, even years, of hard work put in by these ambitious young athletes (and their parents), the issue of child labor has rarely come up, and the laws prohibiting child labor have never been applied to elite youth athletes. This point is forcefully made by the author of a book about young elite gymnasts and figure skaters. She argues: "There simply is no safety net protecting these children. Not the parents, the coaches or the federations. Child labor laws prohibit a thirteen-year-old from punching a cash register for forty hours a week, but that same child can labor for forty hours or more inside a gym or an ice skating rink without drawing the slightest glance from the government."[52]

The extent to which parents, coaches, and young athletes will go, when winning becomes the only thing, has been well documented. The types of behaviors, with the attitudes toward sports to which they have been conditioned, does little to promote personal growth and the "character traits" that are universally endorsed as outcomes of sports involvement.

We wish to reemphasize that we are not denying the quest for victory has its place in youth sports. Striving for victory in a competitive situation is a perfectly legitimate goal. We do think, however, given the organizational nature of many youth sports programs and the emphasis on winning for elite-level young athletes, that there is a tendency to allow winning to become the only goal. When this happens in youth sports, the enormous potential benefit of sport involvement for a healthy self-concept development is jeopardized.

Sports Alternatives for the Young Athlete

Although youth sports programs have many problems, there are few viable alternatives for occupying the enormous free time that young persons have in North American culture. The alternatives that many have adopted, turning to drugs or withdrawing from society, are certainly much more destructive to human potential than sport involvement.

Our major contention is that sports for youth have virtually unlimited potential for promoting personal growth and self-actualization. Therefore the goal of age-group sports should be nothing less than self-fulfillment of the individuals engaged in and influenced by them. The emphasis of such programs should be upon personal expression and the value of participation, upon offering everyone the opportunity to engage in sports in a way that youngsters experience no feeling of humiliation if the contest is lost. Why must sport be justified on the basis that it does things other than providing a lot of joy and self-fulfillment for the participants?

An increasing number of attempts have been made to improve youth sports by designing programs based on principles that place the personal-social needs of the participants first and the ambitions of adults far behind. There is growing literature describing these programs

and discussing ways and means by which parents and coaches can improve the quality of the sporting experience for young boys and girls. Several of the best books on this subject are: *SportParent, Positive Coaching, Coaching Children in Sport, Sports Without Pressure,* and *Parents' Complete Guide to Youth Sport.*[53]

Cooperative Games

Many youth sports leaders believe that one of the objectives of sports and physical activity programs for youth should emphasize the learning of cooperative behavior—how to get along well with others and to share with one another. A number of educators and coaches have experimented with play and games as a means of developing positive cooperative behavior among children. They have found that cooperatively structured games are effective in producing cooperative social interaction among children.[54]

Youth Sports Coaches

It is estimated that there are some 5 million volunteer youth sports coaches in North America, most of whom have had no formal instruction in the developmental or educational aspects of teaching/coaching. There is agreement by almost everyone associated with youth sports that the vast majority of youth sports coaches are ill-equipped for their role. Without them, though, millions of boys and girls would not have the opportunity to participate in organized sports. In an effort to help volunteer coaches become more knowledgeable, some youth sports programs have instituted mandatory clinics, workshops, and certification programs for all of their coaches.

In the United States, the American Coaching Effectiveness Program (ACEP) is a complete education package that has been adopted by many youth sports organizations throughout the country. Since its founding in 1976 ACEP has been a valuable education training tool for youth sport coaches. ACEP participant coaches learn to teach skills and strategies, plan effectively for their season, prepare athletes for competition, and understand the developmental needs of young athletes. Its curriculum is built on the philosophical foundation of "Athletes First, Winning Second."

The National Youth Sport Coaches Association (NYSCA) has been a pioneer in the development of a national training system for volunteer coaches. Over 500,000 coaches have undertaken the three-year, three-level program to qualify for certification.

In Canada, the National Coaching Certification Program (NCCP) is now used from one coast to the other. Many youth sports organizations encourage, some even require, formal training for their coaches. The NCCP attempts to ensure that youth coaches have the necessary knowledge, skill, and values that are prerequisite to effective youth sport coaching.[55]

In addition, Ronald Smith and Frank Smoll at the University of Washington have developed the Coaching Behavior Assessment System (CBAS). They formulated a set of guidelines for desirable coaching behavior and then tested the guidelines effectiveness. They did this by observing a group of youth sports coaches in action, then attempted to modify the coaching behaviors of half of these individuals in accordance with the guidelines they had formulated. Their results showed that the coaches who underwent the training were evaluated more positively by their players and that the players exhibited both a higher level of intrateam attraction for each other and had a significant increase in general self-esteem compared with earlier scores.[56]

Bill of Rights for Young Athletes

In an attempt to protect youth from adult exploitation in sports, a group of medical, physical education, and recreation leaders formulated a Bill of Rights for Young Athletes several years ago. The ten rights are targeted to coaches, leaders of recreation programs, officials, and parents in the hope that their implementation will promote the beneficial effects of athletic participation for all who are involved. These rights are:

1. The right to participate in sports.
2. The right to participate at a level commensurate with each child's maturity and ability.
3. The right to have qualified adult leadership.
4. The right to play as a child and not as an adult.
5. The right to share in the leadership and decision making of their sport participation.
6. The right to participate in safe and healthy environments.
7. The right to proper preparation in sports.

8. The right to an equal opportunity to strive for success.
9. The right to be treated with dignity.
10. The right to have fun in sports.

In Canada, a National Task Force on Children's Play created by the Canadian Council on Children and Youth has formulated Fair Play Codes that emphasize sport's potential for promoting desirable values among youthful participants.

Summary

There has been an enormous increase in community-sponsored youth sports programs. There has also been a growth in elite youth sport in which the children train and compete with aspirations of becoming professional athletes. An estimated 20 million North American and 2.5 million Canadian boys and girls participate in these programs each year. Two of the most salient factors contributing to the growth of these programs are (1) the rise of organized and corporate sport, followed by the desire to participate and to spectate on the part of large numbers of people and (2) the realization by Canadians and Americans of the importance of providing varied opportunities for their children.

The objectives of most youth sports programs are to provide participants with an opportunity to learn culturally relevant sport skills and to develop attitudes and values about such things as competition, cooperation, sportsmanship, discipline, authority, and social relationships. There are, however, programs that are blatantly career-training programs.

The extent to which the attitudes, values, beliefs, and behaviors of participants are actually influenced by organized youth programs is largely unknown. Most studies of attitudes toward youth sports suggest that parents and participants believe that they are more beneficial than detrimental to the development of young boys and girls. Participants in these programs are socialized into them by a variety of social agents and agencies, parents, siblings, peers, coaches, the mass media, and so forth.

The social context of the informal, peer-organized sports activities is vastly different from that of the adult-organized youth sports programs. Thus, the play behavior in the two social contexts is likely to lead to quite different learning.

There are a number of problems in organized youth sports. One is that the intrusion of adults into the play of youngsters may rob the young participants of many of the values of play. A second is that the norm learning involved may actually be at variance with North American social norms. A third is that normal educational experiences may become impossible. A fourth is that intense training and competition for prolonged periods of time may cause both acute and chronic injury. Finally, the overemphasis on winning in some youth programs threatens to overshadow the expressive, self-fulfilling potential of sports participation.

A number of interesting efforts have been made to develop alternative youth sports programs; in most cases the emphasis of these programs is on fun, participation, and skill learning. One group of researchers has developed a system for helping coaches improve their coaching behavior, and in both the United States and Canada, courses have been developed to help coaches become more effective. In an attempt to protect young athletes from adult exploitation in sports, a Bill of Rights for Young Athletes and Fair Play Codes have been formulated.

Notes

1. American Sport Education Program, *SportParent* (Champaign, Ill.: Human Kinetics Publishers, 1994); Ann Hall et al., *Sport in Canadian Society* (Toronto: McClelland & Stewart, 1991).

2. Laurie Werner, "The Venus Mission," *USA Weekend,* 2–4 August 1991, p. 5.

3. Robin Finn, "Camp is a Career for Tennis Prodigies," *New York Times* 21 November 1991, sec. B, pp. 1, 8.

4. James H. Humphrey, *Sports for Children: A Guide for Adults* (Springfield, Ill.: Charles C Thomas, 1993).

5. Bernard R. Cahill and Arthur J. Pearl, eds., *Intensive Participation in Children's Sports* (Champaign, Ill.: Human Kinetics Publishers, 1993); see also George H. Sage, "Sports Participation as a Builder of Character?" *The World and I* 3 (October 1988): 629–41; Heyward L. Nash, "Elite Child-Athletes: How Much Does Victory Cost?" *The Physician and Sportsmedicine* 15, no. 8 (1987): 129–33.

6. Steven A. Riess, *City Games: The Evolution of American Urban Society and the Rise of Sports* (Urbana, Ill.: University of Illinois Press, 1989), 151–52; Jack W. Berryman, "The Rise of Highly Organized Competitive Sports for Preadolescent Boys," in *Children in Sport*, ed. Frank L. Smoll, Richard A. Magill, and Michael J. Ash, 3d ed. (Champaign, Ill.: Human Kinetics, 1988), 3–16.

7. Mary E. Duquin, "Gender and Youth Sports: Reflections on Old and New Fictions," in *Children in Sport*, 39.

8. Public Law 88–378, 88th Congress, 16 July 1964.

9. Eric A. Margenau, *Sports Without Pressure* (New York: Gardner Press, 1990).

10. Andrew L. Cherry, *The Socializing Instincts: Individual, Family, and Social Bonds* (Westport, Conn.: Praeger, 1994); Harry McGurk, ed., *Childhood Social Development: Contemporary Perspectives* (Hillsdale, N.J.: Erlbaum Associates, 1992).

11. Department of Labor, Women's Bureau, *1993 Handbook on Women Workers: Trends and Issues* (Washington, D.C.: U.S. Government Printing Office, 1994), 71.

12. For a good review of this research, see Daniel M. Landers, "Birth Order in the Family and Sport Participation," in *The Dimensions of Sport Sociology*, ed. March L. Krotee (West Point, N.Y.: Leisure Press, 1979), 140–67.

13. For an excellent review of this research, see John H. Lewko and Susan L. Greendorfer, "Family Influences in Sport Socialization of Children and Adolescents," *Children in Sport*, 287–300; see also Thomas G. Power and Christi Woolger, "Parenting Practices and Age-Group Swimming: A Correlational Study," *Research Quarterly for Exercise and Sport* 65 (1994): 59–66.

14. Deborah L. Feltz, Cathy D. Lirgg, and Richard R. Albrecht, "Psychological Implications of Competitive Running on Elite Young Distance Runners: A Longitudinal Analysis," *The Sport Psychologist* 6 (June 1992): 128–38; Christi Woolger and Thomas G. Power, "Parents and Sport Socialization: Views From the Achievement Literature," *Journal of Sport Behavior* 16 (1993): 171–89.

15. Allison R. Parker, "Parental Influence Upon the Socialization of Children Into Sport" (master's thesis, University of North Carolina, 1989).

16. Lewko and Greendorfer, "Family Influences in Sport Socialization of Children and Adolescents," *Children in Sport*, 292–94.

17. "Having Fun is High Priority," *USA Today*, 10 September 1990, sec. C, p. 14; Mike Dodd, "Children Say Having Fun is No. 1," *USA Today*, 10 September 1990, sec. C, pp. 1–2; Mike Dodd, "Parents Give Coaches Benefit of Doubt," *USA Today*, 10 September 1990, sec. C, p. 14.

18. Joan Ryan, *Little Girls in Pretty Boxes: The Making of Elite Gymnasts and Figure Skaters* (New York: Doubleday, 1995).

19. Lewko and Greendorfer, "Family Influences in Sport Socialization of Children and Adolescents," *Children in Sport*, 288–92.

20. Ibid.

21. Dodd, "Children Say Having Fun is No. 1," *USA Today*, sec. C, pp. 1–2. A study sponsored by the Athletic Footwear Association, with over 10,000 youth responding to a questionnaire, found essentially the same thing—"to have fun" was ranked as the most important reason why young boys and girls play organized sport. See "American Youth and Sports Participation" (North Palm Beach, Fla.: Athletic Footwear Association, 200 Castlewood Drive, 1991).

22. Stephen J. Bavolek, *Child Centered Coaching Parent Handbook* (Park City, Utah: The National Institute for Child Centered Coaching, 1993); see also Tara K. Scanlan et al., "Sources of Enjoyment for Youth Sports Athletes," *Pediatric Exercise Science* 5 (1993): 275–85.

23. American Sport Education Program, *SportParent*, 4; Damon Burton, "The Dropout Dilemma in Youth Sports: Documenting the Problem and Identifying Solutions," in *Young Athletes: Biological, Psychological, and Educational Perspectives*, ed. Robert M. Malina (Champaign, Ill.: Human Kinetics, 1988), 245–46.

24. "Athletic Dropouts: Getting Them Back Into Sports," *Journal of Physical Education, Recreation, and Dance* 62 (April 1991): 15; see also Angela Lumpkin, Sharon K. Stoll, and Jennifer M. Beller, *Sport Ethics: Applications for Fair Play* (St. Louis: Mosby, 1994), 55–56.

25. Daniel Gould, "Understanding Attrition in Children's Sport," in *Advances in Pediatric Sport Sciences,* vol. 2, eds. Daniel Gould and Maureen R. Weiss (Champaign, Ill.: Human Kinetics Publishers, 1987), 66–67.

26. Andrew W. Miracle and C. Roger Rees, *Lessons of the Locker Room* (Amherst, N.Y.: Prometheus Books, 1994).

27. Gary A. Fine, *With the Boys: Little League Baseball and Preadolescent Culture* (Chicago, Ill.: University of Chicago Press, 1987), 18, 20.

28. Michael W. Passer, "Psychological Issues in Determining Children's Age-Readiness for Competition," in *Children in Sport,* 68–72.

29. Gary A. Fine, "Organized Baseball and Its Folk Equivalents: The Transition From Informal to Formal Control," in *Cultural Dimensions of Play, Games, and Sports,* ed. Bernard Mergen (Champaign, Ill.: Human Kinetics Publishers, 1986), 181.

30. Jay Coakley, "Social Dimensions of Intensive Training and Participation in Youth Sports," in *Intensive Participation in Children's Sports* eds. Bernard R. Cahill and Arthur J. Pearl (Champaign, Ill.: Human Kinetics Publishers, 1993), 77–94.

31. Fine, *With the Boys,* 41–58.

32. Ibid., 20.

33. Ibid., 51.

34. Sage, "Sports Participation as a Builder of Character?" 629–41.

35. Lawrence Chalip et al., "Variations of Experience in Formal and Informal Sport," *Research Quarterly for Exercise and Sport* 55 (June 1984): 114.

36. Mary J. Kane, "The Influence of Level of Sport Participation and Sex Role Orientation on Female Professionalization of Attitudes Toward Play," *Journal of Sport Psychology* 4, no. 3 (1982): 290–94; Nancy Theberge, James Curtis, and Barbara Brown, "Sex Differences in Orientations Toward Games: Tests of Sport Involvement Hypothesis," in *Studies in the Sociology of Sport,* ed. Aidan O. Dunleavy, Andrew Miracle, and C. Roger Rees (Fort Worth, Tex.: Texas Christian University Press, 1982), 285–308.

37. Miracle and Rees, *Lessons of the Locker Room,* 90–91; E. M. Swift, "Give Young Athletes a Fair Shake," *Sports Illustrated,* 2 May 1994, 76.

38. Lumpkin, Stoll, and Beller, *Sport Ethics;* Jennifer M. Beller and Sharon K. Stoll, "Sport Participation and its Effect on Moral Reasoning of High School Student Athletes and General Students," *Research Quarterly for Exercise and Sport* 65 (March 1994, Supplement): A94; also see David Decker and Kevin Lasley, "Participation in Youth Sports, Gender, and the Moral Point of View," *The Physical Educator* 52 (winter 1995): 14–21.

39. For a summary of this research, see George H. Sage, "Social Development," in *Physical Activity & Well-Being,* ed. Vern Seefeldt (Washington, D.C.: AAHPERD, 1986), 343–71; see also Maureen R. Weiss, "Self Esteem and Achievement in Children's Sport and Physical Activity," in *Advances in Pediatric Sport Sciences,* 87–119; Ronald E. Smith, Frank L. Smoll, and Nathan J. Smith, *Parents Complete Guide to Youth Sports* (Costa Mesa, Calif.: HDL Publishing, 1989), 27–33.

40. Sally Jenkins, "Teenage Confidential," *Sports Illustrated,* 30 March 1992, 26–29; see also Julie Cart, "Ugly Horror Story," *The Arizona Republic,* 29 January 1996, sec. C, p. 8.

41. Dave Scheiber, "Too Much, Too Young," *Sports Illustrated,* 7 May 1990, 52; for a discussion of how this tennis player finally gained her freedom from her abusive father, see Suzanne Gerber, "How a Tennis Star Overcame Her Troubled Past," *Redbook* September 1995, 52, 54.

42. Douglas S. Looney, "Bred to be a Superstar," *Sports Illustrated,* 22 February 1988, 56–63; Denise Tom, "The Marinovich Plan Reaches Its Goal," *USA Today,* 30 April 1991, sec. C, p. 9; see also James S. Thornton, "Springing Young Athletes From the Parental Pressure Cooker," *The Physician and Sportsmedicine* 19 (July 1991): 92–99.

43. Sally Jenkins and Kelly Whiteside, "Lost Weekend," *Sports Illustrated,* 30 May 1994, 17–18; see also Hal Bock, "Pressure Consumes Sport's Young," *The Greeley Tribune* 10 September 1995, sec. B, p. 6; for an alternative to high pressure youth sport, see Margenau, *Sports Without Pressure.*

44. E. M. Swift, "Violence," *Sports Illustrated,* 17 January 1994, 16–21; E. M. Swift, "Look Who's in the Hot Seat," *Sports Illustrated,* 31 January 1994, 62–64; E. M. Swift, "Anatomy of a Plot," *Sports Illustrated,* 14 February 1994, 28–34, 39–41.

45. Cindy Shmerler, "Decision: $$ or Degree," *USA Today,* 26 August 1991, sec. E, p. 6.

46. Wayne Coffey and Filip Bondy, *Dreams of Gold: The Nancy Kerrigan Story* (New York: St. Martin's Press, 1994); Norm Frauenheim, "Skating a Fine Line," *The Arizona Republic,* 17 January 1993, sec. D, pp. 1, 8; Greg Boeck, "Olympic Gymnastics 'Serious Job,' " *USA Today,* 30 July 1992, sec. A, pp. 1–2.

47. Finn, "Camp is a Career for Tennis Prodigies," *New York Times.*

48. Greg Boeck, "Kids Clamor for Lessons from Pros," *USA Today,* 12 September 1990, sec. C, p. 2; see also Joan Ryan, *Little Girls in Pretty Boxes* (New York: Doubleday, 1995).

49. John F. Duff, *Youth Sports Injuries* (New York: Macmillan, 1992), 3; for a good guide on preventing sport injuries, see Jerald D. Hawkins, ed. *Sports Medicine: A Practice Guide for Youth Sports Coaches and Parents* (Canton, Ohio: Professional Reports Corporation, 1992).

50. Jenkins and Whiteside, "Lost Weekend," *Sports Illustrated,* 15–18.

51. Swift, "Look Who's in the Hot Seat," *Sports Illustrated,* 62–64; Swift, "Anatomy of a Plot," *Sports Illustrated,* 28–34, 39–41; see also Frank Coffey and Joe Layden, *Thin Ice: The Complete Uncensored Story of Tonya Harding* (New York: Windsor Publishing Co., 1994).

52. Ryan, *Little Girls in Pretty Boxes,* 11.

53. Martin Lee, ed., *Coaching Children in Sport* (New York: E & FN Spon, 1993); Jim Thompson, *Positive Coaching: Building Character and Self-Esteem Through Sports* (Dubuque, Iowa: Brown & Benchmark, 1993); American Sport Education Program, *SportParent;* Margenau, *Sports Without Pressure;* Smith, Smoll, and Smith, *Parents' Complete Guide to Youth Sports.*

54. Kathleen M. Haywood, "Modifications in Youth Sport: A Rationale and Some Examples in Youth Basketball," in *Sports for Children and Youths,* ed. Jan Broekhoff, Michael J. Ellis, and Dan G. Tripps (Champaign, Ill.: Human Kinetics, 1986), 179–85; John C. Pooley, "A Level Above Competition: An Inclusive Model for Youth Sport," in *Sports for Children and Youths,* 187–93; G. S. Don Morris, "Developing a Sense of Competence in Children Through Game Modifications," in *Sports for Children and Youths,* 195–200; G. D. Morris and James J. Stiehl, *Changing Kids' Games* (Champaign, Ill.: Human Kinetics, 1989); Terry Orlick and Ann Pitman-Davidson, "Enhancing Cooperative Skills in Games and Life," in *Children in Sport,* 149–59.

55. Karen Partlow, "American Coaching Effectiveness Program (ACEP): Educating America's Coaches," *Journal of Physical Education, Recreation, and Dance* 62 (September 1992): 36–39; Fred Engh, "National Youth Sports Coaches Association (NYSCA): More Than Just a Certification Program," *Journal of Physical Education, Recreation, and Dance* 62 (September 1992): 43–45; Geoff R. Gowan, "Canada's National Coaching Certification Program (NCCP): Past, Present, and Future," *Journal of Physical Education, Recreation, and Dance* 62 (September 1992): 50–54.

56. Frank L. Smoll and Ronald E. Smith, "Educating Youth Sport Coaches: An Applied Sport Psychology Perspective," in *Applied Sport Psychology* ed. Jean M. Williams, 2d ed. (Mountain View, Calif.: Mayfield, 1993), 36–57; Smith, Smoll, and Smith, *Parents' Complete Guide to Youth Sports.*

Chapter 5

Interscholastic Sport

Sport and education are inexorably intertwined in American society; virtually every secondary school is engaged in some interschool sport competition. To ascertain the degree to which sport contributes to the educational process, however, is difficult. The conventional view is that participation in sport has educational benefits. High school athletes benefit, it is commonly believed, from adult supervision, by ego enhancement, by learning to play by the rules, by working together with teammates toward a common goal, by being achievement oriented, and by working at school work to stay eligible.

A contrary view, less widely held, is critical of sport as now constituted in our schools. From this perspective, sport is believed to detract from educational goals. Moreover, the critics assert that although athletic participation may lead some individuals to be good sports, it may lead others to be bad sports; although some play by the rules, others circumvent them; and although there is integrity in some sports programs, there is hypocrisy in others. In short, these critics believe that sport and education are incompatible.

The subjects included in this chapter are directly or indirectly related to this controversy. We describe first the status of sport in American education; next, we explore the positive and negative consequences of sport for the school, the community, the individual, and the society; finally, we assess the relationship between sport and education by examining inherent problems and dilemmas.

The Status of Sport in Secondary Schools

Although the main thrust of this book is on corporate sport in society, much of the material in this chapter is devoted to organized sport. That is, sport at the high school level. We shall see, however, that sport in American education varies from organized to corporate.

High school sports are central in U.S. schools. In the 1994–95 school year, about 5.8 million boys and girls in the United States were involved in thirty different sports at the high school level (38 percent of this total were girls and 62 percent boys).[1] This high level of involvement, however, is not the case in most other countries. In most societies (the nations of Europe, for example), sports programs for high school age youth are organized through community-based athletic clubs, *not through the schools*. Canada is somewhat unique because it has both school sports and community sports clubs for adolescents. Hockey, the most popular sport for male participation in Canada, is organized only as a community sport in most areas. The less popular male sports and all of the female sports are organized primarily through the schools.[2]

Interschool high school sports in the United States have become so vitally important that contemporary schools might appear to an outsider to be more concerned with athletics than with scholarly endeavors.

A visitor entering a school would likely be confronted, first of all, with a trophy case. His examination of the trophies would reveal a curious fact: the gold and silver cups, with rare exception, symbolize victory in athletic contests, not scholastic ones. The figures adorning these trophies represent men passing footballs, shooting basketballs, holding out batons; they are not replicas of "The Thinker." The concrete symbols of victory are old footballs, basketballs, and baseballs, not works of art or first editions of books won as literary prizes. Altogether, the trophy case would suggest to the innocent visitor that he was entering an athletic club, not an educational institution.

Walking further, this visitor would encounter teenagers bursting from classrooms. Listening to their conversations, he would hear both casual and serious discussions of the Friday football game, confirming his initial impression. Attending a school assembly that morning, he would probably find a large segment of the program devoted to a practice of school cheers for the athletic game and the announcement of a pep rally before the game. At lunch hour, he would be likely to find more boys shooting baskets in the gymnasium than reading in the library. Browsing through a school yearbook, he would be impressed, in his innocence, with the number of pages devoted to athletics.

Altogether, this visitor would find, wherever he turned, a great deal of attention devoted to athletics. As an impressionable stranger, he might well suppose that more attention is paid to athletics by teenagers, both as athletes and as spectators, than to scholastic matters. He might even conclude, with good reason, that the school was essentially organized around athletic contests and that scholastic matters were of lesser importance to all involved.[3]

A consequence of the extraordinary popularity of sport in United States secondary schools is its generation of status for males and, increasingly for females as well. Foremost, for males, the athlete, regardless of other attributes, is favored over the nonathlete with the highest preference being "scholar-athlete." For young women, popularity is judged more by their being in the "in-group" than their scholarship. Membership in the "in-group" is crucial and being an athlete is not sufficient for inclusion. This is especially true for women in "gender-inappropriate" sports (i.e., sports generally considered not "feminine").[4] Second, the importance of athletics for male status system acts as a deterrent to academic achievement, a most important implication for the goals of schools. It does so because persons are encouraged to divert their energies away from scholarship to athletics and social activities. Thus, groups and individuals in the school (with the aid of the administration and the community) actually work against the academic objectives of the school.

A third generalization, is that achievement in athletics, not social background, is for the most part the basis for status among male peers. For females, social background and being in the "in-crowd" are more important for social status than athletic achievement. This may be changing for high school women as female participation in sports in high schools is becoming more and more acceptable and their participation has increased so rapidly since Title IX. The conclusion by Jay Coakley seems appropriate:

. . . because males and females in North America are still treated and evaluated in different ways, adolescents use different strategies for seeking acceptance, autonomy, and sexual development, and recognition as young adults. As things are now, sport participation for males is an important basis for popularity, as long as the young men don't neglect school. Sport participation is also important for young women, but being an athlete must usually be combined with other things for young women to be popular within the student cultures of most high schools. Young women don't have to conform to traditional definitions of femininity, but to be popular they usually need to show they are something other than just tough and competitive in sports.[5]

The prominence of athletics in the status system of adolescents differs somewhat in Canadian high schools from American high schools. David Friesen's study in nineteen Canadian schools with fifteen thousand students revealed some interesting similarities and differences.[6] Friesen found that, like American adolescents, Canadian high school students are extremely concerned with popularity among their peers. The crucial difference, though, is that Canadians place academics before athletics in their hierarchy of values. Whereas American adolescents prefer athletics, popularity, and then academics, Canadians rank academics first, followed by popularity, and finally athletics.

The Consequences of Sport for Schools, Communities, and Individuals

Clearly, high school and college athletes receive substantial rewards for their activities. They receive fame and acclaim from peers, neighbors, teachers, and even strangers. A high school star (especially a male) can become a legend in his or her own time, a deity canonized in newspapers and immortalized through countlessly retold exploits. Even nonstar athletes have celebrity status. They enjoy praise and honor, special favors from businesses and the community, and popularity with the opposite sex. Moreover, schools and communities are usually much more willing to spend great sums of money for athletic equipment and arenas than they are for academic equipment and buildings. They are also willing to allow a disproportionate amount of time to be spent on athletics and related activities.

Why are athletes and athletics given such extraordinary importance? The answer is because sport has positive consequences for the participants, the schools, and the communities.

The Consequences of Sport for the School

All organizations must have a minimal amount of unity; members must give an organization some allegiance for it to survive. Allegiance can stem from pay, ideology, chances for promotion, or the cooperative need to accomplish a collective goal. Schools, however, do not have the usual means to motivate their members. Grades, the equivalent of pay, do not always work because part of the school population is indifferent to them, and because they are so often dependent on defeating one's peers. Moreover, students are forced by custom and by law to attend school; this ensures their physical presence but not their involvement in the school's academic objectives. Aside from athletic contests, schools do not have collective goals, only individual ones. Therefore, any activity that promotes loyalty to the school serves a useful and necessary purpose. James Coleman showed how athletics provides a unifying function for the school:

> Athletic contests with other schools provide, for these otherwise lifeless institutions, the collective goals that they lack. The common goals shared by all make the institution part of its members and them part of it, rather than an organization outside them and superimposed upon them. The results are evident to any observer: the adolescent social system is centered at the school, not at the drugstore; the name by which the teenagers identify themselves is that of the school ("Those are East High kids; I'm from Tech."); the teenagers think of

the school, the team, and the student body as one and use the pronoun "we" in referring to this entity ("We're playing Parkville Friday.") . . .

> Thus, the importance of athletic contests in both high schools and colleges lies, at least in part, in the way the contests solve a difficult problem for the institution—the problem of generating enthusiasm for and identification with the school and of drawing the energies of adolescents into the school.[7]

Interschool sports competition, then, is a means of unifying the entire school. Different races, social classes, fraternities, teachers, school staff, and students unite in a common cause—the defeat of a common enemy outside the group. An athletic program sometimes keeps potentially hostile segments from fragmenting the school. The collective following of an athletic team can also lift morale, thereby serving to unify the school (although we should remember that unity is usually accomplished when teams win; losing teams may actually increase the possibility of division).

Athletics serves not only to unify student bodies but also to minimize conflict between students and teachers.

> There is a tendency for the school population to split up into hostile segments of teachers and students and to be fragmented by cliques among both groups. The division of students into groups prevents a collective morale from arising and thereby complicates administration; the split between students and teachers is even more serious, for these two groups tend to become definite conflict groups, and conflict group tensions are the very antithesis of discipline. This condition athletics alleviates. Athletic games furnish a dramatic spectacle of the struggle of picked men against a common enemy, and this is a powerful factor in building up a group spirit which includes students of all kinds and degrees and unifies the teachers and the taught.[8]

In addition to the unifying function of athletics, it also serves a social control function. Willard Waller gave the following advice to school administrators:

> The organization of the student body for the support of athletics, though it is certainly not without its

ultimate disadvantages, may bring with it certain benefits for those who are interested in the immediate problems of the administration. It is a powerful machine which is organized to whip all students into line for the support of athletic teams, and adroit school administrators learn to use it for the dissemination of other attitudes favorable to the faculty and the faculty policy.[9]

Assuming that school administrators can manipulate students through sport, what social control functions may be performed? First, athletic activity may make students more tractable because it drains their surplus energies. For athletes and nonathletes alike, sport furnishes a diversion of attention from undesirable to desirable channels. It gives students something to think about and something to do with their time, thereby keeping them from mischief and from questioning the system. Second, athletes, because they must obey school rules and training rules if they want to compete, serve as examples of good behavior. Athletes have high status in the school system, and by virtue of their favored position, they tend to have the conservatism of the privileged classes. If this assumption is correct and nonathletes tend to admire them, then athletes serve to preserve the system as it is.

The school advocates sports participation for self-serving reasons (school and community cohesion, financial support, and social control). Administrators and school boards encourage participation not only because they want to encourage physical fitness but, more importantly, because they believe that sports participation inculcates the values of society into individuals. As David Matza put it, "The substance of athletics contains within itself—in its rules, procedures, training, and sentiments—a paradigm of adult expectations regarding youth."[10] Schools want individuals to follow rules, to be disciplined, to work hard, to fit in. Athletics accomplishes these aims. Thus, athletics is believed by those in authority to be justified.

A final social control function of athletics is its dampening of violent rivalries between towns, neighborhoods, and schools. Athletic contests are often symbolic contests between rivals. The official goal of civil order (minimizing real violence) is believed to be accomplished because the contests are routinized and institutionalized (by the rules of the game and the sanctions that can be applied for violations). The problem is that ritualized violence may erupt into actual violence between players, spectators, or both at any time. It has been generally assumed by school authorities that the benefits outweigh the potential for actual conflict.[11] However, especially in urban areas, sporting events between schools have actually intensified the probability of violence. As a consequence, some contests have been either canceled or held without spectators.

Sports can also be used by the school to encourage intellectual activities among the students. A contingency for participation in sports is the maintenance of a certain grade-point average, so athletes must at least meet this minimum. The existence of sports may also keep some youngsters from dropping out of school because of their desire to participate.

The Consequences of Sport for the Community

We have already noted that school athletics appears to be an effective means for channeling the interest and loyalty of the community. Clearly, this enthusiasm generated by sports is a unifying agent for the community. Regardless of occupation, education, race, or religion, residents can and do unite in backing a school's teams against the common enemy.

Sports provide action in an otherwise humdrum world. They offer not only excitement but also fantasy and escape. Thus, they entertain.

Communities vary in their attachment to high school athletic teams. Most often, individual sports are ignored by communities. The girls' games are often minimized, too. Typically, the community members concentrate their interests around boys' football and basketball. Small communities are generally more involved in high school sports than are large urban communities. The focus on a sport may also vary by geographical location, with high school basketball the rage in Indiana, hockey in Minnesota, and football in Texas. H. G. Bissinger, for example, has written of the importance of high school football in Odessa,

Texas. Bissinger, a Philadelphia reporter, lived in Odessa for a year, chronicling life in that town as it centered on high school football. One excerpt from Bissinger's book *Friday Night Lights* illustrates the importance of football to the town and its inhabitants: "Bob Rutherford, an affable realtor in town, might as well have been speaking for thousands when he casually said one day as if talking about the need for a rainstorm to settle the dust, 'Life really wouldn't be worth livin' if you didn't have a high school football team to support."[12]

The Consequences of Sport for the Participant

Individuals participate in sports for a variety of reasons. Perhaps most important is the desire for high status and the approval of fans, press, peers, parents, teachers, and others. H. G. Bissinger has described just how important it was to be a football player at Permian High School in Odessa, Texas: "[They were] gladiators, the ones who were envied by everyone else, the ones who knew about the best parties and got the best girls and laughed the loudest and strutted so proudly through the halls of school as if it was their own wonderful, private kingdom."[13] They may also participate because they enjoy the activity and being physically fit and because they derive great pleasure from being part of a cohesive unit striving for a common goal. Sometimes forgotten, however, is that many persons participate because all of the normative influences pull them in that direction. There are many pressures to participate, whether an individual wants to or not. Of course, if youngsters are socialized to desire participation, they may not feel the constraints.

Regardless of the motivation for participation in sport, there are some important consequences of participation. Several are considered here: academic benefits, character development, and adjustment to failure and life after sport.

Academic Benefits

The empirical evidence is that high school athletes as a group receive better grades than nonathletes, and they have higher academic aspirations.[14] This consistent finding validates, seemingly, the conventional wisdom

that athletic participation builds discipline, the work ethic, and other achievement-oriented qualities that translate into better students.

Some problems of interpretation exist, however, whenever athletes are compared with nonathletes.[15] The two categories differ not only in physical characteristics but in other significant dimensions as well. First, when grades are compared, athletes may have a higher GPA because they must meet a minimum level to be eligible for sports. This grade barrier keeps some students who are poor in academic performance from ever attempting to participate in athletics. Second, rebellious youth may either choose not to participate in sport or coaches may dismiss them because they do not fit in. Third, we cannot determine whether the relationship between athletic involvement and academic achievement is a casual one. The relationship between high school participation and grades may be the result of other factors, such as receiving extra help from tutors and teachers, taking easier courses in order to handle the rigors of being an athlete, or outright gifts of good grades from sympathetic teachers. The result may be good grades for being an athlete but not because being an athlete makes one a good student.

Most important, athletes may be different from nonathletes, but *not* because of sport. Elmer Spreitzer, analyzed data from a national probability sample of twelve thousand high school students.[16] The information was collected from high school sophomores and seniors and then from these same students over a six-year period after they left high school. Spreitzer summarizes the results:

> In this article, we corroborated the widely shared perception among sport scientists that selectivity factors prevent us from making straightforward conclusions concerning the effects of sports participation during one's youth. We identified two sources of selectivity that prevent such simple conclusions: a filtering process in terms of who enters high school athletics and a filtering process in terms of who drops out of high school athletics between the sophomore and senior years. The data from this national probability sample of American youths clearly show that *those who begin and*

continue with high school athletics tend to be from more advantaged social backgrounds in terms of parental social class, level of cognitive ability, academic achievement, and level of self-esteem.[17] (emphasis added)

In short, high school athletes are more advantaged academically *before* they participate in high school sports than their nonathlete peers. Thus, we should not infer that athletic participation makes one perform better in the classroom.

Building Character

We noted in our earlier discussion that there is a negative side to the conventional assumption that sport builds character, a position that Charles Banham summarized. Such an assumption, he said,

> is not sound because it assumes that everyone will benefit from sport in the complacently prescribed manner. A minority do so benefit. A few have the temperament that responds healthily to all the demands. These are the ones able to develop an attractively active character. Sport can put fresh air in the mind, if it's the right mind; it can give muscle to the personality, if it's the right personality. But for the rest, it encourages selfishness, envy, conceit, hostility and bad temper. Far from ventilating the mind, it stifles it. Good sportsmanship may be a product of sport, but so is bad sportsmanship.[18]

The results of research on whether sport builds character are contradictory. The problem is that sport produces positive outcomes for some individuals and negative ones for others. Terry D. Orlick summed up this dualism:

> For every positive psychological or social outcome in sports, there are possible negative outcomes. For example, sports can offer a child group membership or group exclusion, acceptance or rejection, positive feedback or negative feedback, a sense of accomplishment or a sense of failure, evidence of self-worth or a lack of evidence of self-worth. Likewise, sports can develop cooperation and a concern for others, but they can also develop intense rivalry and a complete lack of concern for others.[19]

There is an important study that examines the larger issue of whether or not participation in high school sports builds character. Frank M. Howell, C. Roger Rees, and Andrew W. Miracle analyzed data collected from a national sample, beginning with twenty-five male sophomores in each of eighty-seven high schools. These students were interviewed at the beginning of the sophomore year and again at the conclusion of the senior year. The data showed that participation in varsity sports tended to increase self-esteem but also increased the negative traits of aggression and irritability. In general, though, the researchers concluded that high school sports do not do much to "build character" in adolescent boys—in either prosocial or antisocial ways.[20]

A longitudinal study surveyed 5,669 female students during their sophomore and senior years to ascertain the effects of sports participation on their development. The results were mixed. The researchers found that athletic participation was modestly related to perceived popularity and slightly related to educational aspiration. Participation was not related to psychological well-being, self-esteem, sociability, academic achievement, or sex-role attitudes.[21]

On the other hand, Herbert Marsh examined data from a random probability sample of 14,825 students, comparing seniors with the data compiled on them as sophomores.[22] Marsh found some consistent positive effects of sport participation, including higher perceived popularity, higher educational aspirations, and subsequent attainment.

Adjustment to Failure and Life After School Sport

Two problems for individual high school athletes are often overlooked. First, for many, sport leads to a series of failures. Either they fail to make the team, or if they make the team they sit on the bench, or their team loses many more times than it wins. In a success-oriented society, what are the effects of all the failures that sport generates? At the individual level, failure can be devastating for some. They may be defined by others and by themselves as losers, which is a strong negative label in a society that places such high value on winning. This may negatively impact their self-esteem, confidence, and assertiveness. It may lead to mental health problems.

box 5.1 *The Pepettes*

At Permian High School in Odessa, Texas, there is an organization called the Pepettes. H. G. Bissinger describes this group and the ways they support the school's football team.

[The Pepettes were] a select group of senior girls who made up the school spirit squad. The Pepettes supported all teams, but it was the football team they supported most. The number on the white jersey each girl wore corresponded to that of the player she had been assigned for the football season. With that assignment came various time-honored responsibilities.

As part of the tradition, each Pepette brought some type of sweet for her player every week before the game. She didn't necessarily have to make something from scratch, but there was indirect pressure to because of not-so-private grousing from

players who tired quickly of bags of candy and not so discreetly let it be known that they much preferred something fresh-baked. . . .

In addition, each Pepette also had to make a large sign for her player that went in his front yard and stayed there the entire season as a notice to the community that he played football for Permian. Previously the making of these yard signs, which looked like miniature Broadway marquees, had become quite competitive. Some of the Pepettes spent as much as $100 of their own money to make an individual sign, decorating it with twinkling lights and other attention-getting devices. It became a rather serious game of can-you-top-this, and finally a dictum was handed down that all signs must be made the same way, without any neon.

A Pepette also had responsibility for making smaller posters, which went up in the school

Another problem is one of adjustment after a career in sport is finished. The odds of making a team at the next level are remote: only 4 percent of high school football players and 2 percent of male high school basketball players will participate in college; the odds of making it from college into the pros is even less likely. Clearly, these long odds mean that most high school athletes will terminate their careers at the conclusion of high school. After the glory years, what happens to former athletes when they are considered has-beens? Does participation in sport have carry-over value to other endeavors where there is no hero-worship, no excitement, and no fame? What happens to the athlete who finds himself or herself suddenly outside the world that has until now been at the center of his or her life and the principal source of identity and social status? Do former athletes become embittered and turn away from sport, or do they fill their time reliving the past, attending games, Monday-morning quarterbacking,

and watching sports on television? How does the athlete, when compared to the nonathlete, adjust to job, marriage, and upward or downward mobility? An ex-athlete from Permian High School in Odessa, Texas, was interviewed by H. G. Bissinger:

He saw the irresistible allure of high school sports, but he also saw an inevitable danger in adults' living vicariously through their young. And he knew of no candle that burned out more quickly than that of the high school athlete.

"Athletics lasts for such a short time. It ends for people. But while it lasts, it creates this make-believe world where normal rules don't apply. We build this false atmosphere. When it's over and the harsh reality sets in, that's the real joke we play on people."[23]

Little research has been done on the effects of this shift away from the athletic limelight.[24]

box 5.1 *Continued*

halls at the beginning of each week and were transferred to the gym for the mandatory Friday morning pep rally. The making of these signs could be quite laborious as well, and one Pepette during the season broke down in tears because she had to stay up until the wee hours of the morning trying to keep up with the other Pepettes and make a fancy hall sign that her player never even thanked her for.

These were the basic Pepette requirements, but some girls went beyond in their show of spirit.

They might embroider the map of Texas on towels and then spell out MOJO [the school nickname] on pillowcases that the players could take with them during road trips. Or they might place their fresh-baked cookies in tins elaborately decorated in the Permian colors of black and white. In previous years Pepettes had made scrapbooks for their players,

including one with the cover made of lacquered wood and modeled on Disney's *Jungle Book*. The book had clippings, cut out in ninety-degree angles as square and true as in an architectural rendering, of every story written about the Permian team that year. It also had beautiful illustrations and captions that tried to capture what it meant to be a Pepette.

"The countryside was filled with loyal and happy subjects serving their chosen panther," said a caption in a chapter entitled "Joy," and next to it was a picture of a little girl with flowers in her hand going up to a panther, the Permian mascot, roaring under a tree. . . .

"It's very revered to be a Pepette or a cheerleader," said Julie Gardner, who had come to Odessa from a small college town in Montana as a sophomore. "It's the closest they can get to being a football player."

Source: Excerpts from H. G. Bissinger, *Friday Night Lights: A Town, A Team, and A Dream* (Reading, Mass.: Addison-Wesley, 1990), 45–46, 138.

Problems, Dilemmas, and Controversies

Although, as we have noted, sport in secondary schools has positive consequences for the schools, the participants, and the spectators, critics wonder about the educational benefits of sport activities. This section focuses on the fundamental problem of interscholastic sport as it is presently organized, that it is not designed to maximize its educational potential. Implicit in this criticism is the assumption that sport participation is a worthwhile school-related activity if it is congruent with educational goals.

The Reinforcement of Gender Roles

Sport in American schools has historically been almost exclusively a male preserve. This is clearly evident as one compares by gender the number of participants and facilities. We will examine sexism in sport to greater detail in chapter 14, therefore, the discussion here is limited to the unintended ways in which school sport works to maintain the conventional expectations for masculine and feminine roles.

What is the impact of a society that encourages its boys and young men to participate in sports while expecting its girls and young women to be spectators and cheerleaders? (See box 5.1.) The answer is that the society thereby uses sport to reinforce societal expectations for males and females. Males are to be dominant and aggressive, the doers, while females are expected to be passive supporters of men, attaining status through the efforts of their menfolk.

With the implementation of Title IX (see chapter 14) and the efforts to bring gender equity to school athletic programs, the number of female sport participants has increased dramatically from 300,000 girls involved in high school sports in 1971 to over 2.2 million in

1994. Although attempts have been made to equalize male and female programs in facilities, equipment, coaching, and transportation, inequities remain. Football, with its high cost and large number of participants, continues to skew budgets in favor of males. The scheduling of games and media attention also stress male sports.

Finally, a major trend in women's sports is that as women have gained in popularity, money, and respect, men have gained more and more control over them. Men are more likely than women to be athletic directors and coaches of women's sports at the high school and college levels. Male athletes see male role models exclusively as coaches and administrators, but more and more female athletes in their formative years are being denied female role models in positions requiring decisiveness, confidence, and self-assurance. Thus, females once again receive the unambiguous message that the more responsible a position in an organization is, the more likely men are to occupy it.[25]

Cheating

Cheating involves a violation of the rules to gain an unfair advantage over an opponent. It occurs at all levels of sport and may be done by individual players, teams, or coaches. The types of cheating depend on the sport and the ingenuity of the participants.[26] Clearly, cheating is antithetical to educational values and should have no place in educational programs.

Some high school players are coached to use illegal but difficult-to-detect techniques. One example is holding or tripping by offensive linemen in football. In basketball it is often advantageous to touch the lower half of the shooter's body because the referee usually watches the action around the ball. A form of cheating often taught basketball players is to fake being fouled. The intent is to fool an official who is out of position.

Coaches sometimes break the spirit of a rule if not the rule itself. For example, teams may not have organized practices before a certain date, yet coaches insist on players practicing, with captains in charge or coaches at a distance yelling orders.

A different form of cheating involves the use of drugs so that an athlete may compete at a higher-than-normal level of ability. This is sometimes done at the insistence of trainers and coaches, sometimes by an athlete's own decision. It has been estimated by the government that about 7 percent of high school senior males have taken anabolic steroids to increase weight and muscle.

Autocratic Coaches

Another criticism of high school sports is the almost total control that coaches exercise over their players' lives. Many coaches, for example, dictate hairstyles, clothing, dating, whom the players associate with, church attendance, and the like. Many also monitor their players' behavior off the field (bed checks) and restrict freedom of choice (what position to play, mandatory off-season weight lifting). Most coaches impose their will on their teams concerning team rules, discipline, play calling, and personnel decisions.

Whether coaches have the right to infringe upon the civil liberties of their charges is certainly a legal question. Beyond that, there is the question of the educational value of controlling these youngsters on and off the field. A system that denies personal autonomy apparently fosters dependence and immaturity rather than the presumed virtues of participation, which are leadership, independence, and self-motivation. Moreover, does subservience to a dictator prepare one for life in a democracy?[27]

Excessive Pressures to Win

Many of the problems found in school sports result from the excessive emphasis on winning. The sociological explanation for the tendency of coaches to be authoritarian, or to cheat, or to be hypocritical lies not in their individual psyches but in the intensely competitive system in which they operate.

In American society the success or failure of a team is believed by most persons to rest with the coach. This pressure to win brings some coaches to use illegal inducements to attract athletes to their schools, or to teach their linemen to hold without getting caught, or to look the other way when athletes (who face the same pressures to succeed) use drugs to enhance performance. The absolute necessity to win also explains why some coaches drive their players too hard. Thus, what some persons might label brutality has been explained by some coaches as a necessity to get the maximum effort from players. Finally, authoritarianism can be explained by the constraints on the coaching role. Democracy is unthinkable to most in the coaching profession because coaches are liable for the outcome in an extremely uncertain situation. They cannot control injuries, officiating, mental lapses by athletes, or the bounce of the ball, so most coaches are convinced that they must seek to control as much else as possible. As Willard Waller has said:

> A more serious indictment of the social system which allows the livelihood of a man and his family to depend upon the athletic achievements of boys is that the coach is so pressed that he uses his human material recklessly. He trains his "men" (aged sixteen) a bit too hard, or he uses his star athletes in too many events, or he schedules too many hard games; all this he does from a blameless desire to gain a better position or a rise in salary for himself, but he often fails to consider the possible effects upon the physical well-being of the rising generation.[28]

Another consequence of the excessive stress on winning is that sports participation becomes work rather than play. The emphasis is on the outcome rather than on enjoyment of the process. Fun has become equated with winning rather than with pleasure in participating.

Elitism

Interscholastic sport programs are elitist. That is, they are for the few, not the many. If sports participation is believed to have educational benefits, how can schools justify limiting teams to the most gifted athletes? Why should participation be restricted almost exclusively to the fast, the strong, or the tall? Further, how can schools justify letting these few have almost exclusive rights to the athletic facilities?

Sport Specialization

A growing trend in high school sports is specialization, that is, athletes limiting their participation to one sport that is trained for on a year-round basis.[29] This has tended to be the case in individual sports (running, swimming, gymnastics, tennis), but it is increasingly found in team sports as well, especially in large

schools. The arguments for this practice are that refined skill levels lead to optimal individual and team performance, it encourages excellence, and it increases the chances for obtaining a college athletic scholarship. The possible negative consequences of this practice include physical and psychological burnout, creation of a professional atmosphere for athletes that is inappropriate for adolescents, friction among coaches who compete for athletes, and the overuse of athletic facilities by a few.[30] Dick Fawcett, assistant director of the National Federation of State High School Associations, summarizes his objection to sport specialization this way: "A good school athletic program ought to create options for kids rather than close them down. If we're shutting kids out, then something's wrong."[31]

Budget Shortfalls

School districts fund sports in their districts, supplemented by ticket sales. Many districts have experienced a fiscal crisis with declining appropriations from the federal and state governments. This has especially affected urban school districts, as wealth has left the city for the suburbs.[32] The trend appears to be for more budget tightening as the federal government shifts more programs to the states and the mode of the electorate is to reduce taxes.

Three strategies to overcome these declining revenues have been employed to continue the financing of sports (and other extracurricular activities), each having negative consequences. First, schools have reacted to budget shortfalls by reducing or eliminating some sports (almost always individual sports with no potential for producing revenue) or the number of teams (eliminating sophomore or junior varsity teams). This solution, of course, reduces the number of participants and makes the sports all the more elitist. Football, by the way, is typically not subject to removal (although the number of players might be reduced). This is ironic because it is the most expensive sport in the number of coaches required, the cost of equipment (about $300 per player), and the cost of insurance. The sacredness of football poses another problem—because it is only for males, and lots of them, as other sports are reduced or eliminated, the proportion of the athletic budget going for males becomes all the more unbalanced.

A second solution to meager budgets is to charge a fee for all participants. Pay-for-play has been tried throughout the country, with the fees varying from $35 per sport to more than $300. The institution of this practice usually has resulted in reduced numbers of participants. Most important, this has created difficulty for students from lower-income families, especially reducing their participation. Thus, sport becomes not only elitist in skill level but elitist in terms of social class.

The third strategy employed by some districts has been to encourage corporate sponsorship. Corporations have been solicited to promote certain events, purchase advertising, buy scoreboards, artificial turf, a track, or a team bus. Two questions arise when this practice occurs. Is the commercialization of high school sport compatible with educational goals? Will those who control the resources of a program ultimately control it? In other words, will companies that donate thousands of dollars to a high school program have an influence on schedules, coach selection, and use of the facilities? Will they encourage a win-at-any-cost philosophy, since they do not want to have their products associated with a loser?

Corporate High School Sport

There are three indicators that sport is already at the corporate level in some schools and moving generally in that direction across the United States.

First, some school districts spend extraordinary amounts of money on their athletic teams, especially football and basketball. At Permian High School in Odessa, Texas, for example:[33]

- The football stadium cost $5.6 million in 1982. It is a sunken artificial-surface field eighteen feet below ground level, with a two-story press box, and poured concrete seating for 19,032. There is a full-time caretaker for this facility who lives in a house on the premises.
- During the football season, $6,400 is spent to rush film prints of the football games to the coaches, but only $5,040 is spent for all of the teaching materials for the English department in the high school.
- About $70,000 a season is spent for chartered jets for travel of the football team.

- The football coach is paid $48,000 (a teacher in the district with twenty years of experience and a master's degree makes $32,000); he teaches no classes; and he receives the free use of a new Ford Taurus each year.

Although this is an extreme example, there are schools in Texas, Ohio, Pennsylvania, and elsewhere with similar budgets, revealing the priority of sport in these schools and that sport has taken on the characteristics of corporate sport.

A second indicator that sport in high school is becoming corporate is the combined effect of increased exposure and commercialization, which is moving high school sport to more closely resemble big-time college programs. High schools used to play games against league rivals and participate in tournaments at the state level. For many schools this continues to be the case, but some now participate in national tournaments in Hawaii, Florida, Las Vegas, and elsewhere. These events are sponsored by corporations (for example, the McDonald's Classic in Honolulu; the Dr. Pepper Classic in Dallas; and the Arby's Classic in Bristol, Tennessee). In the past media attention tended to be local. *USA Today,* however, lists the twenty-five top ranked high schools for the sport in season (separate lists for boys and girls teams) in the nation. *USA Today, Parade,* and other national publications select high school All-American teams and coaches-of-the-year. SportsChannel, MSG (Madison Square Garden), and ESPN now produce weekly "magazine" shows on high school sports. Moreover, the National Federal of State High School Associations receives money from cable stations to televise football and basketball games nationally on cable. Reebok pays the California Interscholastic Federation $1 million for a three-year contract to sponsor all state championships. Nike pays some of the coaches of the nationally ranked teams thousands of dollars to outfit their teams in Nike's products. Alexander Wolff of *Sports Illustrated* summarizes the situation for the elite schools:

> High school basketball, alas, is no longer as you remember it. The cool kids are leaving the unwashed geeks behind. High school teams have been eclipsed by an elite layer of high school

programs, powerhouses that can be found in every corner of the country. . . .

These high-octane high schools now play national schedules. They appear on national television. They float up and down the Super 25 rankings in *USA Today* and wear sneakers provided gratis by shoe companies. . . .

Nor will you find their coaches monitoring the cafeteria. They're in their offices, on the phone—with a tournament director in Hawaii or the parent of some hotshot eighth-grader who lives 20 miles away. The Big Game crosstown? It's for dorks. The scene is now tournaments and the tube, complimentary Nikes and The Nation's Newspaper—be there or be square.[34]

The third indicator of high school sports becoming corporate is the channeling of elite athletes into "professionals." It starts with some promising elementary and junior high school athletes being "red shirted" (held back a year) to give them an extra year before college to increase their skills, size, speed, strength, coordination, and maturity. Many young athletes are recruited to attend certain high schools. The lure of eventually playing for the "big money" means, according to sports columnist Gerald Eskenazi, that "in effect, many children are declaring a major in athletics as early as grade school. And such an emphasis on athletics often comes at the expense of education."[35] These children specialize. They play and train at their sport year-round. During the summers they play in high level leagues and attend camps run by college coaches to hone skills and become recognized by agents, scouts, and coaches. This continues throughout the high school years, with increased pressure to succeed. What was once play has become work.[36]

Finally, the elite high school athletes are the objects of intense recruitment by colleges throughout high school. The experience is flattering to the athletes, but it has a tendency to inflate their egos and get in the way of their education. It also tends to make them cynical about education because of the often sleazy aspects of recruiting.[37] A more important consequence is that these athletes are on the market. As such, they ultimately will be purchased by a university athletic department. For high school athletes to be treated as commodities is the essence of corporate sport.

One of the most significant reforms in high school sports has been in providing opportunities for girls. Over two million girls now participate in high school sports each year.

Efforts to Reform High School Sports

Many educators and others are concerned with the path that high school sports have taken. As we have seen, there are school districts with twenty-thousand-seat stadiums, there are high school coaches who do not teach in the classroom, some high school coaches make thousands from shoe companies, and there are nationally televised games. Under these conditions, the pressure on coaches and athletes becomes heavier. As a result some coaches have become even more demanding. The potential for abuse and exploitation of athletes has increased. There have been more and more scandals involving payments and other gifts to high school players, recruiting, altered transcripts, and pressures on teachers to "give" athletes grades. Clearly, the education of the players tends to become secondary. In short, high school sport is moving in the same direction as sport at the college level, that is, toward commercialization, overemphasis, exploitation, elitism and away from the educational mission of schools. What follows are suggestions for reforming high school sports. The principle guiding these suggestions is that high school sports should be organized to maximize educational goals.

1. *Resist all efforts to "corporatize" high school sports.* High school sports should not be in the entertainment

business. Nor should they allow the encroachment of corporations into their world. Moreover, high school sports should be kept in perspective; that is, they should not put undue pressure on coaches and players. In effect, to counter high school sport becoming corporate several reforms must be instituted:

• Ban the national televising of high school sports. John Eisenberg has argued that such televising is wrong:

> High school should be a time to build an academic foundation; sports, no matter how talented the athlete, should be an extracurricular activity, not a televised, overemphasized spectacle. Now, I am not naive. I know sports is much more than an extracurricular activity to many top high school athletes. But shouldn't we be trying to correct the problem, not worsen it? Isn't it part of the reason college sports is such a cesspool? These kids need to concentrate more, not less, on classwork. They don't need distractions. And the lure of television would, assuredly, be distracting."[38]

• Schedule teams only within your area. As George Vecsey of *The New York Times* has suggested: "Let's pass a bus rule. If a team can get there comfortably in a bus, it's tolerable. But sending high school teams winging around the country is an abuse."[39]
• Eliminate post-season all-star games.
• Do not permit the involvement of athletic shoe companies and other corporations to intrude in high school sports. This means that these corporations must not be allowed to have high school coaches on their payrolls or to sponsor summer camps.

2. *Enforce an educationally defensible standard for school performance for athletes to be eligible to participate in sports.* Many school districts and states have low academic requirements for athletes. Many districts accept a "D" average for sport eligibility. Low eligibility standards do not prepare athletes for college, and they proclaim the message that academics are not important.

In 1983 a committee appointed by the governor of Texas and headed by H. Ross Perot concluded that school districts in that state were spending too much money on extracurricular activities and that students

were spending too much on them (fifteen to twenty hours a week, compared to five hours outside school on academic pursuits). As Perot argued: "Extracurricular activities are about the only place in the public school system where we demand excellence."[40] Among the recommendations of this committee was the controversial "No Pass No Play" rule, which required that players pass (receive grades of 70 or higher) in each subject during each six-week grading period or sit out the next six-week grading period.

The "No Pass No Play" rule became effective in the fall of 1984 against stiff resistance from coaches, parents, and others. There were court challenges, but the Texas Supreme Court upheld the rule. The immediate consequence of the rule was to create havoc on athletic teams (and in other extracurricular activities). In 1985, for example, about 20 percent of varsity football players were unable to play because they had less than the required 2.0 GPA. By 1990, however, less than 8 percent of Texas student-athletes were ineligible.[41] One interpretation for this improvement is that the rule had motivated athletes to perform well in the classroom. Schools may have instituted tutorials and other practices to enhance the learning of marginal students. This decline in failures, though, may indicate problems with the rule. For example, students' improved grades may have been a function of pressure on teachers to pass failing students so that they might retain their eligibility. Marginal students may have taken easier courses to stay eligible. Former athletes may have opted to drop out because they could not meet the tougher educational requirements. Efforts at reform have been attempted in several other states. In addition to Texas, California, Hawaii, Mississippi, New Mexico, and West Virginia now require at least a "C" average before a student is eligible for high school sports participation. In addition, many local school districts throughout the United States have instituted an approximation of this rule.

Another example of efforts intended to help reform school athletics through academic standards was instituted by the NCAA at the behest of the American Council on Education. Proposition 48, although passed by the governing body of intercollegiate athletics, is directed at the high schools. Formerly, entering college students were required simply to have had an overall

2.0 grade-point average in high school to participate in college athletics. Proposition 48, which set new eligibility standards for college athletics, went into effect in the fall of 1986. Entering college students must have (1) a 2.5 high school grade-point average in 13 core courses; and (2) a minimum total Scholastic Aptitude Test (SAT) score of 700, or a 15-point American College Testing (ACT) score. This controversial rule puts the responsibility on the high schools to prepare prospective college athletes academically for college.

The evidence is that Proposition 48 is working; that is, high school athletes are apparently better academically prepared for college than they were a generation ago. The number of new college recruits that are ineligible because of Proposition 48 is diminishing. Again, caution should guide the interpretation of this apparent good news. This lower rate may not be a consequence of better preparation for students. The colleges may be less willing than in earlier years to offer scholarships to marginal students because their scholastic failures are embarrassing to the academic community. Another possibility is that marginal students opted to play in community colleges where Proposition 48 does not apply. Despite these cautions, it appears that the new academic demands are working. High school athletes and their coaches are taking academics more seriously.[42]

3. *Bring coaches back into the teaching profession.* High school coaches should be part of the faculty, teaching courses and being responsible for nonsport duties just as are other faculty members. Coaches should be certified coaches, trained in first aid, the technical aspects of their sport, and the physiological and psychological aspects of adolescence. Coaches must be certified teachers, subject to the same rights and responsibilities as other teachers, including tenure. This will enhance the job security of coaches, thereby lessening, somewhat, the fanatical "win-at-all-costs" attitude.

4. *Minimize the elitism of sports.* Must sports only be for the unusually tall, large, and quick? (See box 5.2.) Schools should provide more school teams in more sports. Why not have two football teams, one for those weighing more than 150 pounds and one for those under that weight? Basketball could be divided into teams over and under a certain height. As Jay Coakley has said: "Too often the focus is on football and basketball rather than a variety of sports suited for a variety of participants. Why not have Frisbee teams, racquetball teams, flag football teams, softball teams, weight lifting teams, or teams in any sports where there is enough interest to get people to try out? With a little guidance, the students themselves could administer and coach these teams and coordinate meets and games with their counterparts in other schools."[43]

5. *Increase student involvement in sports programs.* One of the great ironies of school sports programs is that they are thought to enhance responsibility, autonomy, and leadership qualities in participants. However, as presently organized with autocratic coaches, imposed rules, and all decisions made by adults, these goals are not being achieved.

Could sports be organized so that the athletes are involved in the rule-making? Could they be organized so that elected player representatives could apply punishments for rule violations? Could team captains work with coaches on game strategies and make decisions during games? Again, Jay Coakley has an interesting suggestion: "Why should adult coaches make all the decisions on student sport teams? Ideally, the goal should be to prepare the team to be self-coached. In fact, some leagues should require that for the last two or three games of the season, coaches must sit in the stands and watch while the players coach themselves. This would be real leadership training."[44]

Although rare, there have been some experiments promoting athlete involvement in decision making. One radical experiment with democracy in football was used by George Davis, a football coach at several California high schools and a junior college. At St. Helena High School, his teams won forty-five consecutive games. The Davis system of coaching was unique. His players voted on who should be in the starting lineup; they decided what positions they wanted to play; and they established the guidelines for discipline. In other words, Davis's revolutionary system was democratic. Some critics in Willits, a community where Davis wanted to establish this system, were upset with it. They accused Davis of shirking responsibility, promoting disunity, and aiding Communist agitators. The irony is that these evils were the presumed consequences of a democratic system.

Jerry Goldsberry was cut from his college baseball team. Two decades later, he still remembers: "I was practicing base-running, and the coach called me over and said, 'I don't think you have the talent for baseball.' I don't know why he had to put it that way."

Venetia Faulkenberg was cut from her junior high school cheerleading squad. "It had an impact on the whole family," she says. "Parents feel the rejection almost as much as their kids do."

Geoff Bradley played two years of college basketball but was dropped from the team his junior year. "They said, 'We don't believe you can help our program.'" he recalls. "That's a blow to your ego."

As far as I could tell, Goldsberry, Faulkenberg and Bradley have grown up into happy, well-adjusted adults. But I was struck by the fact that each of them still remembers vividly an incident from youth that—at least for a time—wounded them emotionally. Being cut, for most kids, is a hurtful experience; for some, it can even leave lingering feelings of insecurity and worthlessness.

I went to Plainfield, Ind., recently to find out how one school has helped to put an end to this unnecessary trauma of growing up—Plainfield Community Middle School, where Geoff Bradley is the athletic director, Venetia Faulkenberg is a teacher and cheerleader sponsor and Jerry Goldsberry is the principal.

Plainfield's middle school separated from the high school and moved into its own building last year. Before that, however, for both academics and extracurricular activities, faculty committees recommended something called "Widespread participation"—the idea that schools need to involve more kids in more activities. Their proposal for this town just nine miles from the sports capital of Indianapolis? "They said, 'We want to come up with a no-cut policy,'" recalled Goldsberry.

What this meant is that every child would have an equal chance at feeling like an important part of a team or activity. If a child wanted to sing in the choir, he could; if a student wanted to belong to the swim team or run track, she could. With a little thought and planning, administrators discovered that they could apply the no-cut principle to all except two school activities—volleyball and basketball, where the limited space would allow for teams that were large but still finite.

"We felt, 'How is a student going to know what his strengths or weaknesses, likes and dislikes are, unless he tries?'" says Goldsberry. And under the no-cut system, a child would have the chance to improve or blossom.

The students came out in droves. The last year in the old building, only 13 kids showed up for cross-country; under the first year of the no-cut system, the number went to 78. Instead of 67 students on the track team, there were 120; the swim team grew from 50 to 64. Overnight, more than half of the 800 children at the middle school were taking part in activities. "The biggest problem was that we needed two school buses for everybody on the team," recalls the cross-country coach, Bruce Baker. Parent volunteers help out.

Davis believed that his system would:

1. Increase confidence between players and coaches.
2. Promote team cohesion.
3. Teach responsibility, leadership, and decision making, thereby fostering maturity rather than immaturity and independence rather than dependence.
4. Increase player motivation—instead of being driven by fear, harassment, and physical abuse by the coach, the players would have to impress their peers.
5. Free the coach to teach skills, techniques, and strategies.
6. Allow the players to experience the benefits of democracy.

box 5.2 *Continued*

In track and field events, a school can enter an unlimited number of students—but only the times of the top finishers count toward the final result. In other sports, of course, team sizes are limited. With its 66-member football squad, Plainfield has to be inventive to make all the kids feel included. "We still try to field our best team and, at the same time, balance that with getting more kids to participate," says Geoff Bradley.

When a limited number of students can take part in a meet—as in some track and all wrestling events—the school will hold intramural contests beforehand to select the kids who compete in that week's contest. A student who does not compete early in the season might be a regular starter by the end.

I stopped in as Mike Cummings was conducting a sixth-grade band rehearsal. The students were playing with all their hearts and sounded much like any junior high band. "If someone says, 'I have this trumpet, but I'm not quite sure what to do with it,' we say, 'You're in the band,'" Cummings told me. When the choir began this year, a number of students couldn't match the tune that the others were singing. "We surrounded them with stronger voices," said the co-director, Jonelle Heaton. "Now most of them are matching perfectly. One young man even was given a solo in our Christmas concert."

Surely, I thought, no-cut must have a devastating effect on the success of the athletic teams. Not so, "Last year, we had eight championships," Bradley told me. "And we were county-wide champions in wrestling, boys' cross-country and boys' swimming."

A sampling of parents I spoke with offered nothing but support. "I think it's great that all the kids in the school get to have the experience of participating," said Jim Horstman, summing up the general attitude.

Some people might argue that a no-cut policy is no preparation for the real world, where competition and disappointment happen to everybody. Bruce Baker, who is a counselor as well as a coach, responds, "These are still kids here. They're 11, 12, 13, 14, years old. I've had to cut kids that age from teams in the past, and it's devastating to them, no matter how you explain it. So we decided we wanted to make this a safe place for kids to be. They know it will be different in high school and college, but here they can still be kids."

But the last, and best, argument for no-cut is one I got from an eighth-grader on the school's cheerleading squad—one of the 73 cheerleaders at the school. No, they don't all perform at once; they're broken into three squads, which alternate games. And, no, they're not yet ready for the Rose Bowl, though virtually nobody else is at that age, either. They have lots of spirit, they're proud of what they do—and they're having fun.

Just before she was to perform at a basketball game, this girl told me, "I'm going to high school next year, and I know I won't make the cheerleading squad there. I know there are a lot of girls who are better at it than I am. But at least I got to have the experience. And that's something I can remember all my life."

Source: Michael Ryan, "Here, Everybody Gets to Play," *Parade Magazine* (15 March 1992), 10.

Davis summed up his system this way:

> What does the vote achieve? It takes the problems of discipline and responsibility and puts them where they belong, with the players. The coach becomes a teacher, what he is being paid to do, a resource unit. My job is to teach, to help athletes reach a level of independence. At any level this is how democracy works and why it succeeds.[45]

Summary

The theme of this chapter has been the relationship between school sport and educational goals. Our

Figure 5.1 Attributes of sports at different education levels

Source: Reprinted from Eldon E. Snyder and Elmer A. Spreitzer, "Sport, Education, and Schools," in *Handbook of the Social Science of Sport,* ed. Gunther R. F. Luschen, and George H. Sage (Champaign, Ill.: Stipes, 1981), 138.

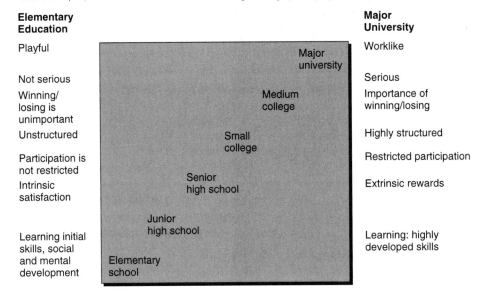

conclusion is that for sport to be compatible with educational goals, it should be structured as organized sport, not corporate sport. The data presented in this chapter, however, suggest that school sport is moving in the direction of corporate sport.

Sport at the elementary school level tends to accomplish educational goals (e.g., fostering good health practices, teaching skills, demonstrating the value of teamwork, and providing the experience of striving for a goal) in a playful, enjoyable atmosphere. At each successive educational level, however, the nature of sport changes; it becomes more serious, bureaucratized, and elitist, and its outcome becomes more crucial. Figure 5.1, provided by sociologists Eldon E. Snyder and Elmer A. Spreitzer, shows the progression in school sports from informal sport to corporate sport.

The serious question for educators is whether there is a place for corporate sport in education. The problem, of course, is not limited to education. As Harry Edwards said: "What's "wrong" with sport and sport in education in America reflects America itself—particularly the relationships between contemporary social, political, and economic realities and this nation's value priorities, its attitudes, and its perspectives."[46]

Notes

1. National Federation of State High School Associations data, reported in the *Denver Post,* 19 September 1995, sec. D, p. 2.

2. Donald Macintosh, "Interschool Sport Programs in Canada," *Journal of Physical Education, Recreation & Dance* 61 (February 1990): 58, 60, 62, 64.

3. James S. Coleman, *The Adolescent Society* (New York: Free Press, 1961), 309.

4. T. J. L. Chandler and A. D. Goldberg, "The Academic All-American as Vaunted Adolescent Role-Identity," *Sociology of Sport Journal* 7, no. 3 (1990): 287–93; Alyce Holland and Thomas Andre, "Athletic Participation and the Social Status of Adolescent Males and Females," *Youth & Society* 25 (March 1994): 388–407.

5. Jay J. Coakley, *Sport in Society: Issues and Controversies,* 5th ed. (St Louis: Times Mirror/Mosby, 1994), 391.

6. David Friesen, "Academic-Athletic-Popularity Syndrome in the Canadian High School Society," in *Canadian Sport: Sociological Perspectives,* ed. Richard S. Gruneau and John G. Albinson (Don Mills, Ont.: Addison-Wesley, 1976), 361–71.

7. James S. Coleman, *Adolescents and the Schools* (New York: Basic Books, 1965), 49.

8. Willard Waller, *The Sociology of Teaching* (New York: Wiley, 1965), 115–16. This was first published in 1932.

9. Ibid., 116. Many of the insights that follow about the social control functions of sport in schools derive from this source.

10. David Matza, "Position and Behavior Patterns of Youth," in *Handbook of Modern Sociology,* ed. Robert E. L. Faris (Chicago: Rand McNally, 1964), 207.

11. Ibid., 205–206.

12. H. G. Bissinger, *Friday Night Lights: A Town, A Team, and A Dream* (Reading, Mass.: Addison-Wesley, 1990), 20. For another, more scholarly, ethnography of sport in a Texas community, see Douglas E. Foley, *Learning Capitalist Culture: Deep in the Heart of Tejas* (Philadelphia: University of Pennsylvania Press, 1990), especially pp. 28–62.

13. Bissinger, *Friday Night Lights,* 127.

14. For a more elaborate analysis of the relationship between athletic involvement and academic achievement, see Eldon E. Snyder and Elmer Spreitzer, "Sport, Education, and Schools," in *Handbook of the Social Science of Sport,* ed. Gunther R. F. Luschen and George H. Sage (Champaign, Ill.: Stipes, 1981).

15. See the excellent summary of the methodological problems found in such studies in Christopher L. Stevenson, "Socialization Effects of Participation in Sport: A Critical Review of the Research," *Research Quarterly* 46 (October 1975): 287–301; and Christopher L. Stevenson, "College Athletics and Character: The Decline and Fall of Socialization Research," in *Sport and Higher Education,* ed. Donald Chu, J. O. Segrave, and B. J. Becker (Champaign, Ill: Human Kinetics Publishers, 1985).

16. Elmer Spreitzer, "Does Participation in Interscholastic Athletics Affect Adult Development: A Longitudinal Analysis of an 18–24 Age Cohort," *Youth and Society* 25 (March 1994), 368–87.

17. Ibid., 384.

18. Charles Banham, "Man at Play," *Contemporary Review* 207 (August 1965): 62.

19. Terry D. Orlick, "The Sports Environment: A Capacity to Enhance—A Capacity to Destroy," (paper presented at the Canadian Symposium of Psycho-Motor Learning and Sports Psychology, 1974), 2.

20. See C. Roger Rees, Frank M. Howell, and Andrew W. Miracle, "Do High School Sports Build Character? A Quasi-Experiment on a National Sample," *The Social Science Journal* 27 (1990): 303–15; and Andrew W. Miracle and C. Roger Rees, *Lessons of the Locker Room: The Myth of School Sports* (Buffalo, N.Y.: Prometheus Books, 1994).

21. Merrill J. Melnick, Beth E. Vanfossen, and Donald F. Sabo, "Developmental Effects of Athletic Participation Among High School Girls," *Sociology of Sport Journal* 5 (March 1988): 22–36.

22. Herbert W. Marsh, "The Effects of Participation in Sport During the Last Two Years of High School," *Sociology of Sport Journal* 10 (March 1993), 18–43.

23. Bissinger, *Friday Night Lights,* xiv.

24. See Donald W. Ball, "Failure in Sport," *American Sociological Review* 41 (August 1976): 726–39; Donald S. Harris and D. Stanley Eitzen, "The Consequences of Failure in Sport," *Urban Life* 7 (July 1978): 275–80; Jay J. Coakley, "Leaving Competitive Sport: Retirement or Rebirth," *Quest* 35, no. 1 (1983): 1–11; JoAnne Drahota, "The Role Exit of Professional Athletes," (Ph.D. diss., Colorado State University, 1996). For an excellent non-social science account of this process, see the documentary film *Hoop Dreams* (1994).

25. M. L. Saneholz, "Should Men Coach Women's Sports?" *Journal of Physical Education, Recreation & Dance* 57 (March 1986): 39–43; D. Stanley Eitzen and Stephen R. Pratt, "Gender Differences in Leadership Styles: The Case of Female Basketball Teams," *The Research Quarterly* 60 (June 1989): 152–58; D. Stanley Eitzen and Stephen R. Pratt, "Comparing Male and Female Women's Basketball Coaches," *Coaching*

Women's Basketball 3 (November/December 1989): 22–25; Stephen R. Pratt and D. Stanley Eitzen, "Differences in Coaching Philosophies Between Male Coaches of Male and Female Teams," *International Review of Sport Sociology* 24, no. 2 (1989), 151–61; and Frank Perna, "Equality in Sport: Are All Men and Women Athletes Treated Equal?" *The Center for the Study of Sport in Society Digest* 2 (summer 1990): 8.

26. For a survey of the literature and numerous insights about the phenomenon of cheating in sports, see D. Stanley Eitzen, "Ethical Problems in American Sport," *Journal of Sport and Social Issues* 12 (spring 1988): 17–30.

27. D. Stanley Eitzen, "Sports and Ideological Contradictions: Learning From the Cultural Framing of Soviet Values," *Journal of Sport & Social Issues* 16 (December 1992): 144–49.

28. Waller, *The Sociology of Teaching*, 114–15.

29. Grant M. Hill and Jeffrey Simons, "A Study of the Sport Specialization on High School Athletics," *Journal of Sport and Social Issues* 13 (spring 1989): 1–13.

30. Grant M. Hill and Gary F. Hansen, "Specialization in High School Sports: The Pros and the Cons," *Journal of Physical Education, Recreation & Dance* 59 (May/June 1988): 76–79.

31. Dick Fawcett quoted in Del Stover, "What to Do When Grown-Ups Want to Spoil the Fun of School Sports," *The American School Board Journal* 175 (July 1988): 20.

32. See Doug A. Timmer, "Urban Problems in the United States," in *Social Problems,* D. Stanley Eitzen and Maxine Baca Zinn, 7th ed. (Boston: Allyn and Bacon, in press), chapter 6; and E. M. Swift, "Why Johnny Can't Play," *Sports Illustrated,* September 1991, 60–72.

33. Bissinger, *Friday Night Lights,* 42, 145–46.

34. Alexander Wolff, "High School Confidential," *Sports Illustrated,* 8 January 1990, 20.

35. Gerald Eskenazi, "Arena of Big-Time Athletics Is Showcasing a Younger Act," *New York Times,* 5 March 1989, 18.

36. For a critique of summer basketball camps for high school stars, see Phil Taylor, "The Summer Game," *Sports Illustrated,* 15 July 1991, 50–53; and Curry Kirkpatrick, "The Big Boys of Summer," *Newsweek,* 7 August 1995, 57.

37. See Alexander Wolff and Armen Keteyian, *Raw Recruits: The High Stakes Game Colleges Play to Get Their Basketball Stars—And What It Costs to Win* (New York: Pocket Books, 1990); Murray Sperber, *College Sports Inc.* (New York: Henry Holt, 1990), 205–296; and Darcy Frey, *The Last Shot* (New York: Houghton Mifflin, 1994).

38. John Eisenberg, "Is Prep TV, 'Final Four' Going Too Far?" *Denver Post,* 4 March 1989, sec. F, p. 6.

39. George Vecsey, "Young Athletes Deserve Good Old School Days," *New York Times,* 10 March 1989, sec. B, p. 11.

40. H. Ross Perot quoted in Ellie McGrath, "Blowing the Whistle on Johnny," *Time,* 30 January 1984, 80.

41. Chris White, "Can Johnny Read? Is No Pass-No Play Working in America's Classrooms?" *Center for the Study of Sport in Society Digest* 2 (summer 1990): 9.

42. See Richard E. Lapchick, "The High School Student-Athlete: Root of the Ethical Issues in College Sport," in *The Rules of the Game: Ethics in College Sport,* ed. Richard E. Lapchick and John B. Slaughter (New York: Macmillan, 1989), 17–28.

43. Coakley, *Sport in Society,* 411.

44. Ibid., 412.

45. Neil Amdur, *The Fifth Down: Democracy and the Football Revolution* (New York: Delta Books, 1972), 218.

46. Harry Edwards, *Sociology of Sport* (Homewood, Ill: Dorsey Press, 1973), 361.

Chapter 6

Intercollegiate Sport

The first intercollegiate sports contest in the United States was a rowing race between Harvard and Yale in 1852. In 1869 the first intercollegiate football contest took place between Princeton and Rutgers. These early collegiate sports were run by students. The faculties, administrators, and alumni were not involved. According to George H. Sage, "The original form of governance was modeled after the well-established sports in the private secondary schools of England. In the British model the sports were for the students, and as student recreations they were expected to be organized, administered, and coached through student initiative, not adult intervention."[1] Students soon began losing control over their sports. The first college faculty athletic committee was formed by Princeton in 1881 and by Harvard a year later. As early as 1883 faculty representatives from several colleges met to discuss common problems surrounding sports. In 1895 the first league (later known as the Big Ten) was formed. By 1905 there was a need for a national organization to standardize rules and address problems associated with college sport. The Intercollegiate Athletic Association was formed in that year. Its name was changed in 1910 to the National Collegiate Athletic Association (NCAA). That organization has controlled college sport ever since, except for small colleges, which later came to be controlled by the National Association of Intercollegiate Athletics (NAIA) and for women's college sport, which it did not control until 1981. All of this is to say, that what was once a student-run activity has been transformed so that now students have virtually no voice in athletic policies, control being vested in coaches, school administrations, athletic corporations, booster organizations, leagues, national organizations, and television. Moreover, college sport has been transformed from an activity for the participants to large scale commercial entertainment.

Along with this transformation of intercollegiate sport have come many abuses, such as illegal recruiting practices, altered transcripts, phantom courses, the physical and psychological abuse of athletes, and the exploitation of athletes.[2] These abuses occur for two related reasons, which are pressure to win on the field and to succeed financially. William F. Reed of *Sports Illustrated* wrote a characterization of college basketball, which is just as relevant for big-time college football, that suggests the magnitude of the problem:

> Every fan knows that underneath its shiny veneer of color, fun and excitement, college basketball is a sewer full of rats. Lift the manhole cover on the street of gold, and the odor will knock you down. Look at this season [1990]: The programs at North Carolina State, Florida, Illinois, Missouri, and Nevada-Las Vegas—to cite only the most prominent examples—are up to their backboards in scandal.
>
> The misdeeds allegedly committed by college basketball programs today are the same stuff that has plagued the game for decades—buying players, cheating in academics, shaving points, etc. And the NCAA is powerless to stop it. Make a statement by coming down hard on a Kentucky or a Maryland, and what happens? Nothing, really. The filth merely oozes from another crack.[3]

If these harsh words are true, and we believe the evidence that they are is irrefutable, then big-time intercollegiate athletics has severely corrupted the goals and ideals of higher education.

The following discussion is limited for the most part to the problems found in "big-time" football and basketball programs in colleges and universities. We will not consider schools with scaled-down athletic programs, few athletic scholarships, regional schedules, small coaching staffs, limited funds from gate receipts, and no television money. We have not considered Canadian universities here because their athletic programs are much less emphasized than those in North American universities. Sport in Canadian universities commands little attention from school administrators, students, communities, or the media, and attendance at sports events is relatively low; there are almost no broadcast revenues from sports. The recruitment of athletes is low key, and very few athletic scholarships are available.[4]

This chapter is divided into four parts: (1) college sport as big business, (2) the NCAA and student-athletes, (3) the education and noneducation of athletes, and (4) efforts to reform big-time college sports.

College Sport As Big Business

Big-time college sport in the United States is organized so that separating the business aspects from the play on the field is impossible. The intrusion of money into collegiate sport is evident in the following representative examples:

- The NCAA projected revenue for the 1995–96 fiscal year was $234,210,000.[5] The NCAA increased ticket prices for the 1997 and 1998 Final Four basketball tournaments to $l00, $80, and $55 (a $30 increase over 1996 prices).[6]
- Each school in the 1995 Rose Bowl received $6.5 million, and each school in the Orange Bowl received $4.2 million. The total amount paid to schools of teams competing in postseason bowls exceeded $68 million. In 1996 the money involved jumped substantially when the Fiesta Bowl paid each participating school $12 million.
- In 1994 CBS agreed to pay the NCAA $1.725 billion ($215.6 million a year) for the rights to televise the men's basketball tournament through 2002.
- One school, Louisiana State University, through its athletic program generates more than $65 million in sales for local firms, another $25.5 million in household earnings, and supports 1,616 jobs in the Baton Rouge area.[7]
- Syracuse University built a 50,000-seat, domed stadium for $26.85 million. The University of Tennessee built a 24,500-seat basketball arena for $43 million. The University of North Carolina constructed the $35 million Dean Smith Arena during a time in the 1980s when there was a faculty pay freeze. In the 1994–95 basketball season, the average attendance at Syracuse men's games was 24,245; the University of Kentucky 23,806; and the University of North Carolina 21,231.
- In 1995 the University of Michigan football team averaged 106,217 in attendance per home game. Penn State averaged 96,289 and Tennessee 95,637.
- A number of bowls have corporate tie-ins. For example, for an annual contribution of $2 million, USF&G sponsors the Sugar Bowl (now the USF&G Sugar Bowl). Similarly, there is now the John Hancock Bowl, the Federal Express Orange Bowl, the Mobil Cotton Bowl, the Mazda Gator Bowl, the IBM OS/2 Fiesta Bowl, the Outback Steakhouse Gator Bowl, and the Sea World Holiday Bowl. At the university level, a school such as San Diego State has corporate sponsors that pay, collectively, $2 million a year to the school. Coors Brewing Company paid $5 million to the University of Colorado when the university agreed to name the new fieldhouse "Coors Events Center." At a lower level, Colorado State University receives about $375,000 from contributors such as First Interstate Bank, Coors, Coca-Cola, McDonald's, Pizza Hut, Continental Airlines, Marriott, and Anheuser-Busch.
- Each year, supporters of university athletic programs donate about $400 million to them.[8] For example, the University of Nebraska athletic department receives $2 million annually from boosters (the Touchdown Club has 2,700 members who each contribute at least $200 annually, and the Husker Beef Club, with another 1,500 members, raises $350,000 a year plus supplies the beef for the athletes' training table).[9] Clemson University through its IPTAY ("I Pay $30 A Year") Club raises about $5 million a year from football season-ticket holders who pay a minimum of $100 extra (inflation has made the name of the club obsolete) and as much as $2,000 for priority seating.
- The University of Florida has "skyboxes" at its football stadium that rent for $30,000 each a year, with a minimum five-year lease for each box.
- Notre Dame has a $38 million contract to televise its football games. The sale of Notre Dame merchandise brings the school another $l million and an appearance in a bowl game raises another $3 to $6 million.
- An estimated $2.5 billion a year in college merchandise is sold under license, generating about $100 million to the schools in royalties. The University of Michigan receives the most income from this source—$5.8 million in 1994.[10]
- In 1992 Penn State University awarded an exclusive contract to Pepsi, meaning that no other sodas will be sold anywhere on the university's twenty-one

campuses. In return, Pepsi gave $14 million to the university, part of which will go for the construction of a new sports arena.

Another set of examples shows how well the coaches of big-time programs are compensated:

- When Jerry Tarkanian was basketball coach at University of Nevada at Las Vegas, he was a tenured member of the faculty with an annual salary of $203,976 (1991), making him the highest salaried state employee. In addition, he received a guarantee of 10 percent of the school's profits from the NCAA basketball tournament and a gift of 234 season basketball tickets (over $40,000 in value). Moreover, he has a lucrative shoe contract and other side deals. Tarkanian's successor at UNLV, Rollie Massimino, was given a salary of $511,000 plus a supplemental contract of $375,000, the last amount hidden from the Board of Regents.
- Summer camps are especially lucrative for well-known coaches, with annual gross revenues exceeding $400,000 in the powerhouse programs.
- Major sporting goods manufacturers, especially those selling shoes, regularly pay coaches to insure that teams wear their brand of equipment (and, therefore, their brand is seen at games, on television, and in photographs—shoes prominently displayed on the cover of *Sports Illustrated* are the most prized). Basketball coaches average twice that of football coaches for shoe deals. At the high end, Mike Krzyzewski, basketball coach at Duke University, signed a fifteen-year shoe endorsement contract for a $1 million bonus plus $375,000 a year. In 1993 North Carolina basketball coach Dean Smith signed an agreement with Nike worth an estimated $4.7 million to Smith and the university over four years. The terms: a $500,000 bonus to Smith; $300,000 annually to Smith, which he will share with his assistants; Nike will provide shoes, clothing, and equipment to twenty-four of the schools athletic teams; and Nike will fund an international trip for the basketball team worth about $200,000.

- John Calipari, head basketball coach of the men's basketball team at the University of Massachusetts, was compensated under these terms: (1) a base salary of $132,000; (2) 94 percent of the estimated $300,000 net from his summer camp; (3) $50,000 from season-ticket revenues; (4) $50,000 provided in the form of a pension; (5) 35 percent of all postseason tournament revenue; and (6) all of the school's share from one road game of his choice. This totalled to about $550,000 *excluding* his personal deals with Nike, Spaulding, and Champion.[11]
- Coaches also are compensated for promoting other products through advertising. According to Murray Sperber, "Penn State's Joe Paterno, a symbol of probity in men's football, charges $25,000 to $100,000 for a television commercial, and $5,000 to $15,000 for a print ad."[12]
- Coaches may also receive gifts of housing, paid country club memberships, cash annuities (Denny Crum, Louisville basketball coach, received a lump-sum $1 million in 1993 for fulfilling his long-term contract), and free cars.[13]

These examples of schools and their coaches demonstrate clearly that college athletic programs are not amateur athletics. Big-time college athletic programs are big business. The average annual budget for an entire athletic program of a school in Division IA (the top 106 football schools) is about $12.5 million, with the largest budgets approaching $25 million. The money is raised from gate receipts, student athletic fees, the budget of the university, booster organizations, individual contributors, television, and league reimbursements for the television and bowl or tournament appearances by league members.

There are two related commonly held beliefs regarding money generated by big-time athletic programs. The first is that these athletic departments are doing very well financially. The second is that winning sports programs translate into increased funds for the universities they represent. Both of these beliefs are myths. In fact, about 70 percent of schools operate in the red and the accomplishments of the athletic departments do not spill over into contributions for academics. Murray Sperber summarizes the situation this way:

One of the most tenacious myths about today's big-time college sports is that they earn huge sums of money for American higher education. In fact, if profit and loss are defined according to ordinary business practices, almost all colleges lose money on their intercollegiate athletics programs. Richard D. Schultz, executive director of the National Collegiate Athletic Association, recently admitted, "You can probably count on your two hands the number of athletic departments that actually have a surplus annually."

Another myth about college sports is that big-time athletics programs generate money for the academic units of their universities. In reality, studies indicate that athletics programs raise dollars only for themselves and that their main donors refuse to contribute to any unit of the institution other than the athletics department. Moreover, when an institution becomes involved in a sports scandal, regular donors to the university—alumni, foundations, and corporations—often withhold contributions.[14]

There are several reasons for the red ink generated by athletic departments. First, the revenue-producing sports (football and men's basketball and occasionally baseball and hockey) are expected to pay for the entire athletic program. Second, whenever a surplus occurs, it is typically spent to "improve" the program by building better training facilities (e.g., the University of Colorado spent $12 million for a multipurpose football team house), adding to the stadium seating, building more "skyboxes," adding office space, improving practice facilities, hiring more fundraisers, spending more on recruiting, and the like. The argument is that you have to spend money to make money. Third, the athletic departments generally spare no expense to fund the revenue-producing sports. Employees in these athletic departments tend to be paid better than employees elsewhere in their universities. Typically, athletic directors in Division I programs make over $100,000 a year plus a car, entertainment allowance, and free travel to away games. Moreover, the salaries for associate and assistant directors average more than the average annual salary for an associate professor in

most university departments.[15] Travel budgets for the teams and for recruiters are generous. A common practice, for example, is for the football team to stay in a local hotel the night before home games. Fourth, universities sponsor pregame football parties for influential alumni, boosters, and legislators. At the University of Colorado the annual cost of brunches and game tickets is about $100,000. Fifth, creative bookkeeping can make the teams seem profitable. Again, using the example of the University of Colorado, the budget shows a high income, but included in this "income" was (in 1995) $900,000 in presidential support, $1,064,331 in chancellor's support, and $1,254,000 in support from mandatory student fees.[16] These amounts, totalling $3.218 million, artificially inflate athletic department income. Moreover, they represent monies given to the athletic program, which could have funded other programs in the university. Also, the university administrations often use their funds for capital improvements for constructing arenas, sports complexes, and the like. As John Silber, president of Boston University said of his former employer, the University of Texas at Austin: "They've got a $50-million to $60-million capital investment in their football plant at U.T. Try amortizing that at 5 or 6 percent and you will see the program is actually losing money."[17]

The Consequences of a Money Orientation in College Sports

First, the lack of adequate monies leads to a reduction in the number of sports offered by these institutions. Football and men's basketball produce revenue, therefore they are exempt from budget cuts. When the cuts are severe, some programs may be eliminated, and these casualties are in the so-called "minor" sports such as wrestling, lacrosse, gymnastics, swimming, water polo, tennis, and golf. Women's sports are less vulnerable than the men's minor sports because of Title IX (see chapter 14), but their programs are also subject to cuts. The point is that the necessity of raising money through sports programs tends to make college sport more elitist (fewer and fewer participants) and limited to certain skills and physical types (the tall or the large or both). They insure the dominance of male sports, at least football and basketball.

The necessity of making more and more money is a major source for the many abuses found in big-time college sport. A team does not make millions and coaches do not make hundreds of thousands, without winning. This necessity of winning is a primary reason why some coaches cheat and dehumanize their players. The pressures to win may be responsible for the use of drugs to enhance performance beyond normal limits. Money has prostituted the university and the purpose of sport. As Maurice Mitchell, former chancellor of the University of Denver, characterized the situation:

> The curse of big-time athletics still plagues the American university. Athletics has nothing to do with the primary purpose of the university. It is an embarrassment and in many cases a demonstration of immorality, of hypocrisy, a reallocation of scarce university resources, and an involvement with a group of people who, in most cases, should not be on a university campus. Big-time athletics demonstrate—to students and faculty alike—that the university is willing to operate under a double standard. Big-time athletics on university campuses may be a symbol of our willingness to use our institutions of higher learning, which were established for sacred purposes, for the least sacred of purposes. Like prostitution, it is accepted but not honored.[18]

Another consequence of an athletic department's search for money is that decision making tends to leave the university and flow toward the sources of revenue. Television money dictates schedules, for example. Booster organizations that supply funds may influence which coaches are hired and when they will be fired. Corporate sponsors may intrude in various ways as they give or withhold their monies. The point, as Murray Sperber says, is that these practices "undermine one of the fundamental tenets of colleges and universities—their independence."[19]

Another result of "going after the money" is that the relatively few seats available in arenas tend to go to big-spending boosters, depriving students of the chance to watch their teams play. For instance, the University of Louisville only allots 10 percent of its seats for basketball games to students. Many schools with successful basketball programs such as the University of Arizona hold a lottery to choose the students that may attend games. The situation worsens during tournament time when each school is allotted relatively few tickets. These, typically, are given to the greatest benefactors of the athletic department rather than to students. This raises the serious question: Should not *school* sports be primarily for *students?*

When the pressure to win becomes too great, the result can be a sub rosa policy of cheating, that is, a policy of offering athletes more than the legal limit to lure them to a school and keep them there or using unethical means to keep them scholastically eligible. As far back as 1929 a report by the Carnegie Foundation decried the widespread illegal recruiting practices of American colleges and universities. Since then, the problem has not only continued but intensified. The scandals involve illegal and immoral behavior of overzealous coaches, school authorities, alumni, and boosters. These recruits are not only suspect academically but sometimes they also go over the line in antisocial behavior. Let's cite a few representative cases of scandals in college sport:

Item: In one celebrated case, Hart Lee Dykes was granted immunity from punishment by the NCAA if he would reveal the improper inducements he was offered when he left high school in 1985. Dykes's testimony resulted in four schools being placed on NCAA probation—Illinois; Texas A&M; Oklahoma; and the school he chose to play for, Oklahoma State.

Item: Sports Illustrated in an open letter to the president of the University of Miami argued that he should dismantle the football program to salvage his school's reputation. The following is part of the rationale for this strong position:

> During the past decade your school enrolled and suited up at least one player who had scored a 200 on his verbal SAT—the number you get for spelling your name correctly. An on-campus disturbance, involving some 40 members of the football team, required 14 squad cars and a police dog to quell. Fifty-seven players were implicated in a financial-aid scandal that the feds call "perhaps the largest centralized fraud upon the federal Pell Grant

program ever committed." And among numerous cases of improper payments to players from agents was one in which the nondelivery of a promised installment led a Hurricane player to barge into the agent's office and put a gun to his head.

The illegal acts with which your Hurricanes have been charged run the gamut from disorderly conduct and shoplifting to drunken driving, burglary, arson, assault and sexual battery. . . . *No fewer than one of every seven scholarship players on last season's team has been arrested while enrolled at your university.*[20]

Item: In 1994 a federal grand jury indicted Baylor University's head basketball coach and three of his assistants, two junior college coaches, and two junior college administrators on charges of violating federal mail fraud, wire fraud, and conspiracy statutes. In effect, Baylor had faxed a term paper to a junior college player it was recruiting so that the player could use that paper in an English composition class he was taking at Westark Community College. Moreover, another Baylor recruit was instructed to take a correspondence course on the Old Testament from Southeastern College of the Assemblies of God because the Baylor coaches had a copy of the final exam from this course and others. Finally, an athlete wanting to enroll at Baylor was provided with a fraudulent transcript by two administrators at his school, Shelton State Community College.[21]

Item: Correspondence credits from Southeastern College (noted previously) were gained fraudulently (not by Southeastern College, but perpetrated by the people taking courses there and their benefactors) by athletes in search of easy credits to stay eligible or to be eligible to enroll at a particular school. To date, as many as sixty junior colleges have accepted these credits from their athletes and fifty-five NCAA schools have eventually given scholarships to these athletes.[22]

Item: Howard Cosell in his book *What's Wrong with Sports* lists 110 schools convicted of cheating and placed on probation by the NCAA during the 1980s.[23] One of these schools, Arizona State, was found guilty in six of its programs: baseball,

gymnastics, wrestling, basketball, football, and track. Several schools were recidivists, that is, they were repeat offenders. Those found guilty twice in the same sport in the 1980s were Auburn, Georgia, Illinois, Kentucky, Memphis State, Oklahoma, Oral Roberts, University of Southern California, Southern Mississippi, Texas, Cincinnati (in both basketball and football), San Francisco, West Texas State, West Virginia, and Wisconsin. Other schools were found guilty three times in one sport (if criminals are found guilty three times, they are labeled "habitual offenders" and by the "three strikes and you're out" rule given life sentences) during this ten-year-period: Memphis State in football (they were also guilty twice in basketball, as noted previously), Oklahoma State in football, and Southern Methodist in football. SMU received the so-called "death penalty" (the harshest punishment ever administered by the NCAA) for illegal payments by boosters to twenty-one football players during the 1985–86 season.

Item: From 1980 to 1995, twelve schools finished first in one of the major polls of football achievement. Of these twelve programs, only three were not sanctioned by the NCAA or faced serious controversies because of alleged criminal wrongdoings or steroid use.[24]

In most instances school administrators, students, and supporters do not demand that guilty coaches be fired for their transgressions—if they win. As John Underwood has characterized the situation: "We've told them that it doesn't matter how clean they keep their programs. It doesn't matter what percentage of their athletes graduate or take a useful place in society. It doesn't even matter how well the coaches teach their sports. All that matters are the flashing scoreboard lights."[25] This insight was also recognized by the judge in the trial of former University of New Mexico men's basketball coach Norman Ellenberger. After the jury found Ellenberger guilty on twenty-one counts of fraud (including bribery of school officials and the altering of transcripts) for which he could have gone to the state penitentiary for twenty-one years, District Judge Philip Baiamonte placed him on unsupervised probation, saying:

I am being asked to sentence a man who is simply one cog in the entire machine, the entire system that exists, not only here but over the entire country, called college ball. In effect, you see, I am being asked to sentence a man because he got caught, not because his conduct was unacceptable. The clear testimony in this case is that everybody looked the other way until he got caught. . . . What's going through my mind at this point is the question, really, of how fair is it to incarcerate in prison a coach who is basically doing what almost everybody in this community wanted him to do. Win basketball games at any cost and by whatever means might be necessary to do that. It seems that the prevailing attitude was, "It's not how the game was played, but whether or not you win or lose that counts."[26]

The pursuit of money has prostituted the university and the purpose of sport. Education is not the goal. The physical and emotional welfare of athletes is secondary to their athletic performances. Sport as a pleasurable activity is an irrelevant consideration in the climate of big-time collegiate sport. Winning and the money generated are paramount. In this milieu the resulting evils are due not to the malevolent personalities of coaches but to a perverse system. Philip Taubman captured the perversion in the following statement:

> At places like Ohio State, Alabama, Texas, Notre Dame, USC, Michigan, and Oklahoma, they've forgotten football is just a game. It has become a big business, completely disconnected from the fundamental purposes of academic institutions. The goal of college ball is no longer for young men to test and strengthen their bodies, to learn about teamwork, and to have a good time. All that matters is winning, moving up in the national rankings, and grabbing a bigger share of the TV dollar that comes with appearances on NCAA's game of the week on ABC. To achieve these aims, schools and coaches not only bend and break the National Collegiate Athletics Association (NCAA) rules governing college football but, far more destructively, violate the intellectual integrity and principles of the American university system.[27]

Perhaps the most serious result of the "winning-at-all-costs" mentality that pervades many athletic departments is that the education of the athletes is secondary. Coaches proclaim that their athletes are students first and athletes only secondarily; this is the typical recruiting speech to prospects and their parents, but in practice the reverse is often true. The relationship between coach and athlete is essentially that of employer and employee. The athlete has signed a contract and is paid for his or her athletic services (but not well). Moreover, because of such enormous demands on their time, athletes frequently must take a reduced course load and thus will not usually graduate in the normal number of years. Study halls and tutors are frequently available, even required, for college athletes, but the primary function of these adjuncts is to ensure athletic eligibility, not necessarily an education. Athletes are often counseled to take easy courses, whether or not those courses fit their educational needs. Achieving an education is incidental to the overriding objective of big-time sports. As Alabama's legendary football coach Paul "Bear" Bryant once put it: "I used to go along with the idea that football players on scholarships were student-athletes, which is what the NCAA calls them. Meaning a student first, an athlete second. We were kidding ourselves, trying to make it more palatable to the academicians. We don't have to say that and we shouldn't. At the level we play, the boy is really an athlete first and a student second."[28]

The cynicism with which some coaches regard education is seen in the revelations concerning the enrollment of athletes in "phantom" courses (correspondence or residence courses that give credit for no work or attendance). Clearly, for a coach to permit this is to admit that the athlete's eligibility supersedes his or her learning. For the athlete, the message is equally clear.

Perhaps the greatest disregard for the education of athletes occurs when those without hope of graduation are recruited. In the words of syndicated columnist George Will:

> The worst scandal does not involve cash or convertibles. It involves slipping academically unqualified young men in the back doors of academic institutions, insulating them from academic expectations, wringing them dry of their

athletic-commercial usefulness, then slinging them out the back door even less suited to society than they were when they entered. They are less suited because they have spent four years acquiring the idea that they are exempt from normal standards.[29]

Although there are exceptions (e.g., Duke and Notre Dame), many institutions recruit academically marginal (or even unqualified) athletes, as measured by high school grades and standardized tests (SAT and ACT).[30] While basketball coach at North Carolina State, Jim Valvano, for example, recruited players who had no reasonable expectation of graduation. According to Barry Jacobs: "Basketball players recruited by Valvano characteristically average 250 points below the student body average on the Scholastic Aptitude Test. Before the NCAA's enforcement in 1986 of Proposition 48, which mandated a minimum score of 700 on the SAT, Valvano brought in 13 players who scored below 700 [including one, Chris Washburn, who scored 470]."[31] We will discuss athlete performance as students later in this chapter.

A Contradiction: Athletes As Amateurs in a Big Business Environment

We have seen that great sums of money are generated by big-time college sports. The university athletic departments act like corporations (indeed, many are organized separately from their universities as corporations), many businesses outside the university make considerable sums from college sports, and many individuals in the athletic departments (athletic directors, coaches, trainers, accountants, groundskeepers, equipment managers, academic advisors) make their living, some as much as $1 million annually, from their involvement in college sport. The irony is that the major labor force in producing college sport, the athletes, is not paid. Young men (and more recently young women) on athletic scholarships are limited by NCAA rules to room, board, books, and tuition to bring honor and lots of dollars to their universities. They are considered to be amateurs who participate for the love of sport untainted by money. But this is a charade, as George Sage has argued:

In reality, the scholarship is nothing but a work contract. What colleges are really doing is hiring entertainers. The deceit of claiming that educational purposes preclude salaried compensation for athletic performances is testimony to the extensive attempts of the collegiate establishment to avoid its financial responsibilities. Athletic scholarships are actually a form of economic exploitation, the establishment of a wage below poverty level for student-athlete-entertainers who directly produce millions of dollars for athletic departments. . . . Paying as little as possible to operate a business is called keeping overhead low; it's what every business owner strives to do. The NCAA and major universities have mastered this principle. No other American business operates so pretentiously, making huge sums of money but insisting the enterprise be viewed as an educational service.[32]

The average male professional basketball player in 1995, for example, earned well over $1 million per year, while the average male college basketball player on full scholarship at a state school earned about $10,000 and at a private school between $15,000 to $20,000 annually (in services rather than money). As an extreme example, basketball star Patrick Ewing brought more than $12 million to Georgetown University during his four years there (a tripling of attendance, increased television revenues, and qualifying for the NCAA tournament each year). The cost to Georgetown totaled $48,600.[33] This issue raises two questions of morality: (1) Should universities use student athletes to hustle money for the universities? and (2) If so, should the athletes be paid wages that are not commensurate with their contributions?[34]

The NCAA and Student–Athletes

The NCAA or an organization like it is necessary to administer college sports. Such an organization is needed to provide a uniform set of rules for each sport, to adjudicate disputes among members, and to organize playoffs and tournaments. Rules must be made and enforced to curb cheating, to eliminate the exploitation of athletes, to enhance the education of student-athletes, to eliminate the use of illicit drugs to enhance performance, and to maintain the integrity of the sports and athletes. What has emerged, however, is a powerful monopoly,[35] a monopoly that controls big-time college sport *for the interests of the universities, not the student-athletes*. This occurs in two ways: the enforcement of "amateurism" and rules that limit athletes' rights.

The Enforcement of "Amateurism"

First, as we have just discussed, the NCAA rules enforce a code of amateurism on the athletes, while the NCAA and its member institutions raise millions off of these athletes. By defining the athletes as amateurs, the schools keep the costs of operation low by not paying athletes what they are worth. Moreover, if the activity is defined as amateur, it permits the monies generated from athletics to be free from taxation. Even though the scholarship appears to be a payment for services rendered, it is called a "grant-in-aid" for educational purposes. The NCAA is on shaky ground in keeping athletic monies tax-free since the rules of the Internal Revenue Service stipulate that any amount received from an employer for educational expenses is taxable income.[36] Therefore, the NCAA has done all it can to retain the "amateur" status of college athletes. Specifically, the NCAA has lobbied in various state legislatures that college athletes should not be included under workmen's compensation because they would then be defined as employees. Similarly, the NCAA has argued strenuously that college athletes should not be paid a stipend in addition to room, board, books, and tuition because this would lessen their case that the athletes are amateurs. Also, they do not want the athletes to be "professional" in any way. Some examples:

• Athletes are not allowed to have a financial advisor (agent) until after their final college game.
• Athletes may not use their athletic ability to make money for themselves. Janet Evans, for example, won three gold medals in the 1988 Olympics as a high school student. As a result, she was offered many commercial opportunities, which she turned down because she wanted to compete in college

and the NCAA rules forbade such commercialism. Thus, Evans forfeited her rare opportunity to make money from swimming. (While the NCAA does not allow this, the Athletics Congress, track and field's national governing body, allows athletes to retain their amateur status by placing income from commercial endorsements in the athlete's trust fund for cost-of-living and training expenses.) Going further, using this principle the NCAA said that a New Mexico State University basketball player, who won a car by making a halfcourt shot at halftime of a World Basketball League game (he was one of two spectators chosen in a random drawing for the shot), could keep the car or his senior year of eligibility, but not both.

• Athletes cannot be used to raise money for others, even charities. For example, the Lions Club of Alachua, Florida, was not allowed to raffle off a football signed by members of the University of Florida football team to raise money for its eye bank because, the NCAA ruled, the players were being exploited by selling their autographs.
• Athletes cannot receive extra compensation from their universities. This has meant, for example, that the NCAA put Seton Hall on probation for buying a suit for a player to attend his father's funeral. On another occasion, James Madison University was not allowed to transport its football team to a teammate's funeral because such a trip at school expense would constitute "an extra benefit."

These examples show the lengths to which the NCAA will go to keep the "amateur" status of college athletes. They also demonstrate the hypocrisy of the NCAA. While keeping their athletes pure, the NCAA, the universities, and the individual coaches, are engaged in a relentless pursuit of revenue. It must be emphasized again, this revenue is generated by the athletes. Athletes literally can be walking billboards by wearing shoes, for which the coach receives thousands of dollars, but the athletes cannot receive anything other than the free shoes. Athletes cannot endorse products or otherwise use their name recognition for economic gain, but universities can use them in their publicity and can license and sell clothing, sports equipment, and souvenirs with the team logo. Athletes cannot sell their complimentary tickets (in fact, they cannot give their tickets to anyone except family members, relatives, and students), yet coaches (some with hundreds of tickets) have no restrictions on their distribution. Coaches typically receive bonuses for taking their teams to a bowl (e.g., Bill McCartney, coach at Colorado, received a $75,833 bonus in 1991 for winning the Orange Bowl and ending the season rated as the number one team), but their players do not. Money is made, lots of it, at the expense of poorly paid workers. In the words of Mike Trope, an agent for professional athletes: "[P]eople have this perception of a benevolent NCAA that protects these poor young lads. What the NCAA protects is its own self-interest. The rules of the NCAA are created artificially to protect the profit structure of [big-time college sports]. I consider the collegiate system one of the greatest forms of labor exploitation in America."[37]

David Glasner has argued:

> In actual fact amateur college sports are a thing of the past, and they have been ever since major colleges realized how profitable sports programs could be in attracting receipts at the gate and alumni support. As television payments have made those programs even more profitable, major colleges and universities have increased their investments in them accordingly. How convenient for them to be able to operate this lucrative business on the side without having to pay their best players even a fraction of what they're worth.[38]

The Restriction of Athletes' Rights
The NCAA rules also work against athletes by restricting their rights. When young persons sign letters-of-intent to play for certain schools, they have made one-sided, disadvantageous agreements. Foremost, these athletes have agreed to play for four years at a given institution. Should they change their minds and switch, they must wait a year to play at a new institution. What if they selected a college because of a particular coach, and the coach leaves? Perhaps the coach may leave even before the student has enrolled in a school. It does not matter, under the NCAA rules,

they have signed with a school, not a coach, and they must stay or lose a year of eligibility. They must also stay or lose eligibility even if they find the coach at the place they have chosen to be abusive, racist, or unethical. The circumstances do not matter, they are stuck. The situation is even more disadvantageous for athletes. What if a player wants to leave but his/her coach does not chose to release him/her? Without the release the athlete must sit out two years instead of the customary one year.

Although the athletes sign a four-year agreement to play for a school, the schools have only a one-year commitment to the athletes. This one-year renewable commitment by the schools gives coaches extraordinary power over athletes.

Each of these rules restrains the freedom of athletes but not their schools. The athletes are bound by a contract, but the schools are not. Coaches may have contracts that allow them to leave at anytime, or their schools may not hold them to their contracts; but there are no exceptions for athletes. Coaches do not have to sit out a year if they move, but players do if they leave for another school. The NCAA rules clearly protect the schools and coaches but not the players.

Most interesting, and disheartening we would add, is the tendency for the NCAA to deflect attention away from the problems resulting from the structure of sport by blaming athletes for them. The passage of Proposition 48 provides a good example of this tendency. Requiring that student-athletes achieve certain minimum test scores before they can participate is good public relations, since it clearly favors academic standards. However, in George Sage's words:

> Actually, what all this charade for academic standards has done is deflect attention away from the commercialized structure of major college athletic programs and focused it on the athletes. The only reason that there is an academic standards problem in college sports is that coaches and other university officials have been willing to admit academically unqualified students and, through various ingenious methods, have been able to keep them eligible for one purpose: to help the university athletic teams maintain competitive

success in the world of commercialized sport. . . . Proposition 48, then, does nothing to alter the major reason why universities recruit academically unprepared athletes; indeed, since it went into effect coaches have found a variety of ways to circumvent its purpose.[39]

The Educational Performance of Student–Athletes

The research indicates that college athletes in big-time football and basketball programs do not perform at the same level academically as other athletes and the general student body. Their grades are lower, and they are much more likely to take easy courses in easy majors. Most significantly, they are much less likely to graduate. Before we examine the college performance of athletes, though, let's look at their preparation for college.

Intellectual Preparation of Student–Athletes for College

There are three standard predictors of college performance—the combined score on the Scholastic Aptitude Test (SAT), the American College Test (ACT) composite score, and high school grade point average. Research on a number of schools shows that in most big-time programs, athletes in the revenue sports (men's football and basketball) are less prepared for college than women athletes, men in the minor sports, and the general undergraduate student population. Before Proposition 48 went into effect in 1986 requiring a minimum SAT score of 700, the revenue athletes (football and men's basketball) that entered Tulane University in 1985, for example, had an average SAT score of 648 (484 points lower than the average student).[40]

After Proposition 48, marginal students who were good athletes continue to be recruited, despite their likely problems educationally. A survey by the *Chronicle of Higher Education* found in 1989 that football and men's basketball players in big-time sports programs are more than six times as likely as other students to have received special treatment in the admissions process, that is, be admitted *below* the standard requirements for their universities. Put another way,

more than one-fourth (27 percent) of these players, compared to only 4 percent of all entering freshmen, were accepted even though they failed to meet their university's regular standards.[41] Apparently schools are willing to take marginal students because of the athletic payoff. As evidence, sixty-six of Colorado's national champion football team's ninety-five scholarship players (69.5 percent) did not meet the university's academic standard but received special admittance through the school's Fall Institute Program, which is targeted to assist underprivileged minority students.[42]

Academic Performance

The data on class grades are somewhat difficult to interpret. The reason is that athletes, especially those in the revenue-producing sports are more likely than other athletes and other students to receive grades fraudulently (e.g., "shady" correspondence courses, "friendly" professors,[43] surrogate test takers or term paper writers) or to take easy courses and cluster in easy majors. In general, it is fair to state that athletes in football and men's basketball in big-time programs tend to not perform as well academically as other athletes or other students.

Graduation Rates

An obvious indicator of their school performance is the overall graduation rate of college athletes. An NCAA study of athletes from 300 Division I schools who entered college in 1985 revealed that after six years student-athletes had just about the same graduation rate (52 percent) as the rest of the student body (54 percent). Table 6.1 reveals, however, that these data are misleading. Some categories of athletes exceed the graduation rates of the student body: women athletes (African American or white) and white athletes. Those categories below the student body rate are: male athletes and African American student athletes (men and women). It is especially instructive to examine the graduation rates of Division I basketball and football players. Here we find that female basketball players far exceed their male counterparts (57 percent to 43 percent); and that white basketball players (62 percent) and white football players (58 percent) surpass their

table 6.1   *A Look at Graduation Rates*

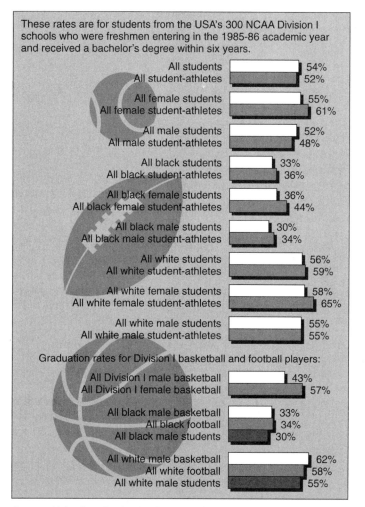

These rates are for students from the USA's 300 NCAA Division I schools who were freshmen entering in the 1985-86 academic year and received a bachelor's degree within six years.

All students	54%
All student-athletes	52%
All female students	55%
All female student-athletes	61%
All male students	52%
All male student-athletes	48%
All black students	33%
All black student-athletes	36%
All black female students	36%
All black female student-athletes	44%
All black male students	30%
All black male student-athletes	34%
All white students	56%
All white student-athletes	59%
All white female students	58%
All white female student-athletes	65%
All white male students	55%
All white male student-athletes	55%

Graduation rates for Division I basketball and football players:

All Division I male basketball	43%
All Division I female basketball	57%
All black male basketball	33%
All black football	34%
All black male students	30%
All white male basketball	62%
All white football	58%
All white male students	55%

Source: "A Look at Graduation Rates," *USA Today,* 20 May 1993, sec. C., p. 10.

African American teammates in basketball (29 percent higher in basketball and 24 percent higher in football). Clearly, gender, race, and we can infer, social class, are very important variables affecting the graduation rates of athletes.

Within these data on graduation rates, there are both positives and negatives. On the positive side, a number of schools have an excellent record of graduating their athletes. Table 6.2 shows that ten basketball programs graduate 88 percent or more of their athletes and ten football programs graduate more than two-thirds of their players. These schools with excellent graduation rates generally have high admission standards, ensuring that their athletes are academically sound upon arrival on campus. The other requirement is a commitment by

table 6.2   *Graduation Rates*

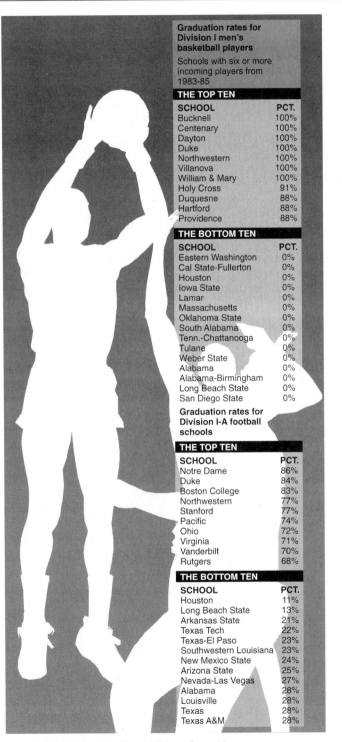

Graduation rates for Division I men's basketball players

Schools with six or more incoming players from 1983-85

THE TOP TEN

SCHOOL	PCT.
Bucknell	100%
Centenary	100%
Dayton	100%
Duke	100%
Northwestern	100%
Villanova	100%
William & Mary	100%
Holy Cross	91%
Duquesne	88%
Hartford	88%
Providence	88%

THE BOTTOM TEN

SCHOOL	PCT.
Eastern Washington	0%
Cal State-Fullerton	0%
Houston	0%
Iowa State	0%
Lamar	0%
Massachusetts	0%
Oklahoma State	0%
South Alabama	0%
Tenn.-Chattanooga	0%
Tulane	0%
Weber State	0%
Alabama	0%
Alabama-Birmingham	0%
Long Beach State	0%
San Diego State	0%

Graduation rates for Division I-A football schools

THE TOP TEN

SCHOOL	PCT.
Notre Dame	86%
Duke	84%
Boston College	83%
Northwestern	77%
Stanford	77%
Pacific	74%
Ohio	72%
Virginia	71%
Vanderbilt	70%
Rutgers	68%

THE BOTTOM TEN

SCHOOL	PCT.
Houston	11%
Long Beach State	13%
Arkansas State	21%
Texas Tech	22%
Texas-El Paso	23%
Southwestern Louisiana	23%
New Mexico State	24%
Arizona State	25%
Nevada-Las Vegas	27%
Alabama	28%
Louisville	28%
Texas	28%
Texas A&M	28%

Source: *USA Today,* 20 May 1993, sec. C., p. 10.

the school and athletic department to the academic progress of their athletes.

On the negative side, a number of schools have abysmal graduation rates for their athletes. Table 6.2 shows that fifteen men's basketball programs graduated *zero* percent of their players while ten football programs graduated 28 percent or less of their athletes.

The record is especially bad for recruited minority athletes. For example, another *USA Today* survey of 149 Division I schools found that twenty schools that had recruited at least ten minority players from 1980 to 1984 had graduated one or none.[44] Finally, although the graduation rate for women athletes is excellent, there are signs that as women's programs become more prominent, the graduation rate deteriorates. There are two indicators of this. First, the more successful teams have lower graduation rates. For example, although 64 percent of players on teams never making the NCAA women's basketball tournament from 1981 to 1990 graduated, only 56 percent did from teams that made it to the tournament at least once. Second, graduation rates declined during the 1980s, a time when women's college basketball annual attendance doubled from 1.2 million to 2.3 million. The rates from three conferences make this point: The graduation rate in the Southeastern Conference declined from 55 percent in 1986 to 36 percent in 1990, in the Big Ten from 78 percent to 60 percent, and in the Big Eight from 62 percent to 40 percent. These rates appear to be negatively correlated with television time; as the TV time increases, graduation rates decrease, following the pattern of big-time men's basketball.[45]

The Impediments to Scholarly Achievement by College Athletes

In addition to many college athletes being ill-prepared for the intellectual demands of college, they face a number of obstacles that impede their scholarly achievement. The pressures on athletes, especially those in big-time, revenue-producing sports, are well known, including physical exhaustion, mental fatigue, media attention, and demanding coaches. The time demands alone are onerous. Harry Edwards has estimated that during the season basketball players spend fifty hours and football players as much as sixty hours a week preparing for, participating in, recovering from, and traveling to games.[46] The athletes in commercialized, professionalized programs have trouble reconciling the roles associated with their dual statuses of athlete and student. Allen Sack and Robert Thiel found in the study of athletes from forty-seven schools that those ranking low in their high school graduating classes were most likely to react to this role conflict by deemphasizing the student role by cheating on tests, taking easy courses, and doing the minimum.[47]

Peter and Patricia Adler conducted a study of the University of Tulsa basketball program from 1980 to 1984.[48] They found that the pressures of big-time sport and the academic demands resulted in the gradual disengagement of the athletes from their academic roles. Most athletes entered the university feeling idealistic about their impending academic performance; that is, they were optimistic about graduating, and they considered ambitious majors. This idealism lasted until about the end of the first year and was replaced by disappointment and a growing cynicism as they realized how difficult keeping up with their schoolwork would be. The athletic role came to dominate all facets of their existence. The athletes received greater positive reinforcement from their athletic performance than from their academic performance. They were isolated increasingly from the student body. They were segregated in an athletic dormitory. They were isolated culturally by their racial and socioeconomic differences from the rest of the students. They were even isolated from other students by their physical size, which others often found intimidating. They interacted primarily with other athletes, and these peers tended to demean academics. In their first year they were given courses with "sympathetic" professors, but this changed as athletes moved through the university curriculum. The academic expectations escalated, and the athletes were unprepared. The resulting academic failure or, at best, mediocre academic performance led to embarrassment and despair. The typical response, according to the Adlers, was role distancing: "To be safe, it was better not to try than to try and not succeed."[49] This attitude, and the resulting behaviors, were reinforced by the peer subculture.

The noneducation and miseducation of college athletes is especially acute for African Americans. Every study that has compared African American athletes to their white counterparts has found them less prepared for college and more likely to fulfill this prophecy in college: African Americans tend to enter college as marginal students and to leave the same way. Harry Edwards has argued that the African American "dumb jock" is a social creation: " 'Dumb jocks' are not born; they are systematically created." [50] This social construction results from several factors. First, African American student athletes must contend with two negative labels: the dumb athlete caricature and the dumb African American stereotype. This double negative tends to result in a self-fulfilling prophecy as teachers, fellow students, and the athletes themselves assume low academic performance. Moreover, as soon as an African American youngster is viewed as a potential athletic star, many teachers, administrators, and parents lower their academic demands because they assume that athletic stardom will be the athlete's ticket out of the ghetto. In junior high school and high school, little is demanded of them academically. The reduced academic expectations continue in college, or in community college if they do not qualify for college. With professors who "give" grades, occasionally altered transcripts, surrogate test takers, and phantom courses, there is "little wonder that so many black scholarship student-athletes manage to go through four years of college enrollment virtually unscathed by education." [51]

African Americans (athletes or not) on mostly white campuses (only 4 percent of the Tulane student body, for example, is African American) are often alienated by the actual or perceived racism they experience and by their social isolation. This compounds the problems for African American athletes.

A major unintended consequence of this situation in which African American athletes find themselves is that their individual adaptations, meaning denigrating education, opting for easy courses and majors, not making progress toward a degree, emphasizing the athlete role, and eventually dropping out of education without a degree, reinforce the very racial stereotypes an integrated education is meant to negate. Thus, unwittingly, the universities with big-time programs that recruit marginal students and do not educate them offer "proof" for the argument that African Americans are genetically inferior to whites in intellectual potential.

The NCAA's Proposition 48, which took effect in 1986, was designed to remedy some of these problems. Specifically, prospective college athletes would not be permitted to participate in athletics unless they met minimum college standards. Most importantly, once athletes enrolled in a university, they must make progress toward a degree to remain eligible.

Even with the implementation of Proposition 48, a strong possibility exists that the gap in educational preparation and achievement between African American and white athletes and between athletes and the rest of the student body will increase. The basis for this prediction is that the composition of the general student body is becoming whiter and more affluent. The ever-higher tuition costs coupled with the drastic reduction in government loans and scholarships are restricting access to higher education to the children of the affluent. Generally, the more affluent the student, the better they are prepared for academia. Thus, average SAT and ACT scores for the student body will be treading upward, increasing the gap between students and student-athletes, particularly ill-prepared African American athletes.

Reform

Big-time college sports pose a fundamental dilemma for educators. [52] On the positive side, the games provide entertainment, spectacle, excitement, and festival, along with excellence in athletics. On the negative side, as we have seen, big-time athletics have severely compromised academe.

Pursuit of educational goals has been superseded by the quest for big money. Winning programs realize huge revenues from television, gate receipts, bowl and tournament appearances, and even legislatures, therefore many athletic departments and coaches are guided by a win-at-any-cost philosophy.

Can this fundamental dilemma be resolved? Can the corporate and corrupt sports programs at colleges and universities be changed to redress the wrongs that are making a mockery of their educational goals? Can the abuses be eliminated without sacrificing the high level of achievement by the athletes and the excitement of college sports?

Reform must be directed at three crucial areas: the way sports are administered, the education of athletes, and the treatment of athletes. We suggest the following reforms.

The Administration of College Sports

As a beginning, athletic departments must not be separated from their institutions in self-contained corporate entities. They must be under the direct control of university presidents and boards of regents. Presidents, as chief executive officers, must be accountable for the actions of their athletic departments. They must set up mechanisms to monitor athletic programs to detect illegal and unethical acts. They must determine policies to maximize the educational experiences of student-athletes.

Coaches must be part of the academic community and the tenure system, to provide them with reasonable job security and to emphasize that they, too, are teachers. As educators with special responsibilities, they should earn salaries similar to those of academic administrators. They should not receive bonuses for winning championships. Such performance incentives overemphasize winning and increase the likelihood of cheating. The outside incomes of coaches should be sharply curtailed. Money from shoe companies should go to the universities, not the coaches. If coaches fail to keep their programs ethical, they should lose their tenure and be suspended from coaching at any institution for a specified period, even, in special cases, forever. Among the important criteria for evaluating coaches' performance should be the proportion of athletes who graduate in five years.

One problem with college sports is that it is run by the NCAA, which, in turn has been run by athletic directors, representing their institutions, rather than by academicians. This is changing somewhat as university presidents, guided by a President's Commission, have, since 1984, become more involved. The presidents must take over the NCAA's rule-making to ensure fairness in the distribution of television and tournament revenues (we favor an equal distribution to all members

to lessen the extraordinary rewards of winning and the accompanying pressures) and the fair treatment of student-athletes. Some NCAA conventions passed some encouraging rules (e.g., the elimination of athletic dorms by 1996 and the limitation of in-season practice time to a maximum of four hours a day and 20 hours a week), but for the most part reform efforts have been timid and do not attack the problems endemic to big-time intercollegiate sport.[53]

It is crucial that athletic departments be monitored and, when warranted, sanctioned externally. The NCAA is not, however, the proper external agent, since it has a fundamental conflict of interest. The NCAA is too dependent on sports-generated television money and bowl contracts to be an impartial investigator, judge, and jury. Accrediting associations should oversee all aspects of educational institutions, including sports, to assess whether educational goals are being met. If an institution is not meeting those goals because of inadequacies in the sports program, then it should lose accreditation, just as it would if the library were below standard or too few professors held doctorates. Also, since big-time sports are engaged in interstate commerce, the investigation and prosecution of wrongdoing, such as fraud, bribery, and the falsification of official records, in college sports should be pursued by federal district attorneys and the courts.

Emphasizing the Education of Student–Athletes

Academic institutions worthy of the name must make a commitment to their athletes as students. This requires, first, that only athletes who have the potential to compete as students be admitted. A few, very few, may be admitted as exceptions, but they and other academically marginal students must receive the benefits of a concerted effort by the university to improve their skills through remedial classes and tutorials so that they can earn a degree.

Second, freshmen should be ineligible for varsity sports. Such a requirement has symbolic value, because it shows athletes and the whole community that academic performance is the highest priority of the institution. More important, it allows freshman athletes time to adjust to the demanding and competitive academic environment before they also take on the pressure that comes from participating in big-time sports.

Third, colleges must insist that athletes make satisfactory progress toward a degree. There should be internal academic audits to determine whether athletes are meeting the grade-point and curriculum requirements for graduation. Schools must now provide the NCAA with graduation rates based on how many athletes graduate in five years. Schools must also be required to make these rates public, including giving them to each potential recruit.

Fourth, the time demands of sports must be reduced. In-season practice time, travel, and team meetings must be kept to a reasonable minimum. Mandatory off-season workouts should be abolished. Spring football practice should be eliminated.

Finally, colleges should grant athletic scholarships on a four-year basis, no strings attached (instead of the one-year commitment that is the present rule). Doing so would dramatically demonstrate the institutions' commitment to their athletes as students. In addition, and this is critical, if scholarship athletes participate in a sport for three years, the scholarship commitment by the institution should be extended automatically from four to five years.

Commitment to Athletes' Rights

The asymmetrical situation, where schools have the power and athletes do not, must be modified. First, student-athletes should have the right to counsel from agents, accountants, attorneys or whatever, just as any other student.

Second, athletes should have the right to fair compensation from the revenues they generate. By already receiving room, board, books, and tuition, athletes are not amateurs. Neither are they well-paid professionals. They should be adequately compensated by a modest monthly stipend for instance, $300 a month. Moreover, they should be allowed to have a job in the off-season (forbidden by the NCAA except for summer employment), just as any other student. Also, because scholarship athletes are in effect employees of the institution, they should be eligible for workmen's compensation if

injured. Most assuredly, they must be fully insured by their institutions for injuries.

If players are dissatisfied with their situation at a school and want to transfer without losing eligibility, they should be able to submit their case to an arbitration panel, independent of the NCAA, which should be established to hear such cases and make binding decisions. Athletes should also have the right to legal assistance and due process in disputes with athletic departments and coaches. Coaches are sometimes right, but when they are wrong they must not be protected at the expense of the athletes, as is the usual case.

Summary

Without designating them all as such, we have examined and demythologized several myths in this chapter. The first myth is that college athletic programs are amateur athletics. Big-time college sport is big business. The second myth is that the athletic programs in the various schools make money. Only about 30 percent do. The rest depend on various subsidies to keep afloat. A related myth is that these programs help the universities. Almost always the surplus monies are kept within the athletic departments. So, too, are the monies that sports attract from contributors. Also, when athletic departments are put on probation or otherwise punished for transgressions, the universities are hurt by the negative publicity.

Another myth is that the NCAA protects student-athletes. As we have seen, the NCAA rules are extremely one-sided in favor of the institutions over the athletes. Clearly, we have shown that the term "student-athlete" is an oxymoron. Scholarship athletes in the revenue-producing sports are employees of their athletic departments. Their role of student is surely secondary to the role of athlete in most big-time programs. Similarly, athletes are not amateurs. They are just poorly compensated professionals.

Finally, the notion that sports builds character is a myth at the big-time, big-business level of intercollegiate sports. Cheating in recruiting is commonplace. Payments to athletes outside the rules are widely dispensed. Athletes are sometimes pampered. Rules for admittance to schools are bent for them. They are enrolled in courses with professors friendly to the athletic department. Athletes hear the rhetoric about sport building character and that education is first, but they see a different reality. In such a climate, cynicism abounds and the possibility of positive character development is diminished.

Notes

1. George H. Sage, *Power and Ideology in American Sport: A Critical Perspective* (Champaign, Ill.: Human Kinetics Publishers, 1990), 170.

2. For excellent summaries of the problems endemic to contemporary college sport, see Murray Sperber, *College Sports Inc.* (New York: Henry Holt, 1990); Rick Telander, *The Hundred Yard Lie: The Corruption of College Football and What We Can Do to Stop It* (New York: Simon and Schuster, 1989); and John R. Thelin, *Games Colleges Play: Scandal and Reform in Intercollegiate Athletics* (Baltimore: The Johns Hopkins University Press, 1994).

3. William F. Reed, "Absolutely Incredible!" *Sports Illustrated*, 26 March 1990, 66.

4. See James E. Curtis and William G. McTeer, "Sport Involvement and Academic Attainment in Universities: Two Studies from the Canadian Case" (paper presented at the Olympic Scientific Congress, Eugene, Oreg., July 1984); William G. McTeer, "Intercollegiate Athletes and Student Life: Two Studies in the Canadian Case," *Arena Review* 11 (November 1987): 94–100; and John C. Pooley, "The Sociology of University Athletic Awards," *Arena Review* 11 (November 1987): 101–107.

5. *The NCAA News*, 16 August 1995, 1, 10.

6. *The NCAA News*, 19 July 1995, 6.

7. "Louisiana State Athletics Show to Be an Economic Catalyst," *The NCAA News*, 5 June 1991, 5.

8. Sperber, *College Sports Inc.*, 67.

9. William C. Symonds, "Big Red's Big Green Machine," *Business Week*, 5 November 1990, 84.

10. Dana Rubin, "You've Seen the Game. Now Buy the Underwear," *New York Times*, 11 September 1994, sec. F, p. 5.

11. Alexander Wolff and Richard O'Brien, "UMess," *Sports Illustrated*, 31 October 1994, 11.

12. Most of the examples on the extra compensation of coaches are taken from Murray A. Sperber, "The College Coach as Entrepreneur," *Academe* 73 (July/August 1987): 30–33; and Jack McCallum, "Foot Soldiers of Fortune," *Sports Illustrated*, 23 January 1984, 56–68.

13. Sperber, *College Sports, Inc.*, 192–200.

14. Murray Sperber, "Despite the Mythology, Most Colleges Lose Money on Big-Time Sports," *Chronicle of Higher Education*, 3 October 1990, sec. B, p. 1. See also Barbara R. Bergmann, "Do Sports Really Make Money for the University?" *Academe* 77 (January/February 1991): 28–30; and James H. Frey, "The Winning Team Myth," *Currents* 12 (January 1985): 33–35.

15. See, for example, Sperber, *College Sports Inc.*, 98.

16. Curtis Eichelberger, "The Party May Be Over At CU," *Rocky Mountain News*, 9 April 1995, sec. B, p. 28.

17. John Silber quoted in Sperber, *College Sports Inc.*, 132.

18. Maurice Mitchell, "Higher Education in Colorado: An Act of Faith Amid the Chaos," *Rocky Mountain News*, 27 August 1978, p. 58.

19. Sperber, *College Sports Inc.*, 65.

20. Alexander Wolff, "Broken Beyond Repair," *Sports Illustrated*, 12 June 1995, 22.

21. Jack McCallum, "Paper Trail," *Sports Illustrated*, 28 November 1994, 45–48.

22. Alexander Wolff and Don Yaeger, "Credit Risk," *Sports Illustrated*, 7 August 1995, 46–55.

23. Howard Cosell with Shelby Whitfield, *What's Wrong with Sports* (New York: Simon and Schuster, 1991), 62–63.

24. Alexander Wolff and Kostya Kennedy, "Winning Ugly," *Sports Illustrated*, 11 September 1995, 14. For a litany of the scandals in college sport, see David Whitford, *A Payroll to Meet: A Story of Greed, Corruption, and Football at SMU* (New York: Macmillan, 1989); Charles Thompson and Allan Sonnenschein, *Down and Dirty: The Life and Crimes of Oklahoma Football* (New York: Carroll and Graf, 1990); Francis X. Dealy, Jr., *Win at Any Cost: The Sell Out of College Athletics* (New York: Carol Publishing, 1990); Wilford S. Bailey and Taylor D. Littleton, *Athletics and Academe: An Anatomy of Abuses and a*

Prescription for Reform (New York: Macmillan, 1991); Tom McMillen, *Out of Bounds* (New York: Simon & Schuster, 1992); John R. Thelin, *Games Colleges Play: Scandal and Reform in Intercollegiate Athletics* (Baltimore: The Johns Hopkins Press, 1994); and James H. Frey, "Deviance of Organizational Subunits: The Case of College Athletic Departments," *Journal of Sport and Social Issues* 18 (May 1994): 110–22.

25. John Underwood, "A Game Plan for America," *Sports Illustrated,* 23 February 1981, 81.

26. Philip Baiamonte, "Baiamonte's Pre-Sentencing Remarks," *Albuquerque Journal,* 9 July 1981, sec. A, p. 6.

27. Philip Taubman, "Oklahoma Football: A Powerhouse That Barry Built," *Esquire* 90, 5 December 1978, 91.

28. Paul W. Bryant and John Underwood, *Bear: The Hard Life and Good Times of Alabama's Coach Bryant* (Boston: Little, Brown, 1974), 325.

29. George Will, "Our Schools for Scandal," *Newsweek,* 15 September 1986, 84.

30. Dean A. Purdy, D. Stanley Eitzen, and Rick Hufnagel, "Are Athletes Also Students? The Educational Attainment of College Athletes," *Social Problems* 29 (April 1982): 439–48; Select Committee on Intercollegiate Athletics, *Report of the Select Committee on Intercollegiate Athletics* (New Orleans: Tulane University, 1986); and D. Stanley Eitzen, "The Educational Experience of Intercollegiate Student-Athletes," *Journal of Sport and Social Issues* 11 (fall/winter 1987–1988): 15–30.

31. Barry Jacobs, "Valvano Asked to Quit as NC State Athletic Director," *New York Times,* 26 August 1989, 31.

32. Sage, *Power and Ideology in American Sport,* 179–80. See also D. Stanley Eitzen, "The Sociology of Amateur Sport: An Overview," *International Review for the Sociology of Sport* 24 (1989): 95–105.

33. Gregg Leslie, "Pick-and-Bankroll," *Regardie's,* January 1986, 17.

34. For arguments on both sides of this issue, see Dick DeVenzio, *Rip-Off U: The Annual Theft and Exploitation of Revenue Producing Major College Student-Athletes* (Charlotte, N.C.: Fool Court Press, 1986); Curry Kirkpatrick, "The Hoops are Made of Gold," *Newsweek,* 3 April 1995, 62; Vincent J. Dooley, "Student-Athletes Well-Compensated," *The NCAA News* (March 1, 1995), 4–5; Dick DeVenzio, "Let Capitalism Apply to the Players," *The NCAA News,* 22 March 1995, 4.; Alexander Wolff and Richard O'Brien, "Conventional Wisdom," *Sports Illustrated,* 16 January 1995, 14; and Walter Byers, *Unsportsmanlike Conduct: Exploiting College Athletes* (Ann Arbor: University of Michigan Press, 1995).

35. Arthur A. Fleisher III, Brian L. Goff, and Robert D. Tollison, *The National Collegiate Athletic Association: A Study in Cartel Behavior* (Chicago: The University of Chicago Press, 1992).

36. Sperber, *College Sports, Inc.,* 205–206.

37. Mike Trope, *Necessary Roughness* (Chicago: Contemporary Books, 1987), 79.

38. David Glasner, "Cheap Labor on Campus," *Newsweek,* 9 November 1987, 12.

39. George H. Sage, "Blaming the Victim: NCAA Responses to Calls for Reform in Major College Sports," *Arena Review* 11 (November 1987): 1–11. See also Sage, *Power and Ideology in American Sport,* 184–87; and Allen L. Sack, "Proposition 48: A Masterpiece in Public Relations," *Journal of Sport and Social Issues* 8 (summer 1984): 1–3.

40. Select Committee on Intercollegiate Athletics, *Report,* 5.

41. Douglas Lederman, "Special Admissions Treatment for Athletes Widespread at Big-Time-Sports Colleges," *Chronicle of Higher Education,* 1 May 1991, sec. A, pp. 1, 31–33.

42. Curtis Eichelberger, "CU Polishes Academic Image," *Rocky Mountain News,* 24 May 1991, p. 96.

43. Murray Sperber, "Flagrant Foul: How Professors Let Jocks Push Them Around," *Lingua Franca* 4 (November/December 1993), 1, 26–31.

44. "Lowest Minority Graduation Rates," *USA Today,* 19 June 1991, sec. C, p. 8.

45. Mark Coomse, "Women's Basketball Suffers Growing Pains," *USA Today,* 20 June 1991, sec. C, p. 8.

46. Harry Edwards, "The Collegiate Arms Race: Origins and Implications of the 'Rule 48' Controversy," *Journal of Sport and Social Issues* 8 (winter/spring 1984): 7.

47. Allen L. Sack and Robert Thiel, "College Basketball and Role Conflict," *Sociology of Sport Journal* 2 (September 1985): 195–209.

48. Peter Adler and Patricia A. Adler, "From Idealism to Pragmatic Detachment: The Academic Performance of College Athletes," *Sociology of Education* 58 (October 1985): 241–250. See also Patricia A. Adler and Peter Adler, *Backboards and Blackboards: College Athletes and Role Engulfment* (New York: Columbia University Press, 1991).

49. Adler and Adler, "From Idealism to Pragmatic Detachment," 247. The conclusions of the Adlers for men's basketball has not been found for women. See Barbara Bedker Meyer, "From Idealism to Actualization: The Academic Performance of Female College Athletes," *Sociology of Sport Journal* 7 (March 1990): 44–57; and Susan Birrell, "The Woman Athlete's College Experience: Knowns and Unknowns," *Journal of Sport and Social Issues* 11 (December 1987): 82–96.

50. Harry Edwards, "The Black 'Dumb Jock': An American Sports Tragedy," *The College Review Board,* no. 131 (spring 1984): 8.

51. Ibid., 9. See also D. Stanley Eitzen, "Racism in College Sports: Prospects for the Year 2000," in *Racism in College Athletics: The African-American Athlete's Experience,* ed. Dana D. Brooks and Ronald C. Althouse (Morgantown, W. Va.: Fitness Information Technology, 1993), 269–85; and Timothy Davis, "The Myth of the Superspade: The Persistence of Racism in College Athletics," 22 *Fordham Urban Law Journal* 615, (1995): 615–98.

52. The following is taken from D. Stanley Eitzen, "How We Can Clean Up Big-Time College Sports," *Chronicle of Higher Education,* 12 February 1986, 86. For some other reform proposals, see James H. Frey, "Hitting the Wall: Breaking the Corporate Hold on Collegiate Sport," (paper presented at the North American Society for the Sociology of Sport, Savannah, Ga., November 1994); and Timothy Davis, "A Model of Institutional Governance for Intercollegiate Athletics," 3 *Wisconsin Law Review* 599, (1995): 599–645.

53. D. Stanley Eitzen, " 'Reforms' Don't Fix Commercialization of College Sports," *The Baltimore Sun* "Perspective," 17 March 1991, sec. N, p. 4.

Chapter 7

Social Problems and North American Sport:
Violence and Drugs

Throughout this book we have emphasized the close relationship between sports and the broader North American society. It is not an exaggeration to say that the United States and Canada are plagued by a number of common major social problems, such as poverty, racism, sexism, health care, environmental destruction, and crime to name just a few. On almost everyone's list of social problems, violence and drug abuse have a prominent place. Given the close connections between sport and society, it should come as no surprise that violent behavior and drug abuse are pervasive problems in North American sports.

Violence in Sport: Which Is It— Violence or Aggression? Confusion in the Literature

A brief excursion into the meaning of two key concepts that will be used in the first part of this chapter is necessary. These two words, violence and aggression, are often found together, and in fact some writers use them as synonyms. On the other hand, there are behavioral and social scientists who differentiate sharply between these two words. There are some who believe that the concepts have come to have so many meanings anymore that they have lost a good deal of their meaning.

In spite of the various definitions and meanings used for the two words, a kind of consensus about them exists: Aggression is the more generic concept. Aggressive behavior is considered to be any behavior that has the potential to, or does, injure, either psychologically or physically, another person. Violence is more specific; it is *physically assaultive* behavior that has the potential to, or does, injure another person or persons. Although there are distinctive conceptual differences, we are still left with the overwhelming amount of literature on this topic that does not use these concepts so distinctly. In this chapter we shall attempt to use these two words in the way described, but when referring to other theorists' and researchers' works, it will be necessary to employ their terminology.

Theories About the Connection Between Violent Behavior and Sport

Two theories of human aggression dominated the scientific literature during the first three-quarters of the twentieth century: the instinct theory and the frustration-aggression theory. The first postulated that aggressive behavior is based in human instincts; indeed, this notion was so popular it has been called the folk theory of aggression. The instinctive theory of aggression owed its popularity to two major proponents: Sigmund Freud, the founder of psychoanalysis, and Konrad Lorenz, a world-renowned ethologist. Both claimed that aggression is instinctive in humans and that humans can do very little to change or control this aggressive impulse. See table 7.1 for additional descriptions of these theories.

Basing this theory of aggression on his studies of various animal species, Lorenz concurred with the outlines of Freud's notion that humans possess an aggressive impulse that requires periodic release. Furthermore, by venting aggressive energy we become less aggressive, an effect known as "catharsis." Aggressive releases of energy can take benign forms or destructive forms, and Lorenz believed that sports can help channel aggressive behavior into benign forms. He even suggested that if nation states would devote more energy to sporting activities the chances for war between countries would be reduced.[1]

This model of aggression has been roundly attacked by both social and biological scientists. One animal behaviorist says: "All our present data indicate that fighting behavior among higher mammals, including man, originates in external stimulation and that there is no evidence of spontaneous internal stimulation."[2]

A second theory of aggression that has generated much interest and research is called the frustration-aggression theory (F-A). First advanced by a group of behavioral scientists at Yale University just before World War II, this theory proposed a specific process by which the underlying instinct to aggression is triggered. They propose that when an individual is frustrated by someone or something, he/she will aggress in order to purge the pent-up frustration. In other words, the existence of frustration leads to some form of

table 7.1   *Theories About Aggression / Violence*

Instinct theory	Aggressive behavior is based in human instincts; humans cannot change or control this aggressive impulse; aggressive impulse requires periodic release; sports can help channel aggressive behavior into benign forms.
Frustration-aggression theory	When an individual is frustrated, he/she will aggress in order to purge the pent-up frustration; the aggression then produces a catharsis, a reduction to further aggression.
Aggression is socially learned	Emphasis on the learning of aggression via vicarious or observational learning and reinforcement through the interaction-socialization process; focus on learning, thinking, and interacting with peers, family, community, social institutions, and cultural practices in shaping aggressive behavior.

aggression, although not necessarily an overt act of violence, which then produces a catharsis, a reduction in the instigation to further aggression.[3]

When examined by the methods of empirical research, the F-A hypothesis, like the Freud-Lorenz theory, has not stood up. Most studies show that aggression does not always occur when a person has been frustrated and that there is no cathartic effect after aggression is employed. One of the most telling arguments against the F-A hypothesis is research that has persuasively shown that not all aggressive behavior stems from prior frustrations and that the linkage between frustration and aggression is not as close as the Yale scientists claimed.[4]

In 1986 a group of eminent social and behavioral scientists met in Seville, Spain, to discuss the roots of human aggression. They concluded not only that the instinct and F-A models of aggression are inaccurate but, more generally, that there is no scientific basis for the belief that humans are naturally aggressive. The document they produced is called "The Seville Statement." Parts of the statement include:

It is scientifically incorrect to say that war or any other violent behavior is genetically programmed into our human nature. Except for rare pathologies the genes do not produce individuals necessarily predisposed to violence. . . . It is scientifically incorrect to say that humans have a "violent brain." While we do have the neural apparatus to act violently, there is nothing in our neurophysiology that compels us to [do so]. . . . We conclude that

. . . violence is neither in our evolutionary legacy nor in our genes.[5]

The most recent theorizing about aggressive behavior has come from scholars who advance theories that postulate that aggression is a learned social behavior (e.g., social learning theory, social cognitive theory, social interaction theory). These theories place emphasis on the learning of aggression via vicarious or observational learning and reinforcement and through the interaction-socialization process. See table 7.1. A major assumption of these models is that individuals who observe esteemed others (parents, teachers, peers, coaches) exhibiting aggressive behavior and being rewarded for it will experience a vicarious reinforcement that will have the same effect as personally receiving the positive reinforcement. Moreover, individuals who exhibit aggressive behavior and receive approval for it, will tend to employ aggressive behavior in future situations that are similar. In both cases, the prediction is that continued rewards for aggressive acts will eventually form a tendency to respond to various situations with aggressive actions. In sum, according to these socially grounded theories, the conditions most conducive to the learning of aggression seem to be those in which the individual is rewarded for his or her own aggression, has many opportunities to observe aggression, and in which the individual is the object of aggression. Individuals

growing up under such conditions will come to assume that violent behavior is normative and, therefore, an appropriate response in many interpersonal situations. Such [individuals] will continually be rehearsing violent sequences both in actual situations and in fantasy, and will dismiss alternative situations as inappropriate or ineffectual. Moreover, they will encounter many situations in which such responses are easily triggered because of the similarity of cues to the original situation in which the violent response was learned.[6]

The converse is also true. That is, if an individual receives, or observes esteemed others receiving, some form of negative sanction, or punishment, that aggressive behavior will be inhibited. Thus, negative reinforcement will eventually form a habit or tendency to respond to various situations nonaggressively.

It may be seen, then, that social learning, social cognition, and social interactionist theories depart drastically from the older models for explaining aggression. Whereas the instinct and F-A models ground aggression in biological explanations, the socially grounded theories focus on learning, thinking, and interacting with peers, family, community, social institutions, and cultural practices in the environment as shaping aggressive behavior.

Socially based theories and cultural explanations have much more research support than the other aggression models, and we will describe some of that research in the next section. This is not to say, however, that the issue of the roots of aggression have been settled once and for all. Scientists of several disciplines continue to probe for answers to the mysteries surrounding the pervasiveness of human aggression.

Aggression Theories and Research on Sports

Advocates of the instinct and F-A theories have often claimed that participation and observation of aggressive activities have a cathartic effect by allowing one to discharge pent-up aggressive energy, and sporting activities have often been suggested as a means of dispelling aggression in a socially healthy way. William James, considered by many as America's first psychologist, suggested that sport is the moral equivalent of war. A disciple of Freud called sports "a salutary purgation of combative instincts which, if damned up within, would break out in a disastrous way."[7] Konrad Lorenz said: "The most important function of sport lies in furnishing a healthy safety valve for that most indispensable and, at the same time, most dangerous form of aggression that I have described as collective militant enthusiasm."[8]

As for the notion that sports provide an outlet for the aggressive instinct, the basic problem with it is that it doesn't have a sound empirical basis. James, Freud, Lorenz, and anyone else can make claims about the connections between instinct, aggression, and sport, but in order for the claims to be credible they need scientific confirmation. No empirical findings, either from James, Freud, Lorenz, or any others, has provided a shred of evidence in support of their claims.

In what has become a classic test of the prediction of instinct and F-A theories about sport having cathartic effects, the researchers assessed the hostility of male spectators before and after a football game and a gymnastics meet. They found that, contrary to the predictions of these theories, hostility actually increased significantly after observing the football game (a violent event), regardless of the preferred outcome of the game. However, there was no increase in hostility from spectators after observing the gymnastics meet (a nonviolent event). In a follow-up to that study, the researchers studied men and women who were exposed to either a professional wrestling match, an ice hockey game, or a swimming event. General support was found for the previous finding of increased spectator hostility as a result of observing violence. Hostility among subjects increased at wrestling and hockey events, but such increases did not occur at the swimming competition.[9]

A number of other studies have tried to test the cathartic effects of sports participation or observation. Overwhelmingly, the findings suggest that, contrary to the predictions of instinct and F-A theories, aggression tends to produce more aggressive predispositions and actions rather than serving as a catharsis. For example, one researcher found that homicide rates in the United States increased immediately after televised broadcasts of highly publicized boxing matches, which is just exactly the opposite of what should happen according to the cathartic effect of aggression.

Several studies seem to corroborate the work of the socially-oriented scientists, meaning that learned cultural behavior patterns explain aggressive behavior rather than aggressive behavior being the result of an innate drive in the humans. A unique and interesting study by an anthropologist focused on the relationship between war and sport forms in different types of cultures. He assessed the correlation between types of societies, warlike and nonwarlike, and the existence of combative sports. Using cross-cultural data on ten warlike and ten nonwarlike cultures, the researcher found that warlike societies and combative sports were positively correlated—90 percent of warlike societies had combative sports, but only 20 percent of nonwarlike societies had combative sports.

This same anthropologist did a time-series case study of the United States to see if the popularity of combative sports (e.g., boxing, hockey, and football) rose or fell during times of war. He found that during wartime, combative sports indeed rose in popularity while noncombative sport declined. Both investigations lead to the conclusion that war and combative sports are found together in societies. Combative sports are not channels for the discharge of aggressive tensions but rather serve to promote aggression.[10]

Further support for the connection between militarism and sports comes from a study that found a positive relationship between national military activity and the popularity of contact sports in countries participating in the Olympic Games. Another of the accumulating pieces of data against the instinct and F-A theories reveals that certain societies do not display aggressive behavior or include aggressive games in their play culture.

Directly and indirectly, sports research studies have found no support for the instinct and F-A theories of aggression. At the same time, support for the socially-oriented theories has accumulated from a variety of sources.

Violence and North America

As we noted early in this chapter, aggression is a more generic concept that includes psychological as well as physical components, while the violence concept is specific to *physical assaultive* actions. In the remaining sections of this chapter our focus will be on physical actions, so we will be using the words violent and violence more often than the word aggression.

Given the state of theories of aggression and the research findings about these theories, we take a socially-oriented perspective as the most viable. Therefore, an assumption underlying the following sections on violence is that violent behavior in sport must be understood within a historical, social, and cultural framework. Understanding the ways and means by which violence has come to play such a salient role in sports requires historically situating and culturally locating it within the larger culture in which sports are embedded.

A History of Violence

In this section we shall emphasize the prominent role that violence has played in North American history, but we want to acknowledge that we do know and understand that violence has been an integral part of much of human history. The reason that our focus in this section is limited to North America is because North America is the focal point of this book.

Canada and the United States were literally born through violence. Early colonists in North America encountered a native population that the colonists systematically imprisoned, killed, or placed in reserved lands. Thus, mostly through violent means European settlers acquired almost all of the land in the North American continent.

Both nations began in a climate of warfare. In the case of the American colonists, the Declaration of Independence was a document that literally furnished the rationale for the legitimate use of violence by the colonists. In Canada, settlers from France and England, principally, contended over the vast northern expanse of land mass for over 200 years, fighting many bloody battles until the Peace of Paris in 1763 finally ceded Canada to Great Britain.

Over the past two centuries, oppressed groups in North America have been subject to the violence of their oppressors as well as using violence to struggle against the oppressors. Quite obviously African Americans brought to North America throughout the colonial period and up to the U.S. Civil War were the subjects of daily violence by the slave owners. Violence against

African Americans continues, as examples of police brutality recorded by citizens with camcorders has vividly shown. At the same time, African Americans have resorted to violence in every era of North American history to redress their grievances; as African American activist H. Rap Brown said in justifying the use of violence: "Violence is as American as apple pie."

Actually, every ethnic minority group in North America has encountered hostility and violence and has also resorted to violent means to protect themselves or to gain a measure of revenge. Asians, Chicanos, Hispanics, Irish, you name it, every newly immigrated ethnic and racial group has been subject to violence in some form.

Throughout the nineteenth century, Canadian and U.S. farmers were subjects of violence by law enforcement officers trying to evict them from their lands and by ranchers who objected to their growing crops on what ranchers considered "grazing" land. The farmers then used violence to protect their land, to protest economic exploitation, and to publicize their demands for fairer treatment.

Also in the nineteenth century, capitalism brought wage labor; horrible working conditions; and autocratic, sometimes brutal, bosses. By the latter nineteenth century workers had begun to organize into unions for collective action against the policies and practices of the industrialists. Such organizations were often met with force, which then turned to violence by both capitalists and workers. During the past hundred years, strikes and labor disputes in the United States have actually been more prevalent and violent than in almost any other country of the world.[11]

The expansion of the United States territories, which began in the early nineteenth century, has been mostly accomplished through violent military actions. Native Americans had most of their land taken away by violent means, Mexicans were driven out of what is now the Southwest United States. Cuba and the Philippines were invaded and subjected to U.S. control. Within two decades the U.S. military invaded three countries—Granada, Panama, and Iraq—without being attacked.[12]

In summarizing the history of violence in American society, two sociologists say: "Violence was necessary to give birth to the United States. Violence was used both to keep the blacks in servitude and to free them. Violence was used to defeat rebellious Indians and to keep them on reservations. Additionally, violence has been a necessary means for many groups in American society to achieve equality or something approaching parity in power and in the rights that all Americans are supposed to enjoy."[13] This heritage of violence is learned in informal and formal ways by each new generation of young people, and it becomes embedded in their understandings about the culture of which they are a part.

A Contemporary Culture of Violence

All anyone has to do is read the newspaper or watch the television news to get the latest stories of gruesome violence. The number of murders in the United States has increased to the point where there are over 25,000 per year, and one criminologist predicts that the increases are going to continue. In an account about criminal violence in the United States, the writer contends:

> Violence on the American level comes to seem like a fact of life, an inevitable feature of modern society. It is not. . . . Most of us are aware that we are worse off, in this respect, than other advanced countries. How much worse, however is truly startling. . . . Americans [face] roughly seven to ten times the risk of death by homicide as the residents of most European countries and Japan. Our closest European competitor in homicide rates is Finland, and we murder one another at more than three times the rate the Finns do. . . . And Canada ranks fairly high, internationally, in homicide rates.[14]

Other serious crimes of violence are prevalent as well. In the United States there are three to six times more rapes and robberies than there are in other industrialized countries. Americans living in cities report an alarmingly high rate of fear of being involved in a violent confrontation; that is, robbed, burglarized, raped. They have good reason to fear![15]

Many popular films and TV programs are violent: "True Lies," "Pulp Fiction," "Mortal Kombat," and "Desperado." One genré of film is called "slasher" films because people are skinned, decapitated, and sliced into parts. People do not have to leave their living rooms to witness massive doses of violence. No other nation comes close to us with respect to TV violence; children's daytime programs average 15.5 violent acts per hour, and evening prime-time programs average 6.2.[16]

More than any other western nation, American culture promotes violence, glorifies violence, and people in other countries are baffled by the levels of violence we allow in our society. Added to a heritage of violence, then, is a contemporary culture of violence that many people throughout the world find astounding. To return to the basic theme that underlies this volume, which is the connections between sport and North American society, sporting practices would be an anomaly if violent behaviors did not play a prominent role.

Violence in North American Sport

Violent actions have been a part of sporting practices for as long as we have records of organized sports. Any doubt about that can be quickly dispelled by a perusal of the book *Combat Sports in the Ancient World: Competition, Violence, and Culture,* which is a compendium of sports with varying degrees of violence that were popular in ancient societies.[17]

In the ancient Olympics Games, the Greeks had boxing and pancration as a regular part of the program of events. In the former, there were no rounds and no weight classifications. The boxers continued to pummel each other until one boxer was hurt so badly that he could not continue or he acknowledged defeat. The pancration was a brutal all-out combination of wrestling and what we would call street fighting. The rules permitted almost anything including kicking, choking, hitting, and twisting of limbs. Gouging of eyes and biting were illegal. The object was to maim the opponent so badly he could not continue or to force him to admit defeat, as in boxing.[18]

Physical tests of strength, endurance, and skill were popular in the Roman civilization and the Middle Ages, and many, such as gladiator spectacles, chariot races, jousts, and tournaments were quite violent; indeed, deaths were common in these events. The irrepressible bare-knuckle boxing and the precursors to team sports, such as soccer and football, were popular in England and Europe during the eighteenth and nineteenth centuries; all were extremely violent.[19]

Violent Behavior by Athletes As Part of the Game

> Just bring along the ambulance,
> And call the Red Cross nurse,
> Then ring the undertaker up,
> And make him bring a hearse;
> Have all the surgeons ready there,
> For they'll have work today,
> Oh, can't you see the football teams
> Are lining up to play.
>
> —*A popular jingle in the 1890s*

Violent actions in sports have always had a special meaning separate from violence in the wider social context. Violent behavior in the larger society, except for a few situations, such as war, typically carries with it negative sanctions in the form of norms or laws; violent behavior is punished. On the other hand, violent actions are actually encoded into the rules of some sports, and there are sport-specific techniques, tactics, and strategies that are quite violent but considered perfectly appropriate in playing the sport.

One major justification for the legitimate use of violence in sport is that participants play knowing the rules and therefore understanding that they will be subject to violent actions against them. Just the opposite is typically true in the larger society: People expect they will not be subject to violence and that there are laws that protect them from violent actions. Of course, as we have previously described, this has not always been the case.

If, as some analysts have suggested, violence is as American as apple pie, violence in North American sport is as natural as the knock-out punch or the "bell-ringing" tackle. Sports and violence are almost inseparable. One example can suffice to illustrate this point. In a *Sports Illustrated* article on violence in football, the following statement is made: "Preliminary numbers . . . are in line with statistics on concussions for the past five years [in the NFL]. According to data supplied by the . . . teams, 445 concussions were suffered by 341 players [in a four-year period]. That is about four concussions per weekend, or 2.5 concussions for every 1,000 plays. . . . Of the 1.5 million high school football players in the U.S., 250,000 suffer a concussion in any given season." [20] A concussion is a bruise on the brain. The size of the bruise and the effects vary, but players who suffer such a bruise may be neurologically damaged for life.

The nature of some sports, the skills required to achieve victory, the strategy and tactics, and the rules, literally demand violent actions. Boxing is perhaps the most obvious example. The entire object of a boxing match is for the two contestants to try to injure the other so severely that one cannot continue. A knockout, in which one's opponent is rendered unconscious (or at least semiconscious), is what every fighter strives for. In the thirty-five-year period between the end of World War II and 1995, some 500 boxers died from injuries sustained in the ring, mostly from cerebral blood clots.

Other sports, classified as "body contact" sports, include football, ice hockey, and lacrosse (some would include basketball). Tackling, body checking, collisions, and legal "hits" of various kinds are inherent to the action of these sports. Indeed, it is taken for granted that when athletes engage in these activities they automatically accept the inevitability of contact, the probability of some bodily injury, and even the prospect of serious injury.

Still, few people realize how frequent the injuries are and how serious some of them are. Injuries are so common in the National Football League that during the season newspapers publish a weekly "casualty" list of each team in the league. In some seasons, up to five hundred NFL players, or 21 percent of the total players, are hurt seriously enough to miss at least one game a year because of injury. In a survey of 100 former NFL football players, 82 percent said they suffer continuing football-related disabilities and 66 percent said they believe that playing football has shortened their life expectancy. [21] In a TV film about injuries in the NFL, former center for the Oakland Raiders, Jim Otto,

when asked about the injuries he had incurred, said "Well, [I've broken] my nose, my jaw, I had both elbows operated on because I tore up the bursas in both elbows, knee surgeries, broken ribs . . . I've had to have back surgery. . . . I think I've had sixteen surgeries." Casualty rates in the Canadian Football League are comparable.

Is it any wonder that casualties are common when you have players like an NFL defensive end who said, after he knocked a quarterback unconscious: "It sounds animalistic, but I got such a rush, I was slobbering. That's the name of the game. It might be crazy, but it goes back to Pop Warner football. At every level, the harder you hit, the more you get patted on the back and the happier you are." [22]

College and high school football violence takes its toll too. According to the National Athletic Trainers' Association, about 37 percent of U.S. high school football players are injured badly enough each year to be sidelined for at least the remainder of the day. About eight high school football players die each year from football-related injuries.

A number of sports, such as baseball, basketball, soccer, and water polo, do not have the inherent violence found in others, but the tactics increasingly employed and the way the rules are being interpreted are increasingly encouraging brutal body contact.

Borderline Violence

What in the sports culture is called "borderline violence" is a category of violent actions that are prohibited by the official rules of a given sport but that routinely occur and are more or less accepted by everyone; they have become the unofficial norms. Included here are such acts as the late hit in football, hockey fist-fighting, the knock-down pitch in baseball, the high tackle in soccer, and the deliberate foul in basketball. All of these actions occasionally produce serious injuries; they also occasionally trigger bench-clearing brawls among the athletes. Although penalties are often meted out for these actions, the punishments are typically not severe enough to deter their future occurrence.

There is often an intent behind much of this type of violence in sport to "get the edge" over an opponent through what is known as "intimidation." The fist-fight in ice hockey, the "brush back" pitch and the "break-up-the-double-play slide" in baseball, "clothes-lining" and hitting wide receivers even when they are not directly involved in the play in football all are done with the intent of breaking athletes' attention and concentration on the tasks they are trying to perform. Indeed, in NHL hockey and NBA basketball it has been a common practice of teams to carry an "enforcer" or "intimidator" on the roster. One general manager of an NHL team acknowledged: "Every team likes to have one or two enforcers or designated hit men so that the rest of the team feels comfortable."[23]

Although the objects of these tactics may not be physically harmed, there are cases in most sports where these tactics have resulted in career-ending injuries: Rudy Tomjanovich, who coached the Houston Rockets to two consecutive NBA championships, was, while he was an NBA player, slugged in the face by another player, ending his playing career in basketball; NFL defensive back Jack Tatum hit wide-receiver Darryl Stingley after a pass play and rendered him quadriplegic (Tatum later said, "It was one of those pass plays where I could not possibly have intercepted, so . . . I automatically reacted to the situation by going for an intimidating hit"); Boston Red Sox batter Tony Conigliaro was hit in the face with a "brush back" pitch, ending his career in baseball; NHL hockey player Dave Forbes hit Henry Boucha in the face with the butt of his hockey stick and then grabbed Boucha's head by the hair and pounded it into the ice until Forbes was restrained—Boucha's career as an NHL player was ended.

These are, of course, the most well-known examples of violent actions that have led to major injuries. There are literally hundreds of other incidents where the quasi-criminal violence shortened the victims sports career or rendered him permanently impaired for the remainder of his career. A study completed at Ball State University revealed that one out of three NFL players leaves the league because of injuries. Whenever current and former pro athletes get together to talk about their trade, stories are recounted about the "dirty play" or the "cheap shot" that had long-term consequences for the victim.

Although comparative figures are hard to come by, there is a widely held perception that all of the types of sports violence previously described are increasing in North America. Articles deploring this trend regularly detail the latest incidents of sports violence, with pleas to everyone, from the athletes to the highest officials in government, to end the growing menace to the good health of athletes, officials, and fans.

Who or What Encourages Player Violence?

Television

One of the most respected researchers of the coverage of violent play by television believes the mass media highlight and foster violence in sports in a number of ways; for example, focusing on rough play, replaying spectacular "hits" over and over, and sportscasters praising violent play are three prominent ways.[24] It is true that broadcast sports tend to be unrestrained odes to violent action; almost any violent behavior—the more spectacular, the better—is highlighted and justified. In one NFL play-off game, the instant replay showed an offensive lineman clearly and deliberately delivering a viciously illegal elbow into the face of an opponent, virtually twisting off the head of the victim. This graphic illegal violence was followed by a comment from one of the sportscasters: "Nobody said this was going to be a tea party!" Camera crews and sportscasters are ever-vigilant to the violent collision, the late hit, the shove in the back that can be replayed over and over via instant replay to the horrified fascination of viewers.

As if actually viewing violent confrontations in person or via television were not enough, television anthology programs have devised videotaped shows of NFL and NHL game segments showing only the most vicious hits and fights. NFL Films Video sells violence through videos with titles like *The NFL's Greatest Hits, Thunder and Destruction,* and *CrunchTime.* On the cover case of the last one is this sales pitch: "For those who love a bone-rattling hit as much as a touchdown and recognize guts as well as glory, *CrunchTime* is a must-see." A regular part of the classified section in *Hockey Stars* is ads for videotapes with titles like *Devastating Hits of Hockey* and *The Best of Hockey's Hardest Hitters.*

Fans

Organized sports are commercial endeavors, and those who produce the sporting events (professional franchise owners, university athletic departments, etc.) are dependent on fan support. Surveys of fans indicate that spectator enjoyment of games is related to the amount of violence in them. In a summary and review of research findings about viewers' enjoyment of televised sports events, a communications researcher, said: "Taken together, the findings from the research that has been presented and reviewed seem to reveal several general features of the enjoyment of viewing sports violence. . . . Most avid sports fans seem to enjoy extremely rough, even violent televised sporting events.[25]

One avid ice-hockey fan believes that efforts to eliminate fighting from the NHL would be a step toward destroying the sport, so he created a newsletter devoted to "the physical aspect of the NHL" titled *Beaver's Mixin' It Up*. Each issue has a detailed compilation of "every on-ice battle that occurred" since the previous issue. One such conflict drew this review: "Great fight; bloody slugfest, both men cut." In one issue he wrote that hockey is "the greatest sport on the face of the earth, and fighting is part of the game."[26]

Given the preferences that fans seem to have for violent action, and given that commercial sports must depend on the fans to stay in business, it should not be surprising that the sports industry is quite willing to make sure that violent play is a salient feature of the games. A frequent exclamation of professional sports executives, coaches, and players is: "We depend on the fans for our existence."

Pressures on Athletes to Be Violent

Pressures exist in sports to use violence, legal and illegal, in the quest for a victory. At all levels of play, coaches teach players the use of intimidating and violent tactics, and peer pressure inspires players to use violence. At all levels incentives exist for athletes to be violent.

The folklore of the sports world is that aggressive play yields positive results. Youth, high school, and college athletes often either secure a place on the team or are cut from the team, depending on the amount of

aggressiveness they display. College athletic scholarships are often awarded by coaches on the basis of the aggressive tendencies shown by recruits. Various financial incentives control the aggressive actions of professional athletes.

Coaches, Owners, Commissioners

Beginning with their first organized sports experience, athletes learn that they must please their coaches if they expect to remain a member of the team. Pleasing the coach often means doing "whatever it takes" to win. Many coaches firmly believe that violent behavior leads to victory, therefore, athletes quickly learn that being aggressive gains the coach's approval. A former NFL player said the message that coaches repeat over and over is if you're going to make a mistake, make an aggressive one.

Shortly before his retirement as commissioner of the NHL, John Ziegler, when asked in a television interview if he thought that fighting in NHL hockey should be eliminated, responded: "It doesn't matter to me. What matters to me is providing a product that people enjoy and want to see . . . because I am in the entertainment business, and the measure to me is, Are people going to pay money to see . . . [fighting]? And they are saying yes to it. . . . So, if it ain't broke, don't fix it."

Professional team owners refuse to condemn violence because they are convinced it attracts spectators. Among owners and general managers of professional sports franchises there is a tacit agreement that it's hard to justify making changes in the rules to reduce violence because the bottom line is that there are a lot of fans who like fighting. The Chairman of the International Bar Association's Sports Law Committee acknowledges, "there is no economic incentive to curb violence on the playing field."[27]

Athletes who refuse to participate in violent actions often find themselves demoted on the team roster or even dropped from the team. In professional ice hockey the expectation that players will participate in fights is so strong that in several instances when a player refused to enter a violent melee, he was sent to the minor leagues or traded.

Violence Against Athletes

Violent attacks on movie stars, television personalities, musicians, and politicians have occurred with some regularity for many decades, but, except for a few very rare incidents of a fan assaulting an athlete, or athletes receiving death threats (Major League baseball great Hank Aaron received many death threats as he approached breaking Babe Ruth's home run record) athletes have been exempt from the kinds of attacks that other celebrities have encountered. However, given the omnipresence, adulation, and celebrity status of elite athletes it was probably inevitable that they would become targets of assaults. Several attacks on high profile athletes have occurred.

In the spring of 1993 Monica Seles, at that time the No. 1 ranked women's tennis player in the world, was stabbed in the back during a match by a German tennis fan who was obsessed with the No. 2 ranked tennis player, Steffi Graf. The assailant's explanation for the attack was that he merely wanted to injure Seles slightly so that Graf would assume the top spot while Seles was recovering. Seles recovered from the wound but did not return to competition for twenty-eight months.[28]

In January 1994, just before the U.S. Figure Skating Association championships in Detroit, on her way to the dressing room after a practice the day before the women's competition began, figure skater Nancy Kerrigan was attacked and savagely hit on the knee by a bludgeon-wielding assailant. Her kneecap and upper-leg tendon were seriously bruised. Kerrigan had to withdraw from the event. Tonya Harding, Kerrigan's main rival for the women's national championship, went on to win the championship.

Subsequent events revealed that Tonya Harding's ex-husband, with whom she was reconciled, and several co-conspirators were responsible for the attack. Harding was implicated in the plot by the conspirators, but she denied any knowledge of it. As part of a plea bargaining agreement Harding admitted "hindering prosecution," terminating any further determination by the legal system of her possible role in the attack on Kerrigan.[29]

These attacks have horrified the sports world. A different social climate now exists for athletes. Many have expressed a feeling of fear that didn't exist before these two incidents. A different atmosphere prevails in sporting venues, where tighter security measures have been put in place. Only time will tell whether these incidents are aberrations or signals of a difffernet form of violence in sports.

Violent Behavior by Athletes off the Field of Play

Most athletes' lives are lived off the field of play. Even on days in which they practice or play sports, these activities will typically take less than 20 percent of their waking hours. Beyond their role as athletes, athletes do most of the same things that other young people do. They have friends they hang out with, they party, they drink, they develop sexual relationships, they marry and have families, and so forth. At one time, what athletes did on their "own" time was little known by the public nor was it reported by the media. Moreover, if athletes got into trouble of any kind, coaches, owners, administrators, and the media covered it up; "taking care of the athlete" was the explanation given for this action (others have called it a "conspiracy of silence"). In effect, athletes' misbehavior, even unlawful actions, were protected from public scrutiny and the criminal justice system.

At the same time that athletes of previous eras were being protected if they ran afoul of the law, they were portrayed as honest, sober, upstanding pillars of the community and heroes to be emulated. The accumulating literature makes quite clear that in reality many of them engaged in behavior ranging from fun-loving mischief to criminal behavior when they were not playing ball.

A book published by a former New York Yankee pitcher and entitled *Ball Four* was the first to break down the invisible barrier between the idealized image of athletes and their real personal worlds. The author described in detail what went on in the club house and what the players did in their free time. What he divulged was athletes getting drunk and going on rampages, doing drugs just before games, married players having sexual liaisons with female "groupies" that hung around the players, and players going on voyeuristic expeditions. A flood of similar books followed.

The private lives and escapades of college and professional athletes in many sports have been spelled out in detail in various mass media. In many cases, it has not been a pretty story because violent criminal behavior, especially sexual assaults and spousal abuse, by the athletes has been a rather persistent theme.

Whether there is more sexual assault and spousal abuse by present-day athletes or whether the private lives of these athletes are just being scrutinized more closely and the behaviors that prevailed for a long time are now being reported, is widely debated. One thing is certain: Available research indicates that athletes are frequently involved in sexual assaults. These examples illustrate this point:

- A three-year study by the National Institute of Mental Health found that athletes participated in approximately one-third of 862 sexual assaults on college campuses.
- A Bucknell University psychologist found that of 26 documented campus gang rapes most of them involved fraternity brothers and varsity athletes, especially football and basketball players.
- A survey of over 1,000 athletes and more than 10,000 students by the Towson State University Center for the Study and Prevention of Campus Violence found that athletes were 5.5 times more likely to admit committing date rape.[30]
- In the best designed study thus far, the researchers examined the relationship between collegiate athletic participation and reported sexual assaults at Division I universities. They found that male college athletes, "compared with the rest of the male student population, are responsible for a significantly higher percentage of the sexual assaults reported to judicial affairs offices on the campuses. . . . Athletes appear to be disproportionately involved in incidents of sexual assault on college campuses."[31]
- And it's not just collegiate athletes who have been implicated in sexual assaults. Professional athletes have been involved as well. Perhaps the most infamous has been Mike Tyson, former World's

Heavyweight Boxing Champion, who was convicted of rape and served time in prison for his crime. A rape suit in Cincinnati implicated twenty Bengal football players. Many other pro athletes have been involved in sexual assault episodes also.[32]

The trial of O. J. Simpson for the murder of Nicole Brown Simpson and Ronald Goldman highlighted what *Sports Illustrated* called "Sport's Dirty Secret"— domestic violence. Evidence in the trial revealed that O. J. beat his wife and did so on more than one occasion. He is not alone among athletes on this count. Hardly a week passes without a collegiate or professional athlete being accused of violence against his wife.[33] In a book written by an NFL player, he confesses to having repeatedly battered his first two wives.[34]

Obviously, athletes are not the only assaultants and abusers of women. We focus on athletes because this book is about sports. An estimated 10 to 12 million women are assaulted each year by their partners, and domestic violence is the leading cause of injury among women ages fifteen to forty-four. Male sexual assault against women and spousal abuse are major national social problems.

Why Do Athletes Assault Women?

What accounts for this rather alarming trail of violence by athletes in their private lives? There is, of course, the fact that they live in a violent culture and that their lives are much more under the media's scrutiny than the average person's. These factors have been previously discussed, but are there other factors? We believe there are. There are at least three factors that might contribute to this subculture of violence: male bonding rituals, preconditioning to aggressive behavior, and steroid use by many athletes.

Male Bonding Ritual

As part of gender development, both males and females learn culturally prescribed attitudes, rituals, symbols, and behaviors for their sex. Much of this learning, and exhibiting the effects of the learning, takes place in sex-segregated activities. Sports teams provide fertile ground especially for male bonding, fostering a spirit of exclusivity, camaraderie, and solidarity among males.[35] Given traditional masculine prescriptions of toughness, dominance, repression of empathy, and competitiveness, athletes may display the effects of this socialization by engaging in reckless and violent behavior as proof of their masculinity. The author of a study carried out by the Association of American Colleges dealing with campus gang rape said that athletes are "really raping for each other," validating, as it were, the code of male bonding.[36]

Preconditioning for Violence Against Women

A number of behavioral and social scientists contend that male socialization is a preconditioning to aggressive behavior as an appropriate response for achieving one's goal, whether it is defending oneself in the streets, making a tackle, or satisfying one's sexual desires against a woman's wishes. Society's concept of masculinity is inextricably woven into aggressive, forceful, physical behavior. One legal expert noted: "Physicality for men has meant male dominance; it has meant force, coercion, and the ability to subdue and subject the natural world, one central part of which has been [women]."[37]

The epitome of socially appropriate physical dominance, use of force, and violent action occurs in various sports. An anthropologist who spent a year in a Texas community studying its high school football team wrote "what the players talked about most was 'hitting' or 'sticking' or 'popping' someone. . . . These were the things that coaches exhorted players to do. . . . The supreme compliment was . . . to be called a 'hitter' or 'headhunter.' A hitter made bone-crushing tackles that knocked out or hurt his opponent."[38] A culture of violence begins on the sporting field. Behavior learned in one context, where it is appropriate, can get transferred to another, where it is not.

Steroids and Violent Behavior

There is plenty of medical as well as testimonial evidence convincingly showing that steroids stimulate aggressive behavior. There is also convincing evidence that steroids are widely used by college and professional athletes, again primarily in the contact sports.[39]

Undoubtedly, these and other factors can interact in any given situation or incident that ultimately leads to violent, even criminal, behavior by athletes. We want to emphasize, though, that we recognize that the actual percentage of athletes at any level and in any sport that are involved in violence off the field is very small. Nevertheless, there are enough incidents, and they are serious enough, for all of us to be concerned. Concerted efforts need to be made by everyone involved in sport to find ways and means to reduce, even eliminate, sexual assaultive and domestic violence by athletes that have become all too familiar.

Sports Fan Violence

Violence on the playing field is often mirrored by sports fans in the stadium, arena, or the surrounding environs, and it is not merely a contemporary phenomenon, nor is it confined to North American sports. In one renowned spectator riot at the chariot races in ancient Rome, some 30,000 fans were killed. In 1969 in a World Cup soccer series between El Salvador and Honduras, spectator violence accompanied each of the games. Finally, the riot that followed the third game resulted in the two countries severing political and economic relations and mobilizing their armies against each other; this has been called the "soccer war" between El Salvador and Honduras.

Soccer hooliganism, common in Britain, is by no means a new phenomenon; it was widely practiced in Britain before World War I. More recently, one of the most infamous soccer hooligan riots occurred at Heysel Stadium in Brussels, Belgium, before a European Championship Cup match between British and Italian teams. Thirty-eight people were killed, and over 400 were injured (the game was played anyway, with dead bodies still in the stadium).

Everyone who follows North American sports is quite aware of the many incidents of spectator violence. Within the past decade, major fan violence has erupted in all of the professional team sports (NFL, NHL, NBA, MLB). It has also penetrated into the university campuses, and collegiate football and basketball games have been marred by riots in the stands. Due to frequent spectator riots, several large city school systems have imposed strict limits on the number of spectators admitted to basketball games in an effort to prevent fights between fans and opposing teams. Several years ago *Sports Illustrated* took what it called an "unscientific poll of fans" and reported that everyone who reported having ever been to a sporting event had witnessed one or more acts of violent behavior by fans.

Newspaper and magazine articles describing, and usually condemning, a seemingly escalating amount of fan violence are common. "Sports in USA Sick: Violence Out of Hand," "Sports No Substitute for War, Sports is War," "War in the Grandstand," and "Fanning the Fury" are examples of article titles found in the popular press.[40] The man who helped author the Sport Violence Arbitration Act, which was introduced into the U.S. House of Representatives, contends that an excessively violent equilibrium exists in sports today at almost all levels.

Factors Associated with Fan Violence

Behavioral and social scientists seeking to understand and explain spectator violence tend to center their explanations around fans' social learning and experiences in the wider society. In support of this, one journalist said: "In society, violence has gone from fistfights to knife fights to gunfights, so it shouldn't be a surprise that violence at stadiums and arenas has increased as well."[41] Scientists uniformly reject cathartic explanations. Instead, they contend that violence in sport contributes to violence in the crowd, as opposed to the notion that viewing violent acts results in reduced feelings of violence. One of the most respected researchers of violent behavior explains that "people learn what they observe, and if what they observe goes unpunished, they are likely to repeat it when they find themselves in similar circumstances."[42] Thus, sports fans learn specific aggressive actions by observing aggressive athletes on the playing field engage in unpunished violence.

The sequence of witnessing violence-learning-acting might proceed in this manner: Fans watching a violent sporting event are likely to become more aggressively inclined themselves; as they witness violent behavior, they may, under just the right circumstances, act violently themselves. Of course, as we emphasized earlier in this chapter, learning the heritage and culture of violence is the lived experience of everyone in North America, so sports fans have more than their immediate experiences in the stadium or arena mediating a mindset for violence.

There are other factors as well that may precipitate spectator violence that go beyond just broad enculturation and witnessing violence on the field. Two forms of "perceived injustice" can trigger fan violence. The first form occurs when fans believe that officials have applied a rule unfairly or inaccurately; the second occurs when fans believe that a rule itself is unfair, regardless of how accurately employed.

Bad calls by officials, such as calling a batted baseball foul when it was fair or calling a made basket from three-point range two points are examples of the first. An example of the second might occur when a penalty kick is awarded near the end of a tie game in soccer; since it is such a high percentage kick, it will almost always result in a victory for the kicking team. The penalty kick in soccer is uniformly condemned as unfair by soccer fans, so a situation as just described may precipitate fan violence.

One social scientist has suggested five social situational factors that can be conducive to spectator violence. They are: (1) a large crowd, because of a perceived power inherent in a mass of people, and the anonymity ferments irresponsible behavior; (2) a dense crowd, because annoyance and frustration builds when one's comfortable space is violated and when one is forced to be near strangers; (3) a noisy crowd, because noise is itself arousing, and arousal is a common precondition to violence; (4) a standing crowd, because standing for long periods is tiring, jostling is common, and the lack of an assigned space is frustrating; (5) crowd composition, because drinking crowds, young male crowds, and crowds made up of people who are oppressed in the larger society are more predisposed toward violent behavior than more diverse crowds.

Reducing Fan Violence

Numerous suggestions for reducing spectator violence have been proposed by fans to researchers of violence.

Some of the suggestions that often appear are: improving the physical facilities and appearances of stadiums and arenas, making them more attractive and less foreboding places; increasing the numbers of security forces at sporting events; limiting the sale of alcohol (already done in some stadiums and arenas); changing the rules of some sports, such as soccer, to make scoring easier; keeping violence under control on the field by preventing fights, excessive displays of anger or aggression by athletes, and arm-waving displays of disapproval of officials' calls by coaches and athletes; and severely punishing offenders.

All of these suggestions might indeed reduce fan violence to some extent. However, none of them deals with the larger, structural issue of the heritage and culture of violence that underlies much of the violence in contemporary North American society beyond the confines of sports but nevertheless affects both athletes and fans alike.

Substance Abuse and Sport

"The High Price of Hard Living." "I Was Killing Myself." "Lost Weekend." "I Lied: I'm Sick and I'm Scared." These are all magazine headlines, all from issues of *Sports Illustrated*. They tersely, but poignantly, tell of personal tragedies, not of criminals or derelicts but of five of North America's superstar athletes who were involved with substance abuse. As for the first headline, sportswriter Tom Verducci tells the story of how "reckless years in the fast lane, fueled by alcohol and cocaine . . . cost former New York Mets phenoms Darryl Strawberry and Dwight Gooden the prime years of their careers."[43]

The second headline captures the heart wrenching story of the great New York Yankee outfielder, Mickey Mantle, who a year before he died of cancer in 1995 explained: "My last four or five years with the Yankees, I didn't realize I was ruining myself with all the drinking. I just thought, 'This is fun.' . . . Today I can admit that all the drinking shortened my career. . . . God gave me a great body to play with, and I didn't take care of it. And I blame a lot of it on alcohol."[44]

The subject of the third headline was Jennifer Capriati, child tennis prodigy, who had just been

arrested for possession of marijuana and accused by two of her cohorts of having used crack and heroin. A week after her arrest, Capriati entered a drug rehabilitation facility for the second time in a year.[45]

The fourth headline is from a *Sports Illustrated* article authored by Lyle Alzado, a former NFL star who played fifteen years in the league. He begins by saying: "I lied. I lied to you. I lied to my family. I lied to a lot of people for a lot of years when I said I didn't use steroids. I started taking anabolic steroids in 1969, and I never stopped."[46] He had just learned that he had cancer, a brain lymphoma, and he and several physicians believed that his history of steroid use may have been the precipitating cause. Alzado died less than a year after the article was published.

The Scope of Substance Abuse in Sport

As anyone who has followed sports in the past few years knows, the athletes discussed previously represent only a speck of dust in the universe of substance abuse in the sports world. Indeed, there are knowledgeable authorities who believe that substance use by athletes is epidemic in scope, all the way from high school to the professional level (we include Olympic athletes as professionals). Several studies reveal that steroid use among male high school students is between 6 and 10 percent; its use among females is about 2 percent, meaning that over 300,000 high school students are using steroids. (See table 7.2 for a description of steroids.) A study by the U.S. Department of Health and Human Services underscores the belief that high school steroid users have about the benefits of the chemical. According to the study, of the adolescent steroid users interviewed, "93 percent said they believe they made 'a good decision' by starting to use steroids, and 87 percent would make the same decision today 'without hesitation.'" A study by a Penn State researcher projected steroid use as high as 29 percent among college football players, 20 percent among men's track and field teams, and 16 percent for women's track and field.[47] Several NFL athletes have claimed that up to 75 percent of NFL players use or have used steroids.[48]

table 7.2 *Steroids: What Are They?*

What they are:	Anabolic-androgenic steroids are synthetic forms of testosterone, which is a male hormone that is naturally present in the human body. They are taken either orally or by injection into the muscle.
Their effects:	They increase lean body mass; they increase strength; they increase muscle definition; they decrease recovery time from exercise; they increase aggressiveness.
Their dangers:	Cause testicular shrinkage; reduce testosterone production; cause benign and malignant liver tumors; cause bizarre and violent personality changes; cause feminized characteristics of males and masculinized characteristics of females.

Actually, an accurate assessment of steroid use by athletes is very difficult. The NCAA has released figures from its drug testing program showing the number of positive test results in Division I football is around 1.1 percent. From this figure, the NCAA claimed steroid use had declined dramatically, thus displaying a complete naivete to the sophisticated methods that athletes use to avoid testing positive. Physicians who have experience with steroid users say they have found numerous ways to beat the drug testing systems; drug testing actually isn't the threat to drug-using athletes that is often portrayed by sport organizations.

Substance Abuse Not New to Sports

The use of substances to enhance performance has been present throughout the history of organized sports. The ancient Greek athletes consumed mushrooms in the belief that they improved performance, and Roman gladiators used a variety of stimulants to hype them up and forestall fatigue. Athletes throughout the nineteenth century experimented with caffeine, alcohol, nitroglycerine, opium, and strychnine. Strychnine, cocaine, alcohol, and caffeine mixtures were used by boxers, cyclists, and British and European soccer players before World War II. Amphetamines and steroids began their rise to the drugs of choice among athletes in the years immediately after World War II. An unofficial poll taken by a member of the U.S. track and field team at the 1972 Munich Olympics revealed that 68 percent of the track and field athletes used some form of steroids in preparing for those Games (there were no accurate tests for detecting steroid use at that time).[49]

The variety of substances athletes use in the hopes of improving their performances has become astounding: Growth retardant hormones are used by female gymnasts to prolong their careers; archers and shooters use beta-blockers to slow the heart rate for steadier aiming; swimmers use nasal decongestants to enhance air flow through their lungs; weight lifters use amphetamines to release vast amounts of adrenalin into the blood and speed up the systems used for strength activities; endurance athletes use recombinant erythropoietin (rEPO) to stimulate the production of red blood cells that transport oxygen throughout the body, thereby improving performance; wrestlers and boxers use diuretics for weight loss to compete at lower weight classes, and drug-using athletes in many sports use diuretics to minimize detection of other drugs by diluting the urine.

In addition to the use of performance-enhancing substances, athletes, like the general population, are deeply involved in what are called "recreational" drugs. The main culprit has historically been alcohol, serious enough, to be sure, but not the deadly, debilitating substance like those that have come on the scene in the forms of: cocaine, crack, heroin, and speed. Athletes at all levels continue to abuse alcohol more than any other substance. The amount of cocaine, crack, heroin, and speed usage is minuscule compared to the use of alcohol. A *USA Today* survey of almost 800 high school coaches asked what they considered the greatest threat to athletes on their teams. The responses: alcohol 88 percent, cocaine/crack 6 percent, marijuana 3 percent, steroids 1 percent. So many professional and intercollegiate athletes have been arrested for drunkenness that it hardly raises eyebrows anymore when reports appear on television or in newspapers. Several high-profile pro and college athletes have been involved in fatal accidents in which alcohol played a role.

Although the use of cocaine, crack, heroin, and speed by athletes may be small compared to alcohol, this does not mean it is insignificant. A study of intercollegiate athletes revealed that 17 percent acknowledged using cocaine in the prior year; two years later, in a study of elite women athletes, 7 percent reported using cocaine, about half of these saying they used it before or during competition. Players representing nearly all the professional sport leagues and dozens of intercollegiate teams have been involved with cocaine use in criminal cases, with some teams having several players arrested.

Eating Disorders: A Unique Form of Substance Abuse

While steroid use is prevalent among male athletes who are trying to bulk up, eating disorders, mainly anorexia nervosa and bulimia, afflict female athletes who want to slim down. World-class gymnast, Christy Henrich, who lost her battle with eating disorders in 1994, weighed 95 pounds at the peak of her sports career but less than 60 pounds shortly before her death.[50] Eating disorders are the gravest health problem for female athletes. They affect gymnasts, distance runners, swimmers and divers, figure skaters, and tennis and volleyball players. The American College of Sports Medicine estimates that up to 62 percent of female athletes in these sports suffer from eating disorders. In an NCAA study, 58 percent of the women and 38 percent of the men were considered to be at risk of developing an eating disorder. One collegiate women's gymnastic team would binge and vomit together following meets; it was considered a "social thing" to do.[51]

Eating disorders are not confined to athletes. The Association of Anorexia Nervosa and Associated Disorders estimates that 18 percent of females in the United States are afflicted with eating disorders. Most experts contend that social norms, media images of females, and advertising portrayals of the "ideal" female body as extremely lean and firmly toned are major contributing factors in the contemporary woman's obsession with thinness.

Female athletes not only have to contend with these forces, they have to cope with additional ones. In some women's sports, such as gymnastics, figure skating, and diving, a significant part of the judging is on "appearance," and an extremely thin silhouette is a definite advantage. Coaches and athletes know this. Many female athletes report that their coaches hammer home the message of "get thin and stay thin" to them in a variety of ways, some of which are quite abusive. Many athletes aspire to be the best, to be a national or an Olympic champion, so they are willing to sacrifice to achieve that goal. The combination of these conditions creates the social climate for the development of eating disorders.[52]

Reasons for Substance Abuse Among Athletes

Why do athletes risk their health and their opportunity to compete by using drugs? There is, of course, no single answer to this question because athletes have different reasons. Athletes are a part of a much larger social community, and substance abuse is rampant in this larger social community. Indeed, some experts on drug abuse refer to the United States as a "Drug Nation," and that portrayal seems accurate. Studies show that "if the world's countries are divided into those with high, medium, and low drug problems, the United States is the *only* developed country that falls into the 'high' category."[53]

Athletes are not immune from the societal influences in which they live. In their world, athletes see drug use all around them: aspirin, tranquilizers, amphetamines, diet pills. They see the almost universal acceptance of alcohol and tobacco. The first, considered by most health professionals to be the most abused drug in North America, is responsible for over half the traffic fatalities annually and for the estimated 15 million alcoholics in North America. The second, tobacco, is the leading cause of lung cancer and is considered addictive by the U.S. Surgeon General. Cigarettes carry a label: "Smoking is dangerous to your health."

Young athletes are especially susceptible to what they see and hear from high-profile athletes. There was a TV commercial for the pain killer Nuprin in which tennis pro Jimmy Conners tells NFL quarterback Joe Montana (now retired) that he overcame his pain and played successfully with Nuprin, suggesting that Montana can do the same. The message was clear: "Drugs can help you play better." Young athletes often hear TV sportscasters report that a given athlete was given pain suppressants, such as morphine, so that he could play in the game that day. During a Monday Night NFL football game between the Buffalo Bills and Miami, one of the sportscasters commented approvingly about Buffalo's quarterback, Jim Kelly: "Here's a guy who probably had to take a pain-killer shot in his lower back so he could play tonight." Many young athletes have seen athletic trainers' rooms, rooms that are filled with all kinds of salves, ointments, and pills, all used to help athletes perform at their best. Is it any wonder that young athletes see that drugs are widely used in sports? The sports culture itself promotes drug usage in sports.

Another factor that motivates young athletes to turn to chemicals for performance enhancement is that there is enormous social status that goes with being an athlete; as we noted in chapter 5, being an athlete is admired by both males and females. Most people do not understand how or the extent to which the system of sport and its status-conferring and rewarding properties, often leads athletes to a commitment in which they are willing to risk anything, even their life, to achieve their goal. Several years ago the following hypothetical situation was posed to a number of elite-level athletes: Suppose there was a special pill that, if you took it, would guarantee you an Olympic gold medal, but the pill would cause your death within a year. Would you take it? Over 50 percent of the responding athletes said yes!

There are other temptations. The best high school athletes are recruited to colleges with "full-ride" scholarships—a college education with all expenses paid. Although there are very few who ultimately become professional athletes or Olympic champions, there are millions of young athletes who devote themselves to years of training and personal sacrifice in attempting to attain this lofty goal. At every level the competition is keen, and athletes know that they must continue to improve if they are to move to the next rung of the ladder. Many literally devote their lives to the quest to move onward and upward, and anything that will aid them in their quest will be tried. Thus, athletes striving to improve often believe that any substance that will provide even the slightest advantage over their opponents is worth trying. Rather than depending upon legitimate training methods and developing a sound psychological approach to their sport, some athletes choose to rely upon drugs to improve their performance.

It is very difficult for young athletes to do their best when they know they might be competing against athletes who are using substances that may be performance enhancing. A Canadian weightlifter described why he felt it was necessary to use steroids in order to attain his objective of competing at the international level in his sport: "To go to international competitions, you have to meet international standards and those are based on what the Russians and Bulgarians do. They are the best weightlifters in the world . . . and they take steroids. So if I go to the Olympics, I must take steroids."[54]

Another factor in substance abuse among athletes is that at the high school, college, and professional levels pressures are put on athletes by coaches to improve their performance and play when injured. To meet these demands, some athletes resort to drugs to enhance their performance or to play when hurt. The editor of one of the most respected books on steroids in sport claims: Coaches like "the benefits of steroids. It gives world records, bigger-than-life humans with tremendous physical capacities that sell television minutes and fill stadiums."[55]

Finally, there is the ambiguity, perhaps hypocrisy is more appropriate, of all that athletes see every day in the way of sports-substance abuse connections. They see the cozy financial connection between alcohol and tobacco and big-time sports. Beer and tobacco companies are the number one sponsors and underwriters of sporting events. Beer ads dominate concession stands and score boards at sports venues; beer commercials dominate TV and radio advertising during sports events. It is virtually impossible to watch or listen to a sporting event in North America without feeling overwhelmed by beer ads. The St. Louis Cardinals baseball team is owned by Anheuser-Busch, which is the largest beer maker in North America, and this beer company is one of the top five media advertisers during sporting events in North America. The Colorado Rockies baseball team plays in Coors (beer) Field.

According to the NFL's drug policy, alcohol is "without question the most abused drug in our sport," and a number of college sport officials acknowledge that alcohol is a much more pervasive problem for collegiate athletes than other substances. The managing editor of *Collegiate Baseball* put it rather bluntly: "Alcohol is much more of a problem [than drugs] on college campuses today. Drugs are only a small pimple on the buttocks of life."[56] Still, professional leagues, Canadian and American Olympic sports organizations, and the NCAA happily accept advertising money generated by alcohol companies.

Is it any wonder that athletes are confused about substance abuse? When the rules and customs governing drug use in both the larger society and the sports world itself seem arbitrary and inconsistent, it is easy to understand why athletes may view drug use as acceptable and normative behavior, in spite of the distortions they bring to the ethics of the social process of competition and their potentially devastating consequences to health and well-being.

Preventing Substance Abuse in Sports

Although the evidence, incomplete as it is, strongly suggests that only a minority of athletes at any level, in terms of percentages, have a substance abuse problem, there is still the question of what is to be done with the small number who are drug abusers. There are several options, but the one that has received the most attention is the drug testing programs of the various sports' governing bodies because the programs have been implemented without fully resolving at least two important questions: (1) What are the athletes individual rights? (2) What are the athletes responsibilities?

With respect to athletes rights, the fourth amendment to the U.S. Constitution forbids any unreasonable searches and seizures, any intrusions on human dignity and privacy, simply on the hunch that incriminating evidence might be found; this protects all U.S. citizens, including athletes. The U.S. Supreme Court has ruled

that extracting bodily fluids constitutes a search within the meaning of this amendment. The U.S. Constitution protects persons only from intrusion by government and because there can be different interpretations of "reasonableness," this has become a complicated issue involving a balancing of the invasion of personal rights and the need for the search.

Although some of the major sport organizations, such as the International Olympic Committee, the NCAA, and the National Football League, have taken the lead in mandatory and random drug testing, considering it necessary and appropriate, there are many critics as well. One critic who is particularly skeptical of the NCAA substance testing policy argues:

> If the NCAA had respected these athletes as students and as sensitive human beings, random drug testing would have been instituted only as a last resort and, even then, only after encouraging athletes to consider the constitutional issues involved.
>
> Efforts to fight substance abuse in college sports must be concerned with more than keeping athletes drug-free in the short term. The goal should be to help athletes understand the role that drugs play in our society and to prepare them to fight drug abuse throughout their lives. The NCAA should take the hundreds of thousands of dollars that are going into random drug testing and undertake a massive program of drug education.[57]

Several unresolved issues exist where drug testing has been implemented. The validity and accuracy of the tests have been a continuing controversy, and rightly so, because the test results are not infallible. Drug testing programs in professional sports have been frequently found to be misleading to the public and unfair to the players. Several sport organizations that now routinely test their athletes do not even have an appellate process in place; thus, an athlete who tests positive does not have a process for appealing the results of the tests.

Two noted authorities on drugs in sports argue that there are sports-specific reasons why teams or other sports organizations may wish to test athletes, such as preventing drug users from gaining an advantage over opponents or protecting them from drugs that might be debilitating. They claim that general reasons, including protecting athletes from long-term physical and mental disability or avoiding possible discipline problems, are also evoked in support of testing. After discussing the pros and cons of drug testing from ethical and legal standpoints, they conclude:

> Where teams or players' associations propose testing of athletes for drugs, one criterion of the legal sufficiency of testing programs should be that there is an empirically demonstrable relationship between use of target drugs and their adverse effects on performance, health, or the quality of competition. If this criterion is not met, it would seem that athletes' interests in freedom from intrusion should outweigh testers' interests in trying to identify users of drugs.[58]

Regarding the responsibilities that athletes have for abstaining from substance abuse, various lists have been compiled that range from the personal responsibility that athletes have for keeping their bodies in excellent physical condition to their responsibilities as society's role models to their responsibilities to spectators who pay money to watch their performances. These appear to be good "common sense" reasons for athletes to abstain from drug abuse, but they ignore a number of related issues. For example, it does not take in-depth investigating into equitable treatment provisions in sports to see how blatantly athletes are victimized by the drug testing system. Although athletes must undergo mandatory, random drug testing, there is no provision for coaches, athletic directors, sports information directors, athletic trainers, athletic secretaries, and various and sundry others who are part of the big business of sports to undergo the same testing. Instead, the public is encouraged to dwell on all the alleged defects of athletes.

Moreover, there seems to be no understanding or acknowledgment by sport organizations that the social conditions of high pressure sports may actually contribute to drug abuse by athletes. Several studies have documented the pressures and incredible time demands that go with being a high school, major university, or professional athlete. It does not appear to be stretching the imagination to think that some of these pressures may actually contribute to substance abuse by athletes. As one Penn State drug abuse researcher says: "We're telling [athletes] in our society that sports are more than a game. Until we change those signals, for the most part we might as well tell people to get used to drug use."[59]

Many medical professionals, health educators, and other knowledgeable professionals who have been critical of drug testing programs acknowledge the social structural factors that cultivate drug abuse by athletes, but they are skeptical about any immediate changes that will address the need to discourage athletes from abusing drugs. They are also scornful about random drug testing as a viable tool for behavior change. Instead, many believe that drug education programs can make a valuable contribution as a key component of drug abuse prevention. Not just any drug education program will do, however; certainly the "one shot" efforts of many universities and professional teams are largely a waste of time. The fundamental strength of any substance abuse prevention program for athletes should be through education, and drug education must include more than just giving information or threatening athletes with punishment for substance abuse.

Efforts should be made to go beyond the single goal of merely restraining athletes from abusing drugs. Programs are needed to help as many athletes as possible avoid making decisions about drugs that they may regret for the rest of their lives.

In the best of all possible worlds—a world we should all be striving for—there would be no place for drug abuse among athletes. Use of performance-enhancing drugs corrupt the essence of fair sporting competition; it is cheating. As serious as this is within the bounded world of sport, performance-enhancing and recreational drug abuse are improper for a more important reason: They are dangerous to personal health; their use is an unnecessary health risk.

The structure of society, especially the political and economic institutions, is responsible for many of the problems associated with drug abuse among North Americans. At a more microsocial level, the political economy of sports has contributed to drug abuse among athletes. Thus, solutions to the drug abuse among athletes must begin with structural modifications in the larger society as well as in sport culture;

when this happens, serious amelioration of drug abuse among athletes will occur.[60]

Summary

It should come as no surprise that violent behavior and substance abuse are conspicuous problems in North American sports, given the close connections between sport and society. Three theories of human aggression dominate the scientific literature: the instinct theory, the frustration-aggression (F-A) theory, and socially grounded theory. Advocates of the instinct and F-A theories have often claimed that participation and observation of aggressive activities have a cathartic effect by allowing one to discharge pent-up aggressive energy, and sporting activities have often been suggested as a means of dispelling aggression in a socially healthy way. The research findings suggest that, contrary to the predictions of the instinct and F-A theories, aggression tends to produce more aggressive predispositions and actions rather than serve as a catharsis.

Another theory about aggressive behavior has come from scholars who advance a socially grounded perspective that postulates that aggression is learned in the social environment. This latter perspective places emphasis on the learning of aggression through the socialization process. Socially based explanations have much more research support than the other aggression models. Directly and indirectly, sports research findings have overwhelmingly supported this perspective of human aggression.

Violent behavior has been a part of sporting practices for as long as we have records of organized sports. The nature of some sports literally demand violent actions. Other sports do not have the inherent violence found in some, but the tactics employed and the way the rules are interpreted are increasingly encouraging violent actions.

Athletes feel pressure to be violent because coaches, owners, and fans all encourage player violence in their own ways. Whether there is actually more violence and criminal behavior by present-day athletes in their private lives or whether they are just scrutinized more closely than in the past is widely debated.

Violence on the playing field is often mirrored by sports fans in the stadium, arena, or the surrounding environs, and it is not merely a contemporary phenomenon, nor is it confined to North American sports. Everyone who follows North American sports is quite aware of the many incidents of spectator violence. Within the past decade, major fan violence has erupted in all levels of competition—high school, collegiate, professional.

The use of substances to enhance performance has been present throughout the history of organized sports. Some behavioral and social scientists believe that drug use by athletes is an epidemic, from the high school to the professional level. The variety of substances athletes use in the hopes of improving their performances has become astounding.

There is no single answer to the question of why some athletes risk their health and their opportunity to compete by using drugs because athletes have different reasons. Athletes are a part of a much larger social community, and substance abuse is rampant in this larger social community. There is enormous social status that goes with being an athlete, and undoubtedly that is one factor that motivates young athletes to turn to chemicals for performance enhancement. There is also the potential of the fulfillment of young athletes' dreams of being a professional athlete or being an Olympic gold medalist.

Only a small minority of athletes at any level have a substance abuse problem. There is still, however, the question of what is to be done with those who are drug abusers. There are several options, but the one that has received the most attention is the drug testing programs of the various sports governing bodies. Two important questions that have been raised about drug testing are what are the athletes individual rights and what are the athletes responsibilities? Also, several unresolved issues exist where drug testing has been implemented. The validity and accuracy of the tests have been a continuing controversy.

Use of performance enhancing drugs corrupts the essence of fair sporting competition. As serious as this is within the world of sport, performance enhancing and recreational drug abuse are unsuitable for another important reason: They are potentially dangerous to personal health.

Notes

1. Konrad Lorenz, *On Aggression* (New York: Harcourt, Brace & World, 1963); see also Robert A. Baron and Deborah R. Richardson, *Human Aggression*, 2d ed. (New York: Plenum, 1994), 15–18.

2. Quoted in Alfie Kohn, "Making Love, Not War," *Psychology Today,* (June 1988): 35.

3. John L. Dollard, et al., *Frustration and Aggression* (New Haven: Yale University Press, 1939); see also Leonard D. Eron, "Theories of Aggression: From Drive to Cognitions," in *Aggressive Behavior: Current Perspectives,* ed. L. Rowell Huesmann (New York: Plenum, 1994), 4–5.

4. Eron, "Theories of Aggression: From Drive to Cognitions," 4–5; see also Leonard Berkowitz, *Aggression: Its Causes, Consequences, and Control* (New York: McGraw-Hill, 1993), 30–46, 337–69.

5. Quoted in Kohn, "Making Love, Not War," 37.

6. Eron, "Theories of Aggression: From Drive to Cognitions," 10; see also Richard B. Felson and James T. Tedeschi, eds., *Aggression and Violence: Social Interactionist Perspectives* (Washington, D.C.: American Psychological Association, 1993); Arnold Goldstein, *The Ecology of Aggression* (New York: Plenum, 1994).

7. A. A. Brill, "Why Man Seeks Sport," *North American Review* (1963): 85–99.

8. Lorenz, *On Aggression,* 281.

9. Berkowitz, *Aggression: Its Causes, Consequences, and Control,* 212, 237.

10. Richard G. Sipes, "Sports as a Control for Aggression," in *Sports in Contemporary Society: An Anthology,* ed. D. Stanley Eitzen, 4th ed. (New York: St. Martin's Press, 1993), 78–84.

11. Lynda J. Hess, *Rage in the Streets: Mob Violence in America* (San Diego: Browndeer Press, 1994); Richard M. Brown, *No Duty to Retreat: Violence and Values in American History and Society* (New York: Oxford University Press, 1991); Reeve Vanneman and Lynn Weber Cannon, *The American Perception of Class* (Philadelphia: Temple University Press, 1987).

12. Richard Slotkin, *Gunfighter Nation: The Myth of the Frontier in 20th Century America* (New York: Atheneum, 1992).

13. D. Stanley Eitzen and Maxine Baca Zinn, *In Conflict and Order: Understanding Society,* 7th ed. (Boston: Allyn and Bacon, 1995), 56.

14. Elliott Currie, "Rethinking Criminal Violence," in *Society's Problems: Sources and Consequences,* ed. D. Stanley Eitzen (Boston: Allyn and Bacon, 1989), 325–26.

15. Gary Kleck, *Point Blank: Guns and Violence in America* (New York: de Gruyter, 1991).

16. Myriam Miedzian, *Boys Will Be Boys: Breaking the Link Between Masculinity and Violence* (New York: Doubleday, 1991), 209; see also Charles R. Acland, *Youth, Murder, Spectacle: The Cultural Politics of "Youth in Crisis"* (Boulder, Colo: Westview Press, 1995).

17. Michael B. Poliakoff, *Combat Sports in the Ancient World: Competition, Violence, and Culture* (New Haven: Yale University Press, 1987).

18. David Sansone, *Anatomy of Sport: Greek Athletics and the Genesis of Sport* (Berkeley: University of California Press, 1988); Vera Olivova, *Sports and Games of the Ancient World* (New York: St. Martin's Press, 1985).

19. Dennis Brailsford, *Sport, Time and Society* (New York: Routledge, 1991).

20. Michael Farber, "The Worst Case," *Sports Illustrated,* 19 December 1994, 43–46; see also Tim Friend, "Alarm About 'Bell-Ringers' on the Rise," *USA Today,* 17 February 1995, sec. C, p. 7; Jarrett Bell, "Players Must Cope With Aftereffects," *USA Today,* 17 February 1995, sec. C, p. 7.

21. Peter King, "The Unfortunate 500," *Sports Illustrated,* 7 December 1992, 20–28; see also Peter King, "Halt the Head-Hunting," *Sports Illustrated,* 19 December 1994, 27–30, 37; John Ed Bradley, "Broken Promises," *Sports Illustrated,* 25 September 1995, 58–69; Rob Huizenga, *"You're Okay, It's Just a Bruise,"* (New York: St. Martin's Press, 1994).

22. King, "Halt the Head-Hunting," 29; see also Kevin Young, "Violence, Risk, and Liability in Male Sports Culture," *Sociology of Sport Journal* 10 (December 1993): 373–96.

23. E. M. Swift, "Hockey? Call it Sockey," *Sports Illustrated,* 17 February 1986, 14.

24. Jennings Bryant, "Viewers' Enjoyment of Televised Sport Violence," in *Media, Sport & Society,* ed. Lawrence A. Wenner (Newbury Park: Sage, 1989), 270–89.

25. Ibid., 287–88.

26. Richard O'Brien, "Fighting Words," *Sports Illustrated,* 15 March 1993, 9.

27. Chris Carlson, "When Violence Rules," *Sports Inc.,* 7 March 1988, 42.

28. Sally Jenkins, "Savage Assault," *Sports Illustrated,* 10 May 1993, 18–21; see also S. L. Price, "The Return," *Sports Illustrated,* 17 July 1995, 22–26; G. Russell "Athletes as Targets of Aggression," in *Targets of Violence and Aggression,* ed. Ronald Baenninger (New York: North-Holland, 1991).

29. E. M Swift, "Violence," *Sports Illustrated,* 17 January 1994, 16–21; E. M. Swift, "Look Who's In the Hot Seat," *Sports Illustrated,* 31 January 1994, 62–64; E. M. Swift, "Anatomy of a Plot," *Sports Illustrated,* 14 February 1994, 28–41; Sonja Steptoe and E. M. Swift, "A Done Deal," *Sports Illustrated,* 28 March 1994, 32–35.

30. Gerald Eskenazi, "The Male Athlete and Sexual Assault," *New York Times,* 14 March 1990, sec. 8, pp. 1, 4; Chris O'Sullivan, "Acquaintance Gang Rape on Campus," in *Acquaintance Rape: The Hidden Crime,* ed. A. Parrot and L. Bechhofer (New York: Wiley, 1991), 120–56; Jill Neimark, "Out of Bounds: The Truth About Athletes and Rape," *Mademoiselle,* May 1991, 196–99, 244–46; Weinberg, "Campus Crime Study Not Kind to Athletes," *USA Today* 21 February 1991, sec. C, p.2; Merrill Melnick, "Male Athletes and Sexual Assault," *Journal of Physical Education, Recreation, and Dance* 63 (May/June 1992): 32–35; Mariah B. Nelson, *The Stronger Women Get, the More Men Love Football: Sexism and the American Culture of Sports* (New York: Harcourt Brace, 1994), see especially chapter 7.

31. Todd W. Crosset, Jeffrey R. Benedict, and Mark A. McDonald, "Male Student-Athletes Reported for Sexual Assault: A Survey of Campus Police Departments and Judicial Affairs Offices," *Journal of Sport and Social Issues* 19 (May 1995): 126–40.

32. Steve Rushin and Sonja Steptoe, "Second Chance," *Sports Illustrated,* 3 July 1995, 34–40; G. Mihoces, "Rape Suit Implicates 20 Bengals," *USA Today,* 9 September 1992, sec. C, p. 1; see also Mike Messner and William Solomon, "Sin & Redemption: The Sugar Ray Leonard Wife-Abuse Story," in *Sex, Violence & Power in Sports: Rethinking Masculinity,* ed. Michael A. Messner and Donald F. Sabo (Freedom, Calif.: Crossing Press, 1994), 53–65; Nelson, *The Stronger Women Get, the More Men Love Football: Sexism and the American Culture of Sports,* see especially chapter 7.

33. Richard Hoffer, "Fatal Attraction?" *Sports Illustrated,* 27 June 1994, 16–31; William Nack and Lester Munson, "Sport's Dirty Secret," *Sports Illustrated,* 31 July 1995, 62–74; Janet Singleton, "Athletes and Abuse," *The Denver Post,* 9 March 1995, sec. E, pp. 1, 3.

34. Vance Johnson, *The Vance: The Beginning and the End* (Dubuque, Iowa: Kendall/Hunt, 1994).

35. Mary P. Koss et al., *No Safe Haven: Male Violence Against Women at Home, at Work, and in the Community* (Washington, D.C.: American Psychological Association, 1994); D. Scully, *Understanding Sexual Violence* (Boston: Unwin Hyman, 1990); Miedzian, *Boys Will Be Boys.*

36. Quoted in Lisa Faye Kaplan, "Sports Linked to Rape," *The Coloradoan,* 19 May 1990, sec. A, p. 8.

37. Catherine A. MacKinnon, *Feminism Unmodified: Discourses on Life and Law* (Cambridge, Mass.: Harvard University Press, 1987), 121; see also Joan Ryan, "Why Sports Heroes Abuse Their Wives," *Redbook,* September 1995, 83–85, 130–32; Jackson Katz, "Advertising and the Construction of Violent White Masculinity," in *Gender, Race and Class in Media,* ed. Gail Dines and Jean M. Humez (Thousand Oaks, Calif.: Sage, 1995).

38. Douglas E. Foley, *Learning Capitalist Culture: Deep in the Heart of Tejas* (Philadelphia: University of Pennsylvania Press, 1990), 52–53.

39. Charles E. Yesalis, ed., *Anabolic Steroids in Sport and Exercise* (Champaign, Ill.: Human Kinetics Publishers, 1993); "Steroids Linked to Violent Moods," *Rocky Mountain News,* 26 May 1994, sec. A, p. 48.

40. Rick Morrissey, "Fanning the Fury," *Rocky Mountain News,* 27 August 1995, sec. B, pp. 16–17.

41. Ibid., sec. B, p. 16.

42. Jeffrey H. Goldstein, "Sports Violence," in *Sport in Contemporary Society,* ed. D. Stanley Eitzen, 3d ed. (New York: St. Martin's Press, 1989), 83–84.

43. Tom Verducci, "The High Price of Hard Living," *Sports Illustrated,* 27 February 1995, 16–35.

44. Mickey Mantle, "I Was Killing Myself: My Life as an Alcoholic," *Sports Illustrated,* 18 April 1994, 66–77.

45. S. L. Price, "Lost Weekend," *Sports Illustrated,* 30 May 1994, 15–18.

46. Lyle Alzado, "I'm Sick and I'm Scared," *Sports Illustrated,* 8 July 1991, 20–24.

47. Charles B. Corbin et al., "Anabolic Steroids: A Study of High School Athletes," *Pediatric Exercise Sciences* 6 (1994): 149–58; see also Jeffrey A. Pottieger and Vincent G. Stilger, "Anabolic Steroid Use in the Adolescent Athlete," *Journal of Athletic Training* 29 (1994): 60–64; Scott E. Lucas, *Steroids* (Hillside, N.J.: Enslow Publishers, 1994); Yesalis, *Anabolic Steroids in Sport and Exercise.*

48. Rick Telander, "In the Aftermath of Steroids," *Sports Illustrated,* 27 January 1992, 103.

49. Terry Todd, "Anabolic Steroids: The Gremlins of Sport," in *Sport in America: From Wicked Amusement to National Obsession,* ed. David K. Wiggins (Champaign, Ill.: Human Kinetics Publishers, 1995), 285–300; see also John M. Hoberman, *Mortal Engines: The Science of Performance and the Dehumanization of Sport* (New York: Free Press, 1992), chapter 4.

50. Merrell Noden, "Dying to Win," *Sports Illustrated,* 8 August 1994, 52–60; see also Kathryn Zerbe, *The Body Betrayed: Women, Eating Disorders, and Treatment* (Washington, D.C.: American Psychiatric Press, 1993).

51. Jack McCallum and Kastya Kennedy, "Small Steps for a Big Problem," *Sports Illustrated,* 22 January 1996, 21–22; see also Nanci Hellmich, "Eating Disorders, A Desperate Dead End," *USA Today,* 2 August 1994, sec. D., p. 6; Herbert A. Haupt, "Substance Abuse by the Athletic Female," in *The Athletic Female,* ed. Arthus J. Pearl (Champaign, Ill.: Human Kinetics Publishers, 1993), 125–40.

52. Rick Morrissey, "Starving for Success," *Rocky Mountain News,* 28 May 1995, sec. B, pp. 1, 10–11; see also Joan Ryan, *Little Girls in Pretty Boxes* (New York: Doubleday, 1995), 9–10, 113–19; Nancy Clark, "Eating Disorders Among Athletic Females," in *The Athletic Female,* ed. Arthur J. Pearl (Champaign, Ill.: Human Kinetics Publishers, 1993), 141–47.

53. Elliott Currie, *Reckoning: Drugs, the Cities, and the American Future* (New York: Hill & Wang, 1993), 11.

54. Quoted in Rob Beamish, "Labor Relations in Sport: Central Issues in Their Emergence and Structure in High-Performance Sport," in *Sport in Social Development,* eds. Alan G. Ingham and John W. Loy (Champaign, Ill.: Human Kinetics Publishers, 1993), 203.

55. Quoted in Skip Rozin, "Steroids and Sports: What Price Glory?" *Business Week,* 17 October 1994, 177.

56. Quoted in "Opinions," *The NCAA News,* 26 September 1988, p. 4.

57. Quoted in "Opinions," *The NCAA News,* 6 July 1988, p. 5.

58. Gary I. Wadler and Brian Hainline, *Drugs and the Athlete* (Philadelphia: F. A. Davis, 1989), 238.

59. Quoted in James E. Wright and Virginia S. Cowart, *Anabolic Steroids: Altered States* (Carmel, Ind.: Benchmark Press, 1990), 196.

60. Currie, *Reckoning: Drugs, the Cities, and the American Future;* Beamish, "Labor Relations in Sport: Central Issues in Their Emergence and Structure in High-Performance Sport."

Chapter 8

Sport and Religion

On the one hand, there may seem to be little in common between sport and religion; going to church on Sunday, singing hymns, studying the Bible, and worshiping God all seem quite alien to the activities that we associate with sport. On the other hand, like religion, contemporary sport symbolically evokes fervent commitment from millions of people. Sports fans worship their favorite athletes much as followers of various religions worship their special deities. Also, sports fans, like religious groups, consider themselves to be part of a community. Finally, the rituals and ceremonies common to religion are paralleled by rituals and ceremonies in sport.

As sport and religion have become increasingly intertwined, each has made inroads into the traditional activities and prerogatives of the other. For Christians of previous generations, Sunday was the day reserved for church and worship, but with the increase in opportunities for recreational pursuits—both for participants and for spectators—and the virtual explosion of televised sports, worship on weekends has been replaced by worship of weekends. As a result, sport has captured Sunday, and churches have had to revise their schedules to oblige sport. At most Roman Catholic churches, convenient Saturday late-afternoon and evening services are now featured in addition to traditional Sunday masses, and other denominations frequently schedule services to accommodate the viewing of professional sports events. In many respects churches have had to share Sundays with sports, and the idea that the Sabbath should be reserved for worship now seems merely an absurd idea of the past.

At the same time that sport appears to be usurping religion's traditional time for worship and services, many churches and religious leaders are attempting to weld a link between the two activities by sponsoring sports events under religious auspices and by proselytizing athletes to religion and then using them as missionaries to spread the Word and to recruit new members. Thus, contemporary religion uses sport for the promotion of its causes.

Sport uses religion as well and in more ways than just seizing the traditional day of worship. People involved in sports—as participants or as spectators—employ numerous activities with religious connotations in connection with the contests. Ceremonies, rituals, taboos, fetishes, and so forth—all originating in religious practice—are standard observances in the world of sport.

In this chapter we shall examine the multidimensional relationship between religion and sport.

Religion and Society

Religion is the belief that supernatural forces influence human lives. There are many definitions of religion, but the one by French sociologist Emile Durkheim has perhaps been cited most. Durkheim said that "religion is a unified system of beliefs and practices relative to sacred things, that is to say, things set apart and forbidden—beliefs and practices which unite into one single moral community called a Church, all those who adhere to them."[1] As a social institution, religion is a system that functions to maintain and transmit beliefs about forces considered supernatural and sacred. It provides codified guides for moral conduct and prescribes symbolic practices deemed to be in harmony with beliefs about the supernatural. For all practical purposes we may assume that religious behavior among human beings is universal in that ethnologists and anthropologists have not yet discovered a human group without traces of the behavior we call "religious."[2]

Societies have a wide range of forms and activities associated with religion, including special officials (priests), ceremonies, rituals, sacred objects, places of worship, pilgrimages, and so forth. In modern societies, religious leaders have developed elaborate theories, or theologies, to explain the place of humans in the universe. Moreover, the world religions, including Christianity, Hinduism, Buddhism, Confucianism, Judaism, and Islam, are cores of elaborate cultural systems that have dominated world societies for centuries.

Social Functions of Religion

The term social functions as used here refers to the contribution that religion makes to the maintenance of human societies.* The focus is on what religion does

*Functionalism, as used in the social sciences, involves applying to social systems the biological notion that every organism has a structure made up of relatively stable interrelationships of parts.

and what it contributes to the survival and maintenance of societies and groups.

One of the first sociologists to write from a functionalist perspective was Emile Durkheim. He was also the first to apply functionalism to religion in a systematic way. According to Durkheim, religions exist because they perform important functions at several levels of human life, including individual, interpersonal, institutional, and societal.

At the individual level, religious experience meets psychic needs by providing individuals with emotional support in this uncertain world. The unpredictable and sometimes dangerous world produces personal fears and general anxiety that revering the powers of nature or seeking cooperation through religious faith and ritual may alleviate. Fears of death, too, are made bearable by beliefs in a supernatural realm into which a believer passes. If one can believe in a God-giving scheme of things, the universal quest for ultimate meaning is validated, and human strivings and sufferings seem to make some sense.

Religion functions at the interpersonal level as a form of human bonding. It unites a community of believers by bringing them together to enact various ceremonies and rituals, and it provides them with shared values and beliefs that bind them together. The need to proclaim human abilities and to achieve a sense of transcendence is met and indeed fostered by many religions through ceremonies and rituals that celebrate humans and their activities.

At the institutional level religion serves as a vehicle for social control; that is, religious tenets constrain the behavior of the community of believers to keep them in line with the norms, values, and beliefs of society. In all the major religions, morals and religion are intertwined, and schemes of otherworldly rewards or punishments for behavior, such as those found in Christianity, become powerful forces for morality. The fear of hellfire and damnation has been a powerful deterrent in the control of Christian societies. The virtues of honesty, conformity to sexual codes, and all the details of acceptable, moral behavior in a society become merged with religious beliefs and practices.

For society Durkheim argued that the paramount function of religion is social integration. It promotes a binding together both of the members of a society and of the social obligations that help unite them because it organizes the individual's experience in terms of ultimate meanings that include but also transcend the individual. When many people share this ordering principle, they can deal with each other in meaningful ways and can transcend themselves and their individual egoisms, sometimes even to the point of self-sacrifice.

Religious ceremonies and rituals also promote integration because they serve to reaffirm some of the basic customs and values of society. Here, the societal customs, folkways, and observances are symbolically elevated to the realm of the sacred. In expressing common beliefs about the supernatural, in engaging in collective worship activities, in recounting the lore and myths of the past, the community is brought closer together and linked with their heritage.

Another important integrative function that religion performs is bringing people with diverse backgrounds into meaningful relationships with one another. To the extent that religious groups can reach individuals who feel isolated and abandoned and who are not being relieved of their problems elsewhere, to that extent religion is serving society.

Another social integrative role of religion is that it tends to legitimize the secular social structures within a society. There is a strong tendency for religious ideology to become united with the norms and values of secular structures, producing, as a consequence, religious support for the values and institutions of society. From its earliest existence, religion has provided rationales that serve the needs and actions of a society's leaders. It has legitimized as "God-given" such disparate ideologies as absolute monarchies and egalitarian democracies.

In contrast to sociologists who emphasize only the beneficial functions of religion for the individual and society, there are others who view the inclinations of people to create gods and believe in supernatural phenomena as instrumentally useful for powerful and wealthy

---

Each of these parts performs a specialized task, or function, that permits the organism to survive and to act. With respect to societies, this notion assumes that societies consist of elements, each of which performs a specific function contributing to the overall survival and actions of the society.

groups to promote their privileged status and justify socially inequitable conditions. This latter approach to religion was articulated most clearly by Karl Marx, who believed that religion was primarily a tool of the rich and powerful to produce a "false consciousness" in the masses of people. One of Marx's most well-known ideas was that religion is a means for legitimating the interests of the dominant class, justifying existing social injustices and inequalities, and, like a narcotic, lulling people into ready acceptance of the status quo. He said: "Religion is the sigh of the oppressed creature, the heart of a heartless world, and the soul of soulless conditions. It is the opium of the people."[3]

The Relationship of Religion and Sport

Primitive Societies

Some historians who have studied the origins of sport claim that sport began as a religious rite.[4] The ball games of the Mayans and Aztecs are examples of primitive societies that included physical activities as part of their religious rituals and ceremonies. The purpose of many games of primitive peoples was rooted in a desire to gain victory over foes seen and unseen, to influence the forces of nature, and to promote fertility among crops and cattle. The Zuni Indians of New Mexico played games that they believed would bring rain and thus enable their crops to grow. In southern Nigeria, wrestling matches were held to encourage the growth of crops, and various games were played in the winter to hasten the return of spring and to ensure a bountiful season. One Eskimo tribe, at the end of the harvest season, played a cup-and-ball game to "catch the sun" and thus delay its departure. In his monumental work on the Plains Indians, Stewart Culin wrote: "In general, games appear to be played ceremonially, as pleasing to the gods, with the objective of securing fertility, causing rain, giving and prolonging life, expelling demons, or curing sickness."[5]

Ancient Greece

The ancient Greeks, who worshiped beauty, entwined religious observance with their athletic demonstrations in such a way that to define where one left off and the other began is difficult. Greek gods were anthropomorphic (humanlike), and sculptors portrayed the gods as perfect physical specimens who were to be both admired and emulated by their worshipers. The strong anthropomorphic conceptions of gods held by the Greeks led to their belief that the gods took pleasure in the same things that mortals enjoyed such as music, drama, and displays of physical excellence. The gymnasia located in every city-state for all male adults (females were not allowed in the Greek gymnasia) provided facilities and places for sports training as well as for the discussion of intellectual topics. Furthermore, facilities for religious worship, an altar and a chapel, were located in the center of each gymnasium.

The most important athletic meetings of the Greeks were part of religious festivals. The Olympic Games were sacred contests, staged in a sacred location and as a sacred festival; they were a religious act in honor of Zeus, king of the gods. Athletes who took part in the Olympics did so in order to please Zeus and the prizes they won came from him. Other Panhellenic games were equally religious in nature. Victorious athletes presented their gifts of thanks upon the altar of the god or gods whom they thought to be responsible for their victory. The end of the ancient Olympic Games was a result of the religious conviction of Theodosius, the Roman emperor of A.D. 392–395. He was a Christian and decreed the end of the games as part of his suppression of paganism in favor of Christianity.[6]

The Early Christian Church

In western societies, religious support for sport found no counterpart to that of the Greeks until the beginning of the twentieth century. The Christian religion was dominated by the Roman Catholic Church until the Reformation in the sixteenth century. Since then Roman Catholicism has shared religious power with Protestant groups. At first Christians opposed Roman sport spectacles such as chariot racing and gladiatorial combat because of their paganism and brutality, but later Christians opposed sport because they came to regard the human body as an instrument of sin.

The early Christians did not view sports as evil per se, for the Apostle Paul wrote approvingly of the benefits of physical activity. He said, for example, "Do you not know that those who run in a race, all indeed run, but one receives the prize? So run as to obtain it" (1 Cor. 9:24–25). In another place, Paul reminded Timothy of the importance of adhering to the rules: "If anyone contends even in the games, he is not crowned unless he has contended according to the rules" (2 Tim. 2:5).

The paganism prominent in the Roman sports events, however, was abhorrent to the Christians. Moreover, early Christianity gradually built a foundation based on asceticism, which is a belief that evil exists in the body and that therefore the body should be subordinate to the pure spirit. As a result, church dogma and education sought to subordinate all desires and demands of the body in order to exalt the spiritual life. Twelfth-century Catholic abbot, Saint Bernard, argued: "Always in a robust and active body the mind lies soft and more lukewarm; and, on the other hand, the spirit flourishes more strongly and more actively in an infirm and weakly body." Nothing could have been more damning for the promotion of active recreation and sport.

Spiritual salvation was the dominant feature of the Christian faith. Accordingly, the cultivation of the body was to be subordinated to the salvation of the spirit, especially since the body, it was believed, could obstruct the realization of this aim. An otherwise enlightened Renaissance scholar, Desiderius Erasmus, while a monk at a monastery (before he became a critic of Roman Catholicism), wrote an essay "On the Contempt of the World," which articulately characterized the Christian attitude of his time toward body and soul:

> The monks do not choose to become like cattle; they know that there is something sublime and divine within man which they prefer to develop rather than cater for the body. . . . Our body, except for a few details, differs not from an animal's body but our soul reaches out after things divine and eternal. The body is earthly, wild, slow, mortal, diseased, ignoble; the soul on the other hand is heavenly, subtle, divine, immortal, noble. Who is so blind that he cannot tell the difference between body and soul? And so the happiness of the soul surpasses that of the body.[7]

The Reformation and the Rise of Protestantism

The Reformation of the early sixteenth century signaled the end of the viselike grip that Roman Catholicism had on the minds and habits of the people of Europe and England. With the Reformation, the pejorative view of sports might have perished wherever the teachings of Martin Luther and John Calvin prevailed. Protestantism had within it, though, the seeds of a new asceticism, and the Calvinism imported to England, in its Puritan form, became a greater enemy to sport than Roman Catholicism had been.

Puritan influence grew throughout the sixteenth century and by the early seventeenth century had come to have considerable influence on English life. Moreover, since Puritans were among the earliest English immigrants to America, they had considerable influence on the social life in the colonies. Perhaps no Christian group exercised a greater opposition to sport than the Puritans. One historian asserted that the Puritans saw their mission to erase all sport and play from men's lives because they "found only sin and error in the people's customary play. . . . Sport and recreation could make no justifiable calls on the time of the virtuous.[8] The Puritans gave to England the "English Sunday" and to the United States its equivalent, the blue laws, which until a few decades ago managed to bar sports on the Sabbath and severely limit the kinds of sports played to those that were considered appropriate for Christians.

As a means of realizing amusement and unrestrained impulses, sport was suspect for the Puritan; as it approached mere pleasure or involved physical harm to participants or to animals (e.g., boxing and cockfighting) or promoted gambling, sport was, of course, altogether evil. The renowned nineteenth-century English historian Thomas B. Macaulay claimed that the Puritans opposed bearbaiting not so much because it was painful for the bear but because it gave pleasure to the spectators.

From the Seventeenth to the Twentieth Century

The principal relationship between the church and sport for the early North American settlers was one of restriction and probation, especially with regard to sports on the Sabbath. Soon after the first English settlement was established in the American colonies, a group of Virginia ministers enacted legislation prohibiting sports participation on Sunday. Such repressive acts are more commonly associated with the Puritans in New England who enacted similar legislation. Actually, most of the colonies passed laws against play and sport on the Sabbath, and it was not until the mid-twentieth century that industrial and economic conditions brought about the repeal of most of these laws, although most had been annulled by custom.[9]

There were a number of reasons for Protestant prejudice against play and sport among the early settlers. One prominent objection was that participation would divert attention from spiritual matters. There was also the belief that play and its resultant pleasure might become addictive because of the inherent weakness of human nature. The practical matter was that survival in the New World required hard work from everyone; thus, time spent in play and games was typically considered time wasted. Finally, the associations formed and the environment in which play and sport occurred conspired to cast these activities in a bad light. The tavern was the center for gambling and table sports, dancing had obvious sexual overtones, and field sports often involved gambling and cruelty to animals.

Church opposition to leisure pursuits was firmly maintained in the first few decades of the nineteenth century, and each effort to liberalize attitudes toward leisure pursuits was met with a new attack on sport as "sinful." Sports were still widely regarded by the powerful Protestant religious groups as snares of the devil himself. However, in the 1830s social problems became prominent concerns of American social reformers, many of whom were clergy and intellectual leaders. There were crusades against slavery, intemperance, and poor industrial working conditions; widespread support for the emancipation of women, for public education, and for industrial reform; and indeed, scrutiny of every facet of American life. One aspect of this comprehensive social-reform movement was the concern for human health and physical fitness.[10]

Social conditions had begun to change rapidly under the aegis of industrialization. The population was shifting from rural to urban residence, and labor changed from agricultural toil to work for wages in squalid working and living conditions. The physical health of the population became a major problem, leading a number of reformers to propose that people would be happier, more productive, and healthier if they engaged in vigorous sports activities. Surprisingly, some of the leading advocates of play and sport were clerics, and from their pulpits they presented forceful arguments that physical prowess and sanctity were not incompatible. Intellectual leaders also joined the movement.

The proposals of support for physical fitness and wholesome leisure had a profound effect on the church. Responding to the temporal needs of the people, the clergy began to shed much of the otherworldly emphasis and sought to alleviate immediate human problems. Recognizing the need for play and the health benefits of leisure amusements, the church began to soften its attitude toward play and sport. Although the development of a more liberal attitude by church leaders toward sport began to appear by the mid-nineteenth century, not all church authorities subscribed to the trend. A staid Congregationalist magazine, the *New Englander,* vigorously attacked sport:

> Let our readers, one and all, remember that we were sent into this world, not for sport and amusement, but for labor; not to enjoy and please ourselves, but to serve and glorify God, and be useful to our fellow men. That is the great object and end in life. In pursuing this end, God has indeed permitted us all needful diversion and recreation. . . . But the great end of life after all is work. . . . It is a true saying. . . . "We come into this world, not for sports." We were sent here for a higher and nobler object.[11]

In official publications and public speeches, some church leaders fought the encroaching sport and leisure mania throughout the late nineteenth century. There was a growing awareness, however, that disapproving churches were fighting a losing war. Church leaders gradually began to reconcile play and religion in response to pressure from medical, educational, and political leaders for games and sport. These activities were believed to aid in the development of physical, mental, and, indeed, moral health.

To meet the social needs of rural and city members, churches adopted sports and sponsored recreations to draw people together, and church leadership played an important part in the promotion of community recreation and school physical education in the latter part of the nineteenth century. Many clergy used their church halls and grounds as recreation centers. The playground movement in America began in 1885 when the sand gardens were opened in the yards of the West End Nursery and the Parmenter Street Chapel in Boston. The New York City Society for Parks and Playgrounds got its start in 1890 with the support of clergymen who delivered sermons to their congregations on children's need for playgrounds.[12]

Support for physical education found its way into denominational journals and meetings, and religious support for physical education helped promote its acceptance by colleges and its eventual adoption by public school boards across the country. The Young Men's Christian College (now Springfield College) at Springfield, Massachusetts, made sport and physical fitness one of the cornerstones of a proper Christian education and lifestyle.

Increasingly, churches broadened their commitment to play and sport endeavors as means of drawing people together. Bowling leagues, softball leagues, and youth groups, such as the Catholic Youth Organization (CYO), were sponsored by churches for their young members. The church's prejudice against pleasure through play had broken down almost completely by the beginning of the twentieth century.

Twentieth–Century North America

Churches have been confronted with ever-increasing changes in the twentieth century; economic pressures, political movements, and social conditions have been the chief forces responsible for the drastically changed relationship between religion and sport. Increased industrialization turned the population into a nation of urban dwellers, and higher wages were responsible for an unprecedented affluence. The gospel of work (the Protestant work ethic) became less credible, and increased leisure has enhanced the popularity of sports. The story of changes in the attitudes of religionists in the twentieth century is largely one of increasing accommodation. Much of both Catholic and Protestant North America have come to view sport as a positive force and even as a useful means of promoting God's work. Sports and leisure activities have become an increasingly conspicuous part of the recreation programs of thousands of churches and many church colleges.

Clergy of many religions and denominations who over the centuries preached that sport is a handmaiden of the devil must be shifting uneasily in their graves at trends of the past half century. Times have certainly changed, the church as well, and the reconciliation between sport and organized religion has approached finality.

Sport As Religion

In the past generation the powers and influence of sport have increased enormously, and at the same time formalized religion and the institutional church have suffered a decline of interest and commitment as society has undergone secularization. During this process of social change, sport has taken on so many of the characteristics of religion that some have argued that sport has emerged as a new religion, supplementing, and in some cases even supplanting, traditional religious expressions. A noted Catholic theologian, claims that "Sports are religious in the sense that they are organized institutions, disciplines, and liturgies; and also in the sense that they teach religious qualities of heart and soul. In particular, they recreate symbols of cosmic struggle, in which human survival and moral courage are not assured. To this extent, they are not mere games, diversions, pastimes. . . . Sports, in a word, are a form of godliness."[13]

A professor in the religious studies program at Pennsylvania State University is even more emphatic on this point:

For me, it is not just a parallel that is emerging between sport and religion, but rather *a complete identity. Sport is religion* for growing numbers of Americans, and this is no product of simply facile reasoning or wishful thinking. Further, for many, sport religion has become a more appropriate expression of personal religiosity than Christianity, Judaism, or any of the traditional religions. . . . It is reasonable to consider sport the newest and fastest growing religion, far outdistancing whatever is in second.[14]

When he was President of the International Olympic Committee, Avery Brundage claimed that the Olympic Movement itself was a religion: "The Olympic Movement is a Twentieth Century religion, a religion with universal appeal which incorporates all the basic values of other religions, a modern, exciting, virile, dynamic religion. . . . It is a religion for which Pierre de Coubertin was the prophet, for Coubertin has kindled a torch that will enlighten the world."[15]

There is no doubt that organized sport has taken on the trappings of religion. A few examples will illustrate this point. Every religion has its gods (or saints or high priests) who are venerated by its members. Likewise, sports fans have gods (superstar athletes) they worship. They also have their saints, those who have passed to the great beyond (such as Jim Thorpe, Knute Rockne, Babe Ruth, and Babe Didrikson Zaharias). The high priests of contemporary sport are the professional, collegiate, and national amateur team coaches who not only direct the destinies of their athletes but also control the emotions of large masses of sports fans.

Sport also has its scribes, the sport journalists and sportscasters who disseminate the "word" of sports deeds and glories; its houses of worship, such as the Astrodome and Yankee Stadium;* and its masses of highly vocal "true believers." Numerous proverbs fill the world of sport: "Nice guys finish last"; "When the going gets tough, the tough get going"; "Lose is a

four-letter word"; and so forth. These proverbs are frequently written on posters and hung in locker rooms for athletes to memorize.

The achievements of athletes and teams are celebrated in numerous shrines built throughout the country to commemorate and glorify sporting figures. These halls of fame have been established for virtually every sport played in North America, and some sports have several halls of fame devoted to them. They preserve the sacred symbols and memorabilia that direct us to rehearse the triumphs of the "saints" who have moved on.[16]

Symbols of fidelity abound in sport. The athletes are expected to give total commitment to the cause, including abstinence from smoking, alcohol, and in some cases, even sex. The devout followers who witness and invoke traditional and hallowed chants show their devotion to the team and add "spirit" to its cause. It is not unusual for these pilgrims to travel hundreds of miles, sometimes braving terrible weather conditions, to witness a game, thus displaying their fidelity.

Like religious institutions, sport has become a function of communal involvement. In an article entitled "The Super Bowl as Religious Festival" the author commented: "There is a remarkable sense in which the Super Bowl functions as a major religious festival for American culture, for the event signals a convergence of sports, politics and myth. Like festivals in ancient societies, which made no distinctions regarding the religious, political and sporting character of certain events, the Super Bowl succeeds in reuniting these now disparate dimensions of social life."[17]

Perhaps the most salient role that sport-as-religion plays for communal involvement is in the sense of belonging and of community that it evokes. In cheering for the Green Bay Packers, the New York Yankees, or the Montreal Canadiens, one belongs to a "congregation." The emotional attachment of some fans to their teams verges on the religious fanaticism previously seen in holy wars against heretics and pagans. Opposing teams and their fans, as well as officials, are occasionally attacked and brutally beaten.

In the past few years, two popular motion pictures, "Field of Dreams" and "Bull Durham," have used

---

*A favorite story of Texans concerns the home field of the Dallas Cowboys. The stadium has a roof that covers most of the stands but is open over the playing field. Fans say that God wants to be able to see his favorite football team more clearly.

numerous religious themes and symbols suggesting baseball-as-religion. They do not claim that baseball is a religion in a traditional theological way with Jesus present, but they do suggest a symbiosis (an intimate association or close union) between the two. "Bull Durham" opens with gospel music in the background and the female lead, Annie, delivering the prologue: "I believe in the church of baseball. I've tried all the major religions and most of the minor ones. . . . I gave Jesus a chance, but it just didn't work out between us. The Lord laid too much guilt on me. . . . There's no guilt in baseball, and it's never boring. . . . The only church that truly feeds the soul, day in and day out, is the church of baseball."

"Field of Dreams" makes clear its baseball-as-religion point of view. In the basic plot a supernatural voice of revelation tells a young farmer and baseball fanatic to plow up part of his corn fields and build a baseball field. The farmer does this, and soon baseball players from the past are playing on the baseball diamond, like saints from a land beyond the first rows of the cornfield. After the farmer has made a pilgrimage and faced his need for forgiveness, he is miraculously reconciled with his long-dead baseball-player father. At the end of the movie, the farmer's baseball field is a shrine that draws flocks of people seeking "the truth." The movie has many religious themes and symbols: life after death, a seeker who hears a voice and has to go on a spiritual quest, an inner healing, becoming a child in order to enter the kingdom, and losing your life to gain it.

In spite of the many seeming parallels between sport and religion, sport does not fulfill what are considered by many to be the key functions of "churchly" religion. For example, why humans are created and continue to wrestle with their purpose here on earth and life hereafter are not addressed by sports. In this regard, one social scientist noted:

> Sport has nothing whatever to do with such questions [of ultimate meaning]. While sport may provide us with examples of belief, ritual, sacrifice, and transcendence, all of them take place in a context designed wittingly and specifically by human beings, for the delight of human

beings. . . . Sport per se cannot tell us where we came from, where we are going, nor how we are to behave while here. Sports exist to entertain and engage us, not to disturb us with questions about our destiny. That is the uncomfortable prerogative of religion.[18]

Other critics of sport-as-religion also emphasize that many activities that humans become deeply committed to can be referred to as a religion, when speaking metaphorically, but if we include in religion all meaningful or spiritual activities, we then wind up including practically all activities into which humans pour their will, emotions, and energy. Although sport does have some religiouslike symbols, rituals, legends, sacred spaces and time, and heroes, it is organized and played by humans for humans without supernatural sanction.

Religion Uses Sport

Churches

From a position of strong opposition to recreation and sport activities, most religions have made a complete reversal within the past century and now heartily support these activities as effective tools to promote "the Lord's work." Social service is a major purpose of the religious leaders who provide play and recreation under the auspices of their churches. Church-sponsored recreation and sport programs offer services to members and sometimes the entire community that are often unavailable in acceptable forms anywhere else. Church playgrounds and recreation centers in urban areas have facilities, equipment, and instruction that municipal governments often cannot provide. The Young Men's Christian Association (YMCA), the Young Women's Christian Association (YWCA), the CYO, and other church-related organizations perform a variety of social services for old and young alike, one of which is the sponsorship of sports leagues.

Promoting sport to strengthen and increase fellowship in their congregations has been beneficial to the churches as well as to their members. In a time of increasing secularization, such as that witnessed by the United States and Canada in the past fifty years, it is understandable that churches would accommodate activities that solidify and integrate church membership.

Religious Leaders

Not content merely to provide recreational and sports opportunities under the sponsorship of the church, some religious leaders outwardly avow the association between religion and sport in their preaching and use sport as a metaphor for the social enterprise of the church. Jerry Falwell, one of the self-styled leaders of fundamental Protestantism in the United States, told an audience: "He [Jesus] wants you to be a victor for God's glory. A champion is not an individual star but one of a team who knows how to function with others." One of the most popular contemporary evangelists, Billy Graham, enthusiastically supports the virtues of sports competition and the sanctity of Christian coaches and athletes. He has made sport a basic metaphor in his ministry. According to Graham, the source of Christianity, the Bible, legitimates sport involvement: "The Bible says leisure and lying around are morally dangerous for us. . . . Sports keep us busy."

Church Colleges and Universities

Intercollegiate sports programs were originally organized and administered by the students merely for their own recreation and amusement. By the early years of the twentieth century, however, the programs gradually changed form and character, and one of the new features that emerged was the use of collegiate sports teams to publicize the school and to bind alumni to their alma mater. Church-supported colleges and universities began to use their athletic teams to attract students, funds, and public attention to impoverished (and sometimes academically inferior) institutions. The classic, but by no means only, example is Notre Dame; many other Roman Catholic colleges and universities, also, have used football and basketball for publicity. Basketball, especially, has become a popular sport for Catholic colleges; indeed, Catholic university teams have played in the NCAA basketball championship games several times.

Protestant institutions have followed the same pattern of using their athletic teams to advertise; Brigham Young University, Texas Christian University, and Southern Methodist University are among the most visible. Of these, BYU has become the most renowned athletic powerhouse. It meshes conservative religious tenets with big-time sports and produces some of the more prominent professional athletes in North America. One All-American football player said: "The athletes bring more attention to the Morman church than anything else. When I came here, the president of the university told me, 'Here's your chance to be a missionary for the church by playing football for us.' "[19]

Liberty University, founded by Jerry Falwell, has aggressively embraced big-time athletics to publicize the school, and, according to Falwell, "use the school as a means of carrying out our higher mission, which is preaching the gospel of Christ to the world." Falwell goes on, "we probably place as high a priority on sports, if not higher, than many of the major universities. Sport to us—we don't deify it—but we nearly do."[20]

Falwell wants to make Liberty University to born-again Christians what Notre Dame is to Catholics and Brigham Young University is to Mormons. To this end, he hired a former NFL coach to lead the football team and a former major leaguer to coach the baseball team. The football coach claims, "[W]e're here to bring the word of Christ to as many people as possible—if we can do it in the Rose Bowl playing UCLA, then fine."[21]

Ironically, it was a church college, Southern Methodist University, that was hit with the most severe penalty ever meted out by the NCAA, the so-called death penalty (abolishment of the football program for a period of time). The NCAA took this drastic action after those connected with the SMU football program continually lied, cheated, and generally violated NCAA rules.[22]

Religious Organizations and Sports

One of the most notable outgrowths of religion's use of sport has been the rise of nondenominational religious organizations composed of coaches and athletes. These organizations provide a variety of programs designed to serve current members and recruit new members to religion. Several major incorporated organizations offer everything from national conferences to services before games. The most well known are Sports Ambassadors, Fellowship of Christian Athletes (FCA), Athletes in Action (AIA), Pro Athletes Outreach (PAO), Sports World Ministries, and Baseball Chapel. The movement that these organizations represent has been labeled "Sportianity" or, more derisively, "Jocks for Jesus." [23]

The prototypical organization for using sport as a tool for evangelism was Venture for Victory, which traces its beginnings back to the early 1950s. Since then, Venture for Victory has gone through a series of organizational changes to emerge as Sports Ambassadors. Sports Ambassadors uses international sports for evangelism and prepares Christian coaches and athletes for competent growth and service for Christ.

The Fellowship of Christian Athletes

The Fellowship of Christian Athletes was founded in 1954 with a focus on high school and college coaches and athletes. Its avowed purpose, which appears on most of its official publications and on the title page of each issue of *Sharing the Victory,* is "to present to athletes and coaches, and all whom they influence, the challenge and adventure of receiving Jesus Christ as Savior and Lord, serving him in their relationship and in the fellowship of the Church." The FCA attempts to combat juvenile delinquency, elevate the moral and spiritual standards of sports in a secular culture, challenge Americans to stand up and be counted for or against God, and appeal to sports enthusiasts and American youth through hero worship harnessed.

The FCA uses older athletes and coaches to recruit younger ones to Christ. It has a mailing list of more than fifty-five thousand persons and a staff of over thirty. Its most important activity is the sponsorship of annual, week-long summer conferences attended by thousands of participants, where coaches and athletes mix religious and inspirational sessions with sport instruction and competition.

Another important facet of the FCA's work is the "huddle fellowship program," in which high school

and college athletes in a community or on a campus get together to talk about their faith, engage in Bible study, and pray. They also take part in projects such as becoming "big brothers" for delinquent or needy children, visiting nursing homes, and serving as playground instructors. There are now some five thousand high school and college huddles in North America, the bulk of which are found in the South, Southwest, and Midwest. Most of the members of the FCA are white, middle-class males; however, female athletes are admitted to the FCA, and their membership in the organization is growing. In addition to these activities, the FCA sponsors state and regional retreats and provides various informational materials such as films, records, and tapes. [24]

Organizations that focus on specific athletic groups supplement the work of the FCA. The National Football League (NFL) and major baseball leagues sponsor chapels and Bible studies for their athletes. Major league baseball, in addition to providing Sunday chapel for all teams, has produced an evangelical film called "God's Game Plan," which relates real-life experiences and the on-field action of many of the ball players who have made a vital commitment to Jesus Christ.

Sport and Missionary Work of Churches

The use of sport as a drawing card has been a major consideration for many religious leaders. An often-used slogan nicely sums up their view: "Many a one who comes to play remains to pray." Getting persons into church recreation and sports programs is often viewed as a first step into the church and into Christian life. Playgrounds and recreation centers in or near churches, and the supervision of these facilities by clergy or laypersons with a strong religious commitment, provide a convenient setting for converting the nonchurchgoing participant. A great deal of informal but successful missionary work is done in these settings. Famous sports figures make effective missionaries because of their prominence and prestige, and virtually every religious group has used coaches and athletes as evangelists to recruit new members.

There are several dozen ministry groups within North America working with international religious groups to mobilize massive recruiting efforts at the site of each Olympic Game. They use the Olympic Games, the most prestigious sporting event in the world—and an event that attracts people from all over the world—as a venue for recruiting people to Christianity. They sponsored a World Congress on Sport prior to the 1988 Seoul Olympic Games and a similar Congress at the 1992 Olympics in Barcelona, Spain. These groups held one of their largest Christian recruiting efforts of all time at the Atlanta Olympic Games.

Athletes in Action

Of all the purposes or consequences or both of religion's association with sport, certainly one of the most important is the use of athletes, coaches, and the sports environment to recruit new members to the church. Evangelical athletes who have made a personal commitment to Christ accept the responsibility of witnessing their faith to others. As a result, the practice of athletes and coaches serving as lay evangelists is so widespread that it has been called a modern crusade.

One of the best known of the sport missionary groups is a division of the Campus Crusade for Christ called Athletes in Action (AIA), an organization made up mostly of former collegiate athletes. Its purpose is "to use the ready-made platform of sports to share the adventure and excitement of following Christ."[25] With a special dispensation from the NCAA, the AIA fields several athletic teams that compete against amateur teams throughout the world each year. As part of each appearance of an AIA team, the AIA athletes make brief evangelical speeches and testimonials to the crowds and distribute free religious materials.

Athletes As Evangelists

One major advantage of using athletes to sell religion is access. They interact closely and for prolonged periods of time with other athletes, and because they are widely admired, they are warmly welcomed by the general public. The missionary techniques of athletes are fairly straightforward. Those who are already committed to religion convert the others. Since athletes are among the most visible and prestigious persons in our society, they may be used for missionary work in spreading the gospel not only to their teammates but to anyone with whom they come in contact. Religious witnessing among athletes is tolerated and has become rather common in all sports in the past decade.[26]

Combining their popular appeal as celebrities with the metaphors of the sports world, athletes are able to catch and hold the attention of large groups of people. As one researcher noted, "as a mode of evangelism, sport has few rivals in modern religious history. Sports fans who wouldn't dream of visiting church to hear the eloquent sermons of a seminarian will listen patiently to an athlete's stammering tribute to God, guts, and glory."[27]

A high profile athlete who understands the basics of his/her faith can reach more people, and especially young people, than a typical priest or minister can ever hope to reach. Many pro teams have a "God Squad," a group of teammates who pray together and make public appearances on behalf of the Christian cause. Several NBA teams have sponsored a God and Country Night for their fans, a mixing of basketball, church, and state that attempts to recognize the role faith and patriotism play in the lives of management, players, and fans associated with the NBA.

The Promise Keepers: Sportianity, Gender, and Sexuality

In 1990 Bill McCartney, the University of Colorado football coach, and a dedicated evangelical Christian, started The Promise Keepers. It has become one of the country's fastest growing religious movements. The first meeting in Boulder, Colorado, in 1990 attracted 70 people; by 1996 over a dozen meetings were held nationwide, with between 20,000 and 75,000 in attendance at each. By the year 2000, Promise Keeper leaders plan to draw 2 million men to its meetings.

The central philosophical message of the Promise Keepers is that God commanded that men be the dominant, the head of the family, and men must reclaim their leadership in the family and in the community, thus becoming better men of God.[28] The traditional patriarchal gender role, with men as the family leader, is said to be dictated by God. McCartney says, "It's always been mandated by God that the spiritual leaders be men. It's always been God's heart that men would set the tone. . . . We are bonded. We are men of God."[29] One journalist summarized the logic of the

Promise Keepers in this way: "Christ is the head of man, and man is the head of the home. And we'll bless and honor our wives. And they'll be a lot better off than they would be as women's liberationists."[30]

The Promise Keepers shares the position of religious fundamental Protestants and the Catholic Church that homosexuality violates God's creative design for males and females. McCartney has publicly denounced homosexuality as "an abomination of almighty God," and he was a member of a group that sponsored a ballot measure in Colorado barring civil-rights ordinances that insure homosexuals' rights.[31] (Colorado voters approved the measure, but it has been declared unconstitutional by the U.S. Supreme Court in 1996.)

The researchers of a study focusing on The Promise Keepers and its connections with sports, Christianity, and masculinity noted:

> The Promise Keepers have used the cultural symbols of sport in their descriptions of proper masculine behavior. The historical and cultural significance of sport carries great weight, and when that is combined with a mandate from God, the Promise Keepers ability to reach men becomes more powerful. McCartney's direct connection with football, as well as many of the metaphors used [by the leaders of The Promise Keepers], help to legitimate the acceptance of God because there is a direct parallel between traditional manliness associated with sport and being a "Godly man."[32]

Sportianity and Social Issues

There is little inclination on the part of religious leaders and the various organizations that make up Sportianity to confront the pressing social issues of sport or of the larger society. Virtually all of the leaders in the Sportianity movement are fundamentalists who preach a conservative theology. They are generally reluctant to take a stand on moral issues within sports or within the wider society. In reviewing the numerous publications circulated by the organizations involved in Sportianity, one thing stands out rather glaringly, namely that little direct effort is being channeled into improving the morality of sports.

There is no noticeable social reform movement on the part of the Sportianity movement. The various organizations and their members have not spoken out against racism, sexism, cheating, violence, the evils of collegiate athletic recruiting, or any of the other well-known unethical practices, excesses, and abuses in the world of sport, with the exception of exhortations about refraining from drugs. Instead, the pervasive theme is stick with the positive, don't deal with the problems in sports. The impression is don't stir the waters. Just publicize the good story about the good ole boy who does good things.

In the final analysis, then, sports morality does not appear to have been improved by the Sportianity movement. Instead, Sportianity seems willing to accept sport as is and seems more devoted to maintaining the status quo than to dealing with sports as a social practice with many of the same problems of the larger society that need attention and resolution.

Value Orientations of Religion and Sport

The value orientations underlying competitive sports in North America may appear only remotely connected with religion, but most values that are central to sports are more or less secularized versions of the core values of Protestantism, which has been a dominant religious belief system throughout American and Canadian history.

The Protestant Ethic

The classic treatise of the Protestant ethic and its relationship to other spheres of social life is Max Weber's *The Protestant Ethic and the Spirit of Capitalism,* originally published near the turn of the century.[33] The essence of Weber's thesis is that there is a parallel relationship between the Calvinist doctrine of Protestantism as a theological belief system and the growth of capitalism as a mode of economic organization. Weber suggested the relationship between Protestantism and capitalism was one of mutual influence; he used the term "elective affinity" (one of his translator's used the word "correlation" in place of elective affinity).

The relationship existed in this way: For John Calvin, God could foresee and therefore know the future; thus, the future was predestined. In a world whose future was foreordained, the fate of every person was preestablished. Each person was, then, saved or doomed from birth by a kind of divine decree; nothing the individual did could change what God had done. Although each person's fate was sealed, the individual was plagued by "salvation anxiety" and craved some visible sign of his or her fate; and since Calvin taught that those elected by God acted in a godly manner, the elected could exhibit their salvation by glorifying God, especially by their work in this world.

According to Weber, "the only way of living acceptably to God . . . was through the fulfillment of obligations imposed upon the individual by . . . his calling." Thus, the best available sign of being among the chosen was to do one's job, to follow one's profession, to succeed in one's chosen career. According to Weber, "In practice this means that God helps those who help themselves." Work per se was exalted; indeed, it was sacred. The clearest manifestation of being chosen by God was success in one's work. Whoever enjoyed grace could not fail since success at work was visible evidence of election. Thus, successful persons could think of themselves, and be thought of by others, as the righteous persons. The upshot was that this produced an extreme drive toward individual achievement, resulting in what Weber called "ascetic Protestantism," a life of strict discipline and hard work as the best means of glorifying God.[34]

Although the Protestant ethic gave divine sanction to the drive to excel and encouraged success in business, industry, and science, it condemned the material enjoyment of success. The chosen person merely used success to document salvation. Persons who used success for personal gratification and luxury merely showed that they were doomed by God. To avoid the accumulation of vast personal wealth, Calvinism promoted the reinvestment of profits to produce more goods, which created more profits and, in turn, represented more capital for investment ad infinitum, the essence of entrepreneurial capitalism.

Weber's study of the relationship between religious beliefs and capitalism investigated the religious principles that provided a rationale for the ideology of capitalism and for the authority of the capitalist. The spirit of capitalism, according to Weber, consisted of several principles, each of which was compatible with Protestant principles. Collectively, they constituted a clear, elective affinity (correlation) between Calvinist Protestantism and the spirit of capitalism. Weber made it quite clear that he was not suggesting that one social process was a causal agent for the other. In his final paragraph, he said: "It is . . . not my aim to substitute for a one-sided materialistic an equally one-sided spiritualistic causal interpretation of culture and history."[35]

What does this have to do with sport? It is rather obvious that Weber's notion about the relationship between the Protestant ethic and the spirit of capitalism can be applied to the "spirit" of sport. Here is how:

> If work has intrinsic worth and carries with it high standards of excellence, the activity of the serious athlete could be seen as reflecting these elements of dedication and striving for excellence. If worldly success is a sign of membership in the elect, sport success could be considered such a sign. If a strongly ascetic approach to life is encouraged, the discipline of athletic training could reflect this value. If salvation is attained with a rational approach to life, the systematic training of the athlete could be understood as a part of this plan.[36]

Anyone who is familiar with contemporary sports and the Protestant ethic cannot overlook the unmistakable link between them (a correspondence also exists between capitalistic ideology and modern sports, but that will not be examined here). The emergence of sport as a pervasive feature of North American life undoubtedly owes its development to various social forces, one of which may be Protestant Christianity, the value orientations of which form the basis of the fundamental doctrine of the North American sport ideology. This ideology suggests that persons involved with sports, especially coaches and athletes, adhere to a particular kind of ideology, the overriding orientation of which is individual achievement through competition. The phrase "ideology of sport" is a generic designation for all ideas espoused by or for those who participate in and exercise authority in sports as they seek to explain and justify their beliefs.

If we place the values inherent in the Protestant ethic and the ideology of sport side by side, it immediately becomes apparent that the two are congruent; that is, they share a significant equivalence. Without attempting to claim a causal link between the two belief systems, it does seem possible to suggest an elective affinity between them. Success, self-discipline, and hard work, the original tenets of the Protestant ethic, are the most valued qualities of an athlete.

Success

The Protestant stress on successful, individual achievement is in keeping with the values of contemporary sport. The characteristics of the good Christian are also those needed by the successful athlete. The temper of organized sport is competitive, with an overriding sense of wins and losses. The notion that achievement separates the chosen from the doomed is seen in the winning-is-everything ideology in sports. Winners are the good people; personal worth, both in this and the other world, is equated with winning. The loser is obviously not one of God's chosen people; failure in one's occupation stamps the Protestant-ethic believer as doomed to hell.

The Protestant ethic recreated in sport was captured by one scholar: "Christians play their games for fun, but more important than fun is the responsibility to play them well and, of course, to win." Elaborating on this point, he continued:

> Anyone close to the sports scene knows that competition, even between the most amicable opponents, often becomes a rite of unholy unction, a sacrament, in which aggression is vented, old scores settled, number one taken care of, and where the discourteous act looms as the principal liturgical device. Even in contests played in the shadow of church walls—the church league softball or basketball game—tempers can flare and the spiritual graces of compassion and sensitivity can place second to winning one for "good ole First Baptist."[37]

One self-described "Christian athlete" told a researcher studying values in sports that to be successful in sports

"you've got to be downright mean sometimes, and . . . you've got to beat your opponent up to do well." The researcher found that for "the majority of the Christian-athletes [there] did *not* appear to [be] any conflict between the values of their Christian faith and the values of their sporting practices."[38]

The importance of winning is legitimized by implying that Christ himself would do whatever it takes to win. As one major league baseball player who was a member of Baseball Chapel said, "If Jesus Christ was sliding into second base, he would knock the second baseman into left field to break up a double play."[39]

Success is not only important in its own right for athletes; it is important in evangelical work. As one writer pointed out: "Few will be inclined to listen and even fewer will believe unless the speaker is a proven winner. Sports writers don't care about the religious beliefs of chronic losers, and bench sitters are notoriously poor draws at Rotary luncheons. As one sport evangelist put it: "We have to win. That's what the world looks at. The world won't listen to our message if we are losers." And of course, he's right. . . . Winning is critical to evangelical enterprises.[40] To the congruent values of Protestantism and sports can be added American societal values. As an AIA basketball player noted: "It's important for us to win, not because God wants winners, but because Americans do."[41]

Although the quest, even the obsession, for victory is congruent with the Calvinistic view as it is manifested in the Protestant ethic, the theology of Christianity contains a worldview that places the unmitigated quest for success in question. As Hoffman noted: "Competitive sport—that which celebrates the myth of success—is harnessed to a theology that consistently stresses the importance of losing. Sport—that which symbolizes the morality of self-reliance and teaches the just rewards of hard work—is used to propagate a theology dominated by the radicalism of grace ('the first shall be last and the last first'). Sport, a microcosm of meritocracy, is used to pay tribute to a God who says all are unworthy and undeserving."[42]

Self-Discipline

The notion that dedication, self-discipline, and sports participation may be an occupational calling is central to the ideology of Sportianity. God is glorified best, so the thinking goes, when athletes give totally of themselves in striving for success and victory. This idea is manifested in the traditional Christian asceticism that emphasizes sacrifice, control, and self-discipline as relevant means to salvation. As one spokesperson for Sportianity put it, no athlete "can afford to discredit Jesus by giving anything less than total involvement with those talents that he has been given in his training and competition." Perhaps the greatest challenge for the Christian athlete's self-discipline is to maintain the desire to win without compromising his or her faith, to "temper competitive enthusiasm with just the right amount of spiritual grace, so that one can engender the requisite competitive disposition without marring one's Christian witness. The eternal quest of the Christian athlete seems to be for spiritual control over their competitive attitudes all the while being careful not to be excessively controlled and thus rendered ineffective as a competitor." [43]

Hard Work

Just as the businessperson is responsible to God to develop his or her talents to the fullest, so is the athlete equally responsible. If God has granted one athletic abilities, then one is obligated to use those abilities to glorify and honor God; anything less than total dedication to the task is insufficient. Major league pitcher Orel Hershiser echoed this sentiment: "I have a responsibility for the talent I've been given, and on the days when I don't give my best, I think God should be upset with me." [44]

Hard work, training, and unremitting dedication by athletes not only lead to success ("workers are winners") but are seen as ways of using God-given ability to glorify God, an important Protestant requirement. Success can be considered as the justly deserved reward of a person's purposeful, self-denying, God-guided activity. Giving less than 100 percent is regarded by some Christian athletes as a direct violation of God's law. National Football League defensive end Reggie White says: "I believe that I've been blessed with physical ability in order to gain a platform to preach the gospel. . . . I've got to do what I do, hard but fair." [45]

Protestantism and Contemporary Sport

Any belief system that can help provide athletes and coaches with a rationale for their deep commitment to sports provides a means of expressing the essence of their striving, and Protestant theology does just that. In short, it is a belief system to which the athlete and coach can hold an elective affinity. Whether they actually do hold such an elective affinity remains a matter of speculation. Moreover, we hasten to add that Protestantism certainly is not responsible for the creation of the sport ideology, but it does provide religious reinforcement for it.

Perhaps it is not coincidental that the belief systems of fundamentalist Protestantism and modern sports are so congruent. The two institutions use similar means to respond to their members' needs. Each tries to enforce and maintain, through a strict code of behavior and ritual, a strict belief system that is typically adopted and internalized by all involved. Each performs cohesive, integrative, and social-control functions for its members, giving them meaningful ways to organize their world. Both religion and sport, because of the sacredness nurtured by these systems, resist social change and, in this way, support the status quo.

Sport Uses Religion

Religious observances and competitive sports constantly impinge on each other, and religious practices of various kinds are found wherever one finds sports. Religion can be viewed from one point of view as an important means of coping with situations of stress. There are several categories of stress situations. One of these comprises situations in which largely uncontrolled and unpredictable forces may imperil the vital personal and social concerns of an individual or group. Sports competition falls into this category of stress because competition involves a great deal of uncertainty about a typically important outcome.

Coaches and athletes have great respect for the technical knowledge required for successful performance, but they are also aware of its limitations. As a supplement to the practical techniques, sports participants often employ religious practices. Coaches and athletes do not believe that these practices make up for their failure to acquire necessary skills or to employ appropriate strategy. However, these practices help them adjust to stress by providing opportunities for them to dramatize their anxieties, thus reinforcing their self-confidence. Religion invokes a sense of "doing something about it" in uncertain undertakings where practical techniques alone cannot guarantee success. The noted anthropologist Bronislaw Malinowski concluded from his research that when the outcome of vital social activities is greatly uncertain, magico-religious or other comparable techniques are inevitably used as a means of allaying tension and promoting adjustment.[46]

The Use of Prayer

Prayer is perhaps the most frequently employed use of religion by coaches and athletes; prayer for protection in competition, prayer for good performance, and prayer for victory are three examples. Sometimes the act of prayer is observed as a Roman Catholic crosses himself or herself before shooting a free throw in basketball or as a team prays in the huddle before a football game. One researcher who studied what he called "Born-Again Sport" said, "most born-again athletes use prayer to influence God to help their team win or to help them perform well."[47]

The first historical example of prayer and the direct intervention of gods in sports competition is described by Homer in the *Iliad*. During the funeral games held in honor of Patroclus, who was killed in battle, one of the events was a footrace in which three men competed. Ajax took the lead from the start, followed closely by Odysseus: "Thus Odysseus ran close behind him and trod in his footsteps before the dust could settle in them, and on the head of Ajax fell the breath of the godlike hero running lightly and relentlessly on." As they neared the finish line, Odysseus prayed for divine assistance, and his prayer was answered by Athena, who not only inspired him to make a last-minute dash but caused Ajax to slip and fall in a mass of cow dung, and Odysseus won the race. Ajax received an ox as second prize: "He stood holding the horns of the ox and spitting out dung, and exclaimed: 'Curse it, that goddess tripped me up. She always stands by Odysseus like a mother and helps him.'"[48]

Very little is known about the actual extent to which individual athletes use prayer in conjunction with their participation, but it seems probable that if some athletes are seen praying, others are doing so without outward, observable signs. Coaches often arrange to have religious services on the Sabbath or on game days. At present, almost every professional major league baseball and football team—more than fifty of them—holds Sunday chapel services, at home and away, and Sunday services are also held in sports as varied as stock-car racing and golf.

One of the claims for religious service and prayer is that it strengthens a group's sense of its own identity, provides unity, and accentuates its "we" feeling. There are probably other reasons why coaches sanction locker-room prayers. Observers who suspect that locker-room prayer is about coaches' only concession to religion imply that one coach does it because the other coaches are doing it, and "you can't let them get the edge." One scholar of sport and religion suggested that it may be "only a sweaty-palmed response to the anxieties and uncertainties of competition . . . [coaches and] athletes are notorious [spur-of-the-moment] converts—pious and repentant in those gut-wrenching moments before a big game, [but] destined to backslide as soon as the ball is put into play. Indeed, the exigencies of many competitive sports require them to leave religion in the locker-room."[49] In *The Prince of Tides,* author Pat Conroy relates the events in one high school locker room before a football game. Although the book is a novel and the locker room is therefore fictitious, the situation as Conroy relates it is very close to the reality found in many real-life locker rooms:

The coach began to speak. "Tonight I'm gonna learn and the town's gonna learn who my hitters are. All you've proved so far is that you know how to put on pads and get dates to the sock hop after the game, but until I see you in action, I won't know if you're hitters or not. Real hitters. Now a real hitter is a headhunter who puts his head in the chest of his opponent and ain't happy if his opponent is still breathing after the play. A real hitter doesn't know what fear is except when he sees it in the eyes of a ball carrier he's about to split in half. A real hitter loves pain, loves the screaming and the sweating and the brawling and the hatred of life down in the trenches. He likes to be at the spot where the blood flows and the teeth get kicked out. That's what this sport's all about, men. It's war, pure and simple. Now tonight, you go out there and kick butt all over that field. If something moves, hit it. If something breathes, hit it. . . .

"Now do I have me some hitters?" he screamed, veins throbbing along his temple.

"Yes, sir," we screamed back.

"Do I have some fucking hitters?"

"Yes, sir."

"Do I have me some goddamn headhunters?"

"Yes, sir."

"Am I going to see blood?"

"Yes, sir."

"Am I going to see their guts hanging off your helmets?"

"Yes, sir."

"Am I going to hear their bones breaking all over the field?"

"Yes, sir," we happy hitters cried aloud.

"Let us pray," he said.

He led the team in the recitation of the Lord's Prayer.[50]

Although there is little empirical work on the use of prayer by athletes and coaches, those who pray in connection with sports are likely to be regular churchgoers with a strong religious orientation. Thus, coaches and athletes who pray at game time probably do it because prayer is something they use in numerous situations of their daily life, not because the contest elicits such prayers any more than other stressful episodes in daily life.

Many athletes who pray believe that the use of prayer might affect the outcome of the game. One athlete asserted, "I never play my best if I haven't recited the Lord's Prayer first." Another said, "My experience tells me that sincere prayer can be the winning factor." Another described the prayer he uses: "Dear Lord, we'd like [you] to bless the players and protect us from injury and hopefully [let us] come out with a win."[51] For many athletes the belief is strong that prayer will

bring forth the intervention of God on the athlete's behalf. In the locker room after the 1991 Super Bowl game in which his New York Giant players prayed for the Buffalo Bills place kicker to miss the field goal attempt (which he did), which would assure a victory for the Giants, the coach of the Giants said: "I realized a long time ago . . . that God is playing some of these games and He was on our side today."[52] After the miraculous 64-yard "Hail Mary" touchdown pass on the last play of the 1994 University of Michigan versus University of Colorado football game, the quarterback for the Colorado team recalled praying to God before the play, "You know, I've done everything you've asked. I have confidence in you." About the play and the victory, Colorado coach Bill McCartney told reporters, "That was the Lord."[53]

Opposition to the use of prayers in the locker room before games, in the sideline huddles preceding games, and as public ceremonies before sports events is growing, especially when they are a part of public school events. One member of the clergy who objected to team prayer said: "God was never intended to be used as a blessing for a particular competitor, or for a particular sport event." A high school athletic director said: "The way I feel about it is that prayers are about as appropriate at football games as the Notre Dame fight song is in church." [54]

Several years ago, at the University of Colorado, the American Civil Liberties Union challenged the head football coach's practice of leading prayers before games. The CU athletic department agreed to a policy to pursue and maintain a course of neutrality toward religion, thus ending the coach-led praying. In Georgia a high school student's father objected to prayers before sporting events. He said, "I don't think local government should establish any religion. If you have one religion dominating, you don't have freedom." The U.S. Supreme Court agreed, ruling that organized prayer before public high school and college sports events violates the constitutional principle of separation of church and state.[55]

Religious services in connection with sporting events are still held at church-sponsored and professional sporting events; indeed, to have an important sports event started by a religious invocation is not unusual. Some invocations are brief and to the point, but others are used by clergy to conduct a religious service or to metaphorically dramatize the relationship between sports and religion.

The Use of Magic

The reader may be surprised, even shocked, that a section on magic is included because many people see no relationship between magical practices and religion. In practice, however, religion and magic, as defined by anthropologists, are closely intertwined. Although magic and religion are alike in assuming the existence of supernatural powers, a significant difference exists between the ends that they seek. Religion is oriented to the otherworldly, toward a supreme supernatural god, and religion typically centers on such overarching issues as salvation and the meaning of life and death; this is not true of magic. The practitioner of magic seeks ends that are in the everyday world of events; magic is oriented toward immediate, practical goals.

There are other ways in which religion and magic differ. Religious worshipers possess an attitude of awe and reverence toward the sacred ends they pursue, but the users of magic are in business for practical and arbitrarily chosen ends. The latter are manipulators of the supernatural for their own private advantage rather than worshipers of it; the attitude of magic users is likely to be utilitarian. In this respect, Bronislaw Malinowski noted that magic has an end in pursuit of which the magical ritual is performed. The religious ritual has no purpose, that is, the ritual is not a means to an end but an end in itself. Malinowski said, "While in the magical act the underlying idea and aim is always clear, straightforward and definite, in religious ceremony there is no purpose directed toward a subsequent event." Furthermore, the content of magic and religion differ. The content of magic has no unified inclusive theory but instead tends to be atomistic, somewhat like a book of recipes. Religion, on the other hand, tends to encompass the whole of life; it often provides the comprehensive theory of both the supernatural and human society.[56]

The Malinowski Thesis

According to Malinowski, magic flourishes in situations of uncertainty and threat; it is most commonly invoked in situations of high anxiety about accomplishing desired ends. The origin of most magical rites can be traced to fears experienced individually or collectively. These rites are associated with human helplessness in the face of danger and unpredictability, which give rise to superstitious beliefs and overt practices to ward off impending danger or failure and to bring good luck. Malinowski reported: "We find magic wherever the elements of chance and accident, and the emotional play between hope and fear have a wide and extensive range. We do not find magic wherever the pursuit is certain, reliable, and well under control of rational methods.[57] In support of this contention, Malinowski compared two forms of fishing among natives of the Trobriand Islands of Melanesia: lagoon and open-sea fishing. "It is most significant that in the lagoon fishing, where man can rely completely upon his knowledge and skill, magic does not exist, while in the open-sea fishing, full of danger and uncertainty, there is extensive magical ritual to secure safety and good results."[58]

Malinowski's thesis about the conditions under which magic appears is applicable to the world of sport. Athletes and coaches are engaged in an activity of uncertain outcome in which they have a great deal of emotional investment. Even dedicated conditioning and practice and the acquisition of high-level skills do not guarantee victory because opponents are often evenly matched and player injury and other dangers are often present. Thus, "getting the breaks" or "lucking out" may be the determining factor in the outcome of a contest. Having a weakly hit baseball fall in for a base hit or a deflected football pass caught by an unintended receiver are examples of luck or "getting the breaks" in sports. Although the cliche "the best team always wins" is part of the folk wisdom of sport, athletes and coaches know that this is not always so and indeed believe that factors leading to a win or a loss are somewhat out of their control.

According to Malinowski's theory, athletes and coaches may use magic to bring them luck and to assure that they "get the breaks," thus supplying themselves with beliefs that serve to bridge over uncertainty and threat in their pursuit of victories. The magic enables them to carry out their actions with a sense of assurance and confidence and to maintain poise and mental integrity in the face of opponents.

Magic and Its Uses in Sports

It is difficult to assess just how extensive the uses of magic are in sport. Newspaper and magazine stories leave little doubt, however, that magical beliefs and practices play a prominent role in the lives of athletes and coaches. They tend to employ almost anything imaginable that might ensure "getting the breaks," and this often involves some form of ritualistic, superstitious behavior. Superstition is a belief that one's fate is in the hands of mysterious external powers, governed by forces over which one has no control. It is a form of magical belief. One sports journalist, after studying the superstitions of athletes, argued that "some athletes turn to superstition for the same reasons that others turn to religion or drugs—to relieve pressure, to convince themselves that results are predetermined, to take the fear out of the unknown."[59]

There have been a few attempts to study empirically the uses of magic in sport. The findings of those studies can be summarized as follows: Sport superstitions are similar for athletes who compete in teams and for those who compete in individual sports, but team athletes indicate greater support for superstitions related to equipment and its use, to the order of entering the sports arena, to dressing-room rituals, to repetitive rituals, and to sports personalities than individual-sport athletes. The latter show greater support for superstitions related to wearing charms, to lucky lane numbers, to team cheers, and to crossing oneself before participation. Pregame superstitions of basketball players center on warm-up rituals; game superstitions are directed toward free-throw shooting, team cheers, and gum chewing. Endorsement of superstitions increase with involvement in sport, in other words, the higher the competitive level and the greater the involvement in a sport, the greater the prevalence of superstition. The gender of the athlete is less important than the level of involvement.

Superstitions are related to the uncertainty and importance of the outcome, as Malinowski indicated.

Applying the Malinowski thesis to baseball, anthropologist George Gmelch, a former professional ball player, published what has now become one of the classic studies of athletes and their uses of magical practices. Gmelch hypothesized that in baseball magical practices would be associated more with hitting and pitching than with fielding; the first two involve a high degree of chance and unpredictability, whereas the average fielding success rate is about 97 percent, reflecting almost complete control over the outcome. From his observations as a participant in professional baseball, Gmelch reported that there was indeed a greater incidence and variety of rituals, taboos, and use of fetishes related to hitting and pitching than in fielding. He concluded: "Nearly all of the magical practices that I participated in, observed, or elicited, support Malinowski's hypothesis that magic appears in situations of chance and uncertainty. The large amount of uncertainty in pitching and hitting best explains the elaborate magical practices used for these activities. Conversely, the high success rate of fielding . . . involving much less uncertainty, offers the best explanation for the absence of magic in this realm."[60]

What emerges in all of these investigations, and others, is that athletes use magical practices extensively in their sport experiences. Among the specific forms of magic practiced in sport are ritual, taboo, fetishism, and witchcraft.

Ritual

Rituals are standardized actions directed toward entreating or controlling the supernatural powers in regard to some particular situation, and sports are infused with ritualistic practices. An almost infinite variety of rituals are practiced in sport, since all athletes are free to ritualize any activity they consider important for successful performance. Typically, rituals arise from successful performances. Unable to attribute an exceptional performance to skill alone but hoping to repeat it in future contests, athletes and coaches single out something they did before the performance as being responsible for their success. That "something" might be a certain food they had eaten before the game, a new pair of socks or sneakers they had put on, or a specific sequence of behaviors preceding the contest. A National Hockey League player described the importance of ritual in preparing for a game following a win:

> When you win, you try not to change anything. Nothing. You do everything exactly as you did the whole day of your win. Beginning from the time you get up, was your window/door open? Get up on the same side of the bed. Eat the same meals, at the same places—home or at the same restaurant—nothing extra. If your salad was dry, order it dry again; if you had a large milk, then again; if your steak was ordered medium, then again; no dessert, and so on. You leave at the same times, take the same routes, park in the same place, enter through the same door, and prepare for the finale—game time—with the accent on precision.[61]

In a story of the rituals of a group of minor league baseball players, the sports reporter who had been observing the team noted that the league's home run champion would not "step into the batter's box until he has swept it clean of other batters' cleat marks" and a pitcher "doesn't make a start without playing a tape from the rock group Boston."[62]

In addition to individual rituals, there are a number of team rituals. In basketball the ritual of stacking hands is frequently employed just before the team takes the floor at the beginning of the game and after time-outs. The most universal hockey ritual occurs just before the start of a game when players skate in front of their goal and tap the goalie on the pads for good luck.

Taboo

A taboo is a strong social norm prohibiting certain actions that are punishable by the group or by magical consequences. There are numerous institutional taboos in each sport and, of course, many personal taboos. Two of the strongest taboos in baseball prohibit crossing the handles of bats and mentioning that the pitcher has a no-hitter in progress. Crossing bats is believed to bring bad luck and mentioning a no-hitter to the pitcher

is believed to break his spell on the batters, ending his chances to complete a no-hit game.

Sports Illustrated writer, Jack McCallum, related how the Salt Lake Trappers of the Class A Pioneer League attempted to prolong their 1987 twenty-nine-game winning streak, a professional baseball record: They "adopted the no-wash superstition. . . . No player washed his socks, and some washed nothing at all" because they feared their good luck might be washed away with the dirt.[63]

Some athletes develop taboos about not stepping on portions of the playing surface, such as the chalk foul lines (just as children avoid stepping on sidewalk cracks) or about not wearing certain parts of the uniform, such as socks.

Fetishism

Fetishes are revered objects believed to have magical power to attain the desired ends for the person who possesses or uses them. Fetishes are standard equipment for coaches and athletes. They include a bewildering assortment of objects: rabbits' feet, pictures of heroes or loved ones, pins, coins, remnants of old equipment, certain numbered uniforms, and so forth. Typically, these objects obtain their power through association with successful performances. For example, if the athlete or coach happens to be wearing or using the object during a victory, the individual attributes the good fortune to the object; it then becomes a fetish embodied with supernatural power. The seriousness with which some athletes take fetishes was described by Gmelch: "I once saw a fight caused by the desecration of a fetish. Before the game, one player stole the fetish, a horsehide baseball cover, out of a teammate's back pocket. The prankster did not return the fetish until after the game, in which the owner of the fetish went hitless, breaking a batting streak. The owner, blaming his inability to hit on the loss of the fetish, lashed out at the thief when the latter tried to return it."[64]

One of the most amusing episodes in the motion picture "Bull Durham" occurs when Annie, the temptress and part-time pitching tutor to the talented young pitcher, Nuke, convinces him that if he wears one of her garter belts when he pitches he will be unbeatable. Despite some delay and reluctance on Nuke's part, when he does finally wear the garter belt he pitches brilliantly. From then on it is a sacred item for him. This episode may seem merely humorous in the movie, but it illustrates a very realistic slice of the sports world. Actually, even more outrageous fetishes can be found among athletes.

Witchcraft

Magical practices that are intended to bring misfortune on others are known as black magic, witchcraft, or sorcery. In sport, those who employ this form of magic believe that supernatural powers are being harnessed to harm or bring misfortune on opponents. In Africa witchcraft dominates some sports. Medicine men who claim that they can make the ball disappear or that they can cast a spell on opposing players are especially active in soccer. It is estimated that about 95 percent of Kenyan soccer teams hire witch doctors to help them win, and matches have been marred by witchcraft-inspired riots.

We laugh when reading about African soccer teams traveling with witch doctors, and we are amused by such practices of witchcraft as players painting their bodies with pig fat to ward off evil spirits, reasoning that sports teams in North America are much too sophisticated to travel with witch doctors or to wear pig fat. Our teams, instead, travel with Catholic priests and Protestant ministers and wear medals around their necks! A number of college football teams have traveling chaplains who accompany the teams on road trips. As one social scientist has noted, "We may not readily recognize that some of our social antics aimed at boosting morale and energy of team and supporters . . . are all acts of sorcery."[65]

Actually, witchcraft is not confined to African sports. During an American League baseball play-off game several years ago, Kansas City player George Brett hit a two-run homer to beat the New York Yankees. Jose Martinez, one of the Kansas City coaches, claimed that the victory was the result of his enlisting the help of his godfather, a practitioner of voodoo.

Martinez revealed that he called his godfather to ask what could be done to ensure that the Royals would win the pennant. Although the godfather was a Yankee fan, he felt obligated to help his godson, and so he told him, "Stick the Yankee line-up card in the freezer," an action that he said would "freeze their bats." Before the game, Martinez dutifully obtained a copy of the New York line-up, went into a back room in Yankee Stadium and placed the card in a freezer. This is why, Martinez suggested, the Yankees scored only two runs.

Summary

In this chapter we have examined the reciprocal relationship between sport and religion. Although sport and religion may appear to have little in common, we have attempted to demonstrate that contemporary sport and contemporary religion are related in a variety of ways. For many centuries Christian church dogma was antithetical to play and sport activities, but over the past century, with the enormous growth of organized sport, churches and religious leaders have welded a link between these two institutions by sponsoring sports events under religious auspices and by proselytizing athletes to religion and then using them as missionaries to convert new members.

Although contemporary religion uses sport for the promotion of its causes, sport uses religion as well. Numerous activities with a religious connotation—ceremonies, rituals, and so forth—are employed in connection with sports contests.

Notes

1. Emile Durkheim, *The Elementary Forms of Religious Life,* trans. J. W. Swain (New York: Free Press, 1965), 62.

2. Malcolm Hamilton, *The Sociology of Religion: Theoretical and Comparative Perspectives* (New York: Routledge, 1994); Robert Wuthnow, *Rediscovering the Sacred: Perspectives on Religion in Contemporary Society* (Grand Rapids, Mich.: W. B. Eerdmans, 1992).

3. Karl Marx, *Selected Writings in Sociology and Social Philosophy,* trans. and ed. Tom B. Bottomore and Maximilien Rubel (New York: McGraw-Hill, 1964), 26–27.

4. Rudolph Brasch, *How Did Sports Begin?* (New York: David McKay, 1970), 1.

5. Stewart Culin, *Games of the North American Indian* (Washington, D.C.: U.S. Government Printing Office, 1907), 34; see also Allen Guttmann, "The Sacred and the Secular," in *Sport Inside Out,* ed. David L. Vanderwerken and Spencer K. Wertz (Fort Worth: Texas Christian University Press, 1985), 298–308.

6. Noel Robertson, "The Ancient Olympics: Sport, Spectacle and Ritual," in *The Olympic Games in Transition,* ed. Jeffrey O. Segrave and Donald Chu (Champaign, Ill.: Human Kinetics Publishers, 1988), 11–25; David Sansone, *Greek Athletics and the Genesis of Sport* (Berkeley: University of California Press, 1988).

7. Desiderius Erasmus quoted in Albert Hyma, *The Youth of Erasmus* (Ann Arbor: University of Michigan Press, 1930), 178.

8. Dennis Brailsford, *Sport, Time, and Society* (New York: Routledge, 1991), 18.

9. Nancy L. Struna, "Puritans and Sport: The Irretrievable Tide of Change," *The Sporting Image: Readings in American Sport History,* ed. Paul J. Zingg (New York: University Press of America, 1988).

10. Kathryn K. Grover, ed., *Fitness in America: Images of Health, Sport and the Body, 1830–1940* (Amherst, Mass.: University of Massachusetts Press, 1989); Harvey Green, *Fit for America: Health, Fitness, Sport, and American Society* (New York: Pantheon, 1986).

11. "Amusements," *New Englander* 9 (1851): 358.

12. Richard Swanson and Betty Spears, *History of Sport and Physical Education in the United States,* 4th ed. (Madison, Wisc.: Brown and Benchmark, 1995).

13. Michael Novak, "The Natural Religion," in *Sport and Religion,* ed. Shirl J. Hoffman (Champaign, Ill.: Human Kinetics Publishers, 1992), 36, 39.

14. Charles S. Prebish, comp., *Religion and Sport: The Meeting of Sacred and Profane* (Westport, Conn.: Greenwood, 1993), 62, 74.

15. *The Speeches of Avery Brundage* (Lausanne: Comite International Olympique, 1968), 80.

16. James A. Vlasich, *A Legend for the Legendary: The Origins of the Baseball Hall of Fame* (Bowling Green, Ohio: Bowling Green State University Popular Press, 1990); Eldon E. Snyder, "Sociology of Nostalgia: Sports Halls of Fame and Museums in America," *Sociology of Sport Journal* 8 (September 1991): 228–38.

17. Joseph L. Price, "The Super Bowl as Religious Festival," in *Sport and Religion,* 13.

18. Joan M. Chandler, "Sport is Not Religion," *Sport and Religion,* 55; see also Robert J. Higgs, "Muscular Christianity, Holy Play, and Spiritual Exercises: Confusion About Christ in Sports and Religion," *Sport and Religion,* 89–103.

19. David L. Moore, "BYU Sports: Mission Accomplished," *USA Today,* 22 October 1986, sec. C, p. 2.

20. Debbie Becker, "Smiting Foes, Saving Souls at Liberty," *USA Today,* 13 September 1989, sec. C, p. 1.

21. Douglas Lederman, "Liberty U. Seeks Success in Football to Spread Fundamentalist Message," *The Chronicle of Higher Education,* 15 March 1989, sec. A, p. 32; see also Leigh Montville, "Thou Shalt Not Lose," *Sports Illustrated,* 13 November 1989, 82–91.

22. David Whitford, *A Payroll to Meet: A Story of Greed, Corruption & Football at SMU* (New York: Macmillan, 1989).

23. J. Cairney, "Jocks for Jesus," *The Spectator,* 6 June 1987, sec. C, p. 16.

24. James A. Mathisen, "Reviving 'Muscular Christianity': Gil Dodds and the Institutionalization of Sport Evangelism," *Sociological Focus* 23 (August 1990): 233–49.

25. Brian W. W. Aitken, "The Emergence of Born-Again Sport," *Religion and Sport,* comp. Charles S. Prebish, 199.

26. Bill Briggs, "God Squads," *The Denver Post Magazine,* 23 October 1994, 12–15.

27. Shirl J. Hoffman, "God, Guts, and Glory: Evangelicalism in American Sport" (paper presented at the National Convention of AAHPER, 1982), 15.

28. B. P. Kaufman, "Promise Keepers Rallies Men to Commitment," *Christianity Today* 36 (14 September 1992): 57; see also Michael Romano, "Keeping the Promise of God," *Rocky Mountain News,* 17 July 1994, sec. A, pp. 16–19.

29. Romano, "Keeping the Promise of God," sec. A, p.16; see also Edward Gilbreath, "Manhood's Great Awakening," *Christianity Today* 39 (6 February 1995): 20–28; Sara Diamond, "The New Man," *Z Magazine* 8 (December 1995), 16–18.

30. Ibid., sec. A, p. 17.

31. Romano, "Keeping the Promise of God," sec. A, p. 19; see also Peter Monaghan, "U. of Colorado Football Coach Accused of Using His Position to Promote His Religious Views," *The Chronicle of Higher Education,* 11 November 1992, sec. A, pp. 35, 37.

32. Becky Beal and John Gray, "Bill McCartney and The Promise Keepers: Exploring the Connections Among Sport, Christianity, and Masculinity," (paper presented at the Annual Meeting of AAHPERD, Portland, Oreg., April 1995).

33. Max Weber, *The Protestant Ethic and the Spirit of Capitalism,* trans. Talcott Parsons (New York: Scribners, 1958). This essay, probably the most famous work on the sociology of religion, has aroused a great deal of controversy among sociologists and historians. For an excellent collection of the views of Weber's critics, see Robert W. Green, ed., *Protestantism, Capitalism and Social Science: The Weber Thesis Controversy* (Lexington, Mass.: Heath, 1973).

34. Ibid., 80, 115.

35. Ibid., 183.

36. Jacqueline H. Gillis, "Olympic Success and National Religious Orientation," *Review of Sport and Leisure* 5 (winter 1980): 4.

37. Shirl J. Hoffman, "Evangelicalism and the Revitalization of Religious Ritual in Sport," in *Sport and Religion,* 114.

38. Christopher L. Stevenson, "The Christian-Athlete: An Interactionist-Developmental Analysis," *Sociology of Sport Journal* 8 (1991): 365, 367.

39. Quoted in "No Comment," *The Progressive* 55 (July 1991): 11; see also Shirl J. Hoffman, "The Sanctification of Sport: Can the Mind of Christ Coexist With the Killer Instinct?" *Christianity Today* 30, 4 April 1986: 17–21.

40. Hoffman, "God, Guts, and Glory," 15.

41. Carol Flake, "The Spirit of Winning: Sports and the Total Man," in *Sport and Religion,* p. 166.

42. Hoffman, "Evangelicalism and the Revitalization of Religious Ritual in Sport," in *Sport and Religion,* p. 122.

43. Hoffman, "God, Guts, and Glory," 12.

44. Rachel Shuster, "Hershiser Tells Costas: I'm Worth What I Ask," *USA Today,* 14 February 1989, sec. C, p. 3; see also Ron Knapp, *Sports Great Orel Hershiser* (Hillsdale, N.J.: Enslow, 1993); David Leon Moore, "Ballplayers Putting Faith in Christ," *USA Today,* 26 July 1991, sec. C, pp. 1–2.

45. Paul Zimmerman, "White Heat," *Sports Illustrated,* 27 November 1989, 68; see also Jim Donaghy, "Religion Taking Hold Among Big Leaguers," *Rocky Mountain News,* 30 June 1991, 63.

46. Bronislaw Malinowski, *Magic, Science, and Religion and Other Essays* (Glencoe, Ill.: Free Press, 1948).

47. Aitken, "The Emergence of Born-Again Sport," *Religion and Sport,* comp. Charles S. Prebish, 208.

48. Louise R. Loomis, ed., *The Iliad of Homer,* trans. Samuel Butler (Roslyn, N.Y.: Walter J. Block, 1942), 368–69.

49. Hoffman, "God, Guts, and Glory," 4–5.

50. Pat Conroy, *The Prince of Tides* (Boston: Houghton Mifflin, 1986), 330–31.

51. "Pregame Prayer Decision Upheld," *USA Today,* 31 May 1989, sec. C, p. 8; see also Betty Kelley, Shirl J. Hoffman, and Diane L. Gill, "The Relationship Between Competitive Orientation and Religious Orientation," *Journal of Sport Behavior* 13 (1990): 145–56.

52. Erik Brady, "God Does Not Take Sides in Football Games," *USA Today,* 29 January 1991, sec. C, p. 10.

53. Briggs, "God Squads," 14.

54. "Quotelines," *USA Today,* 10 October 1989, sec. A, p. 10.

55. Elyzabeth Holford, "Prayer on the Playing Field," *Journal of Physical Education, Recreation, and Dance* 63 (February 1992): 29–32.

56. Malinowski, *Magic, Science, and Religion,* 12–30.

57. Ibid., 116.

58. Ibid., 14.

59. Jack McCallum, "Green Cars, Black Cats and Lady Luck," in *Sport and Religion,* 204.

60. George Gmelch, "Baseball Magic," *Trans-Action* 8 (June 1971): 54.

61. Mari Womack, "Why Athletes Need Ritual: A Study of Magic Among Professional Athletes," in *Sport and Religion,* 196.

62. Norm Clarke, "Zephyrs Depend on Voodoo, Too," *Rocky Mountain News,* 25 June 1989, sec. S, p. 10.

63. McCallum, "Green Cars, Black Cats and Lady Luck," in *Sport and Religion,* 205.

64. Gmelch, "Baseball Magic," 54.

65. Phillips Stevens, Jr., "Table Tennis and Sorcery in West Africa," *Play & Culture* 1 (1988): 138–45; see also B. G. Brooks, "McCarthy Receives Guidance From Unorthodox Minister," *Rocky Mountain News,* 26 December 1990, pp. 93, 100.

Chapter 9

Sport and Politics

The argument of this chapter is that sport and politics are closely intertwined. Several characteristics inherent to sport serve to guarantee this strong relationship.

First, sports participants typically represent and have an allegiance to some social organization (e.g., school, factory, neighborhood, community, region, or nation). Much of the ritual accompanying sporting events (such as slogans, chants, music, wearing of special clothing, and so forth) is aimed at symbolically reaffirming fidelity to the sponsoring organization. Phillip Goodhart and Christopher Chataway argued that there are four kinds of sport: sport as exercise, sport as gambling, sport as spectacle, and representative sport. *Representative sport* is

> a limited conflict with clearly defined rules, in which representatives of towns, regions, or nations are pitted against each other. It is primarily an affair for the spectators: they are drawn to it not so much by the mere spectacle, by the ritual, or by an appreciation of the skills involved, but because they identify themselves with their representatives. . . .
>
> Most people will watch [the Olympic Games] for one reason only: there will be a competitor who, they feel, is representing them. That figure in the striped singlet will be their man—running, jumping, or boxing for their country. For a matter of minutes at least, their own estimation of themselves will be bound up with his performance. He will be the embodiment of their nation's strength or weakness. Victory for him will be victory for them; defeat for him, defeat for them.[1]

This last point requires emphasis. Evidence from the Olympics or from other international competition shows that for many nations and their citizens, victory is an index of that nation's superiority (in its military might, its politico-economic system, and its culture). Clearly, the outcomes of international contests are very often interpreted politically, an argument we will return to later in this chapter.

A second basis for a close relationship between sport and politics is inherent in the process of organization itself. As sport has become increasingly organized, numerous teams, leagues, players' associations, and ruling bodies have been created. These groups acquire certain powers that by their very creation are distributed unequally.[2] Thus, a power struggle may develop between players and owners (e.g., the 1994–95 baseball strike) or between competing leagues (e.g., the NFL versus the USFL in professional football) or between various sanctioning bodies (the AAU versus the NCAA in amateur athletics) or between the organizations governing men's and women's collegiate sports (the AIAW versus the NCAA).

The essence of politics is power. As just elaborated, organizations have power over sports, teams, coaches, and athletes. Power and control over sport also occur in less obvious guises. Sport, for example, has been affected mightily by television. Television networks, paying hundreds of millions for rights, have insisted on changes such as converting golf from match play to medal play and mandatory timeouts in football and in the continuous sports of basketball, soccer, and hockey. The networks have also moved schedules (times and dates) to accommodate them rather than the fans or the teams involved. Behind the scenes, television networks have sometimes determined the opponents in football bowl games and invitational basketball tournaments. Other corporations, most notably those selling beer, soda, cars, and shoes have enormous power over sport. Some of these corporations actually own teams (e.g., Anheuser Busch owns the St. Louis Cardinals, Molson Brewing owns the Montreal Canadiens). Corporations provide the money to television through buying advertising time; they buy scoreboards and other equipment for local teams from professional teams to high school teams; they pay millions to become the official soft drink of the NFL (Coca Cola paid $20 million), or the 1996 Olympics (again Coke, this time paying $40 million; NBC paying $456 million for the television rights); the shoe companies in particular have coaches under contract (college and even some high school coaches), they run summer camps for prospective college athletes, and they have multimillion dollar contracts with star athletes in a number of sports. The shoe companies are so powerful that *Sports Illustrated* and *The Sporting News* both named the chief executive officer of Nike, Phil Knight, as the most powerful person in American sports.[3]

The linkage between sport and politics is quite obvious when the impact of the government on sports is considered. Several illustrations at the federal level make this point: (1) legislation has been passed exempting professional sports from antitrust laws; (2) tax laws give special concessions to owners of professional teams; (3) the blackouts of televised home games have been lifted for professional football under certain circumstances despite the protests of the league commissioner and the owners; and (4) Congress decides which sport organization will have the exclusive right to select and train athletes for the Olympic Games.[4]

Moreover, governments may encourage sport through various forms of funding. As we will see in the next chapter, municipal governments are very generous in subsidizing local teams owned by private entrepreneurs. For now let's consider the case of government subsidies to the Atlanta Committee for the 1996 Olympic Games.[5] The federal government supplied about $92 million to the local Olympic organizing committee in security, transportation assistance, trash pickup, and protection of the environment. The state of Georgia spent more than $150 million on public buildings and road construction related to the Olympics. Atlanta and other local governments spent about $90 million on Olympic related projects.

Another indication of the close relationship between sport and politics is that sports events and political situations have reciprocal effects. A famous example of a sports event affecting politics was the tour of China in 1971 by the American table-tennis contingent. This tour proved to be the prelude to political exchanges between the two nations. Other examples were the wars that erupted between El Salvador and Honduras and between Gabon and the Congo after soccer matches. There are also many examples of political situations that have affected sports. The apartheid policies of South Africa have resulted many times in that nation being barred from sports competitions.[6]

The United States boycott of the 1980 Olympics and Russia's boycott of the 1984 Olympics provide examples of another way in which sport and politics are related. They demonstrate clearly that sport is a tool of foreign policy.[7] Sport is used to achieve legitimacy for a political regime, and sport can be used as a prelude to formal relations between countries. Conversely, refusal by one country to compete against another is a way of pressuring that country.

The institutional character of sport is a final source of the strong relationship between sport and politics. The institution of sport, just as other institutions, is conservative; it serves as a preserver and a legitimator of the existing order. The patriotic pageants that accompany sporting events reinforce the political system. Moreover, sport perpetuates many myths, such as that anyone with talent, regardless of race or social station, has an equal chance to succeed.

We have seen that the very nature of sport makes politics endemic to it. The remainder of this chapter will demonstrate this relationship further by examining: (1) the various political uses of sport; (2) the political attitudes of coaches and athletes; and (3) the politics of the Olympic Games.

The Political Uses of Sport

Sport As a Propaganda Vehicle

Success in international competition frequently serves as a mechanism by which a society's ruling elite unites its citizens and attempts to impress the citizens of other countries. A classic example of this was Adolf Hitler's use of the 1936 Olympic Games to strengthen his control over the German people and to introduce Nazi culture to the entire world. According to Richard D. Mandell in his book *The Nazi Olympics,* the festival planned for these games was a shrewdly propagandistic and brilliantly conceived charade that reinforced and mobilized the hysterical patriotism of the German masses.[8] The success of the German athletes at those Olympics—they won 89 medals, 23 more than U.S. athletes, and more than 4 times as many as any other country won—was "proof" of German superiority.

Before the breakup of the eastern bloc countries, the reunification of the two Germanies, and the demise of the Soviet Union, the Communist nations used sport for promoting their common cause. During their heyday, the Communist countries dominated the Olympics, even though they only constituted about 10 percent of the athletes at those

Figure 9.1 Olympic medals per country and per population in 1992

Source: "Ready, Steady, Go," *The Economist,* 24 July 1993, 90. © 1993 The Economist Newspaper Group, Inc. Reprinted with permission. Further reproduction prohibited.

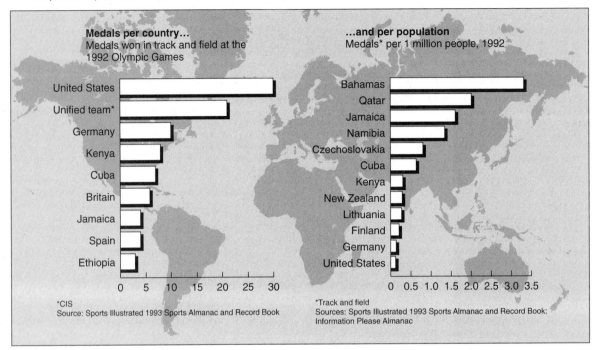

events. This, the Communists argued, provided convincing evidence of the superiority of the Communist politico-economic system. Of the remaining Communist nations, perhaps Cuba takes sport the most seriously, devoting 2 to 3 percent of its budget to its sports ministry. In the Pan American Games, Cuba tends to win about fifteen times more medals than the United States on a per capita basis, and Cuban Premier Fidel Castro has proclaimed to Latin America that this is proof of the superiority of the Cuban people and the Cuban system. Cuba's athletic prowess was demonstrated at the 1991 Pan American Games, held in Cuba, where Cuba with a population less than half the size of California's won 140 gold medals compared to 130 for the United States (see figure 9.1 for an analysis of how the nations ranked in the 1992 Summer Olympics, taking population into account).

The most striking example of success in the modern Olympics before the breakdown of the Communist countries was East Germany. Although it was a nation smaller in population than California (16.6 million compared to 25 million in California), East Germany consistently ranked in the top three nations in total medals and clearly outdistanced the Soviet Union and the United States on a per capita basis. In 1987 East Germany spent about $660 million (about 1 percent of its national budget) on its massive sports program. From the age of seven, children were tested, and the most promising athletes were enrolled in sixteen special schools, where they received special training, medical and scientific expertise, and expert coaching in addition to their normal schooling. After their formal education was completed, the star athletes were given special jobs, permanent military deferments, and apartments.[9] Why did East Germany devote so much money, time, and talent to sport? One reason was the competition between East and West Germany. A second reason was East Germany's goal of international acceptance as a sovereign state. Another reason was the desire to demonstrate the superiority of the Communist way of life. According to Lynn Rosellini, "For the Communist nations, each victory was proof, as East German party General Secretary Erich Honecker put it, of 'their better socialist system.'"[10] East Germany was not unlike the other Communist countries in using sport for the accomplishment of political goals.

National efforts to use sport for political purposes are not limited to Communist countries. International sports victories are just as important to nations such as Canada and the United States. Canada has a federal agency, Sport Canada, and similar organizations at the provincial level that work to promote sports excellence in elite athletes. There is a federal Athlete Assistance Program, which gives living and training grants to outstanding athletes. There is a network of national training centers, with professionalized coaching, and a calendar of events. These efforts are done, according to former elite Canadian athlete and now sociology of sport scholar Bruce Kidd, to "enhance Canadian nationalism and [the Canadian state's] legitimacy."[11]

After the 1972 Olympics, when the Americans fared worse than was expected (especially in track and basketball), many editorial writers and politicians advocated plans whereby American athletes would be subsidized and would receive the best coaching and facilities to regain international athletic supremacy. This did not happen, and the cry arose again after the 1976 Olympics. As a result, Congress then appropriated funds for the United States Olympic Committee and for the establishment of permanent training sites for the Winter and Summer Games. Also, since 1976 the U.S. Olympic Committee has gradually loosened the eligibility rules for participation. By 1984 this meant that athletes could be subsidized by corporations (e.g., Nike) and still compete. Most significantly, athletes were permitted to retain their "amateur" standing even while receiving huge sums of money for appearances, performances, and endorsements, which means that world class athletes make hundreds

of thousands, perhaps surpassing even $1 million, without losing their eligibility.

These changes did not achieve the intended results, that is, United States superiority. Following the 1988 Winter Olympic Games, for example, many Americans were embarrassed by the poor showing of American athletes (6 medals overall, compared to 29 for the Soviet Union and 25 for East Germany). As a result, the U.S. Olympic Committee formed a commission chaired by George Steinbrenner, then owner of the New York Yankees, to investigate the "problem" and to recommend solutions involving money, training, athlete selection, facilities, coaching, and organization. The clear assumption behind this commission was that if we give American athletes the resources and the commitment that the Communist nations have given their athletes, the American athletes will prevail proving the superiority of the free-enterprise system.

The United States government uses athletes to promote international goodwill and to enhance the American image abroad. The State Department, for example, sponsors tours of athletes to foreign countries for these purposes.

Sport as an instrument of national policy is not limited to the industrialized nations of the world. The developing countries use sport even more for this purpose. A study of the 133 members of the United Nations in 1973 showed that although 26 percent of all the nations had a cabinet-level post related to sport, 87 percent of those classified as "developing" had such a position.[12] The probable reason for such keen interest is that sport provides a relatively cheap political tool to accomplish national objectives of prestige abroad and unity at home.

Sport and Nationalism

Success in international sports competition tends to trigger pride among a nation's citizens. As mentioned previously, the Olympics and other international games tend to promote an "us versus them" feeling among athletes, coaches, politicians, the press, and fans. It can be argued, then, that the Olympic Games represent a political contest, a symbolic world war in which nations win or lose. This interpretation is commonly held; that is why citizens of each nation involved unite behind their flag and their athletes.[13] The integral interrelationship of sport and nationalism is easily seen in the blatantly militaristic pageantry that surrounds sports contests. The playing of the national anthem, the presentation of the colors, the jet aircraft flyovers, the band forming a flag or a liberty bell are all political acts supportive of the existing political system.

The irony is that nationalistic displays are not generally interpreted politically. Recognition of the explicit acceptance of the political content of these festival rituals was manifested in 1970, however, by the refusal of the American Broadcasting Company (ABC) to televise a halftime program in which the University of Buffalo band presentation featured three themes: antiwar, antiracism, and antipollution. The network refused on the grounds that the halftime show was a "political demonstration." Later in that same season, however, ABC televised the halftime program of the Army-Navy game in which several Green Berets who had staged a raid on a prisoner-of-war camp in North Vietnam were honored. It is revealing that one of these programs was labeled political while the other was not. Clearly, both were political, but only those demonstrations or ceremonies that were controversial and anti-establishment were so labeled and frowned upon.

Athletes who do not show proper respect for the flag or for the national anthem are subject to stiff penalties. When Tommie Smith and John Carlos raised gloved, clenched fists and bowed their heads during the national anthem at the 1968 Olympics, the U.S. Olympic Committee stripped them of their medals and banned them from further Olympic competition. Vince Mathews and Wayne Collett received the same penalty for their alleged disrespect to "The Star-Spangled Banner" at the 1972 Olympics. The Olympic Committee made such decisions even though they claim the Olympics are nonpolitical events—a claim that could not be further from the truth, as we will see later in this chapter.

During the 1991 war in the Persian Gulf, U.S. sport showed its support of the troops in a number of ways.[14] As examples, the University of North Carolina postponed a basketball game that was scheduled on the day the United States started the ground campaign; the 1991 Super Bowl was dedicated to the troops serving in the Persian Gulf (in addition to the nationalistic pageantry

before the game and at halftime, each spectator received a plastic American flag); and the NCAA permitted teams to wear American flag patches on their uniforms. Regarding this last instance, the players at Seton Hall were each given a choice whether to wear the flag. One player, Marco Lokar, an Italian citizen, refused to wear it. This was reported in the press, and when Seton Hall played St. John's at Madison Square Garden, many of the spectators booed every time he touched the ball. Moreover, he and his wife received threatening phone calls. As a result he left school and returned home to Italy. The various professional leagues had their players wear a flag decal on their uniforms to represent patriotic pride and support of American troops in the Persian Gulf. The National Hockey League also did this but it had a unique problem. Seven of the NHL's twenty-one teams represent Canadian cities. Moreover, many players come from foreign countries. The solution was for each team to choose a flag of the United States, Canada, or the United Nations. The St. Louis Blues, for example, chose the United Nations decal because only one of its players was a U.S. citizen.

Why are patriotic displays commonplace at sports contests but not at most other public events (e.g., plays, lectures, concerts, and movies)? The support for these patriotic rituals is so strong that whenever an occasional administrator decides not to play the national anthem at a sports event, there is, typically, a public outcry. Tom Wicker, of the *New York Times* made the following speculation as to why athletic events are so overladen with patriotic themes:

What is the correlation, if any, between patriotism and people battering one another in the boxing ring or in football games—or for that matter between patriotism and track meets, baseball games and other athletic events that are not so violent?

The explanation probably is that symbols like the flag and the anthem, appropriate as they are to the warlike spirit, are equally appropriate to sports events, with their displays of the instinct to combat and the will to win. Even the so-called "noncontact" sports exalt competition and the pursuit of victory, including the kind of individual heroism and team spirit that are evoked in wartime.[15]

box 9.1 *Sport Unifies Whites and Blacks in South Africa*

South Africa was barred for a time from the Olympic Games and other international competitions, most notably the World Cup of the favorite sport of whites—rugby. With the fall of apartheid and the election of Nelson Mandela, the sports world accepted South Africa. So much so that it was allowed to host the 1995 World Cup in Rugby.

President Mandela used the Rugby World Cup as an opportunity to bring change in South Africa. He visited the training camp of South Africa's team—the Springboks. While there he put on a Springbok cap.

> This was no casual gesture. The nickname Springbok is controversial in South Africa, strongly associated with the proapartheid white regimes of the past. Then Mandela pointedly told the rugby players, "The whole nation is behind you."

> The Springboks (white except for one black player) took that message to heart. The day before their game against Australia the players requested a tour of Robben Island, off Cape Town, where Mandela had been imprisoned for 18 years. They visited his former cell and afterward vowed to dedicate their efforts in the World Cup to their president.

Before one of the matches Mandela gave a speech before a primarily black audience. He said, "This cap does honor to our boys. I ask you to stand by them tomorrow because they are our kind." To which *Sports Illustrated* remarked:

> *Our kind.* Not black. Not white. South African. The rugby team became a symbol for the country as a whole. . . . Given the right time and place, sport is capable of starting such a process in a society. It is only a start, of course. The hard work lies ahead, after the crowds have dispersed and the headlines have ceased. South Africa's racial and economic woes are not behind it. Far from it. But thanks to the common ground supplied by a rugby pitch, those problems appear less imposing than they did only a month ago.

The Springboks won the World Cup defeating the world's two rugby powers, Australia and New Zealand, in the process. For the first time in South Africa's troubled history, whites and blacks found themselves unified by a sport.

Source: E. M. Swift, "Bok to the Future," *Sports Illustrated*, 3 July 1995, 32–33.

For whatever reason, sport competition and nationalism are closely intertwined. When athletes of one country compete against those of another, national unity is the result for both sides, unless the athletes of one do poorly. Citizens take pride in their representatives' accomplishments, viewing them as collective achievements. This identification with athletes and their cause of winning for the nation's glory tends to unite the citizenry regardless of social class, race, and regional differences (see box 9.1). Thus, sport can be used by political leaders whose nations have problems with divisiveness.

Sport As an Opiate of the Masses

We have shown that sport success can unite a nation through pride. This pride in a nation's success, because

it transcends the social classes, serves as an "opiate of the masses." It enables the poor to forget partially the harshness of their lives. In 1994, for example, when Haiti was on the verge of a severe crisis, the embattled military ruler, Raoul Cedras, paid for the broadcasting rights to the World Cup soccer matches. The spirits of the Haitians were raised as their adopted team, Brazil, was successful. Rather than massing in the streets to demonstrate against a political regime that oppressed them, the masses danced in the streets as their favorite team won. Moreover, as the games were played on the government-owned station, the rulers used halftime to inflame anti-American feelings by showing footage of the U.S. invasion of Panama in 1989, focusing on the bombing of residential areas.[16] Thus, sport serves as a

International sport has increasingly been used as an instrument of national diplomacy. National sports teams are portrayed as representatives of the political-economic system of their country.

safety valve for releasing tensions that might otherwise be directed toward disrupting the existing social order.

Retired senator Bill Bradley, also a former Rhodes scholar and professional basketball player, has pointed out that sport deflects us from seeking solutions to such problems as war and racism:

> "Life is full of ironies. . . . It's really ironic the way the fans come out to cheer the Big Game when there's a war on; people being bombed to death; racism, and all the rest of it. . . . It's also ironic that when 100,000 people will be at tomorrow's rally [a New York peace rally], the Knicks and me will be going over tonight's game films." . . . And Bill Bradley wonders hard about the morality of providing what he calls a "fix," a temporary escape from the problems of the world to a sports dreamworld; an escape that is really no escape because it permits those problems to go on just as before.[17]

Sport also acts as an opiate by perpetuating the belief that persons from the lowest classes can be upwardly mobile through success in sports. Chapter 12 will deal with this topic in more detail; meanwhile, it is enough to say that for every major leaguer who came up from poverty, tens of thousands did not. The point, however, is that most Americans believe that sport is a mobility escalator and that it is merely a reflection of the opportunity structure of the society in general. Again, poor youths who might otherwise invest their energies in changing the system work instead on a jump shot. The potential for change is thus impeded by sport.[18]

The Exploitation of Sport by Politicians

Politicians may use athletics and athletes in several ways. First, an athlete can use his or her fame and free publicity as aids to getting elected or appointed to office. In the 1994 election, Steve Largent, seven-time

Pro Bowl wide receiver with the Seattle Seahawks, and J. C. Watts, who quarterbacked Oklahoma to two Big Eight championships, were elected to Congress joining other ex-professional athletes Jim Bunning and Tom McMillen. Of course, these persons may have had the political skills to be successful in political races anyway, but athletic fame undoubtedly helped them. Politicians also find it beneficial to get the approval and active campaign support of sports stars. Athletes, because they are well known and admired, can get votes for either themselves or for candidates whom they support. Sport is so popular in American society that politicians may use examples of sport or sport metaphors to communicate with the public.[19] Moreover, politicians find it useful to identify with teams and to attend sports events. For example, on that special evening in 1995 when Cal Ripken, Jr., broke Lou Gehrig's record of 2,130 consecutive games played, President Clinton attended and was highly visible as he congratulated Ripken publicly and spent time in the television booth during the broadcast. Presidents Ronald Reagan, George Bush, and Bill Clinton have thrived on interaction with athletes and sports teams. Routinely, champions from colleges, the professionals, and the Olympics are invited to the White House. The trend is for presidents, governors, members of Congress, mayors, and other political officials to identify more and more with sports and sports heroes.

Politicians capitalize on the popularity of athletes by using them to support the system. In the United States, for example, athletes are often sent overseas to maintain the morale of service personnel. Athletes appear in advertisements that urge the viewer or reader to join the military or ROTC, to vote, and to avoid drugs. Athletes are also asked to give patriotic speeches on holidays and other occasions.

Use of athletes for the maintenance of the status quo is common in other countries as well. Athletes may be asked to visit factories and villages to hold demonstrations and make political speeches. These activities spread the philosophy of the rulers, help unify the people, and bolster the morale of the factory and farm workers to increase production.

Sport As a Vehicle of Change in Society

A recurring theme of this book is that sport reflects the dynamics of the larger society. It is not surprising, therefore, that the social and political turmoil of American society in the 1960s had its effect on the sports world.

Sport and sporting events were used by revolutionaries and by reformers to attack racism and American involvement in Vietnam, the two major societal problems. Racism was attacked in a number of ways. Most dramatic was the proposed boycott of the 1968 Olympics by African American athletes. Harry Edwards, an African American sociologist and former athlete, was a leader of this boycott. His rationale for the protest was: "The roots of the revolt of the black athlete spring from the same seed that produced the sit-ins, the freedom rides, and the rebellions in Watts, Detroit, and Newark. The athletic revolt springs from a disgust and dissatisfaction with the racism prevalent in American society—including the sports world."[20]

Another boycott was directed against the New York Athletic Club's annual indoor track meet. The goal of this action was to dramatize and to change the club's policy of excluding Jews, African Americans, and other minorities from membership. African American athletes at schools such as San Jose State and the University of Wyoming participated in a symbolic protest in the late 1960s against Brigham Young, a Mormon-supported university (the Wyoming protestors were removed from the team by the coach). These athletes wore arm bands to symbolize their contempt for the racial policies of the Mormon Church, which at that time did not allow African American males into the priesthood.

Two examples from the early 1990s show another avenue for sport changing society; this time by the power structure of sport. In 1990 the Professional Golf Association (PGA) made it a policy to no longer hold its championship at country clubs that excluded minorities as members. This forced Shoal Creek Country Club in Birmingham, Alabama, the site of the 1990 championship, to alter its admissions policies.

Similarly, many country clubs opened their memberships (although a few refused and, as a result, will no longer be eligible to host a PGA championship). The second example of the power structure using its power to reduce racism was a political decision by the National Football League. The League decided to take the 1993 Super Bowl away from Phoenix, after it had been awarded to Phoenix, because Arizona refused to have an official, statewide holiday to celebrate the birthday of Martin Luther King, Jr. In effect, the league was saying to the citizens of Arizona, "If you want to play the game of bigotry, we'll take our millions of dollars in tourist trade and scores of hours of television time someplace else."[21] This ploy worked as Arizona accepted the King holiday, followed by the League awarding Phoenix the 1996 Super Bowl.

These examples are interesting for two reasons: (1) because the power structure of sports has never taken the lead in social causes before (these acts may, therefore, be anomalies or, perhaps, the beginning of a trend); and (2) because they have political potential, ironically, either way (positively, because the leagues hold the power to "blackmail" recalcitrants into line, or negatively, because of a backlash from the public who resent blatant politics [i.e., antistatus quo politics] from sports organizations).

These examples show once again how sport and politics are intertwined. The worldwide popularity of sport and the importance attached to it by fans and politicians alike make sport an ideal platform for political protest. However, the use of sport for protest, especially from the powerless, although an important means of dramatizing social problems, is generally unsuccessful in causing meaningful change. This is a tribute to the institutional character of sport, with its built-in bias for preserving and legitimizing the status quo.

Sport As a Socializing Agent

We have frequently pointed out that sport is a vehicle by which the values of success in competition, hard work, perseverance, discipline, and order are transmitted. This is the explicit reason given for the existence of Little League programs for youngsters and for the tremendous emphasis on sports in the schools. As former vice-president, Spiro Agnew voiced the prevailing view in a speech delivered to the Touchdown Club of Birmingham, Alabama:

Not the least of these values is the American competitive ethic which motivates young Americans . . . to strive toward excellence in everything they undertake. For such young Americans—whether on the athletic field, in the classroom, or on the job—the importance of our competitive ethic lies in the fact that . . . only by trial of their abilities—by testing and challenging—can they discover their strengths and, yes, their weaknesses. Out of this process of self-discovery, painful though it may be at times, those young Americans who compete to excel learn to cope with whatever challenges lie ahead in life. And having given their best, they also emerge from the competitive test with greater ability to determine for themselves where their individual talents lie. Life is a great competition. In my judgment it will remain so despite the efforts of the social architects to make it a bland experience, controlled by their providing what they think is best for us. Success is sweet but it entails always the risk of failure. It is very, very important to learn how to lose a contest without being destroyed by the experience. For a man who has not known failure cannot fully appreciate success. A person cannot know pleasure to any greater degree than he has known pain. And from defeat, from failure, from hardship, something builds within a person. If a person can throw off disappointment and come back and try again, he develops a personal cohesiveness that holds him together as a man throughout his life—and that gives him the durability to convert temporary defeat into ultimate victory. . . .

And so, to me, that is the message of competitive sports: not simply trying to win, and to achieve, but learning how to cope with a failure—and to come back. In this regard, let me say something about my personal philosophy concerning the meaning of success and failure in sports for young Americans.

First, I believe that sports—all sports—is one of the few bits of glue that holds society together, one of the few activities in which young people can proceed along avenues where objectives are clear and the desire to win is not only permissible but encouraged. Opponents of the free-enterprise system tell our young people that to try for material success and personal status is bad; that the only thing worthwhile is to find something to wring your hands about; that the ultimate accomplishment is to make everybody feel better.

I, for one, would not want to live in a society that did not include winning in its philosophy; that would have us live our lives as identical lemmings, never trying to best anybody at anything, all headed in the same direction, departing not from the appointed route, striving not for individual excellence. In short, I would rather be a failure in a competitive society which is our inheritance than to live in a waveless sea of nonachievers.[22]

Agnew, of course, overlooked the noncompetitive aspects of corporate sport, for example, professional teams are exempt from the Sherman Antitrust Act, hence permitting leagues to be monopolies; team owners receive special statutory tax breaks; and professional teams play in tax-subsidized stadiums. In short, he neglected to say that team owners do not compete. He did voice, however, what most people believe.

Whether sport actually transmits these values or whether only the most competitive individuals survive are empirical questions.[23] There is empirical evidence that the more time high school students spend watching sports on television, the more politically conservative they are. The next section looks at this relationship more carefully.

The Political Attitudes of Coaches and Athletes

Sociologists are interested in the political attitudes of individuals in various social categories, such as social classes, occupations, and religious groups. This interest is based on the assumption that individuals in similar social situations are constrained to view the world and to evaluate events and ideas from the same perspective. This section focuses on the political attitudes of coaches and athletes, who face somewhat similar pressures and therefore have congruent attitudes.

Liberalism-conservatism is a multidimensional phenomenon. Some of the many dimensions involved are attitudes about welfare, foreign aid, racial integration, the free-enterprise system, morality, and social change. Few persons, therefore, hold a consistent pattern of thought across these dimensions. This fact makes our analysis difficult and doubtless oversimplified. Nevertheless, the discussion that follows will consider political conservatives to be persons who support the existing socioeconomic-political system. This means that they have a great respect for tradition, authority, law and order, the free-enterprise system, patriotism, and the tried-and-true values of hard work, goal orientation, and Christian morality. It implies, further, that they tend to be intolerant of challenges to these traditional values.

Despite an occasional political protest, athletes as a group are politically conservative. Although some former professional and college athletes have been critical of sport in American society, they are clearly exceptions to the rule. The response of the vast majority of athletes, coaches, reporters, and others in the sports world to critiques of contemporary sport is indicative of this conservative tendency. We will examine and explain this conservatism, focusing particularly on the political attitudes of coaches and athletes. We must note two caveats before we begin. First, there is little empirical research in this area. We will supply what information is available, but much additional research is needed. Second, the available data are mostly about white males.

Coaches

Generalizations about any social category are always difficult because few such groups are homogeneous. The coaching profession is no exception. There are harsh and lenient coaches, bigoted and nonbigoted coaches, and coaches who are hawks and doves on America's military policies. Despite these differences, however, coaches as a category can be characterized as politically conservative. Let us examine the available evidence.

Several studies indicate that physical education teachers (most coaches are trained in this field) tend to be more conservative than teachers in other fields. One study compared prospective high school physical education teachers with prospective high school liberal arts teachers at a large midwestern university. The researcher found the physical educators to be more traditional, dogmatic, and authoritarian, and more conservative in their political and religious values.[24]

Physical education teachers at the college level also appear to be more conservative than professors in other fields. A survey by the Carnegie Commission on Higher Education of the political opinions of over sixty thousand full-time college faculty members found that physical education faculty ranked second out of thirty fields in percentage of respondents who characterized themselves as strongly and moderately conservative (only agriculture faculty members were found to be more conservative).[25]

Unfortunately, little research on the political attitudes of coaches has been done to support the indirect evidence we have cited, but existing research tends to support these notions. One study by sport psychologists Bruce C. Ogilvie and Thomas A. Tutko concluded: "We know that coaches are aggressive people, self-assertive; we know that they are highly organized and ordered . . . they are also inflexible in their profession as coaches; they dislike change and experimentation; and they are extremely conservative—politically, socially and attitudinally."[26]

George H. Sage, in a study comparing college head coaches (football, basketball, and track) with college students and businesspeople, found the coaches to be more conservative than the students but somewhat less so than the businesspeople.[27] The Polyphasic Values Inventory showed the coaches to be significantly more conservative than the college students on fourteen of the twenty items. Of special interest were the items of greatest conservatism: the value of obedience to authority and the value of good conduct. Sage concluded:

> The total response profile of the college coaches showed them to possess moderate-conservative values. . . . Although conservatism is not extreme among coaches, it is more pronounced than it is among college students. . . . The findings of this

study support the notion that coaches possess a greater conservatism than college students. But an item-by-item analysis of the response choices certainly does not support the assertions which have been made recently that coaches are extremely conservative—even reactionary—in value orientation.[28]

The available but sketchy evidence, then, suggests that coaches tend to be conservative. Research has shown, moreover, that coaches, regardless of their sport and their age, tend to have similar political and social outlooks.[29] The question remains, Why is there a tendency for coaches to be politically conservative?

The first of at least six reasons has to do with the particular lifelong socialization of coaches.[30] There is considerable evidence that coaches, when compared with other faculty members, come from markedly lower socioeconomic backgrounds.[31] For example, although 22 percent of the fathers of college professors in general held high-status jobs, only 6 percent of the fathers of college football and basketball coaches had high-status occupations. Moreover, 58 percent of the fathers of basketball coaches and 54 percent of the fathers of football coaches had jobs in the low or very low occupational prestige categories. Two related reasons explain why this is significant for our discussion. Considerable social science research shows that child-rearing practices differ by social class. Working-class parents, for instance, are much more likely than middle-class parents to use physical punishment, to be more authoritarian, and to be more rigidly conventional. In addition, working-class parents tend to hold particular values: those favoring law and order, obedience to authority, and political conservatism. These practices and values held by working-class parents are a result of the particular conditions of life experienced by them.[32] Parental values are transmitted to their offspring and then internalized, therefore it follows that persons growing up in working-class families will themselves tend to possess values stressing political and social conservatism.

The second reason for the propensity for conservatism among coaches is that almost invariably they are former athletes. As we will see in the next section, the ruthless selection process in athletics encourages certain traits and discourages others. Coaches are products of such a system, and the thesis of this chapter is that this system is conservative.

Third, coaching is an occupational subculture, and socialization theory suggests that members of a group tend to possess similar value orientations. The two reasons for this are selection and assimilation. Occupational choice is often made on the basis of compatible values; that is, the individual is attracted to a particular occupation because he or she is in agreement with the values of that occupation. Typically, too, an individual who aspires to a particular occupation will internalize the values, attitudes, and behaviors characteristic of persons in that occupation, especially the characteristics of the most successful ones. This process is called *anticipatory socialization* and leads to *assimilation.*[33]

Fourth, in addition to selection and assimilation, the individual will also feel overt pressure to adopt the attitudes, values, and behaviors of those supporting him or her in the occupation. Communities, school boards, and fans demand that their coaches support the traditional values because coaches are hired to mold the character of youth. Thus, a coach or potential coach who harbors political and social views outside the mainstream will have great difficulty in finding or retaining a job, thereby leaving the vast majority of the available positions to those considered politically safe.

Fifth, the subcultural character of the coaching profession is maintained by open opposition from the academic community, a hostility that strengthens the isolation of coaches by creating alienation and polarization. This opposition stems from the belief that coaches are anti-intellectual, dehumanizing, and insensitive to the individuality of their athletes. Whether these beliefs are accurate or not, the result is an antagonistic relationship that develops solidarity among coaches and tends to reinforce their unity around specific beliefs.[34]

Sixth, and perhaps most crucial, the success or failure of a coach depends almost entirely on whether the coach is considered competent (in other words, whether his or her team wins more than it loses). Thus, there is a strong tendency for coaches to control the situation as much as possible. Since they will be held responsible for the outcome, they will make the decisions (who will play, what plays will be called, and what strategy will be used). Moreover, they will control as much of the players' lives as possible because what the players eat, when they sleep, whom they date, and whether they have long hair may make a difference in the coaches' uncertain world.

The rationale for controlling the lives of players off the field is summed up in this exhortation from a coach to the players on his team: "Our school, our team, our coaches, and our community are judged by your behavior. It is very important that you be gentlemen in all your actions."[35] Apparently this coach felt the need to control an area that is more certain than the outcome of a game and that also has a bearing on whether he keeps his job or not. For all of these reasons, coaches find it difficult to be tolerant of behavior that is outside community norms. As Harry Edwards put it, "The apparent inflexibility of coaches then derives at least in part from the institutionalized demand that they be totally liable for outcomes in a situation fraught with uncertainties."[36] In short, the behaviors of coaches are likely not the results solely of personality but they are also the products of their unique social situation.

Athletes

Existing research that contrasts athletes with nonathletes consistently finds that in the United States the former are the more politically conservative. Walter E. Schafer examined this relationship, especially among high school students, and concluded: "Interscholastic athletics serve first and foremost as a social device for steering young people—participants and spectators alike—into the mainstream of American life through the overt and covert teaching of appropriate attitudes, values, norms and behavior patterns. As a result school sports tend to exert more of a conservatizing and integrating influence in the society than an innovative or progressive influence."[37]

Two studies support Schafer's contention. The first was a study of 937 male seniors from eight high schools in the state of New York. The researchers found

that (1) the greater the participation in extracurricular activities (athletics and others), the greater was the acceptance of authority; (2) athletes were more likely than nonathletes to believe that the American way of life is superior to that of any other country; (3) athletes were less likely than nonathletes to endorse a statement calling for fundamental structural change in American society; and (4) athletes, more than nonathletes, believed that resistance to the draft was basically wrong.[38]

Research on college students has produced essentially the same findings. When compared with college nonathletes, college athletes were found to be more conservative, less interested and active in politics, more tolerant of violations of civil liberties, and more tolerant of repressive reactions to campus unrest.[39]

However, we must qualify the generalization that athletes tend to be conservative. Studies on the political attitudes of athletes have not been separated by race and gender. Minority athletes might differ from their majority counterparts because of the discrimination they have experienced. On the other hand, they may perceive that the system has been good to them so they do not challenge it. This is a charge leveled by some on successful African American athletes such as Michael Jordan. Women athletes, we predict, are more likely to be politically liberal than men athletes because they have had to go against the traditions of society and they have seen that the power structure of sport has tended to fight gender equality. This may change, however, as women athletes become more accepted and rewarded. Obviously, these questions need to be researched.

Another qualification is that the findings for athletes in the United States may not hold for other societies. Brian M. Petrie and Elizabeth L. Reid studied the political attitudes of Canadian athletes and found them to be generally liberal.[40] This may mean that the conservatism of sport is situationally specific, in other words, specific to a particular culture. If true, this would reconfirm the thesis that sport mirrors society.

Why do American athletes (at least white male athletes) tend to be politically conservative? A number of reasons have been advanced. First, athletes are the prestige leaders in their school and community. They rarely criticize the status quo because they benefit from the way things are. Second, since athletes devote substantial time and energy to sports activities, they have less time than nonathletes to become involved in or even to consider social criticism. Third, athletes are more likely to have grown accustomed to accepting, rather than questioning, authority.[41] Fourth, it is almost impossible to remain radical in the sports world. Athletes whose views and behavior are nonconventional will soon be weeded out from the regimented world most coaches insist on.[42]

No research has yet been undertaken contrasting the political attitudes of professional athletes to nonathletes with similar educational backgrounds. Presumably, two factors should operate to make professional athletes especially conservative: (1) They have been successful school athletes with all the attendant pressures from schools and communities to be conventional; and (2) they are successful in both monetary and prestige dimensions, making it difficult to question the system.

The Political Olympics

The motto of the Olympic Games is "Citius, Altius, Fortius" ("Faster, Higher, Stronger"). It implies that athletes should strive for ever better performances. Moreover, the objective of the Olympic movement is "to educate young people through sport in a spirit of better understanding between each other and of friendship, thereby helping to build a better and more peaceful world." However, since the revival of the Olympics in 1896, there has been an erosion of the prominence of athletic accomplishments and the corresponding ascendance of political considerations. This section addresses the political side of the Olympics and offers suggestions for reducing the corrosive effects of politics on the Olympic movement and its ideals.

Political Problems

Politics surrounding the Olympics is manifested in five major ways: (1) excessive nationalism within nations concerning the performance of their athletes in the Olympics; (2) use of the Olympics as a site for political demonstrations and violence by political dissidents in the host country; (3) decisions by ruling bodies to deny participation by certain nations; (4) decisions by nations to boycott the Games for political reasons; and (5) the political organization of the Olympics. Let's examine these in turn.

Excessive Nationalism Within Nations

Nationalism related to the Olympics that goes beyond its appropriate boundaries is expressed in several ways. Foremost, there is the use of athletics to promote political goals. As we have seen, Hitler turned the 1936 Games in Berlin into a propaganda show to legitimate Nazi Germany. Similarly, nations tend to use their showing in international athletic events as an indicator of the superiority of their politico-economic systems. Some nations are quite blatant in their efforts to demonstrate their superiority, offering large prizes to their athletes who win medals.

A second manifestation of excessive nationalism is that in the zeal to win some nations may promote the use of performance-enhancing drugs for their athletes. This was clearly true for the East Germans before 1990. It appears that China has embarked on such a policy. During the 1994 Asian Games, seven Chinese swimmers, along with two canoeists, a cyclist, and a hurdler failed drug tests.[43]

A third indication of national chauvinism has to do with the reporting of international events. Members of the media in reporting the Olympics may let their politics distort their analyses. For example, during the opening ceremonies of the 1988 Winter Olympics in Calgary, as the North Koreans followed by the Danes paraded by the television cameras, ABC's Peter Jennings observed: "What a contrast between North Korea—remote, closed, hostile to westerners— and Denmark, this peace-loving nation of Northern Europe where the emphasis is really on quality of life . . ."[44]

Use of the Olympics by Political Dissidents in the Host Country

This is a common problem associated with the Olympics. At virtually every recent Olympics there have been political demonstrations, threats, and violence by disaffected groups. The host country has usually responded with extra security and police violence (e.g., Mexico City and Seoul). The 1992 Olympics in Barcelona faced this problem as Basque separatists threatened to use the Olympics as a vehicle for worldwide recognition of their plight.

Political Decisions by National and International Olympic Committees

The following are a few examples from the last fifty-five years of decisions made for political reasons by ruling bodies.[45]

- 1936: As a concession to the Nazis, the United States dropped two Jewish sprinters from the 400-meter relay.
- 1948: Israel was excluded from participation after a threat of an Arab boycott.
- 1952: East Germany was denied participation because it was not a "recognized state."
- 1960: The International Olympics Committee (IOC) decreed that North and South Korea should compete as one team, using the same flag, emblem, and uniform. Nationalist China was forced to compete under the name of Taiwan.
- 1964: South Africa was banned from the Olympics for its apartheid policies.
- 1968: Tommie Smith and John Carlos of the United States raised a black power salute during the American national anthem and were banned from Olympic competition for life by the U.S. Olympic Committee.
- 1972: The IOC ruled that Rhodesia would be allowed to participate. Many African nations were incensed by this action because of the racist policies of the ruling elite in Rhodesia and threatened a boycott of the Games unless Rhodesia was barred. The IOC bowed to this pressure and rescinded its earlier action.
- 1991: The International Olympic Committee agreed to let South Africa participate in the 1992 Olympics provided that it meet certain conditions regarding the dismantling of apartheid.

Political Decisions by Individual Nations Regarding the Olympics

International incidents that have nothing to do with the Olympic Games have sometimes caused nations to withdraw their teams from competition. Some examples:

- 1952: Taiwan boycotted the Games when Communist China was admitted to the International Olympic Committee.
- 1956: Egypt, Lebanon, and Iraq boycotted the Olympics because of the Anglo-French seizure of the Suez Canal. Spain, Switzerland, and the Netherlands withdrew from the Olympics in protest after the Soviet Union invaded Hungary.
- 1976: Twenty-eight African nations boycotted the Games because New Zealand, whose rugby team had toured South Africa, was allowed to compete.
- 1980: Some fifty-four nations, including the United States, West Germany, Canada, and Japan, boycotted the Games because of the Soviet Union's invasion of Afghanistan.
- 1984: Fourteen nations, most notably the Soviet Union, East Germany, Cuba, Bulgaria, and Poland, boycotted the Games because it was held in the United States.
- 1988: Cuba boycotted the Summer Games because North Korea was not allowed to cohost the Games with South Korea. North Korea joined in the boycott.

The Political Organization of the Olympics

In addition to the corruptions of the Olympic ideals that have been outlined, the very ways that the Games are organized are political. Nations select which athletes will perform (i.e., no athlete can perform without national sponsorship). The IOC provides ceremonies where athletes march behind their country's flag. After each event, the winner's national anthem is played and the flags of the three medal winners are raised at the awards ceremony. The IOC also considers political criteria in the selection of the site of the Olympics and in the choice of judges, ensuring in the latter case a balance between East and West, especially in the judging of events such as boxing, diving, ice skating, and gymnastics.

A Proposal for Change

To be fair in this appraisal, the Olympic Games do attempt to promote the idea of oneness with the use of the Olympic Hymn and the Olympic flag (five interlaced rings representing "the union of the five continents and the meeting of athletes from all over the world at the Olympic Games in a spirit of fair and frank competition"). However, as Gilbert Cranberg has pointed out, "nationalism not merely intrudes, it dominates." For him, another Olympiad will be another "orgy of flag-waving. Not just literally, but in the way Olympic contests get the patriotic juices flowing."[46]

Is there a way to organize the Olympics to accomplish the aim of neutralizing the crippling political problems that work to negate the Olympic ideals? We offer the following proposals to achieve that aim:

1. *Establish two permanent sites for the Games.* Each permanent site must be neutral, for otherwise the Games will continue to be subject to the influence of power politics. The choices most often mentioned are Greece for the Summer Olympics and Switzerland for the Winter Games. Greece is a natural choice because the ancient Olympian Games were held there every four years for more than one thousand years, ending in A.D. 393. Even better, each of these permanent sites should be in a free zone. A free zone would be land ceded to the International Olympic Committee and therefore land that no nation claims, just as the United Nations is located in a free zone in New York City.

2. *Restrict the events to competition among individuals.* All team sports must be eliminated because each team represents a nation, which makes political considerations inevitable. A second reason for eliminating team sports is that they are inherently unfair; the larger the population base of a nation, the more likely that country will be able to field a superior team.

3. *Athletes must represent only themselves.* Athletes, in actuality and symbolically, should not represent a country, nor should any nation-state be represented by uniforms, flags, national anthems, or political leaders. When an athlete is awarded his or her medal for winning an event, only the Olympic Hymn should be played. Athletes should also be randomly assigned to housing and eating arrangements at the Games to reduce national identification and to maximize cross-national interaction.

4. *Revise the opening ceremonies so that athletes enter the area with other athletes in their events.* As Jay Coakley has argued, "If athletes were grouped by event rather than citizenship, spectators would be less likely to see the Olympics and the athletes in political terms. . . . The emphasis in the opening ceremonies would be on unity and fellowship among athletes, not on the political and economic systems in which the athletes were born through no choice of their own."[47]

5. *All athletes (amateur and professional) are eligible for competition.* The nation-state should not be involved in the selection process because this encourages nationalistic feelings. To ensure that the best athletes of the world are able to compete, a minimum standard for each event should be set by the governing board. Athletes meeting this standard would have all expenses to meet in regional competition paid by the Olympic Committee. At the regionals another and higher standard of excellence would be set for athletes to qualify for the Olympics. Again, for those athletes qualifying for the Olympics, all expenses for travel and per diem would be paid by the Olympic Committee.

6. *Subsidize the cost of the Olympics from revenues generated from spectators' admissions to the regionals, admissions to the Games, and from television.* By establishing permanent sites and eliminating team events, the cost of the Olympics would be reduced significantly. Revenues from admissions and television should cover the costs after the Games are established. During the building of the permanent sites, though, the Olympic Committee may need a subsidy or loan from the United Nations. Television revenues present a particularly thorny problem because the revenue potential is great and this lends itself to threats of overcommercialization, the intrusion of corporations into the decision-making arena, and jingoism by chauvinistic television commentators. To reduce these potential dangers, the events could be televised and reported by a company strictly controlled by the Olympic Committee. The televising of the Olympics would be provided to each country at a cost determined by the existing number of television sets in that country. Each nation would decide how the fee would be paid, but the important point is that no country would have any control over what would be shown or the commentary emanating from the Games.

7. *Establish an Olympic Committee and a secretary-general to prepare for and oversee the Games.* The composition of this committee would be crucial. Currently the members of the IOC are taken from national committees, with an important criterion being the maintenance of a political balance between opposing factions. The concept of a ruling body is essential, but the committee should be reorganized to reduce political considerations. This is a baffling problem because the selection will inevitably involve politics. One possibility would be to incorporate the selection procedures used in the United Nations to select its secretary-general. These procedures have worked, even during the darkest days of the Cold War, toward the selection of a competent, objective, and nonaligned (of neither a pro-western or a pro-eastern bloc) arbitrator. In addition to an Olympic secretary-general, a governing board and a permanent staff would also have to be established.

Now is a propitious time to depoliticize the Olympics. The tensions and paranoia associated with the Cold War are receding. We have seen cooperative efforts between the two superpowers that have not occurred since World War II. The eastern bloc is no longer a force. East and West Germany are now Germany. The European Economic Community will break down nationalistic barriers further. Of course, there will be international tensions, wars, and acts of terrorism, but it appears they will not be as threatening as before. Could we take this turning point in history and reorganize the Olympics to eliminate as much of the politics from it as possible? The task is challenging but not impossible. The Olympic movement is important. That is why it must be radically altered from its present form if its lofty goals are to be realized.

Summary

Two themes have dominated this chapter: Sport is political in character, and persons connected with sport in almost any capacity tend to be conservative. A basic conservatism in sport has two important implications for society. First, the athletic programs of the schools, to which most persons are exposed, will support and reinforce a view of the world and of the society that perpetuates the status quo. In the United States this is accomplished through the promotion of American values and the support of the American politico-economic system.

A second implication, given the institutional character of sport, is that efforts to change sport will rarely come from those who control sport. Moreover, any attack on sport will be defined as an attack on society itself. Thus, change in sport will be slow and congruent with what is happening in society.

Notes

1. Phillip Goodhart and Christopher Chataway, *War Without Weapons* (London: Allen, 1968), 3.

2. See Ralf Dahrendorf, *Class and Class Conflict in Industrial Society* (Palo Alto, Calif.: Stanford University Press, 1959); and Robert Michels, *Political Parties* (New York: Dover, 1959), first published in 1914.

3. Donald Katz, "Triumph of the Swoosh," *Sports Illustrated,* 6 August 1993, 54ff; and Michael Knisley, "The 100 Most Powerful People (in Sports)," *The Sporting News,* 4 January 1993, sec. F, p. 13.

4. See Arthur T. Johnson and James H. Frey, eds., *Government and Sport: The Public Issues* (Totowa, N.J.: Rowman and Allanheld, 1985); and Philip R. Hochberg, "How Congress Looks at Sports," *Sports Inc.,* 1 February 1988, 46–49.

5. Associated Press release, "Millions in Federal Taxes Will be Spent on Olympics Despite Private Funding," *Rocky Mountain News,* 5 September 1995, sec. A, p. 29.

6. See Richard E. Lapchick, "Sports and Apartheid: The World Closes In," in *Fractured Focus: Sport as a Reflection of Society,* ed. Richard E. Lapchick (Lexington, Mass.: Lexington Books, 1986), 369–76.

7. See James A. R. Nafziger, "Foreign Policy in the Sports Arena," in *Government and Sport,* ed. Arthur T. Johnson and James H. Frey, 248–60.

8. Richard D. Mandell, *The Nazi Olympics* (New York: Macmillan, 1971).

9. See Lynn Rosellini, "The Sports Factories," *U.S. News & World Report,* 17 February 1992, 48–59.

10. Ibid., 51.

11. Bruce Kidd, "How Do We Find Our Own Voices in the 'New World Order'?" *Sociology of Sport Journal* 8 (June 1991): 182. See also Donald Macintosh, Tom Bedecki, and C. E. S. Franks, *Sport and Politics in Canada: Federal Government Involvement Since 1981* (Kingston: McGill-Queens University Press, 1987); and Donald Macintosh and Don Whitson, *The Game Planners: Transforming Canada's Sports System* (Kingston: McGill-Queens University Press, 1990).

12. Robert M. Goodhue, "The Politics of Sport: An Institutional Focus," Proceedings of the North American Society for Sport History (1974): 34–35.

13. See Donald W. Ball, "Olympic Games Competition: Structural Correlates of National Success," *International Journal of Comparative Sociology* 13 (September/December 1972): 186–99; and Goodhart and Chataway, *War Without Weapons.*

14. Paula Edelson, "Sports During Wartime," *Zeta Magazine* 4 (May 1991): 85–87.

15. Tom Wicker, "Patriotism for the Wrong Ends," *New York Times,* 19 January 1973.

16. See Tom Squitieri, "Soccer Eases Crisis, Lifts Spirits," *USA Today,* 28 June 1994, sec. A, p. 6 (international edition); Janet Lever, *Soccer Madness* (Chicago: University of Chicago Press, 1983); and Steve Wulf, "Running on Empty: Cuba Maintains a Rich Sports Tradition Despite Shortages of Everything but Pride," *Sports Illustrated,* 29 July 1991, 60–70.

17. Paul Hoch, "The World of Playtime, USA," *Daily World,* 27 April 1972, p. 12.

18. For greater depth on the theme of sport as an opiate, see Paul Hoch, *Rip Off the Big Game* (New York: Doubleday, 1972); Jean-Marie Brohm, *Sport: A Prison of Measured Time*, trans. Ian Fraser (London: Ink Links, 1978); and Jay J. Coakley, *Sport in Society*, 5th ed. (St. Louis: Mosby/Times Mirror, 1994), 30–31.

19. See Sue Curry Jansen and Don Sabo, "The Sport/War Metaphor: Hegemonic Masculinity, the Persian Gulf War, and the New World Order," *Sociology of Sport Journal* 11 (March 1994), 1–17; and Ike Balbus, "Politics as Sports: The Political Ascendancy of the Sports Metaphor in America," *Monthly Review* 26 (March 1975): 26–39.

20. Harry Edwards, *The Revolt of the Black Athlete* (New York: Free Press, 1969), xv.

21. Teri Thompson, "Ban the Klan," *Westword*, 13 November 1993, p. 28.

22. Excerpts from the press release of the address by vice-president of the United States Spiro Agnew, Birmingham, Ala., 18 January 1972, 5–6.

23. For an important theoretical discussion of sport as a socializing agent, see John M. Hoberman, *Sport and Political Ideology* (Austin: University of Texas Press, 1984).

24. Gerald S. Kenyon, "Certain Psychological and Cultural Characteristics Unique to Prospective Teachers of Physical Education," *Research Quarterly* 36 (March 1965): 105–12.

25. S. M. Lipset, M. A. Trow, and E. C. Ladd, *Faculty Opinion Survey* (New York: Carnegie Commission on Higher Education, n.d.).

26. Bruce C. Ogilvie and Thomas A. Tutko, "Self-Perception as Compared with Measured Personality of Male Physical Educators," in *Contemporary Psychology of Sport*, ed. Gerald S. Kenyon (Chicago: Athletic Institute, 1970), 73–77.

27. George H. Sage, "Value Orientations of American College Coaches Compared to Those of Male College Students and Businessmen," in *Sport and American Society*, ed. George H. Sage, 2d ed. (Reading, Mass.: Addison-Wesley, 1974), 207–28.

28. Ibid., 222–23.

29. George H. Sage, "Occupational Socialization and Value Orientations of Athletic Coaches," *Research Quarterly* 44 (October 1973): 269–77.

30. Many of the insights that follow come from George H. Sage, "An Occupational Analysis of the College Coach," in *Sport and Social Order*, ed. Donald W. Ball and John W. Loy, Jr. (Reading, Mass.: Addison-Wesley, 1975), 395–455; John D. Massengale, "Coaching as an Occupational Subculture," *Phi Delta Kappan* 61 (October 1974): 140–42; George H. Sage, "Sociology of Physical Educator/Coaches: Personal Attributes Controversy," *Research Quarterly* 51 (March 1980): 110–21, and George H. Sage, "Socialization of Coaches: Antecedents to Coaches' Beliefs and Behaviors," in *Sport and American Society*, ed. George H. Sage, 3d ed. (Reading, Mass.: Addison-Wesley, 1980), pp. 160–69.

31. John W. Loy, Jr., and George H. Sage, "Social Origins, Academic Achievement, Athletic Achievement, and Career Mobility Patterns of College Coaches" (paper presented at the Annual Meeting of the American Sociological Association, New Orleans, La., August 1972).

32. Melvin L. Kohn, "The Effects of Social Class on Parental Values and Practices," in *Perspectives on the Family: History, Class, and Feminism* (Belmont, Calif.: Wadsworth, 1990), 389–405.

33. See Morris Rosenberg, *Occupations and Values* (Glencoe, Ill.: Free Press, 1967).

34. Massengale, "Coaching as an Occupational Subculture," 141.

35. From a statement on the policies concerning individual conduct, Shawnee Mission East High School, Shawnee Mission, Kans., 1973.

36. Harry Edwards, *Sociology of Sport* (Homewood, Ill.: Dorsey Press, 1973), 140.

37. Walter E. Schafer, "Sport, Socialization and the School: Toward Maturity or Enculturation?" (paper presented at the Third International Symposium on the Sociology of Sport, Waterloo, Ont., August 1971), 6.

38. Richard A. Rehberg and Michael Cohen, "Political Attitudes and Participation in Extra-Curricular Activities with Special Emphasis on Interscholastic Activities" (mimeographed paper, State University of New York at Binghamton, n.d.).

39. Derrick J. Norton, "A Comparison of Political Attitudes and Political Participation of Athletes and Non-Athletes" (master's thesis, University of Oregon, 1971).

40. Brian M. Petrie and Elizabeth L. Reid, "The Political Attitudes of Canadian Athletes," Proceedings of the Fourth Canadian Psycho Motor Learning and Sports Psychology Symposium (Waterloo, Ont.: University of Waterloo, 1972), 514–30.

41. These first three reasons are taken from Walter E. Schafer, "Sport and Youth Counterculture: Contrasting Socialization Themes," in *Social Problems in Athletics*, ed. Daniel M. Landers (Urbana, Ill.: University of Illinois Press, 1976), 183–200.

42. Bruce C. Ogilvie and Thomas A. Tutko, "Sport: If You Want to Build Character, Try Something Else," *Psychology Today* 5 (October 5, 1971): 61–63.

43. Alexander Wolff, "Great Fall of China," *Sports Illustrated*, 19 December 1994, 19.

44. Lynn Rosellini, "The Distorting Lens of Politics," *U.S. News & World Report*, 29 February 1988, 64.

45. For a sample of the sources dealing with the political aspects of the Olympics, see Richard D. Mandell, *The Nazi Olympics*; Richard Espy, *The Politics of the Olympic Games* (Berkeley: University of California Press, 1979); Harry Edwards, *The Revolt of the Black Athlete*; *Arena Review* 6 (December 1982), entire issue; Allen Guttmann, *The Games Must Go On: Avery Brundage and the Olympic Movement* (New York: Columbia University Press, 1984); Harry Edwards, "Sportpolitics: Los Angeles, 1984–'The Olympic Tradition Continues,'" *Sociology of Sport Journal* 1, no. 2 (1984): 172–83; Robert A. Mechikoff, "The Olympic Games: Sport as International Politics," *Journal of Physical Education, Recreation and Dance* 55 (March 1984): 23–25; Richard E. Lapchick, "A Political History of the Modern Olympic Games," in *Fractured Focus*, ed. Richard E. Lapchick, 329–45.

46. Gilbert Cranberg, "Excess Nationalism Harms the Olympics," *USA Today*, 23 September 1988, sec. A, p. 6.

47. Coakley, *Sport in Society*, 373.

Chapter 1 characterized three levels of sport: informal sport, organized sport, and *corporate sport,* the latter referring to levels of sporting activity dominated by factors, economic or political, extrinsic to sport itself. Corporate sport, in which the relatively spontaneous, pristine nature of informal sport has been corrupted, is characteristic of sport in contemporary North America. Money has become the foundation of sport, even at the so-called amateur level. The profit motive shapes the decisions of owners, school administrators, and the corporations that use sport. Lawsuits and strikes have redistributed the wealth and shifted the balance of power in the professional leagues. The money mania has eroded owner and player loyalties. Fans are left with the gnawing sense that they are the victims of the greed of owners and players alike. John Underwood has criticized this trend by saying that sport "has been transformed into economic snake oil. From something wonderful, it has been made grotesque by commerce. It has been distorted and polluted by money, and the never-ending quest for more."[1]

Whether corporate sport is a business is no longer a question, although the owners would like to perpetuate the myth that it is not. In this chapter we will examine the intimate interrelationship between money and sport and the consequences of this trend.

Who Benefits Economically from Sports?

Only a small percentage of the people participating in sport activities derive direct economic benefits from them. (The instrumental use of sports, for example businesses using golf, tennis, and so forth as a means of entertaining clients or customers, is another situation.) As we will document more fully in chapter 12, the number of professional athletes competing in major league competition is extremely small. For instance, the total number of full-time major league players in the four top North American team sports, which are baseball, basketball, football, and hockey, is about three thousand one hundred annually. Add to this the very few professional golfers who earn their living on the tour and a handful of tennis players, race-car drivers, boxers, and jockeys, and it is apparent that the business of professional sport is based on the exploits of a very small group of talented individuals. For those who have attained major league status, the financial benefits can be substantial, but the well-publicized salaries of a handful of superstars have given the public a distorted and inflated idea of professional athletes' incomes. These salaries should be balanced against the brief, often tenuous, careers of professional athletes. For instance, the median length of a professional football player's career is 3.4 years, which does not even qualify the typical player for a pension.

Successful professional athletes receive many additional benefits through product endorsements; speeches and other public appearances; jobs as actors, entertainers, and sports announcers; opportunities for investments in business ventures as diverse as sports camps, real estate developments, quick-order franchises, motels, and restaurants; and many other advantages. In 1995 the top ten athletes in endorsements were Michael Jordan ($35 million), Shaquille O'Neal ($14.5 million), Jack Nicklaus ($13 million), Arnold Palmer ($12.6 million), Joe Montana ($12 million), Wayne Gretzky (8.8 million), Nancy Kerrigan ($4 million), Steve Young ($4 million), Hakeem Olajuwon ($3.8 million), and Bonnie Blair ($3.2 million).[2]

For most whose livelihoods are dependent on athletic abilities, the financial rewards are not nearly so great.

- *Item*: More than twenty-five hundred individuals play minor league baseball, and only 7 percent of them will make it to the major leagues. None of these minor league players are covered by the minimum salary scales of major league baseball.
- *Item*: In professional golf 350 men and 270 women pursue the multimillion dollar prize money, but only about 200 make a living at it. The rest have trouble making expenses.
- *Item*: An individual needs over $1 million a year for expenses to be competitive on the auto racing circuit. This money comes from commercial sponsors who give it, typically, to the already successful and their sons (e.g., some sons of famous drivers who began their careers with considerable corporate sponsorship are Michael Andretti, Al Unser Jr.,

and Kyle Petty). Meanwhile, unknowns, people of color, and women have great difficulty in obtaining sponsorships.

• *Item*: In professional basketball a lucrative sports career awaits the successful athlete but only about 276 players, and approximately 40 rookies, are hired each year.

• *Item*: The scholarship athlete in college is paid virtual slave wages for his or her services. Calculated on the basis of the room, books, meals, and tuition allowed by the NCAA, a college athlete's salary does not greatly exceed the federal government's stated poverty level and is about at the federally established minimum hourly pay scale.

Coaches are in a category of professional athletes frequently overlooked in calculating the economic effects of sport in America. About 200,000 coaches are employed in secondary schools, and 22,000 men and 4,200 women are engaged in coaching at the college level.[3]

Umpires and referees constitute another sports occupational category. Baseball umpires are the best paid. After a threatened strike, an agreement was reached whereby the 1995 salaries of major league umpires ranged from $60,000 for rookies to $200,000, plus expenses, for umpires in their twentieth year. Hockey and basketball also require full-time officials, but the pay is much less. Professional football pays its officials on a part-time, game-by-game basis. Thousands more officiate at the other levels of sport for relatively low fees.

Another occupational category dependent on sport is the specialist in sports medicine. The treatment of sports injuries requires special techniques, and sports medicine clinics are becoming relatively commonplace in metropolitan centers. It would be interesting to know the proportion of the billions spent for health care in the United States that go for the treatment of sports-related injuries.

A relatively new sports job is that of the player agent. With the advent of free agents and accelerated player salaries, agents for the players are performing an ever-greater function in professional sports.[4] They provide a service to the players because they know the tax laws and the market value of the athletes. Their goal is to maximize monetary benefits for the athlete by extracting the most beneficial contract from management. For this service the agent receives a percentage of the agreement (between 5 and 10 percent), which can be a considerable amount in this era of multimillion dollar contracts. This business is so lucrative (and unregulated), therefore, some agents have taken advantage of their naive clients by, for example, having them sign huge contracts with payments deferred over as many as forty years; the agent takes a percentage of the total up front, while the player receives no interest on the deferred money, which is further devalued by inflation. Agents also sometimes violate NCAA amateur rules by signing college athletes and giving them bonuses.

In addition to those directly involved in producing the sport product, many auxiliary businesses benefit from the sports boom. Hotels, taxis, restaurants, and other business establishments can thereby increase their volume of business. The presence of a major league team generates millions of dollars for a city's economy, and this is why cities are so generous to sports teams (in stadium rentals, concessions revenues, and various tax subsidies). Huge sports spectaculars such as the Kentucky Derby, the Indianapolis 500, the World Series, and the Super Bowl are major tourist attractions bringing an economic bonanza to numerous ancillary businesses. The 1994 Super Bowl, for example, poured an estimated $150 million into the Atlanta area economy (see box 10.1).

The concessions business provides sports spectators with food, drink, and merchandise. A concessionaire is typically given a monopoly by a team management, league, or city; in return the grantor receives a percentage of the proceeds. According to Richard Sandomir, "During a typical sold-out New York Rangers game at Madison Square Garden, concessionaire Harry M. Stevens sells 20,000 hot dogs, 15,000 beers, 10,000 sodas, 2,500 programs, 500 yearbooks, and 10,000 pennants, flags, and T-shirts. . . . Stevens' per-game Rangers' gross is about $480,000 [an average of $5 per fan]."[5]

Benefits from sport accrue to some entrepreneurs and collectivities through gambling. In 1989 gambling on sports amounted to $57.1 billion (about 20 percent of the $290 billion bet legally and illegally on everything). In fiscal 1989–90 $1.96 billion was wagered in the legal sports books in Nevada (where the house takes 10 percent of each wager). These sports books have grown enormously (the amount wagered in the Nevada sports books increased from $360 million in fiscal 1980–81 to $1.96 billion ten years later). Nevada is the only state to permit sports books.[6]

As sports mania has pervaded the country, public pressure to legalize sports betting has intensified, pressure exerted both by the financial distress of many state governments and by bet-eager constituents. As a result the majority of states have legal pari-mutuel wagering on horse racing and greyhound racing, and a few even have legal wagering on jai alai.[7]

Corporations are the greatest beneficiaries from sport, both directly, through the sale of sports-related products, and indirectly, through the use of sports to generate interest in their products. Sport is big business. Nike, the largest supplier of sports clothing and shoes, for example, is a $3.7 billion company.

Sport enhances big business. Sports themes and prominent athletes are used in advertisements to sell products. Companies are convinced that through the proper selection of sports and sports personalities, they can reach particular pre-identified consumer categories or strengthen the general visibility of their products.

The commercialization of sport is easily seen in the advertising at the ballparks and arenas. Take, for example, what occurs at the Seattle Coliseum during a SuperSonics basketball game:

A total of ten bulletin boards, advertising companies such as Alaska Airlines, Blockbuster Video, G.T.E. . . . and Safeway . . . circle the outer reaches, blocking scoreboard visibility for fans sitting in the top rows. Illuminated Coca-Cola signs hang above the four courtside exits. The scorer's table rotates a series of new ads every five minutes or so throughout the course of the game, continually catching one's attention with their sudden movements. No matter where the eyes

box 10.1 *Continued*

18 TV cameras were used by NBC, including two overhead end-zone cameras; 16 videotape machines, including two super slo-mo units.

1,500 amplifiers, 212 speakers and enough wire to stretch the length of 30 football fields were used in the halftime show.

$2,600 was the cost of renting a limousine in Atlanta for the three-day weekend.

750 million people worldwide were expected to watch the Super Bowl on TV. One billion are expected to watch the World Cup soccer championship.

2,000 full and part-time Super Bowl jobs were created in Atlanta.

Four days was the average length of visit.

$170 was what the average visitor spent each day in Atlanta; $44.20 went to food and alcohol.

1,200 corporate jets were parked at local airports.

$15 million in licensed NFL merchandise was sold in the Atlanta area during Super Bowl week. $1 million of counterfeit merchandise was confiscated.

73% of men watch the game from start to finish, vs. 46% of women.

$38,000 goes to each winning player; losers get $23,500. Annual U.S. income per person: $21,000.

2,189,007 have attended Super Bowl games; largest crowd was 103,985 at Super Bowl XIV.

$56 million was bet in Nevada on last year's Super Bowl; 50 to 100 times more was bet illegally.

80 percent of the 71,600 at the Super Bowl will be executives, managers, sales representatives or professionals. One in four will be a corporate officer.

6,200 people were fed on game day at the Atlanta Hyatt Regency. Cost: $185 per person, or nearly $500,000, paid for by the host companies.

$250 million was the cost to Coca-Cola to be the NFL's official soft drink through the 1998 Super Bowl. During Super Bowl week in Atlanta, Coca-Cola left 32,000 welcome boxes in hotel rooms, rented more than 140 billboards throughout Atlanta, and hung more than 1,200 Coca-Cola street banners.

Sources: "Super Bowl by the Numbers," *USA Today,* 31 January 1994, sec. B, p. 5; and Del Jones, "Game Ticket: Companies Super Perk," *USA Today,* 28 January 1994, sec. B, p. 1.

might rest, no matter how trivial that spot might be, it seems someone, somewhere, coveted its commercial potential. The folding chairs used to seat the visiting players sport Coca-Cola logos. The sweats worn by the Sonics ball boys carry Avia logos (as do their caps and the backs of their shirts); and there is also an honorary Coca-Cola ball boy at each game. The scoreboard is a whirl of computer-generated graphics, advertising [various] products. . . . In all, sixty-five different product lines flash across the big screen at least once every game—many accompanied by messages broadcast over the public address system. Full-blown advertisements for Coca-Cola, Subaru and Tim's Cascade Style Potato Chips . . . fill the breaks between quarters. The Sonics Dance Team, brought to you courtesy of Nestle Crunch, performs original dance numbers to popular hits between timeouts.[8]

The use of sport to promote business interests takes a number of other forms as well, some reciprocal. Corporations sponsor such sports as running, bowling, golf, rodeo, tractor pulls, tennis, and skiing. In 1993 corporations spent $2.4 billion sponsoring various sports events.[9]

Sponsorship has been especially crucial to the gain in women's professional sports: Virginia Slims, Carlton, Colgate, L'eggs, Bonnie Bell, Sarah Coventry, Sears, S & H Green Stamps, and Sealy have all underwritten women's golf and tennis tournaments and have thus significantly raised the prize money and the visibility of women's sports. Corporate sponsorship has also been instrumental in increasing the prize money available for male athletes. Corporations now underwrite track meets and college bowl games in return for having their names appear prominently in their titles (e.g., the Sunkist Fiesta Bowl and the USF&G Sugar Bowl). Corporations also pay so that stadiums and arenas will bear the corporate name. Some examples: United Airlines signed a 20-year, $17.5 million agreement to put its name on the home of the Chicago Bulls and the Chicago Blackhawks; the name of the Hoosier Dome in Indianapolis has been changed to the RCA Dome, as RCA signed a 10-year $10 million contract for the name change; America West Airlines, Inc. has a 30-year, $26 million name sponsorship for the home of the Phoenix Suns; USAir pays $1 million annually to put its name on the arena where the Washington Bullets play.

The major corporations of the United States have been active in the sponsorship of the United States Olympic team for the presumed benefits of public relations, advertising, and a generous allotment of tickets. Corporate involvement in the 1996 Summer Games in Atlanta reached "Olympic" proportions.[10] Television rights were sold to ABC for $309 million, which in turn sold to other corporations high-cost, thirty-second advertising spots. Corporations paid the organizers of the Atlanta Olympic Games in order to be designated as official sponsors. Some 45 sponsors paid $500 million for that right. There are three levels of sponsorship, with the cost to be in the highest level $40 million (Coca-Cola paid $50 million). For that amount the corporation has the right to use the Olympic logo in advertising and packaging, and prime access to seating and hotel rooms. Most significant, each corporation has a monopoly on the Olympic logo among its competitors. In other words, there is only one official "Olympic" soft drink (Coke), one official credit card (Visa), one official fast food (McDonald's), one official Olympic airline (Delta), one official Olympic insurance (John Hancock), and so on. Other corporations paid to be official licensees, selling items with Olympic logos. Other corporations paid for the designation of official supplier, contributing food, bedding, and other items to the Olympic athletes.

The most blatant use of sport for commercial purposes occurs in automobile racing. Here, drivers and owners of race cars receive a fee for using a corporation's logo on their racing vehicle and on the clothing of the driver. These logos usually represent corporations involved in products for automobiles (e.g., tires, oil, auto parts, mufflers, shock absorbers) but they also include corporations selling chewing tobacco, cigarettes, clothing, soft drinks, and the like.

A special relationship seems to exist between the beer companies and sport. Beer is largely consumed by men, and men are overrepresented among the spectators at sporting events and among the avid followers of sport. The result is that the beer companies have partially subsidized sport. Some have owned teams: Anheuser-Busch owns the baseball Cardinals; Coors is part owner of the expansion baseball team in Denver, the Colorado Rockies. Coors agreed to become one of the owners, putting up about $30 million but only if the stadium would be named Coors Stadium; in hockey, Molson Breweries of Canada owns the Montreal Canadiens. Most sports teams have several sponsors for their local radio and television broadcasts, but a beer company is almost always one of them.

Professional Sport As a Business

Contrary to what some owners would have the public believe, professional sport is big business. This section examines how professional sport is structured to maximize profit. This requires that we examine how sport is profitable, the advantages of monopoly, and the public subsidization of professional teams. We also consider the changes in the owner-player relationship brought about by the players' agitation to increase their power and monetary rewards.

Professional Sport As a Monopoly

The sport industry is not only a monopoly but an unregulated one. Unlike the broadcasting industry, for example, whose monopolistic practices are regulated by the Federal Communications Commission, the sport industry is left to regulate itself. Each professional league operates as a *cartel* (competitors joining together as a self-regulating monopoly). This means that the teams make agreements on matters of mutual interest (e.g., rules, schedules, promotions, expansion, and media contracts). Such agreements are illegal in most other businesses because they lead to collusion, price-fixing, and restraint of trade.

The enormous advantages to the league cartel are several. Foremost, each sports franchise is protected from competition. The owner of the Kansas City Royals, for instance, is guaranteed that no other major league baseball team will be allowed to locate in his or her territory. There are some metropolitan areas with two major league baseball teams, but these exceptions occurred before baseball had agreed to territorial exclusivity. Even in these cases, the teams are in different leagues, ensuring that, for example, a Chicago baseball fan who wants to see American League games can see them only by attending White Sox games.

This protection from competition eliminates price wars. The owners of a franchise can continue to charge the maximum without fear of price cutting by competitors.

The cartel also controls the number of franchises allowed. Each cartel is generally reluctant to add new teams because scarcity permits higher ticket prices, more beneficial media arrangements, and continued territorial purity. In short, the value of each franchise increases by the restriction on the number of teams. When new teams are added, such as the addition of the Denver and Miami franchises in 1993 to baseball's National League, they are selected with economic criteria paramount, especially concerning new television markets (neither the Rocky Mountain time zone nor Florida had a major league team, making them attractive additions to the league). By the way, as a condition of being included in major league baseball, the Colorado Rockies and the Florida Marlins each paid $95 million.

This monopolistic situation enables a league to negotiate television contracts for the benefit of all members of the cartel. The 1961 Sports Broadcast Act allowed sports leagues to sell their national television rights as a group without being subject to the antitrust laws. As a result, the national networks and cable systems may bid for the right to televise, for example, professional football. This gives the football monopoly enormous bargaining power. As a result, one television contract with the NFL, for instance, provided each team with $40 million annually.

The final advantage of the monopoly is that the players are drastically limited in their choices and bargaining power. In football, players are drafted out of college. If they want to play in the NFL, they must negotiate with the team that drafted them. Their other choices are to play in the Arena League or the World Football League (both of which have little prestige and relatively poor pay). Another option is to play in Canada (but Canadian teams limit the number of Americans allowed per team, and the average pay is about one-third that offered by U.S. teams) or not to play that year. We will return to the owner-player relationship later in this chapter.

Public Subsidization
of Professional Team Franchises

The subsidies to franchise owners take two forms—tax breaks and the availability of arenas at very low cost. Let us examine these in turn.

The bleak financial picture typically painted by some owners of professional teams is misleading because it refers only to accounting losses (expenses exceeding income). The tax benefits available to sports promoters have been largely unpublicized. Even in those cases in which owners have not profited directly from their investments, owning a professional team is by no means the liability that publicly stated accounting losses would indicate. In short, for many wealthy individuals owning a sports franchise has lucrative tax advantages.

Investment in professional franchises enables a wealthy owner to offset the team's gate losses or to minimize taxable profits of the team or of other investments by large depreciation allowances. The purchase of a professional sports franchise includes (1) the legal right to the franchise; (2) player contracts; and (3) assets such as equipment, buildings, cars, and so forth. However, since the most valuable assets of a pro sports team are its players, most of the purchase cost will be attributed to player contracts, which, in turn, can be depreciated in the same way a steel company depreciates the investment costs of a new blast furnace. Similarly, acquisition of a player from another team will enable the new owner to depreciate the player's value over a period of years, usually five or less. Thus, the player's status as property is readily apparent, for no other business in America depreciates the value of human beings as part of the cost of its operation. There is an inconsistency here—the team is allowed to depreciate its players but players are not permitted to depreciate themselves for tax purposes. This anomaly indicates the bias in the tax code of owners over players and that players are considered as property.

An excellent example of the manner in which such depreciation operates to provide the appearance of minimum profits and maximum losses from a sports investment is revealed in the 1973 sale of the New York Yankees by the CBS network to a national syndicate of wealthy businessmen (including George Steinbrenner) for $10 million. Assuming that $1 million is attributed to franchise cost and $500,000 to equipment, $8.5 million can be allocated to player costs. This amount can be depreciated over a five-year period at $1.7 million a year. Thus, the Yankees could achieve a $1 million profit a year for five years and still show a tax loss of $700,000 a year, which may, in turn, be prorated to each investor. If the syndicate comprised ten men, each would receive a $70,000 tax loss against his own personal income tax return in addition to the $100,000 tax-free return he received as his share of the profits. It is, in this case, possible for the Yankees to have a profit of $1.7 million a year before the team or its owners pay any income tax on that profit.[11]

Ownership of professional sports franchises provides this kind of tax shelter even if the team shows accounting losses. That is why it has become an attractive investment for many wealthy persons, who can use losses and player depreciation as a means of offsetting other taxes on individual income.

These factors contribute to a high turnover of professional team ownership. Since a team can depreciate the value of its players over a relatively short period (five years or less), expansion teams or newly franchised teams composed of players purchased from other owners can depreciate, but old leagues and established teams cannot, except with players purchased from previously established clubs. Thus, buying and selling teams is more profitable than retaining them for extended periods of time.

The second type of public subsidy of professional sport is the provision of sports facilities to most franchises at very low cost. Adequate facilities are of great concern to sports promoters because they are essential to the financial success and spectator appeal of professional and big-time amateur sports. Conventional wisdom holds that the presence of major league sports teams enhances a city's prestige and generates considerable economic activity. Regarding the former, image is important, at least to civic boosters, and having a major league team gives the impression of being a first-class city.[12] Concerning the latter, the myth is that the presence of a major league team brings substantial economic growth. This is a myth for at least three reasons. First, subsidizing a team drains government resources (the cost of building and maintaining arenas, providing access roads, and the loss of revenues because of "sweetheart deals" [see box 10.2] with team owners). Second, the deflection of government money toward a sports team often means that services to the poor will be reduced or dropped altogether. Third, the economic benefits are not spread equally throughout the community. The wealthy benefit (team owners, owners of hotels and restaurants) while the costs are paid disproportionately by the middle and lower classes.[13] As John Underwood, referring to the major subsidy of a stadium, has summarized: "The point that never quite gets made in this process is that no hard evidence exists to support the notion that building stadiums for professional sports franchises is anything close to economic good sense for a community. The opposite is closer to the truth. Every study not subsidized by those with a stake in the matter indicates that taxpayers invariably get left holding the bag, and that the bag brims over with I.O.U.'s."[14]

As the boom in sports in America has increased, so also has the demand for facilities to accommodate the demands of fans for entertainment and of promoters for profits. Since 1965 at least fifty state and local governments have spent more than $6 billion to build or refurbish stadiums. About 70 percent of these stadiums are publicly financed, generally through revenue bonds that allegedly are to be paid off with the revenue from the project. However, whenever a bond-financed public project cannot pay for itself, the obligation becomes a general public one. Initial estimates of construction costs are usually understated, and estimated revenues from stadium use are often overstated. The New Orleans Superdome provides the most extreme example of this

box 10.2   *A Cozy Arrangment: The Rockies Stadium Deal*

The citizens of the six counties surrounding and including Denver passed a sales tax proposal to fund a new stadium for the Colorado Rockies baseball team. Thus, the team's ownership would have a $215.5 million stadium plus a $9 million scoreboard system provided to them free. (Actually, when the Rockies changed the original plans to increase the seating, they agreed to contribute about $30 million toward the construction costs.) The stadium district board gave its chairperson, John McHale, Jr., the power to negotiate the terms of the stadium lease with the Colorado Rockies. The deal struck between these two parties included the following provisions:

1. The Rockies owners were given the right to name the stadium, which they sold to Coors for $15 million.
2. The team owners will not have to pay rent or maintenance until the year 2000. After that they will pay the stadium district less than 2.5 percent of the team's net profits and $150,000 a year to cover the stadium's operating costs.
3. The team owners receive seat rights, luxury suites, advertising, parking, and concession rights for seventeen years *at no cost.* They

keep 40 percent of all concession sales, which is at least $10 million. All the revenue from 64 private suites (ranging in price from $60,000 to $90,000 annually) goes to the Rockies.
4. The owners will receive all revenues from nonbaseball events for parking, concessions, and rent. For a sold-out rock concert, for example, the owners would receive about $500,000.
5. As stadium managers, the owners will receive an annual fee of $2.65 million.

As George Sage observed: "Incredible as it may seem, the lease gave the Rockies every source of revenue generated by the stadium including concessions, parking, advertising, concerts and control over other non-baseball events there. The agreement sent no revenue streams back to taxpayers who were footing the construction bill through the sales tax hike." (p. 118)

As noted earlier, the taxpayers were represented in these one-sided negotiations by John McHale, Jr. Four months after the lease was signed, McHale joined the Rockies as the team's executive vice-president for baseball operations.

Sources: George H. Sage, "Stealing Home: Political, Economic, and Media Power and a Publicly-Funded Baseball Stadium in Denver," *Journal of Sport & Social Issues* 17 (August 1993): 110–124; Fawn Germer, "Rockies Strike Richest Deal," *Rocky Mountain News,* 28 November 1991, p. 8; Paul Hutchinson, "Coors Field Tab Up to $215.5 Million," *Denver Post,* 3 December 1994, p. 1; and Richard Corliss, "High on the Rockies," *Time* (19 July 1993), 55.

inflationary process. After being told that it would cost $35 million, Louisiana voters in 1966 approved a state constitutional amendment permitting its construction. However, actual costs for the giant facility exceeded $167 million. This stadium runs deficits of $5 million or so annually, which are paid by the state of Louisiana.

In another interesting situation, St. Petersburg, Florida, built a domed stadium for $110 million, *yet had no commitment from a team to play there.* The city's decision makers thought that they would get the Chicago White Sox, but Illinois taxpayers came up

with $150 million to build a new stadium to keep the Sox in Chicago.

These new facilities, most of them publicly financed, are being built at the same time that the human needs for housing, schools, and medical facilities have reached crisis proportions, especially in United States cities. On the same day that New York's Mayor John Lindsay announced that the city would spend $24 million to purchase and renovate Yankee Stadium, the city's board of education announced that it was dropping more than six thousand teachers from its school system for lack of funds. Similar financial problems have afflicted other urban areas, for example, Cincinnati (which built a $45 million sports facility and cut school budgets from $77 million to $62 million), Philadelphia, Kansas City, and Buffalo. As a final example, when the Illinois state legislature agreed to finance the new White Sox stadium for $150 million, that legislature in that same year reduced the increase for funding to education at a much lower level than had been sought.

This sort of stadium funding has not been without public criticism, although it is significant that bond elections for stadium construction have often succeeded when other proposed expenditures (e.g., for education and for municipal facilities) have been defeated. Numerous critics have scorned the priorities demonstrated and have argued that these facilities represent a direct subsidy to the sports industry by the public, many of whom are not even sports fans and few of whom are able to use or to benefit from the facilities their money supports.

An indirect subsidy to the owners involves property taxes. Publicly owned stadiums do not pay property taxes. Another subsidy to the owners involves the 50 percent tax deduction for business entertainment expenses. Professional teams rely on corporations to buy blocks of season tickets and to rent expensive skyboxes (the highest rent is $240,000 a year at New York City's Madison Square Garden).

Clearly, to have the public provide and maintain stadiums is in the interest of franchise owners. No wonder the owners of Mile High Stadium in Denver transferred it to public ownership in 1968. Such a move, seemingly incongruous, meant that the owners were absolved of property taxes and that the city would pick up the tab for future bills. In ensuing years the city paid to install more lights so that the stadium would qualify for "Monday Night Football" telecasts and to enlarge the stadium by 25,000 seats. Meanwhile, the owners were responsible only for a nominal rental fee.

So powerful is the urge by municipal officials and local chambers of commerce to have big-league teams in their cities that they will go to extreme lengths to placate present or future owners.

• *Item*: The owners of the Chicago White Sox threatened to leave Chicago for St. Petersburg or some other location. The Illinois state legislature agreed to build a new $150 million stadium across the street from the old Comiskey Park. The new arena has 82 skyboxes (rented for $60,000 to $90,000 each per season, contributing about $5 million to the owners). Moreover, there are 21,000 box seats that sell for $13 (compared to fewer than 5,000 box seats in the old park at $10.50 apiece—a difference of $220,500 per game if all are sold). Under the favorable lease agreement, the team pays rent to the state, which owns the stadium, on attendance only over 1.2 million.[15]

• *Item*: When the Raiders returned to Oakland in 1995, part of the deal was that *all* of the income from the 175 luxury suites (costing between $40,000 and $85,000 a year) would go to the Raider ownership (netting an extra 7.6 million a year).[16]

• *Item*: In 1994 Cleveland opened a stadium-arena complex (for the Cleveland Indians baseball team and the Cleveland Cavaliers basketball team) called Gateway at a cost to the taxpayers of $434 million. Included in this project is a five-story office complex for the Indians' management (cost of $7 million, including $900,000 in furnishings), and an up-scale double decker restaurant overlooking the baseball field seating 900 (cost of $5.1 million). The profits from this restaurant and the office building go to the Cleveland Indian ownership property-tax free.[17]

• *Item*: The Cincinnati Bengals warned local leaders that the team would leave if they did not get a new stadium. They did get a new stadium. The proposed cost to the people of Cincinnati: $540 million.

In short, the owners are greatly subsidized to provide teams. To what extent do the communities that pay these subsidies benefit? We argue that the benefits are not widespread for the following reasons:

1. The wealthy benefit disproportionately from the letting of building contracts and through the feeding and housing of persons wishing to see the games. Although more jobs may be created, the profits will accrue to the capitalists, not to

the workers. Team owners (and stockholders) especially will profit from attendance without any investment in the land or construction. They cannot lose financially because the burden is on the taxpayers. This is clearly a case of the wealthy receiving a public subsidy.

2. The prices of individual and season tickets are usually too high for the lower classes. Ironically, bringing a major league team to an area (a primary reason for building a new stadium) usually means that the poor see fewer games than before if the home games are blacked out on television. (This ban on televised home football games is lifted if the game is sold out forty-eight hours before game time.) Moreover, building a new stadium or refurbishing an old one invariably raises ticket prices. Underwood states:

> The greatest damage done by this new elitism [expensive stadiums with lavish skyboxes] is that even the cheapest seats in almost every big-league facility are now priced out of reach of a large segment of the population. Those who are most critically in need of affordable entertainment, the underclass (and even the lower-middle class), have been effectively shut out.
>
> And this is especially hateful because spectator sport, by its very nature, has been the great escape for the men and women who have worked all day for small pay and traditionally provided the biggest numbers of a sport's core support. As it now stands, they are as good as disenfranchised—a vast number of the taxpaying public who will never set foot inside these stadiums and arenas. That's not just cynical, it's criminal.[18]

3. New stadiums are often built in suburban or downtown locations rather than in residential areas. The old stadiums, typically in run-down neighborhoods, are abandoned upon completion of the new. One consequence is that the poor living near the old stadiums are deprived of incomes previously derived from the games (e.g., jobs as parking attendants, salespersons,

janitors, cooks, and so forth). They are also deprived of easy access to the games. Their lack of money and the generally insufficient system of mass transportation make their attendance all the more improbable. When the stadiums are built in downtown locations, they often displace old warehouses and cheap hotels with upscale restaurants, apartments, and boutiques. This *gentrification* increases rents and other costs, forcing the poor to live elsewhere.

4. Publicly financed arenas are built for those sports that appeal more to the affluent, for example, baseball, football, basketball, and hockey. "*Prole*" sports, in other words sports for the working classes, tend to occur in privately owned arenas (see chapter 12).

The obvious beneficiaries of subsidized public arenas are the owners of sports teams, plus the owners of hotels, media, commercial modes of transportation, restaurants, construction firms, and property affected by the location of the new arena site. There is a strong relationship between professional team owners and the decision makers at the highest political, corporate, financial, and media levels.[19] These strong ties may explain the commonly found affirmative consensus among the political and economic elite for the building of public sports arenas.

Finally, there is research showing that public subsidization of sports facilities does not have a positive economic impact on the community. Economists Robert A. Baade and Richard F. Dye, after reviewing the literature and their own research, concluded (1) the costs exceed the revenues to the municipal treasury, (2) major league sports often have no significant positive impact on a city's economy, and (3) the promise of increased economic activity during and after the building or renovation of a sport facility is minor if at all.[20]

Ownership for Profit

For those teams owned by individuals, psychic gratifications are inherent in owning a professional team. Many owners derive great personal satisfaction from knowing athletes personally. In addition, owners are feted by the community as service leaders and achieve a degree of prominence otherwise unattainable in their business ventures.

Apart from the "psychic income" of team ownership, there are very substantial economic motives. Indeed, for most investors the primary motivation would seem to be a rationally economic one, sport is a profitable long-range investment. Ownership of a sports franchise also provides celebrity status, social prestige, and publicity that can enhance other facets of an individual's business.

Moreover, the value of sports franchises has consistently increased. Several examples make this point: the Philadelphia Eagles entered the NFL at a cost of $2,500 in 1933. In 1949 the franchise was sold for $250,000. The value of the Eagles franchise in 1996 was estimated by *Financial World* at $182 million.[21] In 1960 Clint Murchison purchased the Dallas Cowboys franchise for $50,000 plus another $550,000 for the players. In 1984 he sold the Cowboys and the Dallas Stadium for $80 million. In 1989 the Cowboys were purchased by Jerry Jones for an unprecedented $140 million. Seven years later that franchise had increased in value by $132 million to $272 million. The New York Mets franchise was purchased in 1960 for $1.8 million, again in 1978 for $16 million, and in 1980 for $21.1 million, and its value in 1996 was estimated at $131 million. In 1979 Jerry Buss purchased the Forum Sports Arena, the Los Angeles Lakers basketball team, and the Los Angeles Kings hockey team from Jack Kent Cooke for $67 million, which was $44 million more than the package originally cost Cooke in 1967. In 1996 the worth of this package was estimated at $252 million. In 1973 the New York Yankees were purchased for $10 million. In 1996 the value of that franchise was estimated at $209 million. In one of the quickest and most lucrative capital gains deals, Edgar Kaiser purchased the Denver Broncos in 1980 for about $35 million and sold the team four years later for $70 million. The new owner, Patrick Bowlen, has seen the value of the Broncos continue to increase from $70 million in 1984 to $164 million in 1996.

The reasons for the great appreciation in franchise value are, as we have seen, the advantages of monopoly, television revenues, tax breaks, and subsidized arenas.

That the structure of professional team sports tends to be lucrative is established, but what about the primary motivations of the owners for their involvement? Are they profit-oriented entrepreneurs or wealthy persons willing to take financial risks to provide a service to their respective communities? This is an important question because its answer should determine whether professional sport is a sport or a business. If it is a business, then special tax concessions, antitrust exemptions, and arena subsidies are inappropriate. If, on the other hand, professional team owners deserve these advantages because they are providing sport as a community service, then their profits should be scaled down and the benefits should accrue to the players and the fans.

Perhaps the best test of the owners' primary motivation involves their policies regarding ticket prices. The test is simple. If the owner is basically civic-minded, then the better the attendance during the season, the lower will be the prices. The data show consistently that the greater the demand for tickets, the higher the prices tend to be. Most illustrative of this tendency to price according to the principle of supply and demand was the case of the Montreal Canadiens, one of the most successful hockey teams and perennially sold out for home games. The ticket prices for the Canadiens were a full two dollars higher than those of the next most expensive team.

The Denver Broncos provide an excellent example of this tendency to charge whatever the market will bear. The Broncos have 75,000 season-ticket holders with a waiting list of thousands. They are invariably sold out for their home games. Management, under these conditions, has systematically raised prices: From 1980 to 1984 the high-priced seats went from $7.70 to $19.25, and the loge boxes from $22 to $80. In 1988, after reaching the Super Bowl for the second consecutive year, the Broncos raised ticket prices again, this time by an average of 13.2 percent. For 1991 the average Bronco ticket was $24.67. In 1994 the average Bronco ticket was $32.

Perhaps the best example of price gouging by professional sports teams is that in 1982—the year the NFL signed a $2.1 billion, five-year television contract guaranteeing each team $15 million annually (up from about $5 million under the previous contract)—fifteen of the twenty-eight teams *increased ticket prices.*

The rationale usually offered to explain ticket price increases is that costs are skyrocketing, especially because of the high salaries of superstars. As a result, fans typically vent their anger on the well-paid athletes rather than on the owners. The anger seems misplaced; apparently the fans do not recognize that greed motivates the owners as well as the players. Profit is, of course, the basic rule of capitalism. Still, the owners should not have it both ways. If they are capitalists, then subsidies are inappropriate. Their monopolies should not be supported by the Congress and the courts. Their tax breaks should be eliminated. If public arenas are provided for professional teams, then the rent should be fair for both the owners of the teams and the citizens of the city.

One thing is clear, owning a team is profitable, very profitable. *Financial World,* after a thorough analysis, concluded that: "The four sports leagues as an industry had an operating profit margin of 17% on $3.7 billion in revenues, an enviable benchmark. . . . For the past 20 years, baseball, football, and basketball teams have had an annual compounded increase of 20% to 25% in their franchise values."[22]

In a facetious vein, a *Denver Post* sports columnist characterized team owners this way: "Christopher Columbus would have made an appropriate club owner. He didn't know where he was going. He didn't know where he was when he got there. He treated people like slaves. *And he did it with other people's money.*"[23]

The Relationship Between Owner and Athlete

Ownership of a professional team has tended to be profitable because the courts have allowed sport exemption from the antitrust laws. In 1922 Supreme Court Justice Oliver Wendell Holmes ruled that baseball was a game that did not involve interstate commerce and was therefore exempt from federal antitrust laws. The special legal status conferred on professional sport by this decision persisted until the mid-1970s. Of special interest has been one consequence of sport monopoly: the right of owners to own and control their players.

The Draft and the Reserve Clause

The 1970s were characterized by a concerted attack by athletes on the employment practices of sport. Unlike employees of other businesses, athletes were not free to sell their services to whomever they pleased. Players' salaries were determined solely by each team's owner. In baseball, before the landmark cases of the mid-1970s, once a player signed a contract with a club, that team had exclusive rights over him, and he was no longer free to negotiate with any other team. In succeeding years, the player had to sell his services solely to the club that owned his contract unless it released, sold, or traded him, or he chose to retire. The *reserve clause* specified that the owner had the exclusive right to renew the player's contract annually, and thus the player was bound perpetually to negotiate with only one club; he became its property and could be sold to another club without his own consent.

Professional football was more restrictive in one respect and more open (at least on paper) in another. Unlike baseball, football had a draft of college players, and the selected athletes had no choice of the team for which they would play. The player would play for the team that drafted him and at the salary offered or else join a team in the Canadian League (the number of Americans allowed to play in Canada is limited, however, so that option was a real one only for the most sought-after athletes). As in baseball, after signing with a team, the football player was bound to that team. He could, however, play out his option, in other words, play a year at 90 percent of his previous salary without signing a contract whereupon he would be free to negotiate with another team. This apparent freedom of movement for the players was severely limited, however, by the "*Rozelle Rule.*" This rule allowed the NFL commissioner at that time, Pete Rozelle, to require the team signing any such "free agent" to compensate (with other athletes or with money of equal value) the club the player had left. This rule made signing free agents rarely in a club's interest; therefore, the free agent did not in reality have full economic freedom.

These provisions in football and baseball (and similar ones in basketball and hockey) were clearly one-sided, giving all the power to the owners. Michael I. Sovern, dean of Columbia University's School of Law, described this asymmetrical relationship: "The reserve clause binds the employee without binding the employer. . . . The owner is free to decide whether to continue the relationship: the player is not."[24] As another observer put it: "After the Civil War settled the slavery issue, owning a ball club was the closest one could come to owning a plantation."[25] The rationale for such a limitation on the freedom of the players is that sports depend on competitive balance for survival. Without binding players to a team, it was argued, talent would soon become maldistributed, with the richest owners in the best markets (e.g., New York, Chicago, and Los Angeles) acquiring a monopoly of superior players. A counterargument, however, is that the ability of professional teams to buy and sell players invites the same possibility: The wealthiest teams acquire the best talent, which is precisely what occurred several times during the extremely successful history of the New York Yankees. Thus, the absolute power of professional sports owners never prevented player movement; it merely ensured that any changes were in the owner's, not necessarily in the player's, interest. The major difference between a free-market system and the reserve system is that in the former the player alone would be paid for a team change; in the latter the owner is paid what should accrue to the player. As Michael I. Sovern argued: "Companies with star salesmen, universities with star professors, law firms with star partners receive no special compensation if their stars leave and cause them financial loss. If they wish to protect themselves, they must offer sufficiently attractive terms to hold their stars; or they can enter into long-term contracts with both parties bound, both the employer and the employee."[26]

Moreover, it is problematic whether the mechanisms of the draft and the reserve clause ever operated effectively to equalize team competition. From an economic standpoint, a single owner would be foolhardy to attempt to monopolize a sport's best players because attendance revenues would suffer from the absence of a real contest between teams.

In other words, the closer the competition between teams, the more fan interest is likely to be generated and, consequently, the greater the attendance revenues.

Surely in a free-market system an owner would have a vested interest in not obtaining a monopoly, not acquiring all the stars, but in ensuring that some remain on other teams. Owners know that the differences in the quality of play must not be too great. Teams cannot be economically successful unless their competitors survive, too. Thus, a balance of competition is in the mutual interest of all concerned—players, fans, and owners.

The question is whether the draft and reserve clause practices are the only ways balance can be achieved. Economists have argued that such a result does not require collusion, only the free operation of market forces. The natural-forces-of-competition argument has also been made: A team overstocked with superstars will probably have morale problems or problems in combining their talents effectively, and those superstars who feel that they are not playing enough (or that their talents are not being sufficiently or adequately utilized or publicized) will sign contracts with other clubs.

The most telling argument against the draft and the reserve clause is that neither has succeeded in distributing talent equitably. If these mechanisms had worked in the anticipated manner, league champions would have been distributed randomly over an extended period of time. In other words, team A would have been a champion as frequently as teams B, C, D, and E. Obviously, this has not been the case in North American professional team sports. Each major sport has had certain long-standing champion teams (and others that have been almost perpetual losers). The dynasties of the New York Yankees from 1921 to 1964, the Boston Celtics during the 1950s and 1960s, the Green Bay Packers during the 1960s, the Pittsburgh Steelers in the late 1970s, the Edmonton Oilers of the 1980s, and the shared dominance of the Dallas Cowboys and San Francisco 49ers are examples. Clearly, the existing rules have resulted in the unequal distribution of talent.

Moreover, it is problematic whether the draft alone can alter a club's situation radically (except, perhaps, in basketball because of the smaller number of team members, the acquisition of a single superstar such as Michael Jordan or a Shaquille O'Neal can have such an effect). The only difference between the teams selecting first and last in a player draft is one player per year, and in most sports the addition of a single outstanding player per year will make little difference in a team's ultimate success. Indeed, the emphasis placed on the draft system has attributed an undue rationality to it.

Sports promoters have argued not only that the common draft and reserve clause are necessary to ensure equal distribution of playing talent and to prevent rich clubs from acquiring a monopoly of outstanding players but also that these mechanisms are the only means of avoiding financial ruin for professional sports, claiming that competitive bidding for players would otherwise become prohibitive. This latter argument led professional football to obtain congressional exemption from the antitrust laws in 1966 and professional basketball leagues to seek a similar exemption in 1971. Although the football-merger bill passed through Congress virtually unopposed, by the time professional basketball promoters sought a similar exemption, players in all major sports had become much more effectively organized and aware of the effect of a merger agreement in reducing player salaries. Their opposition was a major factor in the failure of basketball to receive an exemption from the antitrust laws.

The existence of rival leagues provides a much greater opportunity for athletes to realize their full economic value. Both players and owners agree that salaries increase substantially when two leagues are in competition for player talent and that a merger agreement, because it controls or limits player bargaining power, depresses player salaries. There is little doubt that the financial position of players greatly improves under competitive conditions. In professional football average salaries rose from $4,000 per year in 1946 to $8,000 per year in 1949 when there were two competing leagues, the National Football League and the All-American Conference.

Similarly, in the two years after the USFL was founded in 1982, NFL salaries went up substantially. "Because of competition from the USFL, the NFL paid 58 percent more in first-round base contract money and 96 percent more in first-round aggregate bonus

money in 1983 than it did the previous year. For [1984's] rookies, projections show base contracts up another 40 percent and bonuses up 60 percent."[27]

Free Agency

The late 1960s was a period in American history when various downtrodden groups (racial minorities, women, gays) became militant in attempts to change existing power arrangements. Within the society-wide framework, athletes, too, began to recognize their common plight and organized to change it. Most fundamentally, they felt that because the owners had all the power, the players did not receive their true value in the marketplace. The result was that athletes, singly and together in player associations, began to assert themselves against what they considered to be an unfair system.

Several cases were especially instrumental in the modification of the reserve clause in baseball. First, there was Curt Flood, who was traded by the baseball Cardinals to the Philadelphia Phillies but refused to play for them. He did not play the next year (1970) in protest and brought suit against organized baseball, alleging that the reserve system constituted a system of peonage. The United States Supreme Court ruled five to three against Flood but recognized that the system should be changed by congressional action.[28]

In 1974 Jim "Catfish" Hunter of the Oakland Athletics was allowed by an arbitrator to be released from his contract because the owner had failed to make payments on an insurance policy that was part of the contract. The subsequent bidding for Hunter's services resulted in his signing a multiyear contract with the New York Yankees for $3.5 million. This showed the other athletes very clearly that they were not being paid their true worth and had much to do with increasing their militancy.

Finally, the reserve system in baseball died in December 1975 with the decision by an arbitration panel that two players, Andy Messersmith and Dave McNally, were free agents because they had played out their existing contracts plus an additional year. McNally did not pursue his career because of an injury, but Messersmith signed a three-year, no-cut contract with the Atlanta Braves for about $1 million.

These landmark cases led to an agreement between the owners of professional baseball teams and the Players' Association in July 1976. The provisions allowed (1) players without 1976 or 1977 contracts to become free agents and (2) players with six or more years in the major leagues to become free agents without waiting a one-year option period. Most importantly, there would be no compensation for the free agent's former team.

The first test of baseball's free-agent system occurred in November 1976 when the eligible players entered the reentry draft (called by some the "auction of freed slaves"). What happened had several important implications for the future of baseball. First, contrary to many predictions, only 24 out of the pool of some 600 athletes took the free-agent route. This was probably a consequence of the second result: Salaries had been raised to mollify the athletes under contract. Third, again contrary to expectations, the competitive balance of baseball was generally enhanced. Of the twelve teams with winning seasons in 1976, three signed a total of four new players. Of the twelve with losing records, seven teams purchased fourteen free agents (by the end of 1976, six players remained unsigned). Fourth, the owners' profits were now being shared more equitably with the athletes, especially the star athletes. The first fourteen free agents signed long-term agreements ranging from three to ten years that totaled $20.5 million in bonuses, salaries, and deferred payments. To put this in perspective, Gene Autry purchased the Angels in 1960 for $2.1 million. In 1976 he paid more than $5 million for three athletes: Joe Rudi, Bobby Grich, and Don Baylor. Baseball was still profitable for owners but less so. The attendance at major league baseball games in 1976 was thirty-three million. When this is multiplied by the average cost of tickets ($3.45), the total is $113,850,000, not counting parking and concessions revenues. Moreover, according to Marvin Miller, executive director of the Players' Association, radio and television revenues produce 150 percent of baseball's payroll.[29] While baseball franchise owners continued to make profits, the momentous

decisions in baseball clearly restructured the power relationship between owner and athlete. When the effects on other sports are considered, the year 1976 can truly be considered the year of "jock liberation."

The victories for the baseball players were not won easily. The owners fought them at every instance. There were strikes by the players and lockouts by the owners. Most significant, the owners were found guilty by the courts of *collusion,* that is, they conspired to not sign free agents from 1985 to 1987. This was an attempt to stop the salary spiral in baseball by taking away the players' power. The arbitrator, George Nicolau, in his opinion found that "there was no vestige of a free market [during these years]. It was replaced by a patent pattern of deliberate contravention of baseball's collective bargaining agreement." As a result, the owners had to pay $280 million in damages to the players adversely affected by the owners' collusion.[30] (See box 10.3 for a summary of how the power has shifted in major league baseball.)

Baseball reached an impasse in 1994. The owners and the players could not reach a collective bargaining agreement, resulting in a strike that ended the season prematurely and canceled the World Series. Over the winter the issues were not resolved, resulting in the 1995 season not beginning as scheduled. (See box 10.4 for the economic consequences of this, the longest strike in sports history.) The parties agreed to play a shortened 1995 season without a collective bargaining agreement. At issue was a salary cap for each team (as used in the NFL and NBA). A salary cap, of course, limits the potential income of the athletes and, therefore, controls salary escalation. The owners argued that a salary cap is needed so that the small-market teams such as Milwaukee, Pittsburgh, and Kansas City can compete with the large-market teams that have greater revenues (attendance, local TV and radio, advertising). The players argued that the salary cap makes the players pay for this balance, rather than the owners who should develop ways to divert money from the large-market teams to the small-market teams (revenue sharing by participating equally in *all*

box 10.3 *The Business of Baseball: Shifting Power and Increased Salaries*

1879—Reserved rules instituted.

1922—The Supreme Court decided that baseball was not a trade in interstate commerce and therefore not subject to federal antitrust laws.

1953—A minor league player, George Toolson, wanted to change teams but was denied. The Supreme Court agreed with the owners that the players were bound to a club for life, citing the 1922 decision.

1966—Marvin Miller was elected executive director of the Players' Association. At this time the average player salary was $19,000 and the minimum for a major league player was $6,000 (a rise of only $1,000 since 1947).

1968—Players agreed not to sign 1969 contracts until a benefits plan (pensions and health insurance) agreement could be reached. This was the first mass holdout in baseball history. The minimum salary was increased to $10,000.

1970—The Players' Association negotiated a grievance and arbitration procedure with the owners.

1970—Curt Flood refused to leave the St. Louis Cardinals for Philadelphia.

1972—The Supreme Court ruled 5–3 against Flood.

1972—The first strike in the history of professional sports, lasting 13 days—4 in the preseason and 9 during the season—occurred. As a result the owners added $500,000 to the health care insurance and agreed to a cost-of-living increase in retirement benefits. The average salary was $22,000 and the minimum salary was $13,500.

1974—Jim "Catfish" Hunter became a free agent. As a result he left his $100,000 salary with Oakland for $750,000 with the Yankees.

1975—Andy Messersmith and Dave McNally became free agents.

1976—Free agency rights were created in the contracts of baseball. The average salary at this time was $51,500.

1979—The average salary was $113,558.

1980—A new pension agreement increased all benefits. The owners' contribution to the pension plan was one-third of the national television and radio package.

1981—A strike occurred for 50 days because the owners demanded restricted free agency (compensation for the loss of a free agent), which would have lost what the players had won in 1976. The players lost $34 million (an average of $52,000 each) in the strike, but they won by retaining free agency. The average salary at this time was $186,000.

1985—The average salary was $371,000.

1989—The average salary was $489,000.

1990—The average salary was $597,000, with the minimum salary at $100,000. The combined salaries for major leaguers was $388 million, and the owners combined revenues were $1.5 billion (players, thus, received 26 percent of the revenues they generated).

1992—The average salary was $1,000,000.

1994–95—A 232-day shutdown of major league baseball with no World Series in 1994. After a delay of the 1995 season and still no labor agreement, attendance for the season was down around 18 percent and television audiences were off by 11 percent.

Source: Marvin Miller, *A Whole Different Ball Game: The Sport and Business of Baseball* (New York: Birch Lane Press, 1991).

box 10.4 *The Economic Consequences of the 1994 Baseball Strike*

The 1994 baseball season ended 52 days and 669 games early because of a strike. Some of the estimated costs of the strike:

The baseball teams lost $442 million in revenue and the players lost $236 million in salaries.

NBC and ABC lost about $3 million in advertising for each lost broadcast during prime time.

The major league cities lost an average of $91,000 per game in local and state taxes.

Local businesses in each major league city lost approximately $641,000 in revenue per game (see table 10.1).

About 22,000 jobs, mostly part time, were lost (e.g., cleanup crews, vendors, ticket sellers, ushers, stadium parking workers).

There were also jobs lost in the informal economy (e.g., parking, collecting aluminum cans, gambling).

Delta Air Lines, which flies 12 major league teams, lost 53 charter flights.

The manufacturers and suppliers of beer, soft drinks, ice, hot dogs, and other food and drink items lost considerable sums of money. The 32,000 fans at just one Chicago Cubs game will buy 40,000 cups of beer, 60,000 cups of soft drinks, 5,000 slices of pizza, 3,000 pounds of hot dogs, and 575 baseball caps.

The sales of baseball memorabilia, baseball cards, and clothing with team logos slumped considerably with the strike.

table 10.1 *Effects of Baseball Walkout*

The per-game economic effect of the Major League Baseball strike, estimated after the 1994 season:

Team	Total Loss Per Game	Stadium Revenues	Local Taxes	Local Business	Jobs Lost
		(In Millions)			
Calif. Angels (Anaheim)	$1.9	$0.1	$.441	$1.42	600
Texas Rangers (Dallas)	$2.0	NA	—	—	2,500
Atlanta Braves	$3.0	$2.0	—	$1.00	6,350
Baltimore Orioles	$1.2	$0.1	—	$1.10	2,000
Boston Red Sox	$0.1	NA	$.010	$0.04	400
Chicago Cubs	$0.7	$0.6	$.030	$0.07	1,000
Chicago White Sox	$0.9	$0.8	$.039	$0.03	1,000
Cincinnati Reds	$0.7	$0.1	$.010	$0.64	600
Cleveland Indians	$2.0	$1.2	$.600	$0.24	2,000
Colo. Rockies (Denver)	$2.0	$0.04	$.040	$1.96	1,944
Houston Astros	$1.0	$0.4	$.040	$0.60	1,000
Kansas City Royals	$0.5	$0.3	$.023	$0.25	350
Minnesota Twins (Minneapolis)	$0.9	$0.3	$.036	$0.64	900
New York Mets	$2.1	$2.0	$.063	—	850
New York Yankees	$2.1	$2.0	$.063	—	850
Oakland Athletics	$1.0	$0.03	$.010	$0.94	438
Philadelphia Phillies	$0.3	$0.1	$.042	$0.08	500
Pittsburgh Pirates	$0.5	$0.02	$.020	$0.40	350
St. Louis Cardinals	$0.4	NA	$.030	$0.40	1,180
Seattle Mariners	$0.2	$0.1	$.024	$0.08	327
San Diego Padres	$0.2	$0.02	$.005	$0.18	825
San Francisco Giants	$1.8	$0.5	$.136	$1.10	800

Sources: U.S. Conference of Mayors; *USA Today*, 31 March 1995, sec. A, p. 2.

Sources: Del Jones and Shelly Reese, "Baseball Strike Losses Ain't Peanuts," *USA Today*, 16 October 1994, sec. B, p. 1; Steve Rushin, "Casualties of War," *Sports Illustrated*, 10 October 1994, 37–43; and Beth Belton, "Folks Behind Game Suffer Biggest Loss," *USA Today*, 12 August 1994, sec. B, p. 1.

broadcasting revenues—the Yankees receive about $50 million from local radio and television, while other clubs may receive only $5 million; a 50/50 split in ticket sales instead of the 60/40 split that is now the norm, etc.).

Professional football did not have as far to go as baseball did because players were already allowed to play out their option. The obstacle, as we noted earlier, was the Rozelle Rule, which was voided after two court cases. The first occurred when quarterback Joe Kapp signed a nonstandard contract with the New England Patriots and it was voided by Commissioner Rozelle. Kapp gave up his career and sued the league. A district court judge ruled in Kapp's favor in 1974, saying that the standard player contract violated federal antitrust laws and that the Rozelle Rule was illegal.

Since the Kapp case involved an individual player rather than the entire NFL system and was subject to a prolonged appeal process, the NFL Players' Association brought suit to change the system for all players in December 1975 (*Mackey v. NFL*). A federal court judge decided that the Rozelle Rule was illegal. He directed the NFL and its twenty-six teams to cease enforcing the rule. The result was that in May 1976 twenty-four new free agents began searching for the best offers: Larry Csonka signed for more than $1 million covering four seasons; John Riggins, who as a New York Jet played his option year for $67,500, put his price at $1.5 million for five years, payable at $100,000 a year until 1990.

Another significant case occurred in 1976. In a suit brought by former Washington Redskin Jim ("Yazoo") Smith, the college draft was struck down also because it violated antitrust law. In response to the court cases, fear of additional litigation, and owner-player strife, the owners and the National Football League Players' Association came to terms on a collective-bargaining agreement in 1977. This contract was significant to the players because it recognized the union, voided arbitrary hair and dress codes, set minimum salaries, and awarded the union $13.65 million for damages arising in the *Mackey* case. In return, the union accepted the college draft and killed free agency. That is, they permitted the

Rozelle Rule to continue, although in modified form. Under this arrangement, when a team signs a player entering his third year for $280,000 or more, it owes his old team two first-draft picks; for $230,000 to $280,000, a first and second pick; for $180,000 to $230,000, a first and a third; and so on. The net effect of this rule is that NFL teams almost never sign free agents, thus depressing the potential salaries of the better players. The net effect, according to one critic, is that the union "traded free agency and the abolished draft—unprecedented, monumental breakthroughs for the players—for nothing much more than a healthy union treasury."[31]

In 1982 the NFL Players' Association conducted a fifty-seven-day strike that cost the owners $210 million in lost revenues. The eventual settlement allowed the modified Rozelle Rule to continue but gave considerable overall monetary benefits to the players ($1.6 billion over five years, designating 46 percent of the NFL owners' gross to the players). In 1987 the union again went on strike—missing forty-two games—demanding free agency and $18 million for the pension fund. The strike failed as the owners hired replacement players, the networks televised the games, and public opinion sided with the owners. The strike cost the players $79 million in lost salaries and the owners $42 million in fewer ticket sales and $60 million in rebates to the television networks. Although the players lost this battle, the war is not over. The courts have ruled the Rozelle Rule and the draft in violation of antitrust law before. Without a collective bargaining agreement, the players are free to use the courts again. As of 1995, the NFL and the NFL Players' Association had agreed to a collective bargaining agreement. The important provisions of this agreement are: (1) A modified free-agent system, which increases the mobility for most players but protects a team from losing its most important players (designated as "franchise" and "transition" players). In effect, these special players can receive offers from other teams but his team has the right of first refusal. (2) Minimum salaries are set for these special players as an average of the best players at that position. (3) Pension, life insurance, severance, and medical benefits were increased substantially for the players.

Historically, negotiations within professional basketball, unlike those in football and baseball, have been characterized by considerable cooperation between owners and athletes. Agreements have also been much more progressive. This spirit of cooperation on the part of the owners, however, has been prompted by clear messages of the court decisions in the other sports: Owners may no longer treat their players as highly paid slaves. The most significant provisions of the 1976 NBA settlement were:

1. The option clause was to be eliminated from nonrookie player contracts, beginning with those that expired with the 1976 season. In other words, a veteran was no longer bound to a team for one year after his or her contract ran out.
2. In 1980 the owner of a player whose contract had expired would have the right of first refusal if that player was offered a contract by another team. By equaling the best offer, the owner could keep the player; otherwise, the player would be free to join the new team.

In 1983 the NBA owners and players agreed to revenue sharing and the first salary cap in professional sports. The purpose of this provision was to allow poor teams to compete for star players and to slow the acceleration in player salaries. Some teams, however, were permitted to surpass the cap through a "grandfather" clause for salaries already exceeding the limit, and all teams were permitted to spend any amount to retain their own free agents. The salary-cap agreement granted the players 53 percent of the total league revenues. As a result, the average player salary increased from $240,000 in 1983 to $510,000 in 1987 to $990,000 in 1991 and $1,870,000 in 1994.

In 1995, after the NBA Players' Association negotiated a deal with the league, a number of high profile athletes (e.g., Michael Jordan, Patrick Ewing) led an attempt by the players to decertify the union. The union members voted against this effort, followed by the owners' ratification of the collective bargaining agreement. This new plan will allow a dramatic increase in the salary cap and will take the average player salary to nearly $3 million by the conclusion of the contract, decrease the amount of rookie contracts, and guarantee all first-round choices three-year deals, after which they will become free agents.

Salaries

The legal decisions favoring the athletes had one major impact, which was that salaries increased dramatically (see table 10.2). Football and hockey lag behind the other team sports because they have continued under more restrictive compensation systems. Hockey especially lags behind because of a stronger reserve clause, the lack of a competing league, and much lower television revenues.

These higher average salaries reflect the very high salaries paid to superstars. In 1995, for example, 320 of the 1,590 rostered players in the NFL made $1 million or more. More than 200 of the 650 players made $1 million or more, and 106 hockey players earned more than $1 million.

Athletes of superstar status in individual sports sometimes receive even higher incomes than those in team sports. The most popular heavyweight boxers can make as much as $20 million for a single fight. The elite tennis players make more than $5 million. A few golfers exceed $1 million a year in winnings, as do a few auto racers, jockeys, and "amateur" track athletes.

These huge incomes, which are supplemented by endorsements and personal appearances, raise two important questions: (1) Are athletes paid too much? and (2) How do such enormous salaries for athletes affect the fans?

To the fans, their once-noble athletic heroes are now business people. Athletes demand huge salaries to perform in games. They threaten not to play. They no longer seem to have loyalty to their team or city. Roger Angell observed that fans do not appear to object as much to the large salaries of the superstars as to the across-the-board affluence of athletes.

> Large payments to athletes are not enjoyed or approved of by us, the fans, if the payment is made broadly, to all the athletes engaged in a particular trade at the big-league level—all basketball players,

table 10.2 *Average Salaries in Major Professional Leagues for Selected Years*

Year	National Basketball Association	Major League Baseball	National Football League	National Hockey League
1968	$ 20,000	$ 19,000	$ 21,000	$ 20,000
1976	110,000	51,000	63,200	90,000
1984	246,000	325,900	162,000	130,000
1991	990,000	850,000	355,000	370,000
1994	1,870,000	1,186,000	737,000	463,000

all hockey players, and so on. "The players have gotten too greedy," "They're all paid too much"—these are current grandstand convictions, which I also hear from other people, in and out of the sports world. As I pick up this complaint, however, it seems to apply more to a well-paid journeyman than to the superstar. . . . It would be extremely interesting to measure this, if we could. What it means, I think, is that high pay for athletes is resented if they are seen as employees. And when these employees behave like contemporary workmen, trying to extract the most money and the most favorable working conditions and retirement benefits from a typically reluctant and unsympathetic employer, and forming a union to press their demands—which is what the baseball and football and basketball players have all done in recent years—then they are resented even more deeply, almost to the point of hatred. This is an extraordinary turn of events in a labor-conscious, success-oriented society like ours.[32]

Ironically, the fans have tended to take the side of the team owners in many salary disputes, strikes, and other disruptions, even though the owners over the years have had the monopoly, have taken economic advantage of their athletes, and have had the temerity to move franchises to more lucrative communities. The next few years will provide the data as to whether this resentment toward the businessperson-athletes is a short-lived phenomenon or not.

One irony is that fans resent the high salaries of athletes but take in stride the huge salaries of other entertainers. There are fifteen stars who receive more than $10 million to act in *one* motion picture, with Sylvester Stallone receiving $60 million to appear in three movies. Barbra Streisand receives more than $1 million for a single concert.[33] These examples make the $7 million that Barry Bonds receives for playing 162 games seem relatively meager, yet the fans seem to resent more, much more, his high salary compared to those of an actor or entertainer. For some reason the huge monies collected by these and other entertainers is accepted by the public, but the lesser monies received by athletes tends to foster resentment.

In addition to the entertainment analogy, several other arguments justify the amounts paid to superstars for playing games. The first is that their salaries are paid on the basis of scarcity. If there are 242 professional basketball players in a nation of some 260 million, that makes the athlete less than one in a million, and he or she should be paid accordingly. The second argument is that a sports career is so brief that players should be paid extra (out of the 242 players in the NBA, only 30 or so are 30 years of age or older). Third, the owners are only paying the athletes what they are worth, because the superstars bring out the fans. For example, when Wayne Gretzky was purchased by the Los Angeles Kings for $15 million, the Kings estimated that Gretzky would mean an extra $9 million a year to the franchise ($5.7 million more in season tickets, $2 million more in single-game ticket sales, and at least $1 million more in what they could charge for cable television rights).[34] Finally, related to the last point, salaries have escalated but so to have owners' revenues from television, ticket sales, royalties from the sale of merchandise, and the like. For example, from 1981 to 1990, the total player payroll in the NFL increased from $186 million to $660 million. "But in the same 10 years, NFL revenues leaped too—from $408 million to $1.28 billion, or 213 percent."[35]

A Radical Question: Are Owners Necessary?

Owners receive anywhere from 50 to 75 percent of the profits from professional teams. What have they provided to receive such generous compensation? They did buy the teams from other owners but what else? The stadiums and arenas, except in rare occasions, have been provided by taxpayers. The practice facilities are also. Why don't the municipalities own these teams? They could hire competent general managers to sign players, make schedules, hire coaches and support staff, and work with others for television and radio contracts. David Meggyesy, a former professional football player and now employed by the NFL Players' Association, has argued the following:

You know, people say, "Oh, those jocks are making all that money," but what about the owners? It's a relative thing. Remember, the players are everything in this game. They are both the hired hands and the machinery, both the coal and the coal miners, however you want to say it. In every meeting I have, I tell my guys, "You are the game. You are the people the fans come to see, not the owners sipping their scotch in their luxury boxes."

Those of us who have been around the NFL long enough tend to see that the only irrelevant and expendable element in the equation are these 28 franchise owners. . . . We proved this to ourselves when we put on our two NFLPA all-star games when we were on strike in 1982. The people who should ultimately be putting together a structure and an organization to present the games—and that's all

the owners are, sports entertainment promoters—are the players themselves and their association, much like is done in men's tennis and the professional golfers tour. It's just a great fiction that the owners do anything significant; they don't. In a player's league, the NFLPA could certainly hire competent general managers and coaches, in addition to organizing the league, contracting stadiums, and scheduling games. In this [plan] the municipalities could become partners with the players, and profits from the games could be plowed back to the communities to support the community sports infrastructure, including school athletics. That's professional sports as it should be.[36]

Amateur Sport As a Business

The trend toward greater bureaucratization, commercialization, and institutionalism—the trend toward corporate sport—is not restricted to professional athletics; it is also true of much of organized amateur athletics. Analysis of the sports industry must therefore deal with these two categories of sports participation, although in reality they are often virtually indistinguishable.

The amateur concept was a product of the late eighteenth-century leisure class, whose ideal of the patrician sportsman was part of their pursuit of conspicuous leisure. Consequently, to be a pure amateur required independent wealth, since the true amateur derived no income from his sports participation. Explicit in the amateur ideal is the belief that one's athletic endeavor must be unrelated to one's work or livelihood and that sport itself is somehow sullied, tarnished, or demeaned if one is paid for performing it.[37]

In most cases the distinction between professional and amateur sport is artificial. This has been recognized in tennis, which has laid aside the archaic idea that amateurs and professionals cannot compete against each other. Also, the Olympics, through their various international sport organizations, have eliminated the notion of professional in many sports (e.g., track and field, skiing, basketball, tennis). In other sports, though, the distinction is still made and, usually, applied inconsistently.

The most frequent means of subsidizing amateur athletes is through scholarships to colleges and universities. Ignoring for the moment the long-range value of a college degree, the typical U.S. athletic scholarship (a legal maximum of room, books, board, tuition, and fees, as specified by the NCAA) has an annual value of $10,000 at a state-supported school with low tuition and $20,000 at a private school with high tuition. These sums do not include the widespread illicit payments frequently discovered through NCAA investigations. College scholarships do not constitute incomes comparable to professional contracts; nevertheless, college athletes are being compensated financially for their athletic exploits. Most athletes in highly competitive sports are subsidized in some way, and thus the distinction between amateur and professional sport is primarily one of degree.

The decisions made by various ruling bodies as to who is amateur and who is not results in considerable hypocrisy. As Bill Russell put it:

> The hypocrisy of amateur sports is offensive to anybody who cares. To me, being an amateur is like being a virgin. It is an old idea that has some innocence and charm, celebrated mostly by people to whom it doesn't apply. It doesn't look as good on old people as on young ones. It is impossible to keep partially, though many try to do so. It is associated with deception and pretense. And even if you love the idea, you still can't help being suspicious when you see the pious members of the U.S. Chastity Committee charging the public money to peep at their soiled virgins.[38]

The Economics of Collegiate Sport

The business dimension of amateur sport is most fully developed in the athletic programs of United States colleges and universities. The intercollegiate sports system, initially student-organized and student-run, came under the control of school administrators early in the twentieth century. It has since become a major business proposition, generating, as noted in chapter 6, $25 million budgets, millions for bowl appearances, and lucrative television contracts.

Operating a big-time collegiate athletic program is a business proposition, which means that financial losses are unacceptable. There have been different responses to the financial crisis in intercollegiate sports. The NCAA has responded by permitting first-year students to compete in varsity athletics, by reducing the maximum number of scholarships that each school may annually award, and by eliminating the $15 "laundry" money previously allowed athletes each month. Some schools have reduced their commitment to intercollegiate athletics, either by de-emphasizing the level of competition in their athletic programs or by dropping support of specific (typically minor) sports, such as golf, tennis, swimming, soccer, rugby, and lacrosse.

However, in many instances the sports dropped by a university administration as financially prohibitive are being reinstituted as student-initiated and student-run affairs without any real institutional assistance, thus moving them back to their original level: organized sport.

Financial losses have most frequently prompted the individual athletic programs to redouble their efforts to remain competitive and thus to approach fiscal solvency. One response is to fire the incumbent coach and replace him or her with another who promises to reverse the institution's athletic fortunes, the agreement to coach frequently having been obtained by the university's commitment of greater financial outlays to support the new and invigorated program. The most far-reaching consequences of these escalating costs are that they further intensify the pressures to recruit athletes legally and illegally.

The lure of money affects even teams below the big-time level. A common practice is for lesser teams to schedule big-time teams just for the gate money. The University of Denver, for example, played two Big Ten teams in basketball for a total of $19,000, knowing that it had no chance of winning either game. As former Denver coach Ben Jobe put it: "Athletics is a business. There are only two reasons you are in a game. If you don't win and you don't make money either, you might as well have stayed in bed."[39]

Both schools benefit from such an arrangement. The small school makes relatively big money, and the big-time school adds to its winning record. Again, according to Coach Jobe: "It's called buying and selling games. It's a form of prostitution."[40]

The extensive financial involvement of American colleges and universities in athletics makes it difficult to distinguish their operation from noncollegiate professional enterprises. In fact, the average game attendance of many universities in football and basketball exceeds that of professional teams. As mentioned earlier, the salaries paid college athletes raise the question of how they are to be distinguished (except qualitatively) from professionals. In other words, the money an admitted professional receives is merely greater than that paid the typical college player (although the professional player is not confronted with the necessity of diverting energies to studies, to the hassle of remaining academically eligible; the professional is free to devote himself or herself solely to developing athletic skills).

It is not surprising that collusive practices similar to those employed by professional promoters have infiltrated college athletics because the professional-amateur distinction is difficult to make realistically. As with professional athletes, a free market does not exist for college athletes; they are subject to severe restrictions by the NCAA, the major governing body of college athletics, which functions as a cartel.[41] NCAA regulations regarding recruiting, scholarships, and eligibility are collusive, and like the reserve clause in professional sports, their effect is to prevent one team from raiding another for players. Although colleges have not yet fully rationalized procedures to the point of instituting a draft of eligible high school and community college players, fierce competition exists. The national and conference letters of intent require a player to declare his or her intention of enrolling in and competing for a specific school, which "has the effect of insulating a given university-firm from competition for inputs by other university-firms in its conference."[42]

The effect of such practices are, of course, advantageous for competing schools; it enables them to restrict their feverish recruiting of high school talent to a few months of the year. NCAA rules also preclude "tampering" with players who have already committed their services: A school cannot recruit a player already at another school unless the player is willing to be penalized by being declared ineligible for a year. This rule against transfers has an effect similar to the option clause in professional sports. Only if the player is willing to forgo competing for a year can the student transfer his or her services to another school's team. (The practice does not apply to the coaches of intercollegiate teams, of course, only to the players.)

Other NCAA regulations also seriously limit the freedom of college athletes. First, players may not compete for more than four years in a single sport, nor may they compete in intercollegiate athletics after they have received the baccalaureate degree. This rule has led to the somewhat common situation of players having the requisite number of credits to fulfill the institution's graduation requirements but refusing to accept their degrees until after completing their intercollegiate athletic eligibility. Graduate students in English universities are allowed to compete in British collegiate sports, but graduate students in the United States are prohibited from doing so. Moreover, the NCAA stipulates that an athlete cannot compete more than five years after initially entering college, except in the cases of interruption of college career for military or missionary service (revealing exemptions). The student who drops out of school for any other reason and returns several years later may not participate in intercollegiate athletics.

As James Koch concluded, the effect of these NCAA regulations is to permit American colleges to operate their athletic programs in a monopolistic manner by regulating and limiting the freedom of potential athletes. They establish a ceiling on players' salaries, regulate the length and criteria for participation, and limit player mobility.[43]

Despite the pervasive commercialization of college sport, it still retains (or attempts to retain) an aura of wholesomeness. We must, though, recognize the professional aspect of the big-time college athletic system. Especially in football and basketball, and to a lesser but increasing extent in baseball and hockey, intercollegiate sports serve as the minor league farm systems for major league professional team sports and as sources of free publicity for future pro stars.

Collegiate sports participation has historically been the prelude to professional competition in basketball and football, whereas this has been infrequently (although increasingly) the case in baseball and hockey. Although the minor league system of major league baseball has diminished considerably from its heyday immediately after World War II, it is still much more extensive than that of any other major professional team sport. The primary difference between the baseball and hockey minor leagues and those of the other pro sports is that there is little mobility among the latter. Whereas for a baseball or hockey professional not to have served at least a minimal apprenticeship in the minor leagues is highly atypical, for a professional basketball or football player to have done so is highly atypical.

Awareness of the professionalism of collegiate sports and their function as minor leagues, or training grounds, for future major leaguers has led to the suggestion that the professionalism of collegiate athletics be explicitly recognized. This would be accomplished by having a college athlete's letter of intent be considered a legal contract with the school in the same way that a professional athlete's contract is owned by his or her team. Major league owners desiring the services of such an athlete would have to purchase the contract, thereby reimbursing that school for the cost of player development and training and simultaneously improving the financial position of the school team supplying the pro team with its raw material.

Recognizing this natural source of player development, professional basketball and football teams have entered into informal agreements with colleges and universities. The pro teams promise that they will not tamper or try to negotiate with undergraduate players until they have completed four years of athletic eligibility. Thus, a player like Wilt Chamberlain, who competed for only three of four years at Kansas University, was unable to play in the NBA during the fourth year because he was not yet deemed eligible for the draft. The effect of these arrangements within the professional leagues is clearly collusive, and was legally declared so soon after the fledgling American Basketball Association challenged the rule by signing undergraduate players to contracts in their sophomore and junior years. The National Basketball Association once refused to permit this practice unless the player was deemed a hardship case in which instance, because of his or her family's alleged dire economic condition, he must receive more substantial wages than his university can provide. The NBA now permits anyone to declare their candidacy for the professional draft.

Professional football, reluctantly, has followed the lead of basketball. College players may declare themselves eligible for the draft prior to their senior year. The NCAA has vigorously opposed players leaving early for professional careers. They have allowed this only because their attempts to prohibit this would not stand up in court.

Summary

We have shown the economic side of sport in this chapter. The message is clear: in professional and in big-time collegiate sport, the dollar is king. Sport is used by big business in a multimillion-dollar effort to sell products. Owners squeeze as much money as they can from fans and taxpayers. Players' demands for money seem incapable of satiation. The result is the ultimate corruption of sport as a meaningful, joyous activity in itself into corporate sport. Let us review briefly the various components that demonstrate the businesslike atmosphere of sport.

1. Sport has sold out to the demands of television. In return for large contracts, the leagues and the NCAA allow the television networks to dictate schedules, time-outs, and the like.
2. The principle of supply and demand operates in setting admission charges for athletic events. If sport were truly a game rather than a business, the most successful teams would charge the lowest ticket prices, but this is not the case.
3. The owners of professional teams are in a constant search of better markets and higher profits. The possibility that a franchise will

move increases the probability that municipalities will provide facilities or other inducements at taxpayers expense to entice teams to their city or to encourage them to remain there.

4. Athletes seemingly put self-interest ahead of team play and loyalty to their fans. Players demand very high salaries and other monetary inducements (bonuses, retirement benefits, insurance policies, interest-free loans, and so forth). The frequent result is pugnacious negotiations between owners and athletes.

5. A struggle exists between athletes (through unionlike organizations) and entrepreneurs for the power to regulate sports and to apportion profits. This is manifested in court battles, player strikes, owner lockouts, and press agentry by both sides to sway public opinion.

In sum, instead of being an escape from the workaday world of money-making, strikes, strife, and legal complexities, sport has become similar to the world of work. As such, it reveals, in microcosm, the values of the larger society. As Roger Angell said of baseball (and the same is true of all corporate sport):

Professional sports now form a noisy and substantial, if irrelevant and distracting, part of the world, and it seems as if baseball games taken entirely—off the field as well as on it, in the courts and in the front offices as well as down on the diamonds—may now tell us more about ourselves than they ever did before.[44]

Notes

1. John Underwood, *Spoiled Sport* (Boston: Little, Brown, 1984), 4–5.

2. "Advertisers' Dream Team," *USA Today,* 27 July 1995, sec. B, p. 2.

3. George H. Sage, "Sociology of Physical Educator/Coaches," *Research Quarterly for Exercise and Sport* 51 (March 1980): 112.

4. See *Journal of Sport & Social Issues* 16 (December 1992), which includes five articles on agents and agency.

5. Richard Sandomir, "The Gross National Sports Product," *Sports Inc.,* 16 November 1987, 16.

6. The data on sports books are taken from a two-part series on legalized sports gambling in *USA Today,* 25–26 June 1991.

7. See James H. Frey, "Gambling on Sport: Policy Issues," in *Sport in Contemporary Society,* ed. D. Stanley Eitzen, 5th ed. (New York: St. Martin's, 1996), 193–201.

8. Jacob Weisman, "Acolytes in the Temple of Nike," *The Nation,* 17 June 1991, 811.

9. Michael Hiestand, "Sponsorship: The Name of the Game," *USA Today,* 16 June 1993, sec. C, pp. 1–2.

10. Bruce Horovitz, "Sponsors Warm Up a Year Before Games," *USA Today,* 19 July 1995, sec. C, pp. 1–2.

11. See William Johnson, "Yankee Rx Is Group Therapy," *Sports Illustrated,* 12 February 1973, 46–49.

12. See David Whitson and Donald Macintosh, "Becoming a World-Class City: Hallmark Events and Sports Franchises in the Growth Strategies of Western Canadian Cities," *Sociology of Sport Journal* 10 (September 1993): 221–40.

13. See George H. Sage, "Stealing Home: Political, Economic, and Media Power and a Publicly-Funded Baseball Stadium in Denver," *Journal of Sport & Social Issues* 17 (August 1993): 110–24; and Andrew Zimbalist, *Baseball and Billions.* (New York: Basic Books, 1992).

14. John Underwood, "From Baseball and Apple Pie, to Greed and Sky Boxes," *New York Times,* 31 October 1993, sec. S, p. 11.

15. Anthony Baldo, "Secrets of the Front Office: What America's Teams are Worth," *Financial World* 160 (9 July 1991), 28–41.

16. Steve Wulf, "How Suite It Isn't," *Time,* 10 July 1995, 52.

17. Roldo Bartimole, " 'If You Build It, We Will Stay,' " *The Progressive* 58 (June 1994): 28–31; and Roldo Bartimole, "The Plush Club You Paid For," *Cleveland Free Times,* 23 March 1994, p. 3.

18. Underwood, "From Baseball and Apple Pie, to Greed and Sky Boxes," 22.

19. Sage, "Stealing Home." For a similar analysis in Canada, see Richard S. Gruneau, "Elites, Class and Corporate Power in Canadian Sport," *Sport, Culture and Society,* ed. John W. Loy, Jr., Gerald S. Kenyon, and Barry D. McPherson, 2d ed. (Philadelphia: Lea and Febiger, 1981), 348–71.

20. Robert A. Baade and Richard F. Dye, "Sports Stadiums and Area Development: A Critical View," *Economic Development Quarterly* 2 (August 1988): 265–75.

21. The 1996 estimates in this section are taken from *Financial World* 161 (20 May 1996). Reported in *USA Today* (2 May 1996), sec. C, p. 13.

22. Baldo, "Secrets of the Front Office," 30.

23. Woody Paige, "For Owners in a League of Their Own," *Denver Post,* 20 January 1993, sec. C, p. 1.

24. Michael I. Sovern quoted in Leonard Koppett, "Don't Blame It All on the Free Agents," *Sporting News,* 2 July 1977, 4, 16.

25. Alex Ben Block, "So, You Want to Own a Ball Club," *Forbes,* 1 April 1977, 37.

26. Senate Subcommittee on Antitrust and Monopoly, *Committee on the Judiciary: Hearings,* 92d Cong., 1st sess., 1971, 323.

27. NFL Players' Association figures cited in *USA Today,* 26 June 1984, sec. C, p. 3.

28. See Joan Ryan, "Courage to Fight Back: Curt Flood Risked Career by Suing Baseball," *Denver Post,* 15 February 1995, sec. D, p. 6. For extensive discussions of the legal cases, see John C. Weistart and Cym H. Lowell, *The Law of Sports* (Indianapolis: Bobbs-Merrill, 1979), 477–776; Robert C. Berry and Glenn M. Wong, *Law and Business of the Sports Industries: Professional Sports Leagues,* vol. 1 (Dover, Mass.: Auburn House, 1986); Edward R. Garvey, "From Chattel to Employee: The Athlete's Quest for Freedom and Dignity," *Annals* 445 (September 1979): 91–101; U.S. Congress. House. *Rights of Professional Athletes* (Washington, D.C.: U.S. Government Printing Office, 1975) serial 59; and Marvin Miller, *A Whole Different Ball Game: The Sport and Business of Baseball* (New York: Birch Lane Press, 1991).

29. Marvin Miller quoted in Red Smith, "When Prices Go Up, Up, Up," *New York Times,* 28 November 1976, p. 35.

30. See John Helyar, "How Peter Ueberroth Led the Major Leagues In the 'Collusion Era,'" *Wall Street Journal,* 20 May 1991, pp. 1, 6.

31. Mike Trope, *Necessary Roughness* (Chicago: Contemporary Books, 1987), 169–70.

32. Roger Angell, "In the Counting House," *New Yorker,* 10 May 1976, 109–10. Copyright 1972, 1973, 1974, 1975, 1976, 1977 by Roger Angell. Reprinted by permission of Simon and Schuster, Inc.; see also Rick Morrisey, "Fanning the Fury: Spectators, Athletes on Collision Course in '90s," *Rocky Mountain News,* 27 August 1995, sec. B, pp. 16–17.

33. See Andy Seiler, "Stallone: The $60 Million Man," *USA Today* (August 9, 1995), sec. D, p. 1; and Christopher Farrell, "Why Some Compensation is Clean Outta Sight," *Business Week,* 4 September 1995, 60.

34. Joshua Mills, "Gretsky: Deal with Dividends," *New York Times,* 20 August 1988, pp. 17, 29.

35. Ben Brown, "Business As Usual Is Over the Pro Game," *USA Today,* 11 May 1993, sec. A, p. 2.

36. Matthew Goodman, "David Meggyesy Interview," *Zeta Magazine* 3, September 1990, 88, 89.

37. D. Stanley Eitzen, "The Sociology of Amateur Sport: An Overview," *International Review for the Sociology of Sport* 24, No. 2 (1989): 95–104.

38. Bill Russell and Taylor Branch, "Money & Sports," *Professional Sports Journal* 1 (February 1980): 26.

39. Ben Jobe quoted in the *Rocky Mountain News,* 30 November 1978, p. 112.

40. Ibid.

41. See James V. Koch, "A Troubled Cartel: The NCAA," *Law and Contemporary Problems* 38 (winter/spring 1973): 135–50.

42. James V. Koch, "The Economics of 'Big-Time' Intercollegiate Athletics," *Social Science Quarterly* 52 (September 1971): 253.

43. Ibid.

44. Angell, "In the Counting House," 107.

Chapter 11

Sport and the Mass Media

Social institutions that appear to be independent of one another frequently are found, on closer examination, to be very interdependent. Such is the case of sport and the mass media, even though the former is concerned with physical action, skill in a highly problematic task, and the outcome of a competitive event, while the latter communicates information and entertains. Both commercial sports and the printed and electronic media are preeminently commercial industries that constitute two of the most successful businesses in North America. Thus, the goal (and logic) of both is mainly economic profit. As one mass communication scholar noted:

> Sport and the mass media enjoy a very symbiotic relationship in [North] American society. On one hand, the staggering popularity of sport is due, to no small extent, to the enormous amount of attention provided it by the mass media. On the other, the media are able to generate enormous sales in both circulation and advertising based upon their extensive treatment of sport. Media attention fans the flames of interest in sport and increased interest in sport warrants further media attention.[1]

Social Roles of the Mass Media

The term mass media refers to all of the technically organized means of communication that reach large numbers of diverse people quickly and efficiently. These systems of communication can be grouped into two major categories: printed media—newspapers, magazines, and books; and electronic media—radio, television, and movies.

Prominent and Subtle Roles of the Media

One of the prominent roles of the mass media is the communication of information. Culture depends upon communication; indeed, culture cannot exist without an effective system of transmitting and disseminating information. In small primitive societies information is transmitted by direct one-to-one, face-to-face contact, but this form of information transmission is efficient only in a society of limited size, sparse population, and minimal social differentiation. Modern societies require complex networks of printed and electronic media to keep people informed about other people and events. Information binds people to their neighbors, cities, states, and to other nations and the world.

Another prominent role of the mass media is to provide entertainment for our consumer world. Each medium has its entertainment aspect. Newspapers carry special features and the comics. Magazines and books offer stories of adventure, humor, and mystery. Radio and television provide a wide variety of entertainment, from music to sporting events.

In performing these two roles (communication and entertainment), the mass media fulfills at least two subtle roles: social integration and social change. To the extent that a social institution, such as the media, promotes shared values and norms and secures a common consensus among citizens, it may be said to contribute to social integration. Shared information and entertainment contribute to the socialization of citizens in a particular culture and thus serve to integrate persons in that culture. It may be seen, then, that the mass media is a powerful ideological institution because the messages and images that it creates help shape and mold the national and international cultural atmosphere. In North America a strongly conservative ideology is conveyed in the mass media; indeed, critics of this social role of the media contend that it tends to promote and sustain the unequal distribution of power and wealth, as well as legitimizing existing unequal social relations related to class, gender, and race.

Although the media play an important role in the promotion of the status quo, it nevertheless promotes social change as well. The mere reporting of ideas and events serves as a stimulant for reinterpreting the world, triggering changes in many spheres of life. For example, social change as dramatized on television and in the movies exposes audiences to sex, nudity, and "obscenity." As a result, audiences grow more accustomed to public permissiveness, and community standards change.[2]

The Symbiosis of Mass Media and Sport

The four roles of the media are sustained in its association with sports: information, entertainment, social integration, and social change. First, it supplies information about sports—for example, game results and statistics about individual players and teams. Second, it provides exciting entertainment. Reading about, listening to, or watching sporting events allows individuals opportunities to escape temporarily the burdens and frustrations that bind them to reality. Media sport has the perfect combination of entertainment, including controlled violence, excitement, and lots of audio and visual power.

Social integration, one of the media's subtle roles, is often played out through conversations about sport. One can ask almost any stranger about sports or well-known sporting events and the stranger will likely know the relevant information because he/she has read about it, heard about it, or seen it in the media; consequently, the conversation can be sustained and sometimes transformed into a more enduring social relationship. Media sport, then, provides a communal focus whereby large segments of the population can share common norms, ceremonies, and values.

Finally, the media have played a role in the creation of some sports, the popularity of others, and rule changes of others (more about this later in the chapter). The media have played a significant role in social change as it relates to sports.

Linkages of the Mass Media and Sport

Little did the inventors of our technical means of communication realize how their inventions would become associated with sport. Johannes Gutenberg invented movable type in the mid-fifteenth century. As his invention was refined during the following centuries, the ability of the printing press to produce reading material quickly and cheaply increased and made possible the growth of the publishing industry. Wireless telegraphy, invented at the end of the nineteenth century, served as the technological foundation for radio and television.

Newspapers

In the mid-nineteenth century American newspapers began periodic coverage of sports events, but it was not until the 1890s that the first sports section became a regular feature of a newspaper. It was William Randolph Hearst, publisher of the *New York Journal,* who in 1895 was the first to develop the modern sports section.

By 1900 sports news made up about 15 percent of all general news coverage of the leading newspapers. Over the past ninety years the symbiosis between the newspaper and sport has become so well established that in many of North America's most popular newspapers, sports coverage constitutes almost 50 percent of the space devoted to local, national, and international stories, and the sports pages have about five times as many readers as any other section of the newspaper. The newspaper sports section has not been curtailed by the growth of either radio or television; instead, radio and television have strengthened rather than replaced the sports section of newspapers.[3]

Magazines

Even before the newspaper sports section, magazines and books chronicled the activities of athletes and teams. In the years between the American Revolution and the 1830s, there arose a widespread interest in journals of all kinds, and magazines cropped up everywhere to exploit the popular interest in horse racing, hunting, fishing, and athletic sports. The momentum of sports literature accelerated in the 1830s, and the first prominent sports journal in the United States, *Spirit of the Times,* began publication in 1831. This journal featured horse racing in particular but also reported on other sports and indirectly helped to establish what was to become "the national pastime"—baseball.

Magazines specializing in sports have been standard fare in the publishing business for the past one hundred years, with almost every sport having its own publication. Indeed, one indication that a new sport is rising in popularity is the appearance of a magazine describing its techniques and strategies, profiling its best players, and advertising equipment and accessories for playing or watching the sport. About half the space at every newsstand is filled with sports magazines. *Sports Illustrated* is the largest-selling sport magazine, with a weekly circulation of a little over 3 million copies; in 1996 it was the fifth most-read magazine in North America. *Sport, Inside Sports,* and *The Sporting News* are other highly successful magazines, selling a combined total of some 2 million copies with each issue.

Books

The first massive book wave in the United States began in the two decades before the Civil War as dime novels began to appear in large quantities. Numerous books on field sports, horse racing, boxing, and the increasingly popular team sports poured from the publishing houses throughout the late nineteenth century, but the youth literature contributed most significantly to arousing interest in sports among the youngsters of this era. Undoubtedly the most prolific of the youth-literature authors was Gilbert Patten (whose real name was Burt L. Standish), who in 1896 began turning out a story every week about the greatest of schoolboy heroes, Frank Merriwell. In the early 1900s the Merriwell stories sold about 135,000 copies weekly. Youth athletic stories also streamed from the pens of many other authors.

Serious novelists tended not to mention sport to any extent, although some of the most powerful passages in Ernest Hemingway's novels dealt with blood sports (e.g., bullfighting). A trend has now developed toward serious writing about sport, and North American novelists have increasingly employed sports themes in their works. One indication of this growing interest is that a Sport Literature Association was founded in the early 1980s, and it publishes a journal entitled *Aethlon: The Journal of Sport Literature.*

Perhaps the greatest impact of sport on the literary field has been made by former athletes and sports journalists. The United States has been virtually deluged with books by professional athletes (most of these are actually ghostwritten) who describe their experiences in sports. A number of former athletes have written "kiss-and-tell" books either mocking or criticizing their sports experiences. Sports journalists have also shared in the publishing windfall; several have written what might be called exposé, or muckraking, types of books. Most bookstores have an entire section of sports books.

Radio

In the last fifty years the electronic media—radio, motion pictures, and television—have made dramatic inroads into the traditional information and entertainment functions of the printed media. Whereas centuries separated the invention of the printing press and sport's exploitation of that medium, only a few years separated the invention of wireless broadcasting and the advent of radio sportscasts. The first permanent commercial radio station, KDKA in Pittsburgh, went on the air in 1920. Less than a year later, in July 1921, the first heavyweight championship boxing bout was broadcast. From the mid-1920s to the early 1950s, radio reigned supreme in broadcasting sports news and live sports events.

Radio was dealt a serious blow with the growth of television, but there are still some 9,500 radio stations in North America that broadcast over 500,000 hours of sport annually. Sports call-in shows, interviews with sports celebrities, as well as play-by-play game reporting have sustained the role of radio in sports, and the twenty-four-hour-per-day, all-sports radio stations appear to have created excitement in this industry. There are now over thirty-five all-sports radio stations in the United States.[4] In a *Sports Illustrated* article titled "Yak Attack," the writer noted:

> Sports call-in shows are everywhere these days. Every major city has at least one show, and usually more than one. The programs are also popular in the smaller markets, where there may not be a major league team or an NFL franchise but where college football and basketball are talked about all year long. And . . . they're on around the clock, most conspicuously at "drive time," those hours when the fans—mostly male— are trapped in commuter traffic with only their radios, and increasingly, their cellular phones for company.[5]

Motion Pictures

Thomas Edison's rudimentary motion-picture camera, the kinetoscope, which he patented in 1891, marked the birth of the movie industry. By 1939 an estimated 85 million Americans saw one movie per week. As popular as the movies were, though, sports stories were relatively rare before 1970, although *Knute Rockne-All-American,* the story of the legendary Notre Dame coach, and *The Pride of the Yankees,* the story of the famous New York Yankee first baseman Lou Gehrig, among a few others, had gained some popularity. The number of sports films has increased. Films such as *Bull Durham, Field of Dreams, Rudy,* and *Cobb* are only a few of the recent movies involving sports themes. Several sports films have received critical acclaim; *Rocky* and *Chariots of Fire* were awarded the Oscar for best picture.

Of course, quantity is not good indication of the worth of films, but the quality of sports films has certainly improved. Increasingly, sports films are transcending mere entertainment and attempting to explore broader social issues and problems.

Television

The technology to produce telecasts was developed during the 1930s, but World War II caused the delay of large-scale growth of commercial television for nearly a decade. When television began to grow, however, its rate of growth was staggering. In 1942 there were four commercial television stations in North America; in 1995 there were over 800. In 1950 less than 10 percent of households had television; in the mid-1990s 98 percent of North American homes had at least one set, 38 percent had two sets, and 28 percent have three or more sets.

In 1970 the average television viewer received only four or five channels, three of which were broadcast networks; the average viewer in the 1990s received around thirty-five channels (broadcast and cable), and some received over one hundred. DIRECTV and The United States Satellite Broadcasting (USSB) satellite networks offer over one hundred fifty channels of programming choices. To watch this plethora of TV choices, North Americans own over 200 million television sets, representing more than one-third of the world's total.[6]

The next section is devoted to examining the impact of television because it has had such a multifaceted and powerful impact on sports.

Television: The Monster of Sports World

Television has come to have a dominating grasp on sport, but its influence has been reciprocal; television programming is greatly influenced by sport as well. Sport made a union with television while the tube was still in its infancy. The first televised sports event was a college baseball game between Columbia and Princeton in 1939. The announcer was located in the stands with the spectators; there was only one camera, and its range was so limited that it could not show the batter and the pitcher at the same time. Other technical difficulties made it almost impossible for viewers to know what was happening during the game. In describing the TV coverage, the *New York Times* reported: "The players were best described by observers as appearing like white flies running across the screen. . . . When the ball flashed across the grass, it appeared as a cometlike white pinpoint . . . the commentator saved the day, otherwise there would be no way to follow the play or tell where the ball went except to see the players run in its direction."[7]

In what has become a classic description of sports viewing on television before the use of multiple cameras and instant replays, the author of an amusing book, *Super Spectator and the Electric Lilliputians,* said:

Like a clumsy, myopic robot the camera tried. . . . But its field of vision was like peering down a small drainpipe that was mounted on a swivel. It could not take in both the pitcher and the batter for the same shot. On every pitch, it was swinging constantly back and forth, describing dizzy blurry arcs across the screen as it hurried to follow the path of the ball to the plate. . . . Foul balls set off wild, looping searches by the cameraman seeking the baseball. On a hit, the old Iconoscope would sweep its eye doggedly along the landscape, chasing crazily after the bouncing white sphere.[8]

Despite the many problems encountered by the infant television industry, it grew enormously in a short time, and television is now by far the most popular and most time-consuming leisure activity in the

United States. Average daily viewing of TV by North American households is over seven-and-one-half hours a day.[9] Thus, TV is a dominating influence on the social lives of North Americans.

Increasing TV Sports Coverage

The most dramatic programming trend in television has been the enormous increase in sports coverage. In 1971 television beamed 800 hours of sport into North American homes, by 1995 the major networks (ABC, CBS, NBC) broadcast some two thousand hours of sport, or the equivalent of eighty-three full days of sporting events. In addition, sports accounted for about five thousand hours of cable TV, and countless thousands of hours of local broadcast television on independent television stations. These increases are the result of the popularity of televised sports programs; they draw millions of viewers. Indeed, of the ten top-rated TV shows of all time, five are NFL championship games, and over half of the twenty-five all-time top-rated television programs are sports events.

The trends suggest that the amount of sport on television will continue to increase. All of the major networks are planning to expand their sport coverage. More significant is that the television sports market underwent a significant change. The three major networks (ABC, CBS, NBC) and local stations are no longer the main dispensers of TV sports. Basic cable, satellite, and regional pay services have entered the picture in a big way.

The assault on the "big-three" commercial networks monopoly on sports began in the fall of 1980 when ESPN, North America's first total sports network, began telecasting sports on cable systems twenty-four hours per day, 365 days per year. By 1995 ESPN reached over 63 million households, more than 60 percent of homes. It also spawned a second network, ESPN2. Other national cable networks are emphasizing sports programs, especially the CNN and USA cable channels. Furthermore, regional sports networks, which hardly existed a few years ago, are one of the fastest growing segments in cable TV.[10]

Another development in TV sports that seems destined to become more prominent is "pay-per-view" (PPV), a variant of cable in which the subscriber agrees to pay a specific fee, in advance, so that the signal for a specific event will be beamed to the subscriber's set. Others do not see that event. Television analysts claim that PPV will become a major factor. PPV championship boxing matches have been on the forefront of this trend, but the NBC 1992 Summer Olympics PPV package was the first large-scale effort to test market this type of TV service. In the fall of 1995, DIRECTV began offering via the Digital Satellite System (DDS) up to thirteen NFL football games every Sunday on its NFL SUNDAY TICKET. This service is a form of PPV. Some television executives believe that in the not-so-distant future all of the top sports events, including the Super Bowl, Gray Cup, World Services, Stanley Cup, Kentucky Derby, Indianapolis 500, Olympics, college bowl games, and the like, will be available only via PPV.

Economic Aspects of Televised Sports

Accompanying the enormous expansion in sports programming has been the incredible economic impact of televised sport. Money is the fuel propelling the TV-sports machine, and sport and television are mutual beneficiaries in one of the most lucrative business associations. In return for the rights to telecast sports events, professional and collegiate sports receive free publicity as well as broadcast rights fees. At the same time, television companies profit from the use of their products (the telecasts) by sport consumers.

The system works this way: Television networks pay money for the rights to broadcast a professional (or college) league's (e.g., NFL) games. The networks hope to get that money back, plus a profit, by selling advertising time for the games. Administrators of the sports leagues take the money received from the television network and distribute it to the league members. In essence, then, the television industry is basically a broker, bringing together the sellers (sports leagues), the buyers (advertisers), and consumers (fans). The relationship between media and sport is one of planned, calculated business rationality.

The extent to which the fees for telecasting rights have escalated may be seen in the following examples:

Summer Olympic Games	Television Rights Costs
1960	$394,000
1972	$7,500,000
1976	$25,000,000
1980	$87,000,000
1984	$225,000,000
1988	$300,000,000
1992	$401,000,000
1996	$456,000,000
2000	$705,000,000
2004	$793,000,000
2008	$894,000,000[11]

Winter Olympic Games	Television Rights Costs
1960	$50,000
1980	$15,500,000
1984	$91,500,000
1988	$309,000,000
1992	$243,000,000
1994	$300,000,000
1998	$375,000,000
2002	$545,000,000
2006	$613,000,000

The economics of television are changing because of these escalating rights fees, and the reign of the television networks as the exclusive carrier of the Olympics ended after the 1988 Summer Games in Seoul. Cable television has gotten a larger and larger piece of the Olympic pie. Satellite is just beginning to make its mark in the industry.

Professional sports are able to operate the way they do primarily through the television contracts they have been able to negotiate. In 1995 each NFL team received in excess of $40 million annually as its portion of the NFL's television contract. This means that about 65 percent of all revenues of NFL teams comes from the TV contract. Also in 1995 major league baseball sold TV rights for five years to Fox, NBC, and ESPN for $1.7 billion, which brings in an annual income of over $12 million per team. The NBA contract, when divided up by the teams, brings in some $23 million annually per team. Television effectively subsidizes several professional sports leagues, and many of the league salary structures are based on the flow of television money.[12] One might ask, "Why is television so eager to spend such lavish sums for the rights to telecast sporting events?" It's simple, TV networks expect to benefit from the prestige, ratings, and huge advertising revenues of the predominately male audiences that follow sports.

In order for television networks to remain profitable while televising sports events, they must sell advertising time to companies. The escalating rates of advertising time can be seen from the following examples of Super Bowl rates for a thirty-second commercial:

Year	Advertising Rate
1970	$75,000
1976	$125,000
1982	$400,000
1985	$500,000
1988	$600,000
1990	$700,000
1993	$850,000
1996	$1,200,000[13]

Television's Influence on Sport

Each medium has made an impact on sport in its own way. Newspapers of the late nineteenth century and early twentieth century contributed to the rise of professional and collegiate sports by creating an interest in these activities. Magazines and books helped create and sustain the hero worship of the athlete in succeeding generations. Radio brought live sports action into the home for the first time. It was television, though, that had the most profound impact. Several interpreters of the impact of television on sport have argued that TV has produced more revolutionary and irrevocable changes in sport than anything since such modern sport began in the mid-nineteenth century.

Increases in Sport Revenue

Before the advent of television, professional sport was only a skeleton of what it has become, and the professional franchises that did exist were struggling financially. There were only sixteen major league baseball teams in the 1950s, and no new teams had come into the leagues in over fifty years; now there are twenty-eight teams and plans to expand. This expansion, and baseball's prosperity, have been due to television. Similar patterns can be seen in professional football, basketball, and hockey. All of these sports entered the 1950s as struggling enterprises with less than ten franchises each, and neither the owners nor the players were making much money. These sports now have over twenty-five franchises each, and all have expansion plans. Television contributes a substantial portion of their revenues. Professional golf, tennis, bowling, and other professional sports either did not exist or were inconsequential prior to the infusion of large sums of television money.

The extent to which professional sport has become dependent upon television revenue is captured in remarks frequently made by sports executives, remarks such as: "There is no way we could survive without television" or "If sports lost television revenues, we'd all be out of business." Indeed, so many pro sports organizations have built their budgets around TV income that if television ever did withdraw its money, the entire pro sports structure in its present form would collapse.[14]

Professional sports owners have not been the only beneficiaries of this windfall. Television money has increased the social mobility of athletes as well. Pro athletes' salaries have tripled or even quadrupled; television money has made it possible for them to command their enormous salaries.[15]

The extent to which sport has been influenced by its increasing economic dependence on television was brought into focus by the late sportswriter Leonard Shecter, who was an early interpreter of TV's impact on sports: "Television buys sports. Television supports sports. It moves it with its money and supports sports in a style to which they have become accustomed and then, like a bought lady, sports become so used to luxurious living they cannot extricate themselves. So, slowly, at first, but inevitably, television tells sports what to do. It is sports and it runs them the way it does most other things, more flamboyantly than honestly."[16]

Shecter's comment was made years ago, but he was an accurate prophet. His observation that "television buys sports" is not rhetorical chatter. It is literally true,

as an increasing number of professional sports teams are owned wholly or partly by media companies. Some of them are (in 1995): Atlanta Braves (Turner Broadcasting Company); Philadelphia Phillies (Taft Broadcasting Company); Pittsburgh Pirates (Warner Communications); Chicago Cubs (*The Chicago Tribune*); Miami Dolphins, Florida Marlins, and Florida Panthers (Blockbuster Video); Anaheim Mighty Ducks (Walt Disney Corp.); Denver Nuggets and Colorado Avalanche (Ascent Entertainment Group); and the Colorado Rockies (*Rocky Mountain News* and KOA radio). The New York Knicks and Rangers have been owned by several different media-oriented corporations.

Popularity Shifts

Television's dominating role is demonstrated most clearly in the changing popularity of the various sports. Telecasts have greatly increased the popularity of some sports and decreased interest in others. Football and baseball with their series of crises, tennis with its evolving drama, basketball with its fast action, and boxing with its violence in a confined space are ideal sports for television. Natural breaks in the action permit viewers to contemplate the next moves; more importantly, they provide the opportunity for periodic commercial breaks without seriously disturbing the flow of the sporting event. Other sports, such as soccer, have been less successful because they lack predictable crises, natural breaks, or action in a manageable space.

If television viewing is the criterion of national pastime status, football has replaced baseball as America's national pastime. It has also eroded the popularity of ice hockey in Canada. There is little doubt that football is ideally suited for television, with its fast, violent action confined to a rather restricted area, its periods of inaction between plays, and its rigidly controlled time orientation.[17]

Although televised baseball has not enjoyed the popularity of football, there has been enough interest to erode interest in the minor league system. At the time TV coverage of major league baseball games began, there were 448 minor baseball teams playing in fifty-nine minor leagues, and some 42 million people attended minor league games. Then came television. Minor league attendance plunged, and by 1974 there were only 145 teams in eighteen leagues. Although this decrease may, in part, have been due to major league expansion, the primary culprit was television; few people wanted to see minor league baseball when they could tune in and watch the best—the major leaguers.

Boxing has experienced an escalator existence with television. In the early years of television, boxing matches were the most popular sport on TV; sometimes as many as five bouts a week were telecast by the three major networks. Many fans stopped attending local fights, and boxing clubs declined. However, just as suddenly as it began, television dropped boxing, as sponsors' interest in televised fights declined. Owing to the popularity of champions such as Mike Tyson, televised boxing has made a comeback, but not on the major networks, instead on cable and pay-per-view.

Professional Sports
Franchise Location

Not only has television influenced the popularity and the fortunes of entire sports, but it has, more selectively, come to play a direct role in decisions about the number and locations of professional franchises. The promise of lucrative television contracts explains why the number of professional football, basketball, baseball, and hockey franchises has more than doubled in the past two decades. Moreover, as the NFL, NBA, MLB, and NHL have awarded new franchises, the size of the potential television market in a region has been a major consideration.

Prior to television, professional sports franchises were considered to be permanent fixtures in a city, but the practice of jumping from city to city has become common. There have been over thirteen moves of NFL teams since 1971 (two in 1995 alone, Los Angeles Rams to St. Louis and Los Angeles Raiders back to Oakland) and over a dozen city changes for NBA teams. The fundamental reason for moving in almost every case has been the promise of additional television revenues. Given the economic structure of professional sports, it is not surprising that professional leagues and their franchise owners gravitate toward television money.

Although television revenues have been responsible for the health and expansion of some professional sports enterprises, the lack of network television contracts has been responsible for the demise of others. In the early 1980s the United States Football League failed to secure network sponsorship and folded. Professional track died for similar reasons, and professional volleyball and several women's professional sports have had an off-and-on existence for lack of television contracts. On the other hand, the World League of American Football was created by the NFL and a joint partner, the media giant Fox Inc./Newscorp., primarily to provide spring football to capitalize on the popularity of televised football games.[18]

Intercollegiate Sport

At the same time that television was enhancing the expansion and financial status of the openly professional sports, it was also furthering the professionalization of a self-proclaimed amateur sport enterprise, intercollegiate sport, which has been a professional enterprise for many years. When collegiate football became one of the most popular viewer events on early TV, the NCAA, the controlling organization of intercollegiate athletics, quickly stepped in to regulate television coverage of collegiate football games. Under that system of regulation, the NCAA always limited the number of football games that could be televised each week and the number of times a particular team could appear on television each season. Nevertheless, a few of the football "powers" were seen rather frequently, while most collegiate football teams never appeared on television. Teams that are televised received large payments per appearance, therefore, the television package has had the effect of increasing the gap between the "haves" and the "have-nots" in college football. Moreover, it thrust both big-time college football and college basketball into the professional sports business and made these programs dependent upon television revenue for their very existence. The network manipulation of college football schedules has made a mockery of traditional scheduling. Traditional rivalry game dates have been revised and traditional starting times no longer exist.[19]

The dependence of major university athletic programs on television money led to a challenge of the NCAA's right to negotiate TV contracts on behalf of all of its member institutions. It was settled by a U.S. Supreme Court decision in which the court invalidated the NCAA's exclusive college football TV contract. The effect was to free individual colleges and conferences to negotiate their own television contracts with the networks, cable companies, and local stations. College football broadcasts on national cable and syndication channels has risen over 150 percent since that decision. It appears, however, that the freedom of individual colleges to negotiate fees has been a mixed blessing; television rights fees have not been the windfall that many athletic directors and coaches anticipated. Television companies have been able to pay less to show more games because colleges now do not have an exclusive product.

The Supreme Court decision regarding college football did not affect the NCAA's control over its men's basketball tournament. The growth of the NCAA men's basketball tournament provides a vivid demonstration of television's influence on collegiate sports (see table 11.2). The pattern is quite clear: the more teams in the NCAA basketball tournament, the greater was the television revenue, and the greater was the amount of money paid the participating teams. Therefore, the NCAA continued to increase the number of teams participating in the tournament. In 1990 CBS signed a seven-year $1 billion contract with the NCAA for the rights to televise the men's basketball tournament. In mid-December 1994 that contract was replaced with a new seven-year $1.725 billion deal.[20] What is the financial impact of this television contract on intercollegiate sports? The majority of universities with big-time intercollegiate sports programs run a deficit in their annual budgets; the deficits would be larger were it not for television money, and for those who do not run a deficit it is largely because of television money they receive. Television money is the financial foundation for the administrative agency of college sports—the NCAA. The men's basketball TV contract provides around 85 percent of the NCAA's total revenue![21]

Television has played an important role in molding public interest in intercollegiate football and basketball.

The television industry has televised only college football and basketball on a regular basis, therefore, it has effectively made these two sports dominant on university campuses to the exclusion of others. With a view toward receiving television money and public exposure, universities throughout the country throw enormous human and financial resources into their football and basketball programs while they have been dropping other sports from their offerings. Some universities have dropped as many as six sports in the past decade.

High School Sports

The television industry has reached down to tap a different source, high school athletics. In the fall of 1989, SportsChannel America, a cable network, signed a multiyear agreement with the National Federation of State High School Associations, the administrative organization for high school sports. At the time the negotiations were underway, an executive for SportsChannel said: "We think high school sports are going to be the TV sport of the 90s."[22] This is exactly the attitude that many educators fear. Can pressures for national high school championships be far behind if television becomes the financial support for high school sports? The answer is "no." The Louisiana Superdome officials, in conjunction with ESPN2 and *USA Today,* have proposed a national championship for high school boys basketball. Can national championships in football and other sports be far behind?[23] If that happens, the educational priorities will surely be sacrificed in the interests of keeping the television industry happy.

Television coverage of state football and basketball championships and tournaments has already become an annual event in many states. Minnesota's state ice hockey tournament has brought on a bidding war by local stations. Several state high school activity associations have begun to explore coverage of regular season games.

Television has even become a factor in recruitment of high school athletes. Many athletes are choosing to attend a university because of the TV coverage that university gets. The football games of some universities are carried on national TV much more frequently than others. In the case of big-time collegiate basketball, some athletes are selecting eastern universities because the viewing audiences of the games are much larger than midwestern or western states due to the time the games are played. The athletes in football and basketball believe that greater television exposure helps their chances of being drafted by the pros.

Game Modifications for TV

In order to enhance spectator appeal and to accommodate programming needs, the television industry has increasingly manipulated the structure and the processes of televised sports. In pro football, rule changes, such as moving in the sideline hash marks, reducing defensive backs' contact with receivers, liberalizing offensive holding, and the longer kickoff, have been implemented in order to open up the game and to make it more attractive to television viewers. The "sudden death" tie-breaking rule in the NFL and the extended play-off system (also used in all the professional team sports) are further means of increasing spectator interest. Other modifications have been introduced to permit more commercials: official time-outs at the end of each quarter, time-outs at the discretion of television officials, and of course, the two-minute warning in NFL games is designed solely for additional commercials.

Production innovations, such as multiple cameras and instant replay, make the game more entertaining for viewers. The World League of American Football, a league created primarily to provide televised football games in the spring, introduced the helmet camera to give viewers a sense of actually being on the field and in the action.

Major league baseball officials introduced the designated hitter in the American League, lowered the strike zone, and switched the time-honored afternoon World Series and All-Star games to evenings for television. Many knowledgeable baseball people strongly suspect (in spite of denials by baseball executives and ball manufacturers) that the baseball has been modified to make it more lively, thus producing what spectators like to see: a steady barrage of extra base hits and home runs.

The rules and conventions of other sports have been modified to accommodate TV. In basketball, the shot clock, the "slam dunk," and the three-point shot are now part of the game to keep the action lively and the viewers interested. In golf, match play, in which the golfers compete on a hole-by-hole basis (the golfer winning the most holes is the winner), has been completely replaced by medal play, with golfers playing the field (the golfer with the lowest score over the course wins), and the Skins Game because these forms of play lend themselves more readily to television coverage. The Skins Game involves wagering on each of the eighteen holes (a TV version of gambling that golfers have done for years) but on TV the pro golfers play for the sponsor's money, and the stakes are very high. As much as $100,000 can be riding on a single hole. This, of course, can generate a great deal of interest for TV viewers, the same way that big-money game shows do.

At the request of television producers, tennis tournament officials instituted a tie-breaker system of scoring to be used when sets reach six games for each contestant. This enables matches to be completed within a designated time period. Shoot outs in professional soccer matches and NHL hockey were instituted primarily to fit soccer and ice-hockey contests into the prescribed time-niche scheduled by television programming executives.

There are other ways television has modified sports that could be mentioned, but it suffices to say that most of the changes identified here, and others, are tied directly to television's interest in enhancing the action for television viewers and keeping them in their chairs to watch the commercials. This is, after all, the means by which the television industry makes its profits. As the television industry's investment in sports continues to grow, so does TV's resolution to get the most for its investment by orchestrating the sporting events for maximum viewer appeal.

Redefining the Meaning of Sport

Television has not only revised the way sport is played and the way it is watched, it has redefined the meaning of sport in many ways. Contemporary sport has become part of media culture, meaning that its form and content have been altered to suit the interests of the media.[24] Although the media appear to simply report what is happening, or what has just happened, during a sporting event, they actually construct the events to increase the number of viewers. Television plays a role in shaping opinions and creating images, and it is through these means that TV uses sports programming to draw viewers and to promote commercial messages.

Televised sports are the result of a carefully crafted selection process. Television executives select sports events that make "good television" watching, showing them over and over, while not selecting some sports events for programming at all. For example, team sports such as football, basketball, baseball, and hockey are the "authorized" sports; they dominate TV programming. Also, men's sports events overwhelmingly outnumber women's sports events on television, reflecting the media's bias about what are the "important" sports and that male viewers greatly outnumber female viewers as watchers of sporting events. This selective process is not benign; social value is conveyed through particular choices of coverage. People's attitudes are shaped about sports by what is chosen as well as by what is left out of televised sports.

The selection process is at work within a particular sporting event. Production executives foreground particular aspects of the event for the viewers. In baseball, home runs are highlighted over "routine" singles; in football the quarterback gets the focus, rather than any of the ten other positions; in multiple events, such as track and field, some events get more attention than others, for example, in track and field the sprints get more coverage than most other events. Beyond mere selecting, viewers are provided with descriptions of what has been selected through narrative themes and interpretations of preferred meaning about the action or the event itself. Televised sporting events do not merely consist of pictures, they also involve commentary on the pictures—a commentary that shapes what viewers are seeing and believing.

This selective highlighting is not "natural." It is based on media assumptions about what is good television and what keeps viewers watching. These decisions are socially constructed. They involve preferences about what to reveal to the viewers. Televised sport involves an active process of representation; what viewers see, then, is not the actual event, but a mediated event, in other words, a media event.

The selecting, screening, and filtering of sports events that is carried out by television through images and verbal commentary results in the presentation of a whole new game, a game created from an entertainment perspective, because in essence entertainment is what televised sport is all about. In consequence, the basis for interest in sport has changed from an appreciation of the beauty and style, the skill, and the technical accomplishments of the performers, to a primary concern for titillating excitement and productive action.

The intrinsic, process-oriented participation motive to engage in sport has been redefined by media sport, as it has increasingly become the national definer of meaning in sport and how to "do" sport. Media sport valorizes the obsession with victory above all else. Television executives, camera personnel, sportscasters, and even the vast majority of viewers are not attuned to the aesthetic nuances of a well-executed play; instead the overriding ethos is a win by whatever means it takes. Indeed, the mantra expressed over and over by sportscasters is "Whatever it takes."

John Alt articulately described the consequences of televised sport directed to a mass audience:

> The cultural crisis of modern sport is directly associated with . . . the triumph of the sport spectacle oriented to the commercial and mechanical production of a cult of winning, violent action, physical masculinity, and sensationalized entertainment. . . . Packaging the game, altering the rules and action, is undertaken to create special effects, usually in the form of visual-audio images, which resonate to the new cultural-emotional needs of masses. For instance, rules are changed to allow for more excitement-producing action. A cult of winning dominates the purpose of every sport franchise re-shaping the structure and integrity of the game and its players. Owners and players operate under the fetishized power of money, leaving traditional sports creeds behind. The national media take over the mass distribution of the new games, and interject an entertainment ethic and technical fetishisation, replacing that traditional commentary once important to the meaning of the ritual. In the extreme, the spectacle form reduces

sport to its most banal and sensational elements as standards of excellence are repressed by commercial norms.[25]

Trash Sports

Perhaps the most degrading influence on television sport, at least from a traditional purity of sports perspective, has been the introduction of a number of staged television events that are popularly, and appropriately, known as "trash sports." This trivialization began in the mid-1970s with "Supersports," an ABC program in which outstanding athletes competed in events other than their specialties. The idea of the program, at least as it was promoted, was to find out who were the "best" athletes and which sports developed the "best" athletes. Actually, though, from the TV networks standpoint, an economic motive explained its airing. The point was to take athletes whose status as celebrities had been constructed by the media in the sports in which they regularly competed and use that celebrity status to attract viewers to contrived sports programs, and the commercials shown on those programs.

Once "Supersports" had become a television success, other trash sports followed: "Challenge of the Sexes," in which top male athletes competed against top female athletes (the males were given handicaps to heighten the uncertainty of the outcomes); and "Super Teams," in which members of professional teams in two different sports vied in contrived events; "Battle of the Network Stars" and "Celebrity Challenge of the Sexes," in which television and movie entertainers challenged each other in "sporting" events and sport was blatantly exploited to promote show-business personalities and the programs that they represent. With the growth of all-sport cable networks, networks that have twenty-four hours of programming to fill every day, a variety of "contrived" sports have been created.

According to some media researchers, "made-for-television events are often nothing more than gussied-up program-length commercials for the resort hotel or equipment manufacturers sponsoring the competition. They exist to sell products in as many ways as possible: through endorsements, favorable coverage, demonstrations of the equipment, association with athletes, and public exposure."[26]

As for the widespread criticism leveled at these programs, one of the executives instrumental in bringing them to television said, "As long as some guy who's putting out widgets all week on an assembly line enjoys the program, I don't particularly care what the critics say."[27] Obviously, other TV executives have similar feelings.

Why such programs attract audiences that are, in some cases, comparable in size to more traditional sports programs has attracted the speculations of a number of scholars. For some social scientists, the popularity of such shows is an indication of an alienation, a craving for excitement, perhaps even a pathology in North American society.[28]

The Impact of Sport on the Mass Media

Increased Sport in the Media

The relationship between the mass media and sport is one of financial interdependence. As noted in an earlier section of this chapter, the sports section helps sell newspapers; indeed, a close observer will have noticed that sports are becoming more prominent every year in the papers. In many, sports occupy a special, separate section—a development of recent years. Print media managers like to say they publish what the public wants, and it's obvious that newspaper editors believe that the public wants vast amounts of sports news and that sports information will sell more and more papers.

Sport has also invaded other sections of newspapers. Not too many years ago a sports story or photo on the front page of papers like the *New York Times* would have been unheard of. Now it is a regular occurrence. Several popular comic strips feature sports characters, and strip themes often involve sport. "Doonesbury" and "Peanuts" comic strips frequently portray sports situations. Editorial cartoonists routinely use sport themes to illustrate political, economic, and social issues.

Sports franchise owners and athletes reap vast sums of money from television, but the television corporations in turn are richly remunerated by sports. Network television sells advertisers $1 billion worth of time for sports programs, which greatly contributes to the $30- to $50-million profit that the networks report each year.

Beyond the economic impact, there is the influence of sport on programming. Weekend programming is developed around sports, and even the prime-time evening slots have been invaded by Monday Night Football, All-Star games, the World Series, and the Super Bowl. It was the enormous popularity of any kind of sports program that led television to create the trash sports discussed earlier. It was sports again that led to the creation of entire television networks, for example, the Entertainment and Sports Programming Network (ESPN).

Sports Privileged Treatment by the Media

The mass media are fiercely independent (or claim to be), and reporters staunchly defend their right to freedom of the press. Sport, however, is one arena in which the media's reporting of events is blatantly manipulated. Stories are withheld or distorted, and sports news is edited to ensure a favorable image of the home team. Millions of dollars in free publicity are generously contributed to sports. Indeed, with respect to professional sports, no other privately owned, profit-making business receives as much free publicity for its product. Newspapers carry daily accounts of the activities of local pro teams, and television newscasters keep viewers informed in the same way. The media exposure is enough in itself to promote pro sports, but typically the stories are reported in a blatantly booster fashion, clearly designed to hype local interest in the teams. In a biting commentary on sports news, Elaine Rapping contended: "Sports news is the most repetitious and non-analytical thing on TV. There is no sense that economic or social factors come into play in the sports world. On the contrary, the typical sportscast is predictable to the point of self-parody. Athletes are interviewed about a game coming up or just played. The questions and answers are always the same. 'How do you think you'll do this season, Bud'? 'Well, gee, we're just gonna get out there and give it our best and all,' is recognizably typical."[29]

Of course, the motives of the media are quite clear: The media ethos is rooted in profit maximization, and it is driven by the competition to be number one to reap the power and prestige that accompanies this. The more interest generated in local sports, the more people will buy local newspapers, listen to radio, and watch local television to follow the teams. The result is greater profits for the local mass media.

Sports Consumers and the Mass Media

The home has become the major site of leisure in postindustrial society. The main force for this has been the mass production of cheap home entertainment systems in the form of radio, television, audio, and video equipment. Exact figures on the amount of time people spend with the mass media are not readily available, but the best estimates for both the United States and Canada indicate that newspaper reading accounts for about two and one-half hours per person per week and television viewing for some forty-nine hours per household per week. Televised sports have produced a dramatic shift in the mode of the fans' consumption of sport. In the pretelevision era the only way a fan could see a sports event was to attend, usually paying admission to do so. Television has, of course, changed that. Indeed, television has become the most important source of sports programming for the sports consumer, and television provides this programming at a very low cost to the fan (even assuming the price of the television set and the advertising costs that are passed on to the public). The opportunity to see sports events on television at low cost has also had the effect of creating fans among parts of the population that have traditionally had little interest in sport, especially women and the elderly.

Surveys of adults in the United States conducted by various opinion research agencies have consistently found that professional football and college football were the most frequently watched sports: 60 percent of those polled had watched pro football and 54 percent had viewed major league baseball during the previous year. Next most popular were college football (47 percent), college basketball (32 percent), and pro basketball (32 percent). All other sports had been viewed by less than 30 percent of those polled. Viewing televised sports tended to increase in proportion to the viewer's education level.[30]

Sports regularly attract some of television's largest audiences. Annually, the Super Bowl attracts an enormous number. In the past few years over 125 million people have watched this event each January. An estimated 12.5 billion international TV viewers watched the month-long World Cup tournament in the United States in 1994. Some 3 billion people worldwide tuned in to at least some of the televised coverage of the 1992 Barcelona Olympic Games.

Obviously, people do find enjoyment in watching televised sports events, and televised sports programming is the most important source of sports entertainment. The specific factors that contribute to viewers' enjoyment are not well understood at present, but research into this topic has led to some tentative answers.

Enjoyment has been shown to be related to broadcast commentary, the presence of a crowd, the skill displayed by the athletes, and the viewer's disposition toward the players and the teams in competition. The enjoyment of televised sports closely corresponds to the perception of roughness, enthusiasm, and even violence, and the perceptions of all of these aspects of play are strongly influenced by the commentary of the telecasters. The larger the crowd and the more enthusiastic its responses to play on the field, the more television viewers enjoy a game. Seeing teams battle down to the wire enhances suspense and increases the viewers' enjoyment. Finally, the highest level of fan enjoyment results when a well-liked team defeats an intensely disliked team.[31]

Sports Journalism and the Mass Media

Sports journalism, including sportscasting, is a peculiar occupation. On the one hand, a certain amount of prestige and power is associated with the occupation. Sports journalists' names are seen and heard by the public daily, they control access to the sports information that the public wants, and their stories and commentaries can influence the destinies of franchises and athletes. In the world of journalism, however, sports work is not held in high esteem. Among newspaper staffs, the sports department is often labeled the "toy department" or the "playpen."

Ostensibly, sports journalists are expected to report information about the results of sports events; to provide inside information on particular players, teams, and sports events; and to give opinions that help the public interpret sports news. While accuracy and objectivity in reporting are valued norms in journalism, the image of the sports journalist is one of obsequious appeasement. More than one critic of sportswriters has observed that their work all too often reflects jock worship, press-agentry, and awe rather than solid, in-depth reporting.[32]

Several practices of sports journalists contribute to their disparagement as objective reporters. Some sports writers, through their columns and reports about the local teams, convey the impression that they are extensions of the teams; these are frequently called "housemen" or "housewomen" because their stories often read like public relations on behalf of the local team or teams. The unspoken rule appears to be "see no evil, write no evil." In return the local teams are expected to treat this reporter favorably in obtaining access to coaches and players and obtaining exclusive stories about the team or teams. This practice has declined because of the criticism within the journalism occupation itself, but it is easy to see how such an approach can create a cozy interdependence between journalists and sports teams.

A second practice that contributes to the low status of sport journalism is the TV sports news reporters who usually share the news time with anchors reporting on local, national, and international events and with weather forecasters. Typically, sports news is relegated to a very few minutes filled mostly with reporting scores and hyping upcoming events. In cities where pro teams reside or big-time collegiate sports (or both) are nearby, the TV sports reporters are frequently outright cheerleaders for these local teams, referring to local teams as "our team." In some cases they virtually become public relations agents for them.

In general, there is not any place in the sports news broadcasts for investigative journalism. The major reason for the lack of a commitment to pursuing serious news issues was articulated by Neal Pilson, the president of CBS Sports: "When you are sponsoring sports events and generating profits, you can create conflicts and problems. In CBS Sports, we have major business relationships that are worth in the billions of dollars and are renewable. You cannot use the people associated with CBS Sports to investigate the morals of the people you do business with."[33]

In other words, because of the cozy business relations between the television industry and sports, television news does not operate in a serious journalistic manner; its concern is more with promoting the teams and leagues in which it has invested than operating in a serious journalistic manner.

Another reason for sports journalism's low regard is that the sportscasters who broadcast live events on radio or television typically have no background in journalism, and indeed the journalism profession has disavowed any connection with their work. They are usually selected by radio and television executives for their ability to narrate sports events as much as for their knowledge of the game. Many are former athletes who are articulate in explaining the intricacies of the game or are charismatic. They must satisfy not only the media corporation that employs them but also the league commissioners and team owners whose games are being broadcast. The latter routinely screen the announcers and instruct the media executives as to how the announcers can improve their performances, letting it be known that all comments should cast the league, teams, and players in a favorable light. Consequently, objective reporting takes a backseat to the creation and maintenance of a favorable image of both sport and the media. George Vecsey, sportswriter for the *New York Times,* once noted that "televised sports is not journalism; it is entertainment, shaped to keep people in front of the beer advertisements as long as possible." In *Television Myth and the American Mind,* the author proposes that a more appropriate term for sportscasters would be "sport public-relations agents, whose main function is to elevate the banal."[34]

A few viewers realize that sportscasters, in addition to describing the action, are actually providing a constant commercial for the sport on which they are reporting. Much of their commentary is pure promotion, and memorable terms such as "The Doomsday Defense" and "America's Team" are deliberate public relations concoctions devised to get viewers hooked on the product—in the examples above, the NFL. The elaborate discussions of "matchups" and the "keys to winning" are calculated to get viewers absorbed in the contest. These techniques are no different from those used by advertising agencies in promoting detergents or automobiles.

Several analyses of professional football telecasts have revealed that a sizable portion of the audio narration of the coverage is devoted to dramatic embellishments of the event. In other words, sportscasters serve not only to fill in the lack of viewer knowledge about the sport but also to add histrionics to the human drama of athletic events.

In studies of the impact of commentary on audience perception and appreciation, researchers have exposed subjects to two segments of prerecorded, televised games that have been pretested for perception of roughness. Viewers were exposed to one of two presentation modes: with or without sportscasters' commentary. The results showed that the viewers' perceptions of the play were dramatically influenced by the nature of the accompanying commentary. Thus, through the commentary by sportscasters, viewers can be influenced to "see" fierce competition and roughness where it really does not exist. The researchers have concluded that viewers seem to become "caught up" in the commentary and the sportscasters' interpretation of the game, and they allow themselves to be persuaded by the narration of "drama" in the event. There is, then, overwhelming evidence that sports telecasts can be presented and manipulated to create different levels of enjoyment for viewers.[35]

It is one thing for television networks to employ up to three sportscasters to cover a game; it is quite another to believe that these persons are actually giving viewers an accurate or an inside view of the game. They are, in fact, doing just the opposite. They report actions where they do not exist; they protect owners, coaches, and athletes from serious scrutiny; and they constantly hype the sport and its participants. All of these actions are predicated on obtaining high ratings for the network. Of course, the bottom line is that both professional sport and television are big businesses, each dependent upon the fiscal health of the other. By reporting an exciting game, the sportscasters promote both sport and television.

The rise of celebrity sportscasters can be directly attributed to television. Through their own interpretations, they translate games into mass entertainment while at the same time influencing viewers' perceptions of the action. As a group, sport announcers generally have shared low marks for their banal patter and pompous second-guessing. As faithful employees of both television and sports, sportscasters promote sport; rarely do they go beyond the superficial or the obvious.

What a person sees and reads about sports via the mass media has been deliberately filtered to show the best side of sports. Although a certain amount of criticism may be reported, sports journalists in the main are supportive of the system. Very few report anything that might cause discomfort. By omission and commission, complicity and docility, the media reports seldom stray from the promotion of sport. Despite an occasional exposé, and for all the talk about muckraking, sports journalists have very little to say about the seamier aspects of sports.

The reason for sports journalists' cooperation with the sports establishment may be more fundamental than selling newspapers or obtaining high radio and TV ratings. Those few sports journalists who do not report sport in the traditional way often incur the outrage of committed sports fans. They are often targets of hate letters and ugly phone calls in the middle of the night. In one way, this is understandable because it is almost heretical to attack sport. To attack sport is to impugn the North American value system. To challenge the sanctity of sport is to criticize what for many people is their main anchor for understanding how the real world works.

Women and People of Color in Sport Journalism

Since sport has traditionally been viewed as a male preserve, the message to any female who might have been interested in a career in sports journalism was clear: Women do not understand sports, so they certainly would not know how to report them. However, women have not been willing to accept that attitude, and the revolution in women's sport involvement has spread into print and electronic journalism. Despite the indignities and the discrimination that female sports writers and sportscasters have experienced and the relatively few women in the field, impressive gains have been made; table 11.1 illustrates some of the significant milestones.

Perhaps the most significant event in legitimizing the improved status of female sports journalists was the appointment of LeAnne Schreiber in November 1978 as the first female sports editor in the history of the *New York Times*. That appointment came only after a decade-long struggle by women to be given equal opportunity and access to sports news. During that period they had to overcome policies by sports officials that excluded them from stadium press boxes and locker rooms.[36]

By the early 1980s female sports journalists had won access to locker rooms, press boxes, and any other facilities that pertained to their work. However, an ugly incident that happened in the locker room of the New England Patriots in the fall of 1990 vividly illustrates that sexism still existed in the sports world. Several nude football players approached a female sports writer, positioned themselves inches from her face, made lewd and suggestive comments, and dared her to touch their genitals. The incident became a cause celebré and raised anew the legitimacy of female sports writers having access to the locker rooms—which male sports writers have with no questions asked—so they could do their jobs.[37]

Most, but certainly not all, barriers have fallen by the wayside as females have gained increasing respect for their sports reporting skills. Two very significant events occurred in the late 1980s signaling improved opportunities for women in the mass media. Gayle

table 11.1 Milestones for Women in American Newspaper Sports Journalism

1869	*Midy Morgan* joins the *New York Times* and covers racing.
1884	*Sadie Kneller Miller* covers the Orioles for the *Baltimore Telegram*.
1889	*Nellie Bly* joins the *New York World*.
1906	*Pauline Jacobson* covers sports for the *San Francisco Bulletin*.
1908	*Eloise Young* is sporting editor of the *Chronicle News* of Trinidad, Colorado.
1916	*Nan O'Reilly* starts a golf column in the *New York Evening Post*.
1920	*Mary Bostwick* of the *Indianpolis Star* rides in a race car around the Indianapolis Speedway.
1922	*Dorothy Bough* is a sportswriter for the *Philadelphia Inquirer*.
1924	*Lorena Hickok* covers Big Ten football for the *Minneapolis Morning Tribune*.
	Margaret Goss starts a regular "Women in Sports" column for *New York Herald Tribune*.
	Nettie George Speedy covers sports news for the *Chicago Defender*.*
1929	*Nan O'Reilly* is golf editor of *New York Evening Journal*.
	Cecile Ladu is sports editor of the *Albany* (NY) *Times Union*.
1932	*Maribel Vinson* (Owen) covers sports for the *New York Times*.
1942	*Lois Fegan* of the *Harrisburg* (PA) *Telegraph* covers professional ice hockey.
1943	*Jeane Hofmann* of the *New York Journal-American* covers baseball training camps.
	Zelda Hines is women's bowling editor for the *Chicago Defender*.*
1944	*Mary Garber* is sports editor at *Winston-Salem Sentinel*.
1973	*Karol Stringer* of the Associated Press enters the pits at the Indianapolis 500.
	Betty Cuniberti, San Bernardino Sun-Telegram, covers an NFL team from the training camp to the Super Bowl.
1976	*Betty Cuniberti* is a sportswriter for the *San Francisco Chronicle*.
	Lawrie Mifflin is a sportswriter at the *New York Daily News*.
	Lesley Visser covers the National Football League beat for the *Boston Globe*.
1977	*Carolyn White* is a sportswriter for the *Akron Beacon-Journal*.*
1978	*LeAnne Schreiber* is sports editor at the *New York Times*.
1979	*Alison Gordon* covers American League baseball for *The Toronto Star*.
1982	*Claire Smith* joins the staff at the *Hartford* (CT) *Courant*.*
1985	*Christine Brennan* covers the Washington Redskins for the *Washington Post*.
1988	*Karen Hunter-Hodge* is the only black woman sportswriter on a major New York daily (*Daily News*).*

Note: This is intended to be a list of significant "firsts" for women in sports reporting. We welcome challenges to this list because the more one learns about history, the more one learns that it is never safe to say "first." In addition, almost every newspaper in the country can add its own "first" woman sports reporter to this list.

*Significant firsts for African-American women sports reporters.

Source: Pamela J. Creedon, "Women in Toyland," in *Women, Media, and Sport,* ed. Pamela J. Creedon (Thousand Oaks, Calif.: Sage, 1994), 75.

Gardner, ESPN "SportsCenter" host, was hired by NBC as the first full-time female sports anchor, and Gayle Sierens, a news anchor and former sportscaster at Tampa's WXFL-TV, became the first woman to do play-by-play broadcasting in NFL history during a game between the Kansas City Chiefs and the Seattle Seahawks. In 1993 a major milestone occurred when the Association of Sports Press Editors, with some five hundred members, elected its first female president. That same year, the first two women were elected to the Pro Football Writers Board of Directors.[38] Table 11.2 illustrates other important milestones.

Still, according to the Association for Women in Sports Media (AWSM, pronounced awesome), which was founded in 1988, in 1995 there were only about eight hundred women (8 percent) working in sports

table 11.2 *Milestones for Women in American Sports Broadcasting*

1924	*Judith Carey Waller* produces radio play-by-play of a college football game for WMAQ in Chicago.
1937	*Mrs. Harry Johnson* broadcasts baseball for KFAB radio in Lincoln, Nebraska.
1948	*Sarah Palfrey Cooke* hosts NBC's *Sportswoman of the Week* program.
1965	*Donna de Varona* is an ABC sport commentator.
1973	*Eleanor Riger* is a producer at ABC Sports.
	Anita Martini and *Nelda Pena* cover the baseball All-Star game in Kansas City.
1974	*Jane Chastain* broadcasts NFL games on CBS.
	Anita Martini enters the Los Angeles Dodgers' locker room in the Houston Astrodome.
1975	*Phyllis George* cohosts *NFL Today* for CBS.
	Jane Chastain of CBS and *Jeannie Morris* for NBC appear at the Super Bowl.
1977	*Jayne Kennedy* hosts a CBS sports event.*
	Mary Shane does major league baseball on television play-by-play in Chicago.
1982	*Mary Carillo* and *Andrea Kirby* provide the first all-female tennis tournament coverage at the USA Network.
1983	*Gayle Gardner* is ESPN *SportsCenter* anchor.
1987	*Cheryl Miller* is sports commentator on ABC.*
	Andrea Joyce is sports anchor in a Top 10 market (WFAA-TV in Dallas).
1988	*Gayle Gardner* is an NBC Sports anchor.
	Gayle Sierens is play-by-play announcer of an NFL game for NBC.
1990	*Robin Roberts* is an anchor/reporter at ESPN.*
1991	*Nicole Watson* is a producer at TBS Sports cable.*
	Mimi Griffin broadcasts on-air analysis of a men's NCAA basketball tournament game.
1992	*Robin Roberts* is an Olympic commentator for ESPN.*

Note: This is intended to be a list of "firsts" for women in broadcast sports reporting. Where we have found citations from other authors claiming that an individual was "first," we have made that claim explicit in the text. However, we welcome challenges to this list because the more one learns about history, the more one learns that it is never safe to say "first."

*These are firsts for African-American women. Research on firsts for other women of color is sorely needed.

Source: Pamela J. Creedon, "From Whalebone to Spandex," in *Women, Media, and Sport,* ed. Pamela J. Creedon (Thousand Oaks, Calif.: Sage, 1994), 139.

media out of ten thousand sportswriters and sportscasters. Moreover, they do not receive equal pay for equal work; the highest paid men get over five times the salary of the highest paid women.[39]

Sports journalism was virtually an all-white occupation until not too long ago. In 1988 on a "MacNeil/Lehrer News Hour" one sociologist called the mass media "the most segregated corner in sport," and a *New York Times* columnist said, "The hiring practices within the media have been deplorable."[40] Conditions for minorities in all areas of the mass media have changed some since these remarks were made. However, according to the American Society of Newspaper Editors, in 1995 of almost fifty-seven thousand full-time newsroom supervisors, copy editors, reporters, and photographers

on dailies, less than 8 percent were minorities; only 4.5 percent were African American. Conditions in the electronic media are not much different. Surveys have found that radio and television newsrooms are about 90 percent white.

Many viewers have formed the impression that African Americans represent a substantial portion of sports journalism because fans watching televised sports see African American former professional athletes in the broadcast booths of professional and intercollegiate sports events. Nothing could be farther from the truth. The reality is something quite different. The National Association of African-American Sportwriters and Broadcasters, founded in 1994, reports a membership of 1,000, which is less than 5 percent of the total professionals in print and electronic sports journalism. Thus, the few well-known ex-players whose fame as great athletes enabled them to parlay their sports celebrity status into a career in sports journalism are exceptions.

Summary

A symbiotic relationship exists between sport and the mass media; each is a commercial industry whose success has been greatly influenced by the other. The printed media contributed to the rise of sport during the nineteenth century. At the same time, the interest in sports information assisted in the growth of newspapers, magazines, and books. The electronic media—radio and television—have been instrumental in the promotion of big-time intercollegiate sports and professional sports. Indeed, without these media, collegiate and professional sports could not function as they presently do.

The dominating role that the mass media play in the economic aspects of sport has a number of effects. Televised sport has produced a dramatic shift in the mode of fans' consumption of sport; the popularity of several sports has been greatly influenced by television; and television has furthered the professionalization of amateur sport enterprises, such as intercollegiate athletics and the Olympic Games. Television has also manipulated the structure, meaning, and process of sports.

Figures on the amount of time people spend with the mass media are scarce, but studies estimate that television viewing accounts for some forty-nine hours per household per week. Televised sports programs are some of the most popular on TV. The networks alone telecast more than two thousand hours of sport each year; and ESPN, USA, and CNN, as well as regional sports networks and satellite networks, telecast countless additional hours of live sports.

With the rise of media coverage, sports journalists have grown in number, but they have a rather low status among other journalists. The sports department of a newspaper, a radio, or a television newsroom is commonly referred to as the "toy department."

One reason for the news reporters' low regard for sports journalists (especially sportscasters) is that they are not actually professionally trained reporters; they are, instead, employees of professional teams or of television networks, and their jobs are basically promotional. They do not merely report the events; instead, they manage the accounts of the events to make them more interesting, more dramatic, and more important than they really are. Their role, rather than to provide information, is to translate games into mass entertainment aimed at high ratings. In doing so, they promote the media and the sports in which they are employed.

Discrimination, both gender and racial, has been present in the ways in which the mass media report sports and in the hiring practices of media corporations. There are, however, encouraging signs that conditions are improving for women and minorities.

Notes

1. Robert W. McChesney, "Media Made Sport: A History of Sports Coverage in the United States," in *Media, Sports, & Society,* ed. Lawrence A. Wenner (Newbury Park, Calif.: Sage, 1989), 49.

2. Hal Himmelstein, *Television Myth and the American Mind,* 2d ed., (New York: Praeger, 1994); Dennis Mazzocco, *Networks of Power: Corporate TV's Threat to Democracy* (Boston: South End Press, 1994); David Croteau and William Noynes, *By Invitation Only: How the Media Limit Political Debate* (Monroe, Maine: Common Courage Press, 1994); Jeff Cohen and Norman Solomon, *Adventures in Medialand: Behind the News, Beyond the Pundits* (Monroe, Maine: Common Courage Press, 1994).

3. John Stevens, "The Rise of the Sports Page," *Gannett Center Journal* 1 (1987): 1–11; see also Mark Inabinett, *Grantland Rice and His Heroes: The Sportswriter as Mythmaker in the 1920s* (Knoxville: University of Tennessee Press, 1994); Jeff Neal-Lunsford, "Sport in the Land of Television: The Use of Sport in Network Prime-Time Schedules 1946–50," *Journal of Sport History* 19 (spring, 1992): 56–76; Janet Lever and Stanton Wheeler, "Mass Media and the Experience of Sport," *Communication Research* 20 (1993): 125–43.

4. Richard A. Lipsey, *Sports Marketing Place* (Princeton, N.J.: Sportsguide, 1995); see also M. Hiestand, "Sports Radio Scores with Ardent Fans," *USA Today,* 28 July 1993, sec. C, p. 1.

5. Geoffrey Norman, "Yak Attack," *Sports Illustrated,* 8 October 1990, 111.

6. "Facts and Figures," *Rocky Mountain News,* 13 May 1994, sec. D, p. 41; see also Lever and Wheeler, "Mass Media and the Experience of Sport," 131–37.

7. "First Television of Baseball Scene," *New York Times,* 18 May 1939, p. 29.

8. William O. Johnson, *Super Spectator and the Electric Lilliputians* (Boston: Little, Brown, 1971), 36–37.

9. "Facts and Figures," *Rocky Mountain News.*

10. Chris Roush, "ESPN Wants to Reinvent the Couch Potato," *Business Week,* 23 May 1994, 88; David Lieberman, "Fox, Cable Giant to Team Up for Sports," *USA Today,* 2 November 1995, sec. A, p. 1.

11. "NBC Pays $1 Billion-Plus for Upcoming Games," *Rocky Mountain News,* 8 August 1995, sec. B, p. 12; Sally Jenkins, "Peacock Power," *Sports Illustrated,* 25 December 1995 and 1 January 1996 (Double Issue), pp. 52–65.

12. Andrew Zimbalist, *Baseball and Billions* (New York: Basic Books, 1992); Kenneth M. Jennings, *Balls and Strikes: The Money Game in Professional Baseball* (New York: Praeger, 1990); Ronald Blum, "TV, Baseball Make Up With $1.7 Billion Pact," *Rocky Mountain News,* 7 November 1995, sec. B, pp. 1–5.

13. "Super Bowl Ad Spots Fetch Record Sums," *Rocky Mountain News,* 30 December 1993, sec. A, p. 47; Dottie Enrico, "Oscar Mayer Spells Halftime At Super Bowl," *USA Today,* 8 January 1996, sec. B, p. 1.

14. Zimbalist, *Baseball and Billions,* see especially chapter 7.

15. William O. Johnson, "For Sale: The National Pastime," *Sports Illustrated,* 17 May 1993, 32–39.

16. Leonard Shecter, *The Jocks* (New York: Paperback Library, 1970), 79.

17. "For Fans, Football Still Favorite," *USA Today,* 23 July 1993, sec. C, p. 10.

18. "World League Kickoff," *USA Today,* 7 April 1995, sec. C, p. 1; Austin Murphy, "As the World Turns," *Sports Illustrated,* 22 May 1995, pp. 62–65.

19. Arthur A. Fleisher, Brian L. Goff, and Robert D. Tollison, *The National Collegiate Athletic Association: A Study of Cartel Behavior* (Chicago: University of Chicago Press, 1992).

20. "CBS, Final Four Make a Deal," *Rocky Mountain News,* 7 December 1994, sec. B, p. 15.

21. Ibid.; see also Debra E. Blum, "Sports Programs Continue to Lose Money, Survey Finds," *Chronicle of Higher Education,* 7 September 1994, sec. A, p. 58.

22. Mike Lardner, quoted in Gerald Eskenazi, "Arena of Big-Time Athletics is Showcasing a Younger Act," *New York Times,* 5 March 1989, sec. 1, p. 1; see also Peter Brewington, "TV's Focus: What's Good in Prep Sports," *USA Today,* 1 September 1989, sec. C, pp. 1–2; Rick Reilly, "Give This Plan An F," *Sports Illustrated,* 18 September 1989, 100.

23. Peter Brewington, "Louisiana Superdome Proposes National Basketball Tournament," *USA Today,* 17 February 1995, sec. C, p. 4.

24. Robert P. Snow, *Creating Media Culture* (Beverly Hills, Calif.: Sage, 1983), 125; see also Michael Real, "Sport and Spectacle," in *Questioning the Media: A Critical Introduction,* ed. John Downing, Ali Mohammadi, and Annabelle Sreberny-Mohammadi (Newbury Park, Calif.: Sage, 1990), 345–56; Himmelstein, *Television Myth and the American Mind,* 288–307.

25. John Alt, "Sport and Cultural Reification: From Ritual to Mass Consumption," *Theory, Culture & Society,* 1, no. 3 (1983) pp. 97–98; for an interesting discussion of how the use of TV cameras changes the way viewers see a game, see Julie Talen, "How the Camera Changes the Game," *Channels,* 6 (April 1986): 50–55.

26. David A. Klatell and Norman Marcus, *Sports for Sale: Television, Money, and the Fans* (New York: Oxford University Press, 1988), 20; see also Terry O'Neil, *The Game Behind the Game: High Pressure, High Stakes in Television Sports* (New York: Harper & Row, 1989).

27. CBS Sales Promotion Office, quoted in Klatell and Marcus, *Sports for Sale,* 152.

28. Norbert Elias and Eric Dunning, *Quest for Excitement: Sport and Leisure in the Civilizing Process* (Cambridge, Mass.: Blackwell, 1993).

29. Elaine Rapping, *The Looking Glass World of Nonfiction TV* (Boston: South End Press, 1987), 57–58.

30. "Football Remains America's Number One Spectator Sport," *The Gallup Poll Monthly* (October 1992): 36–38.

31. Lawrence A. Wenner, "The Audience Experience With Sports on Television," in *Media, Sports & Society*, 241–69; see also Jennings Bryant, "Viewers' Enjoyment of Televised Sports Violence," in *Media, Sports & Society*, 270–89; Walter Gantz and Lawrence A. Wenner, "Fanship and the Television Sports Viewing Experience," *Sociology of Sport Journal* 12 (March 1995): 56–74.

32. Douglas A. Anderson, *Contemporary Sports Reporting*, 2d ed., (Chicago: Nelson-Hall, 1994).

33. Terry O'Neil, *The Game Behind the Game: High Pressure, High Stakes in Television Sports* (New York: Harper & Row, 1989), 242.

34. Himmelstein, *Television Myth and the American Mind*, 295; see also Dan C. Hilliard, "Televised Sport and the (Anti) Sociological Imagination," *Journal of Sport and Social Issues* 18 (February 1994): 88–99.

35. Bryant, "Viewers' Enjoyment of Televised Sports Violence," 270–89; see also Gantz and Wenner, "Fanship and the Television Sports Viewing Experience," 56–74.

36. Pamela J. Creedon, "Women in Toyland: A Look at Women in American Newspaper Journalism," in *Women, Media and Sport*, ed. Pamela J. Creedon (Thousand Oaks, Calif.: Sage, 1994), 67–107.

37. Ibid., 89–96; see also Mary Jo Kane and Lisa J. Disch, "Sexual Violence and the Reproduction of Male Power in the Locker Room: The 'Lisa Olson Incident,' " *Sociology of Sport Journal* 10 (December 1993): 331–52; Susan Fornoff, *"Lady in the Locker Room"* (Champaign, Ill.: Sagamore, 1993); Michael Messner, "Women in the Men's Locker Room?" in *Sex, Violence and Power in Sports*, eds. Michael A. Messner and Donald F. Sabo (Freedom, Calif.: Crossing Press, 1994), 42–52.

38. Pamela J. Creedon, "From Whalebone to Spandex: Women and Sport Journalism in American Magazines, Photography and Broadcasting," in *Women, Media and Sport*, 138–47.

39. Judith A. Cramer, "Conversations With Women Sports Journalists," in *Women, Media and Sport*, 159–80.

40. "Edwards: Only the Ink is Black," *USA Today*, 21 January 1988, sec. C, p. 2; see also Clint C. Wilson, *Black Journalists in Paradox: Historical Perspectives and Current Dilemmas* (New York: Greenwood Press, 1991); Ash Corea, "Racism and the American Way of Media," in *Questioning the Media: A Critical Introduction*, ed. John Downing, Ali Mohammadi, and Annabelle Sreberny-Mohammadi (Newbury Park, Calif.: Sage, 1990), 266; Arelo Sederberg, "Black Journalists Hit Wall," *Editor & Publisher*, 123 (18 August 1990): 14–15.

Chapter 12

Sport, Social Stratification, and Social Mobility

Sport is generally assumed to be an egalitarian and a meritocratic institution. Sport is accepted as egalitarian because it promotes interaction across social class and racial lines and because interest in sport transcends class and social boundaries. Sport is believed to be meritocratic because within it persons who have talent, regardless of social background, can be upwardly mobile. A speech by former president Ronald Reagan at the NCAA Honors Banquet in 1990 illustrates these commonly held beliefs: "When men and women compete on the athletics field socioeconomic status disappears. Black or white, Christian or Jew, rich or poor . . . all that matters is that you're out there on the field giving your all. [It's the same way in the stands, where] corporate presidents sit next to janitors . . . and they high-five each other when their team scores . . . which makes me wonder if it [status] should matter at all."[1] The thrust of this chapter is to show that these widely held assumptions are myths.

The empirical examination of the sports world demonstrates that sport, like the larger society, is highly stratified. Like all institutions, sport accommodates and reinforces the existing structure of social inequality. There are exceptions, as we will note, but as exceptions they prove the rule.

For much of North American history, sports were engaged in mainly by the affluent. Only the wealthy had the time and the money for such nonproductive activities. However, in this century, the average workweek has decreased from sixty to thirty-seven hours. Assuming fifty weeks of work per year, this difference means, in effect, that the average worker has 1,150 more hours a year for leisure than his or her counterpart did in 1900. Innovations such as the four-day work week, paid vacations, and the scheduling of many holidays to coincide with weekends have left the average person with time to devote to family activities, hobbies, and recreation including watching or participating in sports events. Moreover, with greater disposable income, individuals can purchase sports equipment more readily. The result has been a high rate of participation in sports. Also, attendance figures at sports events from high school through the professional levels show that many people take the time and spend the money to watch gifted athletes perform. We also know that the most popular television programs are typically sports events (125 million Americans watch the Super Bowl on television, for example). All of these facts suggest that North Americans, regardless of their socioeconomic status, enjoy sports either as participants or as spectators.

Has this twentieth-century phenomenon of increased interest and activity in sport across class lines diminished the relationship between social class and sport?

Social Class and Sport

North Americans enjoy playing and watching sports. Is what they do or prefer to do related to their socioeconomic status or not? Looking first at participation, the evidence from empirical studies provides consistent support for the generalization that the higher the socioeconomic status of the individual, the more likely that individual will be to participate actively in leisure activities.

Adult Participant Preferences for Sports by Socioeconomic Status

Research has shown that the preferences for types of sport vary consistently according to socioeconomic status (see table 12.1). One difference is that members of the upper social classes tend to engage in individual sports such as golf and tennis, and blue-collar workers tend to be more active in organized team sports such as basketball, volleyball, softball, and baseball. These team sports may be sponsored by community recreation departments, churches, local businesses, unions, and employers. Many industries, for example, have elaborate recreation facilities for their employees and schedule leagues and tournaments for their off-work hours.

There are four probable explanations for the participation of the affluent in individual sports. The most obvious is that many such activities (e.g., sailing, skiing, golf, or sports-car racing) are too expensive for the less well-to-do. In addition, the use of community facilities for golf and tennis is often restricted to members of the local country club.

table 12.1
Participation in Selected Sports Activities by Household Income: 1992 (In percent, for persons 7 years of age or older, based on a sampling of 10,000 households)

Sport	% of Total Participants in the Activity by Household Income	
	Under $15,000	$75,000 and Over
Baseball	14.6%	8.3%
Basketball	13.5	10.1
Bowling	15.7	8.1
Football	16.5	8.7
Softball	13.0	7.4
Hunting (with firearms)	13.5	6.9
Fishing (fresh water)	17.5	7.2
Tennis	10.3	18.6
Skiing	6.5	25.1
Skiing (cross country)	8.8	17.2
Exercising with equipment	12.4	13.2

Source: Adapted from *Statistical Abstract of the United States: 1994* (Washington, D.C.: U.S. Census Bureau, 1994), 258.

A second reason is that organizations for the affluent, such as country clubs, emphasize three individual sports: golf, tennis, and swimming.

An interesting speculation as to why the affluent are disposed toward individual sports was presented by Thorstein Veblen in 1899. He argued that the affluent engaged in leisure activities in order to impress upon observers that they can afford expensive and wasteful activities. In other words, sport is used by these persons as a form of *conspicuous consumption,* to prove that they can spend great amounts of time away from work.[2] This rationale explains why the upper class have held amateur sport as an ideal and why Olympic competition has traditionally been limited to the more well-to-do. That the affluent have been overrepresented on the International Olympic Committee and the national Olympic committees may explain why there has been a reluctance to include team sports in the Olympics.

The fourth explanation of the socioeconomic levels of individual and team sports is the difference by occupation in the amount of time one can devote to a rigid schedule of team practices and games. Lower-level white-collar workers and skilled and semiskilled workers typically work a set number of hours per week. They do not bring additional work home. When their daily shift is over, they are free to engage in other activities. Businesspersons, executives, and professionals, on the other hand, work at their jobs more hours per week, and their schedules fluctuate. Individual sports participation for this group is more practical than participation in team sports because it is more difficult for them to participate in scheduled sports activities.

The affluent individual is attracted to individual sports because that is what friends, relatives, and the influential people in his or her community are doing. An interesting difference between white-collar and blue-collar workers involves participation in workplace-centered fitness programs. Many corporations provide sports equipment and facilities for their workers and encourage them to participate. The typical reaction is enthusiastic support from the salaried professionals and relative nonsupport from the hourly workers.[3] There are several reasons for this. First, the lower the social status, the less likely the individual will be to exercise regularly, to participate in wellness programs, and to stop smoking. Second, white-collar workers (especially professionals) are generally more self-directed, while blue-collar workers are accustomed to being told what to do on the job. Third, the activities provided (e.g., running, swimming, and racquetball) are of more interest to higher-status workers. Fourth, blue-collar workers may mistrust such programs because they interpret them as management tools. They suspect that management provides exercise programs because they serve the interests of management, not the workers. Finally, many blue-collar workers may resent the money spent on exercise equipment and the like because it does not address their real needs (e.g., the monotony of repetitive work, the exposure to toxic chemicals or other dangers, and the effects of shift work). "Health promotion offers a luxury but fails to provide a necessity: relief from the physical harshness of much blue-collar work."[4] In other words, when blue-collar workers are encouraged to become more self-reliant and to take charge of their health, they see this as "blaming the victim" because it refocuses the need for change from the job environment to the individual.

At the lowest end of the stratification hierarchy—the working poor or the unemployed poor—participation in organized team sports is practically nonexistent. Their access to organized sports is severely limited by their lack of resources and the unavailability of teams, equipment, or facilities.

Youth Sport Participation by Socioeconomic Status

There are several tendencies concerning sports participation by the children of the poor. First, they are more likely than the children of the affluent to engage in sports. This is a social arena where they can be somebody, where they can achieve the respect they otherwise do not get.[5] Second, they are more likely than their wealthier counterparts to participate in physical/contact sports (wrestling, boxing, football). Evidence from the United States, Canada, and Germany confirms the generalization that athletes from lower social origins are much more likely to compete in contact sports. Related to that inclination is the tendency of such persons to gravitate to sports that emphasize physical strength (e.g., weight lifting or arm wrestling) and physical toughness (e.g., boxing or wrestling).

A third tendency for children of the poor is to engage in sports that require little equipment or that are publicly funded such as community youth programs and schools. Basketball, both the playground variety and school teams, is the sport at which urban children of the poor tend to excel. Prowess in basketball begins for these youngsters not in organized leagues or teams, but as individuals joining with individuals to challenge another loosely organized group of individuals. Pete Axthelm sensitively characterized it in this way:

> Basketball is the city game. Its battlegrounds are strips of asphalt between tattered wire fences or crumbling buildings; its rhythms grow from the uneven thump of a ball against hard surfaces. It demands no open spaces or lush backyards or elaborate equipment. It doesn't even require specified numbers of players; a one-on-one confrontation in a playground can be as memorable as a full-scale organized game.
>
> Basketball is the game for young athletes without cars or allowances—the game whose drama and action are intensified by its confined spaces and chaotic surroundings. . . .
>
> The game is simple, an act of one man challenging another, twisting, feinting, then perhaps breaking free to leap upward, directing a ball toward a target, a metal hoop ten feet above the ground. But its simple motions swirl into intricate patterns, its variations become almost endless, its brief soaring moments merge into a fascinating dance. To the uninitiated, the patterns may seem fleeting, elusive, even confusing; but on a city playground, a classic play is frozen in the minds of those who see it—a moment of order and achievement in a turbulent, frustrating existence. And a one-on-one challenge takes on wider meaning, defining identity and manhood in an urban society that breeds invisibility.[6]

The fiscal crisis at all levels of government (federal, state, and local) is having a negative impact on sports programs for the children of the poor. Municipal governments often cannot fund recreational programs at an

Basketball, the city game, requires no expensive equipment, is learned on playgrounds, and provides an outlet for acquiring sporting prowess.

appropriate level. City schools are especially hard hit as their funds, which come mostly from property taxes, diminish and federal and state assistance programs are reduced or eliminated.

The children of the affluent, on the other hand, either go to private schools or they attend public schools in wealthier districts. Wealthy districts provide more sports opportunities, more coaches, and better facilities and equipment than do the poorer districts. In the metropolitan Chicago area, for example, suburban schools in 1992 had sports budgets in excess of $200,000 while the city schools each had sports budgets of only $750. While the wealthy suburban schools had as many as twenty-three sports and state-of-the-art weight training facilities, the have-nots, the schools in Chicago, had to do without adequate gymnasiums and weight rooms. They use public transportation to get to games. Their equipment is shabby. They have to eliminate sophomore and junior varsity and some varsity teams.[7] When sports in the more affluent areas are threatened by cuts, the shortfall can usually be saved by "participation fees," which increases the gap between sports participation possibilities for the children of the poor and the nonpoor.

For youngsters growing up in a country club milieu, interest in the sports provided there is natural, and they tend to develop the skills, enhanced by coaches at the clubs, important to the successful performance of these individual sports. Children of the poor, on the other hand, do not have access to golf courses, tennis courts, and swimming pools. Nor do they receive coaching in these individual sports. The only individual sports in which they tend to receive coaching outside of schools are in track and field (through community track clubs), and boxing because gyms are located in the poorest and racially segregated urban areas.[8]

Spectator Preferences for Sports by Socioeconomic Status

The mass media have been instrumental in generating an interest in professional football, basketball, baseball, and hockey that transcends social class. Although lacking precise data, we may reasonably assume that since over 98 percent of all U.S. homes have at least one television set, those tuning in to the Super Bowl or the World Series will not be disproportionately from one social class.

There are two kinds of spectators—those who attend in person and those who watch or listen on television or radio.[9] Examining first the attendance at a live sporting event, the data show a consistently strong relationship between sports attendance and social class. Foremost, the higher the income, the educational attainment, or both, the more likely the individual will attend.[10] This is not surprising, given the relatively high cost for travel, tickets, parking, and concessions. A family of four in 1994 attending an NFL game paid $184.19 for four average-priced tickets, two small beers, four sodas, four hot dogs, parking for one car, two game programs, and two caps.[11] The only exception to this generalization, is attendance at professional wrestling and other pseudosports, where the near poor are overrepresented among those attending.

Statistics on sports watching on television reveal these patterns: (1) The affluent are much more likely than the poor to watch golf and tennis; (2) the college-educated are more likely to watch college sports than those who did not attend college; and (3) high school graduates are overrepresented among those watching auto racing, demolition derbies, tractor pulls, bowling, and professional wrestling.

An excellent indicator of what type of audience watches a sporting event on television is the sponsor who has purchased advertising for them. Advertisers for golf events include corporations such as IBM, Xerox, Prudential, and United Airlines; professional wrestling is typically sponsored by used-car dealers, beer distributors, and country-music record companies. Clearly, advertisers have researched sports audiences and have discerned that for some sports activities, the audiences are disproportionately from certain social classes.

While simple logic suggests why college graduates appreciate college sports, there is no ready explanation for why the working classes gravitate toward *"prole"* sports, a name derived from Karl Marx's term for the working class, *proletariat.*

Prole Sports

Why are blue-collar workers especially attracted to particular kinds of sport activities? On the surface, it would appear that these sports have several common attributes: speed, daring, physical strength, and violence. Let us examine such activities more closely to see why these and other characteristics make them so appealing to this socioeconomic category. However, the possible reasons are speculative because no systematic research has yet been undertaken to assess the actual motivations of blue-collar fans.

The various forms of automobile and motorcycle racing appeal to working-class members for several reasons. First, the artifacts (the machines, the necessary tools, and the equipment) are part of lower-class experience. Blue-collar workers easily identify with these sports because they have accessibility to the machines and the skills to drive them. A second reason is that these vehicles and their drivers represent speed, excitement, and daring to persons whose work is often dull and repetitive. Another possible symbolic reason is that automobiles and motorcycles are symbols of liberation to the working-class person who otherwise feels trapped by his or her situation. The image is one of human and machine united in rebellion against a hostile environment. Two sociologists, Thomas Martin and Kenneth Berry, have suggested that motocross racing is especially attractive to working-class persons because it offers them a chance to prove their worth in aggressive, competitive situations. Such opportunities are not found in their work situations, so they seek them elsewhere.

The demolition derby, one type of motor sport that especially appeals to the lower classes, is interesting because it is so blatantly violent. The contest is designed to encourage crashes among dozens of cars until only one car is left. Tom Wolfe argued that this sport, in its wanton aggression and destruction, is culturally the most important ever originated in the United States because of what it symbolizes:

> The unabashed, undisguised, quite purposeful sense of destruction of the demolition derby is its unique contribution. The aggression, the battering, the ruination are there to be enjoyed. The crowd at a demolition derby seldom gasps and often laughs. It enjoys the same full-throated participation as Romans at the Colosseum. After each trial or heat at a demolition derby two drivers go into the finals. One is the driver whose car was still going at the end. The other is the driver the crowd selects from among the 24 vanquished on the basis of his courage, showmanship or simply the awesomeness of his crashes.[13]

Why would there be interest in such an event? Judging by the popularity of certain kinds of movies and of sports such as football and hockey, Americans appear to be fascinated by violence. This may be especially true of those persons who work at relatively low-paying and monotonous jobs. Their latent hostility toward the more well-to-do may explain why blue-collar workers might be especially fascinated by the destruction of cars too expensive for them to own.

Pseudosports

The Roller Derby, American Gladiators, and professional wrestling, which we have characterized as *pseudosports* because their competition is contrived, depend in very large measure on the interest and attendance of blue-collar workers and their families. These types of shows have several common characteristics that may offer some clues as to why the lower classes are especially attracted to them. First, they emphasize strength, power, and violence rather than agility, strategy, and finesse. Second, the actors are easy to identify with. Some emphasize their ethnic or racial background; some are fat; some are muscular; some are heroes (often wrapped in patriotic symbols); and some are villains (often representing the nation's enemies). Unlike other sports, these activities (especially the Roller Derby) give equal billing to female athletes, allowing lower-class women someone with whom they can identify. There is a strong propensity for spectators to become physically and emotionally involved in the events because of the drama ("good" vs. "evil"). They shout encouragement to their heroes, boo the villains, and occasionally throw things when they get upset with the officiating or with the outcome of the event. The intensity of their feelings is also occasionally manifested in arguments or fights among themselves. The crowd behavior at these events is exactly the opposite of behavior found at country club events such as golf or tennis. Unlike the passivity of spectators at those sports, the fans at wrestling matches and Roller Derbies are intensely involved. One observer characterized the typical crowd at a Roller Derby this way: "You can't call the crowd of 10,000 an audience. It is an organized mob—near hysterical men and women writhing in great paroxysms of emotion, by turns ecstatic, argumentative, despairing and vindictive. But never silent. If the action on the rink is sport, the behavior is spectacle. The two spheres are at times competitive, leaving the spectators to choose between Aristotelian catharsis and just plain raising hell."[14]

Symbolically, wrestling matches are morality plays. As sociologist Gregory Stone put it: "There is always the 'hero' who attempts to defeat the 'villain' within the moral framework of the rules of the game. It is a case of law versus outlaw, cops and robbers, the 'good guys' versus the 'bad guys.'"[15] Although not so pronounced, the Roller Derby scenario also has participants who abide by the rules and those who flaunt them. In both pseudosports, the fans tend to identify with the virtuous hero. When justice prevails and the hero triumphs, the fans' belief in law and order is reinforced. When the villain wins, the victory is attributed to foul play; when the rematch occurs, justice will finally reign. If it does not, then an alternate view of the world is reinforced. In this view, which Arthur Shostak posited as a major working-class belief, the world operates so that some persons take advantage of others and get away with it.[16]

In summary, the prole sports and pseudosports have several characteristics in common that make them especially attractive to the working classes:

1. The necessary equipment (such as automobiles or muscles) and skills (driving, mechanical aptitude, or self-defense) are part of working-class life.
2. The sports emphasize physical prowess and manhood (machismo).
3. They are exciting and therefore serve as an emotional outlet and an antidote to otherwise routine lives. Some focus on the danger of high speed and powerful machines. Others stress violence to machines or human beings. Still others contrive events to excite the crowds (e.g., wrestling events such as tag teams, Texas Death Matches, and the Battle Royales).
4. There is strong identification with heroes who are like the spectators in ethnicity, language, or behavior.
5. The sports are not school related.
6. With few exceptions, working-class spectator sports, as opposed to working-class participation sports, are individual rather than team-oriented.

Segregation in Sports by Social Class

We have noted that the different social strata have some unique preferences in sport. Although they enjoy some sports in common (especially the mass-media presentations of professional football, basketball, and baseball), the self-selection process in sports tends to segregate by social class. Let us look beyond this process to ascertain whether there are any other barriers that separate the social classes.

At the participatory level, some barriers serve to segregate the social classes. In sports such as swimming, golf, and tennis, the affluent compete in private clubs or at facilities limited to residents in an exclusive neighborhood or condominium complex (at some of these, access is controlled by fences, walls, and even armed guards). The middle classes and lower classes may participate in these sports only at public facilities. In a given city, then, a dual system of competition often exists—tournaments or competitions for the wealthy and a separate set of events for the general public. The quality of play at these two levels varies, with the wealthy usually rated better because of their access to better facilities, equipment, and private tutors. This difference in skill also serves to segregate affluent from less-affluent players.

Spectators, too, are often segregated by social class at general-interest sporting events. This is accomplished in several ways. First, ticket prices often exclude the poor, especially when season tickets are considered. The common practice of different prices according to seating location also tends to segregate persons by socioeconomic status (contrary to the image suggested by former President Reagan of the corporate executive sitting next to a janitor at a game). The affluent rarely sit in the relatively low-cost bleacher seats, and the poor rarely purchase reserved seats or box seats and do not have access to seats in the skyboxes.

The ultimate in differentially priced seating locations, and thus segregation by social class, is the purchase of exclusive skyboxes. These rooms are typically outfitted with expensive furniture, a bar, and other luxuries. They are purchased by individuals or corporations for very high prices, as noted in chapter 10.

This ostentatious display of wealth is an example of *conspicuous consumption,* the purchase and display of expensive items to flaunt one's high status. This phenomenon is found among the wealthy, the near-wealthy, and those who fake wealth. Although all sports offer this opportunity, conspicuous consumption is most commonly found at the premier events, for example, at the Super Bowl, the World Series, the Kentucky Derby, and especially heavyweight boxing championship matches. Many status-conscious persons use these highly visible events to impress others. They buy the expensive seats, wear costly jewelry and furs, and are driven in limousines to the arena.

At the other end of the stratification hierarchy, the poor and near poor cannot afford to attend sports. The high costs likely keep the poorest away from the sports arenas except as workers (vendors, janitors). Even if the poor could afford seats for regular events, they are priced out completely from premier events. Since these games are sold out (with corporate sponsors holding huge blocks of seats), scalpers sell the precious few remaining seats at premium prices (e.g., a 1994 Stanley Cup finals ticket with a face value of $125 brought as much as $5,000 at Madison Square Garden).[17] To repeat John Underwood's observation in chapter 10, the high cost of going to sports events has denied the poor and the working poor from attending them.[18]

Social Mobility and Sport

Typically, North Americans believe that the United States and Canada have "open" class systems, in other words, positions of high pay and prestige are open to those with the requisite talents and aptitudes, regardless of their social origin. The world of sport has done more than its share to give substance to this belief as poor boys (not girls) from rural and urban areas, whether white or black, have skyrocketed to fame and fortune through success in sports. Our task in this section is to investigate the extent to which social mobility actually operates in the sports world. Let us first examine the arguments and evidence supporting this belief.

Sport As a Mobility Escalator

The most obvious examples of sports participation facilitating upward social mobility are persons from low socioeconomic backgrounds who become wealthy and famous because of their athletic ability. This happens in almost all sports except those largely restricted to the upper class, such as polo, yachting, and, to a great extent, golf and tennis. Most typically, it occurs in boxing, in which the athletes are recruited almost exclusively from the lower socioeconomic levels and some will earn many millions of dollars during their careers.

Successful athletes in some sports (football and basketball in particular) must attend both high school and college. In this way, sports participation has the effect of encouraging or (in some cases) forcing persons to attain more education than they might otherwise achieve. This, in turn, increases their opportunities for success outside the sports world.

At the high school level, athletic participation requires only that athletes stay out of trouble and maintain some minimum grade-point average to remain eligible. Walter E. Schafer's research substantiated this but indicated that these requirements are most striking when athletic and nonathletic sons of blue-collar fathers are compared. He found that athletes from blue-collar families are more likely to be nondelinquent and to achieve higher grades than their nonathletic peers from blue-collar families. The athletes are more successful, therefore, they will likely have better self-concepts and higher aspirations than their nonathletic peers of the same social class. Thus, boys who would be less academically oriented than sons of white-collar fathers are encouraged to do well and even to aspire to attain a college education. This effect is heightened by their inclusion in the school's "inner circle" (because of their athletic achievements) and in subsequent associations and by their identification with white-collar and college-bound members of the school's leading crowd.[19] The best high school athletes will probably go to college on athletic scholarships, thereby increasing their likelihood of upward social mobility. The athletic experience, even for those not good enough to play in college, increases the probability that they, too, will attend college and have widened opportunities for attaining jobs of higher prestige than those of their parents. In concluding research on this subject, Richard A. Rehberg and Walter E. Schafer said:

> [Our] data have shown that a greater proportion of athletes than non-athletes expect to enroll in a four-year college, even when the potentially confounding variables of status, academic performance, and parental encouragement are controlled. This relationship is especially marked among boys not otherwise disposed toward college, that is, those from working-class homes, those in the lower half of their graduating class, and those with low parental encouragement to go to college.[20]

Research on the consequences of high school sports participation on socioeconomic attainment has found long-term positive effects on educational, occupational, and income achievements.[21] Picou, McCarter, and Howell, in their study of southerners eleven years after high school graduation, found some interesting subgroup differences in upward mobility.[22] They found that white males received substantial payoffs from their high school athletic participation. The success of black males, on the other hand, depended more on background and discrimination than on athletic participation. The adult career achievements and income of black females tended to be adversely affected by their participation in high school sports. Further research is needed to determine whether these findings are limited to the South or are common across regions.

Athletes at the college level, if from a family of low social status, will almost automatically surpass their parents because of their superior educational attainments. (This comparison of children's status with that of their parents measures *intergenerational mobility*.) This has been confirmed by John Loy's study of 1,020 athletes who had competed at UCLA for four years.[23] The data from this study suggest several interesting relationships. First, although the job prestige of former college athletes is fairly stable regardless of the sport played, the occupational prestige of fathers varies a good deal. Apparently, a college education (remember, these athletes had played at least four years) makes the attainment of upper-middle-class jobs possible, regardless of the student's social origin. Second, sons surpassed their fathers in occupational prestige regardless of the sport. Thus, these data indicate the increased social mobility achieved by college athletes when they are compared with their fathers.

This seemingly great mobility by college athletes compared to their fathers may be spurious, however. First, the comparison guarantees that the sons will have exceeded the fathers. Not all of the fathers have graduated from college, but the sample is composed of sons who have. Second, a gap between fathers and sons will always exist because of the general trend to upgrade educational levels. The best method to determine whether athletes have more potential for social mobility, therefore, is to compare them with nonathletes.

We have seen that success in sports enhances the possibility of attending college. This, in turn, increases the probability of attaining a high-status job, as the Loy study and several other studies have demonstrated. Let's examine two representative studies.

In an important study, Allen L. Sack and Robert Thiel compared football players with nonathletes who had graduated from Notre Dame between 1946 and 1965.[24] They found that (1) although the football players had come from poorer backgrounds, they had achieved equivalent incomes with the nonathletes; (2) nonathletes were more likely to have higher-status jobs and to have obtained advanced degrees; and (3) first-string players had much higher incomes than nonstarters and were overrepresented among top-ranking executives in their companies. This study provided strong evidence that athletic participation in college plus graduation does enhance upward social mobility.

Clifford Adelman compared the mobility of college athletes with nonathletes at a number of colleges and universities.[25] This research followed a group of 1972 high school seniors through 1986, looking at a subsample of those males who played football and basketball in college and those males who did not. He found that the athletes (1) were more likely to be home owners; (2) were less likely to be unemployed; and (3) had earnings 10 percent above the average for the nonfootball and nonbasketball group. We should be cautious in generalizing from these data, however, because the study did not differentiate athletes who participated in big-time football and basketball programs from those at smaller colleges.

These representative studies lead to the tentative conclusion that college athletes are upwardly mobile. There are at least three possible reasons for this. First, athletic participation may lead to various forms of "occupational sponsorship." The male college athlete is a popular hero, therefore, a greater likelihood exists that he will date and marry a woman who comes from a higher socioeconomic background than if he were a nonathlete. If this occurs, then the chances are that the college athlete's father-in-law will provide him with benefits in the business world much greater than those available to the average nonathlete. Another form of sponsorship may come from well-placed alumni who offer former athletes positions in their businesses after graduation. This may be done to help the firm's public relations, or it may be part of a payoff in the recruiting wars that some alumni are willing to underwrite.

A second reason why athletes may fare better is that the selection process for many jobs requires the applicant to be "well-rounded," that is, to have had a number of successful experiences outside the classroom. An extreme example of this is in the selection of Rhodes Scholars, which requires, in addition to superior grades, participation in extracurricular activities and demonstrated athletic ability.

Finally, there is the possibility that participation in highly competitive sports situations may lead to the development of attitudes and behavior patterns highly valued in the larger occupational world. If attributes such as leadership, human relations skills, teamwork, good work habits, and a well-developed competitive drive are acquired in sports, they may ensure that athletes will succeed in other endeavors. (See chapter 5.) Considerable debate surrounds the issue of whether sports builds character or whether only certain kinds of personalities survive the sport experience. There may be a self-fulfilling prophecy at work here, however: If employers assume that athletes possess these valued character traits, they will make their hiring and advancement decisions accordingly, giving athletes the advantage.

Demythologizing the Social Mobility Through Sport Hypothesis

The belief that sport is a mobility escalator is built on a succession of myths. These *myths* include: (1) sport provides a free college education; (2) sport leads to a college degree; (3) a professional sports career is possible; (4) sport is a way out of poverty especially for racial minorities; (5) because of Title IX women now have many opportunities for upward mobility through sport; and (6) a professional sports career provides security for life.

Myth: Sport Provides a Free Education

One assumption of the "social mobility through sports participation" position is that involvement in high school sport leads to college scholarships, which is especially helpful to poor youth who could not afford

college otherwise. The problem with this assumption is that so few high school athletes receive full ride scholarships. Consider the following facts:

- *Item:* Participation in football provides the easiest avenue toward a college scholarship. However, this avenue is exceedingly narrow. In Colorado there were 3,481 high school seniors who played football during the 1994–95 season. Of these young men, 31 received full ride scholarships at Division I-A schools (0.0089 percent).[26]
- *Item:* Of all the varsity athletes at all college levels in 1993 only about 15 percent to 20 percent had full scholarships. Another 15 percent to 25 percent have partial scholarships, which "means that 55 percent to 70 percent of all intercollegiate athletes participate in sports without any sport-related financial assistance."[27]
- *Item:* While women comprise about 52 percent of all college students, they make up only 35 percent of intercollegiate athletes and receive only about 31 percent of the athletic scholarship money.[28]
- *Item:* If you are a male athlete in a so-called minor sport (swimming, tennis, golf, gymnastics, cross-country, wrestling), the chances of a full-ride scholarship are virtually nil. The best hope is a partial scholarship, if that, since these sports are underfunded and in danger of being eliminated at many schools.

Myth: Participation in Sport Leads to a College Degree

A problem with the assumption that sports participation leads to a college degree is that relatively few athletes actually receive college degrees (see chapter 6). This is especially true for those athletes who believe that they will become professional athletes. Football, basketball, and increasingly, baseball players, play college ball for at least a while before turning to the professional level. This practice of using college sport as preparation for a professional career should have the benefit of encouraging athletes to graduate, which would help their careers after sports. Data show, however, that relatively few professional athletes do graduate from college (for example, only one-fifth of those in the NBA and one-third in the NFL have college degrees; the rate is even lower for professional baseball where 86 percent have not graduated and in hockey where 92 percent of NHL players have not graduated).

There are a number of barriers to graduation for athletes. One obvious problem is the inordinate demand on their time and energy for practice, meetings, travel, and other sport-related activities. Many athletes, because of these pressures, are counseled to take easy courses that maintain eligibility but that may not meet graduation requirements. The result is either to delay graduation or to make graduation an unrealistic goal.

Another barrier to graduation for many college athletes is that they are recruited for athletic prowess rather than for academic ability. About 12 percent of recruited athletes in Division I schools failed to meet the regular admission standards of their universities.[29] Athletes from the ghetto who have attended inferior high schools, for example, are generally not prepared for the intellectual demands of college. As noted in chapter 6, after six years, only 34 percent of black football players and 33 percent of black basketball players have graduated, compared to 58 percent of white football players and 62 percent of white basketball players. Put another way, *whereas a little less than one-half of white players do not graduate, two-thirds of black players do not graduate.*

A third barrier to graduation for college athletes is themselves as they do not take advantage of their scholarships to work toward graduation. This is the case for those who perceive their college experience only as preparation for their professional careers in sport. Study for them is necessary only to maintain their eligibility. Such a view is unrealistic for all but the superstars, as we will see shortly. It is also short-sighted because even a successful professional athletic career is limited to a few years, and not many professional athletes are able to translate their success in the pros to success in their postathletic careers. Such a problem is especially true for blacks, who often face employment discrimination in the wider society.

Myth: A Professional Sports Career Is Probable

Forbes magazine asked several years ago, "Where does a young man go to get rich today? Wall Street?

Law? Big Business?"[30] The answer was to enter professional sports, and the argument was buttressed by the examples of Arnold Palmer, Jack Nicklaus, and Joe Namath. This article, illustrative of a persistent media message, perpetuates the hope of upward mobility through sport for many youngsters and their parents. The youth of North America, especially black youth, believe this dream. A Louis Harris poll conducted in 1990 asked 1,865 high school students, 71 percent of them athletes, about their future plans. Fifty-five percent of black athletes expected to play in college, and 43 percent said they could make it in the pros. In contrast, but still unrealistic nonetheless, 39 percent of the white athletes thought they would play in college, and 16 percent said they would play as professionals.[31]

If athletes could play as professionals, the economic rewards are excellent. The average salaries per year for the four major North American team sports in 1994 were $1,870,000 in basketball, $737,000 in football, $1,186,000 in baseball, and $463,000 in hockey. Bonuses for signing, playoff checks, endorsements, and other benefits also accrue to the professional athlete.

However, this dream of financial success through a sports career is just that for all but an infinitesimal number. A career in professional sports is nearly impossible to attain because of the fierce competition. Consider the following evidence:

- *Item:* In 1992 there were approximately 1,900,000 American boys playing high school football, basketball, and baseball. That same year about 68,000 men were playing those sports in college, and 2,490 participated at the major professional level. In short, one in twenty-seven high school players in these three sports will play at the college level, and *only one in 736 high school players will play at the major professional level (0.14 percent).*
- *Item:* In baseball, for instance, the potential free-agent pool of players (high school seniors, college seniors, collegians over twenty-one, junior-college graduates, and foreign players) is 120,000 persons each year. Only about 1,200 (1 percent) are actually drafted, and most of those will never make it to the major leagues. Many will play in the minors for

small salaries and hope for the majors some day, but injuries and lack of talent will deny their chances for a major league career for all but a very few. In any one year, only about 100 new personnel are added to major league baseball rosters from newly drafted players and minor leaguers.

• *Item:* While signing a professional baseball contract would seem to be the culmination of the dream to be a major league player, only one in ten of these players will play in the major leagues for at least one day.[32]

• *Item:* The same rigorous condensation process occurs in football. About 15,000 players are eligible for the NFL draft each year. Three hundred thirty-six are drafted, and about 160 actually make the final roster. Each year only about forty new players are added to the rosters in the National Basketball Association. The total number of players in the National Hockey League is 504. About sixty rookies make the final rosters in a typical year. In tennis only about 100 males and 100 females make enough money as professionals to cover expenses.

Myth: Sport Is a Way out of Poverty Especially for Racial Minorities

We have shown that social mobility directly through sport is largely a myth, yet many North Americans accept it. One variant of the myth was stated by Frederick Rudolph: "Eventually football would enable a whole generation of young men in the coal fields of Pennsylvania to turn their backs on the mines that had employed their fathers."[33] To which Jack Scott replied:

> To put it politely, Rudolph is full of patriotic exaggeration. I make this statement as one who "escaped" an eastern Pennsylvania coal-mining town through the assistance of an athletic scholarship. My high school produced some of the finest athletic teams in the state, yet few of my teammates found athletics to be a means for social advancement. Yearly, close to two hundred athletes at my school would base their lives around varsity athletics, but at most only three or four individuals would be rewarded with athletic

scholarships. . . . School boys who spend four years of high school dreaming of collegiate gridiron glory are suddenly confronted by reality on graduation day. For every Broadway Joe Namath there are hundreds of sad, disillusioned men standing on the street corners and sitting in the beer halls of Pennsylvania towns such as Scranton, Beaver Falls, and Altoona.[34]

This quotation points to one negative consequence of believing that sport offers upward mobility. Many boys work very hard to become great in sport, but only a very few will be successful.[35]

Sport appears to be a major way for African Americans to escape the ghetto. The major professional sports are dominated numerically by blacks. While only 12 percent of the population, African Americans comprise around 80 percent of the players in professional basketball and about 60 percent of the players in professional football. Moreover, blacks lead the list of the highest moneymakers in sport (salaries, commercial sponsorships). These facts, while true, are illusory. Consider the following:

• *Item:* Blacks are rarely found in certain sports (automobile racing, tennis, golf, bowling, hockey).

• *Item:* Blacks are rarely found in positions of authority in sport (head coaches, athletic directors, general managers, owners).

• *Item:* Only a very small percentage of African Americans make it to the professional level as athletes. Of the 40,000 young blacks who play high school basketball, only thirty-five will make the NBA and seven will be starters. In sum, using the words of Harry Edwards, as he referred to the slim chances for young black athletes: "Statistically, you have a better chance of getting hit by a meteorite in the next 10 years than getting work as an athlete."[36]

The myth is so pervasive. That is why many boys spend many hours per day developing their speed, strength, or "moves" to the virtual exclusion of those abilities that have a greater likelihood of paying off in upward mobility—mathematical reasoning and communication skills. Although this is true for many lower-class boys, it is especially damaging for blacks whose heroes are almost exclusively in music or in sports. As Scott asked: "Gifted black athletes will usually make out all right, but what happens to the thousands of young unathletic black children whose only heroes are sports stars? How many brilliant doctors, lawyers, teachers, poets, and artists have been lost because intelligent but uncoordinated black youths had been led to believe by a racist society that their only chance for getting ahead was to develop a thirty foot jump shot or to run the hundred [yards] in 9.3?"[37]

This futile pursuit of sports stardom is of serious consequence to the black community, according to Harry Edwards. Blacks, spending their energies and talents on athletic skills, are not pursuing occupations that would help them meet their political and material needs. Thus, because of belief in the sports myth, they remain dependent on whites and white institutions.[38]

As Jay Coakley has said: "Young blacks seem to have accepted American achievement values, and as they perceive obstacles to conventional success, they simply try to avoid failure by focusing on other routes to achievement. What they don't realize and haven't been told is that there are nearly 22,000 black lawyers and over 15,000 black physicians in the United States. They need to know there are 12 times as many jobs for blacks in law and medicine as in professional sports as athletes."[39] Put another way, this time argued by the late African American tennis star Arthur Ashe:

Unfortunately, our most widely recognized role models are athletes and entertainers—"runnin' " and "jumpin' " and "singin' " and "dancin'." While we are 60 percent [now 80 percent] of the National Basketball Association, we are less than 4 percent of the doctors and lawyers. While we are about 35 percent [actually, about 22 percent] of major league baseball, we are less than 2 percent of the engineers. While we are about 40 percent [now 60 percent] of the National Football League, we are less than 11 percent of construction workers such as carpenters and bricklayers.

Our greatest heroes of the century have been athletes—Jack Johnson, Joe Louis and Muhammad Ali. Racial and economic discrimination forced us to channel our energies into athletics and entertainment. These were the ways out of the ghetto, the ways to get that Cadillac, those alligator shoes, that cashmere sport coat. Somehow, parents must instill a desire for learning alongside the desire to be a Walt Frazier. . . . We have been on the same roads—sports and entertainment—too long. We need to pull over, fill up at the library and speed away to Congress, and the Supreme Court, the unions and the business world.[40]

For a few poor whites and racial minorities sport has been a mechanism for upward mobility. This has been accomplished by achieving a college education, a goal unattainable without sport, or by becoming a professional athlete. As we have seen, though, only one-third of black college athletes graduate. The rest either did not take advantage of the situation or they were exploited by their institutions. Exploitation can occur in two major ways. First, by recruiting athletes who have no realistic way of achieving a college education, these athletes are used as long as they remain eligible and are then discarded, to return to the poor economic circumstances from which they came. A second form of exploitation is for the coaching staff to insist that their players are athletes first and students second. Thus, they demand too much of their athletes and channel their athletes' academic activities to keep them eligible but not necessarily moving them toward graduation.

We have focused on the limited possibilities in the major sports of football, baseball, and basketball. Many persons in these sports, however, have attained a formal education, and this in the long run is the greatest contributor to upward social mobility. When sports participation does not involve educational attainment, the already slim chances for mobility are reduced further.[41] Boxers, for example, are typically from a low socioeconomic background. Schools do not have interscholastic boxing so, often, young boxers drop out to devote their time to that sport. For the few who succeed, the rise in status is abrupt, with some fighters getting several million dollars for a single fight. That quick upward mobility, however, is usually followed by plummeting fortunes:

The successful boxers have a relatively quick economic ascent at a relatively young age in terms of earning power. But the punitive character of the sport, the boxers' dependence upon their managers, and their carefree spending during their boxing careers contribute to a quicker economic descent for many boxers. Their economic descent is accompanied by a drop in status and frequently by temporary or prolonged emotional difficulties in readjusting to their new roles.[42]

Most boxers do not achieve big-time status. Herbert Goldman, managing editor of *Ring,* the authoritative magazine on boxing, says that of the 18,000 boxers who fought in 1985, only a few made a living.

We rank the top 10 fighters in each of the weight classes, depending upon how you class them, that's about 150 fighters. You read a lot about multimillion-dollar winnings for a fight. No more than four or five fighters in a generation make that kind of money. I'd say that less than half of the ranked fighters even make a decent living. In the best year of his career, a good fighter is lucky to make $30,000. A 10-year career is several lifetimes for a professional boxer.[43]

Myth: Women Now Have Sport As a Vehicle for Upward Mobility Because of New Opportunities

Since the passage of Title IX in 1972 (see chapter 14), sports participation by women in high school and college has increased dramatically. In 1973, for example, while 50,000 men received some form of college scholarship for their athletic abilities, women received only fifty. By the mid-1990s women received about 35 percent of the money allotted to athletic scholarship (still less than half, but a considerable improvement). This has allowed many women to attend college who otherwise could not have afforded it. That is positive because of the indirect educational benefits accruing from athletic ability. The other plus is that professional golf, tennis, and bowling offer women an opportunity, albeit limited.

- *Item:* Aside from beach volleyball, women in team sports have no professional opportunities in the United States.
- *Item:* The proportion of women coaches of women's teams and women administrators of women's sports

programs in high schools and colleges is declining.[44] This trend is ironic given the increase in women's participation in sports. With success of women's programs, however, men have tended to take them over (see chapter 14).

- *Item:* Another irony is that the sports of the middle- and upper-classes (tennis and golf) offer women virtually the only chance for involvement and financial success in professional sport. In short, sport does not offer poor women, even in a very limited way, the potential for upward mobility. Speaking of African Americans in this regard, Harry Edwards has observed, "We must also consider that to the extent that sport provides an escape route from the ghetto at all, it does so only for black males . . . and the escape of a few black men does not mean that an equal number of black women will go with them as their wives or girlfriends; consequently there is no guarantee that even a few black women will benefit from the success achieved by black male professional athletes."[45]

Myth: A Professional Sports Career Provides Life–Long Security

Even when a professional sport career is attained, the probabilities of fame and fortune are limited. The average length of a career in professional sport is short, between three and five years. This leaves, on average, about forty additional years before retirement. The pay may be relatively high, but the employment does not last very long. Even those few athletes with careers exceeding ten years face the reality that by their middle thirties they are no longer employable as athletes.

Loss of status is another problem faced by the retiring athlete.

For most, the real world is a big step down. Big-time pro athletes are pampered like royalty. They fly first class while hired hands pay the bills and tote the luggage. High-powered executives and heads of state fawn over them. "You begin to feel like Louis XIV," says Wilbert McClure, a two-time Golden Gloves boxing champion who is now a psychologist and counselor to basketball players.

Step off the pedestal, and everything changes. McClure likens it to "being dipped into hell."[46]

The result is that many ex-athletes have problems adjusting. A survey of 645 former NFL players in 1988 found that 42 percent had made three or more career changes and that 62 percent had "some" emotional problems during the first six months. Moreover, 62 percent said they had "permanent injuries" from football.[47]

There is some potential for a sports-related career after one's playing days are over: coaching, managing, scouting, sportscasting, public relations, and administration are all possibilities for the former athlete, but the opportunities are severely limited, especially if the athlete is a minority group member (see chapter 13) or a woman.

Summary

Two themes dominate this chapter. The first theme is that sport, like the larger society, is stratified. Socioeconomic status is related to the types of sports one participates in and watches. The lower one's status, the more one is inclined toward contact sports and such pseudosports as professional wrestling and the Roller Derby. The socioeconomic strata are segregated in sport not only by preferences but also by such barriers as entrance requirements and prohibitive costs.

The second theme is that sports participation has limited potential as a social mobility escalator. There is evidence that being a successful athlete enhances self-confidence and the probability of attending college. Thus, social mobility is accomplished through sport indirectly because of the increased employment potential from educational attainment. Social mobility through sport is limited, however, if one is provided an inferior education, as is often the case. It is also limited by failure to graduate and the very low number of positions in professional sport. It is limited, even almost nonexistent for women. Even for those who attain major league status, the probabilities of fame and fortune are small because of the relatively short careers and injuries.

The myth that sport is a mobility escalator is especially dangerous for minority youth. Ghetto youngsters who devote their lives to the pursuit of athletic stardom are, except for the fortunate few, doomed to failure in sport and in the real world where sports skills are essentially irrelevant to occupational placement and advancement.

Notes

1. Ronald Reagan quoted in "Athletics a Great Equalizer, Reagan Tells NCAA," *NCAA News* (10 January 1990): 1.

2. Thorstein Veblen, *Theory of the Leisure Class* (New York: Macmillan, 1899).

3. Kerry Pechter, "Corporate Fitness and Blue-Collar Fears," *Across the Board* 23 (October 1986): 14–21.

4. Ibid., 17.

5. Michael A. Messner, *Power at Play* (Boston: Beacon Press, 1992).

6. Pete Axthelm, *The City Game: Basketball in New York* (New York: Harper and Row, 1970): ix–x.

7. T. Bell, "Chicago High School Have-Nots of Sports," *Chicago Sun-Times*, 11 October 1992, sec. A, pp. 42–43.

8. L. J. D. Wacquant, "The Social Logic of Boxing in Black Chicago: Toward a Sociology of Pugilism," *Sociology of Sport Journal* 9 (September 1992): 221–54.

9. For a scholarly historical analysis of sports spectators, see Allen Guttmann, *Sports Spectators* (New York: Columbia University Press, 1986). For a less scholarly, but nevertheless insightful analysis of sports fans, see Bill Stokes, "Take Me Out of the Crowd," in *Sport in Contemporary Society*, ed. D. Stanley Eitzen, 5th ed. (New York: St. Martin's Press, 1996), 5–18.

10. Findings here and following are from Marc L. Yergin, "Who Goes To The Game?" *American Demographics* 8 (July 1986): 42–43.

11. "NFL Fan Costs," *Greeley Tribune*, 11 September 1994, sec. B, p. 10.

12. Thomas W. Martin and Kenneth J. Berry, "Competitive Sport in Post-Industrial Society: The Case of the Motocross Racer," *Journal of Popular Culture* 8 (summer 1974): 107–20.

13. Tom Wolfe, "Clean Fun at Riverhead," in *Side-Saddle on the Golden Calf,* ed. George H. Lewis (Pacific Palisades, Calif.: Goodyear, 1972), 40.

14. Joan Grissim, "Nobody Loves Us but the Fans," *Rolling Stone,* 15 March 1969, 18.

15. Gregory P. Stone, "American Sports: Play and Display," in *Sport: Readings from a Sociological Perspective,* ed. Eric Dunning (Toronto: University of Toronto Press, 1972), 59.

16. Arthur B. Shostak, *Blue Collar Life,* (New York: Random House, 1969): 202.

17. D. Stanley Eitzen, "Classism in Sport: The Powerless Bear the Burden," *Journal of Sport and Social Issues* 20 (February 1996): 113–16.

18. John Underwood, "From Baseball and Apple Pie, to Greed and Sky Boxes," *New York Times,* 31 October 1993, sec. A, p. 22.

19. Walter E. Schafer, "Some Social Sources and Consequences of Interscholastic Athletics: The Case of Participation and Delinquency," in *Aspects of Contemporary Sport Sociology,* ed. Gerald S. Kenyon (Chicago: Athletic Institute, 1969), 41–42; Walter E. Schafer and J. Michael Armer, "Athletes Are Not Inferior Students," in *Games, Sport and Power,* ed. Gregory P. Stone (New Brunswick, N.J.: Transaction Books, 1972), 106–109.

20. Richard A. Rehberg and Walter E. Schafer, "Participation in Interscholastic Athletics and College Expectation," *American Journal of Sociology* 73 (May 1968): 739.

21. Luther B. Otto and Duane F. Alwin, "Athletics, Aspirations, and Attainments," *Sociology of Education* 50 (October 1977): 102–33; Michael Hanks, "Race, Sexual Status, and Athletics in the Process of Educational Achievement," *Social Science Quarterly* 60 (December 1979): 482–96; Jomills Henry Braddock, "Race, Athletics, and Educational Attainment: Dispelling the Myths," *Youth and Society* 12 (March 1981): 335–50.

22. Steven Picou, Virginia McCarter, and Frank M. Howell, "Do High School Athletics Pay? Some Further Evidence," *Sociology of Sport Journal* 2 (April 1985): 72–76.

23. John W. Loy, Jr., "The Study of Sport and Social Mobility," *International Review of Sport Sociology* 7 (1972): 5–23.

24. Allen L. Sack and Robert Thiel, "College Football and Social Mobility: A Case Study of Notre Dame Football Players," *Sociology of Education* 52 (January 1979): 60–66.

25. Douglas Lederman, "Students Who Competed in College Sports Fare Better in Job Market Than Those Who Didn't, Report Says," *Chronicle of Higher Education,* 26 September 1990: sec. A, pp. 47–48.

26. Scott Stocker, "Don't Bank on Earning a Division I-A Football Scholarship," *Rocky Mountain News,* 7 February 1995, sec. B, p. 16.

27. Jay J. Coakley, *Sport in Society,* 5th ed. (St. Louis: Mosby, 1994), 296.

28. Ibid., 297.

29. "Recruited Athletes Found Much More Likely than Others to be Admitted as 'Exceptions,' " *Chronicle of Higher Education,* 26 September 1990, sec. A, pp. 47–48.

30. "Superstars! Supermoney!" *Forbes,* 15 September 1972.

31. "Young Black Athletes Rely on Sports for Careers," *NCAA News* (19 November 1990): 16.

32. *NCAA News* (21 October 1991): 16.

33. Frederick Rudolph, *The American College And University* (New York: Random House Vintage Books, 1962), 378.

34. Jack Scott, *The Athletic Revolution* (New York: Free Press, 1971), 178–79.

35. See Darcy Frey, *The Last Shot, City Streets, Basketball Dreams* (Boston: Houghton Mifflin, 1994).

36. Harry Edwards quoted in Bob Oates, "The Great American Tease: Sport as a Way Out of the Ghetto," *New York Times,* 8 June 1979, sec. A, p. 32.

37. Scott, *The Athletic Revolution,* 178–79.

38. Harry Edwards, "The Black Athletes: 20th Century Gladiators for White Americans," *Psychology Today,* 7, November 1973, 43–52.

39. Coakley, *Sport in Society,* 290–91.

40. Arthur Ashe, "Send Your Children to the Libraries," *New York Times,* 6 February 1977, sec. S, p. 2.

41. Rudolf K. Haerle, "Education, Athletic Scholarships and the Occupational Career of the Professional Athlete," *Sociology of Work and Occupations* 2 (November 1975): 373–403.

42. S. Kirson Weinberg and Henry Arond, "The Occupational Culture of the Boxer," in *Sport, Culture and Society,* ed. John W. Loy, Jr. and Gerald S. Kenyon (Toronto, Ont.: The Macmillan Company, 1969), 452.

43. Herbert Goldman quoted in Michael Stanton, "Playing for a Living: The Dream Comes True for Very Few," *Occupational Outlook Quarterly* 31 (spring 1987): 7.

44. R. V. Acosta and L. J. Carpenter, "Women in Intercollegiate Sport: A Longitudinal-Fifteen Year Update" (New York: Brooklyn College, 1992).

45. Edwards, "The Black Athletes," 47.

46. Andrea Rothman and Stephanie Anderson Forest, "The Thrill of Victory, the Agony of Retirement," *Business Week,* 3 June 1991, 54–55.

47. Gary Mihoces, "Less-Visible Players Find Little Glory After Football," *USA Today,* 10 May 1988, sec. C, p. 12.

Chapter 13

Race and Sport

Racial minorities in the United States continue to face systematic and pervasive discrimination against them. While most Americans agree with this sociological fact, they also tend to believe that sport is an oasis free of racial problems and tensions. After all, the argument goes, sports are competitive; fans, coaches, and players want to win; clearly, the color of the players involved is not a factor, only their performance. A further argument is that the proportion of African Americans in the major team sports, which far exceeds their proportion in the U.S. population, indicates an absence of racism (*racism* is defined as discriminatory and demeaning acts by one racial group against another racial group). The facts, however, lead to a very different conclusion. Rather than being free from racism, sport as a microcosm of the larger society reflects the same racial problems as society.

The objective of this chapter is to document the facts showing that racism is prevalent in sport. We hope to alert the reader to this continuing societal problem and to bury the belief that sport is a meritocracy in which skin color is disregarded.

This chapter describes and explains the situation of African Americans in sport in the United States. A *minority group* is a socially identified group that differs from the *majority group,* has much less power, and is discriminated against by them. African Americans were selected because blacks are by far the most prominent racial minority in American sport. For example, in 1990, while blacks were 47 percent of men's college basketball teams, less than 1 percent of the male players were minorities other than black.[1] The modes of discrimination against blacks are not exclusive to them, however. Various racial and ethnic minorities such as Native Americans, Chicanos, Puerto Ricans, Jews, Irish Americans, and Polish Americans have also experienced discrimination in sport (exclusion, blocked opportunities, derisive action, and other forms of abuse).

The History of African American Involvement in Sport

Despite systematic and pervasive discrimination against African Americans throughout their history in North America, they have played a continuing and significant role in the rise and development of modern sport. The history of black involvement in sport can be divided roughly into four stages: (1) exclusion before the Civil War; (2) breakthroughs following the Emancipation Proclamation; (3) racial segregation between the two World Wars; and (4) racial integration after World War II. This last period is especially interesting and significant from a sociological standpoint, and we will focus on it during this chapter.

Africans were brought to North America as slaves throughout the colonial period and into the first half of the nineteenth century. They were concentrated in the southern states because of the plantation system. Plantation owners often used black slaves to stage boxing matches, and they used them as jockeys in horse races. Occasionally in boxing, when a slave boxer won an important bout and won his owner a lot of money, he might be set free. Tom Molineaux, a black slave, was a beneficiary of such an arrangement. In the early nineteenth century, after gaining his freedom, he made quite a name for himself in boxing circles in the northern states and in England.

After the Civil War African Americans made contributions to the rise of spectator sport as boxers, jockeys, and team players, but they were clearly exceptions. Society and sport remained racially segregated by custom and in some places by law (e.g., Jim Crow laws in the South). Between the first Kentucky Derby in 1875 and about 1910, black jockeys dominated the sport of horse racing. Of the fifteen jockeys in the first Kentucky Derby, fourteen were African Americans, including the winner. By the first decade of the twentieth century, however, horse owners and trainers had succumbed to the segregationist doctrine and no longer employed black jockeys. Blacks did remain in much lower status positions around racing, exercising the horses, grooming the horses, and cleaning out their stalls.

When blacks were barred from professional baseball, football, and basketball in the late nineteenth and early twentieth centuries, they formed all-black teams and leagues.[2] The Harlem Globetrotters and the famous players of the black baseball leagues such as Satchel Paige and Josh Gibson emerged from this segregated situation. When Jackie Robinson broke the color barrier, first in 1946 in the minor leagues (the first black in the International League in fifty-seven years) and then in 1947 in the majors, he received much verbal and physical abuse from players and fans who resented a black playing on an equal level with whites. The great major league player Rogers Hornsby uttered the common attitude of the time: "They've been getting along all right playing together and they should stay where they belong in their league."[3]

Although some champions would not fight them, African Americans made early gains in boxing and increased their numbers over the years, even when they were excluded from other professional sports. Perhaps boxing was the exception because it has typically recruited from the most oppressed urban groups. In 1908 Jack Johnson became the world heavyweight champion, the first African American to win this title. Throughout the twentieth century blacks have steadily increased their numbers in boxing. Though blacks were allowed by the boxing establishment to participate continuously during the early 1900s, they were still the objects of discrimination. White boxers tended to receive more money than blacks. The white promoters, because of the great-white-hope myth, liked to match whites against blacks in the ring, and blacks often consented to lose just to obtain a match.[4] The observers of black boxers often referred to them in racist terms. Consider, for example, the following from Paul Gallico, a noted sportswriter, writing of the great black boxer Joe Louis:

> Louis, the magnificent animal. . . . He eats. He sleeps. He fights. . . . Is he all instinct, all animal? Or have a hundred million years left a fold upon his brain? I see in this colored man something so cold, so hard, so cruel that I wonder as to his bravery. Courage in the animal is desperation. Courage in the human is something incalculable and divine.[5]

Sportswriters referred to blacks in other sports in racist terms as well. Consider, for example, the prediction of Jimmy Powers, sports editor of the *New York Daily News:* "[Jackie] Robinson will not make the grade in major league baseball. He is a thousand-to-one shot at best. The Negro players simply don't have the brains or skills."[6]

African Americans were absent, with a few exceptions, from intercollegiate sports for the first half of this century. A few Ivy League and other eastern schools had black athletes at an early time, but they were exceptions. For the most part, though, prior to World War II African Americans played at all-black colleges in black leagues. Although the system was segregated, it did provide many blacks with the opportunity to engage in organized sport.

Paralleling the situation in professional sports, college sports remained segregated, except for isolated instances, until after World War II. In 1948, for example, only 10 percent of college basketball teams had one or more blacks on their rosters. This proportion increased to 45 percent of the teams in 1962 and 91 percent by 1990.[7] The last major conference to integrate was the Southeastern Conference (SEC). The University of Tennessee broke the barrier by signing a defensive back in 1966, and Vanderbilt signed a black basketball player in that same year. By 1975, black athletes were common in the SEC and in all the other conferences. The transition from a segregated program to an integrated one is perhaps best illustrated by the University of Alabama: In 1968 there were no blacks on any of its teams, but its 1975 basketball team had an all-black starting lineup.

As more and more schools searched for talented blacks to bolster their athletic programs, black schools lost their monopoly on black athletic talent. The best black athletes found it advantageous to play at predominantly white schools because of greater visibility, especially on television. This visibility meant, for the best athletes, a better chance to become a professional athlete. The result of this trend was a depleted athletic program at black schools, forcing some to drop their athletic programs and some previously black leagues to disband.

Another consequence of black athletes attending white schools has been their increased exploitation by their schools. Many of them have been kept eligible, as shown in chapter 6, without moving them toward graduation. In the decade of the 1970s, for example, no black basketball player graduated from Memphis State or the University of Houston. At Georgia the graduation rate for black athletes during that decade was only 4 percent. Harry Edwards has called this "a case of the farmer caring for his turkeys—right up until Thanksgiving Day. Then it's back to the ghetto, without an education, without a prayer."[8]

Since World War II, blacks have made tremendous strides in professional team sports (except for hockey). From 1940 to 1994 the percentages of blacks in professional football went from zero to 65 percent; professional basketball from zero to 77 percent; and from zero to 18 percent in baseball (with another 18 percent Latino in baseball).[9] There are now black head coaches in professional football, basketball, and baseball. Blacks now officiate games; they are now part of the media reporting the games in newspapers, magazines, and television (see table 13.1 for a partial list of breakthroughs). Discrimination remains, however, as we will document in the final part of the chapter.

Black Dominance in Sport

We have seen that since World War II African Americans have dramatically increased their numbers in major team sports. The increase during the first fifteen years or so, however, was relatively slow. The watershed year in professional sports (when the proportion of blacks approximated their proportion in the national population) was, for baseball, 1957; for basketball, 1958; and for football, 1960. Since then, however, the rate has virtually exploded. By 1994, as already noted, although African Americans only constituted 12 percent of the general population, they were 77 percent of all professional basketball players, 65 percent of all professional football players, and 18 percent of major league baseball players.

There are three possible explanations (genetic, cultural, and social) for this disproportionate presence of blacks in American team sports. We examine the genetic hypothesis first.

Race–Linked Physical Differences

A common explanation for the overrepresentation of African Americans in certain sports is that they are naturally better athletes than whites and that their predominance in sports is therefore attributable to innate physical supremacy. There are some problems with this biological determinism argument. First, there is the issue of who is black. Racial categories in any society, but particularly in the United States, where amalgamation of Africans, Caucasians, and Native Americans continues, are ill-defined and even socially defined. The point is that racial categories are not fixed, unambiguous, and dichotomous. Second, the studies that have found physical differences between the races have often used faulty methodology.[10] Because blacks, like whites, exhibit a wide range of physical builds and other physiological features, sampling becomes a problem. Does the scientist compare randomly selected whites with randomly selected blacks? More logically, to answer the question of athletic superiority, does the researcher compare a random selection of superior white athletes with superior black athletes? Unfortunately, the latter has not been the case. The key is that blacks are not a homogeneous physical category.

> The word "black" provides little information about anyone or any group. Of the 100,000 genes that determine human makeup, only one to six regulate skin color, so we should assume almost nothing about anyone based on skin color alone. West Africans and East Africans are both black, but in many physical ways they are *more unlike each other* than they are *different from most whites.*
>
> When it comes to assumptions about Africans, we should make just one: That the peoples of Africa, short and tall, thick and thin, fast and slow, white and black, represent the fullest and most spectacular variations of humankind to be found anywhere.[11]

Another problem in comparing races on some behavioral pattern is the impossibility of eliminating social variables (social, cultural, and political factors) from consideration. Why, for example, do blacks from Kenya tend to excel in distance running while blacks from Nigeria do not? Is this major difference explained by differences in diet, cultural emphasis, geography, or what? Whatever the explanation, it is not racial difference. Also, as Laurel Davis has pointed out, the emphasis on biological differences ignores the differences in performance that occur because of differences in effort: "Biological determinist explanations for complex human behavior obscure both human agency and the sociocultural context of behavior. Human agency is obscured when racially linked genetic traits are used to explain black success in sport. Black athletic success is explained as natural, ignoring the black athletes as active agents who work to shape their own performances."[12]

The biological determinist explanation for black athletic superiority also has racist implications.[13] First, the assumption that biological differences exist by race (i.e., blacks are "physically superior" and whites are "mentally superior") reinforces stereotypes of blacks as "naturally" suited for physical activities and, by implication, not suited for activities requiring discipline, intelligence, and judgment. Second, such beliefs reinforce an ideology that seeks to explain and justify the political status quo where blacks are second to whites in power, authority, and resources. Third, this explanation implies that black athletes do not have to work hard to be successful in sport and that white athletes achieve success due to hard work and intelligence.

The problems with existing empirical studies on racial differences lead us to conclude that they are meaningless on the one hand, that is, they make assumptions that obscure the realities of race as a social rather than biological category, and dangerous, that is, racist, on the other. Moreover, whatever differences found to exist among the races are explained not by genetic advantages of one social category over another but because of cultural and social reasons.

Race-Linked Cultural Differences

African Americans may be overrepresented in sport because of the uniqueness of the black subculture in the United States. James Green argued that black subculture places a positive emphasis on the importance of physical (and verbal) skill and dexterity. Athletic prowess in men is highly valued by both black women and black men. The athletically superior male is comparable to the successful hustler or blues singer; he is something of a folk hero. He achieves a level of status and recognition among his peers, whether he is a publicly applauded sports hero or not.[14] There is ample evidence of just such adulation accorded black basketball players, regardless of age, in the urban playgrounds of the United States.[15]

Cultural differences probably do account for the differences in sport performance between black Africans and black Americans. Here, where physical differences are more or less controlled (although black Americans are more racially mixed), we find great variances. At elite level track events, for instance, black Africans excel in distance running but not in the sprints and jumping events. Black Americans, on the other hand, have dominated the sprints, hurdles, and the long jump but have had negligible success in the distance events. Clearly, something other than the physiology of race must explain this variance. Cultural differences, along with differences in history and geography, account for much of the sharp contrast.

Unique forms of dance, music, art, and humor have emerged from the black subculture. Perhaps that subculture also accounts for the interest and ability of black Americans in basketball where moves, speed, and aggression predominate. The interest of other groups in particular sports is easily explained that way. For example, Japanese Americans, who constitute less than 0.3 percent of the total population, make up over 20 percent of the top Amateur Athletic Union (AAU) judo competitors.[16] Although black culture might similarly contribute to black excellence in athletics, especially in certain sports, there is little systematic empirical evidence at present to substantiate the claim.

Social Structure Constraints

The most plausible reasons for black dominance in some sports are found in the structural constraints on blacks in American society. These constraints can be divided into two types: (1) occupational structure and (2) sports opportunity structure.

African Americans may perceive sport to be one of the few means by which they can succeed in the highly competitive American society because their opportunities for vertical mobility in American society are limited. A young black male's primary role models are much more likely to be athletic heroes than are a young white male's models. The determination and motivation devoted by the black adolescent to the pursuit of an

table 13.1 *Black Breakthroughs in U.S. Sport*

Year	Breakthrough
1800	Tom Molineaux, a slave, was the first recognized heavyweight boxing champion.
1875	Oliver Lewis, a black jockey, rode in the Kentucky Derby.
1884	Moses and Weldy Walker (brothers) were the first blacks to play major league baseball.
1904	George Poage became the first black to compete in the modern Olympic Games.
1908	Jack Johnson won the heavyweight boxing championship.
1911	Henry McDonald was the first black professional football player.
1916	Fritz Pollard of Brown became the first black to play in the Rose Bowl.
1945	Kenny Washington and Woody Strode of the Los Angeles Rams became the first blacks to play in the National Football League (NFL).
1947	Jackie Robinson broke the racial barrier in modern major league baseball when he played for the Brooklyn Dodgers.
1947	Harvard University and the University of Virginia played in a precedent-setting football game as Chet Pierce of Harvard became the first black to participate in an integrated game involving a white southern university.
1948	Three black golfers—Bill Spiller, Ted Rhodes, and Madison Gunter—challenged the "Caucasians only" clause in the Professional Golf Association (PGA) constitution. The PGA agreed to rescind the policy in return for the suit being dropped.
1950	The rule limiting the American Bowling Congress membership to white males was abolished. Similarly, the Women's International Bowling Congress ended its membership restrictions against nonwhites.
1950	Althea Gibson became the first black to be accepted to play for the national championship of tennis.
1950	The first case before the Supreme Court involving blacks in sport occurred when the court ruled that a public golf course in Florida could not limit black players to one day of golf per week.
1950	Chuck Cooper became the first black drafted and signed to play in the National Basketball Association (NBA). Earl Lloyd, however, because of a quirk in the schedule became the first black to play in the NBA (by one day).
1952	Emmett Ashford became the first black umpire in organized baseball when he was authorized as a substitute in the Class C Southwest League.
1953	Willie Thrower of the Chicago Bears became the first black to play quarterback in the NFL. However, he was never a starter.
1956	Nell Johnson became the first black head coach of a U.S. Olympic team (women's track and field).
1956	Lowell Perry became the first black assistant coach for an NFL team (Pittsburgh Steelers).
1957	Willie O'Ree of the Boston Bruins became the first black to play in the National Hockey League.
1958	Prentiss Gault became the first black football player signed at a major southern white school (University of Oklahoma).
1959	A Louisiana ban on boxing matches between blacks and whites was declared unconstitutional by the U.S. Supreme Court.
1961	Charlie Sifford became the first black golfer to play on the PGA tour.
1961	John McLendon became the first black head coach of a professional basketball team (Cleveland Pipers of the American Basketball Association).
1963	Buck Buchanan became the first player from an historically black college to be a number one NFL selection.
1964	Arthur Ashe became the first black to play on the American Davis Cup team.
1965	Emmett Ashford became the first black umpire in major league baseball.
1965	Burl Tolar became the first black to officiate in the NFL.
1965	The Sugar Bowl and the Blue-Gray games, both located in the South, allowed blacks to play for the first time.
1966	Bill Russell became the first black head coach in the NBA (Boston Celtics).
1966	Oscar Robertson became the first black elected president of the NBA Players Association.
1966	The last major college conference, the Southeastern Conference (SEC), integrated.

table 13.1 Continued

Year	Breakthrough
1967	Renee Powell became the first black woman on the Ladies Professional Golf Association tour.
1971	Wayne Embry became the first black general manager of a professional team (Milwaukee Bucks of the NBA).
1971	Bill White became the first full-time black radio announcer doing play-by-play in professional sports (New York Yankees).
1971	Ronnie Loudd became the first black director of player personnel for an NFL team (New England Patriots).
1972	Will Robinson became the first black head basketball coach at a predominantly white Division I school (Illinois State University).
1974	Billy Hill became the first head trainer at a major school when hired by Ohio State University.
1974	Frank Robinson became the first black field manager in baseball (Cleveland Indians).
1975	James Harris of the Los Angeles Rams became the first black starting quarterback for a season in the NFL.
1975	Lee Elder became the first black to play in the Master's Golf Tournament in Augusta, Georgia.
1976	Willie Wood became the first black head coach in modern professional football (Philadelphia Bells of the World Football League).
1977	Milt Davis became the first black scout for an NFL team (Miami Dolphins).
1979	Willie Jeffries became the first black football coach in Division I-A (Wichita State).
1981	Dennis Green became the first black head football coach at a college in a major conference (Northwestern University).
1985	Jim Allen became the first black to do the play-by-play of a regionally televised NFL football game (CBS).
1986	Anita De Frantz became the first black from a non-black nation appointed to the International Olympic Committee.
1986	Walter Payton, the NFL's all-time rushing leader, became the first black signed by General Mills, Inc., to appear on Wheaties cereal boxes to sell "The Breakfast of Champions."
1988	John Thompson became the first black head coach of the U.S. Olympic basketball team.
1988	Gil Marchman became the first black referee and crew chief of a major bowl game (Rose Bowl).
1988	Johnny Grier became the first black referee and crew chief in the NFL.
1989	Bill White became the first black to head a major sports league when he was elected by the owners as president of the National League.
1989	Wade Houston became the first black head coach in either basketball or football in the fifty-eight year history of the Southeastern Conference (basketball at the University of Tennessee).
1989	Art Shell became the first black head coach in modern NFL history (Los Angeles Raiders).
1989	Bertram Lee and Peter Bynoe became the first black owners of a major professional franchise (the Denver Nuggets). Although they owned 37.5 percent of the franchise (Comsat Video Enterprises owned 62.5 percent), they managed the franchise on a day-to-day basis.
1989	Andre Ware (University of Houston) became the first black quarterback to win the Heisman.
1990	The Professional Golf Association (PGA) required that all tournaments be played only at clubs that do not discriminate (at that time seventeen of its thirty-nine tour courses were private clubs with no black members).
1991	Willy T. Ribbs became the first black to drive in the Indianapolis 500.
1992	For the first time in history one NFL team, the Green Bay Packers, had a black offensive coordinator (Sherman Lewis) and a black defensive coordinator (Ray Rhodes).
1992	Leroy Walker became the first black president of the U.S. Olympic Committee.
1992	Rob Evans became the first black head basketball coach at the University of Mississippi.
1992	Jim Caldwell became the first black head football coach in the history of the Atlantic Coast Conference (at Wake Forest).
1994	John Merchant became the first black member of the U.S. Golf Association's executive committee. Another black, Leroy C. Richie, became general counsel (lead lawyer) to the USGA.

athletic career may, therefore, be more intense than those of the white adolescent, whose career options are greater. As Harry Edwards argued:

> Black society, as does the dominant white society, teaches its members to strive for that which is defined as the most desirable among potentially achievable goals—*among potentially achievable goals*. Since the onset of integrated, highly rewarding sports opportunities and the impact of television in communicating to all the ostensible influence . . . glamour, affluence, and so forth, of the successful black athlete, the talents of Afro-American males (and females, again, to a lesser extent) are disproportionately concentrated toward achievement in this one area. In high-prestige occupational positions outside of the sports realm, black role models are an all but insignificant few. These are not readily visible, and they seldom have contact or communications with the masses of blacks. . . . Thus, given the competition among athletic organizations for top-flight athletes, it is to be expected that a high proportion of the extremely gifted black individuals would be in sports. Whites, on the other hand, because they have visible alternative role models and greater potential access to alternative high-prestige positions, distribute their talents over a broader range of endeavors. Thus, the concentration of highly gifted whites in sports is proportionately less than the number of blacks. Under such circumstances, black athletes dominate sports in terms of excellence of performance, where both groups participate in numbers.[17]

Occupational limitations for African Americans do not explain why they tend to gravitate toward some sports, such as boxing, basketball, football, track, and baseball, and why they are underrepresented in others, such as swimming, golf, skiing, tennis, and polo. John C. Phillips argued that the reason blacks tend to participate in certain sports lies in what he called the "sports opportunity structure."[18] Blacks tend to excel in those sports in which facilities, coaching, and competition are available to them: in the schools and community recreation programs. Blacks are rarely found in those sports that require the facilities, coaching, and competition usually provided only in private clubs. There are few excellent black golfers, for example, and they had to overcome the disadvantages of being self-taught and limited to playing at municipal courses. Few blacks are competitive skiers for the obvious reasons that most blacks live far from snow and mountains and that skiing is very expensive.

Structural reasons clarify why blacks outperform whites in certain sports. Basketball provides an excellent example because the style of black basketball players differs so significantly from that of white players. The former tend to be more aggressive, better jumpers and rebounders, better at playing close to the basket, better at performing individual moves, and more flamboyant. Whites, on the other hand, tend to be better outside shooters and free throwers, more disciplined, and better grounded in the fundamentals. Donal Carlston has provided a plausible structural explanation for these differences.[19] Most black college and professional players learned the game under substantially different conditions than white players. The inner-city basketball courts frequented by blacks are generally crowded with large numbers competing for valuable playing time on the limited facilities. The norms that prevail under these conditions shape the skills and behaviors of the inner-city players in predictable ways. The games are intensely competitive with winning teams staying on the court to meet the next challengers. Players must learn to dribble, pass, and shoot in close quarters against a tight person-to-person defense. Players in these circumstances learn to fake and to alter shots in midair. Players are expected to score without much help from teammates. They accept contact as routine. The spectators often present at inner-city games encourage flair and flamboyance.

Most white college and professional players developed their basketball talents in rural, small-town, and suburban communities. Basketball in these settings is characterized by player scarcity rather than a crowding of teams and players on the courts. For those who maintain a year-round interest in basketball, play is limited to many hours of solitary practice in one's own driveway and to occasional pick-up games. The noncity player develops playing skills largely free from intense competition, honing excellent shooting skills but not the moves necessary to defeat an aggressive defender one-on-one. The paucity of players leads to rules that encourage the participation of marginal players, make use of skills developed in solo practice, and keep the pace relatively slow. Thus, whites develop pure shooting skills and the ability to score when wide open. In sum, Carlston's analysis suggests that the differences in play between whites and blacks are not found in racial differences but in the structural conditions under which they develop their basketball skills.

Another structural basis for racial differences in participation is that African Americans have been denied membership in private clubs (thus, they are denied access to the best facilities and coaching in sports such as swimming, golf, and tennis) for economic and social reasons. The economic barrier to membership is the result of the discriminatory practices (in types of jobs, salaries, and chances for promotion) that deny most blacks affluence. The social barriers have occurred because of the discriminatory practices of many private clubs that exclude various racial and ethnic groups. Sports in private organizations have been particularly resistant to racial integration. As Jay J. Coakley has noted:

Exclusionary policies are least likely to be maintained in sports in which there is little off-the-field social interaction, especially interaction between men and women. However, when sports directly involve informal, personal, and sexually mixed social contact either on the field or off, desegregation has been very slow. This is one of the reasons why golf, tennis, swimming, bowling, and other sports learned and played in social clubs have been slow to open doors for blacks or other minorities. When sport participation is accompanied by informal social contact between family and friends and by intimate and personal interaction, dominant racial ideology among whites is likely to keep doors closed—or only partially open.[20]

There is, however, another type of discrimination implied in the sports opportunity structure: The powerful in some sports have denied access to blacks, even to blacks with the requisite skills and financial support.

Certain golf tournaments (the Masters, for instance) have been reluctant to admit blacks. Lee Elder became the first black to play the Masters in 1975. Just as golf has allowed black caddies but not golfers, horse racing has allowed blacks as exercise boys but not as jockeys (in this century). Automobile racing is another sport in which blacks have had great difficulty in participating. The Indianapolis 500 waited until 1991 for its first black driver. The explanation for this delay in having a black driver surely lies not in the limitations of blacks in driving fast and with inferior skills but in the reluctance of corporate sponsors to give financial support to black drivers.

Racial Discrimination in Sport

Sport is not free of racial discrimination. However, the dominant presence of African Americans in the three major team sports appears to belie the existence of racism in sport. Moreover, the prominence and huge salaries of black superstars such as Deion Sanders and Michael Jordan have led many Americans, black and white, to infer that collegiate and professional athletics have provided an avenue of upward mobility for blacks unavailable elsewhere.

Many commentators—social scientists, journalists, and black athletes themselves—have argued, however, that black visibility in collegiate and professional sports has merely served to mask the racism that pervades the entire sport establishment. According to these critics, the existence of racism in collegiate and professional sports is especially insidious because the promoters of and commentators on athletics have made sport sacred by projecting its image as the single institution that is relatively immune from racism.

This section focuses on three aspects of the athletic world that have been alleged to be racially biased, the assignment of playing positions, rewards and authority structures, and performance differentials. The analysis is limited to the three major professional team sports (baseball, basketball, and football) in which blacks are found most prominently. In addition to describing and explaining the current situations, we assess whether any substantial changes have occurred or can be anticipated in the future.

Stacking

One of the best-documented forms of discrimination in both college and professional ranks is popularly known as "*stacking*." The term refers to situations in which minority group members are disproportionately found in specific team positions and underrepresented in others. Typically, for example, there are twice as many pitchers on a baseball team as there are outfielders, yet there are about three times as many black outfielders as black pitchers.

Examination of the stacking phenomenon was first undertaken by John W. Loy, Jr., and Joseph F. McElvogue, who argued that racial segregation in sports is a function of centrality, that is, spatial location in a team sports unit.[21] To explain positional racial segregation in sport, they combined organizational principles advanced by Hubert M. Blalock and Oscar Grusky. Blalock argued that (1) the lower the degree of purely social interaction on the job, the lower will be the degree of (racial) discrimination and (2) to the extent that performance level is relatively independent of skill in interpersonal relations, the degree of (racial) discrimination is lower.[22] Grusky's notions about the formal structure of organizations are similar: "All else being equal, the more central one's spatial location: (1) the greater the likelihood dependent or coordinative tasks will be performed and (2) the greater the rate of interaction with the occupants of other positions. Also, the performance of dependent tasks is positively related to frequency of interactions."[23]

Combining these propositions, Loy and McElvogue hypothesized that "racial segregation in professional team sports is positively related to centrality."[24] Their analysis of football (in which the central positions are quarterback, center, offensive guard, and linebacker) and baseball (in which the central positions are catcher, pitcher, shortstop, second base, and third base) demonstrated that the central positions were indeed overwhelmingly held by whites and that blacks were overrepresented in the peripheral (noncentral) positions. Empirical research has found this relationship consistently (the one exception is basketball where stacking has broken down with the increased proportion of blacks) in racially mixed team sports. For example:

- In women's intercollegiate volleyball, blacks are overrepresented at the hitter position and whites at setter (the central position) and bumper.[25]
- In Canadian hockey, French Canadians are overrepresented at goalie (the central position), and English Canadians are disproportionately represented in defensive positions.[26]
- In British soccer, black West Indians and black Africans are overrepresented in the wide forward positions, and whites are overrepresented at goal and midfielder (both central positions).[27]
- In Australian rugby, whites are overrepresented in the central team positions, and Aborigines are found disproportionately in the wide positions.[28] (For the special case of stacking in Canada, see box 13.1.)

The situation for professional football and baseball is found in table 13.2. Examination of these tables reveals: (1) that stacking continues twenty-six years after the Loy and McElvogue research; (2) looking at football, blacks are found more commonly on defense (where the requisite requirement is "reacting" to the offense) than offense (which is control-oriented); and (3) whites are found disproportionately at the thinking, leadership, and most central positions, while blacks are found at those peripheral positions requiring physical attributes (speed, quickness, strength).

Football and baseball have stacking, but basketball, which once did, is no longer characterized by racial segregation by position (both in college or in the pros). This change appears to be related to the proportion of a minority in a sport. When college and professional basketball were dominated numerically by whites, stacking occurred (with whites disproportionately at the point guard and blacks overrepresented at the strong forward position).[29] This trend is no longer the case in college men's basketball, where blacks are now a majority. It still exists in college women's basketball, where blacks continue as a numerical minority.[30] In professional basketball, where more than 77 percent of the players are black, stacking has ceased to exist. These patterns substantiate the hypothesis of Rosabeth Moss Kanter that the greater the numerical proportion of a minority in a social organization, the more likely genuine integration will occur.[31]

box 13.1 *"Stacking" in Canadian Football*

Stacking refers to the assignment of a player to a position, an achieved status, on the basis of ascribed status. In American sport, players are disproportionately assigned to playing positions on the ascriptive basis of race. In professional football in Canada, national origin is the salient ascribed status determining position assignment.

National origin is significant in Canadian football because the Canadian Football League has tried to maximize the number of Canadian players by restricting each team to no more than fourteen imported players. Canadian teams tend to fill this "quota" with Americans, who are typically more skilled at football than Canadians. This is because American youngsters, compared with Canadian youth, have devoted more years to playing football, have played against stronger competition, and have received better coaching. Thus, one would expect Canadian teams to use their limited number of imported players at the positions requiring the most skill.

Donald Ball has analyzed the distribution of Americans and Canadians by position and has found that the pattern of stacking differs from the American "centrality" model. The imported Americans were predominantly at what he calls "primary" positions—those most responsible for accomplishing the team goal of moving the ball and scoring (on offense) or preventing scoring (on defense). The primary positions on offense are quarterback, running backs, and pass receivers; the secondary or supporting positions on offense are center, guards, and tackles. On defense the primary positions are the defensive linemen and linebackers; supporting positions are the defensive backs and safeties.

In sum, Ball found Canadians to be discriminated against in professional Canadian football. They are the least likely to play the primary positions. Even those Canadians with American collegiate experience, although more likely than other Canadians to be at primary positions, are not assigned to them to the same extent as imported players. Further, the average salaries of Canadians are lower than those of Americans.

Source: Summarized from Donald W. Ball, "Ascription and Position: A Comparative Analysis of 'Stacking' in Professional Football," *Canadian Review of Sociology and Anthropology* 10 (1973): 97–113.

Explanations for Stacking

Several explanations have been advanced to account for the stacking phenomenon.[32] The Loy and McElvogue interpretation rested primarily on a position's spatial location in a team unit. However, Edwards argued that the actual spatial location of a playing position is an incidental factor; according to him, the crucial variable involved in positional segregation is the degree of outcome control or leadership responsibility found in each position. For example, quarterbacks have greater team authority and ability to affect the outcome of the game than players who occupy noncentral positions. Thus, it is the leadership and the degree of responsibility for the game's outcome built into the position that accounts for the paucity of blacks in central positions.

Edward's explanation is consonant with the stereotype hypothesis advanced by Jonathan J. Brower (specifically for football, but it applies to other sports as well):

The combined function of centrality in terms of responsibility and interaction provides a frame for exclusion of blacks and constitutes a definition of the situation for coaches and management. People in the world of professional football believe that various football positions require specific types of physically—and intellectually—endowed athletes. When these beliefs are combined with the stereotypes of blacks and whites, blacks are excluded from certain positions. Normal organizational processes when interlaced with racist conceptions of the world spell out an important

table 13.2 *Percentage of Black Players by Position: 1983 and 1994*

Position	1983	1994
A. Stacking in the NFL		
Offense		
Quarterback	1%	7%
Running back	88	92
Wide receiver	77	90
Center	3	18
Guard	2	32
Tight end	48	60
Tackle	32	47
Kicker	2	0
Defense		
Cornerback	92	99
Safety	57	80
Linebacker	47	72
Defensive end	69	71
Defensive tackle	53	63
Nose tackle	n/a	58
Punter	0	3
B. Stacking in Major League Baseball		
Pitcher	7%	7%
Catcher	0	3
First base	38	29
Second base	21	21
Third base	5	13
Shortstop	11	8
Outfield	46	51

Source: Adapted from Richard E. Lapchick and Jeffrey R. Benedict, *1994 Racial Report Card,* 1994, Boston: Center for the Study of Sport in Society.

consequence, namely, the racial basis of the division of labor in professional football.[33]

In this view, then, it is the racial stereotypes of blacks' abilities that lead to the belief that they are more ideally suited to those positions labeled "noncentral." For example, Brower compared the requirements for the central and noncentral positions in football and found that the former require leadership, thinking ability, highly refined techniques, stability under pressure, and responsibility for the outcome of the game. Noncentral positions, on the other hand, require athletes with speed, aggressiveness, "good hands," and "instinct."[34] Evidence for the racial-stereotype explanation for stacking was found in the paucity of blacks at the most important positions of outcome control in football: quarterback, kicker, and placekick holder. It is inconceivable to us that blacks lack the ability to play these positions at the professional level. Placekick holders (mostly whites) must, for example, have good hands, an important quality for pass receivers (who are mostly blacks). Nine out of ten of the pass receivers were black, but not one was selected as a placekick holder. Kicking requires a strong leg and the development of accuracy. Are blacks unable to develop strong legs or to master the necessary technique? The conclusion seems inescapable: Blacks are relegated to noncentral positions that require speed, strength, and quick reactions and are precluded from occupying leadership positions (such as quarterback or defensive signal-caller) because subtle but widely held stereotypes of black intellectual and leadership abilities still persist in the sports world.

Another explanation for stacking was advanced by Barry D. McPherson, who argued that black youths may segregate themselves into specific sport roles because they wish to emulate black stars.[35] Contrary to the belief that stacking can be attributed to discriminatory acts by members of the majority group, his interpretation holds that the playing roles to which black youths aspire are those in which blacks have previously attained high levels of achievement. The first positions to be occupied by blacks in professional football were in the offensive and defensive backfield and in the defensive line, therefore, subsequent imitation of their techniques by black youths has resulted in blacks being overrepresented in these positions.

McPherson produced no empirical support for his explanation, so Stanley Eitzen and David C. Sanford sought to determine whether black athletes changed from central to noncentral positions more frequently than whites as they moved from high school to college to professional competition.[36] Their data from a sample of 387 professional football players indicated that there had been a statistically significant shift by blacks from central positions to noncentral ones. Blacks in high school and in college occupying central positions held primarily by whites in professional football casts doubt on McPherson's socialization model. Athletic role models or heroes will most likely have greater attraction for younger individuals in high school and in college than for older athletes in professional sports. Furthermore, professional players were found distributed at all positions during their high school playing days. The socialization model also assumes a high degree of irrationality on the part of the players. It assumes that as they become older and enter more keenly into competitive playing conditions, they will more likely seek positions because of their earlier identification with black stars rather than make rational assessments maximizing their ultimate athletic skills.

It is possible, however, that socialization variables do contribute to the racial stacking patterns in baseball and football but in a negative sense. That is, given discrimination in the allocation of playing positions (or at least the belief in its existence), young black males may consciously avoid those positions for which opportunities are (or are believed to be) low (e.g., catcher, pitcher, quarterback) and will select instead those positions where they are most likely to succeed (e.g., outfielder, running or defense back).

The Consequences of Stacking
The effects of stacking are far-reaching. First, the stacking of whites in "thinking/leadership" positions and blacks in "physical" positions reinforces negative stereotypes about blacks and the ideology of white supremacy. Second, athletes in those positions requiring speed, quickness, and agility have shorter careers than those in highly skilled positions requiring technique and thinking. The shortened careers for blacks that result mean lower lifetime earnings and more limited benefits from the players' pension fund, which provides support based on longevity. Also, as we will see shortly, playing at noncentral positions reduces significantly the chances of a career as a coach or manager.

Rewards and Authority
One obvious place to look for discrimination is in salaries. The evidence here is mixed. Research shows that there is salary discrimination in basketball and football but not in baseball. James Koch and C. Warren Vander Hill examined the 1984–85 salary structure of professional basketball (NBA) and found that "equal pay for equal work" does not exist. They found that when performance is identical, blacks receive less salary than equivalent white players.[37]

In professional football, the average income gap between whites and blacks, was a difference of about $19,000 in 1988 with whites making the greater amounts.[38] There are two problems with this finding, however. First, it may reflect indirect discrimination resulting from whites being stacked in the better paying positions. Second, it does not control for performance as the Koch and Vander Hill study did for basketball. Studies in baseball have statistically controlled for performance by position and found that salary discrimination does not exist in that sport.[39]

This unequal salary for equal ability may be even more pronounced in boxing, where "great white hopes" are given opportunities and financial packages well beyond their abilities.[40]

Another case of monetary discrimination concerns the athletes' extra income from endorsements, speeches, public appearances, and the like. Some black athletes do extraordinarily well in outside income (e.g., Michael Jordan and Shaquille O'Neal), but others have done less well than their white counterparts. For example, black tennis player Zina Garrison, a highly ranked player, has experienced difficulty in acquiring endorsement contracts.

African Americans also do not have the same opportunities as whites when their playing careers are finished. This is reflected in media positions, where blacks are rarely found in radio and television sportscasting, even rarer as play-by-play announcers, and infrequently as sportswriters.

Officiating is another area that is disproportionately white. "[In 1993] there are fourteen officials in the NBA who are black, as well as one who is Latino. Combined, they make up 28 percent of the officials in the league. On the other hand, major league baseball has just three umpires who are black (5 percent) and two umpires who are Latino (3 percent). Meanwhile the NFL has 13 officials out of 107 who are black."[41]

Although the percentage of black players in each of the three most prominent American professional sports greatly exceeds their percentage of the total population, ample evidence indicates that few opportunities are available to them in managerial and entrepreneurial roles. For example, in 1994 only four of the twenty-eight major league baseball managers and only two of the twenty-eight NFL head coaches were black. Professional basketball was the exception with five head basketball coaches.

Assistant coaches are also conspicuously white. In 1994 the NFL had a black player composition of 65 percent but only 23 percent of the assistant coaches were black. Of these, only three were offensive or defensive

coordinators. Significantly, only fifteen of the twenty-eight teams had more than one black assistant. The few black coaches there are in the league tend to be assigned to coach receivers, running backs, and defensive backs, positions dominated by blacks.[42] In major league baseball only 14 percent of the coaches were black. Moreover, black coaches have been relegated to the less significant coaching jobs. In 1995, of the eighteen minorities coaching the baselines, fourteen were coaching first base. Frank Robinson, the first black major league manager, says: "It's a matter of teams not having confidence in [blacks] to coach third base."[43] This is significant because the third base coach is the most important on-the-field coach and when managing jobs open up, third base coaches have had the best experience to move up.

The dearth of the black coaches in professional sports is paralleled at the college level. Using data from 1995, when blacks made up 51 percent of Division I-A football players, less than 6 percent of the head coaches were black (six out of 108 schools).[44] Only three of the Division I schools (1 percent) had black athletic directors and only 13 percent of the 296 Division I basketball teams had black head coaches. There were no black baseball head coaches and only five black head track coaches.

A 1990 survey of sixty-three of the top Division I athletic programs (based on the Top 25 polls for men's and women's basketball and the Top 25 football poll) found the following minority representation (African American, Latino, Native American, and Asian): two athletic directors, twenty-eight assistant athletic directors, forty-three head coaches, 236 assistant coaches, twenty-one trainers, forty-four academic advisors, and ten sports information directions.[45] In short, of the 3,083 positions in these athletic departments, only 384 (12.5 percent) were held by racial minorities. This leads to the question asked by Richard Lapchick and Joe Panepinto: "What will happen to black athletes who play at these schools and graduate with degrees in physical education or sports administration? This is what most black athletes major in today, yet who is going to hire them? That, of course, is if they graduate; an estimated 80 percent of black Division I basketball and I-A football players don't graduate. . . ."[46]

Black women who aspire to coaching and management positions are victims of double jeopardy—their race and their gender. The barriers are especially difficult because black women have had so few opportunities to participate in high quality programs and because few persons in the position to hire are willing to take what they consider to be high risks. Anita DeFrantz provides ample proof of the lack of opportunities for black women as coaches and administrators:[47]

- Of 106 Division I schools that field women's basketball teams, only eleven are coached by black women and only one athletic director is a black woman.
- There are no black women among the executive directors of the fifty governing bodies for U.S. Olympic sports.
- There has never been an African American woman on any U.S. Olympic basketball coaching staff.

The paucity of black coaches and managers could be the result of two forms of discrimination. Overt discrimination occurs when owners ignore competent blacks because of their prejudices or because they fear the negative reaction of fans to blacks in leadership positions. The other form of discrimination is more subtle. Blacks are not considered for coaching positions because they did not, during their playing days, play at high interactive positions requiring leadership and decision making. For example, Wilbert Leonard, II, Tony Ostrosky, and Steve Huchendorf, found that major league baseball managers between 1876 and 1984 were recruited heavily from the positions of catcher and infield.[48] Blacks, because of stacking, have tended to be in the outfield and therefore do not possess the requisite infield experience that traditionally has provided access to the position of manager. The situation is similar in football. A study by John D. Massengale and Steven R. Farrington revealed that 65 percent of head coaches at major universities played at the central positions of quarterback, offensive center, guard, or linebacker during their playing days. The researchers concluded that "about one-third of the playing positions are producing about two-thirds of the major college head football coaches."[49] Blacks rarely play at these positions and are thus almost automatically

excluded from head coaching responsibilities. And the same pattern has been found for basketball, in which two-thirds of professional and college head coaches played at guard (the most central position). Once again, since black athletes in the past were underrepresented at guard, they are less likely than whites to be selected as coaches when vacancies occur.

Blacks are also underrepresented in the management positions in the organizations that govern sports. In 1991 the management positions in the front offices of the twenty-eight NFL teams were 7 percent black; in the twenty-six major league baseball teams, these positions were 4 percent black; and blacks held 9.2 percent of the front office management positions in professional basketball.[50]

Following the scandalous remarks in 1987 by Al Campanis, a Los Angeles Dodger executive, on national television that "blacks lacked the necessities to be leaders," a number of sports leaders vowed that the hiring of black executives and coaches was a top priority. However, subsequent vacancies tended to be filled by whites. Professional basketball is the most progressive in hiring blacks in leadership positions, but even there the powerful positions remain predominantly white.

Ability and Opportunity

Another form of discrimination in sport is unequal opportunity for equal ability. This means that entrance requirements to the major leagues are more rigorous for blacks; therefore, black players must be better than white players to succeed in the sports world. Aaron Rosenblatt was one of the first to demonstrate this mode of discrimination. He found that in the period 1953–57 the mean batting average for blacks in the major leagues was 20.6 points above the average for whites; in the 1958–61 period the difference was 20.1 points; and in the 1962–65 period, 21.2 points. He concluded: "Discriminatory hiring practices are still in effect in the major leagues. The superior Negro is not subject to discrimination because he is more likely to help win games than fair to poor players. Discrimination is aimed, whether by design or not, against the substar Negro ball player. The findings clearly indicate that the undistinguished Negro player is less likely to play regularly in the major leagues than the equally undistinguished white players."[51] Rosenblatt's analysis has been repeated for subsequent years and for other sports, always with the same results. Blacks outperform whites.[52]

The pattern also exists at the college level, where it is manifested in several ways. First, blacks must exhibit higher athletic skills than most of their white teammates in order to receive a scholarship.[53] Second, blacks are more likely to be recruited from community colleges, which means that universities make a relatively smaller investment in blacks and that the universities are relatively assured of getting athletes with proven athletic abilities. Third, compared to white players, blacks are less likely to play in reserve roles. In sum, whether in college or in the professional ranks and regardless of the sport, blacks must excel in order to participate. The data consistently confirm Jonathan Brower's conclusion that in sport "mediocrity is a white luxury."[54]

Summary

Black participation in the three major professional team sports continues to increase. This has led many observers to conclude incorrectly that sports participation is free of racial discrimination. As our analysis has demonstrated, stacking in football and baseball remains pronounced. Blacks are disproportionately found in those positions requiring physical rather than cognitive or leadership abilities. Moreover, the data indicate that although the patterns have been substantially altered in collegiate and professional basketball, black athletes in the two other major team sports have been and continue to be found disproportionately in starting roles and relatively absent from substitute roles.

Nearly as dramatic is the dearth of blacks in administrative, managerial, and officiating roles. Although black athletes have made significant advances in the past quarter-century, they have not gained comparable access to decision-making positions. With the exception of professional basketball, the corporate and decision-making structure of professional sports is virtually as white as it was before Jackie Robinson entered major league baseball in 1947. The distribution of blacks in the sports world is therefore not unlike that in the larger society. Blacks are admitted to lower-level occupations but virtually excluded from positions of authority and power.

Despite some indications of change, discrimination against black athletes continues in American team sports. Sport is not a meritocratic realm where race is ignored. Equality of opportunity is not the rule if race is a variable. Even where there have been significant positive changes, discrimination continues. In the words of Harry Edwards:

> Jim Crow has evolved into the thoroughly modern "Mr. James Crow, Esquire," The "White Only" and "Colored Only" signs are gone but the fundamental reality remains for the masses of black people both within and outside of sport, that is, subjugation within a two-tiered society predicated upon white superiority and black subordination.[55]

Notes

1. Norman R. Yetman and Forrest J. Berghorn, "Racial Participation and Integration in Intercollegiate Basketball: A Longitudinal Perspective," *Sociology of Sport Journal* 10 (September 1993): 302.

2. See John Holway, *Black Diamonds: Life in the Negro Leagues From the Men Who Lived It* (Westport, Conn.: Meckler, 1989).

3. Rogers Hornsby quoted in Ocania Chalk, *Pioneers of Black Sport* (New York: Dodd, Mead, 1975), 78. See also Jules Tygiel, *Baseball's Great Experiment: Jackie Robinson and His Legacy* (New York: Oxford University Press, 1983).

4. Robert H. Boyle, *Sports: Mirror of American Life* (Boston: Little, Brown, 1963), 103.

5. Paul Gallico quoted in Jay J. Coakley, *Sport in Society,* 4th ed. (St. Louis: Times Mirror/Mosby, 1990), 204.

6. Jimmy Powers quoted in Phillip M. Hoose, *Necessities: Racial Barriers in American Sports* (New York: Random House, 1989), xviii.

7. Forrest J. Berghorn and Norman R. Yetman, "Black Americans in Sport: The Changing Patterns of Collegiate Basketball" (University of Kansas, 1976). See also Adolph H. Grundman, "The Image of Intercollegiate Sports and the Civil Rights Movement: A Historian's View," in *Fractured Focus*, ed. Richard E. Lapchick (Lexington, Mass.: Lexington Books, 1986), 77–85; and Hoose, *Necessities;* and Yetman and Berghorn, "Racial Participation," 303. For the

changing racial composition of teams in the Southeastern Conference, see William F. Reed, "Culture Shock in Dixieland," *Sports Illustrated,* 12 August 1991, 52–55.

8. Harry Edwards quoted in John Underwood, "On the Playground," *Life* 11 (spring 1988), 104.

9. Richard E. Lapchick and Jeffrey R. Benedict, "1994 Racial Report Card," in *Sport in Contemporary Society,* ed. D. Stanley Eitzen, 5th ed. (New York: St. Martin's Press, 1996), 324.

10. Harry Edwards, *Sociology of Sport* (Homewood, Ill.: Dorsey, 1973), 193. See John C. Phillips, *Sociology of Sport* (Boston: Allyn and Bacon, 1993), 158–60.

11. Amby Burfoot, "White Men Can't Run," *Runner's World* (August 1992), 94.

12. Laurel R. Davis, "The Articulation of Difference: White Preoccupation With the Question of Racially Linked Genetic Differences Among Athletes," *Sociology of Sport Journal* 7 (June 1990): 184.

13. The following is taken from Ibid., 179–87.

14. James Green, letter to Norman R. Yetman and D. Stanley Eitzen, 1971.

15. Pete Axthelm, *The City Game* (New York: Simon and Schuster Pocketbooks, 1971).

16. John C. Phillips, *Sociology of Sport* (Boston: Allyn and Bacon, 1993), l73.

17. Edwards, *Sociology of Sport,* 201–202; see also Terry Bledsoe, "Black Dominance of Sports: Strictly from Hunger," *The Progressive* 37 (June 1973): 16–19.

18. Phillips, *Sociology of Sport,* l73–79.

19. Donal E. Carlston, "An Environmental Explanation for Race Differences in Basketball Performance," *Journal of Sport and Social Issues* 7 (summer/autumn 1983): 30–51.

20. Jay J. Coakley, *Sport in Society: Issues and Controversies,* 5th ed. (St. Louis: Times Mirror/Mosby, 1994), 265–66.

21. John W. Loy, Jr., and Joseph F. McElvogue, "Racial Segregation in American Sport," *International Review of Sport Sociology* 5 (1970): 5–24.

22. Hubert M. Blalock, Jr., "Occupational Discrimination: Some Theoretical Propositions," *Social Problems* 9 (winter 1962): 246.

23. Oscar Grusky, "The Effects of Formal Structure on Managerial Recruitment: A Study of Baseball Organization," *Sociometry* 26 (September 1963): 345–53.

24. Loy and McElvogue, "Racial Segregation in American Sport."

25. D. Stanley Eitzen and David Furst, "Racial Bias in Women's Intercollegiate Sports," *Journal of Sport and Social Issues,* 13 (spring 1989): 46–51.

26. Marc Lavoie, "Stacking, Performance Differentials, and Salary Discrimination in Professional Ice Hockey," *Sociology of Sport Journal* 6 (March 1989): 17–35.

27. Joe A. Maguire, "Race and Position Assignment in English Soccer," *Sociology of Sport Journal* 5 (September 1988): 257–69; and Merrill Melnick, "Racial Segregation by Playing Position in the English Football League," *Journal of Sport and Social Issues* 12 (fall 1988): 122–30.

28. Christopher Hallinan, "Aborigines and Positional Segregation in the Australian Rugby League," *International Review for the Sociology of Sport* 26, no. 2 (1991): 69–81.

29. See D. Stanley Eitzen and Irl Tessendorf, "Racial Segregation by Position in Sports: The Special Case of Basketball," *Review of Sport and Leisure* 3 (fall 1978): 109–28.

30. Norman R. Yetman, Forrest J. Berghorn, and William E. Hanna, "Racial Participation and Integration in Men's and Women's Intercollegiate Basketball: Continuity and Change, 1958–1985" (University of Kansas, 1987).

31. Rosabeth Moss Kanter, "Some Effects of Proportions on Group Life: Skewed Sex Ratios and Responses to Token Women," *American Journal of Sociology* 82 (March 1977): 965–90.

32. For a more detailed description of the possible explanations for stacking, see James E. Curtis and John W. Loy, Jr., "Race/Ethnicity and Relative Centrality of Playing Positions in Team Sports," *Exercise and Sport Sciences Review* 6 (1979): 285–313.

33. Jonathan J. Brower, "The Racial Basis of the Division of Labor Among Players in the National Football League as a Function of Stereotypes" (paper presented at the annual meeting of the Pacific Sociological Association, Portland, Oreg., 1972), 27. This argument is also advanced by R. Williams and Y. Youssef, "Division of Labor in College Football Along Racial Lines," *International Journal of Sports Psychology* 6 (1975): 3–13.

34. Brower, "The Racial Basis of the Division of Labor Among Players," 3–27.

35. Barry D. McPherson, "The Segregation by Playing Position Hypothesis in Sport: An Alternative Hypothesis," *Social Science Quarterly* 55 (March 1975): 960–66.

36. D. Stanley Eitzen and David C. Sanford, "The Segregation of Blacks by Playing Position in Football: Accident or Design?" *Social Science Quarterly* 55 (March 1975): 948–59.

37. James V. Koch and C. Warren Vander Hill, "Is There Discrimination in the 'Black Man's Game'?" *Social Science Quarterly* 69 (March 1988): 83–94.

38. Richard E. Lapchick, "Blacks in the NBA & NFL," *Center for the Study of Sport and Society Digest* 1 (summer 1989), 4.

39. Dean A. Purdy, Wilbert M. Leonard, II, and D. Stanley Eitzen, "A Reexamination of Salary Discrimination in Major League Baseball by Race/Ethnicity," *Sociology of Sport Journal* 11 (March 1994): 60–69.

40. Salim Muwakkil, "Off-the-Court Games and Unwritten Rules of Race," *In These Times,* 24 June– 7 July 1987, 9.

41. Lapchick and Benedict, "1994 Racial Report Card," 324.

42. Richard Demak, "Slow Going," *Sports Illustrated,* 10 June 1991, 13.

43. Frank Robinson quoted in Jack McCallum and Kostya Kennedy, "Baseball's Subtle Prejudice," *Sports Illustrated,* 25 September 1995, 15.

44. Harry Blauvelt and Jack Carey, "Black Coaches Still Find Doors Closed," *USA Today,* 2 August 1995, sec. C, p. 3.

45. "How Colleges Compare in Minority Hiring," *USA Today,* 19 March 1991, sec. A, p. 11.

46. Richard E. Lapchick and Joe Panepinto, "The White World of College Sports," *New York Times,* 14 November 1987, sec. E, p. 3.

47. Anita DeFrantz, "We've Got to Be Strong," *Sports Illustrated,* 12 August 1991, 77.

48. Wilbert M. Leonard, II, Tony Ostrosky, and Steve Huchendorf, "Centrality of Position and Managerial Recruitment: The Case of Major League Baseball," *Sociology of Sport Journal* (September 1990): 294–301.

49. John D. Massengale and Steven R. Farrington, "The Influence of Playing Position Centrality on the Careers of College Football Coaches," *Review of Sport and Leisure* 2 (June 1977): 107–15.

50. Richard E. Lapchick, "Professional Sports: The Racial Report Card," in *Sport and Contemporary Society,* ed. D. Stanley Eitzen, 5th ed. (New York: St. Martin's Press, 1996).

51. Aaron Rosenblatt, "Negroes in Baseball: The Failure of Success," *Transaction* 4 (September 1967): 53.

52. See Paul Kooistra, John S. Mahoney, and Lisha Bridges, "The Unequal Opportunity for Equal Ability Hypothesis: Racism in the National Football League?" *Sociology of Sport Journal* 10 (September 1993): 241–55.

53. Norman R. Yetman and D. Stanley Eitzen, "Black Americans in Sports: Unequal Opportunity for Equal Ability," *Civil Rights Digest* (August 1972): 20–34; Arthur Evans, "Differences in Recruitment of Black and White Football Players at a Big-Eight University," *Journal of Sport and Social Issues* 3 (fall/winter 1979): 1–10; and Charles M. Tolbert, "The Black Athlete in the Southwest Conference" (Ph.D. diss., Baylor University, 1975).

54. Jonathan J. Brower, "The Quota System: The White Gatekeeper's Regulation of Professional Football's Black Community" (paper presented at the annual meeting of the American Sociological Association, New York, August 1973).

55. Harry Edwards, "Review of Invisible Men and Baseball's Great Experiment," *Journal of Sport and Social Issues* 9 (winter/spring 1985): 43.

Chapter 14

Gender in North American Sport:
Continuity and Change

One may question the need for a separate chapter dealing with gender and sport, particularly since we have included gender issues with the other topics we have addressed throughout this book. We believe that in spite of the tremendous social change that has taken place over the past fifteen years sport still promotes and preserves traditional gender differences in many ways. As a consequence, a focused and in-depth consideration needs to be given to gender in a way that has not been possible in the other chapters.

American and Canadian societies pride themselves in their concern for the fullest development of each person's human potential, but they have been quite insensitive to the social injustices imposed by gender inequality. A most fundamental feature of both societies is the pervasiveness of male privilege. Male/female disparities in wealth, power, and prestige are ubiquitous social phenomena. Men have greater material rewards, a higher level of deference and esteem, and a more dominant position in the control of both their personal lives and their social activities.[1]

That is only one of the issues that requires attention. An analysis of the social construction of gender relations also involves understanding how meanings about masculinity and femininity serve to promote and sustain gender inequities and injustices, thus creating problems for both men and women. One of the North American cultural practices that is most influential in the construction of meanings about masculinity and femininity is sport. Historically, it has been a significant cultural practice in constructing and reproducing gender relations.

The Heritage of Gender Inequality

In order to develop an understanding about contemporary gender relations, it is helpful to place social relations between the sexes in historical perspective. For the past three thousand years western cultural ideology has been firmly grounded in patriarchy, which is a set of personal, social, and economic relations that enable men to have power over women and the services they provide. Patriarchical ideology defines females as inferior to and dependent on men, and their

primary gender role prescriptions are seen as child-bearers, child-rearers, homemakers, and sex objects. The traditions of western civilization have been perpetuated in North America with respect to the status of women. When the framers of the U.S. Declaration of Independence wrote that "all men are created equal" (excluding black and Native American men, of course), that is literally what they meant, and it was not until 144 years later that women were even considered worthy of the right to vote.

Thus, cultural definitions of female role expectations are embedded in the traditions of western civilization that are foundational to North American society. The overemphasis on protecting women and girls from the experiences of achievement and success and the underemphasis on developing physical skills fits the historical socialization pattern of preparing women for their adult role as passive helpmates of men, standing on the sidelines of history, cheering men on to their achievements and successes.

As modern sport developed in the latter nineteenth century, it served as one of the most powerful cultural forces for reinforcing the ideology of male superiority and dominance. Organized sport created symbols and values that preserved patriarchy and women's subordinate status in society. By celebrating the achievements of males through their sporting achievements and marginalizing females into the roles of spectators and cheerleaders, sport reproduced the male claim to privileged status. The overriding societal attitude with respect to sport was that it was for males and not for females.[2]

A North American woman's place in the nineteenth century was without question in the home. Indeed, the combined role of woman and athlete was virtually unthinkable. Women who wished to participate in competitive sports and remain "feminine" faced almost certain social isolation and censure. By choosing the physically active life, a woman was repudiating traditional female gender-role expectations. It might seem, therefore, that females would have little role to play in the burgeoning expansion of sport. Notwithstanding the cultural obstacles women had to overcome, their increasing presence and persistent involvement in sport in the late nineteenth and early twentieth centuries actually made a significant contribution to the rise of modern sport.

The latter nineteenth century brought many social changes, and industrialization brought more wealth and leisure to more Americans. Middle- and upper-class women experienced more freedom than they had ever known. Their interests expanded to activities outside the home, and as organized sport grew, women were often some of the most ardent participants. Croquet, roller-skating, ice-skating, bowling, archery, lawn tennis, golf, and bicycling were a few of the sports that captured the interest and enthusiasm of women during the latter part of the nineteenth century.[3]

The sport that revolutionized life-styles for both American and Canadian women was bicycling. It was one of the most significant factors in liberating attitudes of North American women and men toward the capabilities and needs of females. Its popularity as a means of social recreation began in the mid-1880s and stayed in vogue for about ten years. Beyond its role as a recreational pursuit, the bicycle was an important agent of social change for females, especially for middle-class women who were denied by lack of social status, money, and leisure time the opportunities to participate in sports like archery, tennis, golf, and croquet. Those with only modest economic means could afford bicycles, and they were soon bicycling by the thousands. The bicycle craze helped prepare American and Canadian women for their emergence as serious sports figures in the early twentieth century.[4]

Another important trend in sport in the latter nineteenth century took place at women's colleges. Several of the best-known women's colleges began including sports as part of their physical education programs. Boating, skating, bowling, horseback riding, swimming, tennis, and golf were all popular on campuses, and they were respectable because participants were protected from public view while they played. When basketball was developed as a sport in the 1890s, it quickly became popular at women's colleges. The English game of field hockey was introduced into the United States in the early twentieth century, and it too became immediately popular in the eastern women's colleges.

A sport historian summarized the state of sports for women at the beginning of the twentieth century: "When the 19th century ended American women enjoyed a freer life. . . . they could run, cycle and take part in a great variety of athletic games without being less a woman. This growth of women's athletics coincided closely with women's struggle for equality, freedom and independence. . . . Sports gave 19th century women the chance to demonstrate the physical side of their nature. . . . Women soon discovered that self-fulfillment, confidence, and self-esteem were other outcomes of sport."[5]

While that portrayal of conditions for females paints a rather optimistic picture, they actually faced a continuing struggle for equality and justice in sports. As is obvious from the following statement made by two *Sports Illustrated* writers, even in 1973 females still encountered oppression and inequality in the world of sport: "There may be worse (more socially serious) forms of prejudice in the United States, but there is no sharper example of discrimination today than that which operates against girls and women who take part in competitive sports, wish to take part, or might wish to if society did not scorn such endeavors."[6]

This statement makes it quite clear that the world of sport was pretty much the exclusive domain of males. Men typically engaged more often in sports and manifested greater interest in sporting achievements. Sports heroes and superstars were mostly males, and male dominance was notable in the administrative and leadership branches of sports, where men clearly overshadowed women in power and numbers. Female athletes did not suit the ideal of femininity, and those who persisted in sport suffered for it. These same *Sports Illustrated* writers characterized the prevailing view in the 1970s: "Sports may be good for people, but they are considered a lot gooder for male people than for female people."[7]

Women have turned to the unfinished business of gender equality, and North America has witnessed a social revolution—a women's liberation movement. As one dimension of this movement, women have responded to inequalities in organized sport by demanding their rightful place as equals. They are no longer content to be the cheerleaders and the pompom girls, urging on male athletes to glory, prestige, and power. Their targets for change vary from the kinds of legal and extralegal restrictions that prevent females from having equal access to sport opportunities, to attempts to elevate the social and political consciousness of women as a group. Coming under special attack are stereotypes of the ways males and females are supposed to behave. One writer summarized the progress that has occurred in this way:

> As a result of Title IX as well as the fitness movement of the eighties, more women and girls play sports, including highly competitive sports, than ever before. . . . They are getting pleasure out of sheer physical competence. . . . Women athletes now have female stars to model themselves after, and those stars are gaining more fame and fortune than would have been thought possible twenty years ago. Sports participation has given millions of women new self-confidence and has taken them to where they never were before—onto what used to be male turf.[8]

Sport opportunities for girls and women have increased tremendously—mainly because of court decisions and federal laws. However, prejudices are not altered by courts and legislation, and culturally conditioned responses to gender ideology are ubiquitous and resistant to sudden changes. Therefore, laws may force compliance in equality of opportunity for females in the world of sport, but inequities in sport continue, albeit in more subtle and insidious forms, as has been the case with racism.

The subject of gender inequities in North American sport is sociologically significant from the standpoint of the social structure and processes that have excluded females from this form of social activity. It is also significant from the standpoint of the social changes that have occurred in the past two decades and that are likely to continue in the future. In the remaining sections of this chapter we examine the social bases for the inequality and injustices in sports that confront both females and males, and we suggest some of the consequences of these processes.

Social Sources of Gender Inequality in Sport

The ultimate basis of gender inequality in North American sport is embedded in the sociocultural milieu of society and in the traditions of western civilization that are foundational to North America. The historical foundations of the North American gender system and how it has specified behaviors, activities, and values of the sexes was described previously. We showed how the gender system has operated as a mechanism of inequality by ranking women as inferior and unable and by conferring privilege and status to males. In addition to the historical sociocultural influences, more specific socialization agents and agencies tend to reproduce the gender system with each new generation. We now turn to an examination of some of these influences, emphasizing the role of social institutions in gender socialization.

Parental Child–Rearing Practices and Gender Construction

Sex is a biological characteristic while gender refers to an ongoing cultural process that socially constructs differences between men and women. Each culture *constructs and teaches its young* the social role expectations for males and females, about what is considered masculine and what is considered feminine. Thus, humans are immersed in a complex network of sex and gender norms throughout life, and all societies have attitudes, values, beliefs, and expectations based on sex.[9]

The teaching of gender-role ideology comes from a range of social sources, including peers, teachers, ministers, mass media, and so forth, but the earliest and most persistent instruction comes from parents. Parents are major contributors to the shaping of gender-role ideology by acting differently toward sons and daughters as early as their first exposure to them and throughout the remaining years of their rearing. From infancy there are both marked and subtle differences in the way parents speak to sons and daughters, the way children are dressed, the toys they are given, and the activities in which they are encouraged and permitted to engage. A certain amount of aggression is not only permitted but it is encouraged in boys; much less is tolerated in girls. Techniques of control tend to differ also: praise and withdrawal of love are used more often with girls, physical punishment relatively more often with boys.[10]

Children rapidly learn the difference in parental expectations concerning gender appropriate behavior. The traditional parental message has been that desirable qualities for males are aggressiveness, independence, and individual achievement striving and that desirable qualities for females are passivity, affiliation, nurturance, and dependence. Studies of the childhood experiences of male and female athletes, have found that in a variety of ways, parents, especially fathers, encouraged the sport involvement of their sons more than of their daughters.[11]

The School and Gender Construction

The school serves to reinforce and extend the gender-role stereotyping that begins in the home. Teachers are in close contact with students throughout the day, day-after-day, year-after-year, therefore they are the major school influence on children and youth. The presence of teachers molds the traditional role differences both directly and indirectly. Two educational researchers found that teachers foster an environment in which children learn that boys are aggressive and physically capable, while girls are submissive and passive. With regard to the social climate of the classroom and its effects, they write:

> Sitting in the same classroom, reading the same textbook, listening to the same teacher, boys and girls receive very different educations. From grade school through graduate school female students are more likely to be invisible members of classrooms. Teachers interact with males more frequently, ask them better questions, and give them more precise and helpful feedback. Over the course of years the uneven distribution of teacher time, energy, attention, and talent, with boys getting the lion's share, takes its toll on girls.[12]

An indirect means by which the school reinforces traditional gender roles is through its own authority structure. While some 80 percent of all elementary school teachers are women, over 77 percent of the elementary school principals are men, and about 90 percent of secondary school principals are men, even though some 45 percent of the teachers at this educational level are women. Less than 2 percent of all superintendents are women. Thus, schoolchildren learn the differential status of men and women simply by attending school.

Another mechanism of gender-role reinforcement is sex-segregated, or at least single-sex dominated, classes. Classes that teach cooking, sewing, and other homemaking skills are considered to be primarily for girls, classes in woodworking or shop primarily for boys. In high school, certain subjects such as math and science are often viewed as male subjects, and English and fine arts regarded as female subjects.

Some textbooks, one of the basic sources of learning in schools, perpetuate gender-role ideology. The kind of history they purvey, the kinds of suggestions they present for adult occupational choices and leisure-time pursuits, suggest a negative image of women as unimportant and unable. In studies of the treatment of gender roles in textbooks, investigators have found that women tend to be marginalized in the world of politics, science, and sports, and their future presented as consisting primarily of glamour and service.[13]

Much of every school day is lived outside the classrooms in hallways, on the playgrounds, and going to and from school. It is during these times that a great deal of interaction takes place between same-sex classmates and between opposite-sex classmates. Much of this time is spent in conversations, informal fun and games, and just plain "horsing around." These interactions between boys and girls turn out to be what one researcher calls "power play." By that she means that through these school-related ritualized interactions gender is socially constructed.[14]

A lot has changed in high school sports in the past twenty years, and we will discuss those changes in more detail later in this chapter. Suffice it to say that in spite of the greater opportunities for females in interschool sports, these programs are still testimony to the importance of boys and the secondary status of girls. Thus, extracurricular activities, like school athletics, play an important role in the production and reproduction of gender differences. Having said that, this gender differentiation in school sports is not nearly as conspicuous as it once was.

The Mass Media and Gender Construction

As we emphasized in chapter 11 on sport and the mass media, social contexts and descriptions of women in the mass media, including newspapers, magazines, radio, television, and motion pictures, generally reinforce the gender-role stereotypes. A persistent and consistent finding in studies of the coverage of women's sports in the mass media is that women's sports are underreported and underrepresented in print, audio, and visual media.

Newspapers do little to enhance an attitude of respect for the female athlete. Overall, coverage of female sports in newspapers constitutes only about 15 percent of the sports section. In many newspapers it is less than that. However, it's not just lack of newspaper coverage. When women's sports are reported, they are rarely located on the front page of the sport section; instead, they are relegated to the back pages. Photos of female athletes seldom accompany the stories.

Magazine stories about women in sport tend to reinforce the stereotypes firmly embedded in the cultural heritage of women. Stories about female athletes, when they do appear, often center on a discussion of figures and fashions, something that never happens with stories about male athletes. In one study of 1,369 magazine photographs featuring women athletes, the investigator identified a variety of ways in which the photographs emphasized differences between male and female athletes. Among them were: (1) female athletes who embody the traditional feminine ideal (e.g., sexy, glamorous) are more popular subjects of photographs than those who do not; (2) female athletes are often photographed in what can be considered soft-core pornography poses; (3) in the framing of photos, male athletes are more likely to be photographed in dominant/masculine positions and female athletes in submissive/feminine positions; (4) camera angles typically focus up to male athletes and focus down upon female athletes; (5) female athletes are more likely to be shown displaying emotions, such as crying. The

researcher argued that sports photographs are "one kind of cultural text among many that shape the way we think about femininity and masculinity. Photographic images build on understanding of gender relationships that already have social currency."[15]

Motion pictures are also a powerful influence in keeping women in their place. Movie producers have tended to project two identities for women, that as a sex object or as a wife/mother figure but seldom as a physically active athlete. There have been numerous movies about male athletes, but very few about female athletes.

Television, because of its omnipresence, plays a powerful role in depicting gender relations, and its coverage of sport powerfully reinforces the traditional cultural privilege of males and the subordinate status of females. Many studies extending over twenty years convincingly show the unequal treatment of women's sports on TV. Several studies show that men's sports receive about 92 percent of the air time, women's sports about 5 percent. Even television commercials where sports figures are used to endorse or advertise products are overwhelming male sports figures. In a study of television advertising and sports figures, ninety-seven percent of the athletic figures employed in commercials were males.[16]

Gender stereotyping and sexist commentary are still used in reports on women athletes. Media coverage of women's sporting events is more often found in individual (tennis, golf) rather than team (basketball, softball) sports and there are few photos or visual images of women doing traditionally "masculine" events (shot putting). Women athletes are frequently trivialized through various characterizations and representations.[17] One TV announcer commenting on a female basketball center noted that she would probably "raise a big family" and make someone "a good cook one day." Women athletes are frequently referred to as "girls," while men athletes are hardly ever referred to as "boys." Commentary during a women's sports event frequently focuses on the physical attractiveness of the performers, their fashionable attire, their grooming, or their "cute" personality characteristics; commentary on such subjects is rarely part of a men's event.[18]

Another way in which females in sports are trivialized is through the nicknames and mascots that are used for high school girl's and college women's teams. Although the nicknames and mascots are chosen by the institutions, it is through the mass media that they are largely communicated to the public. Tigerettes, Rambelles, Teddy Bears, and other "cutesy" mascot names may seem harmless but they have the effect of defining female athletes and female's athletic programs as frivolous, insignificant, even trivial.[19]

The Gendered Nature of Athletes As Role Models

An individual or group of individuals whose behavior in a particular role provides a standard or model by which other persons can determine appropriate attitudes and actions is said to be a role model. There are few feminine counterparts to the fictional athletes Frank Merriwell, Jack Armstrong, and Joe Palooka, or to the actual sport stars Michael Jordan, Wayne Gretsky, Emmitt Smith, Pete Sampras, and Cal Ripken, Jr. Boys are bombarded with daily accounts of high school, college, and professional athletes, but girls rarely read, hear, or see reports about the feats of outstanding female athletes. However, the remarkable achievements of female professional, collegiate, and elite amateur athletes are providing a foundation for role modeling by young female athletes. "Name" female athletes do exist in several sports, and girls of the present generation are beginning to have sport heroines to admire.

Social Barriers to Female Participation in Sport

Gender inequality directed against females, like prejudice and discrimination of any kind, is insidious and denigrating. It takes many forms. First, the perpetuation of myths about the biological and psychological weaknesses of females stereotypes what is deemed appropriate and inappropriate female behavior. Unequal opportunity for participation in many activities is a second form of injustice. Third is the unequal access to the authority and power structure. Each of these forms of gender inequality has been used to discourage women and girls from participating in sports and to deny them equal access to the rewards that sport has to offer.

Negative Stereotypes

A variety of folklore, myths, and slogans traditionally prevalent in North American society have supported sport as an exclusively masculine activity and served as barriers to female participation in sport.

Athletic Participation Masculinizes Females

One of the oldest and most persistent notions about female participation in sport, and a main deterrent, is the idea that vigorous physical activity tends to "masculinize" the physique and behavior of girls and women. For years, women of physical competence were stigmatized as "masculine" by claims that women who engaged in physical activities were not "feminine." This was like a doomsday weapon to discourage female interest and involvement in sport.

Every culture defines appropriate and inappropriate male and female appearance and behavior (and these vary from culture to culture) and establishes severe negative sanctions for those who do not meet cultural standards of masculinity and femininity. From the beginning of modern sport, sport was a male preserve, and images of ideal masculinity for males were culturally constructed through sports. The cultural script was that males validated their masculinity through athletic endeavors. Females had no place there; it could only make them masculine, like it makes males. The founder of the modern Olympic Games and an influential leader in sport, Pierre de Coubertin, opposed what he called the "indecency, ugliness and impropriety of women in . . . sports [because] women engaging in strenuous activities were destroying their feminine charm and leading to the downfall and degradation of . . . sport."[20] At another time, de Coubertin drove home the same point: "Would . . . sports practiced by women constitute an edifying sight before crowds assembled for an Olympiad? Such is not [the International Olympic Committee's] idea of the Olympic Games in which we have tried . . . to achieve the solemn and periodic exaltation of male athleticism with internationalism as a base, loyalty as a means, art for its setting, and female applause as its reward."[21]

The impression that physical activity produces masculine body types is undoubtedly because of some females who become serious athletes do indeed develop muscular and movement characteristics appropriate for performing the skills of a sport. Such muscle development and movement patterns have nothing to do with maleness or femaleness but are merely the most efficient use of the body to accomplish movement tasks. Nevertheless, the threat of masculinization has been sufficiently terrifying to discourage many females from becoming physically active, and those who did become athletes often lived with the fear of becoming "masculine." In 1980 a sport psychologist noted: "The negative sanctions that discourage women and girls from serious participation in athletics apparently stem from two basic fears: the fear that their behavior will become masculinized and the fear that their physiques will become masculinized."[22]

Even in the 1990s many female athletes attempt to maintain a "ladylike" appearance in deference to the ideology that sport masculinizes females. They often compensate for the perceived threat to their femininity by wearing feminine artifacts with their athletic attire. By wearing ruffles, pastel colors, or lacy designs and styles they seem to be saying, "Even though I'm a highly skilled athlete, I'm still feminine."

There is, of course, no evidence to support the notion that vigorous physical activity alters the basic biological constitution of a female, making her more "male." This is not to suggest that no physical or psychological differences exist between female athletes and female nonathletes. Prolonged physical training in a sport alters the female physique, physiological support systems, and psychosocial characteristics just as it does in the male. Indeed, athletes as a group seem to have somewhat special physical and psychological characteristics, but these personal characteristics may have existed before the individual became involved in sport. Actually, these traits may have attracted them to sport in the first place.

There is another social sanction used against active females that is closely linked to the "sports masculinizes females" argument, and that is a charge about female athletes and their sexuality. This takes the form of claiming that sports participation either changes the sexual orientation of females leading them to become lesbians, or females who are lesbians are attracted to sport. In either case, so the argument goes, most female athletes are lesbians. Olympian Jackie Joyner-Kersee said, "It's something they do to keep you from playing sports. That's what it's about."[23] Given the widespread homophobic (meaning dislike and intolerance of homosexuals) public attitudes that prevail in North American societies, this charge has had ominous consequences for females who might wish to become involved in sports and for those who are involved in sports. It has certainly had a profound stigmatizing affect on them.[24]

The claims about sport's presumed "masculinizing" and "lesbianizing" of females has been vigorously attacked by a broad spectrum of scholars and scientists who have exposed the ideological foundations of these arguments. They have emphasized that definitions of feminine and masculine behavior are culturally constructed—that they are not natural, biological characteristics at all. Moreover, they emphasize that sexual orientation is irrelevant with regard to sport participation; and there are heterosexual as well as homosexual males and females in sport just as there is in every other sector of social life. Martina Navratilova, one of the greatest tennis players of all time, was the first well-known female athlete to openly acknowledge she was a lesbian. Since then, a number of other top women athletes have done likewise.[25] These women maintain that contemporary women are no longer willing to have traditional definitions of masculine/feminine and sexuality imposed on them, especially when such definitions prevent females from experiencing highly valued social activities.[26]

It is now quite clear that the presumptions that women become masculinized and their sexual orientation is influenced by sports participation have served as social weapons to reinforce cultural traditions of male privilege and female subordination, and they are now being widely rejected. Indeed, some women have completely repudiated the traditional definitions that identify muscles with masculinity and homosexuality, and such sports as bodybuilding and weightlifting are growing rapidly among sportswomen. Just like male bodybuilders, the women are "judged on the symmetry and proportions of their physiques, on their muscularity and definition, and on their posing routines," and women weightlifters are judged by how much weight they can lift, just like men. Furthermore, their sexuality is no more important than is men's.[27]

Gender-role reconceptualization is taking several forms, but in all its variations a prominent place is reserved for the active woman. In a book describing evolving trends in sports and gender roles, the author said: "Women's presence in weight rooms and gyms, like women's presence in boardrooms and bars, is subtly and insistently challenging men to see women as peers, and to adapt their playing style to what women want and need. By playing sports, women are challenged to see themselves not as the same as men but as equally entitled to define the nature of the games and the relationships between and among players."[28]

It may be seen, then, that contemporary women will not be locked into outmoded role prescriptions and baseless assertions, especially those that limit their physical potential.

Sports Participation Is Harmful to the Health of Females

Another well-entrenched traditional canard is that sports participation is harmful to female health. Principally concerned with physical injury to the reproductive organs and the breasts and with possible effects on the menstrual cycle, pregnancy, and the psychological well-being of females, the literature of the past one hundred years is laden with such opinions. Early in the twentieth century Dudley Allen Sargent, a noted physical educator and actually a promoter of women's physical education, was concerned about competitive sports because of, according to him, "the peculiar constitution of [a female's] nervous system and the greater emotional disturbances to which she is subjected."[29] A few years later, another well-respected physical educator claimed: "Natural feminine health and attractiveness . . . are impaired if not destroyed by the belligerent attitudes and competitive spirit and development which intense athletics inevitably fosters."[30]

Women themselves reinforced the view that female health was harmed by competitive sports. The height of the women's objection to stressful competition for females came in the 1920s and 1930s, but its effects were felt as late as the 1970s. Agnes Wayman, president of the American Physical Education Association in the early 1920s, described her reasons for opposing competitive sports for high school and college women: "External stimuli such as cheering audiences, bands, lights, etc., cause a great response in girls and are apt to upset the endocrine balance. Under emotional stress a girl may easily overdo. There is widespread agreement that girls should not be exposed to extremes of fatigue or strain either emotional or physical."[31]

In 1928 the chairperson of the Executive Committee of the Women's Division of the National Amateur Athletic Federation, voiced her opposition to women's Olympic participation: "Girls are not suited for the same athletic programs as boys. The difference between them cannot be ignored. . . . Under prolonged intense physical strain a girl goes to pieces nervously. . . . The fact that a girl's nervous resistance cannot hold out under intensive physical strain is nature's warning. A little more strain and she will be in danger both physically and nervously."[32]

Although physicians and educators were able to convince the public of the health dangers of sports for females, the health dangers to male sport participants never became the focus of public scrutiny and discussion the way the dangers to females did. Placing the focus of health dangers exclusively on females had an ideological foundation grounded in the preservation of male privilege. Its purpose was the maintenance and continuation of gender differentiation, with exclusive male access to a socially esteemed activity—sport.

It is now clear that intensive sports training and competition, especially at the elite levels of sport have a number of health risks for both men and women. The increased participation of females in high levels of sport competition combined with the growth of the sport sciences has helped to clarify some specific potential health risks for female athletes. As noted previously, the stress of intense training and sport competition has a number of health risks for both males and females, but there are some health risks that are unique to females. Some of them are amenorrhea (cessation of menstrual function without menopause) and related effects (pregnancy, osteoporosis, stress fractures), delayed menarche, high frequency of knee injuries, relationship of reduced body fat to eating disorders. These health risks increase as the intensity, duration, and frequency of the training and competition increases.[33] There are individual and sex specific physiological and psychological differences and responses to sport participation but that is no reason not to provide equal access and opportunity to sporting experiences to females. Furthermore, for the vast majority of females the physiological, psychological, and social benefits gained through physical activity and sports competition by females is pretty much the same as it is for males.

Women Are Not Interested in Sports and Do Not Play Well Enough to Be Taken Seriously

Historically, contempt for the physically active female was shown by the contention that women were not really interested in nor very good at sports. Those who made this point typically referred to the paucity of women in sports, and claimed that the best performances of those who did participate in sport were inferior to mens' performances. Such arguments, like all cultural norm explanations of social regularities, tended to ignore social structure. Women in the past chose to pursue certain roles and not others not just because that was the cultural norm, though it certainly was the norm, but because males and females were related to each other in a relatively stable social structure of power and differential status. This was a structure in which males appropriated the roles they preferred because they had the power to do so and could thus promote more status for themselves. Women's roles were residual, and the norm merely sustained the existing structure of power and status. As we have pointed out throughout this chapter, the role of "athlete" was culturally associated with male-role enactment. Females were simply socialized out of sport by a variety of powerful social agents and agencies; was it any wonder they took little interest in sport? Without interest and encouragement, few indeed could play very well.

With respect to the failure of women to perform up to the athletic standards set by males when records are considered, this is true in many sports. Although women's performances as a group may be less spectacular than those of men as a group, some top-level female athletes individually surpass male athletes in certain sports, and women seem to be as competent as men to fulfill even the most strenuous sport roles. In ultradistance running, swimming, and cycling, as well as equestrian events, dog sled racing, and horse and auto racing women and men now compete together, even at the highest levels of competition. Women win their share of those events, too.[34] World and Olympic records once set by male athletes in swimming, distance running, cycling, and other sports as well, have been broken by female athletes.

People who have been unimpressed by women athletes have typically evaluated women's performances in relation to men's. This is, of course, a nonsensical comparison. Perhaps Simone de Beauvoir, one of the twentieth century's most esteemed writers, best described the absurdity of comparing male and female sports performances: "In sports the end in view is not success independent of physical equipment; it is rather the attainment of perfection within the limitations of each physical type; the featherweight boxing champion is as much a champion as is the heavyweight; the woman skiing champion is not the inferior of the faster male champion; they belong to two different classes."[35]

Female achievements in sport in the 1990s are too numerous and too remarkable to list. Clearly, the argument that females are not interested in sports and that they do not play them well enough to be taken seriously has been put to rest for even the most hardened skeptics of women's potential.

Attitudes Toward Female Athletes

Attitudes involve what people think and how they feel about and behave toward other people or objects. They are learned rather than being innate, and they are enduring but changeable. One consequence of the traditional cultural views toward female involvement in sport was that many people did disapprove of females' involvement in competitive sports, and females who participated experienced role conflict in fulfilling the dual roles of female and athlete. This was especially true for those who participated in what was considered less socially "appropriate" sports for females—softball, basketball, volleyball, and track and field—than for athletes competing in what was considered more socially "appropriate" sports for females—tennis, golf, swimming, and gymnastics.

However, attitudes toward female athletes and active women have changed rapidly. Enlightened persons have come to recognize that negative attitudes toward female athletic participation of any kind are incongruent with the realities of female potential. Moreover, many are realizing that attitudes that sort sports into "appropriate" and "inappropriate" for females are embedded in a cultural ideology of gender inequality and injustice.

There is a high level of acceptance and support for female sports participants among general segments of the population. Moreover, female athletes themselves are increasingly reporting very positive self-images in general; a concept of femininity exists that combines fitness, strength, and health through physical activities with a firm belief that this in no way diminishes their potential or capability to fulfill whatever other roles they wish to pursue.

The Opportunity and Reward Structure for Females in Sport

Denial of equal access to various opportunities and unequal rewards for achievements are the two most ubiquitous injustices that females have historically experienced in relation to sport. Although the opportunity and reward structures for female sports participants have greatly improved (more females are involved in sports and receiving more rewards for their achievements than ever before), an entire book would be required to catalog the numerous ways in which girls and women are still deprived of equal opportunity and receive inferior rewards. In this section we will describe some of the torment females have suffered, and continue to suffer, as well as some of the changes that have opened up opportunities for women to experience the access and rewards of sports participation at all levels.

From Boys-Only Youth Sports to Opportunities for Both Sexes

As we noted in chapter 4, youth sports programs introduce most children to the experience of organized sports. The Little League, Babe Ruth, and Connie Mack baseball leagues are three of the most popular baseball programs. Pop Warner football, Junior Hockey, and Biddie basketball initiate youngsters to tackling, blocking, ice skating, and jump shooting. Age-group programs in swimming, track and field, and gymnastics are only a few of the over twenty-five youth sports programs that involve more than 20 million children annually. Not so long ago, all but a very small percentage of the participants were males, and many of the organizations had formal policies excluding females.

Little League is a baseball organization that operates twenty thousand leagues in thirty-one countries for 3 million boys from eight to twelve years of age. Until the mid-1970s, an all-male policy that prevented girls from playing on its teams was part of its federal charter. This policy was challenged by several girls or their representatives, and it was reluctantly rescinded by Little League officers. Nevertheless, prejudices die hard. One example will illustrate the extent adult male leaders of one Little League program went to discourage girls from playing in the league: In the summer of 1975 a Little League organization in a small city in Michigan made what was clearly a veiled attempt to circumvent court rulings and national Little League policy. The local league established a rule requiring girls as well as boys to wear athletic supporters and protective cups, and coaches made "cup" inspections before each game. One girl's parents tried to ridicule the rule by pinning a toy teacup to their eight-year-old daughter's jersey. The coach benched the child and said that she "won't play until she wears a cup like the other kids."[36] The situation was finally resolved in favor of the girl when a lawsuit was threatened.

Public opinion as well as the laws rapidly turned against those who wished to perpetuate the traditional gender differentiation in physical activities. By the mid-1990s over a million girls were playing youth soccer, some two hundred thousand were playing Little League baseball; and another half million were playing

box 14.1   *Sexism and Soccer in Seattle*

Twelve-year-old Eve Russell likes playing soccer with boys. She prefers their rough and competitive style of play to the girls' more passing-oriented game. So rather than join the girls' soccer team, Russell became a member of the boys' team. Her teammates are glad she did; they say they play better when she's there. They think her decision was fine.

Unfortunately, the Seattle Youth Soccer Association (SYSA) and its president, Robin Chalmers, don't agree. They believe that Russell could get roughed up by a boy angry at losing to a girl, and that she needs to bond with other females in the game. What's more, Chalmers sees her choice as a threat and an insult to the girls' program, which he has worked hard to make one of the best in the country. And he resents charges of discrimination. "Our rules are there to protect the female," he argues. He fears that if Russell is allowed to stay on the boys' team, kids all over the city will want to switch too, ultimately damaging the girls' program. So far, though, no other children have shown an interest in switching teams.

The kids don't understand what all the fuss is about. They have a deep sense of team loyalty and fairness, and they want to stay together. "Just because you're not the same sex doesn't mean you can't do the same things," points out Russell's teammate Ethan Borsak, 12. Russell herself says, "I wouldn't be doing this if one person on the team didn't want me there. I'm not making a personal statement or saying anything bad about *the girls' program; there's nothing wrong with it. I just need to do what's right for me.*"

The controversy came to a head in 1994 when SYSA banned Russell from playing boys' soccer for the third year in a row (in the mean time, she continued to play but was not rostered). In response, the Seattle Parks Department revoked SYSA's permit to use public playing fields until it reinstated Russell on her team. SYSA, in turn, is now threatening to sue the city. Through it all, the team rallied, determined to stay together. "It's not just for Eve," says 12-year-old Dan Cahir, another teammate. "We need her on the team."

Parents rallied, too, concerned about the message their sons would receive if Russell were taken off the team for good because of her gender. But it seems they needn't have worried:

---

softball. Young girl gymnasts outnumbered boys ten to one, and age-group swimming had as many girls as boys participating. In spite of these improvements in young girls' opportunities, there are more youth sports teams available for boys, and about 63 percent of the total participants are boys.

Opportunities in youth sports for girls has been the fastest growing sector of sports. To a large extent this is because the young parents of these children are the first generation of parents since the women's movement began. They are the first generation to renounce the traditional cultural edicts of strict gender differentiation in social life. They tend to have a more favorable attitude toward gender equity, including equity in sport. (However, see box 14.1 for an example of how traditional attitudes remain inspite of more enlightened attitudes of young boys and girls.)

Toward Gender Equity in High School Sports

Prior to the mid-1970s discrimination in sports opportunities for females in high schools was scandalous. The national governing body of high school sports, the Federation of State High School Associations, actually listed nine states that prohibited interschool sports for girls. Little more than twenty years ago, a high school with ten or twelve teams for boys might have no teams, or only a few teams, for girls. Boys' sports seasons might run three months with fifteen or twenty

box 14.1 *Continued*

Since the controversy began, many parents have noticed an increase in their kids' sensitivity and maturity. "My son has deeply internalized what he's learned," says Helene Ellenbogen. "He's taken a stand on the playground and in the classroom when he's felt there was discrimination. He's now willing to take risks in situations where he doesn't have to." As for Russell, she's philosophical. "Things change," she explains. "Who knows, maybe next year I won't want to play because the boys will be a heck of a lot taller and stronger than me. I take it a day at a time."

—*Erika Dillman*

Source: *Women's Sports & Fitness* (April 1995), 75.

scheduled contests; the season for a girls' sport typically extended a mere three to four weeks, with two or three contests.

However, when the Educational Amendments Act of 1972 was passed, Title IX, a key provision, required schools that receive federal funds to provide equal opportunities for males and females. Title IX specifies: "No person in the United States shall, on the basis of sex, be excluded from participation in, be denied the benefits of, or be subjected to discrimination under any education program or activity receiving Federal financial assistance." Title IX constituted a considerable weapon against sex discrimination in the American public school and collegiate sports programs, since some sixteen thousand public school districts and over two thousand six hundred colleges and universities benefit from federal funds.

In Canada nothing comparable to Title IX has existed, but sex equality issues have been dealt with in several ways. However the Fitness and Amateur Sports Women's Program was established in 1980, and it provides government programs, training, and policy standards for females. The publication *Women in Sport: A Sport Canada Policy* in 1986 defined a national policy for women in sport. It established goals of equality of opportunity for women in sport and called for specific action-based programs to achieve the goals.

Title IX proved to be the beginning of a sports revolution for girls and women in the United States. Within the next ten years, the number of female high

table 14.1 *Sports Participation Survey Totals*

Year	Boy Participants	Girl Participants
1971	3,666,917	294,015
1973–74	4,070,125	1,300,169
1975–76	4,109,021	1,645,039
1980–81	3,503,124	1,853,789
1989–90	3,398,192	1,858,659
1994–95	3,536,359	2,240,461

Source: *National Federation Handbook, 1994–95* (Kansas City, Mo.: National Federation of State High School Associations, 1995).

school athletes in the United States jumped from 294,000 to just under 2 million. Table 14.1 illustrates the staggering increases that have occurred in girls' high school athletic participation. In the past twenty-five years the number of girls participating in high school athletic programs throughout the nation has increased a resounding 600 percent. By the mid-1990s, 39 percent of all high school participants were female, and the number of sports available to them was more than twice the number available in 1980.[37]

In spite of a federal law requiring schools to treat the sexes equally, the transition from a predominantly male athletic program to a two-sex program did not occur without controversy and litigation. Title IX was silent or vague on some issues, therefore, high school girls had to challenge the discrimination in their school sports programs through legal and legislative action. A number of lawsuits were brought by girls against school districts or state high school athletic regulatory bodies. In general, the cases fell into two categories: (1) a girl desired to participate on the boys' team when a girls' team was not provided at her school, or (2) a girl wished to be on the boys' team even though her school provided a girls' team. In the first type of case, the courts generally ruled in favor of the girl, though some of these suits required appeals. In the second type of case, the girl was usually not successful because the court reasoned that equal opportunity had not been denied her.

Although many positive strides have been made, issues about participation still persist. Each fall a few girls (in 1995 it was over one hundred nationally) go out for high school football teams. Some states have ruled that they may not become members of the team. Others have ruled that if they can make the team, they may remain.

High school wrestling illustrates the trend that has been taking place with regard to girls participation. When high school girls first came out for the wrestling team, they found various legal and policy barriers. They also found less formal objections. In the case of one girl who was a member of a high school wrestling team in Arizona, a fundamentalist religious group protested, saying it was immoral for a boy to wrestle a girl, one coach filed a protest because the girl did not weigh in stripped with the rest of the boys, and one of her opponents refused to wrestle her because of "strong moral convictions."[38] Despite such barriers and objections, several hundred girls are now members of high school wrestling teams across the country.

A development that has shown increasing strength involves requests by boys to be allowed to participate on girls' high school teams. In almost every case, the boys have wanted to take part on the girls' team because the school did not have a boys' team in that sport. Volleyball, soccer, gymnastics, and swimming have been the sports that have most commonly drawn requests. In several instances the boys have won the right to play on the girls' team. It is now clear, however, that boys will not wish to play on girls' teams in large numbers, but the situation does illustrate the unintended consequences of efforts to address discrimination against one group.

Towards Gender Equity in Intercollegiate Sports

The past twenty years have been tumultuous for women in intercollegiate sports. Prior to the passage of Title IX, only about 15 percent of college athletes were women. In colleges with a female enrollment nearly equal to male enrollment, women's intercollegiate athletic budgets accounted for only 2 percent of the total budget. While females needed bake sales, bazaar nights, and Christmas tree sales to finance their athletic programs, male programs in the same institutions provided new and expensive uniforms and equipment, disbursed generous per diem travel expenses, and never requested the male athletes to help raise money or to spend any of their own. Facilities for female college programs were most often second-rate. The newer and larger gyms routinely went to the men; the older gyms were routinely given to the women. Where men and women used the same facilities, the women were expected to wait for the off-hours, which were mealtime, before sunrise, and late at night. The women got cheaper equipment and were expected to keep it longer.

One aspect of the struggle of gender equity in intercollegiate athletics has revolved around governance and control. Conditions in college sport began to improve for women with the founding of The Association for Intercollegiate Athletics for Women (AIAW), a counterpart to the National Collegiate Athletic Association (NCAA). By 1981 it had over nine hundred and fifty members. Thirty-nine championships were contested in 1980–81 under AIAW's aegis. AIAW estimated that more than one hundred twenty thousand women were taking part in intercollegiate sports, compared with one hundred eighty thousand men.[39]

The NCAA, a bastion of male dominance in collegiate athletics, fought the development of the women's intercollegiate athletics with every resource at its command, including litigation against applying Title IX in collegiate athletics. In 1980, however, in a surprising and controversial move, the NCAA voted to begin sponsoring women's championships the next year in five sports in the NCAA's medium- and small-size schools (Division II and III). The AIAW denounced the decision as an attempt by the men's association to seize control of all women's sports and as a direct threat to the AIAW, claiming that permitting the women's NCAA tournaments, the AIAW would be driven out of intercollegiate athletics.

This was indeed an accurate prophecy. In 1981, despite protests by the AIAW, the NCAA established women's championships in twelve sports for Division I (the major universities). This was an action clearly designed to destroy the AIAW and to integrate women into the NCAA. The AIAW filed an antitrust suit against the NCAA, claiming that its action was a "massive effort to buy women's athletics and add it to its conglomerate interests." The suit charged the NCAA with "conspiracy to restrain trade and commerce in the governance, program, and promotion of women's athletics." The AIAW had to capitulate. Beset by loss of income, loss of members (35 percent of its members switched to the NCAA in the 1981–82 school year), and loss of championships, the AIAW ceased to offer programs and services in mid-1982.[40]

Since then, governance of the women's sport in colleges has been male-dominated. The NCAA, and the much smaller National Association of Intercollegiate Athletics (NAIA), are governing college sports for women. Leadership opportunities for women in these associations have been token at best. Women have been relegated to less than 37 percent representation on the NCAA Council and from 20 to 30 percent membership on other important NCAA structures. The institutional or member vote via one faculty representative from each member institution is 95 percent male.[41]

As women became incorporated into the structure of male-dominated intercollegiate athletics, concern arose that an elite, professionalized approach similar to that of the men's athletic programs would develop. Events indicate quite clearly that despite some protests by women's coaches and athletic directors, many of them actually embrace the NCAA commercial model of college sports and see the NCAA as providing the best avenue for getting on with the "business" of women's collegiate athletics. Indeed, this is exactly the direction that most major university athletic programs have taken. The University of Tennessee has an average attendance at its women's basketball games of over ten thousand; several other universities have reported average attendance over seven thousand.[42]

However, as the popularity of women's collegiate basketball has risen, graduation rates have gone down dramatically. The director of the Center for the Study of Sport in Society at Northeastern

University, places this trend in context: "Ironically, as women's sports become more successful, they become more like the men's programs, which have always placed too much emphasis on the athlete part of student-athlete."[43]

With the professionalization of women's intercollegiate athletics, involving money, prestige, and popularity, has come violations of NCAA rules similar to the kind prevalent in men's programs. Since the NCAA took over women's athletics, several schools have been placed on probation for recruiting violations, and over a dozen have received reprimands. An incident in the spring of 1995 seemed to illustrate the extent to which women's intercollegiate sport has come to model men's sports. An Australian softball pitcher came to UCLA long after the spring semester was underway, and the UCLA team had already played twenty of its fifty-six game schedule. She compiled a 17–1 record, including four wins at the NCAA women's softball national tournament. She was instrumental in UCLA winning the NCAA softball championship. Two days after the final game she left UCLA and returned to Australia, with no college credits earned. Her total stay at UCLA was ten weeks. Clearly, the purpose of her stay at UCLA was to help the UCLA team win a national championship.[44]

Some sportswomen are distressed about what has happened to women's collegiate sports. They see a danger that women will be absorbed into male-dominated sporting structures and lose their chance to advance a different ethic and form for intercollegiate sport. It appears such a structure is already well advanced, and there is no discernible sign that women's athletic leaders have any plan for creating a different model of college sports.[45]

Title IX and Subsequent Legal and Legislative Incidents

As significant as the various individuals and groups have been in dismantling barriers to equal access for females to the world of sport, the most formidable ally college women athletes and coaches have had in their drive for equitable athletic programs is Title IX. Still, we must emphasize that Title IX has not actually brought about the goal of gender equality. A variety of legal challenges to it have been mounted by various groups, including the federal government, the NCAA, and individual universities, many of which still resist complying with the intent of the legislation.

Delay in enforcement has been a major obstacle. Over two years after the final policy for Title IX was formulated in 1979, at least one hundred and fifty complaints accusing colleges and universities of sex discrimination in athletics were still pending, meaning no action had been taken on the complaints.

However, delay was not the most ominous threat to Title IX. One major objection to it had always been its application to athletics. The Office of Civil Rights in the Department of Education took the position that if any part of the school received federal funds, the entire school must come up to Title IX standards. Opponents claimed that only those programs specifically receiving federal funds were bound by the law. No athletic programs receive federal aid directly, so those who favored the narrow definition argued that no athletic program was liable under Title IX. This narrow interpretation of Title IX was supported by the Reagan administration, and vigorous and sustained actions were coordinated through several branches of the government to cripple the law.

A devastating setback for advocates of a broad interpretation of Title IX came in 1984 when the U.S. Supreme Court ruled in the case of *Grove City College v. Bell* that the Title IX language applied only to a specific program or department that received federal funds. This decision negated the original intent of the law: that an educational institution receiving federal funds must provide equal opportunity in all of its programs and activities. In effect, the court's decision said that women could be denied equality in sports. Indeed, that is what happened; within a year of Grove City, the Office of Civil Rights suspended sixty-four investigations, more than half involving college athletics. As one lawyer said, "The discrimination is so apparent, so blatant. Without the support and nourishment of the law, we see how fragile the support to maintain women's athletics really is."[46]

Immediately after the Grove City decision, various women's groups began to lobby Congress to pass legislation restoring weakened civil rights. After four years, both houses of Congress overrode President Reagan's veto, and the Civil Rights Restoration Act became law. The act is designed to assure that federal funds are not used to subsidize discrimination based on sex, race, age, or physical disability. One of its implications is the restoration of the original broad interpretation of Title IX.[47]

Resistance to full compliance with Title IX and the achievement of gender equity in college sport has continued throughout the 1990s. An NCAA survey of Division I universities in 1992 (twenty years after passage of Title IX!) revealed that although undergraduate enrollment was nearly evenly divided between males and females, males constituted 70 percent of all intercollegiate athletes, females 30 percent. Men's programs received 70 percent of the athletic scholarship funds, 83 percent of the dollars allocated for recruiting, and 77 percent of the operating budgets. In some universities women's sports received as little as 10 percent of the operating funds. A follow-up survey by *The Chronicle of Higher Education* that same year reported essentially the same results.[48]

Two years later, in 1994, *The Chronicle of Higher Education* surveyed these same universities and found "slight increases in the proportion of athletes who are women and in female athletes' share of athletic scholarships. However, sports opportunities and grant money for women continue to lag far behind those for men, even though women made up more than half of the colleges' undergraduates." Specifically, women made up 50.8 percent of the undergraduates but only 33.6 percent of the varsity athletes, and female athletes received 35.7 percent of the money spent on athletic scholarships. After reading this report, one director of a women's university athletic program said: "There's been legal action, and a great many promises, committees, and panels, and yet the national picture is still as it is. . . . I think the rate of change is totally insufficient, and my observation is that women have been too patient for too long."[49]

Resistance to gender equity in intercollegiate athletics has been met by complaints filed with the Department of Education's Office of Civil Rights and by legal action through the courts. In the twenty years between 1972, when Title IX became law, and 1992,

over one thousand complaints were filed with the Office of Civil Rights involving sports. Dozens of lawsuits have been filed on behalf of gender equity in college sports, and in most cases the party or parties claiming discrimination have won.

A few examples will give the reader a "feeling" for what has taken place. In 1992 Colorado State University dropped several sports because of budgetary constraints. Among them was the women's softball team. Nine members of the softball team filed suit against CSU claiming the university violated Title IX. The Colorado Supreme Court supported lower court rulings to reinstate women's softball at CSU. In another case, in 1993 the California chapter of the National Organization of Women filed a sex-discrimination lawsuit against the California State University system, claiming that only 30 percent of its participants in sports are women and women's sports receive less than 25 percent of the athletics budget. Nine months later the California State University system agreed to increase significantly its athletics opportunities for women.[50]

In 1994 Brown University lost a sex discrimination suit brought by women athletes seeking reinstatement of women's gymnastics and volleyball teams that Brown had dropped from varsity status to cut athletic costs. The U.S. District court judge ordered the university to reinstate the teams and provide "equal treatment" to women's athletics.[51]

Not all gender equity complaints and lawsuits have come on behalf of women. University officials, principally presidents and athletic directors, have refused to rein in the extravagant expenditures of football and basketball, therefore athletic budgets have been under pressure as women's sports teams have been added to the programs to meet gender equity provisions of Title IX. Consequently, universities throughout the country have been dropping men's "minor" sports (e.g., swimming, gymnastics, golf, wrestling, etc.) at an alarming rate.[52]

These cuts in men's sports have led to reverse discrimination lawsuits, with men relying on Title IX, claiming that the cuts are based illegally on gender. The argument that most universities advance for the privileged status of football and basketball is that they are "revenue producing" sports. However, for the vast majority of institutions the revenue those two sports generate falls far short of their expenses; in fact, they are by far the greatest financial drain of athletic department budgets, when revenue and expenditures are both considered.[53]

What can we say about gender equity in intercollegiate sport at this point? First, it is clear that significant strides have been made towards providing more equitable opportunities and rewards for women college athletes. There is now an average of about 7.5 women's teams per institution; in 1977 there were 5.5. There is still room for improvement. There are still several issues that need to be resolved about what constitutes achieving gender equity. Undoubtedly, these issues will challenge universities, the Office for Civil Rights, and the courts in the years to come.[54]

Gender Equity and High School and College Women's Coaching and Athletic Administration

One ironic consequence of Title IX is that as opportunities for female athletes opened up and programs expanded, a large number of the positions in coaching and athletic administration formerly held by women were sought and filled by men. In high school, for example, in the early 1970s, 80 to 90 percent of high school girls' sports were coached by women; by the late 1980s, just 35 to 42 percent were coached by women.

This trend has slowly begun to reverse itself as an increasing percentage of girls' sports are being coached by women. In a very few high schools, women are coaching boys' teams. In the mid-1990s there were more than two dozen women among the eighteen thousand or so coaches of boys' high school basketball teams across the United States.

The coaching pattern that has just been described for high school girls' teams has been duplicated at the collegiate level. In the early 1970s almost all coaches of women's intercollegiate teams were women, but the situation changed rapidly during the 1980s, and by 1990 only 48 percent of coaches of women's intercollegiate teams at four-year institutions were women (see figure 14.1); at two-year colleges the percentage of female coaches for the nine most popular women's sports teams decreased from 49 to 43 percent between 1984 and 1990.[55]

Figure 14.1 Percentage of College Women's Teams Coached by Women
Source: R. Vivian Acosta and Linda J. Carpenter, "Women in Intercollegiate Sport: A Longitudinal Study—Seventeen Year Update, 1977–1994" (New York: Department of Physical Education, Brooklyn College, 1994).

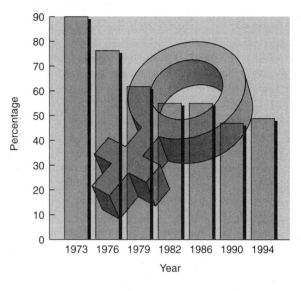

By 1994 the percentage of women coaches of women's teams had inched back up to 49.4 percent, still less than half of the coaches of women's college teams. It is still an open question as to the long-term trend in hiring practices, but every year there are more women who are experienced and successful coaches, and it will be increasingly difficult for higher education officials to hire men for positions that women are as qualified for (or better qualified for) as male applicants. Indeed, there is a handful of women coaching men's teams, and a growing belief that in the not-too-distant future one of the highly successful women basketball coaches will be hired to coach a men's college basketball team.[56]

Another issue for women college coaches involves payment for services rendered. In the 1992 NCAA survey that was discussed above, the average salary for men coaches was almost twice as much as that of women coaches. That shocking finding caused universities throughout the country to reassess their salary structures because gender equity can never be achieved as long as there are such wide differences in salary for men and women doing essentially the same tasks.

Female athletic administrators have lost out too during the past twenty years. Women's intercollegiate athletic programs in the mid-1970s were administered almost exclusively by women with the title of athletic director. Then, as women's programs grew, many colleges combined their men's and women's athletic departments into one. Most such mergers followed a pattern: After the merger, there emerged a male athletic director and several assistant directors, one of which was often a woman in charge of women's athletics or the less-visible sports.

According to two Brooklyn College researchers, who have been conducting a longitudinal study of colleges and universities for over seventeen years, in 1972 more than 90 percent of women's intercollegiate programs were headed by a female administrator; in 1994 only 21 percent were headed by a female. Some 24 percent of all intercollegiate programs for women have no female involved in the administrative structure. While these latter figures may be shocking, they actually represent a slight improvement over the preceding four years. Thus, the trend of institutions to hire men as athletic administrators, which began in the 1970s, may be turning around.

There are signs that the trends may be reversing. In 1995 four women in the country headed athletic departments at Division I universities. Their demonstrated competence and accomplishments show quite convincingly that in this career, just as in many others that have opened up to women, they are quite capable of performing just as well as men. Nevertheless, it seems likely that men will hold the vast majority of these key athletic positions for the foreseeable future.[57]

Leadership opportunities for women in other types of collegiate governance were greatly reduced with the demise of the AIAW, leaving only the NCAA and NAIA. As we noted, leadership in these two groups has been, and continues to be, overwhelming male; women are only slowly wresting leadership positions from the well-entrenched male dominance in these organizations.

The U.S. Olympic Committee continues to be a bastion of male dominance. In 1994 only 15 percent of the Executive Committee were women, 19 percent of the Board of Directors were women, and 24 percent of the committee chairs/vice chairs were women, and 21 percent of the senior staff were women.[58]

Canadian high schools and colleges, as well as elite levels of sport, have experienced a similar pattern of declining percentages of female coaches and athletic administrators. Moreover, the percentage of women coaches decreases in proportion to men as the level of competition increases. However, as with American sports, that has begun to slowly turn around in the past few years.[59]

Why Have Men Been Hired to Coach and Administer Women's Sports?

Considerable speculation has centered on why girls' and women's sports coaching and administration have become dominated by men. Some have suggested that higher salaries are attracting men into high school and collegiate athletics, others have suggested that men have greater access to the hiring system through an "old boys" network, and others contend that when men and women apply for sports jobs, men are perceived to be better qualified because sport has traditionally been a male domain. A study by several sport sociologists comparing the characteristics of male and female high school coaches showed that uncritically believing that men coaches are always better qualified can be a big mistake. In their study the researchers found that the female coaches were actually more qualified than the male coaches with respect to coaching experience with female teams, professional training, and professional experience, and as qualified as male coaches with regard to intercollegiate playing experience.[60] A survey of college administrators by the NCAA found that 93 percent of them believe that "old-boy networking" is a factor affecting women in athletic administration, and 78.5 percent said there are many qualified women who apply but who are not selected for openings in athletic administration.[61]

Gender and Careers at the Top Levels of Sport

As one might expect, opportunities for women to engage in sports at the highest levels have been severely restricted historically, and differential rewards have been the norm, with professional female athletes gaining less public recognition and less money for their performances. Progress has been made, however, during the past decade. Greater opportunities now exist. In 1977 there were only eighty to ninety professional women tennis players; in 1996 there were over three hundred. The total prize money for women on the pro tennis circuit is now over twenty million dollars for major tournaments. Still, in 1995 the top prize money winners on the Men's Professional Golf Association tour win twice as much money as the top Ladies Professional Golf Association money winners, and many of the golf courses on the Ladies Professional Golf Association tour still have policies that prohibit full membership to women, or they have course playing restrictions that apply to females but not to males.

Attendance and national television exposure has increased significantly for the top women's golf and tennis events. Charismatic figures have emerged on the women's tours to capture the interest of the public. Overall, however, women professionals in these two sports earn less than men for comparable performance.

The most popular professional sports for women have been individual sports, especially golf and tennis, because they have been "socially approved" sports for women, particularly by the upper social classes. Professional women's team sports have been less successful in their struggle for acceptance. As far back as World War II, though, there was a professional baseball—yes, baseball—league. During World War II Philip Wrigley, the owner of the Chicago Cubs, started the All-American Girls Professional Baseball League, and it remained a viable league until the early 1950s. Professional baseball for women was revived in 1994 when Coors Brewing Company formed the Colorado Silver Bullets. The Bullets were organized as a touring team that played against both men's and women's teams.[62]

The Women's Professional Softball League was formed in the mid-1970s but was disbanded after about four years. A professional volleyball league with teams comprising both men and women was popular for a couple of years in the late 1970s, but it folded. A new league known as Major League Volleyball began in early 1987, but it too failed within two years. The Women's Professional Volleyball Association, with a touring format, began its pro beach tournaments in 1986 and was still very much alive in 1996.[63]

Several attempts have been made to make a go of women's professional basketball in the United States. In the late 1970s and early 1980s a Women's Basketball League operated for three years before it folded. A new league, the Women's American Basketball Association, began with great expectations in the fall of 1984, but it did not survive the first full year. Another new league, the National Women's Basketball Association, was formed in 1986 with eight teams and planned to play a forty-eight-game schedule. It collapsed before the first game was played. Two women's professional leagues began in 1996 and 1997.

Opportunities to play on foreign teams in Italy, Spain, Sweden, Germany, and Japan, for example, have opened up for women basketball players, and as of 1996 approximately three hundred American female basketball players participated in foreign leagues. Top players can earn up to $200,000 for a six-month season.

Professional opportunities in sports are beginning to diversify for women. Professional ice skating has provided a chance for a few skaters to make very high salaries, and over one hundred women are doing well as jockeys in thoroughbred horse racing. A few female distance runners and triathletes are making six-figure salaries, and Susan Butcher was the first person, man or woman, to win the Alaskan Iditarod sled-dog race three times in a row. Women's Olympic sports are beginning to pay salaries to athletes. For example, members of the U.S. Women's Olympic Basketball team were paid $50,000 annually in preparation for the Atlanta Olympics.[64]

Gender inequality has prevailed in the Olympic Games since the modern Games began in 1896. The quotes by the founder of the modern Olympics in an earlier section of this chapter makes quite clear his belief that females did not belong. While female events have gradually been added to the Olympics over the years, there are still vast gender inequities. In the 1992 Barcelona Summer Olympics there were 159 events open to men and only eighty-six open to women. Females composed 28.5 percent of the total participants in those Games. The situation was not much better for

Figure 14.2 Number of Athletes Competing in Winter Olympic Games

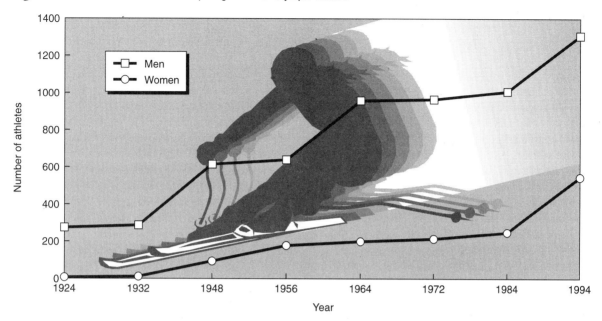

the Winter Games at Lillehammer, Norway that year; 1,302 men competed and only 542 women. See figure 14.2 for an illustration of the participation pattern during Winter Olympic Games. Ironically for Americans, all five of the Gold Medals won by U.S. athletes at the 1992 Winter Games were won by women.

New opportunities are opening up for women in the Olympics. Women's ice hockey was added for the 1994 Winter Games in Lillehammer, and women's softball and soccer were part of the 1996 Summer Games in Atlanta.

The world of sport has discriminated against females not only as professional athletes but in other professional sport occupations as well. As we pointed out in chapter 11, newswomen are greatly underrepresented as sportswriters. Despite the addition of a few women sports reporters to the staffs of television networks and of a few newspapers, there are still relatively few women in the field.

Women are also underrepresented as sports officials, judges, commissioners, athletic trainers, racehorse trainers, and most other sports-related occupations. In the spring of 1988 it appeared that Pam Postema, the

only woman umpire in professional baseball, had a good chance to make it to major league baseball, but just before the season began she was sent to the minor leagues. In 1989 she was released from professional baseball altogether, and major league baseball still awaits its first woman umpire. Several women have vied for work as NBA officials, believing that their successful officiating careers in various basketball leagues qualified them for a shot at the NBA, but none has been given that opportunity.[65]

Fortunately, many barriers to women's involvement in sport careers are falling, and it is becoming more difficult each year to keep women from fulfilling their sport career goals.

Sport and Gender Identity for Males

Gender issues are not just about inequality, injustice, and sexuality involving females. Attention has been focused on these issues as in this chapter, while in other chapters in the book we have examined gender issues related to males as part of other topics of the sports world. However, in this section we do wish to discuss the role of sports in the social construction of masculinity and its consequences for males. Traditional gender role prescriptions have perpetuated problems for males as well as for females.

At the same time that various social barriers discouraged females from sport involvement to preserve their feminine identity, males have been socialized into attitudes, values, and behaviors in which sport plays a dominate role in actually shaping their masculine identities. Sport has been the cultural activity that makes it seem natural to equate masculinity with competition, physicality, aggressiveness, movement skills, and physical achievements. Two of the best known slogans that reinforce this are: "Sports makes men out of boys" and "Sport builds character."

The competitive structures of the sports world socialize young boys into the exciting world of physical skills, tactics, and strategy in the pursuit of victory, but they also introduce them into the structured world of autocratic leadership, hierarchical organization, and bureaucratic relations. That is how the institution of sport is organized at every level. Teams are commanded by strong, forceful male coaches, whose word is taken as incontestable. Sports rules and coaches orders are understood to be followed without question. Athletes are expected to sacrifice their individual interests, skills, and goals for the benefit of the team. Personal relations are structured around competition against teammates for positions on the team as well as, of course, competition against opponents. While friendships and feelings of connection often develop among teammates, these are not deliberately structured in sport organizations. Instead, what develops from an interpersonal connectedness standpoint is a conditional self-worth, meaning masculine identity and personal value are dependent upon one's individual achievements.[66]

Along with other attitudes and values boys acquire through their sport experiences, they also learn about masculine sexuality. One of the most profound things they learn about masculine sexuality through the sport culture is that to be homosexual, or even be suspected of it, is detestable. As one sport sociologist said, "the extent of homophobia in the sports world is staggering."[67] Although there is growing evidence that gay athletes have competed, and continue to compete, at all levels of sport, mostly closeted, the sports world has remained steadfastly homophobic. In 1995, when Olympic diving champion Greg Louganis revealed he was gay, a flood of testimonials came from other gay athletes in other sports, illustrating that sport is no different than other sectors of life, notwithstanding the stigma about homosexuality in sport culture.[68] Indeed, a major Associated Press article carried in newspapers throughout North America was titled "Sports Poised to End Taboo on Open Gays." That view may be too optimistic, but some barriers have fallen with respect to attitudes and behaviors related to this issue.[69]

For males who have been uninterested in sport or unwilling to allow dominant gender definitions of masculinity force them into sport, or into "appropriate" masculine attitudes, values, and behaviors, they have often faced gender bigotry from both males and females. They have been the butt of jokes about their "effeminance," and they have been labeled "fags," "queers," and "fairies." Many times they have been physically abused in various ways. Thus, gender inequality and injustice have been directed at males who for one reason or another do not conform to dominant cultural definitions of masculinity.

Summary

In this chapter we have examined the social bases for the gender inequality and injustice that have traditionally confronted the females in sport, the consequences of the processes, and the developments in this topic. Gender inequality and injustice against females in sport have taken many forms. First, a number of myths about the biological and psychological effects on women of competitive sports effectively discouraged their participation. Second, unequal opportunity for participation in sports existed for a long time. Finally, women had unequal access to the authority and power structure of sport. Patriarchical ideology has been employed to socialize females out of sports and to deny them equal access to its rewards.

Legislation and court decisions have made it more difficult for discrimination to be imposed on women and girls in sports. Greater opportunities are now available for those who wish to compete.

Making discrimination illegal does not eliminate it, however, as previous experiences with civil rights legislation so clearly illustrate. Socially conditioned attitudes are slow to change. In some individual cases, they cannot be changed. Stereotypes are persistent and feed on the examples that confirm them. Nevertheless, attitudes and behaviors have changed in remarkably significant ways in response to challenges and demands as well as to federal legislation.

Gender inequality and injustice involves males as well as females. Traditional masculine identity is closely bound with sport culture, and males who do not conform to the social prescriptions face a variety of negative social sanctions.

Notes

1. Donald Tomaskovic-Devey, *Gender and Racial Inequality at Work* (Ithaca, N.Y.: ILR Press, 1993); see also "Labor Report Says White Males Still Running Corporate America," *The Tuscaloosa News,* 19 March 1995, sec. E, p. 6.

2. Richard A. Swanson and Betty Spears, *History of Sport and Physical Education in the United States,* 4th ed. (Madison, Wis.: Brown & Benchmark, 1995); see also Don Morrow, Mary Keyes, Wayne Simpson, Frank Cosentino, and Ron Lappage, eds., *A Concise History of Sport in Canada* (Toronto: Oxford University Press, 1989).

3. J. A. Mangan and Roberta J. Park, eds., *From "Fair Sex" to Feminism: Sport and the Socialization of Women in the Industrial and Post-Industrial Eras* (Totowa, N.J.: F. Cass, 1987); see also Patricia Vertinsky, "Women, Sport, and Exercise in the 19th Century," in *Women and Sport: Interdisciplinary Perspectives,* ed. D. Margaret Costa and Sharon R. Guthrie (Champaign, Ill.: Human Kinetics Publishers, 1994), 63–82.

4. Mary Keyes, "Women and Sport," in *A Concise History of Sport in Canada,* 231; Swanson and Spears, *History of Sport and Physical Education in the United States.*

5. Margery A. Bulger, "American Sportswomen in the 19th Century," *Journal of Popular Culture* 16 (fall 1982): 14; see also Nancy Theberge, "Women's Athletics and the Myth of Female Frailty," in *Women: A Feminist Perspective,* ed. Jo Freeman, 4th ed. (Mountain View, Calif.: Mayfield, 1989), 507–22.

6. Bil Gilbert and Nancy Williamson, "Sport Is Unfair to Women," *Sports Illustrated,* 28 May 1973, 90.

7. Ibid., 88.

8. Mariah Burton Nelson, *Are We Winning Yet? How Women Are Changing Sports and Sports Are Changing Women* (New York: Random House, 1991), 4; see also Mariah Burton Nelson, *The Stronger Women Get, The More Men Love Football: Sexism and the American Culture of Sports* (New York: Harcourt Brace, 1994).

9. Lana Rakow, *Women Making Meaning: New Feminist Directions in Communication* (New York: Routledge, 1992).

10. For an extended discussion of this topic, see Myriam Miedzian, *Boys Will Be Boys: Breaking the Link Between Masculinity and Violence* (New York: Doubleday, 1991), 177–206; see also John H. Lewko and Susan L. Greendorfer, "Family Influences in Sport Socialization of Children and Adolescents," in *Children in Sport,* ed. Frank L. Smoll, Richard A. Magill, and Michael J. Ash, 3d ed. (Champaign, Ill.: Human Kinetics Publishers, 1988), 287–300.

11. Michael A. Messner, *Power at Play: Sports and the Problem of Masculinity* (Boston: Beacon Press, 1992); Michael A. Messner and Donald F. Sabo, *Sex, Violence and Power in Sports: Rethinking Masculinity* (Freedom, Calif.: The Crossing Press, 1994).

12. Myra Salkers and David Salkers, *Failing at Fairness: How America's Schools Cheat Girls* (New York: Charles Scribner's, 1994), 1.

13. Jane Gaskell and John Willinsky, *Gender In/forms Curriculum* (New York: Teachers College Press, 1995); Myra Salkers and David Salkers, *Teachers, Schools, and Society* (New York: McGraw-Hill, 1994).

14. Barrie Thorne, *Gender Play: Girls and Boys in School* (New Brunswick, N.J.: Rutgers University Press, 1993).

15. Margaret Carlisle Duncan, "Sports Photographs and Sexual Difference: Images of Women and Men in the 1984 and 1988 Olympic Games," *Sociology of Sport Journal* 7 (March 1990): 40.

16. Edward Turner et al., "Television Consumer Advertising and the Sports Figure," *Sport Marketing Quarterly* 4 (March 1995): 27–33.

17. Mary Jo Kane and Susan L. Greendorfer, "The Media's Role in Accommodating and Resisting Stereotyped Images of Women in Sport," in *Women, Media, and Sport,* ed. Pamela J. Creedon (Thousand Oaks, Calif.: Sage, 1994), 34–39; Gina Daddario, "Chilly Scenes of the 1992 Winter Games: The Mass Media and the Marginalization of Female Athletes," *Sociology of Sport Journal* 11 (September 1994): 275–88; Catriona T. Higgs and Karen H. Weiller, "Gender Bias and the 1992 Summer Olympic Games: An Analysis of Television Coverage," *Journal of Sport and Social Issues* 18 (August 1994): 234–46; Jane Crossman, Paula Hyslop, and Bart Guthrie, "A Content Analysis of the Sport Section of Canada's National Newspaper With Respect to Gender and Professional/Amateur Status," *International Review for the Sociology of Sport* 29, No. 2 (1994): 123–34.

18. Kane and Greendorfer, "The Media's Role in Accommodating and Resisting Stereotyped Images of Women in Sport." See also Christy Halbert and Melissa Latimer, " 'Battling' Gendered Language: An Analysis of the Language Used By Sports Commentators in a Televised Coed Tennis Competition," *Sociology of Sport Journal* 11 (September 1994): 298–308; Michael A. Messner, Margaret C. Duncan, and Kerry Jensen, "Separating the Men from the Girls: The Gendered Language of Televised Sports," *Gender & Society* 7 (March 1993): 121–37.

19. D. Stanley Eitzen and Maxine Baca Zinn, "The De-athleticization of Women: The Naming and Gender Marking of Collegiate Sport Teams," *Sociology of Sport Journal* 6 (December 1989): 362–70.

20. Pierre de Coubertin quoted in Sheila Mitchell, "Women's Participation in the Olympic Games, 1900–1926," *Journal of Sport History* 4 (summer 1977): 211.

21. Pierre de Coubertin quoted in Ellen Gerber, Jan Felshin, and Waneen Wyrick, *The American Woman in Sport* (Reading, Mass.: Addison-Wesley, 1974), 137–38.

22. Dorothy V. Harris, "Femininity and Athleticism: Conflict or Consonance?" in *Jock: Sports and Male Identity,* ed. Donald F. Sabo and Ross Runfola (Englewood Cliffs, N.J.: Prentice-Hall, 1980), 224.

23. Jackie Joyner-Kersee quoted in Mariah Nelson, "Label Inhibits Some Women," *USA Today* 18 September 1991, Sec. C, p. 10.

24. Alexander Wolff and Christian Stone, "She Said, He Said," *Sports Illustrated,* 22 May 1995, 16.

25. Martina Navratilova, *Martina* (New York: Knopf, 1985); Sandra Faulkner, *Love Match: Nelson vs. Navratilova* (Secaucus, N.J.: Carol Publications, 1993); Marcia Chambers, *The Unplayable Lie* (New York: Pocket Books, 1995).

26. Pat Griffin, "Changing the Game: Homophobia, Sexism, and Lesbians in Sport," *Quest* 44 (August 1992): 251–65; Steve Wilstein, "Sports Poised to End Taboo on Open Gays," *Rocky Mountain News,* 21 June 1995, sec. A, p. 25; Helen Lenskyj, "Sexuality and Femininity in Sport Contexts: Issues and Alternatives," *Journal of Sport and Social Issues* 18 (November 1994): 356–76.

27. Alan Klein, *Little Big Men: Bodybuilding Subculture and Gender Construction* (Albany, N.Y.: State University of New York Press, 1993).

28. Nelson, *Are We Winning Yet?,* 211; see also Nelson, *The Stronger Women Get, The More Men Love Football;* Susan Birrell and Nancy Theberge, "Feminist Resistance and Transformation in Sport," in *Women and Sport: Interdisciplinary Perspectives,* 361–76.

29. Dudley A. Sargent, "Are Athletics Making Girls Masculine?" *Ladies Home Journal* 29 (1912): 72. For a good discussion of how the same ideas were being promulgated in Canada, see Helen Lenskyj, "Common Sense and Physiology: North American Medical Views on Women and Sport, 1890–1930," *Canadian Journal of History of Sport* 21 (May 1990): 49–64.

30. Frederick R. Rogers, "Olympics for Girls," *School and Society* 30 (10 August 1929): 191.

31. Agnes Wayman quoted in Marjorie S. Loggia, "On the Playing Fields of History," *Ms.,* July 1973, 64.

32. Ethel Perrin, "A Crisis in Girls Athletics," *Sportsmanship* 1 (December 1928): 10–12; see also Lenskyj, "Common Sense and Physiology: North American Medical Views of Women and Sport, 1890–1930."

33. Arthur J. Pearl, ed., *The Athletic Female* (Champaign, Ill.: Human Kinetics Publishers, 1993); Christine L. Wells, *Women, Sport, & Performance,* 2d ed. (Champaign, Ill.: Human Kinetics Publishers, 1991); Jacqueline L. Puhl and C. Harmon Brown, eds., *The Menstrual Cycle and Physical Activity* (Champaign, Ill.: Human Kinetics Publishers, 1986).

34. Stuart Miller, "Playing With the Big Boys," *Women's Sports & Fitness* (April 1995): 72–79, 95.

35. Simone de Beauvoir, *The Second Sex* (New York: Bantam Books, 1952), 311; for an analysis of the ideological role that female sports performance has played in reinforcing the common-sense assumption that "women are different and inferior," see Paul Willis, "Women in Sport in Ideology, in *Women, Sport, Culture,* ed. Susan Birrell and Cheryl L. Cole (Champaign, Ill.: Human Kinetics Publishers, 1994), 31–45.

36. *Rocky Mountain News,* 14 June 1975, p. 148.

37. *1995–96 National Federation Handbook* (Kansas City, Mo.: National Federation of State High School Associations, 1995).

38. Richard Obert, "You Just Can't Pin Her Down," *The Arizona Republic,* 12 February 1993, sec. A, pp. 1, 16; see also "Lupton Girls Banned From Meet," *The Greeley Tribune,* 11 December 1994, p. 3.

39. Joan S. Hult, "The Philosophical Conflicts in Men's and Women's Collegiate Athletics," in *Sport in America: From Wicked Amusement to National Obsession,* ed. David K. Wiggins (Champaign, Ill.: Human Kinetics Publishers, 1995), 301–17; see also Swanson and Spears, *History of Sport and Physical Education in the United States.*

40. Ibid.

41. *NCAA Directory, 1995–96* (Overland Park, Kans.: National Collegiate Athletic Association, 1995).

42. Rachel Zuk, "On the Ball and Off the Wall," *The Women's Sports Experience* (Newsletter of Women's Sport Foundation) (July/August 1994), 6.

43. Quoted in Debbie Becker, "Women Fare Better Come Diploma Time," *USA Today,* 20 June 1991, sec. C, p. 1; see also Mark Coomes, "Women's Basketball Suffers Growing Pains," *USA Today,* 20 June 1991, sec. C, p. 8.

44. Leigh Montville, "Ringer From Down Under," *Sports Illustrated,* 12 June 1995, 76.

45. Elaine Blinde, "Unequal Exchange and Exploitation in College Sport: The Case of the Female Athlete," in *Women, Sport, and Culture,* ed. Susan Birrell and Cheryl L. Cole (Champaign, Ill.: Human Kinetics Publishers, 1994), 135–48.

46. Quoted in Debbie Becker, "Title IX Has Lost Its Clout on Campuses," *USA Today,* 16 September 1986, sec. C, p. 2; see also Peter Brewington, "Women Fight to Keep Door From Closing," *USA Today,* 4 February 1988, sec. C, pp. 1–2.

47. Craig Neff, "Equality at Last, Part II," *Sports Illustrated,* 21 March 1988, 70–71; "Discrimination Complaints in Athletics Foreseen," *NCAA News,* 6 April 1988, pp. 4–5.

48. "Survey Shows Progress With Gender Equity," *NCAA News* 29, 11 March 1992, pp. 1, 20–21; Douglas Lederman, "Men Outnumber Women and Get Most of Money in Big-Time Sports Programs," *Chronicle of Higher Education,* 8 April 1992, sec. A, pp. 36–40; see also Alexander Wolff, "The Slow Track," *Sports Illustrated,* 28 September 1992, 52–66.

49. Quoted in Debra E. Blum, "Slow Progress on Equity," *Chronicle of Higher Education,* 26 October 1994, sec. A, pp. 45, 47; see also Laurie Tarkan, "Unequal Opportunity," *Women's Sports & Fitness,* September 1995, 25–27.

50. Steve Porter, "High Court Keeps Softball Safe at CSU," *The Coloradoan,* 30 November 1993, sec. A, pp. 1, 6; Debra E. Blum, "Judge Tells Colorado State to Reinstate Women's Softball," *Chronicle of Higher Education,* 3 March 1993, sec. A, p. 40; Debra E. Blum, "Big Step for Sex Equity," *Chronicle of Higher Education,* 27 October 1993, sec. A, p. 35.

51. Debra E. Blum, "Brown Loses Bias Case," *Chronicle of Higher Education,* 7 April 1995, sec. A, pp. 37–38.

52. Debra E. Blum, "Men Turn to Federal Anti-Trust Laws to Protect Teams From Chopping Block," *Chronicle of Higher Education,* 11 August 1993, sec. A, p. 33–34; Jack McCallum, "Squeeze Play," *Sports Illustrated,* 15 November 1993, 15; Mike Zapler, "Protecting Men's Sports," *Chronicle of Higher Education,* 6 January 1995, sec. A, pp. 43–44.

53. Peter L. Shaw, "Achieving Title IX Gender Equity in College Athletics in an Era of Fiscal Austerity," *Journal of Sport and Social Issues* 19 (February 1995), 6–27; Alexander Wolff and Richard O'Brien, "The Third Sex," *Sports Illustrated*, 6 February 1995, 15.

54. Ellen J. Staurowsky, "Examining the Roots of a Gendered Division of Labor in Intercollegiate Athletics: Insights Into the Gender Equity Debate," *Journal of Sport and Social Issues* 19 (February 1995), 28–44.

55. R. Vivian Acosta and Linda J. Carpenter, "Women in Intercollegiate Sport: A Longitudinal Study-Seventeen Years Update 1977–1994," (New York: Department of Physical Education, Brooklyn College, 1994); see also Donna L. Pastore, "The Status of Female Coaches in Two-Year Colleges," *Journal of Physical Education, Recreation, and Dance,* 62 (February 1991): 22–26.

56. Ibid.; Phil Taylor, "No Skirting This Issue," *Sports Illustrated,* 12 April 1993, 102.

57. Ibid., 11–13; Jill Yesko, "All in the Family," *Women's Sports & Fitness,* April 1995, 27.

58. Mike Dodd, "Survey Points to Disparity in Boardrooms," *USA Today,* 10 November 1994, sec. C, p. 14.

59. Ann Hall et al., *Sport in Canadian Society* (Toronto: McClelland & Stewart, 1991), 169–71.

60. Cynthia A. Hasbrook et al., "Sex Bias and the Validity of Believed Differences Between Male and Female Interscholastic Athletic Coaches," *Research Quarterly for Exercise and Sport* 61 (September 1990): 259–67.

61 . "Women's Athletic Survey Published," *NCAA News,* 12 June 1991, pp. 1–2; see also Jane M. Stangl and Mary Jo Kane, "Structural Variables That Offer Explanatory Power for the Underrepresentation of Women Coaches Since Title IX: The Case of Homologous Reproduction," *Sociology of Sport Journal* 8 (March 1991): 47–60.

62. Gai I. Berlage, *Women in Baseball: The Forgotten History* (Westport, Conn.: Praeger, 1994); see also Karen H. Weiller and Catriona T. Higgs, "The All American Girls Professional Baseball League, 1943–1954: Gender Conflict in Sport?" *Sociology of Sport Journal* 11 (September 1994), 289–97; Susan Johnson, *When Women Played Hardball* (Seattle: Seal Press, 1994); Lois Browne, *Girls of Summer: In Their Own League* (New York: Harper Collins, 1992). Stuart Miller, "Playing With the Big Boys," *Women's Sports & Fitness,* April 1995, 72–77, 95.

63. Preston Lerner, "Sand Blasting," *Women's Sports & Fitness,* July/August 1995, 62–65.

64. Tony Jackson, "Hard Work Pays Big As Lobo Makes USA Women's Team," *Rocky Mountain News* 26 May 1995, sec. B, p. 8; see also Karen L. Hill, "Women in Sport: Backlash or Megatrend?" *Journal of Physical Education, Recreation, and Dance* 64 (November–December 1993): 49–52; Richard Obert, "A Race for the Money," *The Arizona Republic,* 2 February 1996, p. 9.

65. Lars Anderson, "I Know I'm Qualified," *Sports Illustrated,* 1 May 1995, 10; William F. Reed, "Stalled at the Gate," *Sports Illustrated,* 24 September 1990; "Goodbye to a Pioneer," *Sports Illustrated,* 1 January 1990, 24.

66. Messner, *Power at Play: Sports and the Problem of Masculinity;* Michael A. Messner and Donald F. Sabo, eds., "Sex, Violence & Power in Sports: Rethinking Masculinity* (Freedom, Calif.: The Crossing Press, 1994); J. A. Mangan and James Walvin, eds., *Manliness and Morality* (New York: St. Martin's Press, 1987).

67. Messner, *Power at Play: Sports and the Problem of Masculinity,* 34.

68. Greg Louganis, *Breaking the Surface* (New York: Random House, 1995); see also Brian Pronger, *The Arena of Masculinity: Sports, Homosexuality, and the Meaning of Sex* (New York: St. Martin's Press, 1990); Don Sabo, "The Politics of Homophobia in Sport," in *Sex, Violence & Power in Sports: Rethinking Masculinity,* 101–12; Mike Messner, "Gay Athletes and the Gay Games: An interview With Tom Waddell," in *Sex, Violence & Power in Sports: Rethinking Masculinity,* Michael A. Messner and Donald F. Sabo, eds., 113–19.

69. Wilstein, "Sports Poised to End Taboo on Open Gays," sec. A, p. 25.

Chapter 15

Contemporary Trends and the Future of Sport in North America

"We live in a changing society" is an often-heard cliché. It is voguish to depict contemporary society as dynamic and progressive, the pace of life as fast, growth and change as the only constants, and an accelerating rate of change as likely to inflict "future shock" on many of us. These ideas are buttressed by an apparent obsession with the future. Business leaders look for predictions about population trends and shifts in consumer preferences; young adults seek information about trends in occupations in hopes that the career for which they prepare will be a gateway to opportunity rather than a dead-end street; and even video games have a definite futuristic orientation, as much of the simulated action takes place in outer space. Several of the most popular books of the past few years have been futuristic: *The Age of Paradox; The World in 2020: Power, Culture and Prosperity; Visions for the 21st Century;* and *Future Tense: The Business Realities of the Next Ten Years.*[1]

Meanwhile groups of social forecasters, societal scientists who are actively involved in forecasting societal activity, have also been busy with futuristic studies under the auspices of private foundations and government agencies. Some of the most well known are the Commission on the Year 2000, Forecasting International, the Hudson Institute, and the Institute for Futures Forecasting. The World Future Society is a thriving organization of 32,000 members that sponsors regular conventions throughout the world. Finally, the publication of at least five periodicals on futurism (e.g., *The Futurist* and *Omni*) indicates that people like to read speculation about the twenty-first century.

Notwithstanding the cliché, change in North America is a ubiquitous fact. Today's social and physical environments are vastly different from those of only a generation ago, to say nothing of those of three or four generations ago. The changes over the past three decades have been in direction as well as in rate, and the total amount of change has been so vast and thorough that it can only be conceptualized as a social and cultural revolution. Therefore, we conclude this volume with a chapter that examines the trends and the future of sport in North America, for as we have frequently argued, sport reflects society, and as the society changes, sport will also undoubtedly undergo some transformations.

Trends in Population Growth

One of the most significant trends in North America is the changing nature of its population—total numbers, composition, and location. Futurists are much concerned about population trends. Although improved birth control measures and a vague social commitment to zero population growth has partially controlled the numbers of newborns, a continued increase has occurred as the "baby boom" generation reached adulthood and began producing families of its own. Indeed, during the 1980s, the U.S. population grew by 22.2 million, an increase of 9.8 percent. Estimates are that by the year 2000 the population of the United States will increase from 262 million in 1996 to around 326 million by 2020. Canadian population, presently 27 million, is expected to increase to 32 million by 2025.[2]

Population Composition

During most of the twentieth century North America has had a young population because the birthrate has remained high for an increasing number of people of childbearing age. This condition is now changing rapidly because the long-term trends for birthrates and death rates are expected to decline. Thus, the proportion of young people will diminish, and the proportion of older people will increase, markedly affecting population composition. The average age in the United States will rise dramatically from 33 in 1996 to about 44 in 2050. By 2010, one-quarter of the U.S. population will be at least 55, and one in seven Americans will be at least 65. Even more dramatic will be the average life expectancy, which will climb from the current 76.3 to an estimated 82.6 years of age by 2050. Persons aged 65 and older currently make up 11 percent of Canada's population; that will rise to between 20 and 25 percent in 2025. Not only will there be many more older persons, but they will be healthier and more active than ever before.[3]

Both the United States and Canada have long been havens for immigrants, but the nationalities of those who have come to these two countries have changed with the political and economic winds. Political oppression or economic hardship was the incentive for millions of people to migrate, legally or illegally. Due to both immigration and high birth rates, the Hispanic population in the United States grew from 14.6 million in 1980 to 24 million in 1996, about 50 percent in sixteen years. At the anticipated rate of growth, Hispanics will be the largest ethnic minority by 2010, surpassing African Americans. Even more remarkable, while the United States as a whole grew 9.8 percent, growth in the Asian population from 1980 to 1992 was 108 percent, mostly due to immigration.

By 2050 the U.S. population will be almost evenly divided between non-Hispanic whites and minorities. This rapidly changing ethnic and racial complexion in North America will alter everything in society, from politics and education to industry, values, and culture.

In an effort to preserve its essentially loyal British character, immigration from countries outside Europe was severely curtailed in Canada right up until the reforms of the Trudeau administration in the 1960s. Consequently, prior to the 1960s, 80 percent of all immigrants came from Europe. In the past two decades, 70 percent of immigrants to Canada have been Asian or "nontraditional" (mostly Africans and Latin Americans).[4]

Location of Population

North Americans continue to gravitate toward large metropolitan areas, with about 80 percent of Americans living in central cities and their surrounding suburbs, and the majority of Canadians living within 100 miles of the U.S.-Canadian border are urbanites. Over the next quarter century Americans will probably continue to congregate in at least three gargantuan population centers, or megalopolises, that futurists have labeled "Boswash," "Chipits," and "Sansan." Boswash will extend between Boston and Washington, D.C., Chicago and Pittsburgh will be the centers for Chipitts, and Sansan will stretch from San Francisco to San Diego. These megalopolises appear likely to contain about one-half of the total United States population, including the majority of the most technologically and scientifically advanced, prosperous, intellectual, and creative elements. The growth of these giant centers of population will be accompanied by the continuing trend toward new regional centers, such as Charlotte, North Carolina; Nashville, Tennessee; and

Denver, Colorado, resulting in an urban population of between 80 and 90 percent of the total population within the next two decades.

In the United States the migration from the Northeast and Midwest into states in the South and West has been the most pronounced demographic shift in the past two decades. The surge of newcomers helped the population of the South jump by 20 percent and of the West by 26 percent between 1980 and 1996; indeed, the Sun Belt has absorbed virtually all the U.S. population growth since 1975, and the trend is expected to continue. The West and South are projected to be the fastest growing regions in the United States, and the two regions combined are projected to account for 82 percent of the 68 million persons added to the nation's population between the mid-1990s and 2020.[5] In Canada, population in the Atlantic provinces is slipping significantly, and the big gains have been in Alberta and British Columbia. Ontario and Quebec have substantially more than half the country's population (62 percent), and they will still have a majority in the year 2000, but the winds from the West are rising.

Population Trends and Sport

The giant metropolitan areas, stretching out over hundreds of miles and engulfing many small communities as well as large cities, may very well require the reorganization of professional sports organizations on some feature other than a city name. Indeed, professional sports managements are already preparing for a future in which state and regional considerations will take precedence over city loyalties. Within the past few years the names of professional team sport franchises demonstrate that the leagues and owners are aware of the outmoded practice of single-city affiliation. Most of the newer franchises have adopted state or regionalistic team names: the California Angels, Minnesota Twins, Texas Rangers, Florida Marlins, and Colorado Rockies in major league baseball; the New England Patriots, Arizona Cardinals, and Carolina Cougars of the NFL; the Golden State Warriors, New Jersey Nets, and the Indiana Pacers of the NBA; and The New Jersey Devils, Florida Panthers, and Colorado Avalanche of the NHL.

Professional sport has been one of the most financially successful and growing industries during the past twenty years, riding the crest of a huge population of young people. Consumer-spectator interest appears to have no limit. New franchises spring up all over North America to be greeted by sell-out crowds. Expansion has continued throughout the 1990s. Major league baseball expanded by two teams in 1992, the National Hockey League added three new franchises in the same year, the NFL and NBA expanded by two teams in 1995, and a ten-team World League of American Football began in the spring of 1991 with teams in the United States and Europe. Although it folded in 1993, it began again in 1995 with six teams, all based in Europe. The future trajectory seems quite clear: Professional sports will become another global industry in the next two decades. The NFL, NBA, MLB, and NHL will all have franchises in Europe and Asia.[6]

The owners of professional soccer teams anticipate that the World Cup, held in the United States in 1994, will greatly stimulate the growing popularity of soccer at the amateur level, ultimately justifying expansion. In addition, a number of sports are gaining a professional foothold (e.g., cycling, triathlon, racquetball, distance running, etc.) and may challenge the more established sports for fans. Within twenty years the total number of professional sports could double.

The rising costs of attending a sporting event over the next two decades may prove significant. Figures compiled by various sources have begun to show that rapidly escalating ticket prices of five and six times the cost of living at a time when real income has increased very little for the average fan means, if this trend continues, that the cost of a family outing to a sports event in the late 1990s could be hefty enough to threaten the base of fan support. A family outing to professional sporting events has jumped 167 percent, while consumer prices have risen just 64 percent.

Some of the biggest sports stories of the past few years have been about older athletes: Nolan Ryan pitching a no-hitter at age 44, George Foreman fighting for the world's heavyweight boxing championship at age 42, and tennis pro Jimmy Conners capturing the hearts of sports fans throughout the nation by winning his way to the semifinals at the 1991 U.S. Open at the age of 39. The senior tours of the Professional Golfers Association and the Professional Tennis Association illustrate quite well that older athletes can perform at high levels, and that sports fans will pay to see them compete in their sport.

There is little doubt that people are remaining physically active later in their lives, and more and more sports programs are being created to allow the aging population to participate. Within the past decade the Masters Sports Tournaments and Senior Olympics have become major forces in organizing competitive sports for the elderly. These are only the most visible programs. Retirement communities are typically built to encourage the sport interests of their citizens. Many community recreation departments have expanded their programs to include senior leagues in several sports; indeed, in some communities these leagues are the fastest growing. In all likelihood, participant sports will be a major growth industry wherever large groups of older persons settle.[7]

The change toward greater opportunity for minority groups in sports is one of the most salient trends at the present and will, if futurists' predictions are correct, continue in the coming years. One of the main reasons to expect that minorities will secure increasing access and opportunities is, as we described previously, that their percentage of the population is increasing dramatically. There is no question that organized sports, from youth programs to the professional level, have made great strides toward equalizing opportunities in the past decade, but the goal has not yet been achieved. In chapters 13 and 14 we demonstrated that overt discrimination against African Americans and females, such as denying them access to sports, has been gradually eliminated, but that inequalities and injustices continue in subtler forms. Even these are giving way, however, as more and more African Americans and females achieve positions of prestige, power, and leadership within sport.

In general, minorities are underrepresented in many of the most popular high school, college, and professional sports, but each year new inroads are made into more and more sports. They are taking their rightful place among teammates, and they hold coaching and management positions in a number of sports programs. The future for minorities in North American sports appears to be quite promising.

Trends in Industry and Technology and Sporting Activities

For the vast majority of people, involvement in sport is closely tied to their work. Whether they are participating in sport themselves or watching others perform, the extent to which they can do either depends upon the nonwork time (so-called free time) available to them. In brief, the less time they must work, the more free time they have available for sporting activities; thus, trends in the work life of people will be instrumental in trends that take place in sport.

Industrialization and technology changed not only the way that goods are produced but also the conditions under which they are produced. At first, factories brought workers into sweatshops to toil literally from sunrise to sunset. Later, as steel and other large industries grew, workers were attracted to the plants by the prospect of steady work and a livable wage. Hours were long, but until the emergence of labor unions, workers could do little about that if they wished to remain employed. However, beginning in the early twentieth century, a gradual reduction in the average workweek began for nonagricultural workers from about sixty-five hours to just under forty hours.

Accompanying and supporting industrial trends over the past century have been remarkable technological innovations and the growth of large corporate organizations. Combined, these forces form the most salient feature of North American institutional life, and their effects are manifested in the contours of occupational life. During the past 100 years the proportion of American workers involved in agriculture and manufacturing declined from 83 percent to less than 30 percent, while service occupations have enormously expanded. Some futurists predict that the proportion of the work force employed in manufacturing will fall to about 3 percent in the next fifty years.[8]

An Information/Service North American Society

The ways in which the economy is being transformed and the occupational system reworked suggest that North Americans have entered what is called an "information-based" society, or an information-producing service economy, rather than a goods-producing manufacturing economy.

Futurists predict that computers and other technological innovations will change the nature of work and the balance between jobs and personal lives. In the next ten years, four out of five people will be doing jobs differently from the way they have been done in the last thirty years. Computer networking will be one reason for this trend. We will, in essence, become a computer-connected society, as computer networking enables work to be done anywhere, at any time, at any distance from the office or factory.[9]

Robotics and computer integrated manufacturing will create entirely new industries, employing millions of people in jobs that don't exist today. The use of robots in the United States has been growing by 30 percent per year in the past decade, and it has been estimated that by the late-1990s fifty thousand robots will be installed in the United States and that applications will skyrocket between 1996 and 2010.

Careers in information services are well under way. Some 55 percent of North American workers are currently in information industries. More people are involved in information and communication occupations than in mining, agriculture, manufacturing, and personal services combined; by the year 2010, over three-fourths of the work force will be information workers.[10]

Technological developments have brought about, on an ever-increasing scale, giant organizations, the depersonalization of social relationships, and the eclipse of personalized community. Although most North Americans would not wish to give up many of the products of technological creations—television, central heating, air conditioning, automobiles, and so forth—there are, nevertheless, many people who find that the technocratic/bureaucratic society is dehumanizing. There has been a growing hostility to many forms of technological innovation and bureaucratic organization, and a wide range of spontaneous, activist, and democratic actions in an effort to recapture some sense of control over daily activities.[11]

table 15.1 *Annual Hours of Paid Employment, Labor Force Participants*[a]

	1969	1987	Change 1969–87
All Participants	1,786	1,949	163
Men	2,054	2,152	98
Women	1,406	1,711	305

[a]Includes only fully employed labor force participants.

Source: Juliet B. Schor, *The Overworked American: The Unexpected Decline of Leisure* (New York: Basic Books, 1991), 29.

The Information/Service Workplace and Sporting Activities

One promise made by industry and technology, at least covertly if not overtly, has been that modernization and technological advances will ultimately free the ties that bind workers to their jobs. Accompanying this promise has been the prediction that there will be a great flowering of leisure-time activities for the common person. Despite the promises about the diminishing workweek, the "flowering of leisure" has not yet materialized, and some people question whether it will occur in the near future.

To a great extent, the prediction of a "leisure society" is based on a misperception of the amount of leisure time available at present. The work-nonwork cycle created by modernizing the work place has been altered over the past century so that there now appears to be more time away from work, but U.S. workers work about one hundred sixty hours longer annually than they did in 1969 (see table 15.1). Seven million workers hold multiple jobs (moonlight) to make ends meet.[12] A poll by *USA Today*/CNN/Gallup found that more than half of adults say they have less free time than a few years ago, and over 40 percent believe they work longer hours than their parents did at the same age.[13]

Four-Day and Flextime Workweeks and Free Time

Many private and public organizations have experimented with four-day and flextime workweek schedules. The number of firms using flexible work hours has more than doubled in the past twenty years. These take different forms such as satellite work centers, customized work schedules, staggered shifts, and telecommuting with personal computers to the place of work. By 2010 over half the work force could be on flextime.

These work schemes have been hailed as important steps toward creating a leisure society. However, in all four-day and flextime schemes tried so far the workweek remains near forty hours, so this trend has little to do with a reduction in working time; it is merely a rescheduling of the workload. It fails to even touch upon the more important issue of the desirability of a reduction in the overall length of the workweek.

Although the hours of the workweek remain about the same under the various nontraditional plans, several potential benefits accrue with respect to leisure time. The extra-long weekends make travel and other extended leisure activities possible, and commuting time may be reduced, some of which might be used for leisure activities. On the other hand, the extra time afforded by the four-day workweek may be a mixed blessing. For example, many people use the time working at a second job because continuing inflation tends to require more money to maintain the current living standard. Increases in free time, then, are often used primarily as an opportunity to perform extra work of some kind. It appears that the emergence of a true leisure society will require a respiritualization of our society and the rise of a fundamentally different valuation of work and leisure.[14]

Ignoring for the moment that the greater amount of free time that technology was supposed to have provided has not materialized, how then can we account for participation rates in leisure activities and expenditure on leisure pursuits being at an all-time high? Leisure accounts for about one in every eight dollars spent by North American consumers. Explanations for the leisure pursuits of North Americans tend to converge on the idea that people are just cramming more activities into each twenty-four hours. The tendency to do several things simultaneously and many things in a short period of time has been called "time deepening." It has also been called "the more, the more"—meaning that under the pressure of expanding interests and motivations, the more people do, the more they wish to do, and vice versa. The consequence is that many people suffer from "leisure-time stress." Despite feeling "free" during their free time, many people worry about leisure and hurry from one activity to another, leaving little time to stop and think. Moreover, obsessive consumer attitudes about leisure time do not allow personal initiative and doing one's own thing.[15]

A Future Society and Sport

The twenty-first century society is expected to become increasingly more of a "learning society." In part, this will be a function of the "information explosion"; thus, information (its acquisition and use) will become extremely important. A major problem will be the adequate supply of educated persons with professional and technical competence, therefore futurists expect education, especially college and graduate education, to be acquired by a much greater proportion of the population than at present.[16]

What are the implications for sport of a "cerebral" population? Two diametrically opposed predictions have been proposed. The first suggests that there will be a trend away from violent forms of sport with a greater emphasis upon "intellectual" sports; the other suggests that violent sports will increase.

Intellectual Sports of the Future

Some futurists propose that as we become more cerebral, our choices will tend away from such violent sports as football, hockey, boxing, and auto racing. In addition, greater attention may be paid to the technical competence of the performers rather than just the outcome of the contest.

Perhaps one indication that intellectual or cerebral activities are gaining in popularity is that the latest forms of indoor recreation for young people are "smart" board games and computer games in which the players are expected to outwit or to outthink each other, or, in the case of the latter, beat the computer program. Such games pose daunting intellectual challenges requiring detailed strategy, role-playing, and simulations, and these appeal to an increasing number of people.

The best of the computer-driven video games are called "simulations" because of their capability to re-create the strategic requirements and sensuous experiences of the real sports. About one-fourth of the products sold by video game companies are simulated sports games. Players of simulations games say that "your muscles tighten, your pulse quickens, you feel you're actually in the game." Even more realistic simulation sports games will be developed in the future. As one Microsoft program manager said, "The goal is true-to-life experience."[17]

Fantasy sport leagues have emerged as an extremely popular form of "intellectual" sport, especially among young men. This form of sport involvement enables a "player" to get involved in selecting a team of athletes from a league, such as the NFL, to compete in a fantasy league. After each of the games played by the "real" players, the members of the fantasy league compile the statistics for each of the athletes the members of the fantasy league players have drafted. Those statistics determine how each of the fantasy league "players" have "performed." All of this involves accumulating an extensive knowledge about athletes in "real" leagues, creatively thinking about their use, and out-smarting the others in the fantasy league.

Violent Sports of the Future

Violence continues as a prominent part of both our real world and our fantasy world. High homicide rates plague our cities and even small towns; indeed, it is dangerous to be on the streets in some urban areas after dark. Some of the most popular television programs and movies feature gratuitous violence, and the high tech violence of TV and movies may foretell of future violent societies.

Given the broad societal violence, the possibility of continued or even increased violence in sports certainly exists. As we noted in chapter 7, there are those who believe, as psychologist William James once said, that "sports are the moral equivalent of war." Others have argued that sport provides a cathartic discharge of aggressive urge, and, therefore, violence done under the auspices of sports keeps the cap on social violence. Still others propose that the meaning of sport may be in the "quest for excitement in an unexciting society," and vigorous and violent sport may serve to restore tension and excitement.[18]

The popularity of football, hockey, boxing, and auto racing validates the public interest in violent sports. The public image of these sports projected through radio and television commercials promotes the idea of violence. For example, the National Hockey League has consistently marketed its games through television commercials as violent, almost promising fans that they can expect to see lots of fighting. The opening commercial for Monday Night Football shows a helmet of each of the competing teams for that night; the helmets turn to face each other and smash together, with fragments of each flying away. The message of the imagery is clear: The viewer can expect to see some violent collisions.

Several years ago, in a frightening book entitled *Blood & Guts,* the author summarized the state of modern sport, and made a sobering prediction about the future:

> Against [a] background of rising social violence, the level of violence in sport has also increased dramatically until it has now, in many instances, reached Roman proportions. Under the dictates of our exploitive age we have turned great areas of play into theaters of blood, attracting an audience which is even more Roman than the Romans. Our sportsmen no longer purposely strive to slaughter each other, but we often attend in the hope that they will. We do not callously use "subhuman" slaves to entertain us with their blood, but we distance ourselves from our own gladiators through television so that they are deemed expendable, something less than human. We do not force athletes into blood sports against their will, but we have made the rewards so enticing that there are now any number of participants willing to risk their limbs and their lives for our benefit. Whether press-ganged or paid, they provide the same end result: violence and bloodshed for the delectation of others. Our sporting entertainments give the lie to the popular belief that blood spectacles are the sole prerogative of civilizations that are losing their grip.

> We the sophisticates of the modern age have become super connoisseurs of sporting violence. The future of violent sports seems assured. Games will grow harder and bloodier to feed the rising appetite of an audience which will grow both increasingly more jaded and sated with violence, and increasingly more violent itself.[19]

Nothing has happened in the years since that book was written to suggest that the author was misguided with his observations and predictions.

Uses of Technology in Sport

The world of sports has made tremendous use of technology, and much in current sport is the product of technological innovation. The type of sport that emerges from technological advances has sometimes been called technosport.

Technosport and the Future

A *Sports Illustrated* writer has correctly described the linkage between sport and technology: "Technology has always altered the way sports are played and observed. Scientific advances have been applied to sports equipment and techniques: protective gear, the composition of tennis rackets and golf clubs, high-tech training methods to increase leg strength and foot speed."[20]

To a great extent, the emergence of superior athletic performance is a consequence of a pool of specialized experts who are knowledgeable about the newest biotechnologies. These are sport scientists—biomechanists, exercise physiologists, biochemists, nutritionists, orthopedists—whose expertise is being widely used by trainers and coaches. One of the areas in which sports scientists have been involved is in attempting to select potentially superior athletes more deliberately and rationally. In recent years, biochemical, biomechanical, and behavioral sciences have been used with young children in an effort to sort out the potential future champions from the average athlete.

We may expect that scientific selection of future athletes during their early childhood on the basis of their physical and psychological attributes will become commonplace. Once potential athletes have been identified, they will receive special training in preparation for their ultimate careers in sport. There are already programs of this type underway in North America in the form of elite youth clubs, and the successes in Olympic Games of some of the athletes from these programs are publicly attributed to the early selection procedures.

At perhaps the most futuristic extreme, sport-technologists might turn to "genetic engineering," that is, the breeding of superior athletes. Given moral as well as biotechnical problems, this possibility is not likely within the next generation or so. Nevertheless, one sport sociologist claims: "It is genetic engineering . . . that promises to bring about the most profound biological transformations of the human being, and it is likely that this technology will be used to develop athletes before it is applied to the creations of other kinds of human performers." [21]

Many of the record-breaking feats of the past few years can be attributed to advanced training techniques and better equipment and facilities, but a growing trend among athletes and their coaches is to resort to various chemical substances in order to enhance sports performance. As performance standards increase in every sport, substance abuse will probably escalate. It is likely that new biotechnology will enable biochemists to perfect substances that will increase athletes' chances of winning and will be undetectable in the fluids of the body. In spite of increased sophistication in drug-testing procedures, some new drugs are undetectable before or after competition. Futurists expect that the development of new substances might enable a runner, for example, to shave seven- or eight-tenths of a second off his or her 100-meter dash or a javelin thrower to gain an extra seven or eight feet on his or her throw.[22]

Technosport will be evident in the playing arenas of the future. The domed stadiums built during the past twenty years are miniature prototypes of the giant arenas on the drawing boards. The new edifices will be equipped with many spectacular accouterments, including push-button vending machines and individual television consoles for instant replays at each seat. Seats will be equipped with earphones so that spectators can listen to press-box scouts giving advice to the bench, to conversations at the pitching mounds, to quarterbacks' calls in the huddle, and even to locker-room pep talks.

The Rose Garden built in Portland, Oregon in 1995 provides a glimpse of the future sports facilities. Its luxury suites are equipped with teleconferencing gear capable of displaying channels full of computer-generated sports statistics. The concourses are draped with blazing video screens, and eventually tiny TV monitors will be located at every seat.[23]

Computers will be the central objects because future society will be an information-based society. Computers will be a staple for technosport, just as they will be for technoindustry. Coaches and athletes will be able to receive instant information about their own teams and their opponents. Professional football teams have used computers for several years for the selection of athletes and as an aid in scouting opponents, and such computer use will proliferate. In football a few college and professional teams have experimented with computers to print out tables about opponents' tendencies and to help coaches and athletes make decisions during the game. This trend will undoubtedly accelerate during the next decade, perhaps to the point where each play in football will be called on the basis of printouts, and baseball coaches will use computers to call each pitch and each infield shift.

The fascination with enhanced sports performances and the obsession with winning has meant that technological innovations have been eagerly sought and employed in sports. However, thoughtful people within and outside the sports world are raising important questions such as: Just because science and technology makes it possible for athletes and teams to set new speed, distance, and weight records, should they? Are the higher risks to the life and limbs of athletes' worth using whatever is scientifically and technologically possible?

Many times people simply accept the idea that if it can be done, it should be done; the question of whether something should be done is seldom asked. There are compelling reasons for why that question, and others like it, will be increasingly asked and with good reason. For example, there is no doubt that one of the consequences of employing the latest technological innovations is that various injuries and illnesses are increasing for athletes. Their incidence and seriousness are rising in many sports at the elite levels.[24]

Scientific and technical terminology when used in sport often conceives of athletes as objects, little different than inanimate machines. Indeed, the terms "human machine" or "mortal engine" have been favorite metaphors for athletes' bodies among sport technicians. However, the human-as-machine notion has inherent dangers. Humans are not machines, and acting as if they were can be a source of major problems. After all, when a machine ceases to function properly, or quits working altogether, it can be discarded or scraped. Humans are their body, and they have only one body, and it must last a lifetime; if it is damaged or parts of it destroyed, the quality of life is irreparably damaged.

There is another dimension to questioning the unqualified acceptance of scientific and technical developments in the interest of enhanced performances and sporting victories. The scientific-technical ethos gives priority to the product—the outcome; but the aspect of sport that has always been its prevailing essence is its process—its fun, its spontaneity, its creativeness, its expressiveness. Scientizing and technocizing sport subverts what has always been sport's most endearing features.

It is likely that over the next twenty years a major debate will center around the questions that have been raised here about the scientific-technical directions of sport. The dominate view that prevails in the sports world is not guaranteed. Resistance, opposition, even rejection, of that dominant view has already begun, and will probably continue in some form for the foreseeable future.

A Counterpoint to Technosports: Ecosports

Ecosports involves natural play and unstructured games; many of them are done out-of-doors, without boundaries, and without codified rules. Ecosports also includes a variety of what have been called "nontraditional" or "alternative" indoor physical activities. The various forms of ecosports tend to emphasize cooperation rather than competition, the struggle rather than the triumph; the main point of many of them is to play, to enjoy, to exist.

Ecosports and the Future

The outdoor form of the ecosport movement is well under way, manifested in activities such as hiking,

orienteering, rock climbing, scuba diving, rafting, sailing, hang gliding, skydiving, and Frisbee throwing. Late twentieth century society confronts us with a congested urban life-style. Houses are jammed tightly against each other, apartments are stacked story on story, offices and factories are made up of steel and concrete, and our jobs are forcing us to work among multitudes of our fellow human beings. Thus, many North Americans yearn for the out-of-doors, to be away from the crush of people. The mountains, oceans, lakes, rivers, and the sky all beckon.

In the past decade the number of North Americans participating in outdoor ecosport activities has grown dramatically. Cross-country skiers increased from a few thousand in 1980 to over 4 million in 1996. The number of hikers has more than doubled in the past ten years, and now some 22 million persons hike. At the national parks, backpacking increased by more than 100 percent between 1975 and 1995. The number of mountaineers has been doubling about every five years. High schools and colleges offer courses in scuba diving, sport parachuting, hang gliding, and many other nontraditional sport activities. As young people acquire knowledge and skills of these activities, there is a high likelihood that they will pursue them in their adult years.[25]

Nontraditional or "alternative" indoor ecosports includes several of the Oriental martial arts, such as aikido, karate, judo, and tai-kwon-do, as well as various forms of yoga. Most do not require elaborate equipment and organization; also competition is not important to their mastery (indeed, in aikido, competition is forbidden). Skilled movements in these activities are frequently like dances, and the performers achieve a transcendent beauty in the whirling, throwing, kicking, and jumping common to these activities.[26]

Most ecosports do not attract the publicity of the technosports, and most of them certainly do not attract masses of spectators. The essence of ecosport is participation, so the fanfare and hoopla associated with technosport are not missed. That is precisely what is attractive about these sports for many of the participants.

Some view these forms of sport as a reaction not only against the technocorporate form of organization characteristic of North American social institutions but

Non-traditional and alternative forms of ecosports will gain in popularity in the 21st century.

also against the organized and corporate levels of sport described in chapter 1, where the outcome supersedes the process. Ecosport has its affinities with informal sport, in which participating has top priority.

Ecosport has been a booming form of sport during the past decade. Will the momentum carry into the twenty-first century? Many social dynamics influence the popularity of sports, but most forecasters of sport in the twenty-first century are in agreement that this form of sport will increase in popularity.

The Future and Personal Fitness and Healthy Lifestyles

During the past twenty-five years personal physical fitness and healthy lifestyle changed from being almost inconsequential to most North Americans to being a

goal of recreational activities, employee health programs, and a focus of mass media advertising. However, despite the public perception, fostered by the mass media, of a fitness and health craze, it has become increasingly clear that only a small percentage of adults are doing most of the participating. Only 17 to 30 percent of the population exercises regularly (at least three times a week). Moreover, several large-scale surveys of adult exercise patterns indicate that the percentage of regular, frequent exercisers is remaining about the same. However, 70 percent of adults say they engage in a sport or physical exercise at least once a week.[27]

Many regular, as well as the not-so-regular, adults prefer to do their exercising outside the home. As a result, there are some twenty-five thousand fitness centers and health clubs in the United States with more than 3 million men and women as members. Adult exercisers favor machines and devices, with stair-climbers, step equipment, and treadmills the favorite pieces of equipment.

Runners and Walkers

Perhaps the most visible sign of the fitness and health quest is the runners and walkers who can be observed along the streets and in the parks of every community. An estimated 26 million runners, including a group of more than 7 million "hard-core" runners (they prefer not to be called joggers) who run at least 120 days a year and are sophisticated about training and equipment, constitute the largest single group of fitness and health enthusiasts. Long-distance races, which used to draw a small number of contestants, now attract hundreds, even thousands, of runners. In 1970 there were less than twenty-five marathons held annually; in 1996 there were over 250. Organized road races of less than marathon distance have increased from 4,100 in 1980 to over 20,000 in 1996.[28]

Walking has surpassed swimming in popularity and has become the number one fitness activity of the 1990s, according to the National Sporting Goods Association. The public has taken its cue from medical reports that suggest that walking is just as good as aerobic forms of exercise for general health benefits, and is actually less stressful to the joints and muscles. Given the population trends for the next fifty years, most forecasters expect that walking will greatly increase in popularity among older adults.[29]

One of the latest fitness/health crazes is the so-called "ultra" competitions, which test the limits of human endurance and pain tolerance, and make ordinary marathons seem like cakewalks: 50- and 100-mile road races, Iron Man Triathlons, long-distance bicycle races, and the like. These events have become so popular that officials sometimes have to limit the contestant field. The future of this form of exercise is uncertain; it is not a form that will attract large numbers because of the time and stressful nature of the training necessary to perform in these events.

Employee Fitness Programs

Accompanying and supporting the personal fitness/health movement are employee fitness programs.

Partly as an effort to attract and retain employees and partly to improve employee health and thus offset the staggering increase in costs of employee medical insurance, over 35 percent of North American companies with more than one hundred employees offer employees some kind of fitness/wellness/sport program. The Association for Fitness in Business is a rapidly growing professional association. This is evidence that this industry is flourishing.

Most employee fitness programs were originally designed to keep top-level executives physically fit, but many companies have begun to extend their programs to the rank-and-file employees. It is estimated that corporate fitness programs will become more common, with an annual 10 to 25 percent growth rate.

In the public sector Texas was on the forefront of providing fitness programs for its state employees. In the mid-1980s, the Texas Legislature passed the State Employee Health Fitness and Education Act, which enables Texas state agencies and educational institutions to finance health and fitness programs. This may become a prototype for other similar actions on behalf of public-sector employees.

During the past decade, public employees throughout North America have been pushing for fitness/health facilities at their work sites. There will undoubtedly be increasing pressures for public employers to provide such facilities, especially since there is mounting evidence that fitness/wellness programs are a key to containing health care costs. Private companies and public agencies that operate employee fitness/wellness programs see health care costs drop an average of $300 per person annually.

The U.S. Department of Health and Human Services has undertaken a Healthy People 2000 campaign, and one of its goals is that 80 percent of all large companies will provide fitness/wellness programs by the year 2000. The future of corporate fitness/wellness programs seems destined to expand.[30]

In Canada a national approach to physical activity has been adopted called "Active Living." It is a new way of thinking about the relationship between physical activity, fitness, health, leisure, and recreation. It draws together many professionals having ties to the fitness movement and focuses on a common goal: active living becoming an integral part of Canadian lifestyle—a Canadian cultural trademark.[31]

Trends in the Economy and Future Sports

The North American economic systems are complex mixtures of capitalism and socialism, and the free trade agreements between the United States, Canada, and Mexico tend to integrate the individual economies. Throughout the world during the twentieth century there has been steady movement away from laissez-faire (virtually unregulated) capitalism and toward managerial capitalism, with the adoption of many socialistic features, which has caused some observers to predict that capitalism will die in North America. This view is not shared by most futurists, however. Capitalism has proved extremely adaptable, and despite the growth in social entitlement programs and the growth in government over the past twenty years, there has been no fundamental challenge to the capitalist economy in North America.[32]

Given the enormous influence of the corporate rich and the tendency for most North Americans to accept the present economic structure as proper, capitalism will undoubtedly remain a pillar of society in the United States and Canada. At the same time, many people are expressing increasing dissatisfaction about the privilege and power concentrated among a select few under capitalism, and many North Americans believe that national priorities must be reordered to provide greater assistance to the average citizen as well as redirecting the economy toward community and the environment.[33]

The future economy, barring nuclear holocaust, unforeseen energy problems, or other catastrophic events, will probably continue to go through its cycles of prosperity, recession, and prosperity. According to economic forecasters, economic growth should average about 2.5 percent per year over the next two decades, the inflation rate should range between 3 and 6 percent, gain in personal income will be about 2 percent, and unemployment will average between 5 and 8.5 percent during this period. North America will face increasing international economic competition and will

be challenged to find better ways to accommodate the emerging global economy rather than trying to dominate international economic competitors.[34]

The Future of Professional Sports

The professional sports industry in North America has grown at an unprecedented rate in the past twenty years. It is now a sprawling, multibillion-dollar-a-year industry that is clearly big business, and in which winning and losing count far less than making a profit. Professional sport franchise owners once generally had a deep emotional commitment to the sport and believed that the administration and financial operations were merely necessary adjuncts to owning a team. Current owners are increasingly media conglomerates and think primarily of maximizing profit through rational business procedures. Providing sports entertainment for loyal hometown fans is only a secondary consideration. The most visible example of this is found in the numerous threats by ownership to move franchises if demands for new stadiums, better lease deals, and so forth are not met. They are not idle threats as can be seen in the number of franchise moves.[35]

As we indicated in an earlier section in this chapter, the unmistakable trend appears to be toward an expansion of professional sports in the foreseeable future. In a wide-ranging look at sport in the year 2001, a *Sports Illustrated* writer predicted that the NBA will be "the global game with 128 teams in 30 countries and . . . more popular than soccer ever was.[36] However, fan support depends on adequate disposable income. Should a prolonged economic downturn occur, people will have less disposable income, and this could adversely affect professional sports. Moreover, as noted earlier, if ticket prices outstrip cost of living, professional sports may price themselves out of the market.

The Future of Televised Sports

Television Viewing

Conditions will be just as hi-tech for the fans at home. One forecaster constructed a scenario in 2001 in which he has a Home Control Truck (HCT) in his living room that allows him to call up his own pictures, sound, and instant replays as network directors currently do. His HCT system includes a wall of sixteen small TV monitors, plus his own director's microphone, and a console to select whatever pictures and sounds he wants to appear on his central eight-foot, high-definition TV screen.[37]

Television Coverage

Before television rescued the professional sports industry, professional sports owners were beset with decreasing attendance and the prospect of failure. The importance of television and radio markets has been a prominent factor in the growth and expansion of all professional sports. Professional sport and television enjoy a reciprocal relationship. Both pro sport and television executives realize that if any of the professional sports lost television revenues, their industry would be devastated. Therefore, for professional sports to maintain their entertainment status and to continue to expand, they will have to depend on the benevolence of television. As long as the television networks consider pro sports a money-maker, pro sports will prosper. Should television executives decide that sports are not good business, the pro sport industry would have to drastically restructure.

What could cause such a change of interest on the part of the television networks? First, a declining interest in televised sports—a real possibility—could force such a change. Hours scheduled for network sports increased so dramatically from 1980 to 1996 that the prospect of television saturation looms. Whether saturation will occur is problematic, but if it does, there is little doubt that television will adapt to changing viewer interests, perhaps at the expense of the sport industry. Another possibility is that technosport and/or ecosport innovations will reduce television viewing. Finally, perhaps the indifference and callous way with which professional sport owners and players treat fans will destroy the fans' loyalty, and therefore, public interest in the games.

Television Technology and Sports Viewing

There is another scenario for televised sports. New trends in electronic technology promise to have a

dramatic economic impact on both sport and television. One trend seems clear, sports fans will have greater options in TV viewing in the future. The prospect of the 500-channel universe has many sports fans excited. The prospect that is the most exciting is interactive TV. One form of interactive innovation will give viewers the ability to be a part of sports events through virtual reality. According to one forecaster, "By 2005, it could be possible to put on a masked helmet and merge with the action. Football, among other games, would have a three-dimensional feel to it, and a viewer could see and hear everything the quarterback would see and hear."[38]

Forecasters of future TV sports also see sports fans having various other means of interacting with the coverage and with the game itself. One form of interacting will give viewers control over what aspect of the event they wish to watch. They will be able to call up certain cameras to focus on a single player or a part of the field or court, or they will be able to ask for statistics and personal background on the players. Another form of interactive TV will enable viewers to participate in the event at home, even calling certain plays and making substitutions.

As we noted in chapter 11, pay-per-view (PPV) television is going to become a major factor by 2005. There appears to be little doubt that within ten years sports fans will have to pay for many events they now see on free TV or basic cable. Some forecasters predict that as costs to attend sports events escalate and as television increasingly makes viewing of all important sports events available at low cost, attendance at sports facilities will dwindle.

Regardless of the trends in viewing options and interactivity, high-definition television will give sports viewers a much sharper view of the action than is currently possible. Those who have experienced high definition prototypes say the images are so incredibly clear and lifelike that current TV pictures look like blurred, out-of-focus scenes.[39]

A number of futurists have expressed concern that TV technology will become so exciting, so mesmerizing, that it will have an isolating effect. They fear that masses of sports fans may choose to remain in the comfort of their homes with their TV sets rather than actually attending sports events. A number of social scientists have been warning that "the privatization of leisure," through the retreat into the home for entertainment, has the danger of bringing about "a collapse of a civic ethic within society, the sense of belonging to a society."[40]

Intercollegiate Athletics and the Future

As we have noted at several places in this volume, professional sport is not limited to privately owned sport franchises. Big-time collegiate sports constitute a professional industry in every sense of the word. They are every bit as dependent on economic considerations as other professional sports, and one can confidently predict that as television goes, with respect to buying rights to broadcast intercollegiate sports events, so will go the big-time collegiate programs.

Even with the bonanza of television money, intercollegiate athletic programs have had increasing financial problems. The major problem is money or the lack of it. Growth in attendance has drastically slowed as competition, from both professional sports and other attractions, has increased. Meanwhile, increased costs have taken a brutal toll on the athletic budgets of many colleges. Adding an eleventh and twelfth game to the traditional ten-game football schedule, permitting first-year students to play on varsity teams, expanding play-off schedules in basketball and bowl games in football, limiting the size of coaching staffs, and deemphasizing or dropping so-called "nonrevenue sports" are all economic measures that have been adopted to add revenue or to reduce expenses in intercollegiate athletics.

All is still not well on the campuses. For example, many state-supported universities receive substantial support for collegiate athletics from tax funds, and public opposition to this is growing. Legislatures are weighing the athletic appropriations against, for example, faculty salaries and state aid for disadvantaged students. Other educational considerations include more spending for community colleges and expansion of vocational education. Needs are also being considered in other fields, such as mental health, welfare, law enforcement, and the general administration of government.[41]

What does the future hold for intercollegiate athletics? A polarization has already begun, with a few major universities dominating collegiate TV programming, while most of the other colleges struggle with budgeting problems. As a result, sports club programs are growing on college campuses. These are student-oriented sports teams coached by older students or interested persons with a love for the sport (they typically receive no pay) and are funded by the participants or by small sums from the institution's student activity funds. Some higher education administrators have even predicted that over the next twenty years most of the athletic teams on a college campus will be of the sports club type, with the university having only one or two sports of the high visibility, commercial type.

Secondary School Sports and the Future

The 1980s and 1990s have not been prosperous decades for high school sports. Inflation, the increasing reluctance of taxpayers to support education, and the hesitancy of many state legislatures to raise taxes combined to force many school systems to curtail or even to abolish some of their athletic programs. In a period of austerity, school administrators invariably look to the extracurricular activities as a source of savings, and because the athletic program is typically the most expensive extracurricular function, it is an obvious target. Between 1985 and 1995 over one thousand high schools dropped their football programs.[42]

If financial difficulties continue to plague schools, modifications in the funding of the programs will probably occur. Indeed, one trend of the past decade is the "pay-for-play" plans that require athletes to assume some of the costs of equipment and other expenses associated with their participation. This trend is likely to grow, as it has been successful in many communities. Other means may be tried in the next decade to salvage high school sports programs. More active booster clubs, corporate sponsorship, television contracts have all been tried, but further development is likely. As an alternative to high school athletics, some communities are seriously discussing phasing sports out of the schools entirely and having the municipal recreation departments administer sports programs for all age groups.

Gambling and Sports

Gambling is an economic activity with a history that dates back into antiquity. Humans have been willing, even anxious, to wager on almost anything. Americans wager an estimated $400 billion legally each year, and $100 billion is bet illegally. An acknowledged authority on gambling, says that "gambling is growing at a phenomenal rate in the United States."[43] One reason it is growing is because there are now more opportunities to gamble than ever before. Since 1988, more than one hundred seventy casinos have opened nationwide, and casino gambling is legal in about twenty-five states. Lotteries, a form of gambling, is a state sanctioned business in most of the states.

Moral sanctions against gambling and laws outlawing gambling are simply not around anymore. Forecasters predict "The next frontier in the gambling boom is coming someday to a living room near you. Interactive television will allow viewers to wager on horseracing, dog racing, sporting events, bingo, the lottery and anything else that could involve a bet."[44]

Sporting events have always been subject to wagering because the outcomes are uncertain. With the enormous increase of interest in spectator sports over the past two decades, a corresponding explosion in gambling on sports has occurred. Bookies and betting syndicates handle an estimated $20 billion worth of sports bets a year. The two biggest sports gambling events are the Super Bowl, on which some $3.5 billion is wagered, and the NCAA men's basketball tournament, where around $2.5 billion is bet illegally plus another $50 million is wagered legally. In 1995 *Sports Illustrated* ran a three-part series detailing what it called "the dirty little secret on college campuses," which is that sports gambling is rampant and prospering on campuses throughout the country.[45]

The legalization of gambling and the issue of the profits as a source of income to help support sports organizations and state, provincial, and national governments has been proposed in a number of states and provinces in recent years, but Nevada, Montana, North Dakota, and Oregon remain the only states permitting some form of legalized sports gambling. Given the economic crisis in sport and in government, the prospect of the enormous windfall that could be generated from legalized betting is very attractive to some sports organizations and to politicians. There are also fears about legalizing betting on sports events. First, some think that it would stimulate excessive betting, that persons would bet money that they could ill afford to lose. Second, there is the prospect that athletes and coaches would be corrupted. The point-shaving scandals of collegiate basketball come easily to mind. What of the heightened pressures on athletes resulting from the inevitable dropped pass, strikeout, or missed free throw? A suspicion that perhaps the action was deliberate and charges of dumping the game or shaving points would follow. In spite of these potential problems, one sports writer has proposed this scenario for 2001:

> Sport gambling is now legal in all 52 states (he believes two new states will be added by 2000) and is heavily taxed by the federal government, bringing in $30 billion a year that was unavailable back when most betting was outlawed. These days, the government encourages gambling. There is a new Department of Bookmaking & Wagers in the U.S. Cabinet, headed by the Bookmaker General. Bookmaking & Wagers oversees the whole American gambling system and will install Home Betting Window, Robo-Bookie and Tele-Tout free in any American home.[46]

With the increase in gambling that futurists see, will come the inevitable—compulsive, addictive gambling. Just in one year, between 1994 and 1995, calls to The Center for Compulsive Gambling increased nearly 100 percent. Extensive research at the Center clearly show that where you have availability and opportunity for gambling, compulsive gambling problems increase accordingly. Thus, current trends and future predictions suggest that a growing social problem for both sport and the larger society will likely be large numbers of tragic compulsive gamblers.[47]

Trends in Social Values and Future Sport

In chapter 3 we identified the dominant values in Canadian and American societies. These mainstream values include an entire constellation of beliefs involving the importance of personal effort and accomplishment in defining one's status and worth, both economic and social, and one's relation to social institutions. These values, like other aspects of North American life, have been undergoing rather radical change; indeed, some social scientists claim we are on the verge of a cultural crisis that will ultimately revolutionize our values and institutions. The roots of this crisis reside in a strong disillusionment with traditional values.

The Quest for Democracy and Equality

During the past twenty years a continuing debate has taken place in North America, as well as in countries throughout the world, over the issue of democracy and equality. We have witnessed the downfall of autocratic governments on every continent. Leaders of almost every political revolution or of countries with substantial chronic social unrest, have vowed to provide greater democracy and equality; indeed, there is said to be a worldwide yearning for a "democratic revolution." This is a theme with great appeal to people throughout North America who have been disadvantaged by their ascribed statuses (women, blacks, and other minorities) and they are demanding to be considered as full members of society.[48]

North Americans have actually been in the forefront of those seeking a democracy and equality revolution, and futurists expect that there will continue to be demands for more autonomy, more democracy, and greater participation in places of work and in government. All of these demands add up to a quest for more control over one's life and for the reduction of economic, political, and social inequalities that now prevent people from improving their quality of life.[49]

The essence of the quest for social change is related to new ideas about humanity and methods of interpersonal relations. A more optimistic, democratic, humanistic conception of human nature is emerging. These new values have already had an impact on such social institutions as education, politics, and religion, and they are making their presence felt in the business world.

There is no longer only one acceptable life-style; nor is there one set of moral values. We find, because of this, many changes in economic and political organization and a variety of leisure patterns. The result has been a shift in consciousness. A shift in personal goals and priorities and in the ways of perceiving and ordering the world outside the individual. As a consequence, futurists expect the next twenty years to be characterized by more humane, expressive, and creative approaches to life. Futurists predict that many young people will discover satisfaction in the opportunity to become involved with activities that test their talents, give them more responsibility for their behavior, and let them stretch their minds and bodies.

Trends in Sports Values

Social institutions are based on traditional norms and values and are therefore vulnerable to the effects of value changes among significant segments of the society. Many traditional values have come under attack in the past decade, and since sport is a social institution, it too has been challenged by emerging values.

Democracy and Equality in Sport

Traditional athletic priorities and practices have begun to be challenged by a new set of standards premised on the notion that democratic processes have relevance in sport as well as other sectors of life. Consequently, athletes are demanding changes in sports at all levels; they are especially pressing for greater participation in the decisions that affect their athletic lives and for a greater responsiveness on the part of coaches and athletic administrators. They have also pressed for more autonomy, for the freedom to be what they want to be and to choose how they will live.

Although some athletes have called for a change toward greater freedom and personal responsibility within the structure and functioning of sport, they have been a minority, and it is unlikely that athletes will be in the vanguard of social change in the future. The world of sports generates a fundamental acceptance of the established norms and values. North American physical education faculties and coaches—the two most powerful socializing agents of the sports world—are conservative and typically accept traditional values.[50]

Even if athletes as a group do not catalyze much change, they are nevertheless members of their own youth culture, a culture that is pressing for change. The old athletes tended to confront authorities infrequently; current professional and collegiate athletes are more likely to challenge the management establishment. This attitude is demonstrated by the strikes in pro baseball, hockey, and football. Directions in sport, then, suggest increased egalitarianism, democracy, and humanism, but these are trends that will occur only gradually and only as they become a part of society.

Opportunity and Equality for Special Groups in Sport

Historical inequalities and injustices for females and African Americans were described in chapters 13 and 14. As part of each chapter, we also highlighted the remarkable changes that have taken place in sports world in the past generation that have given greater access and opportunity to African Americans and women in sport. Other groups as well have experienced historical discrimination in sport, but here too conditions are changing for the better and will likely continue to do so.

One of those groups is the disabled, which make up about 20 percent of the population. Disabled people have historically been subjected to systematic prejudice and injustice, and it has only been in the past twenty-five years that national laws and enlightened public attitudes have reversed the practices that treated the disabled as outcasts. Until quite recently the disabled were discouraged from participating in sports. They were made to feel their condition precluded sports involvement; sports equipment and facilities were unavailable to them.

Dramatic changes have occurred in the past two decades for disabled athletes, and athletes with disabilities now have access and opportunities not only to participate in sport, but to become elite athletes competing for gold medals and large sums of money. A *Sports Illustrated* article details the state of sports for disabled athletes:

> There is now an ESPN program, *Break Away,* that features sport for the disabled. There are magazines, from *Sports 'n Spokes* to *Palaestra,* that treat disabled athletes as authentic sports figures. There is a circuit for wheelchair road racers that offers the

best of them a decent living ($30,000 or more annually). There is corporate sponsorship, with Home Depot kicking in $4 million to the Paralympics and other companies such as IBM, United Airlines and Coca-Cola contributing to disabled sports. . . . And, of course, there is the national imperative guaranteed by the . . . Paralympics.[51]

The Paralympic Games are the world's second largest sporting event, attracting athletes with physical disabilities from over 100 nations.

Another group that has faced pervasive injustice is homosexuals. Historically, there has been little toleration for homosexuality in North America. Despite substantially improved attitudes over the past decade, gays and lesbians still suffer various forms of social stigma and injustice. As we noted in chapter 14, sport has been a bastion of homophobia; indeed, sport has been a cultural practice where homophobic attitudes have actually been socially constructed and reproduced.

As with other sectors of society, attitudes and values about human sexuality are gradually changing, and there is a greater acceptance of individuality in sexual orientation. In sport, as well, gays and lesbians have been "coming out," acknowledging their homosexuality (e.g., Martina Navratilova, Greg Louganis). While there is still a deep division in attitudes toward homosexuality among North Americans, the taboo about homosexuality that once prevailed in sport is beginning to vanish.

Gay and lesbian athletes compete at all levels of sport from novice to Olympic champions. To provide a special sporting event for homosexual athletes and improve public attitudes about homosexuality, leaders of the homosexual community have organized the Gay Games, which are patterned after the Olympic Games. Four of those Games have been held. Gay Games IV took place in New York City in 1994; more than ten thousand athletes from over forty countries entered and competed in thirty-one events. At the time the Games were held, the mayor of New York City said he hopes "the Games will be a lesson in tolerance and equality." He helped secure Yankee Stadium for the closing ceremony.[52]

The kinds of value changes that are taking place in North America and the adoption of new values in sport point quite clearly to enhanced opportunities for disabled athletes and gay and lesbian athletes to have an integral role in sports of the future.

New Emphasis on Participation and Cooperation

Traditional youth and high school sports programs were practically built on a foundation in which a few athletes play on a few "varsity" teams, while the vast majority of people became "substitutes" or spectators. A new, active, participative orientation is gaining adherents. One visible trend in youth sports programs is the structuring of play to foster participation, cooperation, and sportsmanship. For example, rules decreeing that every child who registers should be assigned to a team and that every child on a team should play in every game are becoming more common. Some leagues feature no-win games, that is, no points are awarded for a win or loss and no records are kept of league standings or of leading scorers. Those who conduct such programs report that the youngsters appear to have a lot more fun than under the traditional format.[53]

New Forms of Intramural Sports

College students are increasingly rejecting the traditional offerings of campus intramural programs and demanding more innovative programs with greater potential to satisfy their immediate and long-term needs. As a consequence, intramural programs have had to devise new and different activities that deemphasize championships, eliminate trophies, sponsor sports clubs, include equal sports opportunities for women, and provide greater use of facilities for open recreation. Several colleges have experimented with the abolishment of all extrinsic rewards; no point systems or awards of any kind are employed. The importance of victory is deemphasized by doing away with championships and limiting protests to on-the-spot, right-or-wrong, final decisions by activity supervisors. Any combination of undergraduate and graduate students and faculty are allowed to form teams. Women may participate on teams that compete in the men's division.[54]

Questioning Winning As the "Only Thing"

The past decade has witnessed a growing disillusionment with the intensive competition that nurtures a "winning is the only thing" ethos. There is an ever-widening belief that such an orientation subordinates important values that should be inspired by sport, such as fun, teamwork, self-discipline, and a sense of fair play. It is also believed that the "winning is the only thing" ethos tends to generate feelings of conditional self-worth, role-specific relationships, excellence based on competitive merit, perception of self as a means, and subjection of self to external control.

There is growing support for games that emphasize inclusion and cooperation rather than competition and that can be played by large groups and by all ages. By using alternative activities to those that require unusual physical prowess or developed sports skills, the advocates of alternative approaches try to create an atmosphere of fun and relaxed voluntary participation. The motto is: "Play hard, play fair, nobody hurt."

Advocates of these approaches to sports and games see a bright future because physical activities that promote intrinsic rather than extrinsic rewards provide individually meaningful experiences, and move people away from the role of spectators and toward "depth" in sport involvement. They believe such approaches have the potential to become the dominant sport forms of the twenty-first century.[55]

It is not clear just which trajectory this particular trend will take in the future. No doubt the hypercompetitiveness that is promoted via the mass media will be a powerful influence on sports at all levels and in all forms, but a number of societal trends suggest a rejection of these values for sports below the professional levels.

Summary

This is an era of rapid change in North America, and sport, like other social institutions, is undergoing changes in form and content—changes related to those of the larger society. We have identified a number of the more salient social changes and speculated about how current and future trends may affect sport.

Trends in population suggest that the rapid expansion of professional sports is continuing and that pro franchises may soon organize along regional rather than single-city lines. As the average age of the population increases, men and women are going to continue to stay active longer, even in high-level competitive sport. The proportion of minorities in the population is increasing rapidly, and the different cultural traditions of minority groups will influence the trends and patterns of sport involvement. Minorities have gained greater opportunities in the world of sport, and the egalitarian trend suggests that sport opportunities will increase in the years ahead for all persons.

Industrialization and technology have reduced the average workweek, but other conditions have arisen to nullify the actual leisure time of adults. The leisure time available in the future may be used in sports of either a more "intellectual" nature or a more violent nature; moreover, technological developments will probably result in technosport forms, and human reactions against technology will result in ecosports.

Professional and big-time intercollegiate sports have become successful business enterprises, mainly because of television involvement. Their future rests heavily upon the directions dictated by television. Gambling, as it becomes legalized, will probably become more prominent in sports.

Changes in value orientations over the past decade have emphasized equality and pluralism, and the world of sport has experienced protest and even violent revolt as athletes have rebelled against traditional authoritarian leadership and the "win" ethic. A new orientation has begun to make inroads into sport, and innovative programs and practices are beginning to incorporate this new vision.

Notes

1. Charles Handy, *The Age of Paradox* (Cambridge, Mass.: Harvard Business School Press, 1994); Hamish McRae, *The World in 2020: Power, Culture and Prosperity* (Cambridge, Mass.: Harvard Business School Press, 1994); Ian Morrison and Greg Schmid, *Future Tense: The Business Realities of the Next Ten Years* (New York: W. Morrow, 1994); Sheila M. Moorcroft, *Visions for the 21st Century* (Westport, Conn.: Greenwood Press, 1993); Richard A. Slaughter, *The Foresight Principle: Cultural Recovery in the 21st Century* (Westport, Conn.: Greenwood Press, 1995); Howard Snyder, *EarthCurrents: The Struggle for the World's Soul* (Nashville, Tenn.: Abingdon Press, 1995).

2. Paul R. Campbell, *Population Projections for States, By Age, Race, and Sex: 1993 to 2020*, U.S. Bureau of the Census, Current Population Reports, P25–1111, (Washington, D.C.: U.S. Government Printing Office, 1994); Randolph E. Schmid, "Census Bureau Looks at an Aging Nation and at Recent Trends," *The Tuscaloosa News,* 23 January 1995, sec. A, p. 4; Kelvin Pollard, "Faster Growth, More Diversity in U.S. Projections," *Population Today* 21 (February 1993): 3, 10; "Canada Charts Its Demographic Future," *Population Today* 19 (January 1991): 8.

3. Scott A. Bass, Francis G. Caro, and Yung-Ping Chen, eds., *Achieving a Productive Aging Society* (Westport, Conn.: Auburn House, 1993). Figures cited here have been adjusted to include the United States and Canada.

4. "Bigger, More Diverse Population Projected," *The Spokesman-Review,* 29 September 1993, sec. A, p. 4; Campbell, *Population Projections for States, By Age, Race, and Sex: 1993 to 2020;* Kelvin Pollard, "Faster Growth, More Diversity in U.S. Projections, *Population Today* 21 (February 1993): 3, 10; Nicholas Bradbury, "Out of the Frying Pan: New Worries About Asian Newcomers in Canada," *Far Eastern Economic Review* 151 (31 January 1991): 28–29.

5. Campbell, *Population Projections for States, By Age, Race, and Sex: 1993 to 2020.*

6. Austin Murphy, "As the World Turns," *Sports Illustrated,* 22 May 1995, 62–65.

7. Ben Brown, "Discovering Ageless Truth About Sport," *USA Today,* 1 March 1990, sec. C, pp. 1–2; Charles Leershen and Elizabeth Ann Leonard, "Silver-Haired Athletes Reaching for the Gold," *Newsweek,* 25 June 1990, 62–63.

8. Roger Herman, *Turbulence: Challenges and Opportunities in the World of Work: Are You Prepared for the Future?* (Akron, Ohio: Oakhill Press, 1995); Stanley Aronowitz and William DiFazio, *The Jobless Future: Sci-Tech and the Dogma of Work* (Minneapolis: University of Minnesota Press, 1994); David B. Bills, ed., *The New Modern Times: Factors Shaping the World of Work* (Albany: State University of New York Press, 1994).

9. Peter Lloyd, ed., *Groupware in the 21st Century* (Westport, Conn.: Greenwood Press, 1994); Harold A. Linstone and Ian I. Mitroff, *The Challenge of the 21st Century: Managing Technology in a Shrinking World* (Albany: State University of New York Press, 1994); Don Tapscott and Art Caston, *Paradigm Shift: The New Promise of Information Technology* (New York: McGraw-Hill, 1993).

10. Herman, *Turbulence: Challenges and Opportunities in the World of Work: Are You Prepared for the Future?;* Tapscott and Caston, *Paradigm Shift: The New Promise of Information Technology.*

11. Aronowitz and DiFazio, *The Jobless Future: Sci-Tech and the Dogma of Work;* see also Olivia S. Mitchell, ed., *As the Workforce Ages: Costs, Benefits, and Policy Challenges* (Ithaca, N.Y.: ILR Press, 1993); David B. Bills, ed., *The New Modern Times: Factors Reshaping the World of Work* (Albany, N.Y.: State University of New York Press, 1995).

12. Juliet B. Schor, *The Overworked American: The Unexpected Decline of Leisure* (New York: Basic Books, 1991); "The Case for a Shorter Work Week With No Loss in Pay," *Labor Notes,* April 1995, 6; Patricia Edmonds, "Families Running on Overdrive, in Overtime," *USA Today,* 10 April 1995, sec. A, p. 4.

13. "Poll: Few Would Choose Leisure Over Pay," *USA Today,* 10 April 1995, sec. A, p. 2.

14. Edmonds, "Families Running on Overdrive, in Overtime"; see also Joan Greenbaum, *Windows on the Workplace* (New York: Cornerstone Books, 1995).

15. Alvin Toffler, *Powershift: Knowledge, Wealth, and Violence at the Edge of the 21st Century* (New York: Bantam, 1990).

16. James Radlow, *Computers and the Information Society* (Danvers, Mass.: Boyd and Fraser Publishing Co., 1995); Linstone and Mitroff, *The Challenge of the 21st Century: Managing Technology and Ourselves in a Shrinking World.*

17. Donald Katz, "Welcome to the Electronic Arena," *Sports Illustrated,* 3 July 1995, 62; see also Michael Meyer, "Fight to the Finish," *Newsweek,* 12 December 1994, 56–57.

18. Norbert Elias and Eric Dunning, *The Quest for Excitement: Sport and Leisure in the Civilizing Process* (Cambridge, Mass.: Blackwell, 1993).

19. Don Ateyo, *Blood & Guts: Violence in Sports* (New York: Paddington Press, 1979), 375, 377.

20. Katz, "Welcome to the Electronic Arena," 62.

21. John Hoberman, *Mortal Engines: The Science of Performance and the Dehumanization of Sport* (New York: Free Press, 1992), 286.

22. Hoberman, *Mortal Engines: The Science of Performance and the Dehumanization of Sport*; see also T. H. Murray, "The bioengineered competitor," *National Forum* 69 (Winter 1989): 41–42.

23. Katz, "Welcome to the Electronic Arena," 60–61.

24. David Bjerklie, "High-Tech Olympians," *Technology Review* 96 (January 1993): 22–30; Abe Dane, "The Mechanics of Skiing," *Popular Mechanics* 169, February 1992, 34–37; Fred W. Hadley, "Sports and Technology," *Technology Teacher* 52, March 1993, 23–29; Hoberman, *Mortal Engines: The Science of Performance and the Dehumanization of Sport;* Howard L. Nixon, "Accepting the Risks of Pain and Injury in Sport: Mediated Cultural Influences on Playing Hurt," *Sociology of Sport Journal* 10 (June 1993): 183–96.

25. Richard G. Kraus, *Leisure in a Changing America: Multicultural Perspectives* (New York: Macmillan, 1994); see also Randy B. Swedburg and Bill Izso, "Active Living: Promoting Healthy Lifestyles," *Journal of Physical Education, Recreation, and Dance* 65 (April 1994): 32–35; Andrew Brookes, "Reading Between the Lines—Outdoor Experience as Environmental Text," *Journal of Physical Education, Recreation, and Dance* 65 (October 1994): 28–33; Wayne G. Pealo, "Leisure & Active Lifestyles: Moving Into the Twenty-First Century," *Journal of Physical Education, Recreation, and Dance* 63 (October 1992): 26–27.

26. Linda Castrone, "Yoga Goes Hip," *Rocky Mountain News* 5 September 1995, sec. D, pp. 3, 5.

27. Kim Long, *The American Forecaster Almanac: 1994 Business Edition* (Ithaca, N.Y.: American Demographics Books, 1994), 241.

28. *Runner's World* regularly cites participation figures on the number of runners who are taking part in many of the road races that are being held each week.

29. Long, *The American Forecaster Almanac: 1994 Business Edition*, 242.

30. Linda Castrone, "Exercising a Productive Option," *Rocky Mountain News* 22 August 1995, sec. D pp. 3, 6.

31. Government of Canada, *Active Living: A Conceptual Overview* (Ottawa: Fitness and Amateur Sport, 1992); Government of Canada, *Minister's Steering Committee on Active Living—Final Report* (Ottawa: Minister of State, Fitness and Amateur Sport, 1993); Administration Bureau for Active Living Canada, *Making it Work* (Ottawa: Fitness and Amateur Sport, 1993).

32. William E. Halal and Alexander I. Nikiten, "One World: The Coming Synthesis of a New Capitalism and a New Socialism," *The Futurist* 24 (November/December 1990): 8–14.

33. Robert H. Frank and Philip J. Cook, *The Winner-Take-All Society* (New York: Free Press, 1995); Richard J. Barnet and John Cavanagh, *Global Dreams: Imperial Corporations and the New World Order* (New York: Simon & Schuster, 1994).

34. Morrison and Schmid, *Future Tense: The Business Realities of the Next Ten Years*.

35. Tim Crothers, "The Shakedown," *Sports Illustrated*, 19 June 1995, 78–82; see also John Steinbreder, "The Owners," *Sports Illustrated*, 13 September 1993, 64–86; Jack McCallum, "Blame the Bosses," *Sports Illustrated*, 10 October 1994, 30–35; George H. Sage, *Power and Ideology in American Sport: A Critical Perspective* (Champaign, Ill.: Human Kinetics Publishers, 1990), chap. 7.

36. William O. Johnson, "Sports in the Year 2001," *Sports Illustrated*, 22 July 1991, 46.

37. Ibid., 40–52.

38. Rick Morrissey, "In the Viewers Hands," *Rocky Mountain News* 17 September 1995, sec. B, pp. 5, 6.

39. Rick Morrissey, "High Tech Sharpens TV Sports," *Rocky Mountain News* 17 September 1995, sec. B, pp. 7; Rick Morrissey, "In the Viewers Hands," *Rocky Mountain News* 17 September 1995, sec. B, pp. 5 6; Donald Katz, "Welcome to the Electronic Arena," *Sports Illustrated,* 3 July 1995, 61–71, 77.

40. Rick Morrissey, "Getting Close to the TV Can Isolate Fans," *Rocky Mountain News* 17 September 1995, sec. B, p. 9.

41. John R. Thelin, *Games Colleges Play: Scandal and Reform in Intercollegiate Athletics* (Baltimore: Johns Hopkins Press, 1994); Murray Sperber, *College Sports Inc.* (New York: Henry Holt, 1990); Barbara R. Bergmann, "Do Sports Really Make Money for the University?" *Academe* 77 (January/February 1991): 28–30.

42. National Federation of State High School Associations, *1994–95 Handbook* (Kansas City, Mo.: NFSHSA, 1995).

43. Quoted in Tim Layden, "Better Education," *Sports Illustrated,* 3 April 1995, 71; see also Katz, "Welcome to the Electronic Arena," 68.

44. Rick Morrissey, "Interactive Technology Could Mean Trouble for Compulsive Gamblers," *Rocky Mountain News* 17 September 1995, sec. B, p. 8.

45. Gary Mihoces, "Billions Bet on Basketball Tournament," *USA Today* 30 March 1995, sec. C, pp. 1–2; Layden, "Better Education," 69–90; Tim Layden, "Book Smart," *Sports Illustrated,* 10 April 1995, 68–79; Tim Layden, "You Bet Your Life," *Sports illustrated,* 17 April 1995, 46–55.

46. Johnson, "Sports in the Year 2001," 46.

47. Morrissey, "Interactive Technology Could Mean Trouble for Compulsive Gamblers."

48. Edward N. Wolff, *Top Heavy: A Study of the Increasing Inequality of Wealth in America* (New York: The Twentieth Century Fund, 1995); Holly Sklar, *Chaos or Community? Seeking Solutions, Not Scapegoats for Bad Economics* (Boston: South End Press, 1995); Philip Slater, *A Dream Deferred: America's Discontent and the Search for a New Democratic Ideal* (Boston: Beacon Press, 1991).

49. Herbert Gans, *The War Against the Poor* (New York: Basic Books, 1995); William E. Connolly, *The Ethos of Pluralism* (Minneapolis: University of Minnesota Press, 1995); see also Frank and Cook, *The Winner-Take-All Society.*

50. For an example of the coaching methods and philosophy of life of Indiana University's basketball coach Bobby Knight, one of North America's most noted coaches, see John Feinstein, *A Season on the Brink* (New York: Macmillan, 1986); for an example of the subculture of high school football in Texas, see H. G. Bissinger, *Friday Night Lights: A Town, a Team, and a Dream* (Reading, Mass.: Addison-Wesley, 1990).

51. Richard Hoffer, "Ready, Willing and Able," *Sports Illustrated,* 14 August 1995, 69; see also Karen P. DePauw and Susan J. Gavron, *Disability and Sport* (Champaign, Ill.: Human Kinetics Publishers, 1995).

52. "Gay Games Huge Athletic Event," *Greeley Tribune* 18 June 1994, sec. A, p. 8; "The Political Side of The Gay Games 1994," *The Advocate,* 26 July 1994, 20–26; Mike Messner, "Gay Athletes and the Gay Games: An Interview with Tom Waddell," in *Sex, Violence & Power in Sports: Rethinking Masculinity,* ed. Michael A. Messner and Donald F. Sabo, (Freedom, Calif.: The Crossing Press, 1994), 113–19.

53. G. D. Morris and James Stiehl, *Changing Kids' Games* (Champaign, Ill.: Human Kinetics Publishers, 1989).

54. Alan Tower, "Consider a 'Spirit of Competition' and a Rating System for Your Intramural-Recreation Program," *NIRSA Journal* 20 (Fall 1995): 46–47.

55. Susan Kasser, *Inclusive Games: Movement for Everyone* (Champaign, Ill.: Human Kinetics Publishers, 1995); Peggy M. Tomme and Janice C. Wendt, "Affective Teaching: Psycho-Social Aspects of Physical Education," *Journal of Physical Education, Recreation, and Dance* 64 (October 1993): 66–69.

CREDITS

Footnotes

P. 83, footnote 5: From Jay J. Coakley, *Sport in Society: Issues and Controversies,* 5th edition. Copyright © 1994 Mosby-Yearbook, Inc., St. Louis, MO. Reprinted by permission.

P. 95, footnotes 43 and 44: From Jay J. Coakley, *Sport in Society: Issues and Controversies,* 5th edition. Copyright © 1994 Mosby-Yearbook, Inc., St. Louis, MO. Reprinted by permission.

P. 164, footnote 50: From THE PRINCE OF TIDES by Pat Conroy. Copyright © 1986 by Pat Conroy. Reprinted by permission of Houghton Mifflin Company. All rights reserved.

P. 189, footnote 47: From Jay J. Coakley, *Sport in Society: Issues and Controversies,* 5th edition. Copyright © 1994 Mosby-Yearbook, Inc., St. Louis, MO. Reprinted by permission.

P. 253, footnote 27: From Jay J. Coakley, *Sport in Society: Issues and Controversies,* 5th edition. Copyright © 1994 Mosby-Yearbook, Inc., St. Louis, MO. Reprinted by permission.

P. 256, footnote 39: From Jay J. Coakley, *Sport in Society: Issues and Controversies,* 5th edition. Copyright © 1994 Mosby-Yearbook, Inc., St. Louis, MO. Reprinted by permission.

P. 269, footnote 20: From Jay J. Coakley, *Sport in Society: Issues and Controversies,* 5th edition. Copyright © 1994 Mosby-Yearbook, Inc., St. Louis, MO. Reprinted by permission.

Photographs

Chapter 1 Opener: Corel Photo CD; p. 7:© Steve Skjold

Chapter 2 Opener: Bettmann Archive

Chapter 3 Opener: © James L. Shaffer; p. 45: © Steve Skjold

Chapter 4 Opener: David Frazier Photolibrary; p. 66: © James L. Shaffer

Chapter 5 Opener: © James L. Shaffer; p. 93: © Steve Skjold

Chapter 6 Opener: © James L. Shaffer

Chapter 7 Opener: © Al Messerschmidt

Chapter 8 Opener: © Al Messerschmidt

Chapter 9 Opener: © Corel Photo CD; p. 180: Corel Photo CD

Chapter 10 Opener: Michael Yelman/Active Images

Chapter 11 Opener: Reuters/Corbis-Bettmann

Chapter 12 Opener: Tom Moser/Terra; p. 247: © James L. Shaffer

Chapter 13 Opener: Corel Photo CD

Chapter 14 Opener: Corel Photo CD; p. 291: © Colin Meagher

Chapter 15 Opener: David Frazier Photolibrary; p. 317: Digital Stock Photo CD

Academic performance
  and intercollegiate athletes, 108–109, 112
  and interscholastic athletes, 86–87, 94–95
  and youth sports, 73–74
Achievement
  means to achieve as value, 46
  means to achieve in sport, 52
Acland, Charles R., 129
Acosta, R. Vivian, 257, 296
Active Living, 316
Active Living: A Conceptual Overview, 317
Adelman, Melvin L., 24
Adelman, Melvin M., 28
Adler, Patricia A., 115
Adler, Peter, 115
Advertising
  at stadiums, 196–197
  television, 174
The Advocate, 322
Aethlon: The Journal of Sport Literature, 224
Africa, witchcraft and sport, 168
African Americans
  athletic ability and physical superiority, 264–265
  black breakthroughs in U.S. sports, 266–267
  black subculture and sports, 265
  dominance in sports, 264
  exploitation in sports, 256
  racial discrimination in sports, 269–276
  salary discrimination, 273–274
  social constraints and sports participation, 265, 268–269
  social mobility and sports, 255–256
  in sport, historical view, 262–264
  in sport journalism, 239
Age, older athletes, 308
Aggression
  effect of sports on, 126–127
  frustration-aggression theory, 124–125, 126
  instinct theory, 124, 126
  social learning theory, 125–126, 127
  See also Violence and sports
Agnew, Spiro, 183
Airplane, and rise of sport, 37
Aitken, Brian W. W., 158, 163

Albinson, John G., 31, 83
Albrecht, Richard R., 62
Alexander, Charles C., 28
Alienation, meaning of, 48
All-American Girls Professional Baseball League, 298
Alt, John, 233
Althouse, Ronald C., 116
Alwin, Duane F., 252
Alzado, Lyle, 137
Amateur sport
  business of, 214–215
  intercollegiate sports as, 109, 215
Amdur, Neil, 97
American Coaching Effectiveness Program (ACEP), 76
The American Forecaster Almanac, 316
American Gladiators, 249
"American Youth and Sports Participation," 64
Ancient era
  sports and religion, 150
  sports and violence, 129, 135
Anderson, Douglas A., 235
Anderson, Lars, 299
Andre, Thomas, 83
Angell, Roger, 213, 218
Animal Locomotion (Muybridge), 32
Anticipatory socialization, 185
Antitrust laws, 175
  baseball exemption from, 205
Arena League, 199
Armer, J. Michael, 251
Arond, Henry, 257
Aronowitz, Stanley, 309
Artibise, Alan F., 27
Ash, Michael J., 60, 283
Ashe, Arthur, 256
Assimilation, 185
Association for Intercollegiate Athletics for Women (AIAW), 293, 297
Association for Women in Sports Media, 238
Association of Sports Press Editors, 238
Ateyo, Don, 312
Athlete Assistance Program, 177

Athletes
    owner control of player issue, 205–208, 211–212
    political orientation of, 185–186
Athletes in Action (AIA), 157, 158
Athletic club, history of, 28
Atlantic cable, 31
Automobile
    development of, 36–37
    and rise of sport, 37
Automobile racing
    advertising through, 198
    and African Americans, 269
    historical view, 37
    working class attraction to, 248–249
Axthelm, Pete, 246, 265

Baade, Robert A., 203
Baca Zinn, Maxine, 4, 8, 10, 11, 91, 128, 285
Baenninger, Ronald, 133
Baiamonte, Philip, 108
Bailey, Wilford, 107
Baker, Frank, 35
Balbus, Ike, 181
Baldo, Anthony, 202, 205
Ball, Donald W., 88, 178, 184
Ball, James, 34
Banfield, Edward C., 46
Banham, Charles, 87
Barnet, Richard J., 317
Barnett, Battling, 38
Barney, Robert K., 29
Baron, Robert A., 124
Bartimole, Roldo, 202
Barton, Richard L., 22
Baseball
    African Americans in, 264, 270, 272, 275
    in Canada, 28, 31
    free-agent system, 208, 211
    history of, 28, 30, 36, 39
    minor league attendance, 228–229
    night baseball, 39
    salaries, 209, 213
    strike, economic consequences of, 210
    televised, modifications to sport, 231
    women in, 298
Baseball Chapel, 157
Basketball
    African Americans in, 264, 268, 270
    economic agreements in, 212
    salaries in, 212, 213
    televised, modifications to sport, 231
    as urban poor game, 246, 268
    women in, 298

Bass, Scott A., 306
Bavolek, Stephen J., 64
Beal, Becky, 159
Beamish, Rob, 140, 142
Bechhofer, L., 134
Becker, B. J., 86
Becker, Debbie, 156, 294
Bedecki, Tom, 177
Beecher, Catharine, 29
Beer companies, and sport, 198
Beldsoe, Terry, 268
Bell, Alexander Graham, 31
Bell, Jarrett, 130
Bell, T., 247
Beller, Jennifer M., 64, 70
Benedict, Jeffrey R., 134, 264, 274
Benedict, Ruth, 52
Berberoglu, Berch, 26
Berger, Peter L., 4, 5, 8
Berghorn, Forrest J., 262, 263, 270
Bergmann, Barbara R., 105, 319
Berkowitz, Leonard, 125, 126
Berlage, Gai I., 298
Berry, Kenneth J., 249
Berry, Robert C., 207
Berryman, Jack W., 60
Bicycling, women in, 281
Big Ten, 102
Bill of Rights for Young Athletes, 76–77
Bills, David B., 309
Biological determinism, and African American physical
        superiority, 264–265
Birrell, Susan, 115, 287, 288, 294
Bissinger, H. G., 16, 86, 88, 92, 321
Bjerklie, David, 313
Blackouts, 175
Blair, Bonnie, 194
Blalock, Hubert M., Jr., 270
Blauvelt, Harry, 274
Blinde, Elaine, 294
Block, Alex Ben, 206
Blum, Debra E., 230, 295
Blum, Ronald, 227
Bock, Hal, 72
Boeck, Greg, 74
Bonds, Barry, 213
Bondy, Filip, 74
Books
    by professional athletes, 224
    on sports, historical view, 224
Borderline violence, 130–131
Bottomore, Tom B., 150
Bowen, Edward L., 24
Bowlen, Patrick, 204

Boxing
    African Americans in, 263
    historical view, 29, 31, 38
    socioeconomic status of boxers, 256–257
    televised events, 229
Boycotts
    Olympic Games, 187–188
    of Olympics, 175
    racially-based, 181
Boyle, Robert H., 263
Bradbury, Nicholas, 307
Braddock, Jomills Henry, 252
Bradley, John Ed, 130
Brady, Erik, 164
Brailsford, Dennis, 129, 151
Branch, Taylor, 215
Brasch, Rudolph, 150
Brett, George, 168
Brewington, Peter, 230, 294
Bridges, Lisha, 276
Briggs, Bill, 158, 164
Brill, A. A., 126
Brodeur, Pierre, 35
Brody, David, 23
Broekhoff, Jan, 76
Brohm, Jean-Marie, 54, 180
Brookes, Andrew, 314
Brooks, B. G., 168
Brooks, Dana D., 116
Brower, Jonathan J., 272, 276
Brown, Barbara, 70
Brown, Ben, 214, 308
Brown, C. Harmon, 288
Brown, Richard M., 128
Browne, Lois, 298
Bryant, Jennings, 131, 235, 236
Bryant, Paul W., 108
Bryce, James, 34
Bryson, Lois, 15
Bulger, Margery A., 281
"Bull Durham," 155, 167, 225
Bunning, Jim, 181
Bureaucracy, and conformity, 48
Burfott, Amby, 264
Burke, Glenn, 300
Buss, Jerry, 204
Butler, Samuel, 163
Butsch, Richard, 33
Byers, Walter, 109

Cahill, Bernard R., 59, 66
Caillois, Roger, 16
Cairney, J., 157
Calhoun, Kirk, 35

Calipari, John, 104
Campbell, Paul R., 306, 307
"Camptown Races," 24
Campus Crusade for Christ, 158
Canada
    baseball in, 28, 31
    history of sport, 22, 24, 26, 27, 28, 31
    history of violence, 127, 128
    interscholastic sports, 82, 83
    sports organizations, 177
    stacking in, 271
    values of Canadians, 44
    wellness programs, 316–317
    youth sports, 77
Cannon, Lynn Weber, 128
Cantelon, Hart, 28, 35
Capriati, Jennifer, 71, 72, 75, 137
Carey, Jack, 274
Carlos, John, 178, 187
Carlson, Chris, 132
Carlston, Donald E., 268
Caro, Francis G., 306
Carpenter, Linda J., 257, 296
Cart, Julie, 71
Cartel, league cartel, 198–199
Caston, Art, 309
Castro, Fidel, 176
Castrone, Linda, 314, 316
Catharsis, and aggression, 124
Catherwood, Ethel, 34
Catholic Youth Organization (CYO), 153, 155
Cavanagh, John, 317
CBS Sales Promotion Office, 233
Cedras, Raoul, 179
Census of Manufacturers, 34
Chalip, Lawrence, 69
Chalk, Ocania, 263
Chamberlain, Wilt, 217
Chambers, Marcia, 286
Chandler, Joan M., 155
Chandler, T. J. L., 83
Character building, and interscholastic sports, 87, 253
Chariots of Fire, 225
Chase, Francis, Jr., 38
Chataway, Christopher, 174, 178
Cheating
    and interscholastic sports, 90
    and need to win, 46, 49–50
Chen, Yung-Ping, 306
Cherry, Andrew L., 61
Chicago Bears, 36
Christianity, and sport, 150–151, 156, 157–158, 161, 162
The Chronicle of Higher Education, 47
Chronicle of Higher Education Almanac, 254

Chu, Donald, 86, 150
Clark, Nancy, 139
Clarke, Norm, 167
Clinton, Bill, 181
Coaches
    autocratic and interscholastic sports, 90
    compensation of, 104
    emphasis on winning, 49
    number of professional coaches, 195
    political orientation of, 183–185
    racial discrimination in coaching, 274
    salaries, 104
    sports socialization, 63
    training programs for, 76
    and violence in sports, 132
    women, 296–297
    youth sports, 65, 66–67, 76
Coaching Behavior Assessment System (CBAS), 76
Coakley, Jay J., 11, 13, 66, 83, 88, 95, 180, 189, 253, 256, 263, 269
Cobb, 225
Coffey, Wayne, 74, 75
Cohen, Jeff, 222
Cohen, Michael, 186
Cole, Cheryl L., 288, 294
Coleman, James S., 83, 84
College sports. *See* Intercollegiate sports
Collett, Glenna, 34
Collett, Wayne, 178
Collins, Randall, 4
Colonial era
    popular sports, 23
    religious institutions against sport, 22–23, 152–153
Committee on the Judiciary, 206
Communications advancements, and development of sport, 25–26, 31–32, 37–39
Communism, use of sports, 175–177
Community, and interscholastic sports, 85–86
Competition
    as American value, 45–46
    and career in sports, 254–255
    cross-cultural view, 51–52
    and interscholastic sports, 90–91
    negative aspects of emphasis on, 50–51
    as value in sports, 48–52
    and youth sports, 74–75
Competitiveness, and sport, 14
Computers, and intellectual sports, 311
Concessions, economics of, 195
Conflict, and power, 15
Conflict theory, 10–13
    elements of, 10, 12
    compared to functionalism, 11, 13
    view of sport, 11

Conformity
    as American value, 47–48
    levels of, 47
    as value in sports, 53–54
Conners, Jimmy, 308
Connolly, William E., 321
Conroy, Pat, 164
Conservatism, of coaches and athletes, 183–186
Conspicuous consumption, 245, 250
Cook, Philip J., 45, 317, 321
Cooke, Jack Kent, 204
Coomes, Mark, 115, 294
Cooperation, emphasis in youth sports, 76
Corbett, James J., 29
Corbin, Charles B., 137
Corea, Ash, 239
Corporate sports
    interscholastic sports as, 92–93
    nature of, 16–17
Corporations
    media companies ownership of teams, 228
    and Olympic team, 198
    profits from sports, 196
    sponsorship of sports events, 197–198
    sports/wellness programs of, 245–246, 316–317
    team ownership by, 174
Cosell, Howard, 107
Cosentino, Frank, 280
Costa, D. Margaret, 281
Coubertin, Pierre de, 50–51, 285
Country clubs, discrimination by, 181–182
Course of Calisthenics for Young Ladies (Beecher), 29
Cowart, Virginia S., 142
Cramer, Judith A., 239
Cranberg, Gilbert, 188
Crawford, Craig, 44
Creedon, Pamela J., 237, 238, 284
Cross-country skiing, 314
Crosset, Todd W., 134
Crossman, Jane, 284
Croteau, David, 222
Crothers, Tim, 317
Crowther, Samuel, 37
Crum, Denny, 104
Csonka, Larry, 211
Cuba, sports in, 176
Cub Scouts, 45
Culin, Stewart, 150
Currie, Elliott, 9, 128, 139, 142
Curtis, James E., 44, 70, 102, 271

Daddario, Gina, 284
Dahrendorf, Ralf, 174

Dane, Abe, 313
Darwin, Charles, 33
Davis, Laurel R., 265
Davis, Timothy, 116
Dealy, Francis X., Jr., 107
de Beauvoir, Simone, 288
Decision-making, by interscholastic athletes, 95–97
Decker, David, 70
de Coubertin, Pierre, 285, 286
Dedmon, Emmett, 26
Deferred gratification, nature of, 46
DeFrantz, Anita, 275
Degler, Carl N., 33
Demak, Richard, 274
Democracy, and sport, 321–322
Demolition derby, working class attraction to, 249
Dempsey, Jack, 34
Denver Post, 82
DePauw, Karen P., 322
Development, society, impact on, 4–5
DeVenzio, Dick, 109
Deviant behavior
    cheating, 46, 49–50
    in sports, 15–16, 72, 75
Diamond, Sara, 158, 159
DiFazio, William, 309
Digital Satellite System (DDS), 226
Dines, Gail, 135
DIRECTV, 225, 226
Disabled and sports, 322
Disch, Lisa J., 237
Dodd, Mike, 63, 64, 297
Dollard, John L., 125
Donaghy, Jim, 162
Donaldson, Ann, 29
Dooley, Vincent J., 109
Downing, John, 231, 239
Draft clause, provisions of, 205–207
Drahota, JoAnne, 88
Drug testing, of athletes, 141, 142
Drug use. *See* Substance abuse and sport
Dubois, Cora, 44
Dudley, William, 51
Duff, John F., 74
Duncan, Margaret Carlisle, 284
Dunleavy, Aidan O., 70
Dunning, Eric, 233, 249, 312
Duquin, Mary E., 60
Durick, William G., 31
Durkheim, Emile, 148
Dye, Richard F., 203
Dyreson, Mark, 34

East Germany, sports programs of, 176–177
Eastman Kodak, 32
Eating disorders, and athletes, 139
Economics and sport
    amateur sport, 214–215
    auxiliary businesses and profits, 195–198
    big business of sport, 198
    draft/reserve clause, 205–207
    free agency, 207, 211–212
    individual ownership, 203–205
    intercollegiate sport, 215–217
    league cartel, 198–200
    non-athletic monetary activities of athletes, 194
    occupational categories in sports, 195–196
    professional franchise, 199–200
    public subsidy of sport, 200–203
    salaries, 212–214
Ecosports, 314–315
Edelson, Paula, 178
Edison, Thomas A., 32, 224
Edmonds, Patricia, 310
Edwards, Harry, 8, 16, 98, 115, 116, 181, 185, 187, 255, 256, 257, 264, 268, 276
Eichelberger, Curtis, 105, 112
Eisen, George, 29
Eisenberg, John, 94
Eitzen, D. Stanley, 4, 8, 10, 11, 13, 46, 50, 88, 90, 91, 109, 116, 117, 127, 128, 136, 196, 214, 248, 251, 264, 265, 270, 273, 274, 275, 276, 285
Elder, Lee, 269
Elias, Norbert, 233, 312
Elitism
    and interscholastic sports, 91
Ellis, Michael J., 76
Emerson, Ralph Waldo, 29
Engh, Fred, 76
Enrico, Dottie, 227
Erasmus, Desiderius, 151
Eron, Leonard D., 125, 126
Eskenazi, Gerald, 93, 134, 230
ESPN, 226
Espry, Richard, 187
Evans, Arthur, 276
Evans, Janet, 110
Ewing, Patrick, 109, 212

Failure, adjustment to, and interscholastic sports, 87–88
Fair Play Codes, 77
Falwell, Jerry, 156
Family
    and gender-role socialization, 282–283
    and sports socialization, 62–63

Fan violence, 135–137
    examples of, 135–136
    factors related to, 135–137
    preference for violence in sports, 132
    reduction of, 136–137
Farber, Michael, 130
Faris, Robert E. L., 85
Farrell, Christopher, 213
Farrington, Steven R., 275
Faulkner, Sandra, 286
Fawcett, Dick, 91
Feinstein, John, 321
Fellowship of Christian Athletes (FCA), 157
Felshin, Jan, 286
Felson, Richard B., 126
Feltz, Deborah L., 62
Fetishes, in sports, 167–168
Field, Cyrus, 31
"Field of Dreams," 154–155, 225
Fiesta Bowl, 103
Financial World, 204
Fine, Gary A., 65, 66, 67
Finn, Robin, 58, 74
Fisher, Douglas, 24
Fistfighting, 23
Fitness and Lifestyle at the Workplace, 35
Flag, disrespect towards, 178
Flake, Carol, 161
Fleisher, Arthur A., III, 110, 229
Flood, Curt, 207
Foley, Douglas E., 86, 135
Football
    African Americans in, 264, 270, 272
    free-agent system, 211
    historical view, 30, 36
    salaries in, 213
Forbes, 254
Ford, Henry, 37
Foreman, George, 308
Forest, Stephanie Anderson, 258
Fornoff, Susan, 237
Franchises. *See* Professional franchise
Frank, Robert H., 45, 317, 321
Frank Leslie's Illustrated Newspaper, 31
Franks, C. E. S., 177
Fraser, Ian, 180
Frauenheim, Norm, 74
Free agency, 207, 211–212
    example of system, 208
    landmark cases, 207–208
Freedman, Warren, 36
Freeman, Jo, 281

Freud, Sigmund, 124
Frey, Darcy, 93, 255
Frey, James H., 10, 13, 105, 107, 116, 175, 196
Friedrichs, Robert W., 14
Friend, Tim, 130
Friesen, David, 83
Frustration-aggression theory, 124–125, 126
Fulton, Robert, 25
Functionalism
    compared to conflict theory, 11, 13
    elements of, 10, 12
    view of religion, 149
    view of sport, 11
Furst, David, 270
Future view
    economic structures, 317
    ecosports, 314–315
    flextime workweeks, 310–311
    forecasting associations, 306
    gambling, 320
    health/fitness lifestyle, 315–317
    industrialization, 309
    information services, 309
    intellectual sports, 311
    intercollegiate sports, 319
    interscholastic sports, 319
    leisure time, 310
    population, 306–308
    for professional sports, 317
    social values and sport, 320–323
    special groups, opportunities for, 322–323
    technosport, 312–314
    for televised sports, 317–319
    violent sports, 311–312

Gallico, Paul, 263
The Gallup Poll Monthly, 235
Gambling and sport, 195–196
    future view, 320
    legalization issue, 196, 320
Gans, Herbert, 321
Gantz, Walter, 235, 236
Gardner, Gayle, 237–238
Garrison, Zina, 274
Garrity, John, 52
Garvey, Edward R., 207
Gaskell, Jane, 283
Gateway, 202
Gavron, Susan J., 322
Gay Games, 322
Gender inequality, historical view, 280–282

Gender inequality in sport
    gender-role socialization, 282–283
    and governance bodies, 293
    and lack of role models, 285
    and mass media, 284–285
    and Olympic Games, 298–299
    and schools, 283–284
    social barriers to females, 285
    See also Women in sports
Gender roles
    reinforcement and sports, 89–90, 300
    socialization of, 282–285
Gerber, Ellen, 286
Gerber, Suzanne, 71
Gibreath, Edward, 158, 159
Gibson, Josh, 262
Giddens, Anthony, 4
Gilbert, Bill, 16, 281
Gill, Diane L., 164
Gillis, Jacqueline H., 160
Glasner, David, 111
Gmelch, George, 166, 167
God and Country Night, 158
"God's Game Plan," 157
God Squad, 158
Goff, Brian L., 110, 229
Goldberg, A. D., 83
Goldman, Herbert, 257
Goldstein, Arnold, 126
Goldstein, Jeffrey H., 136
Goldstein, Warren J., 28
Golf
    and African Americans, 269
    Skins Game, 231
    televised, modifications to sport, 231
    women in, 298
Goodhart, Phillip, 174, 178
Goodhue, Robert M., 177
Goodman, Matthew, 214
Goodyear, Charles, 32
Gorman, Jerry, 35
Gorn, Elliott J., 23
Gould, Daniel, 64
Government, involvement in sports, 175
Gowan, Geoff R., 76
Graf, Steffi, 133
Graham, Billy, 156
Grant, Carol B., 35
Gray, John, 159
The Greeley Tribune, 248, 292, 322
Green, Gareth M., 35
Green, Harvey, 29, 152
Green, James, 265

Green, Robert W., 159, 160
Greenbaum, Joan, 310
Greendorfer, Susan L., 13, 62, 63, 283, 284
Gretzky, Wayne, 194, 213
Griffin, Pat, 286
Griffo, Young, 38
Grissim, Joan, 249
Groups, as micro level for analysis, 6–7
Grove City College v. Bell, 294–295
Grover, Kathryn K., 152
Grundman, Adolph H., 263
Gruneau, Richard S., 28, 31, 83, 203
Grusky, Oscar, 270
Guthrie, Bart, 284
Guthrie, Sharon R., 281
Guttmann, Allen, 16, 23, 150, 187, 248
Gymnastics, historical view, 29

Hadley, Fred W., 313
Haerle, Rudolf K., 256
Hainline, Brian, 142
Halal, William E., 317
Halbert, Christy, 284
Hall, Ann, 297
Hallinan, Christopher, 270
Hamilton, Malcolm, 148
Handbook on Women Workers, 62
Handy, Charles, 306
Hanks, Michael, 252
Hanna, William E., 270
Hansen, Gary F., 91
Harding, Tonya, 15–16, 72, 75, 133
Hardy, Stephen, 28, 33
Harlem Globetrotters, 262
Harper, William Rainey, 30
Harrington, Michael, 9, 13
Harris, David, 36
Harris, Donald S., 88
Harris, Dorothy V., 286
Hart, M. Marie, 16
Harvey, Jean, 28, 35
Hasbrook, Cynthia A., 297
Haupt, Herbert A., 139
Hawkins, Jerald D., 74
Haywood, Kathleen M., 76
Hearst, William Randolph, 31, 223
Hellmich, Nanci, 139
Helyar, John, 208
Herman, Roger, 309
Hess, Lynda J., 128
Hiestand, Michael, 197, 224
Higgs, Catriona T., 284, 298
Higgs, Robert J., 155

High school sports. *See* Interscholastic sports
Hill, Grant M., 91
Hill, Karen L., 298
Hilliard, Dan C., 236
Himmelstein, Hal, 222, 231, 236
History of sport (in North America)
    business/labor organizations, role in, 35
    Canada, 22, 24, 26, 27, 28, 31
    and class system, 28–29, 34
    colonial era, 22–23
    and communications advancements, 25–26, 31–32, 37–39
    immigrants, role of, 29
    and industrialization, 23–27
    intercollegiate athletics, 29–30, 39, 102
    large-scale organized sport, 24–25
    Muscular Christianity Movement, 29
    nineteenth century, early, 23–25
    nineteenth century, late, 26–34
    professional sports, 35–36
    social philosophy, impact of, 33–34
    and technological advancements, 32–33, 39
    and transportation, 25, 30–31, 36–37
    twentieth century, 34–39
    and urbanization, 27–28, 34
Hoberman, John M., 138, 183, 313
Hoch, Paul, 11, 13, 180
Hochberg, Philip R., 175
Hockey
    in Canada, 82
    salaries in, 213
Hoffer, Richard, 134, 322
Hoffman, Shirl J., 153, 158, 161, 162, 163, 164
Holford, Elyzabeth, 164
Holland, Alyce, 83
Holmes, Oliver Wendell, 29
Holway, John, 262
Homosexuality
    female athletes, 286
    in organized sports, 322
Hoop Dreams, 88
Hoose, Phillip M., 263
Hornsby, Rogers, 263
Horovitz, Bruce, 198
Horse racing, historical view, 23, 24, 31
Howell, Frank M., 87, 252
Huchendorf, Steve, 275
Huddle fellowship program, 157
Huesmann, L. Rowell, 125
Hufnagel, Rick, 109
Hughes, Thomas, 32
Huizenga, Rob, 130
Huizinga, Johan, 16

Hult, Joan S., 293
Humber, William, 28
Humez, Jean M., 135
Humphrey, James H., 59
Hunter, Jim "Catfish," 207
Hyma, Albert, 151
Hyslop, Paula, 284

Ideology of sport, meaning of, 160–161
Iliad (Homer), 163
Immigrants, and development of sport, 29
Inabinett, Mark, 223
Indianapolis 500, 195
Industrialization, and development of sport, 23–27
Industrial Revolution, 23
Informal sport, nature of, 16
Ingham, Alan G., 140
Injuries, and youth sports, 74
Inside Sports, 223
Instinct theory, of aggression, 124, 126
Institutions
    function of, 8–9
    nature of, 8
Intellectual sports, 311
Intercollegiate Athletic Association, 102
Intercollegiate sports
    and academic performance, 108–109, 112
    administration of, 117
    African Americans in, 263–264, 276
    amateur status of athletes, 109, 215
    business of, 103–104, 215–217
    buying and selling games, 216
    of church-sponsored colleges, 156
    collusive practices in, 216
    educational emphasis for student-athletes, 117–118
    eligibility of players for professional teams, 217
    future view, 319, 323
    graduation rates, 112–115, 254
    historical view, 29–30, 39, 102
    impediments to scholarly achievement, 115–116
    money orientation, effects of, 105–109
    National Collegiate Athletic Association (NCAA), 109–112, 216
    professionalization issue, 217
    reform of, 116–117
    rights of athletes, 118
    scandals in, 106–109
    scholarships, 109, 215
    and social mobility of athletes, 252–253
    and television, 229–230
    women in, 292–294, 295
Intergenerational mobility, 252

International Olympics Committee, 187, 188, 245
Interscholastic sports
    and academic performance, 86–87
    academic standing issue, 94–95
    and adjustment to failure, 87–88
    Canada, 83
    and character building, 87
    and cheating, 90
    and coaches, control factors, 90
    and competition, pressure of, 90–91
    consequences for community, 85–86
    consequences for school, 84–85
    corporate nature of, 92–93
    decision making by athletes model, 95–97
    and elitism, 91
    and females, 89–90, 290–292
    future view, 319
    and male status, 83
    no-cut policy, 96–97
    No Pass No Play rule, 94
    participation levels in, 82–83
    reform efforts, 93–97
    and school budget limitations, 91–92
    and social mobility for athletes, 251–252
    specialization in, 91
    and television, 230–231
Izso, Bill, 314

Jackson, Tony, 298
Jacobs, Barry, 109
James, William, 126
Jansen, Sue Curry, 181
Jenkins, Sally, 71, 72, 75, 133, 227
Jennings, Kenneth M., 35, 227
Jenson, Kerry, 284
Jim Crow laws, 262
Jobe, Ben, 215, 216
Jobling, Ian F., 31
Johnson, Arthur T., 175
Johnson, Jack, 263
Johnson, Susan, 298
Johnson, Vance, 134
Johnson, William O., 200, 225, 228, 317, 318, 320
Jones, Bobby, 34
Jones, Jerry, 204
Jordan, Michael, 194, 206, 212, 269, 274
Journal of Physical Education, Recreation, and Dance, 64
Journal of Sport & Exercise Psychology, 6
Journal of Sports & Social Issues, 195
Joyner-Kersee, Jackie, 286
Junior Olympics Sports Program, 58

Kaiser, Edgar, 204
Kane, Mary Jo, 70, 237, 284, 297

Kanter, Rosabeth Moss, 270
Kaplan, Lisa Faye, 135
Kapp, Joe, 211
Kasser, Susan, 323
Katz, Donald, 174, 311, 312, 313, 318, 320
Katz, Jackson, 135
Kaufman, B. P., 158
Kaye, Howard L., 33
KDKA, 224
Keller, Albert Galloway, 33
Kelley, Betty, 164
Kengon, Gerald S., 257
Kennedy, Kastya, 139
Kennedy, Kostya, 107, 274
Kentucky Derby, 195, 262
Kenyon, Gerald S., 13, 16, 184, 203, 251
Kerrigan, Nancy, 15–16, 72, 75, 133, 194
Keteyian, Armen, 93
Keyes, Mary, 280, 281
Kidd, Bruce, 177
King, Peter, 130
Kirkpatrick, Curry, 93, 109
Kirsch, George B., 28
Klatell, David A., 233
Kleck, Gary, 128
Klein, Alan, 287
Knapp, Ron, 162
Knickerbockers of New York, 28
Knisley, Michael, 174
Knute Rockne-All-American, 225
Koch, James V., 216, 273
Kohlsaat, H. H., 37
Kohn, Alfie, 51, 124, 125
Kohn, Melvin L., 184
Kooistra, Paul, 276
Koppett, Leonard, 206
Koss, Mary P., 134
Kraus, Richard G., 35, 314
Krotee, March L., 62
Krzyzewski, Mike, 104

Labor unions, sports activities of, 35
Lacrosse, 24
Ladd, E. C., 184
Landers, Daniel M., 62, 186
Lapchick, Richard E., 95, 175, 187, 263, 264, 273, 274, 275
Lappage, Ron, 280
Lardner, Mike, 230
Largent, Steve, 180
Lasley, Kevin, 70
Latimer, Melissa, 284
Laurie, Bruce, 23
Lavoie, Marc, 270
Layden, Joe, 75

Layden, Tim, 320
Lederman, Douglas, 112, 156, 252, 295
Lee, Martin, 76
Leershen, Charles, 308
Leisure society, 310–311
Lenskyj, Helen, 286, 287
Leonard, Elizabeth Ann, 308
Leonard, George B., 51
Leonard, Wilbert M., II, 274, 275
Lerner, Preston, 298
Leslie, Gregg, 109
Lever, Janet, 179, 223, 225
Lewis, George H., 249
Lewko, John H., 62, 63, 283
Lieberman, David, 226
Liebow, Elliot, 3
Linstone, Harold A., 309, 311
Lipset, S. M., 184
Lipsey, Richard A., 224
Lirgg, Cathy D., 62
Little League
    girls in, 60, 289
    level of participation in, 58
Littleton, Taylor D., 107
Lloyd, Peter, 309
Loggis, Marjorie S., 287
Lokar, Marco, 178
Long, Kim, 315
Loomis, Louise R., 163
Looney, Douglas S., 72
Lorenz, Konrad, 124, 126
Louganis, Greg, 300, 322
Louis, Joe, 263
Lowell, Cym H., 207
Lowenfish, Lee, 35
Loy, John W., Jr., 13, 16, 140, 184, 203, 252, 257, 270, 271
Lucas, Scott E., 137
Lumpkin, Angela, 64, 70
Luschen, Gunther R. F., 86

Macintosh, Donald, 39, 82, 177, 200
Mackey v. NFL, 211
MacKinnon, Catherine A., 135
Madison Square Garden, 32, 202
Magazines and sports
    historical view, 223
    most popular magazines, 223
    and women in sport, 284
Magic, 165–168
    fetishism, 167–168
    Malinowski thesis, 165–166
    compared to religion, 165
    rituals, 166–167
    taboos, 167
    use in sport, 166–168

Magill, Richard A., 60, 283
Maguire, Joe A., 270
Mahoney, John S., 276
Making it Work, 317
Male bonding, and sports, 134–135
Male dominance, in sport, 15
Male status, and interscholastic sports, 83
Malina, Robert M., 64
Malinowski, Bronislaw, 163, 165
Management, racial discrimination in, 275
Mandell, Richard D., 175, 187
Mangan, J. A., 281, 300
Mantle, Mickey, 137
*Manual of Physiology and Calisthenics for Schools
    and Families, A* (Beecher), 29
Marconi, Guglielmo, 37
Marcus, Norman, 233
Margenau, Eric A., 60, 72
Marinovich, Marv, 71–72
Marsh, Herbert W., 87
Martial arts, 314
Martin, Thomas W., 249
Martinez, Jose, 168
Marv Marinovich Performance Training Institute, 72
Marx, Karl, 150
Marxist view, of religion, 150
Massengale, John D., 184, 185, 275
Massimino, Rollie, 104
Mass media
    prominent and subtle roles of, 222
    and violence, 129, 131
Mass media and sports
    books, 224
    close relationship of, 222–223, 233–234
    and consumption of sports, 234–235
    and gender inequality, 284–285
    historical view, 223–225
    increased sport in media, 233–234
    magazines, 223
    manipulation in reporting of events, 234
    most frequently watched sports, 234–235
    movies, 224–225
    newspapers, 223
    radio, 224
    sports journalism, 235–240
    and sports socialization, 64
    television, 225–233, 234–235
Masters Sports Tournaments, 308
Materialism
    as American value, 47
    emphasis on, 14–15
    as value in sports, 52–53
Mathews, Vince, 178
Mathisen, James A., 157

340   *Index*

Matza, David, 85
Mazzocco, Dennis, 222
McCallum, Jack, 104, 107, 139, 166, 167, 274, 295, 317
McCarter, Virginia, 252
McCartney, Bill, 158–159
McChesney, Robert W., 26, 31, 38, 222
McDonald, Mark A., 134
McElvogue, Joseph F., 270
McGee, Reece, 5
McGrath, Ellie, 94
McGurk, Harry, 61
McMillen, Tom, 107, 181
McNally, Dave, 207
McPherson, Barry D., 13, 16, 203, 273
McRae, Hamish, 306
McTeer, William G., 102
Mechikoff, Robert A., 187
Media companies, ownership of teams, 228
Melnick, Merrill J., 14, 87, 134, 270
Mergen, Bernard, 66
Merriwell, Frank, 32, 224
Meschery, Tom, 53
Messersmith, Andy, 207
Messner, Michael A., 134, 237, 246, 283, 284, 300, 322
Metcalfe, Alan, 24, 26, 28
Meyer, Barbara Bedker, 115
Meyer, Michael, 311
Michels, Robert, 174
Miedzian, Myriam, 129, 134, 283
Mihoces, Gary, 134, 258, 320
Mile High Stadium, 202
Miller, Marvin, 207, 208
Miller, Stuart, 288, 298
Mills, C. Wright, 4
Mills, Joshua, 214
Minister's Steering Committee on Active Living, 317
Minorities
    definition of, 262
    social mobility and sports, 255–257
    in sports journalism, 239–240
    See also African Americans
Miracle, Andrew W., 10, 65, 70, 87
Missionaries, and sports, 157–158
Mitchell, Maurice, 106
Mitchell, Olivia S., 309
Mitchell, Sheila, 285
Mitroff, Ian I., 309, 311
Mohammadi, Ali, 231, 239
Molineaux, Tom, 262
Monaghan, Peter, 159
Monkkonen, Eric H., 27

Monopoly
    baseball exemption from antitrust laws, 205
    league cartel, 198–199
    owner control of player issue, 205–208, 211–212
Montague, Susan P., 52
Montana, Joe, 194
Montville, Leigh, 156, 294
Moody, Helen Willis, 34
Moorcroft, Sheila M., 306
Moore, David Leon, 156, 162
Morais, Robert, 52
Moral reasoning, athletes versus nonathletes, 70
Morenz, Howie, 34
Morris, G. D., 323
Morris, G. S. Don, 76
Morrison, Ian, 306, 317
Morrissey, Rick, 136, 139, 213, 318, 319, 320
Morrow, Don, 23, 24, 28, 32, 280
Motion pictures
    historical view, 224–225
    and rise of sports, 38
    about sports, 154–155, 225
    and women in sport, 284
Motocross racing, working class attraction to, 249
Munson, Lester, 134
Murchison, Clint, 204
Murphy, Austin, 229, 308
Murray, T. H., 313
Muscular Christianity Movement, 29
Muwakkil, Salim, 274
Muybridge, Eadweard, 32

Nack, William, 134
Nafziger, James A. R., 175
Nash, Heyward L., 59
National anthem, disrespect toward, 178
National Association of African-American Sportwriters and
        Broadcasters, 239
National Association of Intercollegiate Athletics (NAIA), 102, 293
National Basketball Association (NBA), economic agreements
        of, 212
National Coaching Certification Program (NCCP), 76
National Collegiate Athletic Association (NCAA), 10, 102,
        109–112
    on amateurism and athletes, 110–111
    on employment and athletes, 118
    and freedom of players, 216
    limitations of, 117, 216
    penalty against Southern Methodist University, 156
    restriction of athletes' rights, 111–112
    on televised broadcasts, 229–230

National Federation Handbook, 292

National Federation of State High School Associations, 319

National Football League (NFL), Players' Association strike, 211

National Industrial Basketball League, 35

Nationalism
    and Olympic Games, 187, 188
    and sport, 177–179

National League, beginning of, 30

National Task Force on Children's Play, 77

National Women's Basketball Association, 298

National Youth Sport Coaches Association (NYSCA), 76

Native Americans, games of, 24

Navratilova, Martina, 286, 322

Nazis, in Olympics of 1936, 175

NCAA Directory, 293

The NCAA News, 103, 141, 254, 255, 295, 297

Neal-Lunsford, Jeff, 223

Neff, Craig, 295

Neimark, Jill, 134

Nelson, Mariah Burton, 15, 134, 282, 286, 287

New Englander, 152

Newspapers and sports
    coverage of female sports, 284
    historical view, 223
    scope of coverage, 233, 234

New York Athletic Club, 181

New York Journal, 223

New York Times, 225

Nick Bollettieri Tennis Academy, 58, 74

Nicklaus, Jack, 194

Nike, 196

Nikiten, Alexander I., 317

The 1990 Nielson Report on Television, 38

Nixon, Howard L., II, 13, 313

No-cut policy, interscholastic sports, 96–97

Noden, Merrell, 139

No Pass No Play rule, interscholastic sports, 94

Norman, Geoffrey, 224

Normative research, 13
    types of, 13

Norm learning
    deviant norm behavior, 72
    and sports socialization, 72

Norton, Derrick J., 186

Novak, Michael, 153

Noverr, Douglas A., 39

Noynes, William, 222

Oates, Bob, 255, 256

Obert, Richard, 292, 298

Objectivity, in sociological research, 13–14

O'Brien, Richard, 104, 109, 132, 296

Ogilvie, Bruce C., 184, 186

Olajuwon, Hakeem, 194

Oldfield, Barney, 37

Olivova, Vera, 129

Olsen, Marvin E., 5

Olympic Games, 186–190
    American deficiencies, 177
    ancient, 129, 150
    boycotts, 175, 187–188
    corporate sponsorship of, 198
    flag of, 188
    founder of, 50–51
    gender inequality, 298–299
    missionaries at, 158
    motto of, 186
    nationalism, excessive, 187, 188
    Nazi era, 175, 187
    political decision-making by ruling bodies, 187
    political demonstration problem, 187
    political organization of, 188
    proposals for depolitization of, 188–189
    subsidies by government, 175, 177

O'Neal, Shaquille, 194, 206, 274

O'Neil, Terry, 233, 236

Orange Bowl, 103

Organizations, and rise of sport, 35

Organized sport, nature of, 16

Orlick, Terry D., 76, 87

Ostrosky, Tony, 275

O'Sullivan, Chris, 134

Otto, Luther B., 252

Ownership, 203–205
    benefits of, 204
    necessity issue, 214
    and price of tickets, 204–205
    of professional franchise, 199–200
    profitability of, 204–205, 214
    right to own/control players, 205–208, 211–212
    and violence in sports, 132

Packers, 36

Paige, Satchel, 262

Paige, Woody, 205

Palmer, Arnold, 194

Pan American Games, 176

Panepinto, Joe, 274

Paralympic Games, 322

Park, Roberta J., 281

Parker, Allison R., 62

Parrot, A., 134

Parsons, Talcott, 159, 160

Participant sports, history of, 36

Participation fees, 247

Partlow, Karen, 76

Passer, Michael W., 65
Pastore, Donna L., 296
Paterno, Joe, 104
Patriotism, and athletic events, 178–179
Patten, Gilbert, 32, 224
Patton, Robert W., 35
Pay-per-view events, 226, 318
Pealo, Wayne G., 314
Pearl, Arthur J., 59, 66, 139, 288
Pechter, Kerry, 245, 246
Peers, sports socialization, 63
Perna, Frank, 90
Perot, H. Ross, 94
Perrin, Ethel, 287
Persian Gulf War, 178
Personal-social development, and sports participation, 70–71
Petrie, Brian M., 186
Phillips, John C., 13, 264, 265, 268
Photography, development of, 32
Picou, Steven, 252
Pitman-Davidson, Ann, 76
Play
    informal games, dimensions of, 68–69
    spontaneous play, dimensions of, 68–69
    sports as peer play, 65–67
Player agent, role of, 195
Playgrounds, beginning of, 153
Poliakoff, Michael B., 129
Political office, sports figures in, 180–181
Politics and sport
    government involvement in sports, 175
    Olympics, political aspects, 186–190
    opiate of the masses concept, 179–180
    political orientation of athletes, 185–186
    political orientation of coaches, 183–85
    politician use of athletes, 180–181
    socialization function of sport, 182–183
    sport and nationalism, 177–179
    sport and propaganda, 175–177
    sport and social change, 181–182
    types of links between, 174–175
Pollard, Kelvin, 306, 307
Pooley, John C., 76, 102
Pope, Steven W., 34
Population
    composition of, 306–307
    growth trends, 306
    location of population, 307
    trends and sport, 307–308
Porter, Steve, 295
Pottieger, Jeffrey A., 137

Power, Thomas G., 62
Power
    and conflict, 15
    distributions in organizations, 15
    and politics, 174
Powerhouse programs, 104
Powers, Jimmy, 263
Pratt, Stephen R., 90
Prayer, 163–165
    historical reference to, 163
    opposition to, 164
    use by athletes, 163–164
Prebish, Charles S., 154, 158, 163
Prevention Magazine, 36
Price, Joseph L., 154
Price, S. L., 133, 137
Pride of the Yankees, 225
Primitive societies
    competition in, 51–52
    religion and sport in, 150
Pro Athletes Outreach (PAO), 157
Product endorsements, top ten athletes, 194
Professional franchise, 199–200
    aspects of purchase, 199
    changing locations of, 229
    depreciation of player value, 199–200
    tax shelter aspects, 199–200
Progress
    as American value, 46–47
    as value in sports, 52
The Progressive, 161
Prole sports, 203, 248–249
    working class attraction to, 248–249, 250
Promise Keepers, 158–159
Pronger, Brian, 300
Propaganda, and sport, 175–177
Proposition 48, 94–95, 109, 112, 116
Protestant ethic, 153, 159–162
    on hard work, 162
    nature of, 159–160
    relationship to sport, 160–162
    on self-discipline, 161–162
    on success, 161
Protestant Ethic and the Spirit of Capitalism, The (Weber), 159
Protestantism, and sport, 151, 156, 162
Pseudosports, 17, 249–250
    types of, 249
    working class attraction to, 249–250
Puhl, Jacqueline L., 288
Purdy, Dean A., 109, 274
Puritans, against sports, 22–23

Racial discrimination in sport, 15, 269–276
  black women, 275
  boycotts against, 181
  in coaching, 274
  discriminatory hiring practices, 275–276
  in management positions, 275
  masking of, 269
  salary discrimination, 273–274
  stacking, 270–273
Rader, Benjamin G., 23, 28, 29, 32
Radio
  development of, 37–38
  and sports, historical view, 224
Radlow, James, 311
Railroad, and development of sport, 25, 30–31, 36
Rakow, Lana, 282
Randall, Ivan, 37
Rapping, Elaine, 234
Reagan, Ronald, 244
Real, Michael, 231
Redmond, Gerald, 29
Reed, William F., 102, 263, 299
Rees, C. Roger, 10, 65, 70, 87
Reese, Gary, 300
Reformation, 151
Rehberg, Richard A., 186, 251
Reid, Elizabeth L., 186
Reilly, Rick, 230
Religion
  activities associated with, 148
  definition of, 148
  functionalist view, 149
  and history of sports, 22–23, 29
  Marxist view, 150
  social function of, 148–150
Religion and sport
  in ancient era, 150
  church-sponsored sports, 155–156
  church-supported university athletics, 156
  and early Christian Church, 150–151
  evangelist athletes, 158
  Fellowship of Christian Athletes, 157
  magic, 165–168
  missionary work and sport, 157–158
  prayer, 163–165
  in primitive societies, 150
  Promise Keepers, 158–159
  and Protestant ethic, 159–162
  and Protestantism, 151, 162
  and religious leaders, 156
  seventeenth to nineteenth century, 151–153
  sportianity movement, 159
  sport as religion, 153–155
  twentieth-century, 153

Report of the Select Committee on Intercollegiate Athletics, 109, 112
Representative sport, meaning of, 174
Reserve clause, provisions of, 205–207
Richardson, Deborah R., 124
Riesman, David, 47
Riess, Steven A., 28, 29, 34, 60
Riggins, John, 211
Rights of Professional Athletes, 207
Ripken, Cal, Jr., 181
Rituals, in sports, 166–167
Ritzer, George, 13
Robertson, Noel, 150
Robinson, Frank, 274
Robinson, Jackie, 263
Rockne, Knute, 34
Rocky, 225
Rocky Mountain News, 135, 175, 225, 226, 227, 230, 289
Rogers, Frederick R., 287
Roles, nature of, 7
Roller Derby, 249
Romano, Michael, 158, 159
Rose Bowl, 103
Rosellini, Lynn, 176, 177
Rosenberg, Morris, 185
Rosenblatt, Aaron, 276
Rossellini, Lynn, 187
Rothman, Andrea, 258
Roush, Chris, 226
Rozelle Rule, 205, 211
Rozin, Skip, 140
Rubber, vulcanization of, 32
Rubel, Maximilien, 150
Rubin, Dana, 103
Rudolph, Frederick, 255
Rudy, 225
Runfola, Ross, 286
Runner's World, 316
Running, popularity of, 316
Rushin, Steve, 134
Russell, Bill, 215
Russell, G., 133
Ruth, Babe, 34
Ryan, Joan, 63, 74, 75, 135, 139, 207
Ryan, Nolan, 308
Ryan, William, 46

Sabo, Donald F., 18, 87, 134, 237, 283, 286, 300, 322
Sack, Allen L., 112, 115, 252
Sage, George H., 10, 13, 59, 67, 71, 86, 102, 109, 112, 184, 195, 200, 203, 317

Salaries of athletes, 53, 212–214
    in baseball, 209, 213
    in basketball, 212, 213
    fan reaction to, 212–213
    in football, 213
    in hockey, 213
    justification of, 213–214
    1968–1994 average salaries, 213, 254
    and racial discrimination, 273–274
    and superstar status, 212
Salaries in sports
    athletic directors, 105
    colleges coaches, 104
    umpires, 195
Salkers, David, 283
Salkers, Myra, 283
Sanctions, and conformity, 47
Sanders, Deion, 269
Sandomir, Richard, 195
Saneholz, M. L., 90
Sanford, David C., 273
Sansone, David, 129, 150
Sargent, Dudley A., 287
Satellite networks, 225
Scanlan, Tara K., 64
Schafer, Walter E., 185, 186, 251
Scheiber, Dave, 71
Schmid, Greg, 306, 317
Schmid, Randolph E., 306
Scholarships, athletic, 109, 215
Schools
    and gender role socialization, 283–284
    and sports socialization, 63–64
Schools for sports, 58, 74
Schor, Juliet B., 35, 310
Schreiber, LeAnne, 237
Scott, Jack, 255
Scully, D., 134
Sederberg, Arelo, 239
Seefeldt, Vern, 71
Segrave, Jeffrey O., 86, 150
Segregation, social class and sport, 250–251
Seiler, Andy, 213
Seles, Monica, 133
Self-discipline, Protestant ethic on, 161–162
Senior Olympics, 308
Seville Statement, 125
Sharing the Victory, 157
Shaw, Peter L., 296
Shawnee Mission East High School, 185
Shecter, Leonard, 228
Sherif, Carolyn W., 3
Sherif, Mazufer, 3
Sherman, Howard J., 26

Shirley, Bill, 51
Shmerler, Cindy, 74
Shoe companies, power of, 174
Shostak, Arthur B., 250
Shuster, Rachel, 162
Siblings, and sports socialization, 63
Sierens, Gayle, 238
Silber, John, 105
Simon, David R., 46
Simons, Jeffrey, 91
Simpson, O. J., 16, 134
Simpson, Wayne, 280
Singleton, Janet, 134
Sipes, Richard G., 127
Skins Game, 231
Sklar, Holly, 321
Skolnick, Jerome H., 9
Skyboxes, 103, 105, 202
Slater, Philip, 44, 321
Slaughter, John B., 95
Slaughter, Richard A., 306
Slotkin, Richard, 128
Smith, Jim, 211
Smith, Nathan J., 71, 76
Smith, Red, 208
Smith, Ronald A., 30
Smith, Ronald E., 71, 76
Smith, Tommie, 178, 187
Smoll, Frank L., 60, 71, 76, 283
Snow, P., 231
Snowshoeing, 24
Snow train, 36
Snyder, Eldon E., 14, 49, 52, 53, 86, 154
Snyder, Howard, 306
Soap Box Derby, 49
Soccer, violence during games, 135, 175
Social agency, meaning of, 5
Social change
    and mass media, 222
    sports as impetus for, 181–182
Social class and sport
    and history of sport, 28–29, 34
    and individual sports, 244–245
    prole sports, 248–249
    pseudosports, 249–250
    segregation in sports, 250–251
    social mobility and sport, 180, 251–258
    spectator preferences and social class, 248–250
    sports preferences and social class, 44–246
    and team sports, 246–248
    and youth sports, 246–248
Social Darwinism, and development of sport, 33–34
Social determinism, elements of, 4–5
Social integration, and mass media, 222

Socialization
    anticipatory socialization, 185
    of gender roles, 282–285
    process of, 61
    See also Sports socialization
Social learning theory, aggression, 125–126, 127
Social location, meaning of, 3
Social mobility and sport, 180, 251–258
    basis of, 251–253
    myths about, 253–258
Social order, sports and maintenance of, 179–180
Social-psychological approach, nature of, 6
Societal norms, nature of, 7
Sociobiology, elements of, 3
Sociological research, 13–14
    normative research, 13
    value-neutral approach, 13–14
Sociology
    basic assumptions in, 4–5
    conflict theory in, 10–13
    functionalism in, 10
    limitations of perspective, 5–6
    macro level of analysis, 7–9
    micro level of analysis, 6–7
    social-psychological approach, 6
    study of, 2–3
Solomon, Norman, 222
Solomon, William, 134
Sonnenschein, Allan, 107
Southeastern Conference, 263
Sovern, Michael I., 206
Spalding, Albert G., 32–33
Spears, Betty, 153, 280, 281, 293
Spectators
    sports preferences and social class, 248–250
    types of, 248
The Speeches of Avery Brundage, 154
Spencer, Herbert, 33
Sperber, Murray, 93, 102, 103, 104, 105, 106, 110, 112, 319
Spirit of the Times, 223
The Spokesman-Review, 307
Sport, 223
Sport
    as big business, 2
    corporate sport, 16–17
    definition of, 16
    historical view. *See* History of sport (in North America)
    informal sport, 16
    organized sport, 16
    pervasiveness of, 2
    pseudosport, 17
    reasons for study of, 44
    and society, common elements in, 14–16
Sport Canada, 177

Sportianity movement, 157, 159, 162
Sport in Canadian Society, 58
Sporting goods
    historical view, 32–33
    and intercollegiate sports, 104
    shoe companies, 174
Sporting News, The, 223
Sport Literature Association, 224
SportParent, 58, 64, 76
Sports Ambassadors, 157
Sports Broadcast Act, 199
Sportscasting. *See* Sports journalism
SportsChannel America, 230
Sports facilities
    advertising at, 196–197
    economic importance of, 200
    and property taxes, 202
    public financing of, 200–203
Sports Illustrated, 39, 223
Sports journalism, 235–240
    disparagement of, 235–236
    embellishment of commentary, 236–237
    history of, 26, 38
    housemen/housewomen, 235
    minorities in, 239–240
    promotional function of, 236
    role of journalists, 235
    women in, 237–239
Sports medicine, economics of, 195
Sports socialization
    coaches, 63
    and family, 62–63
    and mass media, 64
    peers, 63
    and schools, 63–64
    and siblings, 63
    strong experiences, factors in, 65
Sports Violence Arbitration Act, 136
Sports World Ministries, 157
Spreitzer, Elmer, 14, 86, 87
Squitieri, Tom, 179
Sreberny-Mohammadi, Annabelle, 231, 239
Stacking, 270–273
    in Canadian football, 271
    consequences of, 273
    examples of, 270
    explanations of, 271–273
    meaning of, 270
Stadiums. *See* Sports facilities
Stagg, Amos Alonzo, 30
Standish, Burt L., 224
Stanford, Leland, 32
Stangl, Jane M., 297
Stanton, Michael, 257

Statistical Abstract of the United States, 36
Status, nature of, 7
Staurowsky, Ellen J., 296
Steamboat, 25
Steinbreder, John, 317
Steinbrenner, George, 177, 200
Stelter, Gilbert A., 27
Steptoe, Sonja, 133, 134
Steroid use, 50, 90
    dangers of, 138
    effects of, 138
    and high school students, 137
    and violence, 135
Stevens, John, 223
Stevens, Phillips, Jr., 168
Stevenson, Christopher L., 86, 161
Stiehl, James J., 76, 323
Stilger, Vincent G., 137
Stocker, Scott, 253
Stokes, Bill, 248
Stoll, Sharon K., 64, 70
Stone, Christian, 286
Stone, Gregory P., 249, 251
Storr, Richard J., 30
Stover, Del, 91
Strikes
    baseball, 210
    NFL Players' Association, 211
Struna, Nancy L., 23, 24, 152
Substance abuse and sport, 137–143
    drug testing, 141, 142
    and eating disorders, 139
    examples of, 137
    historical view, 138–139
    prevention of, 141–143
    reasons for, 139–141
    scope of, 137–138
    steroid use, 50, 90, 135, 137–138
    types of drugs used, 138–139
Success
    as American value, 44–45
    Protestant ethic on, 161
Sugar Bowl, 103
Sullivan, John L., 29, 31
Summer camps, 104
Sumner, William Graham, 33
Super Bowl, 154, 195
    economics of, 196–197
    gambling on, 320
    size of audience, 235
Superdome, 200–201
Supersports, 233
Superstitions, of athletes, 166

Swain, J. W., 148
Swanson, Richard A., 153, 280, 281, 293
Swedburg, Randy B., 314
Sweetheart deals, 200, 201
Swift, E. M., 16, 70, 72, 75, 91, 131, 133
Symonds, William C., 103

Taboo, in sports, 167
Taketak, 51
Talen, Julie, 233
Tangu, 51
Tapscott, Don, 309
Tarkan, Laurie, 295
Tarkanian, Jerry, 104
Taubman, Philip, 108
Tax shelter, and professional franchise, 199–200
Taylor, A. W., 39
Taylor, Phil, 93, 296, 297
Technosport, 312–314
Tedeschi, James T., 126
Telander, Rick, 102, 137
Telegraph, invention of, 25–26
Telephone, invention of, 31
Television
    average daily viewing time, 226
    historical view, 225
Television and sports, 225–233
    advertising, 174
    cable/satellite broadcasts, 226
    changing popularity of sports, 228–229
    economic aspects, 226–227
    future view, 317–319
    game modification for TV, 231
    high school sports, 94, 230–231
    increase in sports coverage, 226
    and increases in sports revenue, 227–228
    and intercollegiate sport, 103, 229–230
    and location of professional franchises, 229
    network profits from, 234
    reciprocal relationship of, 225–226
    and redefinition of sports, 231–232
    and rise of sport, 38
    spectators, socioeconomic status of, 248
    television influence on sports, 227
    trash sports, 233
    and violence and sports, 129, 131
    and women in sport, 284
Tessendorf, Irl, 270
Theberge, Nancy, 70, 281, 297
Thelin, John R., 102, 107, 319
Thiel, Robert, 115, 252
Thompson, Charles, 107
Thompson, Jim, 76
Thompson, Teri, 182

Thorne, Barrie, 283
Thornton, James S., 72
Ticket price
    price gouging, 204–205
    setting of, 204–205
    and social class segregation, 250–251
Tilden, Bill, 34
Timmer, Doug A., 91
Title IX, 10, 83, 89–90, 105, 257, 294–296
    and increase of female participation, 291–292
    legal challenges to, 294–295
Todd, Terry, 138
Toffler, Alvin, 311
Tolbert, Charles M., 276
Tollison, Robert D., 110, 229
Tom, Denise, 72
Tomaskovic-Devey, Donald, 280
Tom Brown at Oxford (Hughes), 32
Tom Brown at Rugby (Hughes), 32
Tomme, Peggy M., 323
Tower, Alan, 323
Transportation, and development of sport, 25, 30–31, 37
Trash sports, televised events, 233
Triathlons, 316
Tripps, Dan G., 76
Trope, Mike, 111, 211
Trow, M. A., 184
Turner, Edward, 284
Turnverein, 29
The Tuscalossa News, 280
Tutko, Thomas A., 184, 186
Tygiel, Jules, 263

Ultra competitions, 316
Umpires, salaries, 195
Underwood, John, 16, 107, 108, 194, 200, 203, 251, 264
United States Olympic Committee, 177
United States Satellite Broadcasting (USSB), 225
Urbanization, and development of sport, 27–28, 34
USA Today, 63, 115, 164, 194, 196, 207, 228, 229, 239, 274, 310

Values, meaning of, 7, 44
Values and sport
    competition/success, 48–52
    conformity, 53–54
    future view, 320–323
    materialism, 52–53
    means to achieve, 52
    progress, 52

Value system of Americans, 44–48
    competition, 45–46
    conformity, 47–48
    irregularities in, 44
    materialism, 47
    means to achieve, 46
    progress, 46–47
    success, 44–45
Valvano, Jim, 109
Vander Hill, C. Warren, 273
Vanderwerken, David L., 150
Vanfossen, Beth E., 87
Vanneman, Reeve, 128
Veblen, Thorstein, 245
Vecsey, George, 94
Venture for Victory, 157
Verducci, Tom, 137
Vertinsky, Patricia, 281
Violence
    aggression, theories of, 124–127
    and contemporary culture, 128–129
    historical view, 127–128
    and steroid use, 135
Violence and sports
    aggression, theories of, 124–126
    athletes assaults on women, 134–135
    borderline violence, 130–131
    career-ending injuries, 131
    and coaches/owners/commissioners, 132
    and fan expectations, 132
    fan violence, 135–137
    future view, 311–312
    historical view, 129
    and nature of sports, 129–130, 132
    off the field violence by athletes, 133–134
    and television, 131
    violence against athletes, 133
    violence versus aggression view, 124
Vlasich, James A., 154

Wacquant, L. J. D., 248
Wadler, Gary I., 142
Walking, popularity of, 316
Waller, Willard, 84, 85, 91
Walton, John, 4
Walvin, James, 300
Watts, J.C., 181
Wayman, Anges, 287
Weber, Max, 159, 160
Weiller, Karen H., 284, 298

Weinberg, S. Kirson, 257
Weisman, Jacob, 197
Weiss, Maureen R., 64, 71
Weistart, John C., 207
Wellness programs, 245–246, 316–317
Wells, Christine L., 288
Wendt, Janice C., 323
Wenner, Lawrence A., 26, 131, 132, 222, 235, 236
Werner, Laurie, 58
Wertz, Spencer K., 150
Wheeler, Stanton, 223, 225
White, Chris, 94
White, Reggie, 162
Whiteside, Kelly, 72, 75
Whitfield, Shelby, 107
Whitford, David, 107, 156
Whitson, David, 28, 200
Whitson, Don, 177
Whorton, J. C., 29
Whythe, William H., Jr., 48
Wicker, Tom, 178
Wiggins, David K., 23, 24, 29, 34, 138, 293
Will, George, 109
Williams, Jean M., 76
Williams, R., 272
Williams, Robin M., Jr., 44, 45
Williams, Trevor, 31
Williamson, Nancy, 281
Willinsky, John, 283
Willis, Paul, 288
Wilson, Clint C., 239
Wilson, Edward O., 3
Wilson-Smith, Anthony, 22
Wilstein, Steve, 286, 300
Winning
    as American value, 48–51
    cheating to win, 46, 49, 90
    deviance related to, 72–73
    emphasis in youth sports, 74–75
    ideas by coaches on, 48–49
    reinforcement by coaches, 49
    slogans on, 49
Wireless communication, development of, 37
Wise, S. F., 24
Witchcraft, in sport, 168
Wolfe, Tom, 249
Wolff, Alexander, 93, 104, 107, 109, 187, 286, 295, 296
Wolff, Edward N., 321
Womack, Mari, 167

Women, athletes assaults on, 134–135
Women in sports
    attitudes toward, 288–289
    careers at top levels, 297–299
    coaches, 296–297
    discrimination and African Americans, 275
    eating disorders, 139
    female health and sports myth, 287–288
    health effects and sports, 289–290
    inferior female athlete myth, 288
    and intercollegiate sports, 292–294, 295
    and interscholastic sports, 89–90, 290–292
    masculinization of women myth, 285–287
    reverse discrimination suits, 295–296
    sex-discrimination suits, 295
    social mobility and sports, 257
    sports in colleges for, 281
    in sports journalism, 237–239
    and Title IX, 83, 89–90, 294–295, 296
    and youth sports, 60, 289–290
    See also Gender inequality in sport
Women's American Basketball Association, 298
Women's Professional Softball League, 298
Women's Professional Volleyball Association, 298
Wong, Glenn M., 207
Woolger, Christi, 62
World Congress on Sport, 158
World Cup, 308
    size of audience, 235
World Football League, 199, 231
World Series, 195
Wrestling
    historical view, 23
    working class attraction to, 249–250
Wright, James E., 142
Wright, Orville and Wilbur, 37
Wulf, Steve, 179, 202
Wuthnow, Robert, 148
Wyrick, Waneen, 286

Yaeger, Don, 107
Yergin, Marc L., 248
Yesalis, Charles E., 135, 137
Yesko, Jill, 297
Yetman, Norman R., 262, 263, 265, 270, 276
Yiannakis, Andres, 13
Young, Kevin, 130
Young, Steve, 194
Young Men's Christian Association (YMCA), 155

Young Women's Christian Association (YWCA), 155
Youssef, Y., 272
Youth sports
    and academic performance, 74
    adult intrusion in, 71–72, 73
    adult-sponsored, emphasis of, 66–69
    Bill of Rights for Young Athletes, 76–77
    books on topic of, 76
    coaches, 65, 66–67, 76
    cooperation emphasis in, 76
    deviation from norm behavior in, 72–73
    and disruption of education, 73–74
    dropping out, reasons for, 64
    and females, 60
    growth, factors in, 59–60
    improvement of, 75–76
    inappropriate competitive ethic in, 74–75
    injury risks in, 74
    most popular programs, 289
    objectives of, 60–61

    parents view of, 62–63
    participant attitudes about, 64–65
    as peer play, 65–67
    and personal-social development, 70–71
    scope of participation in, 58
    and socialization, 61–70
    socioeconomic status and participation, 246–248
    sponsors of, 58, 59
    sport schools, 58, 74
    See also Interscholastic sports

Zapler, Mike, 295
Zerbe, Kathryn, 139
Ziewacz, Lawrence E., 39
Zimbalist, Andrew, 200, 227, 228
Zimmerman, Paul, 162
Zingg, Paul J., 23, 152
Zuk, Rachel, 293
Zuni, 51–52, 150